FIVE RESTORATION
COMEDIES

THE NEW MERMAIDS

General Editor
BRIAN GIBBONS
Professor of English Literature,
University of Zurich

Previous General Editors
PHILIP BROCKBANK
BRIAN MORRIS
ROMA GILL

Five Restoration Comedies

Introduced by
BRIAN GIBBONS

THE MAN OF MODE
THE PLAIN DEALER
LOVE FOR LOVE
THE PROVOKED WIFE
THE RECRUITING OFFICER

A & C BLACK · LONDON

First published in this form 1984
by A & C Black (Publishers) Limited
35 Bedford Row, London WC1R 4JH
© 1984 A & C Black (Publishers) Limited

Five Restoration comedies.—(The new mermaids)
I. Etherege, *Sir* George   II. Series
822'.4'08   PR1266
ISBN 0-7136-2610-0

ISBN 0-7136-2610-0

Printed in Great Britain by
Richard Clay (The Chaucer Press) Ltd,
Bungay, Suffolk

NOTE

NEW MERMAIDS are modern-spelling, fully annotated editions of important English plays. Each play in this anthology is also available individually, with a critical introduction, biography of the author, discussions of dates and sources, textual details, and a bibliography. The reader is recommended to consult these editions for fuller information.

CONTENTS

ABBREVIATIONS

ed.	editor
O.E.D.	*The Oxford English Dictionary*
om.	omit
s.d.	stage direction
s.p.	speech prefix
Tilley	M. P. Tilley, *A Dictionary of the Proverbs in England in the Sixteenth and Seventeenth Centuries*, Ann Arbor, 1950

Names of periodicals abbreviated:

E.L.H.	*English Literary History*
E.S.	*English Studies*
E & S	*Essays and Studies*
J.E.G.P.	*Journal of English and Germanic Philology*
M.L.N.	*Modern Language Notes*
M.L.R.	*Modern Language Review*
N & Q	*Notes & Queries*
P.M.L.A.	*Publications of the Modern Language Association of America*
P.Q.	*Philological Quarterly*
R.E.S.	*Review of English Studies*
S.P.	*Studies in Philology*
T.L.S.	*The Times Literary Supplement*

INTRODUCTION

THIS ANTHOLOGY OFFERS five plays representing the central tradition of Restoration Comedy, only one among many types of play evolved in the years 1660–1700, but the only one to have survived changes in taste since. Restoration theatre had a repertory system, and played to fairly small audiences in which there was a substantial core of regulars. The playhouses were not large, and due to the style of acting on the thrust stage a direct and lively relationship existed between the actors and the spectators. The chief actors had long careers which gave continuity to theatre practice, acting style, and certain types of play; playwrights were thus encouraged to develop a style in successive plays, and could write with particular performers and audiences in mind. Among the surprisingly large number of new playwrights who emerged in this period there were half a dozen whose work is fine enough to have lasted to the present day, being regularly performed in our theatres and read as imaginative literature.

* * *

The comedies in this collection may be arranged in various ways by the reader for the purpose of contrast and comparison; the plays share generic and formal elements and all deal with love intrigue and with a critical display of social behaviour. The playwrights followed current neo-classical comic theory in aiming to represent general features and types in the society of their own times; the plays are all set in the present time of their first performance and invite applause for their truthful representation of it. Thus Wycherley in the Prologue to *The Plain Dealer*:

> But the coarse dauber of the coming scenes
> To follow life and nature only means:
> Displays you as you are: (32–4)

Dryden in the Epilogue to *The Man of Mode* commends Etherege's character Sir Fopling Flutter for his generic, his typical representativeness, not his uniqueness:

> Yet none Sir Fopling him, or him, can call —
> He's knight o' the shire and represents ye all   (15–16)

Dryden cannot quite forget the deliberately recognisable

satiric portrait of himself as Mr Bayes in Buckingham's malicious burlesque *The Rehearsal* (1671); yet his neo-classical view is only reinforced by the subsequent neglect into which Buckingham's too limitedly personal satire has fallen.

Restoration comic playwrights invite the audience's commendation of their truthfulness, but this needs to be understood in the context of their admiring imitation of Ben Jonson and their exploitation of the resources of theatres which had significant affinities, so far as comedy was concerned, with the pre-Civil War stages. Ben Jonson, like his contemporaries, requires no close visual relationship between the action performed on the thrust stage and the façade of the tiring house, with its doors and gallery, behind. The fore-stage is an unparticularised acting area, given temporary localised significance by the action in any scene where the playwright chooses to stress location, otherwise being neutral. The Restoration stage retained a thrust stage, served by four doors, two on either side of its new feature, an open space behind a proscenium arch in which acting was also possible, and in which scenery was arranged. This important innovation was not much used in comedy, for although the spectacular resources of the new perspective scenes were formidable, the decorum of comedy excluded them, and in any case, for comedy, a close, strong relationship between actors (under the bright lighting of the candle-hoops above the thrust stage) and the surrounding audience in the Pit and Boxes, was crucial to success. The area behind the proscenium arch with its flats running in grooves to meet in the centre of the stage, its rows of scenery wings, relief and cut scenes, ground rows, water-rows, and perspective back-scenes, was only lit by candles behind the flats; there was no lighting from above, which must have made the area relatively dim by contrast with the fore-stage, and thus rendered action played behind the proscenium arch comparatively remote. This might well be an advantage in certain tragedies or dramatic operas, but is only very rarely required in Restoration Comedy — or for that matter in Jonson.

Given these playing conditions it is possible to understand in what sense the playwrights claimed truthfulness for their selective, stylised representation of society at the time and in what sense therefore their insight and criticism go beyond that of the gossip columnist or the documentary journalist or filmmaker of today:— even though the actors wore contemporary clothes, spoke prose dialogue, and were to be imagined in specific named streets and places in the surrounding city, engaged in fashionable and familiar activities. Even more dominant than the stylisation already noted, however, is the fact that Restoration

Comedy is based on Romance: that is to say its essential concern is with the ideals of spiritual fulfilment in love, and with the anxious relationship of those ideals to the institution of marriage. As in the case of later writers influenced by Restoration Comedy, such as Henry Fielding, Jane Austen, Oscar Wilde, and George Bernard Shaw, social satire is prominent: it is not merely a by-product but an essential element in the quest for ideal fulfilment in real life, which constitutes the raison d'être of Restoration Comedy as a dramatic genre.

The enforced closing of the theatres during the Civil War had imposed an eighteen-year suspension of regular professional theatre. Immediately after the Restoration, acting began again at several places, including the old Elizabethan Red Bull, but soon rivals were crushed by two royal patent holders, Davenant and Killigrew, and only two companies played thereafter. Before the Civil War there had been several open-air theatres and smaller, indoor playhouses, and the Court Masque had been developed to extravagant and spectacular heights. Thus once theatre got into its stride again after the Restoration it was on a considerably reduced scale and in playhouses differing in significant ways from those of the past.

Only two dramatic companies, then, emerged after the Restoration, formed by the patent holders, Thomas Killigrew and William Davenant, who held responsibility for the choice of plays, hiring of actors, and for casting; these responsibilities were passed on to their successors. Both companies included women, and this presence of professional actresses for the first time in English theatre may be reflected in the range and interest of women's parts in the plays of the period. Killigrew named his company The King's, Davenant his The Duke's. Davenant had experience of the pre-Civil War Court Masque, and his own spectacular work, using movable scenery, *The Siege of Rhodes*, had been presented in 1656 at Rutland House. After becoming patent-holder of the Duke's company Davenant was eager to present this work in public, and in his first theatre, the converted Lisle's Tennis Court in Lincoln's Inn Fields, he established the first professional theatre in England equipped to present, regularly, shows with movable scenery before the general public. Hence developed the vogue for Dramatic Opera as well as Heroic Tragedy, for both of which elaborate scenery and scenic effects were developed. In 1671 Davenant moved to a new, purpose-built theatre designed by Sir Christopher Wren in Dorset Garden (just south of Fleet Street). The greatest actor of the period was Thomas Betterton (1635–1710), a member of the company formed by Davenant in 1661. Killigrew established his company, which included a number of actors with professional experience of the pre-Civil War theatre, first in Gibbons's Tennis Court and then, in 1663, in a converted riding school off Drury Lane. Killigrew had the performance rights to a large number of pre-Civil War plays, which aided him in his rivalry with Davenant. In a wider perspective we can note the importance for Restoration dramatic writers of the frequent revivals throughout the period of plays by Shakespeare (often adapted), Ben Jonson, and, curiously, Beaumont & Fletcher. These dramatists were commended by Dryden in his influential *Essay of Dramatic Poesy*. Killigrew's theatre burned down in 1672 and Sir Christopher Wren designed a purpose-built replacement on the same site off Drury Lane. Difficulties in the King's company led to the two companies combining in 1682, and they continued so reduced to one until in 1695 the leader, Betterton, quarrelled with the Drury Lane manager and took a group of actors with him to perform in the old Lincoln's Inn Fields Theatre, now renamed The New Theatre. The opening of this theatre was marked by the first night of Congreve's latest play *Love for Love*: it was a great success and ran for the exceptional period of thirteen nights in a row.

Estimates based on theatre income indicate perhaps 300, at most 500 spectators on an average night at one playhouse. Even in the early years, when the king and his most favoured courtiers frequently attended, the composition of the audiences seems to have been quite heterogeneous rather than exclusively privileged and fashionable, as has sometimes been maintained. The audience was, nevertheless, separated into categories according to the following system: Gentlemen sat on benches in the Pit, from where they could be seen and heard by the Ladies of Quality who were in the first row of Boxes near the stage itself. In the Lower Gallery were the citizens, their wives and daughters, and above them the Gallery, with common people and footmen. On a vastly enlarged scale this seating pattern can still be recognised in existing Victorian theatres in the English provinces, or at Covent Garden Opera House; Richmond in Yorkshire has an actual Georgian theatre small enough to convey the intimate atmosphere made possible in Restoration Theatre auditoria and so vividly described by Pepys. Prices were a half a crown for the Pit, four shillings for a Box, one and sixpence for the Lower Gallery and a shilling for the Gallery. Although tradesmen and other humbler citizens seem always to have taken tickets and enjoyed performances by the two Restoration companies, nevertheless the part of the audience that mattered to the dramatists, determining their rewards in money and prestige, was predominantly that in the Pit and the Boxes, and spectators in those seats were fashionable, well into the eighteenth century. Dramatists show no inclination to conciliate the city, maintaining the arrogant contempt as a standing convention; but perhaps their mockery failed to give enough offence to drive the citizens away.

The actors in the Restoration companies were on contract; here there was a change from the pre-Civil War period, where the chief actors of a company, the Sharers, had joint responsibility for management. There were on the other hand some important kinds of continuity with the theatre of Shakespeare's day. Many of the chief actors had long and unbroken careers, and they worked, as had the Elizabethans, in a repertory system, and in theatres supported by regular audiences whose judgement of their professional skill might often be supplemented, in the small world of London at the time, by knowledge of the actors as real people off-stage. The dramatists, furthermore, wrote plays with the tastes of their specific audiences in mind and with particular actors in mind for certain roles. A spectator's understanding and enjoyment of a play have added richness and complexity when he has seen a writer's successive plays performed by the same group of actors — as we know from repertory theatres such as the Royal Shakespeare Company, or the work of certain film directors today (Joseph Losey, or Federico Fellini, or Mike Leigh, for example).

For the dramatists who succeeded Etherege, and who had not yet even been born when Charles II acceeded to the throne in 1660, there was every reason for retaining the conventions of Restoration Comedy. It was a kind audiences still liked; it had been evolved for performance in theatres that were still in use, and that had not been developed until after the Restoration. A number of the best actors still working had created the key roles in the early comedies of the genre, and they went on working for many years. When Congreve put on his last comedy *The Way of the World* in 1700 he saw it performed by a cast that included Betterton, the creator on stage of Etherege's Dorimant twenty-four years earlier, as well as Mrs Barry, who had created Mrs Loveit. Millamant was played by Mrs Bracegirdle who had created all Congreve's earlier heroines, and was in fact his mistress too. Among the comic roles Underhill had been a success with many buffoon roles, which included Sancho Panza in Durfey's *Don Quixote* and the Gravedigger in *Hamlet*.

Now the fact that these actors had already created so many roles for which they were still remembered may have contributed to the sense one gets from the later plays that the genre is acquiring, increasingly, a metaphoric status. The range of roles, situations and sentiments is stereotyped to constitute almost a symbolic statement: they also measure, when repeated, a widening historical gap.

The plays in this anthology represent distinct phases of the genre. The first two, *The Man of Mode* and *The Plain Dealer*, were performed in 1676; the next, by Congreve and Vanbrugh, in 1695 and 1696, a gap of twenty years which is registered in subtle rather than in obvious ways in the structure, style and handling of themes. Farquhar's comedy appeared a decade later still, in the reign of Queen Anne, and is remarkable for having a setting not in London but in the provincial town of Shrewsbury—something that would have been simply unthinkable for Etherege, whose plays are committed to an ideal of metropolitan exclusiveness.

* * *

Restoration Comedy is deliberately confined in its scope. Its first playwrights faithfully accepted the precepts of neo-Classical literary theory, which required comedy to observe an aesthetic decorum based on a study of the Roman dramatists Plautus and Terence (and of their commentators) and modified by the contributions of Sir Philip Sidney in his *Apology of Poetry*; of Ben Jonson in his own practice in his comedies, especially *Epicoene*, and in his theoretical assertions in Prefaces, Epilogues, and his *Discoveries*; and especially of John Dryden. Dryden absorbed French neo-classic doctrine in his *Essay of Dramatic Poesy*, where, having emphasised that Restoration writers should honour the achievement in creating character of their great predecessor Shakespeare, and Jonson's correctness in design and manly vigour in critical, satiric comedy, Dryden commended Fletcher for a gaiety anticipating something of the polish and witty grace in dialogue of Dryden's own age, particularly as exhibited in the conversation of the best bred and most witty gentlemen. Dryden dedicated his comedy *Marriage à la Mode*, 1672, to the Earl of Rochester, attributing whatever fineness the play's dialogue might have to his experience of the Earl's conversation. Nature, to which the mirror of art is to be held, is therefore already highly civilised and polished to maintain effortlessly the rules of refined decorum. Such an ideal of behaviour is reflected in the popularity throughout the seventeenth century of Courtesy Books: manuals with instructions in extraordinary detail and thoroughness for correct polite behaviour, including graceful gesture and movement, even analysing walking, sitting down and rising. Life at the French Court, which had been a kind of ideal for the defeated, dispossessed, humiliated and exiled English royalists during the Interregnum, remains a potent influence even when parodied as it is in the fops of Restoration Comedy, of whom Etherege's Sir Fopling Flutter is an unusually strong example, by no means a crass caricature.

The case of the Fop is an appropriate one with which to begin a discussion of the relation between manners, wit, and moral worth in the plays. Congreve, in his Dedication to *The Way of the World*, reminds us of orthodox doctrine on the question of the ridiculous in comedy, as we find it expressed in Sidney's *Apology of Poetry*. Congreve writes 'Those characters which are meant to be ridiculous in most of our comedies are of fools so gross, that in my humble opinion they should rather disturb than divert the well-natured and reflecting part of an audience; they are rather objects of charity than contempt'. Ben Jonson, who was the key exponent of critical comedy in the Elizabethan period, designed his plays so that there was a graduated range of characters exhibiting differing kinds and degrees of folly, presented by progressively large-scale characterisation—from subtle fissures in the patina of wit and judgement in his young gallants, through the graver faults that mark mature, sinful characters such as Morose or Zeal-of-the-Land Busy, down to the completely farcical, the distorted prisoners of their obsession with poetic fame, or fashionable clothes, or other merely outward signs of worth. Congreve's own first comedy *The Old Batchelor* displays this system with graphic clarity and efficiency, but since he wrote the play when very young, perhaps before his twenty-first birthday, it does not absorb the mature art with which Etherege and Wycherley had already developed the Jonsonian model. Congreve himself came to understand their achievement, as his further remarks in the Dedication to *The Way of The World* make clear, when he explains his concern not with natural folly— 'which is incorrigible, and therefore not proper for the stage' — but with 'an affected wit: a wit, which at the same time that it is affected, is also false'. It is a matter of the perversion of judgement and intelligence, then, not of their congenital deficiency, that is the source of ridiculousness.

Since dramatic comedy is not merely exemplary didacticism, we do not find any faultless characters in these plays; as John Dennis wrote in defence of Etherege's achievement in *The Man of Mode*: 'How little do they know of the Nature of true Comedy, who believe that its proper business is to set us patterns for Imitation'. Comedy deals with the whole range of human folly, of which the fop is only an extreme instance, but one which especially focuses the dangers of an exclusive social system in which finer human relationships are sought through conscious regulation and codification of behaviour. Etherege's play offers the comedy of manners in its most concentrated form; other plays in the present anthology betray a generalised debt to the exact depiction of polite behaviour in *The Man of Mode,* both in the subtle wit-combats of the dialogue and the consistent critical position from which characters suffering from different degrees of folly are depicted, as in the scene where one man of mode, Fopling, visits a rake who has just risen from bed, in the company of a more straightforward gallant, Medley:

YOUNG BELLAIR
See Sir Fopling dancing.

DORIMANT
You are practising and have a mind to recover, I see.

SIR FOPLING
Prithee, Dorimant, why hast not thou a glass hung up here? A room is the dullest thing without one!

YOUNG BELLAIR
Here is company to entertain you.

SIR FOPLING
But I mean in case of being alone. In a glass a man may entertain himself—

DORIMANT
The shadow of himself, indeed.

SIR FOPLING
—Correct the errors of his motions and his dress.

MEDLEY
I find, Sir Fopling, in your solitude you remember the saying of the wise man, and study yourself.

SIR FOPLING
'Tis the best diversion in our retirements. Dorimant, thou art a pretty fellow and wearest thy clothes well, but I never saw thee have a handsome cravat. Were they made up like mine, they'd give another air to thy face. Prithee, let me send my man to dress thee but one day. By heavens, an Englishman cannot tie a ribbon!

DORIMANT
They are something clumsy-fisted.

Medley's comment is devastating; Fopling, either uncomprehending of the true significance of the rebuke ('know thyself' means 'recognise and strive to correct your faults') or too committed to making an impression to be able to afford acknowledging it, finds fault with Dorimant's cravat. Dorimant, still in his gown (having just risen from bed with Bellinda) has had more urgent preoccupations, as the audience well knows; still, Dorimant's rejoinder has a surface tone of acquiescence beneath which a sharp irony bites; for Fopling *himself* is an

Englishman, and his efforts at wit and an elegant manner *are* clumsy, as Dorimant implies. The version of the Narcissus myth offered in this diptych of the two men of mode gives no cause for reassurance to anyone. Dorimant's dignity in manner implies a right to respect; he affects an effortless superiority, the achievement of aristocratic courtesy; yet his conduct in the play denies him any such right. His education and intelligence are real — he is more fully aware, more controlled, and more able to impose authority than anyone else in the play, yet he has no more than the air of a man of genuine integrity, since he lives an indolent and useless existence without the courage or commitment apparent in Molière's Don Juan or the real Earl of Rochester. Thus Dorimant's absorption of French manners is, as Sir Fopling asserts, in its own way an achievement; but it is no more than a matter of style, a luxury import. Unlike the real Rochester, Dorimant does not write poems but recites other people's (and remarkably feeble poems they are too). As Dennis justly notes, '*Dorimont* is a young Courtier, haughty, vain and prone to Anger, amorous, false, and inconstant. He debauches *Loveit*, and betrays her; loves *Belinda*, and as soon as he enjoys her is false to her'.

Elsewhere in *The Man of Mode*, Bellair and Harriet give a witty exhibition of 'professional acting' as accepted on stage and hence in the beau monde at the time:

YOUNG BELLAIR
    Now for a look and gestures that may persuade 'em I am saying all the passionate things imaginable.
HARRIET
    Your head a little more on one side. Ease yourself on your left leg and play with your right hand.
YOUNG BELLAIR
    Thus, is it not?
HARRIET
    Now set your right leg firm on the ground, adjust your belt, then look about you.
YOUNG BELLAIR.
    A little exercising will make me perfect.
HARRIET
    Smile, and turn to me again very sparkish.
YOUNG BELLAIR
    Will you take your turn and be instructed?
HARRIET
    With all my heart.
YOUNG BELLAIR
    At one motion play your fan, roll your eyes, and then settle a kind look upon me.   (III.i, 130–42)

Since Harriet and Young Bellair can imitate fashionable manner so accurately and so objectively, their detachment invites favourable contrast with Sir Fopling, whose whole life is no more than an unconvincingly performed role. Young Bellair and Harriet understand that the ideal is something very different: it is to have a manner so absorbed, so completely possessed as part of oneself as to seem effortless in its grace—like a dancer's, a horseman's or a fencer's, only more complexly expressive of moral quality. Since both of them are very young still, their imperfections may be pardoned, as Sir Fopling's may not. The play shows Harriet in the process of moving across the threshold into full adulthood, and because she has fallen in love with Dorimant we have to make a judgement of her at the very end of the play, acknowledging that her choice of unconventionality requires courage, though it is shown to be to an extent an expression of reckless competitiveness, with Dorimant and with her female rivals. Dorimant's affair with Bellinda is still unknown to Harriet, and may not be over; Dorimant tells Mrs Loveit he is marrying to repair his ruined estate, and it is certain that Harriet is rich. These unstable elements are stressed in the play's conclusion, which is thus equivocal; Etherege's resistance to the reconciling spirit implicit in the normal comic plot, where such threads are tied in to a resolution, points to his final determination to aim at a kind of honesty close to modern existentialism, and certainly sympathetic to the spirit of Rochester's lyric and satiric poetry.

Rochester the satirist is to be recognised in the sudden sadistic outburst of Dorimant when he wishes to punish Mrs Loveit, 'pluck off this mask and show the passion that lies panting under'. This somewhat unstable and impure impulse is the general subject of *The Plain Dealer*, which provides an extended panorama of contemporary hypocrisy and corruption in the Third Act, set in Westminster Hall, with its bustle of typical lawyers, unhappy clients, and city people—an alderman, an officer of the Treasury, someone who owes Novel a hundred pounds—all put in the shade by the memorable central image announced in the stage direction

> Enter WIDOW BLACKACRE *in the midle of half a dozen lawyers, whispered to by a fellow in black;* JERRY BLACKACRE *following the crowd* [*which includes* SERJEANT PLODDON, QUAINT, BLUNDER, *and* PETULANT]

The contrast between this episode, this image of the city altogether, and the more earthy, inclusive scene of Jonson's *Bartholmew Fair* (1614) is probably a fair indication of the alteration in atmosphere—and in the scope of dramatic comedy—from the early to the late seventeenth century in London.

Manly is conceived according to the Jonsonian 'humours' recipe, as a blunt man; as the New Mermaid editor of the play, James L. Smith notes, Wycherley's originality is in placing such a character at the centre of the play, so focussing in its love intrigue the stress of idealism united with misanthropic impulses, of hatred of the world and commitment to marriage. The play's conclusion, in which Fidelia rewards Manly with herself and her fortune, leaves every spectator uneasy; Wycherley's use of the components of the comic tradition shows this was deliberate.

In Act III of *The Plain Dealer* Wycherley offers much visual experience to an audience, and his handling of the various small groups of characters obviously shows his indebtedness to Jonson's example, especially in *Bartholmew Fair*. The scenery flats probably depicted Westminster Hall, and perhaps a three-dimensional bookseller's shop, table or booth was used; in front of this scenery the types whom Wycherley propels on and off stage—the sailors, the fine gentlemen, the gowned lawyers, citizens, aldermen, Jerry laden with trinkets (like Jonson's idiotic Cokes), the sharp bookseller's boy, not to mention Widow Blackacre—this gallery of Londoners anticipates the satiric London scenes of Hogarth.

In Wycherley it is the plot-action that imposes critical meanings on the bustle of people entering, leaving, or just sauntering about the stage. Emphasis is on fact, on the collision of differing selfish interests, on the common appetites masquerading in various guises, yet all so modern and familiar. Comedy's decorum at this time deliberately insisted on a more restrained artifice than the one actually practised by Ben Jonson. Visual interest for the audience at Restoration Comedy, by the account of such witnesses as Colley Cibber, was overwhelmingly concentrated on the persons on stage: bodily gesture and movement, facial expression, the texture, cut and colour of costume which closely corresponded with what the audience themselves wore. The few props were unobtrusive and routine.

The restricted visual resources of such staging mean, of course, that dramatists make their points through subtler distinctions and emphases, and dialogue acquires much greater importance, and registers increasingly complex psychological action. Such a development of seventeenth century drama towards naturalism threatens to suppress the essential ritual action without which theatre ceases to be art, and so to deny an audience a shaped, absorbing, imaginatively transforming experience. Restoration Comedy's repeated use of the same group of character types, in a restricted grammar of motives and intrigue plots, does in fact produce a distinct and new myth. It is significant that the later plays make an audience conscious of the conventional outline, and often play variations on the anticipated course of action; the dramatists, that is to say, will not sacrifice the deep ritual structure implicit in the dramatic myth, on the contrary they realise instinctively that it is essential, and are content to indicate obliquely, marginally, and through minor adjustments of style and characterisation, that they are writing for new generations and altered political circumstances.

Vanbrugh is ready to adopt the Restoration Comedy myth as a basis for his comedy *The Provoked Wife,* and it is only because he can rely on an audience's familiarity with it that he can manipulate their expectations, provoke them by challenging stock responses, and place the myth in a critical perspective by his own new treatment, which consists in giving an edge of caricature—that is, an injection of destabilising energy, altered and accelerated pace—and this reinvigoration, or, to look at it another way, this distortion, begins in his decision to make the central action concern not the wooing of a young pair of lovers but a miserably married older couple. They have a formidable adult candour, all the more painful for its uninhibited absoluteness:

LADY BRUTE
  What reason have I given you to use me as you do of late? It once was
  otherwise; you married me for love.
SIR JOHN BRUTE
  And you me for money; so you have your reward, and I have mine.

Lady Brute is determined to face truths, among which is her conscientious inability to ignore her marriage vows; as Sir John puts it, 'I believe my wife's religion will keep her honest'. Himself despairing, he abandons himself to the humiliating squalor of the drunken company of Lord Rake and Colonel Bully, from whom he imitates a tone and manner of hard brutishness which his somewhat cowardly nature cannot live up to. Vanbrugh makes a brilliant and complex episode to focus the frustration, humiliation, impulsiveness and cowardice of Sir John when the drunken trio encounter a tailor in Covent Garden and rob him of his parcel, which turns out to contain the clergyman's gown. Sir John puts on the gown of the hated institution which dispenses marriage, and when he encounters the Watch he strikes the Constable who promptly knocks him down and arrests him. Sir John thus expresses his rage at the

Law in characteristic style: he breaks through all inhibition, but at the cost of considerable humiliation. Returning home after a hilarious scene of farce before the Justice, and another when he encounters his wife and another lady masked, takes them for a pair of whores, and almost discovers their indiscretion, at last the drunken, beaten, sexually disappointed and exhausted Sir John blunders into the drawing room, vacated just in the nick of time by his wife's lover. He kisses and tries to embrace his wife; there is much spite in this:

> SIR JOHN
> I see it goes damnably against your stomach—and therefore—kiss me again.

His drunkenness produces sharp emotional clarity, and Vanbrugh is mercilessly accurate about the physicality of the man:

> So; now, you being as dirty and nasty as myself, we may go pig together. But first I must have a cup of your cold tea, wife.

He goes to get it from the closet, discovers the gallants hiding there, and is convinced he has been cuckolded. He is too drunk, however, to fight; the gallants escape; Sir John turns on his wife, candid in confession of cowardice, impotence, and quite soon, extraordinarily and yet simply, he exhausts his capacity to react at all and just falls asleep. The surprise for an audience is complete; yet instead of proving a lame conclusion the scene invites comparison with Shakespeare for its revelation of character and its true insight into squalid human nature:

> Wear a sword, sir? And what of all that, sir?—He comes to my house, eats my meat, lies with my wife, dishonours my family, gets a bastard to inherit my estate, and when I ask a civil account of all this—Sir, says he, I wear a sword! Wear a sword, sir? Yes sir, says he, I wear a sword! It may be a good answer at cross purposes, but 'tis a damned one to a man in my whimsical circumstance.—Sir, says he, I wear a sword! (*to* LADY BRUTE) And what do you wear now, ha? Tell me. (*Sitting down in a great chair*) What! You are modest, and can't? Why then, I'll tell you, you slut you. You wear—an impudent lewd face—a damned designing heart—and a tail—and a tail full of —(*He falls asleep, snoring*)   (V.ii, 93–104)

This is revolutionary, but it uses conventions to rediscover riot, the ancient comic mode, masks and all—and Sir John is still wearing the clergyman's gown! When asked to remove this offence to the church by revising the play, Vanbrugh made the gown a woman's, Lady Brute's; this makes the episode in its way even more offensive.

Farquhar's comedy *The Recruiting Officer* was written ten

years later, in the reign of Queen Anne and after that landmark in British history, the Battle of Blenheim. As if to mark his sense of the moment, Farquhar begins the play with a drummer beating 'The Grenadier March', Sergeant Kite in uniform, and a 'mob' of Shropshire rustics, with russet names like Appletree and Pearmain, representing the nation's resources; so routinely ridiculed in the theatre, so formidably successful on the battlefield. Certainly Farquhar's presentation of the Shropshire rustics is neither sentimental nor idealising; for if the mode is comic, yet we recognise the guiding influence of Shakespeare in the *King Henry IV* plays in the dramatic technique. Farquhar is always praised for the matter-of-fact tone and texture of these scenes, which derive from his balanced presentation of a range of attitudes embodied in well-contrasted characters. The recruiting scenes in Shakespeare's *King Henry IV* involved the bringing together of simpletons, cunning and unscrupulous predators, doddering justices, upright yeomen; a kaleidoscope of domestic, local and national interests by no means harmoniously related, in which bribery, corruption and naive idealism confuse the scene, the dark clouds of terror in the shape of civil war, mutilation and death hang in the background, while the recruiting officer, Falstaff, at once casual and fiercely purposeful, presents a bluff appearance of warm-hearted patriotic assurance and encourages the low comedy of the rustics along its well-worn path. It is an ancient and familiar routine with its own folk-lore, as is military service itself, and one in which bitterness long since became as ingrained as humour. Recruiting, like patriotism, is perhaps an instance of the proverbial tendency of hope to triumph over experience, and precisely out of this absolute ambivalence Farquhar makes his play.

It is instructive to pause for a moment to compare the opening of *The Recruiting Officer* with the opening of *The Man of Mode*. Dorimant's social rank entitles him to the deference of orange-women, shoemakers, and the like, but mutual interests bring them together, and both sides manipulate and exploit one another. The lower social orders in Etherege's play are clearly depicted, their social and economic circumstances make them too opportunist to bother with political convictions. There is no sense at all of common humanity as a shared value; the metropolitan setting and mood excludes it. In Shrewsbury, almost a symbol in Restoration Comedy for provincial life, a warmer and less calculating mode of human relationship is apparent, but its ham-fisted and somewhat oppressive nature always looks ridiculous from a London perspective. In *The Way of the World* Sir Wilful Witwoud, come fresh from Shropshire, is

simply delighted to meet his half-brother, the London society
fop Witwoud:

WILFUL

Hum! What, sure 'tis not—yea, by'r Lady, but 'tis—'sheart I know not
whether 'tis or no—yea but 'tis, by the Wrekin! Brother Anthony! What
Tony i'faith! What, dost thou not know me? By'r Lady nor I thee, thou art so
becravated and beperiwigged! 'Sheart, why dost thou not speak? Art thou
o'erjoyed?

WITWOUD

Odso brother, is it you? Your servant, brother.

WILFUL

Your servant! Why, yours sir. Your servant again— 'sheart, and your friend
and servant to that—and a—(puff) and a flapdragon for your service, sir! And
a hare's foot, and a hare's scut for your service sir, an you be so cold and so
courtly!

                                                              (III. i, 447–58)

Farquhar had actually served as a recruiting officer in the
midlands and in Shrewsbury, but from a longer perspective it
appears that his setting *The Recruiting Officer* in Shrewsbury is a
gesture in the spirit of Vanbrugh—it is an inversion of the
expected, by means of which a refreshing and salutary truth is
asserted. The truthful, and therefore complex and somewhat
ambivalent characterisation of Sergeant Kite, is a feature which
attracted the modern German playwright Bertolt Brecht, who
made an adaptation of the play. Brecht is strongly anti-war;
Farquhar records accurately and factually a balance of contradictory attitudes, allowing some suprisingly adventurous
switches of mood, as when the Articles of War are read out in the
comic atmosphere of the Court-room scene (V.v, 161); this
feature of Farquhar's style is signalled in the opening scene,
when the rustic takes the Grenadier cap, goes to put it on and
exclaims 'It smells woundily of sweat and brimstone', a touch
which will be reinforced a few moments later when a travel-
stained Captain Plume arrives in his riding cloak, fresh from the
banks of the Danube and the field of Blenheim.

    Shrewsbury and Shropshire are fertile pastures to fatten
possible recruits; the plays of Farquhar's predecessors show little
interest in connecting consumer goods to their producers, being
all too content, like the sophisticated Gwendolen of *The Importance of Being Earnest*, to retort 'I am glad to say that I have never
seen a spade'. As the New Mermaid editor of *The Recruiting
Officer*, John Ross, notes, the recruits Plume gives Brazen can all
too plausibly be visualised being marched to fight at Ramillies in
May 1706, or to join Farquhar's own unit which 'would cross to
Flanders in 1708 and take part the following year in "the very
murdering battle" of Malplaquet'.

In this wide-awake awareness of realities of the time Farquhar tests the strength and validity of a comic form concerned with ideal personal fulfilment in married love. Orchards of fruit trees, bonny bastard babies, good ale, open-hearted if spiritually limited affection, support a community which cannot be separated from its bleaker aspects: rigid class and economic divisions, harsh laws, harsh instincts. The focus on the blacksmith and the butcher in Act IV scene ii has emblematic importance: in Shrewsbury they are essential to the sustenance of life and good cheer, making farm implements and providing meat; in the Army they become agents of death and terror. It is the aim of comedy as practised by Jonson and by Shakespeare to engage truths as profound and contradictory as these.

In many ways Congreve's *Love for Love* can be seen, from this perspective, to be a summation of the strictly orthodox conventions of the genre at its most high-spirited and witty, with verbal artifice and intricacy of plotting wrought to fantastic heights. Congreve shows more sympathy with the earlier tradition, with Dryden, with the pleasures of civility and gaiety. Because of its self-conscious re-working of set patterns, *Love for Love* seems less interested in its time, the mid-sixteen-nineties, and most hospitable to the critic who admires brilliant fantasy and exact artistry. Yet, as this brief survey of the selected plays indicates, each play makes a strongly individual shape out of the available conventions, and the more closely the plays are compared, the more strong these differences will be seen to be. The playwrights have new imaginative experience to communicate, and the genre goes on proving responsive to their needs.

FURTHER READING

A. Stages, Actors, Theatre History

1 Allardyce Nicoll, *A History of English Drama, 1660–1900*, I *1660–1700* (Cambridge 1923), later revised

2 *The London Stage, 1660–1800*, ed. W. Van Lennep, E. L. Avery, A. H. Scouten, G. Winchester Stone Jnr, and C. B. Hogan (Carbondale, Illinois 1960–68)

3 John Loftis, Richard Southern, Marion Jones, and A. H. Scouten, *The Revels History of Drama in English, V: 1660–1750* (1976)

B. Earlier Critical Responses

4 Sir Richard Steele, *The Spectator*, No. 65 (15 May 1711)

5 Horace Walpole, 'Thoughts on Comedy; written in 1775 and 1776' in *The Works* (1798), vol. 2, 315–22

6 William Hazlitt, *Lectures on the English Comic Writers* (1819)

7 Charles Lamb, 'On the Artificial Comedy of the Last Age' in *The Essays of Elia* (1821)

8 T. B. Macaulay, 'The Dramatic Works of Wycherley, Congreve, Vanbrugh and Farquhar', *Edinburgh Review* LXXII, 1841

C. Modern Criticism on General Issues

9 Bonamy Dobrée, *Restoration Comedy: 1660–1720* (London 1924)

10 Thomas H. Fujimura, *The Restoration Comedy of Wit* (Princeton 1952)

11 Harriet Hawkins, *Likenesses of Truth in Elizabethan and Restoration Comedy* (Oxford 1972)

12 Norman N. Holland, *The First Modern Comedies, the Significance of Etherege, Wycherly, and Congreve* (Bloomingdale, Indiana 1959)

13 Peter Holland, *The Ornament of Action: text and performance in Restoration Comedy* (Cambridge 1979)

14 Robert D. Hume, *The Development of English Drama in the late Seventeenth Century* (Oxford 1976)

15 Robert D. Hume, 'The Myth of the Rake in "Restoration" Comedy', *Studies in the Literary Imagination*, vol. 10 (1977), 25–55

16 L. C. Knights, 'Restoration Comedy: The Reality and the

Myth', *Explorations*, (London 1946)

17 Joseph Krutch, *Comedy and Conscience after the Restoration* (New York 1924)

18 Kathleen Lynch, *The Social Mode of Restoration Comedy*, University of Michigan Publications, *Language and Literature*, vol. 3 (New York and London 1926)

19 Clifford Leech, 'Restoration Comedy: The Earlier Phase', *Essays in Criticism*, vol. 1 (1951), 165–84

20 John Harrington Smith, *The Gay Couple in Restoration Comedy*, (Cambridge, Mass. 1948)

21 Virgina Woolf, 'Congreve's Comedies', in *The Moment* (1947)

22 John Russell Brown and Bernard Harris, ed., *Restoration Theatre, Stratford-upon-Avon Studies 6* (London 1965)

23 Earl Miner, ed., *Restoration Dramatists* (Englewood Cliffs, N.J. 1966)

D. Individual Dramatists

Congreve

24 John C. Hodges, *William Congreve: Letters and Documents* (London 1964)

25 Clifford Leech, 'Congreve and the Century's End', *PQ* (1962)

26 John Loftis, *Comedy and Society from Congreve to Fielding* (Stanford, California 1959)

27 Brian Morris, ed., *William Congreve: Mermaid Critical Commentaries* (London 1971)

28 Maximillian Novak, *William Congreve* (New York 1971)

See also 1, 3, 5, 6, 7, 8, 9, 10, 11, 12, 13, 16, 20, 21, 22.

Etherege

Ronald Berman, 'The Comic Passions of *The Man of Mode*', *Studies in English Literature, 1500–1900*, vol. 10 (1970), 459–68

Paul C. Davies, 'The State of Nature and the State of War: A Reconsideration of *The Man of Mode*', *University of Toronto Quarterly*, vol. 39 (1969), 53–62

John Dennis, *A Defense of Sir Fopling Flutter* (1722), in *The Critical Works of John Dennis*, ed. E. N. Hooker, 2 vols. (Baltimore 1939–43)

Maximillian Novak, 'Margery Pinchwife's "London Disease": Restoration Comedy and the Libertine Offensive of the 1670's', *Studies in the Literary Imagination*, vol. 10 (1977), 1–25

Jocelyn Powell, 'George Etherege and the Form of a Comedy', *Restoration Theatre, Stratford-upon-Avon Studies 6,* (London 1965)

Dale Underwood, *Etherege and the Seventeenth-Century Comedy of Manners* (New Haven, Conn. 1957)

See also 1, 3, 7, 9, 11, 12, 13, 15, 20.

Farquhar

Raymond A. Anselment, ed., *George Farquhar: 'The Recruiting Officer' and 'The Beaux' Stratagem'. A Casebook* (London 1977)

Willard Connely, *Young George Farquhar. The Restoration Drama at Twilight* (New York 1930)

Eugene Nelson James, *The Development of George Farquhar as a Comic Dramatist* (The Hague 1972)

Sybil Rosenfeld, 'Notes on *The Recruiting Officer*', *Theatre Notebook*, XVIII (1963–64), 47–8

Eric Rothstein, *George Farquhar* (New York 1967)

Charles Stonehill, ed., *The Complete Works of George Farquhar*, 2 vols. (Bloomsbury 1930)

Albert Wertheim, 'Bertolt Brecht and George Farquhar's *The Recruiting Officer*', *Comparative Drama*, VII (1973), 179–90

See also 3, 14, 18, 25, 26.

Vanbrugh

Paul Mueschke and Jeannette Fleisher, 'A re-evaluation of Vanbrugh', *PMLA*, XLIX (1934), 848–89

Bernard Harris, *Sir John Vanbrugh,* Writers and their Work, No. 197 (1967)

See also 3, 8, 9, 14, 22, 25, 26.

Wycherley

Ronald Berman, 'The Ethic of *The Country Wife*', *Texas Studies in Literature and Language*, IX (1967), 47–55

A. M. Friedson, 'Wycherley and Molière: satirical point of view in *The Plain Dealer*', *Modern Philology*, LXIV (1967), 189–97

Charles Perromat, *William Wycherley, Sa Vie—Son Oeuvre* (Paris 1921)

Ann Righter, 'William Wycherley', available both in *Restoration Theatre,* ed. John Russell Brown and Bernard Harris (London 1965) and *Restoration Dramatists,* ed. Earl Miner

Katharine M. Rogers, *William Wycherley* (New York 1972)

Rose. A. Zimbardo, *Wycherley's Drama. A link in the development of English satire* (New Haven and London 1965)
See also, 1, 3, 7, 8, 9, 10, 12, 13, 15, 16, 19, 20.

The Man of Mode

SIR GEORGE ETHEREGE

Edited by
JOHN BARNARD

ABBREVIATIONS

B   *The Dramatic Works of Sir George Etherege*, ed. H. F. B. Brett-Smith (Oxford, 1927).

CA   *The Man of Mode*, ed. W. B. Carnochan, Regents Restoration Drama Series (Lincoln, Neb., London, 1966, 1967).

CO   *The Man of Mode*, ed. John Conaghan, Fountainwell Drama Series (Edinburgh, 1973).

Q1   *The Man of Mode* (1676). Quarto.

Q2   *The Man of Mode* (1684). Quarto.

Q3   *The Man of Mode* (1693). Quarto.

Thorpe *The Poems of Sir George Etherege*, ed. James Thorpe (Princeton, N.J., 1963).

V   *The Works of Sir George Etherege*, ed. A. W. Verity (1888).

W   *The Works of Sir George Etherege* (1704). Octavo.

THE

Man of Mode,

OR,

Sʳ Fopling Flutter.

A

COMEDY.

Acted at the *Duke's Theatre*.

By *George Etherege* Esq;.

LICENSED,

June 3.
1676.

Roger L'Eſtrange.

LONDON,

Printed by *J. Macock*, for *Henry Herringman*, at the Sign of
the *Blew Anchor* in the Lower Walk of the
New Exchange, 1 6 7 6.

TO HER ROYAL HIGHNESS
THE DUCHESS

MADAM,

Poets, however they may be modest otherwise, have always too good an opinion of what they write. The world, when it sees this play dedicated to your Royal Highness, will conclude I have more than my share of that vanity. But I hope the honour I have of belonging to you will excuse my presumption. 'Tis the first thing I have produced in your service, and my duty obliges me to what my choice durst not else have aspired.

I am very sensible, Madam, how much it is beholding to your indulgence for the success it had in the acting, and your protection will be no less fortunate to it in the printing; for all are so ambitious of making their court to you, that none can be severe to what you are pleased to favour.

This universal submission and respect is due to the greatness of your rank and birth; but you have other illustrious qualities which are much more engaging. Those would but dazzle, did not these really charm the eyes and understandings of all who have the happiness to approach you.

Authors on these occasions are never wanting to publish a particular of their patron's virtues and perfections; but your Royal Highness's are so eminently known that, did I follow their examples, I should but paint those wonders here of which everyone already has the idea in his mind. Besides, I do not think it proper to aim at that in prose which is so glorious a subject for verse, in which

---

9 *sensible* aware
9 *beholding* Q1 (beholden W)

Her ... Duchess Mary Beatrice of Modena (1658–1718), became Duchess of York in 1673. On her husband's accession as James II she became Queen.
7 *service ... duty* this is the only evidence that Etherege served the Duchess in some capacity at this date. Gildon reported that she held the dramatist 'in particular esteem'. In 1682 her husband gave Etherege a pension of £100 and, as King, appointed him envoy to the Diet at Ratisbon in 1685. That appointment was due to the good offices of Lord Sunderland rather than the Queen as Gildon claimed (*The Letterbook of Sir George Etherege*, ed. Sybil Rosenfeld (1928), pp. 15–16). What form the Duchess's 'indulgence' (l.10) took in helping the comedy's success on the stage is not known.

4

hereafter if I show more zeal than skill, it will not grieve me much,   25
since I less passionately desire to be esteemed a poet than to be
thought,
       Madam,
          Your Royal Highness's
             most humble, most obedient,   30
              and most faithful servant,

                        GEORGE ETHEREGE

PROLOGUE

By Sir Car Scroope, Baronet

Like dancers on the ropes poor poets fare:
Most perish young, the rest in danger are.
This, one would think, should make our authors wary,
But, gamester-like, the giddy fools miscarry;
A lucky hand or two so tempts 'em on,   5
They cannot leave off play till they're undone.
With modest fears a Muse does first begin,
Like a young wench newly enticed to sin;
But tickled once with praise, by her good will,
The wanton fool would never more lie still.   10
'Tis an old mistress you'll meet here tonight,
Whose charms you once looked on with delight.
But now, of late, such dirty drabs have known ye,
A Muse o'the better sort's ashamed to own ye.
Nature well-drawn and wit must now give place   15
To gaudy nonsense and to dull grimace;
Nor is it strange that you should like so much
That kind of wit, for most of yours is such.
But I'm afraid that while to France we go,
To bring you home fine dresses, dance, and show, ⎫   20
The stage, like you, will but more foppish grow. ⎬
Of foreign wares why should we fetch the scum, ⎭
When we can be so richly served at home?
For, heav'n be thanked, 'tis not so wise an age
But your own follies may supply the stage.   25
Though often ploughed, there's no great fear the soil
Should barren grow by the too-frequent toil,
While at your doors are to be daily found
Such loads of dunghill to manure the ground.
'Tis by your follies that we players thrive,   30
As the physicians by diseases live;
And as each year some new distemper reigns,

9 *will* puns on the name, Will
13 *drab* slatternly woman or prostitute
14 *ye* Q2–3, V, CA (you Q1)

Sir Car Scroope wit, courtier, and poet (1649–80). He wrote Dorimant's song in
V.ii.

DRAMATIS PERSONAE

MR DORIMANT
MR MEDLEY [*his friend*]
OLD BELLAIR
YOUNG BELLAIR [*his son, in love with Emilia*] } *Gentlemen*
SIR FOPLING FLUTTER   5
LADY TOWNLEY [*sister of Old Bellair*]
EMILIA
MRS LOVEIT [*in love with Dorimant*]
BELLINDA [*in love with Dorimant*] } *Gentlewomen*
LADY WOODVILL, *and*   10
HARRIET, *her daughter*
PERT
and } *Waiting women*
BUSY
A SHOEMAKER   15
AN ORANGE-WOMAN
FOUR SLOVENLY BULLIES
TWO CHAIRMEN
MR SMIRK, *a parson*
HANDY, *a valet de chambre*   20
PAGES, FOOTMEN, *etc.*

---

17 FOUR ed. (*Three* Q1)

17 FOUR ... BULLIES see notes to III.iii, 201 s.d.
20 *valet de chambre* see note to IV.ii, 98

THE MAN OF MODE,
or,
Sir Fopling Flutter
a Comedy

Act I

A dressing room. A table covered with a toilet; clothes laid ready.

Enter DORIMANT *in his gown and slippers, with a note in his hand made up, repeating verses*

DORIMANT

> 'Now, for some ages, had the pride of Spain
> Made the sun shine on half the world in vain'.

Then looking on the note

'For Mrs Loveit'. What a dull, insipid thing is a billet doux written in cold blood after the heat of the business is over! It is a tax upon good nature which I have here been labouring to pay, and have 5 done it, but with as much regret as ever fanatic paid the Royal Aid or church duties. 'Twill have the same fate, I know, that all my notes to her have had of late—'twill not be thought kind enough. Faith, women are i' the right when they jealously examine our

---

1 s.d. *made up* normally means sealed up, but see I, 173 ff.
3 *'For Mrs Loveit'* CA (Q1, etc., centre above Dorimant's speech without quotation marks)

---

1 s.d. *toilet* cloth cover for a dressing-table, of rich material and workmanship. *OED* cites *London Gazette* (1683), No. 1811/4: 'Stolen the 20th Instant, a Toilet of blew Velvet, with a Gold and Silver Fringe'.
1–2 *Now . . . vain* opening couplet of Waller's 'Of a War with Spain, and a Fight at Sea' (*Poems*, ed. G. Thorn Drury (1901), vol. 2, 23). John Dennis reported that contemporaries, in identifying Rochester with Dorimant, instanced his 'repeating, on every Occasion, the Verses of *Waller*, for whom that noble Lord had a very particular Esteem' (*Defence of Sir Fopling Flutter* (1722) in *Critical Works*, ed. E. N. Hooker (Baltimore, Md., 1939–42), vol. 2, 248).
6 *fanatic* in the latter part of the seventeenth century a hostile epithet applied to Nonconformists. *OED* cites John Gaule (1657), 'Enthusiasts, Anabaptists, Fanaticks, and Familists'. Nonconformists opposed both the Crown and the established Church.
6–7 *Royal Aid . . . church duties* 'Royal Aid' was an extraordinary subsidy or tax made by Parliament for the King. Church duties were levied locally for the services of the parish church.

letters, for in them we always first discover our decay of 10
passion.—Hey! Who waits?

Enter HANDY

HANDY
  Sir—
DORIMANT
  Call a footman.
HANDY
  None of 'em are come yet.
DORIMANT
  Dogs! Will they ever lie snoring abed till noon?   15
HANDY
  'Tis all one, sir: if they're up, you indulge 'em so, they're ever
  poaching after whores all the morning.
DORIMANT
  Take notice henceforward who's wanting in his duty—the next
  clap he gets, he shall rot for an example. What vermin are those
  chattering without?   20
HANDY
  Foggy Nan, the orange-woman, and swearing Tom, the
  shoemaker.
DORIMANT
  Go, call in that overgrown jade with the flasket of guts before
  her. Fruit is refreshing in a morning.

                                              Exit HANDY

            'It is not that I love you less,   25
              Than when before your feet I lay—'

            Enter ORANGE-WOMAN [*and* HANDY]

  How now, double-tripe, what news do you bring?
ORANGE-WOMAN
  News! Here's the best fruit has come to town t' year. Gad, I was
  up before four o'clock this morning and bought all the choice i'
  the market.   30

---

21 *Foggy* unwholesomely bloated, puffy
23 *flasket* 'a long shallow basket' (Johnson), or, possibly, a small flask

---

17 *poaching after* taking game illegally (which carries on the hunting imagery), but
   possibly containing a sexual pun on the meaning 'poke' (from OF *pocher*, to
   thrust or dig out with the fingers).
25–6 *It . . . lay* Waller, 'The Self-Banished', ll. 1–2 (*Poems*, ed. G. Thorn Drury
   (1901), vol. 1, 101).

DORIMANT
The nasty refuse of your shop.

ORANGE-WOMAN
You need not make mouths at it. I assure you, 'tis all culled ware.

DORIMANT
The citizens buy better on a holiday in their walk to Tot'nam.

ORANGE-WOMAN
Good or bad, 'tis all one; I never knew you commend anything.
Lord, would the ladies had heard you talk of 'em as I have done.   35
Here—

Sets down the fruit

Bid your man give me an angel.

DORIMANT [*to* HANDY]
Give the bawd her fruit again.

ORANGE-WOMAN
Well, on my conscience, there never was the like of you—God's
my life, I had almost forgot to tell you, there is a young gentle-   40
woman, lately come to town with her mother, that is so taken
with you.

DORIMANT
Is she handsome?

ORANGE-WOMAN
Nay, gad, there are few finer women, I tell you but so, and a
hugeous fortune, they say. Here, eat this peach, it comes from   45
the stone. 'Tis better than any Newington you've tasted.

DORIMANT
This fine woman, I'll lay my life (*taking the peach*), is some
awkward, ill-fashioned country toad, who, not having above
four dozen of black hairs on her head, has adorned her baldness

33 *citizens ... Tot'nam* Tottenham then lay some 4 miles north of the suburbs
beginning to grow outside the City, and so was convenient for tradespeople's
outings. Shadwell distinguishes the different classes of Londoner in *The Vir-
tuoso* (1676)—'your Glass-Coach will to *Hide-Park* for Air. The Suburb-fools
trudge to *Lamb's-Conduit* or *Totnam*; your sprucer sort of Citizens gallop to
Epsom; your Mechanick gross Fellows, shewing much conjugal affection, strut
before their Wives, each with a Child in his Arms, to *Islington*, or *Hogsdon*'
(*Complete Works*, ed. M. Summers (1927), vol. 3, 164).

37 *angel* gold coin, originally called angel-noble, with the archangel Michael and
the dragon as its device. Its value varied from 6*s*. 8*d*. to 10*s*.

38 *bawd* fruit-women were well-known go-betweens. Conaghan cites Dryden's
The Assignation (1673), 'Why, if you will have it, you are little better than a
procuress: you carry messages betwixt party and party, and, in one word Sir,
she's as arrant a Fruit-woman as any is about *Rome*' (*Dramatic Works*, ed. M.
Summers (1931–32), vol. 3, 303).

45–6 *peach ... Newington* presumably a variety of peach from Newington, Kent.
The flesh of a freestone (as opposed to clingstone) separates from the stone.

with a large white fruz, that she may look sparkishly in the   50
forefront of the King's box at an old play.

ORANGE-WOMAN
Gad, you'd change your note quickly if you did but see her!

DORIMANT
How came she to know me?

ORANGE-WOMAN
She saw you yesterday at the Change. She told me you came and
fooled with the woman at the next shop.   55

DORIMANT
I remember, there was a mask observed me, indeed. Fooled, did
she say?

ORANGE-WOMAN
Ay; I vow she told me twenty things you said too, and acted with
her head and with her body so like you—

Enter MEDLEY

MEDLEY
Dorimant, my life, my joy, my darling sin! How dost thou?   60
[*Embraces him*]

ORANGE-WOMAN
Lord, what a filthy trick these men have got of kissing one
another!   *She spits*

58–9 *with her head* W, V, B, CA (with head Q1)
59 *like* Q1 (W, V omit)

50 *fruz* clearly means a wig with short curled hair. Not recorded in *OED* which
gives 'fruz' as meaning 'A collection of short and small branches, producing a
frizzy appearance'. However, there are several contemporary examples of the
word as a verb meaning 'to frizz out the hair'. Thackeray uses 'fuzz-wig' (1848).

50 *sparkishly* a rare adverb: *OED* cites four examples, of which this is the earliest.
When used of a woman, 'spark' meant one of great beauty, elegance, or wit.
Applied to a man it is usually depreciative, and meant a young man of elegant or
foppish character.

54 *Change* the New Exchange, an arcade on the south side of the Strand, with two
long double galleries of shops, one above the other. Etherege had used it as a
setting in *She Wou'd if She Cou'd*, III.i. Fashionable London bought ribbons,
knots, and essences there; consequently lodgings in the Strand over against the
Exchange were popular with country visitors (see Bellinda's remarks at V.i,
48–51). Brett-Smith points out that Herringman, Etherege's publisher, had
his shop there.

61–2 *a filthy trick . . . another* (compare with IV.i, 184). Shadwell's *Sullen Lovers*
(1668) gives a further example of this exaggerated custom when Woodcock is
described as 'A Familiar loving Coxcombe, that embraces and kisses all men
. . .'

MEDLEY

Why do you suffer this cartload of scandal to come near you and
make your neighbours think you so improvident to need a bawd?

ORANGE-WOMAN [to DORIMANT]

Good, now we shall have it! You did but want him to help you.   65
Come, pay me for my fruit.

MEDLEY

Make us thankful for it, huswife. Bawds are as much out of
fashion as gentlemen-ushers: none but old formal ladies use the
one, and none but foppish old stagers employ the other. Go, you
are an insignificant brandy bottle.   70

DORIMANT

Nay, there you wrong her. Three quarts of canary is her business.

ORANGE-WOMAN

What you please, gentlemen.

DORIMANT

To him! Give him as good as he brings.

ORANGE-WOMAN

Hang him, there is not such another heathen in the town again,   75
except it be the shoemaker without.

MEDLEY

I shall see you hold up your hand at the bar next sessions for
murder, huswife. That shoemaker can take his oath you are in
fee with the doctors to sell green fruit to the gentry, that the
crudities may breed diseases.   80

ORANGE-WOMAN

Pray give me my money.

DORIMANT

Not a penny! When you bring the gentlewoman hither you spoke
of, you shall be paid.

ORANGE-WOMAN

The gentlewoman! The gentlewoman may be as honest as your
sisters, for aught as I know. Pray pay me, Mr Dorimant, and do   85

65 *Good ... You* V, CA (Good now, we shall have it, you Q1; Good now, we shall
   have it; you Q3; Good, now we shall have it, you W)
65 *want* need
69 *stagers* Q1 (strangers W, V) veterans, old hands
80 *crudities* undigested (or indigestible) matter in the stomach
84 *honest* honourable, chaste   85 *sisters* Q1 (sister W, V)

---

71 *canary* a light sweet wine from the Canary Islands. Visitors to the bawdy houses
   of the day were usually put to the expense of a few bottles of wine. Possibly
   there is also a pun on the abbreviation of thieves' slang, 'canary-bird'—'a Rogue
   or Whore taken, and clapp'd into the Cage or Round-house' (*A New Canting
   Dictionary* (1725)).

not abuse me so. I have an honester way of living—you know it.

MEDLEY

Was there ever such a resty bawd?

DORIMANT

Some jade's tricks she has, but she makes amends when she's in
good humour. Come, tell me the lady's name, and Handy shall
pay you.   90

ORANGE-WOMAN

I must not, she forbid me.

DORIMANT

That's a sure sign she would have you.

MEDLEY

Where does she live?

ORANGE-WOMAN

They lodge at my house.

MEDLEY

Nay, then she's in a hopeful way.   95

ORANGE-WOMAN

Good Mr Medley, say your pleasure of me, but take heed how
you affront my house. God's my life, in a hopeful way!

DORIMANT

Prithee, peace. What kind of woman's the mother?

ORANGE-WOMAN

A goodly, grave gentlewoman. Lord, how she talks against the
wild young men o' the town! As for your part, she thinks you an   100
arrant devil: should she see you, on my conscience she would
look if you had not a cloven foot.

DORIMANT

Does she know me?

ORANGE-WOMAN

Only by hearsay. A thousand horrid stories have been told her of
you, and she believes 'em all.   105

MEDLEY

By the character, this should be the famous Lady Woodvill and
her daughter Harriet.

ORANGE-WOMAN [aside]

The devil's in him for guessing, I think.

87 *resty* restive or indolent, sluggish
88 *jade* contemptuous name for an inferior horse, applied pejoratively to women
98 *Prithee* I pray thee

---

100 *wild* a keyword in the play. See John Barnard (ed.) *The Man of Mode* (London,
1979), pp. xxix–xxxi.
101 *arrant* (a) wandering, as in 'knight errant', hence with the sense of genuine, (b)
downright or manifest, and hence, unmitigated.

DORIMANT

Do you know 'em?

MEDLEY

Both very well. The mother's a great admirer of the forms and   110
civility of the last age.

DORIMANT

An antiquated beauty may be allowed to be out of humour at the
freedoms of the present. This is a good account of the mother.
Pray, what is the daughter?

MEDLEY

Why, first, she's an heiress, vastly rich.   115

DORIMANT

And handsome?

MEDLEY

What alteration a twelvemonth may have bred in her, I know
not, but a year ago she was the beautifullest creature I ever
saw—a fine, easy, clean shape, light brown hair in abundance,
her features regular, her complexion clear, and lively, large,   120
wanton eyes; but, above all, a mouth that has made me kiss it
a thousand times in imagination—teeth white and even, and
pretty, pouting lips, with a little moisture ever hanging on them,
that look like the Provence rose fresh on the bush, ere the   125
morning sun has quite drawn up the dew.

---

111 *civility* Q1 (civilities Q2–3)
124 *Provence* V (Province Q1; Provins CA)

110–11 *forms and civility of the last age* i.e., the manners and social decorum of the
previous generation (those of Charles I's Court). 'Forms' carries the sense of a
set method of outward behaviour according with etiquette. *OED* gives its last
example of 'forms' meaning 'manners' from 1639, but it is common in Restoration comedy, usually in a pejorative sense and with an old-fashioned flavour.
See Lady Wishfort, *The Way of the World* (1700), III.i., 'I shall never break
Decorums ... I hope Sir *Rowland* is better bred, than to put a Lady to the
necessity of breaking her Forms'.
119 *easy* a word conveying several meanings in the play. See Barnard (op. cit.), p. xxxiii.
Here (as at III.iii, 28) the sense is graceful, attractive (a meaning not recorded
in *OED*).
121 *wanton* the meaning goes beyond Carnochan's 'lively, roguish'. Medley's libertine values set the wide range of the word's senses in tension. At the primary
level, Harriet's eyes are sexually alive and playful. The context inverts the
morally condemnatory sense of lascivious, unchaste, and remembers other
meanings—free, unrestrained (poet.); capricious, giddy; reckless of decorum.
124 *Provence rose* the cabbage rose (*rosa centifolia*). 'The misnamed Provence rose
was first introduced into France by the Crusaders at Provins (Seine and
Marne)' (*Westminster Gazette*, 31 July 1905). Carnochan emends to 'Provins
rose', now used to describe *rosa gallica*.

DORIMANT
Rapture, mere rapture!

ORANGE-WOMAN
Nay, gad, he tells you true. She's a delicate creature.

DORIMANT
Has she wit?

MEDLEY
More than is usual in her sex, and as much malice. Then, she's as
wild as you would wish her, and has a demureness in her looks　130
that makes it so surprising.

DORIMANT
Flesh and blood cannot hear this and not long to know her.

MEDLEY
I wonder what makes her mother bring her up to town? An old,
doting keeper cannot be more jealous of his mistress.

ORANGE-WOMAN
She made me laugh yesterday. There was a judge came to visit　135
'em, and the old man (she told me) did so stare upon her and,
when he saluted her, smacked so heartily—who would think it of
'em?

MEDLEY
God-a-mercy, Judge!

DORIMANT
Do 'em right, the gentlemen of the long robe have not been　140
wanting by their good examples to countenance the crying sin o'
the nation.

MEDLEY
Come, on with your trappings; 'tis later than you imagine.

DORIMANT
Call in the shoemaker, Handy!

ORANGE-WOMAN
Good Mr Dorimant, pay me. Gad, I had rather give you my fruit　145
than stay to be abused by that foul-mouthed rogue. What you
gentlemen say, it matters not much, but such a dirty fellow does
one more disgrace.

DORIMANT [to HANDY]
Give her ten shillings. [To ORANGE-WOMAN] And be sure you tell
the young gentlewoman I must be acquainted with her.　　　150

126 *mere* pure, sheer
139 *Judge* Q1 (a judge V)
140 *gentlemen . . . robe* members of the legal profession

130 *wild* see note to I, 100.
139 *God-a-mercy* 'God reward you', hence used as an exclamation of thanks (here
　　ironically).

ORANGE-WOMAN
  Now do you long to be tempting this pretty creature. Well,
  heavens mend you!

MEDLEY
  Farewell, bog!   *Exeunt* ORANGE-WOMAN *and* HANDY
  Dorimant, when did you see your *pis aller*, as you call her, Mrs
  Loveit?   155

DORIMANT
  Not these two days.

MEDLEY
  And how stand affairs between you?

DORIMANT
  There has been great patching of late, much ado—we make a
  shift to hang together.

MEDLEY
  I wonder how her mighty spirit bears it?   160

DORIMANT
  Ill enough, on all conscience. I never knew so violent a creature.

MEDLEY
  She's the most passionate in her love and the most extravagant in
  her jealousy of any woman I ever heard of. What note is that?

DORIMANT
  An excuse I am going to send her for the neglect I am guilty of.

MEDLEY
  Prithee, read it.   165

DORIMANT
  No, but if you will take the pains, you may.

MEDLEY (*reads*)
  'I never was a lover of business, but now I have a just reason to
  hate it, since it has kept me these two days from seeing you. I
  intend to wait upon you in the afternoon, and in the pleasure of
  your conversation forget all I have suffered during this tedious   170
  absence'.—This business of yours, Dorimant, has been with a

---

153 *bog* bugbear (*OED*, sb. 2, cites this example)
154 *pis aller* last resource, makeshift
158 *late . . . we* V, B, CA, CO (late, much Ado we Q1; late; with much ado we Q3)

---

162 *extravagant* see Barnard (op. cit.), pp. xxxi–iii.
170 *conversation* although the word carries the more limited modern meaning, it
     includes the idea of social intimacy. Medley may be playing on a further
     meaning, sexual intercourse.

vizard at the playhouse; I have had an eye on you. If some
malicious body should betray you, this kind note would hardly
make your peace with her.

DORIMANT

I desire no better.   175

MEDLEY

Why, would her knowledge of it oblige you?

DORIMANT

Most infinitely; next to the coming to a good understanding with
a new mistress, I love a quarrel with an old one. But the devil's
in't, there has been such a calm in my affairs of late, I have not
had the pleasure of making a woman so much as break her fan, to 180
be sullen, or forswear herself, these three days.

MEDLEY

A very great misfortune! Let me see, I love mischief well enough
to forward this business myself. I'll about it presently, and
though I know the truth of what you've done, will set her
a-raving. I'll heighten it a little with invention, leave her in a fit o' 185
the mother, and be here again before you're ready.

DORIMANT

Pray, stay; you may spare yourself the labour. The business is
undertaken already by one who will manage it with as much
address and, I think, with a little more malice than you can.

MEDLEY

Who i' the devil's name can this be?   190

DORIMANT

Why, the vizard, that very vizard you saw me with.

MEDLEY

Does she love mischief so well as to betray herself to spite
another?

DORIMANT

Not so neither, Medley; I will make you comprehend the
mystery. This mask, for a farther confirmation of what I have   195
been these two days swearing to her, made me yesterday at the
playhouse make her a promise, before her face, utterly to break

---

172 *vizard* mask, hence a woman wearing a mask; often used of a masked prostitute.
      Masks were fashionable in the early Restoration period, but fell into disfavour
      because of their use by courtezans. In *She Wou'd if She Cou'd* (1668), III.iii, Mr
      Rakehell, 'a Knight of the Industry', is expected with a 'Coach full or two of
      Vizard-masks and silk Petticoates'.

186 *mother* hysteria. Compare *King Lear*, II.iv, 56–7, 'O! how this mother swells
      up toward my heart, /*Hysterica passio!* down . . .' Kenneth Muir cites Edward
      Jordan (1605): '. . . the Mother of the Suffocation of the Mother, because, most
      commonly, it takes them with choking in the throat; and it is an affect of the
      mother or wombe . . .' (New Arden).

off with Loveit; and because she tenders my reputation and
would not have me do a barbarous thing, has contrived a way to
give me a handsome occasion.   200

MEDLEY

Very good.

DORIMANT

She intends, about an hour before me this afternoon, to make
Loveit a visit; and having the privilege, by reason of a professed
friendship between 'em, to talk of her concerns—

MEDLEY

Is she a friend?   205

DORIMANT

Oh, an intimate friend!

MEDLEY

Better and better! Pray proceed.

DORIMANT

She means insensibly to insinuate a discourse of me, and artificially raise her jealousy to such a height that, transported with
the first motions of her passion, she shall fly upon me with all the   210
fury imaginable as soon as ever I enter. The quarrel being thus
happily begun, I am to play my part: confess and justify all my
roguery, swear her impertinence and ill humour makes her
intolerable, tax her with the next fop that comes into my head,
and in a huff march away, slight her, and leave her to be taken by   215
whosoever thinks it worth his time to lie down before her.

MEDLEY

This vizard is a spark, and has a genius that makes her worthy of
yourself, Dorimant.

Enter HANDY, SHOEMAKER, *and* FOOTMAN

DORIMANT [*to* FOOTMAN]

You rogue there, who sneak like a dog that has flung down a dish,
if you do not mend your waiting, I'll uncase you and turn you   220
loose to the wheel of fortune.—Handy, seal this and let him run
with it presently.

Exeunt HANDY *and* FOOTMAN [: HANDY *re-enters after a few
                                               moments*]

198 *tenders* regards, treats with tenderness
204 *'em, to ... concerns*—Q1 ('em) to ... concerns. W, V)
208–9 *artificially* artfully   217 *genius* prevailing character or spirit
220 *uncase you* strip you (of your livery)   222 *presently* immediately
222 s.d. *Exeunt ... moments*] ed. (*Exeunt ...* FOOTMAN Q1; *Exit Footman* CA)

---

222 s.d. *Exeunt ...* FOOTMAN Handy leaves with the footman to seal the note, but
    returns before l. 272. His entry is unmarked, but there is no need to emend with
    Carnochan (see above).

MEDLEY

Since you're resolved on a quarrel, why do you send her this kind
note?

DORIMANT

To keep her at home in order to the business. (*To the* 225
SHOEMAKER) How now, you drunken sot?

SHOEMAKER

'Zbud, you have no reason to talk. I have not had a bottle of sack
of yours in my belly this fortnight.

MEDLEY

The orange-woman says your neighbours take notice what a
heathen you are, and design to inform the bishop and have you 230
burned for an atheist.

SHOEMAKER

Damn her, dunghill! If her husband does not remove her, she
stinks so, the parish intend to indict him for a nuisance.

MEDLEY

I advise you like a friend, reform your life. You have brought the
envy of the world upon you by living above yourself. Whoring 235
and swearing are vices too genteel for a shoemaker.

SHOEMAKER

'Zbud, I think you men of quality will grow as unreasonable as
the women: you would engross the sins o' the nation. Poor folks
can no sooner be wicked but they're railed at by their betters.

DORIMANT

Sirrah, I'll have you stand i' the pillory for this libel. 240

SHOEMAKER

Some of you deserve it, I'm sure. There are so many of 'em that
our journeymen nowadays, instead of harmless ballads, sing
nothing but your damned lampoons.

DORIMANT

Our lampoons, you rogue?

---

225 *in order to* for the sake of (obs.)   227 *'Zbud* 'Sblood, i.e. 'God's blood'
227 *sack* a class of white wines formerly imported from the Canaries and Spain
238 *engross* monopolize, wholly absorb   242 *harmless* inoffensive

---

242-3 *harmless ballads . . . your damned lampoons* the city journeymen's traditional
    taste for popular ballads has been corrupted by the flood of scurrilous satires
    and lampoons which the Shoemaker identifies with the wits. According to the
    OED 'lampoon' first occurs in 1649. Lampoons and libels circulated widely
    through manuscript copies in Restoration London, but also found their way
    into print as well as being sometimes nailed to the victim's door. Etherege
    himself was regarded as the writer of 'airy songs and soft lampoons' (Thorpe, p.
    vi).

SHOEMAKER

Nay, good master, why should not you write your own commen-   245
taries as well as Caesar?

MEDLEY

The rascal's read, I perceive.

SHOEMAKER

You know the old proverb—ale and history.

DORIMANT

Draw on my shoes, sirrah.

SHOEMAKER

Here's a shoe—   250

DORIMANT

Sits with more wrinkles than there are in an angry bully's forehead.

SHOEMAKER

'Zbud, as smooth as your mistress's skin does upon her. So,
strike your foot in home. 'Zbud, if e'er a monsieur of 'em all make
more fashionable ware, I'll be content to have my ears whipped   255
off with my own paring knife.

MEDLEY

And served up in a ragout, instead of cockcombs, to a company
of French shoemakers for a collation.

SHOEMAKER

Hold, hold! Damn 'em caterpillars! Let 'em feed upon cab-

---

251 *bully* blustering gallant, swashbuckler
257 *ragout* highly flavoured stew
258 *collation* light repast

248 *ale and history* 'Truth is in ale as in history' (M. P. Tilley, *A Dictionary of
   Proverbs in England in the Sixteenth and Seventeenth Centuries* (1950), T578).
   But G. L. Apperson, *English Proverbs and Proverbial Phrases* (1929), p. 4,
   regards the evidence as too slight for the sentence to be regarded as a proverb.
   However, the phrase was current in the seventeenth century, occurring in
   Bishop Corbett's *Iter Boreale* (*Poems of Richard Corbett*, ed. J. A. W. Bennett
   and H. R. Trevor-Roper (1955), p. 43), while Fielding quotes an unidentified
   couplet in *Tom Jones*, IV.i.—'While history with her comrade ale, /Soothes the
   sad series of her serious tale'—and also refers to Butler's couplet, 'Thou that
   with Ale, or viler Liquors, /Didst inspire *Withers*, *Pryn* and *Vickars*' (*Hudibras*
   (1663–78), Part I, Canto i, 645–6).
257–8 *ragout . . . collation* cockscombs can be used in French cooking as a garnish or
   in a sauce. The joke was still current in 1733: James Bramston satirizes a
   Frenchified taste for '. . . frogs fricasseed, and coxcomb pies' (*The Man of Taste*,
   p. 14).

bage!—Come master, your health this morning!—next my   260
heart now!

DORIMANT

Go, get you home, and govern your family better! Do not let
your wife follow you to the alehouse, beat your whore, and lead
you home in triumph.

SHOEMAKER

'Zbud, there's never a man i' the town lives more like a gentleman   265
with his wife than I do. I never mind her motions; she never
inquires into mine. We speak to one another civilly, hate one
another heartily, and because 'tis vulgar to lie and soak together,
we have each of us our several settle-bed.

DORIMANT [to HANDY]

Give him half a crown.   270

MEDLEY

Not without he will promise to be bloody drunk.

---

260 *morning!—next* ed. (Morning next Q1, CA; morning! next B)
266 *motions* either, movements, or emotions, inner promptings (obs.)
269 *several* separate
269 *settle-bed* wooden bench used as a bed
271 *without* unless

260–1 *Come ... now* Carnochan suggests that the Shoemaker asks Dorimant for
money to drink his health: but 'next my heart' is used by Sir Frederick Frollick
when he embraces Jenny, Wheadle's maid (*Love in a Tub*, I.ii), and Brett-
Smith thinks the Shoemaker uses the phrase insolently.
271 *bloody drunk* the adverbial use of 'bloody' in colloquial language was recent, and
the *OED* cites this as its earliest example. However, the word appears in
Dryden's *The Wild Gallant*, I.i, 68–9, where Bibber, using tavern slang, says
'... I was drunk; damnably drunk with Ale; great Hogen Mogen bloody Ale; I
was porterly drunk ...' (*Works of John Dryden*, vol. 7, ed. J. H. Smith, D.
MacMillan, *et al.* (Berkeley and Los Angeles, 1962), p. 11). The modern usage
as a mere intensifier or as an adjective only dates from the nineteenth century.

SHOEMAKER

Tope's the word, i' the eye of the world. [*To* HANDY] For my
master's honour, Robin!

DORIMANT

Do not debauch my servants, sirrah.

SHOEMAKER

I only tip him the wink; he knows an alehouse from a hovel.   275
                                                Exit SHOEMAKER

DORIMANT [*to* HANDY]

My clothes, quickly!

MEDLEY

Where shall we dine today?

                        Enter YOUNG BELLAIR

DORIMANT

Where you will. Here comes a good third man.

YOUNG BELLAIR

Your servant, gentlemen.

MEDLEY

Gentle sir, how will you answer this visit to your honourable   280
mistress? 'Tis not her interest you should keep company with
men of sense, who will be talking reason.

YOUNG BELLAIR

I do not fear her pardon, do you but grant me yours for my
neglect of late.

272–3 *Tope's . . . Robin* CA (Q1, CO have no punctuation; Q2–3, B give a comma
       after 'honour'; W, V give commas after 'world' and 'honour')
275 *tip . . . wink* give a private signal (orig. rogue's cant)

272–3 *Tope's . . . Robin.* Brett-Smith suggests that the Shoemaker rebukes Medley's vulgarism 'bloody drunk': 'tope' is the gentlemanly word. The
Shoemaker, with a wink at Handy, then performs the motions of drinking
Dorimant's health. 'Tope' was a relatively new word (*OED* cites its first
example from 1654), but was less recent than 'bloody'. But 'tope' may be used
as an exclamation, 'I pledge you' (from Fr. *tope,* to accept an offer or proposal,
or, in gambling, to cover a bet, accept a challenge): Palmer uses the word in
this sense in Etherege's *The Comical Revenge* (1664)—'Tope—here, pledg me'
(II.iii, 48). 'In that case, the Shoemaker accepts Medley's conditions, as (he
asserts) would the *world*' (Carnochan). This meaning would make the reading
of the early edd. possible though difficult. Some support may be given to this
by a recent emendation of Suckling's *The Goblins,* I.iv, 6 (*The Works of Sir John
Suckling,* ed. Thomas S. Clayton and Lester Beaurline (Oxford, 1971), vol. 2,
133)—'TAYLOR. Oh no! He seldome wears his Sword. SERGEANT. *Tope* is the
word if he do . . .' Suckling's play was written between 1637 and 1641, so that
this occurrence would precede the *OED*'s first example.

MEDLEY

Though you've made us miserable by the want of your good   285
company, to show you I am free from all resentment, may the
beautiful cause of our misfortune give you all the joys happy
lovers have shared ever since the world began.

YOUNG BELLAIR

You wish me in heaven, but you believe me on my journey to ·
hell.   290

MEDLEY

You have a good strong faith, and that may contribute much
towards your salvation. I confess I am but of an untoward
constitution, apt to have doubts and scruples; and in love they
are no less distracting than in religion. Were I so near marriage, I
should cry out by fits as I ride in my coach, 'Cuckold, cuckold!'   295
with no less fury than the mad fanatic does 'Glory!' in Bethlem.

YOUNG BELLAIR

Because religion makes some run mad, must I live an atheist?

MEDLEY

Is it not great indiscretion for a man of credit, who may have
money enough on his word, to go and deal with Jews, who for
little sums make men enter into bonds and give judgments?   300

YOUNG BELLAIR

Preach no more on this text. I am determined, and there is no
hope of my conversion.

DORIMANT (*to* HANDY, *who is fiddling about him*)

Leave your unnecessary fiddling. A wasp that's buzzing about a
man's nose at dinner is not more troublesome than thou art.

HANDY

You love to have your clothes hang just, sir.   305

DORIMANT

I love to be well-dressed, sir, and think it no scandal to my
understanding.

---

292 *untoward* awkward, perverse
300 *judgments* judicial assignment of chattels, hence the certificate of such a judgment used as security

---

296 *mad fanatic . . . Bethlem* Brett-Smith identifies as Oliver Cromwell's porter,
Daniel, imprisoned in Bethlehem Hospital, the London lunatic asylum usually
known as Bedlam. He cites the dialogue in 'A New Song of the Times, 1683'
between 'Olivers Porter, Fidler, *and* Poet *In* BEDLAM' in which the porter
begins, 'O Glory! Glory! who are these Appear?' (*A Second Collection of . . .
Poems . . . against Popery* (1689), p. 12). There are other contemporary references: the Prologue to D'Urfey's *Sir Barnaby Whigg* (1681) has, 'Like *Lunaticks*
ye roar . . . Like Oliver's Porter, but not so devout'.

HANDY

Will you use the essence, or orange-flower water?

DORIMANT

I will smell as I do today, no offence to the ladies' noses.

HANDY

Your pleasure, sir.   [*Exit* HANDY]   310

DORIMANT

That a man's excellency should lie in neatly tying of a ribbon or a cravat! How careful's nature in furnishing the world with necessary coxcombs!

YOUNG BELLAIR

That's a mighty pretty suit of yours, Dorimant.

DORIMANT

I am glad 't has your approbation.   315

YOUNG BELLAIR

No man in town has a better fancy in his clothes than you have.

DORIMANT

You will make me have an opinion of my genius.

MEDLEY

There is a great critic, I hear, in these matters lately arrived piping hot from Paris.

YOUNG BELLAIR

Sir Fopling Flutter, you mean.   320

MEDLEY

The same.

YOUNG BELLAIR

He thinks himself the pattern of modern gallantry.

DORIMANT

He is indeed the pattern of modern foppery.

MEDLEY

He was yesterday at the play, with a pair of gloves up to his elbows and a periwig more exactly curled than a lady's head   325 newly dressed for a ball.

YOUNG BELLAIR

What a pretty lisp he has!

DORIMANT

Ho, that he affects in imitation of the people of quality of France.

MEDLEY

His head stands for the most part on one side, and his looks are

308 *essence* perfume, scent

---

308 *orange-flower water* see note to III.ii, 207.
316 *fancy* taste, critical judgment in matters of art or elegance. *OED* cites Mrs Hutchinson's *Memoirs of Colonel Hutchinson* (1665), p. 23, 'He was . . . genteel in his habit [i.e., dress] and had a very good fancy in it'.

more languishing than a lady's when she lolls at stretch in her   330
coach or leans her head carelessly against the side of a box i' the
playhouse.

DORIMANT

He is a person indeed of great acquired follies.

MEDLEY

He is like many others, beholding to his education for making
him so eminent a coxcomb. Many a fool had been lost to the   335
world, had their indulgent parents wisely bestowed neither
learning nor good breeding on 'em.

YOUNG BELLAIR

He has been, as the sparkish word is, brisk upon the ladies
already. He was yesterday at my Aunt Townley's and gave Mrs
Loveit a catalogue of his good qualities under the character of a   340
complete gentleman, who (according to Sir Fopling) ought to
dress well, dance well, fence well, have a genius for love letters,
an agreeable voice for a chamber, be very amorous, something
discreet, but not over-constant.

MEDLEY

Pretty ingredients to make an accomplished person!   345

DORIMANT

I am glad he pitched upon Loveit.

YOUNG BELLAIR

How so?

DORIMANT

I wanted a fop to lay to her charge, and this is as pat as may be.

YOUNG BELLAIR

I am confident she loves no man but you.

DORIMANT

The good fortune were enough to make me vain, but that I am in   350
my nature modest.

YOUNG BELLAIR

Hark you, Dorimant.—With your leave, Mr Medley—'tis only a
secret concerning a fair lady.

MEDLEY

Your good breeding, sir, gives you too much trouble. You might
have whispered without all this ceremony.   355

YOUNG BELLAIR (*to* DORIMANT)

How stand your affairs with Bellinda of late?

334 *beholding* Q1 (beholden Q3)
338 *brisk* sharp

DORIMANT

She's a little jilting baggage.

YOUNG BELLAIR

Nay, I believe her false enough, but she's ne'er the worse for your purpose. She was with you yesterday in a disguise at the play.   360

DORIMANT

There we fell out and resolved never to speak to one another more.

YOUNG BELLAIR

The occasion?

DORIMANT

Want of courage to meet me at the place appointed. These young women apprehend loving as much as the young men do fighting   365 at first; but once entered, like them too, they all turn bullies straight.

Enter HANDY

HANDY (*to* YOUNG BELLAIR)

Sir, your man without desires to speak with you.

YOUNG BELLAIR

Gentlemen, I'll return immediately.   *Exit* YOUNG BELLAIR

MEDLEY

A very pretty fellow, this.   370

DORIMANT

He's handsome, well-bred, and by much the most tolerable of all the young men that do not abound in wit.

MEDLEY

Ever well-dressed, always complaisant, and seldom impertinent. You and he are grown very intimate, I see.

DORIMANT

It is our mutual interest to be so. It makes the women think the better of his understanding and judge more favourably of my   375 reputation; it makes him pass upon some for a man of very good sense, and I upon others for a very civil person.

357 *baggage* used familiarly or playfully of any young woman (1672–), but the earlier meaning, a worthless good-for-nothing woman, a strumpet, remained current. *OED* cites W. Robertson, *Phraseologia Generalis* . . . (1693 ed.), p. 197, 'A baggage, or Souldier's Punk'.

366 *bullies* probably plays on different senses of the word—1) sweetheart (of either men or women), 2) blustering gallant, swashbuckler, 3) the 'gallant' or protector of prostitutes.

373 *complaisant* obliging, courteous, accommodating. Cf. Hobbes, *Leviathan*, I.xv, 76, 'Compleasance; that is to say, That every man strive to accomodate himselfe to the rest', and Johnson's *Dictionary*, 'Civility, desire of pleasing . . .' A recent word (first example in *OED* dated 1647). See Barnard (op. cit.), pp. xxxiii–iv.

MEDLEY

What was that whisper?

DORIMANT

A thing which he would fain have known, but I did not think it fit   380
to tell him. It might have frighted him from his honourable
intentions of marrying.

MEDLEY

Emilia, give her her due, has the best reputation of any young
woman about the town who has beauty enough to provoke
detraction. Her carriage is unaffected, her discourse mod-   385
est—not at all censorious nor pretending, like the counterfeits of
the age.

DORIMANT

She's a discreet maid, and I believe nothing can corrupt her but a
husband.

MEDLEY

A husband?   390

DORIMANT

Yes, a husband. I have known many women make a difficulty of
losing a maidenhead, who have afterwards made none of making
a cuckold.

MEDLEY

This prudent consideration, I am apt to think, has made you
confirm poor Bellair in the desperate resolution he has taken.   395

DORIMANT

Indeed, the little hope I found there was of her, in the state she
was in, has made me by my advice contribute something towards
the changing of her condition.

Enter YOUNG BELLAIR

Dear Bellair, by heavens I thought we had lost thee! Men in love
are never to be reckoned on when we would form a company.   400

YOUNG BELLAIR

Dorimant, I am undone. My man has brought the most surprising news i' the world.

DORIMANT

Some strange misfortune is befallen your love?

---

385 *carriage* either, deportment, or habitual manner of conduct

---

379–82 *that whisper ... marrying* the 'whisper' is the exchange between Young
    Bellair and Dorimant (ll. 356–67), from which Medley has been excluded.
    Thus, Dorimant first disguises his relationship with Bellinda from Young
    Bellair (l. 357), so protecting her reputation (cf. IV.ii, 73–4), and then uses
    Emilia as a blind when speaking to Medley.

YOUNG BELLAIR

My father came to town last night and lodges i' the very house
where Emilia lies.   405

MEDLEY

Does he know it is with her you are in love?

YOUNG BELLAIR

He knows I love, but knows not whom, without some officious
sot has betrayed me.

DORIMANT

Your Aunt Townley is your confidante and favours the business.

YOUNG BELLAIR

I do not apprehend any ill office from her. I have received a   410
letter, in which I am commanded by my father to meet him at my
aunt's this afternoon. He tells me farther he has made a match for
me, and bids me resolve to be obedient to his will or expect to be
disinherited.

MEDLEY

Now's your time, Bellair. Never had lover such an opportunity   415
of giving a generous proof of his passion.

YOUNG BELLAIR

As how, I pray?

MEDLEY

Why, hang an estate, marry Emilia out of hand, and provoke
your father to do what he threatens. 'Tis but despising a coach,
humbling yourself to a pair of galoshes, being out of countenance 420
when you meet your friends, pointed at and pitied wherever you
go by all the amorous fops that know you, and your fame will be
immortal.

YOUNG BELLAIR

I could find in my heart to resolve not to marry at all.

DORIMANT

Fie, fie! That would spoil a good jest and disappoint the well-   425
natured town of an occasion of laughing at you.

YOUNG BELLAIR

The storm I have so long expected hangs o'er my head and
begins to pour down upon me. I am on the rack and can have no
rest till I'm satisfied in what I fear. Where do you dine?

---

420 *galoshes* CA (goloshoes Q1; goloshes V). '*Galloches*, high wooden Pattins or
   Clogs ... It also means a Sort of Slipper worn over the Shoes' (Ozell's *Rabelais*
   (1737), vol. 2, 219: cited *OED*)

---

409 *confidante* this should perhaps be regarded as another instance of a French
   word. First instance, from Lady Mary Wortley Montagu, in *OED* dates from
   1709. The word may have been formed to represent the sound of Fr. *confidente*.

DORIMANT

At Long's or Locket's.   430

MEDLEY

At Long's let it be.

YOUNG BELLAIR

I'll run and see Emilia and inform myself how matters stand. If
my misfortunes are not so great as to make me unfit for company,
I'll be with you.   *Exit* YOUNG BELLAIR

Enter a FOOTMAN *with a letter*

FOOTMAN (*to* DORIMANT)

Here's a letter, sir.   435

DORIMANT

The superscription's right: 'For Mr Dorimant'.

MEDLEY

Let's see. [*Looks at the letter*] The very scrawl and spelling of a
true-bred whore.

DORIMANT

I know the hand. The style is admirable, I assure you.

MEDLEY

Prithee, read it.   440

DORIMANT (*reads*)

'I told a you you dud not love me, if you dud, you would have
seen me again ere now. I have no money and am very malicoly.
Pray send me a guynie to see the operies. Your servant to
command, Molly'.

MEDLEY

Pray let the whore have a favourable answer, that she may spark   445
it in a box and do honour to her profession.

DORIMANT

She shall, and perk up i' the face of quality. [*To* HANDY] Is the
coach at door?

HANDY

You did not bid me send for it.

---

430 *Long's or Locket's* well-known eating-places. There was a tavern called Long's
   in the Haymarket and another in Covent Garden, kept by two brothers.
   Locket's, named after its landlord, Adam Locket, is continually referred to in
   Restoration comedies, and was frequented by Etherege himself. Lord Foppington speaks of going 'to Dinner at *Lacket*'s; where you are so nicely and
   delicately serv'd, that, stap my Vitals, they shall compose you a Dish no bigger
   than a Saucer, shall come to Fifty shillings' (*The Relapse* (1697), II.i).
447 *perk up* assume or have a lively or self-conceited attitude or air; lift one's head,
   or thrust oneself forward briskly, boldly, or impudently. But possibly 'perk'
   (*OED*, V. 2), to perch, used of birds, though also transferred to people.

DORIMANT
Eternal blockhead! (HANDY *offers to go out*) Hey, sot!   450
HANDY
Did you call me, sir?
DORIMANT
I hope you have no just exception to the name, sir?
HANDY
I have sense, sir.
DORIMANT
Not so much as a fly in winter.—How did you come, Medley?
MEDLEY
In a chair.   455
FOOTMAN
You may have a hackney coach if you please, sir.
DORIMANT
I may ride the elephant if I please, sir. Call another chair and let
my coach follow to Long's.
              'Be calm, ye great parents, etc.'
                              Exeunt, [DORIMANT] *singing*

457 *I ... elephant* Professor Harold Brooks informs me that there are several
      contemporary references to elephants exhibited in London from 1675 to 1682.
      He kindly provides a citation from the *City Mercury*, No. 3, 11–18 Nov. 1675,
      where an advertisement headed 'The Elephant' reads, 'That Wonderful Beast
      lately sent from *East-India* to the Right Honourable *George Berkley*, And since
      sold for Two thousand pounds sterling: Is now to be seen at the *White Horse*
      Inn over against *Salisbury* Court in Fleet-Street ...' (Further, see Professor
      Brooks's D.Phil. on Oldham, Bodleian Library.)
459 *Be ... parents, etc.* Conaghan identifies as from the song 'My Lord: Great
      Neptune, for my Sake' in the final scene of Shadwell's operatic version of *The
      Tempest* (1674). ll. 17–18 run: 'Be calm, ye great Parents of the Flouds and the
      Springs, /While each *Nereide* and *Triton* Plays, Revels, and Sings' (*Complete
      Works*, ed. M. Summers (1927), vol. 2, 266).

Act II, Scene i
[LADY TOWNLEY's *house*]

Enter my LADY TOWNLEY *and* EMILIA

LADY TOWNLEY
I was afraid, Emilia, all had been discovered.
EMILIA
I tremble with the apprehension still.
LADY TOWNLEY
That my brother should take lodgings i' the very house where
you lie!
EMILIA
'Twas lucky we had timely notice to warn the people to be secret.   5
He seems to be a mighty good-humoured old man.
LADY TOWNLEY
He ever had a notable smirking way with him.
EMILIA
He calls me rogue, tells me he can't abide me, and does so bepat
me.
LADY TOWNLEY
On my word, you are much in his favour then.   10
EMILIA
He has been very inquisitive, I am told, about my family, my
reputation, and my fortune.
LADY TOWNLEY
I am confident he does not i' the least suspect you are the woman
his son's in love with.
EMILIA
What should make him then inform himself so particularly of   15
me?
LADY TOWNLEY
He was always of a very loving temper himself. It may be he has a
doting fit upon him, who knows?
EMILIA
It cannot be.

Enter YOUNG BELLAIR

LADY TOWNLEY
Here comes my nephew.—Where did you leave your father?   20

YOUNG BELLAIR

Writing a note within. Emilia, this early visit looks as if some
kind jealousy would not let you rest at home.

EMILIA

The knowledge I have of my rival gives me a little cause to fear
your constancy.

YOUNG BELLAIR

My constancy! I vow— 25

EMILIA

Do not vow—our love is frail as is our life, and full as little in our
power; and are you sure you shall outlive this day?

YOUNG BELLAIR

I am not, but when we are in perfect health, 'twere an idle thing
to fright ourselves with the thoughts of sudden death.

LADY TOWNLEY

Pray, what has passed between you and your father i' the garden? 30

YOUNG BELLAIR

He's firm in his resolution, tells me I must marry Mrs Harriet, or
swears he'll marry himself and disinherit me. When I saw I could
not prevail with him to be more indulgent, I dissembled an
obedience to his will, which has composed his passion and will
give us time—and I hope opportunity—to deceive him. 35

Enter OLD BELLAIR *with a note in his hand*

LADY TOWNLEY

Peace, here he comes.

OLD BELLAIR

Harry, take this and let your man carry it for me to Mr Fourbe's
chamber, my lawyer, i' the Temple.

[*Exit* YOUNG BELLAIR]

(*To* EMILIA) Neighbour, adod, I am glad to see thee
here.—Make much of her, sister. She's one of the best of your 40
acquaintance. I like her countenance and her behaviour well; she
has a modesty that is not common i' this age, adod she has.

LADY TOWNLEY

I know her value, brother, and esteem her accordingly.

---

37 *Fourbe's* Q1 varies spelling to 'Furb' at V.ii, 11, 28, but 'fourbe' (from the
French) meant a cheat, an impostor, or a trick, imposture. A short-lived word:
OED gives examples of the noun and verb from 1654 to 1761, and cites
Denham's *Passion of Dido* (1668), l. 107, 'Thou art a false Impostor and a
Fourbe'.

38 *Temple* the Inner and Middle Temple of London's Inns of Court are so-called
because they stand on the site of the buildings of the Knights Templar.

OLD BELLAIR

Advise her to wear a little more mirth in her face. Adod, she's too
serious.   45

LADY TOWNLEY

The fault is very excusable in a young woman.

OLD BELLAIR

Nay, adod, I like her ne'er the worse; a melancholy beauty has
her charms. I love a pretty sadness in a face which varies now and
then, like changeable colours, into a smile.

LADY TOWNLEY

Methinks you speak very feelingly, brother.   50

OLD BELLAIR

I am but five-and-fifty, sister, you know—an age not altogether
insensible. (*To* EMILIA) Cheer up sweetheart, I have a secret to
tell thee may chance to make thee merry. We three will make
collation together anon. I' the meantime, mum! [*Aloud*] I can't
abide you; go, I can't abide you—   55

Enter YOUNG BELLAIR

Harry! Come, you must along with me to my Lady Woodvill's.—-I am going to slip the boy at a mistress.

YOUNG BELLAIR

At a wife, sir, you would say.

OLD BELLAIR

You need not look so glum, sir. A wife is no curse when she
brings the blessing of a good estate with her. But an idle town   60
flirt, with a painted face, a rotten reputation, and a crazy fortune, adod, is the devil and all; and such a one I hear you are in
league with.

YOUNG BELLAIR

I cannot help detraction, sir.

---

47 *adod* equivalent to 'egad', 'By God'
54 *meantime . . . I* CA (meantime mum, I Q1; meantime, mum, I Q3). Conaghan
   cites two further contemporary texts for the emendation
57 *slip* release (a greyhound or hawk) from a leash or slip

---

54 *mum* two meanings are possible. 1) Hush, be silent! (the meaning assumed by
   this text). 2) A vulgar variant of 'madam'.
61 *flirt* woman of loose character (1600–1703, *OED*, which cites this e.g.). The
   first example of the modern sense (one who flirts or plays at courtship) given by
   the *OED* is from Richardson in 1748.

OLD BELLAIR

Out a pize o' their breeches, there are keeping fools enough for   65
such flaunting baggages, and they are e'en too good for 'em. (*To*
EMILIA) Remember 'night. [*Aloud*] Go, you're a rogue, you're a
rogue. Fare you well, fare you well. [*To* YOUNG BELLAIR] Come,
come, come along, sir.

                              Exeunt OLD *and* YOUNG BELLAIR

LADY TOWNLEY

On my word, the old man comes on apace. I'll lay my life he's   70
smitten.

EMILIA

This is nothing but the pleasantness of his humour.

LADY TOWNLEY

I know him better than you. Let it work; it may prove lucky.

                              Enter a PAGE

PAGE

Madam, Mr Medley has sent to know whether a visit will not be
troublesome this afternoon?   75

LADY TOWNLEY

Send him word his visits never are so.   [*Exit* PAGE]

EMILIA

He's a very pleasant man.

LADY TOWNLEY

He's a very necessary man among us women. He's not scandalous i' the least, perpetually contriving to bring good company
together, and always ready to stop up a gap at ombre. Then, he   80
knows all the little news o' the town.

EMILIA

I love to hear him talk o' the intrigues. Let 'em be never so dull in
themselves, he'll make 'em pleasant i' the relation.

---

65 *keeping fools* fools who keep mistresses (cf. Dryden's title, *Mr Limberham, or,
    The Kind Keeper*)

---

65 *pize* imprecation of uncertain meaning. It may be an arbitrary substitute for
    'Pest!' or 'Pox!', the latter being used in the same way as 'pize' from 1600
    onwards.
66 *baggages* see note to I, 357.
80, 92 *ombre* a card-game, fashionable in the seventeenth and early eighteenth
    centuries. Played by three people, with forty cards, the eights, nines, and tens
    of the ordinary pack being thrown out. A Spanish game according to Cotgrave,
    so-called because 'he who undertakes to play [for the stake] saith *Jo soy
    L'Ombre*, i.e., I am the man . . .' Matadore (l. 101) was the name given to the
    principal cards (the black aces and variable card).

LADY TOWNLEY

But he improves things so much one can take no measure of the
truth from him. Mr Dorimant swears a flea or a maggot is not   85
made more monstrous by a magnifying glass than a story is by his
telling it.

Enter MEDLEY

EMILIA

Hold, here he comes.

LADY TOWNLEY

Mr Medley.

MEDLEY

Your servant, madam.   90

LADY TOWNLEY

You have made yourself a stranger of late.

EMILIA

I believe you took a surfeit of ombre last time you were here.

MEDLEY

Indeed I had my bellyful of that termagant, Lady Dealer. There
never was so insatiable a carder; an old gleeker never loved to sit
to 't like her. I have played with her now at least a dozen times,   95
till she's worn out all her fine complexion and her tour would
keep in curl no longer.

LADY TOWNLEY

Blame her not, poor woman. She loves nothing so well as a black
ace.

MEDLEY

The pleasure I have seen her in when she has had hope in   100
drawing for a matadore!

EMILIA

'Tis as pretty sport to her as persuading masks off is to you, to
make discoveries.

LADY TOWNLEY

Pray, where's your friend Mr Dorimant?

---

94 *carder* card-player (obs.: *OED* gives examples *c.* 1530–1712)

---

94 *gleeker* player of gleek, a card-game (rare). The game was played by three
people; forty-four cards were used, twelve being dealt to each player, the
remaining eight forming a common 'stock'.

96 *tour* a crescent of false hair. Another word of French extraction (cf. *tour de
cheveux*) newly brought into English (*OED* gives first e.g. from 1674). Chambers's *Cyclopaedia* (1724–41) describes as 'a tress or border of hair, going round
the head, which mingled dextrously with the natural hair, lengthens and
thickens it'.

MEDLEY

Soliciting his affairs. He's a man of great employment—has   105
more mistresses now depending than the most eminent lawyer in
England has causes.

EMILIA

Here has been Mrs Loveit so uneasy and out of humour these
two days.

LADY TOWNLEY

How strangely love and jealousy rage in that poor woman!   110

MEDLEY

She could not have picked out a devil upon earth so proper to
torment her. He's made her break a dozen or two of fans already,
tear half a score points in pieces, and destroy hoods and knots
without number.

LADY TOWNLEY

We heard of a pleasant serenade he gave her t'other night.   115

MEDLEY

A Danish serenade, with kettledrums and trumpets.

EMILIA

Oh, barbarous!

MEDLEY

What, you are of the number of the ladies whose ears are grown

---

106 *depending* pending, like a lawyer's cases (causes)
112 *He's* ed. (Has Q1; h'as Q3, B, CO; H'as CA; he has W, V)
113 *points* pieces of tagged lace or cord for fastening clothes
113 *knots* bows made of ribbon

115, 116 *serenade . . . Danish serenade* 'serenade' was a recent word from the French
(first e.g. in *OED* is from 1649). Medley indicates that French wind instruments were an expected part of the ensemble (ll. 119–20), as they are of Sir
Fopling's *equipage* (see IV.i, 253). Dorimant's 'Danish serenade' is a drunken
practical joke. Carnochan aptly cites *Hamlet*, I.iv, 8–12, 'The King doth wake
tonight and takes his rouse, /Keeps wassail, and the swaggering upspring reels;
/And as he drains his draughts of Rhenish down, /The kettledrum and trumpet
thus bray out /The triumph of his pledge'.

so delicate since our operas, you can be charmed with nothing
but flutes douces and French hautboys?   120

EMILIA

Leave your raillery and tell us, is there any new wit come
forth—songs, or novels?

MEDLEY

A very pretty piece of gallantry, by an eminent author, called *The
Diversions of Brussels*—very necessary to be read by all old ladies
who are desirous to improve themselves at questions and com-   125
mands, blindman's buff, and the like fashionable recreations.

EMILIA

Oh, ridiculous!

MEDLEY

Then there is *The Art of Affectation*, written by a late beauty of
quality, teaching you how to draw up your breasts, stretch up
your neck, to thrust out your breech, to play with your head, to   130
toss up your nose, to bite your lips, to turn up your eyes, to speak
in a silly soft tone of a voice, and use all the foolish French words

120 *flutes douces* ed. (Flute doux Q1; *flutes douces* V, CA)

---

119 *operas* the production of the altered versions of *Macbeth* (1673) and *The Tempest*
(1674) along with Shadwell's *Psyche* (1675), all of them elaborate spectacles
which had musical elements, marked a new stage in the development of
Restoration 'opera'. Brett-Smith cites Evelyn's *Diary*, 5 Jan. 1673/74, 'I saw an
Italian opera in musiq, the first that had been seen of this kind'.

120 *flutes douces* Q1's 'doux' is an erroneous formation from the French. The flute
douce (i.e., the recorder) with its eight holes and two octaves succeeded the
flageolet (see note to III.iii, 228) in popularity, but was a recent introduction to
England. Evelyn's *Diary*, 20 Nov. 1679, records, 'There was also a flute douce,
now much in request for accompanying the voice'.

121 *raillery* imported from the French. First recorded instance in *OED* dates from
1653—'The word Raillery you return'd me for interpretation . . . is now grown
here so common with the better sort, as there are few of the meaner that are not
able to construe it' (R. Loveday, *Letters* (1663), p. 245).

123–4 *The Diversions of Brussels* identified by R. S. Cox as Richard Flecknoe's *A
Treatise of the Sports of Wit* (1675). See 'Richard Flecknoe and *The Man of
Mode*', *Modern Language Quarterly*, vol. 29 (1968), 183–9.

125–6 *questions and commands* a game in which one person addressed ludicrous
questions and commands to each member of the company. The game is seen as
similarly unfashionable in Wycherley's *Gentleman Dancing-Master* (1673), 'He
is as dull as a country-squire at questions and commands' (II.ii).

128 *The Art of Affectation* Medley is mocking Hannah Woolley's *The Gentlewoman's
Companion* (1675). Conaghan notes that the book advises the raising of the eyes
heavenwards ('Of the Government of the Eye', p. 39) and refers to washing and
painting as 'innocently helpful to the beauties of modest women' (p. 240).
Medley's attribution to 'a late beauty of quality' may be based on the portrait at
the front of the book.

that will infallibly make your person and conversation charming;
with a short apology at the latter end, in the behalf of young
ladies who notoriously wash and paint, though they have natur-   135
ally good complexions.

EMILIA

What a deal of stuff you tell us!

MEDLEY

Such as the town affords, madam. The Russians, hearing the
great respect we have for foreign dancing, have lately sent over
some of their best baladines, who are now practising a famous   140
ballet which will be suddenly danced at the Bear Garden.

LADY TOWNLEY

Pray forbear your idle stories, and give us an account of the state
of love as it now stands.

MEDLEY

Truly, there has been some revolutions in those affairs—great
chopping and changing among the old and some new lovers,   145
whom malice, indiscretion, and misfortune have luckily brought
into play.

LADY TOWNLEY

What think you of walking into the next room and sitting down,
before you engage in this business?

MEDLEY

I wait upon you; and I hope (though women are commonly   150
unreasonable), by the plenty of scandal I shall discover, to give
you very good content, ladies.   *Exeunt*

---

135 *wash* use cosmetic washes
141 *suddenly* soon

---

140 *baladine* a theatrical dancer; a mountebank, buffoon (from the French). This
   occurrence is the *OED*'s first clear example of the word being restricted to
   dancers, though it occurs as early as 1599.
141 *ballet* originally employed to illustrate dramatically the costumes and manners
   of other nations. A new word from the French: the only earlier occurrence in
   the *OED* is from Dryden's *Essay of Dramatick Poesie* (1667).
141 *Bear Garden* a hit both at the contemporary craze for music and dancing by
   foreign troupes, and at the proverbial barbarity of the Russians—the Bear
   Garden, on Bankside, was a venue for bear-baiting and prizefighting with
   swords. (Perhaps the bears there danced?)
145 *chopping and changing* the phrase originally meant buying and selling, bartering. As Carnochan observes, the words keep something of that force here.

Act II, Scene ii
[MRS LOVEIT's]

Enter MRS LOVEIT *and* PERT. MRS LOVEIT *putting up a letter, then*
pulling out her pocket-glass and looking in it

MRS LOVEIT

Pert.

PERT

Madam?

MRS LOVEIT

I hate myself, I look so ill today.

PERT

Hate the wicked cause on't, that base man, Mr Dorimant, who
makes you torment and vex yourself continually.   5

MRS LOVEIT

He is to blame, indeed.

PERT

To blame to be two days without sending, writing, or coming
near you, contrary to his oath and covenant! 'Twas to much
purpose to make him swear! I'll lay my life there's not an article
but he has broken—talked to the vizards i' the pit, waited upon   10
the ladies from the boxes to their coaches, gone behind the
scenes and fawned upon those little insignificant creatures, the
players. 'Tis impossible for a man of his inconstant temper to
forbear, I'm sure.

MRS LOVEIT

I know he is a devil, but he has something of the angel yet   15
undefaced in him, which makes him so charming and agreeable
that I must love him, be he never so wicked.

PERT

I little thought, madam, to see your spirit tamed to this degree,
who banished poor Mr Lackwit but for taking up another lady's
fan in your presence.   20

MRS LOVEIT

My knowing of such odious fools contributes to the making of me
love Dorimant the better.

PERT

Your knowing of Mr Dorimant, in my mind, should rather make
you hate all mankind.

MRS LOVEIT

So it does, besides himself.   25

1 s.d. *putting up* putting away

PERT
Pray, what excuse does he make in his letter?

MRS LOVEIT
He has had business.

PERT
Business in general terms would not have been a current excuse
for another. A modish man is always very busy when he is in
pursuit of a new mistress.   30

MRS LOVEIT
Some fop has bribed you to rail at him. He had business; I will
believe it, and will forgive him.

PERT
You may forgive him anything, but I shall never forgive him his
turning me into ridicule, as I hear he does.

MRS LOVEIT
I perceive you are of the number of those fools his wit has made   35
his enemies.

PERT
I am of the number of those he's pleased to rally, madam; and if
we may believe Mr Wagfan and Mr Caperwell, he sometimes
makes merry with yourself, too, among his laughing companions.   40

MRS LOVEIT
Blockheads are as malicious to witty men as ugly women are to
the handsome; 'tis their interest, and they make it their business
to defame 'em.

PERT
I wish Mr Dorimant would not make it his business to defame
you.   45

MRS LOVEIT
Should he, I had rather be made infamous by him than owe my
reputation to the dull discretion of those fops you talk of.

Enter BELLINDA

Bellinda!   *Running to her*
BELLINDA
My dear!

MRS LOVEIT
You have been unkind of late.   50

28 *current* genuine
35 *has* W, V, B, CA (had Q1)
47 *of* Q3, V, B, CA (off Q1)

---

29 *modish* from the French, *mode*, a recent importation. First example in *OED*
dates from 1660.

BELLINDA

Do not say unkind, say unhappy.

MRS LOVEIT

I could chide you. Where have you been these two days?

BELLINDA

Pity me rather, my dear, where I have been so tired with two or
three country gentlewomen, whose conversation has been more
insufferable than a country fiddle.   55

MRS LOVEIT

Are they relations?

BELLINDA

No, Welsh acquaintance I made when I was last year at St
Winifred's. They have asked me a thousand questions of the
modes and intrigues of the town, and I have told 'em almost as
many things for news that hardly were so when their gowns were   60
in fashion.

MRS LOVEIT

Provoking creatures, how could you endure 'em?

BELLINDA (aside)

Now to carry on my plot; nothing but love could make me
capable of so much falsehood. 'Tis time to begin, lest Dorimant
should come before her jealousy has stung her.   65

                        (Laughs, and then speaks on)

I was yesterday at a play with 'em, where I was fain to show 'em
the living, as the man at Westminster does the dead. That is Mrs
Such-a-one, admired for her beauty; this is Mr Such-a-one,
cried up for a wit; that is sparkish Mr Such-a-one, who keeps
reverend Mrs Such-a-one; and there sits fine Mrs Such-a-one,   70
who was lately cast off by my Lord Such-a-one.

MRS LOVEIT

Did you see Dorimant there?

BELLINDA

I did, and imagine you were there with him and have no mind to
own it.

59 *intrigues* liaisons, recently imported from the French. *OED* cites Charleton,
   Ephesian and Cimmerian Matrons (1668), 'She in like manner falls into an
   Intrigue (as they nowadays call it)'. Also Dryden, *Marriage à-la-Mode* (1673),
   'Intrigue, Philotis! that's an old phrase; I have laid that word by; amour sounds
   better' (II.i).

67 *man at Westminster* a guide at Westminster Abbey. Conaghan cites Walter
   Pope, 'It is a Custom for the Servants of the Church upon all Holidays, *Sundays*
   excepted, betwixt the Sermon and Evening Prayers, to shew the Tombs, and
   Effigies of the Kings and Queens in Wax, to the meaner sort of People, who
   then flock thither from all the corners of the Town, and pay their Twopence to
   see *The Play of the Dead Volks*, as I have heard a *Devonshire* Clown not
   improperly call it' (*The Life of Seth Lord Bishop of Salisbury* (1697), p. 157).

MRS LOVEIT
What should make you think so? 75
BELLINDA
A lady masked, in a pretty dishabille, whom Dorimant enter-
tained with more respect than the gallants do a common vizard.
MRS LOVEIT (*aside*)
Dorimant at the play entertaining a mask! Oh, heavens!
BELLINDA (*aside*)
Good!
MRS LOVEIT
Did he stay all the while? 80
BELLINDA
Till the play was done, and then led her out, which confirms me
it was you.
MRS LOVEIT
Traitor!
PERT
Now you may believe he had business, and you may forgive him
too. 85
MRS LOVEIT
Ungrateful, perjured man!
BELLINDA
You seem so much concerned, my dear, I fear I have told you
unawares what I had better have concealed for your quiet.
MRS LOVEIT
What manner of shape had she?
BELLINDA
Tall and slender. Her motions were very genteel. Certainly she 90
must be some person of condition.
MRS LOVEIT
Shame and confusion be ever in her face when she shows it!
BELLINDA
I should blame your discretion for loving that wild man, my

---

76 *dishabille* ed. (dishabillié Q1; *déshabillé* V, CA)
90 *genteel* graceful, elegant

---

76 *in . . . dishabille* a dress of negligent style. Wycherley's *Gentleman Dancing-
Master* (1673) has 'her dishabillie, or flame-colour gown called Indian' (V.i).
Another word newly taken over from the French: the spellings in Wycherley
and Q1 indicate that the word was in the process of being naturalized, though
there is no need to give as French as do Verity and Carnochan.
93 *wild man* possibly a reference to the traditional figure of the wild or 'salvage'
man (Q1 capitalizes 'wild': both words are capitalized in *Works* (1704)). On the
range of meanings of 'wild' in the play see Barnard (op. cit.), pp. xxix–xxxi.

dear—but they say he has a way so bewitching that few can
defend their hearts who know him.   95

MRS LOVEIT

I will tear him from mine, or die i' the attempt!

BELLINDA

Be more moderate.

MRS LOVEIT

Would I had daggers, darts, or poisoned arrows in my breast, so
I could but remove the thoughts of him from thence!

BELLINDA

Fie, fie, your transports are too violent, my dear. This may be   100
but an accidental gallantry, and 'tis likely ended at her coach.

PERT

Should it proceed farther, let your comfort be, the conduct Mr
Dorimant affects will quickly make you know your rival—ten to
one let you see her ruined, her reputation exposed to the
town—a happiness none will envy her but yourself, madam.   105

MRS LOVEIT

Whoe'er she be, all the harm I wish her is, may she love him as
well as I do, and may he give her as much cause to hate him!

PERT

Never doubt the latter end of your curse, madam!

MRS LOVEIT

May all the passions that are raised by neglected love—jealousy,
indignation, spite, and thirst of revenge—eternally rage in her   110
soul, as they do now in mine!

> *Walks up and down with a distracted air*
>
> *Enter a* PAGE

PAGE

Madam, Mr Dorimant—

MRS LOVEIT

I will not see him.

PAGE

I told him you were within, madam.

MRS LOVEIT

Say you lied, say I'm busy, shut the door—say anything!   115

PAGE

He's here, madam.   [*Exit* PAGE]

> *Enter* DORIMANT

DORIMANT

'They taste of death who do at heaven arrive,
But we this paradise approach alive'.

117–18 *They ... alive* from Waller's 'Of her Chamber', ll. 1–2 (*Poems*, ed. G.
Thorn Drury (1901), vol. 1, 26). Dorimant has 'who' for Waller's 'that'.

(*To* MRS LOVEIT) What, dancing the galloping nag without a
fiddle? (*Offers to catch her by the hand; she flings away and walks*   120
on) I fear this restlessness of the body, madam, (*pursuing her*)
proceeds from an unquietness of the mind. What unlucky accident puts you out of humour—a point ill-washed, knots spoiled
i' the making up, hair shaded awry, or some other little mistake
in setting you in order?   125

PERT

A trifle, in my opinion, sir, more inconsiderable than any you
mention.

DORIMANT

Oh, Mrs Pert! I never knew you sullen enough to be silent.
Come, let me know the business.

PERT

The business, sir, is the business that has taken you up these two   130
days. How have I seen you laugh at men of business, and now to
become a man of business yourself!

DORIMANT

We are not masters of our own affections; our inclinations daily
alter. Now we love pleasure, and anon we shall dote on business.
Human frailty will have it so, and who can help it?   135

MRS LOVEIT

Faithless, inhuman, barbarous man—

DORIMANT [*aside*]

Good. Now the alarm strikes—

MRS LOVEIT

—Without sense of love, of honour, or of gratitude! Tell me, for
I will know, what devil masked she was, you were with at the
play yesterday.   140

DORIMANT

Faith, I resolved as much as you, but the devil was obstinate and
would not tell me.

MRS LOVEIT

False in this as in your vows to me! You do know!

DORIMANT

The truth is, I did all I could to know.

MRS LOVEIT

And dare you own it to my face? Hell and furies!   145

Tears her fan in pieces

DORIMANT

Spare your fan, madam. You are growing hot and will want it to
cool you.

119 *galloping nag* country dance, according to Carnochan.

MRS LOVEIT

Horror and distraction seize you, sorrow and remorse gnaw your
soul, and punish all your perjuries to me!   *Weeps*

DORIMANT (*turning to* BELLINDA)

'So thunder breaks the cloud in twain,   150
    And makes a passage for the rain'.

(*To* BELLINDA) Bellinda, you are the devil that have raised this
storm. You were at the play yesterday and have been making
discoveries to your dear.

BELLINDA

You're the most mistaken man i' the world.   155

DORIMANT

It must be so, and here I vow revenge—resolve to pursue and
persecute you more impertinently than ever any loving fop did
his mistress, hunt you i' the Park, trace you i' the Mall, dog you
in every visit you make, haunt you at the plays and i' the drawing
room, hang my nose in your neck and talk to you whether you   160
will or no, and ever look upon you with such dying eyes till your
friends grow jealous of me, send you out of town, and the world
suspect your reputation. (*In a lower voice*)—At my Lady Townley's when we go from hence—   *He looks kindly on* BELLINDA

BELLINDA

—I'll meet you there.   165

DORIMANT

Enough.

MRS LOVEIT (*pushing* DORIMANT *away*)

Stand off! You shan't stare upon her so!

DORIMANT [*aside*]

Good! There's one made jealous already.

MRS LOVEIT

Is this the constancy you vowed?

150–1 *So . . . rain* from Matthew Roydon's 'An Elegie, or friend's passion for his
Astrophill', ll. 59–60: identified by R. G. Howarth, 'Untraced Quotations in
Etherege', *N & Q*, vol. 188 (June 1945), 281. Dorimant has 'breaks' for the
original's 'rends'. Roydon's elegy for Sir Philip Sidney was published in *The
Phoenix Nest* (1593).

158 *Park* either Hyde Park or St James's Park, which were both fashionable
meeting-places, but probably the latter.

158 *the Mall* a broad avenue with four lines of trees laid out on the border of St
James's Park by Charles II as a place to play pall mall (hence the name). Q1
regularly spells 'Mail', reflecting the French origin of 'mall' (avenue, mallet
used in the game). It is likely that Etherege intended the French pronunciation: cf. Blount's *Glossographia* (1656), '*Pale Maille*, This game was heretofore
used at the Alley near St Jameses, and vulgarly called Pel-Mel'.

DORIMANT

    Constancy at my years? 'Tis not a virtue in season; you might as   170
    well expect the fruit the autumn ripens i' the spring.

MRS LOVEIT

    Monstrous principle!

DORIMANT

    Youth has a long journey to go, madam. Should I have set up my
    rest at the first inn I lodged at, I should never have arrived at the
    happiness I now enjoy.   175

MRS LOVEIT

    Dissembler, damned dissembler!

DORIMANT

    I am so, I confess. Good nature and good manners corrupt me. I
    am honest in my inclinations and would not, wer't not to avoid
    offence, make a lady a little in years believe I think her young,
    wilfully mistake art for nature, and seem as fond of a thing I am   180
    weary of as when I doted on't in earnest.

MRS LOVEIT

    False man!

DORIMANT

    True woman.

MRS LOVEIT

    Now you begin to show yourself!

DORIMANT

    Love gilds us over and makes us show fine things to one another   185
    for a time, but soon the gold wears off, and then again the native
    brass appears.

MRS LOVEIT

    Think on your oaths, your vows, and protestations, perjured
    man!

DORIMANT

    I made 'em when I was in love.   190

MRS LOVEIT

    And therefore ought they not to bind? Oh, impious!

DORIMANT

    What we swear at such a time may be a certain proof of a present
    passion; but to say truth, in love there is no security to be given
    for the future.

MRS LOVEIT

    Horrid and ungrateful, begone! And never see me more!   195

174 *rest* abode
181 *of as* Q2–3, V, B, CA (off as Q1)

DORIMANT

    I am not one of those troublesome coxcombs who, because they
were once well-received, take the privilege to plague a woman
with their love ever after. I shall obey you, madam, though I do
myself some violence.

              He offers to go, and MRS LOVEIT *pulls him back*

MRS LOVEIT

    Come back, you shan't go! Could you have the ill nature to offer 200
it?

DORIMANT

    When love grows diseased, the best thing we can do is to put it to
a violent death. I cannot endure the torture of a lingering and
consumptive passion.

MRS LOVEIT

    Can you think mine sickly? 205

DORIMANT

    Oh, 'tis desperately ill! What worse symptoms are there than
your being always uneasy when I visit you, your picking quarrels
with me on slight occasions, and in my absence kindly listening
to the impertinences of every fashionable fool that talks to you?

MRS LOVEIT

    What fashionable fool can you lay to my charge? 210

DORIMANT

    Why, the very cock-fool of all those fools, Sir Fopling Flutter.

MRS LOVEIT

    I never saw him in my life but once.

DORIMANT

    The worse woman you, at first sight to put on all your charms, to
entertain him with that softness in your voice and all that wanton
kindness in your eyes you so notoriously affect when you design a 215
conquest.

MRS LOVEIT

    So damned a lie did never malice yet invent. Who told you this?

DORIMANT

    No matter. That ever I should love a woman that can dote on a
senseless caper, a tawdry French ribbon, and a formal cravat.

MRS LOVEIT

    You make me mad! 220

DORIMANT

    A guilty conscience may do much! Go on, be the game-mistress
of the town and enter all our young fops, as fast as they come
from travel.

MRS LOVEIT

    Base and scurrilous!

211 *cock-fool* a nonce formation

DORIMANT

A fine mortifying reputation 'twill be for a woman of your pride,   225
wit, and quality!

MRS LOVEIT

This jealousy's a mere pretence, a cursed trick of your own
devising. I know you.

DORIMANT

Believe it and all the ill of me you can. I would not have a woman
have the least good thought of me that can think well of Fopling.   230
Farewell. Fall to, and much good may do you with your coxcomb.

MRS LOVEIT

Stay! Oh stay, and I will tell you all.

DORIMANT

I have been told too much already.   *Exit* DORIMANT

MRS LOVEIT

Call him again!   235

PERT

E'en let him go. A fair riddance!

MRS LOVEIT

Run, I say! Call him again, I will have him called!

PERT

The devil should carry him away first, were it my concern.

                                                   Exit PERT

BELLINDA

He's frighted me from the very thoughts of loving men. For
heaven's sake, my dear, do not discover what I told you. I dread   240
his tongue as much as you ought to have done his friendship.

                        Enter PERT

PERT

He's gone, madam.

MRS LOVEIT

Lightning blast him!

PERT

When I told him you desired him to come back, he smiled, made
a mouth at me, flung into his coach, and said—   245

MRS LOVEIT

What did he say?

231 *to* Q2–3, W, V, CA (too Q1)   231 *may* Q1 (may [it] V)

---

231 *much good may do you* a conventional ironic formula. Brett-Smith cites Ravens-
croft's *London Cuckolds* (1682), I.i: '*Wiseacre*. You have a witty wife, much
good may doe you with her./ *Doodle*. And much good may doe you with your
fool'. There is no need for Verity's emendation.

PERT

    'Drive away'—and then repeated verses.

MRS LOVEIT

    Would I had made a contract to be a witch when first I enter-
tained this greater devil. Monster, barbarian! I could tear myself
in pieces. Revenge, nothing but revenge can ease me. Plague,   250
war, famine, fire—all that can bring universal ruin and misery
on mankind—with joy I'd perish to have you in my power but
this moment!

Exit MRS LOVEIT

PERT

    Follow, madam. Leave her not in this outrageous passion.

PERT *gathers up the things*

BELLINDA

    He's given me the proof which I desired of his love, but 'tis a   255
proof of his ill nature too. I wish I had not seen him use her so:

        I sigh to think that Dorimant may be
        One day as faithless and unkind to me.   *Exeunt*

255-6 *but ... so* Q1 (W, V, B print as verse: But ... too;/ I ... so)

Act III, Scene i
LADY WOODVILL's *lodgings*

Enter HARRIET *and* BUSY, *her woman*

BUSY
Dear madam! Let me set that curl in order.
HARRIET
Let me alone. I will shake 'em all out of order!
BUSY
Will you never leave this wildness?
HARRIET
Torment me not.
BUSY
Look! There's a knot falling off.   5
HARRIET
Let it drop.
BUSY
But one pin, dear madam.
HARRIET
How do I daily suffer under thy officious fingers!
BUSY
Ah, the difference that is between you and my Lady Dapper!
How uneasy she is if the least thing be amiss about her!   10
HARRIET
She is indeed most exact. Nothing is ever wanting to make her
ugliness remarkable.
BUSY
Jeering people say so.
HARRIET
Her powdering, painting, and her patching never fail in public to
draw the tongues and eyes of all the men upon her.   15
BUSY
She is indeed a little too pretending.
HARRIET
That women should set up for beauty as much in spite of nature
as some men have done for wit!

5 *knot* decorative ribbon

---

3 *wildness* restiveness. See note to I, 100.
14 *patching* it was fashionable for women to wear small patches, normally of black
silk, on the face.

BUSY

I hope without offence one may endeavour to make one's self
agreeable.   20

HARRIET

Not when 'tis impossible. Women then ought to be no more fond
of dressing than fools should be of talking. Hoods and modesty,
masks and silence, things that shadow and conceal—they should
think of nothing else.

BUSY

Jesu! Madam, what will your mother think is become of you?   25
For heaven's sake, go in again.

HARRIET

I won't.

BUSY

This is the extravagant'st thing that ever you did in your life, to
leave her and a gentleman who is to be your husband.

HARRIET

My husband! Hast thou so little wit to think I spoke what I   30
meant when I overjoyed her in the country with a low curtsy and
'What you please, madam; I shall ever be obedient'?

BUSY

Nay, I know not, you have so many fetches.

HARRIET

And this was one, to get her up to London. Nothing else, I assure
thee.   35

BUSY

Well, the man, in my mind, is a fine man!

HARRIET

The man indeed wears his clothes fashionably and has a pretty,
negligent way with him, very courtly and much affected. He
bows, and talks, and smiles so agreeably, as he thinks.

BUSY

I never saw anything so genteel.   40

HARRIET

Varnished over with good breeding many a blockhead makes a
tolerable show.

BUSY

I wonder you do not like him.

HARRIET

I think I might be brought to endure him, and that is all a

33 *fetches* dodges, tricks

28 *extravagant'st* see Barnard (op. cit.), pp. xxxi–iii.

reasonable woman should expect in a husband; but there is duty   45
i' the case, and like the haughty Merab, I
       'Find much aversion in my stubborn mind',
   which
       'Is bred by being promised and designed'.

BUSY
I wish you do not design your own ruin! I partly guess your   50
inclinations, madam. That Mr Dorimant—

HARRIET
Leave your prating and sing some foolish song or other.

BUSY
I will—the song you love so well ever since you saw Mr Dorimant.

SONG

When first Amintas charmed my heart,   55
My heedless sheep began to stray;
The wolves soon stole the greatest part,
And all will now be made a prey.

Ah, let not love your thoughts possess,
'Tis fatal to a shepherdess;   60
The dang'rous passion you must shun,
Or else like me be quite undone.

HARRIET
Shall I be paid down by a covetous parent for a purchase? I need
no land. No, I'll lay myself out all in love. It is decreed—

Enter YOUNG BELLAIR

YOUNG BELLAIR
What generous resolution are you making, madam?   65
HARRIET
Only to be disobedient, sir.

---

48 *which* B, CA, CO (omitted Q1, V; Q2–3, W include 'Which' but place it at the
   beginning of the couplet, 'Which is ... designed'; in Q1 'which' is given as a
   catchword on p. 32, and is clearly meant to link the two quotations)
64 *lay ... out* spend myself

46–49 *Merab ... designed* Merab, elder daughter of Saul, who should have been
    given to David, but was married to Adriel (I Samuel 18.19). Harriet adapts
    Abraham Cowley's description in *Davideis* (1656), Book III: 'And much
    aversion in her stubborn mind /Was bred by being *promis'd* and *design'd*'
    (*Poems*, ed. A. R. Waller (1905), p. 341).
55–62 SONG often reprinted; see Thorpe, p. 102, who also points out that Amintas
    has something of the charm and dangerousness of Dorimant. For Dr Staggins's
    setting, published in 1684, see Appendix A.

YOUNG BELLAIR
  Let me join hands with you in that.
HARRIET
  With all my heart. I never thought I should have given you mine
  so willingly. Here, [*they join hands*]—I, Harriet—
YOUNG BELLAIR
  And I, Harry—   70
HARRIET
  Do solemnly protest—
YOUNG BELLAIR
  And vow—
HARRIET
  That I with you—
YOUNG BELLAIR
  And I with you—
HARRIET, YOUNG BELLAIR
  Will never marry.   75
HARRIET
  A match!
YOUNG BELLAIR
  And no match! How do you like this indifference now?
HARRIET
  You expect I should take it ill, I see.
YOUNG BELLAIR
  'Tis not unnatural for you women to be a little angry you miss a
  conquest—though you would slight the poor man were he in   80
  your power.
HARRIET
  There are some, it may be, have an eye like Bart'lomew, big
  enough for the whole fair, but I am not of the number, and you
  may keep your gingerbread. 'Twill be more acceptable to the
  lady whose dear image it wears, sir.   85
YOUNG BELLAIR
  I must confess, madam, you came a day after the fair.
HARRIET
  You own then you are in love?

79 *for you* Q1 (for young Q2–3)
86 *you . . . fair* too late (proverbial)

82–3 *an eye . . . fair* an allusion to Cokes in Jonson's *Bartholmew Fair* (1614), Act
    III. The fair was held annually on 24 August in Smithfield.
84 *gingerbread* from 'gingimbrat' (M.E.), preserved ginger. The final syllable was
    early confounded with 'bread', and gingerbread, made into various shapes and
    often gilded, was a staple item at fairs. From 1605 the word also carried the
    figurative meaning, 'anything showy and unsubstantial'.

YOUNG BELLAIR

I do.

HARRIET

The confidence is generous, and in return I could almost find in
my heart to let you know my inclinations.   90

YOUNG BELLAIR

Are you in love?

HARRIET

Yes—with this dear town, to that degree I can scarce endure the
country in landscapes and in hangings.

YOUNG BELLAIR

What a dreadful thing 'twould be to be hurried back to Hampshire!   95

HARRIET

Ah! Name it not!

YOUNG BELLAIR

As for us, I find we shall agree well enough. Would we could do
something to deceive the grave people!

HARRIET

Could we delay their quick proceeding, 'twere well. A reprieve is
a good step towards the getting of a pardon.   100

YOUNG BELLAIR

If we give over the game, we are undone. What think you of
playing it on booty?

HARRIET

What do you mean?

YOUNG BELLAIR

Pretend to be in love with one another. 'Twill make some dilat-
ory excuses we may feign pass the better.   105

HARRIET

Let us do't, if it be but for the dear pleasure of dissembling.

YOUNG BELLAIR

Can you play your part?

HARRIET

I know not what it is to love, but I have made pretty remarks by
being now and then where lovers meet. Where did you leave
their gravities?   110

93 *hangings* wall-tapestries
108 *remarks* observations

102 *playing . . . on booty* joining with confederates to 'spoil' or victimize another
    player; to play into the hands of confederates in order to share the 'plunder'
    with them.

YOUNG BELLAIR

I' the next room. Your mother was censuring our modern gallant.

Enter OLD BELLAIR *and* LADY WOODVILL

HARRIET

Peace! Here they come. I will lean against this wall and look bashfully down upon my fan, while you, like an amorous spark, modishly entertain me.   115

LADY WOODVILL [*to* OLD BELLAIR]

Never go about to excuse 'em. Come, come, it was not so when I was a young woman.

OLD BELLAIR

Adod, they're something disrespectful—

LADY WOODVILL

Quality was then considered, and not rallied by every fleering fellow.   120

OLD BELLAIR

Youth will have its jest, adod it will.

LADY WOODVILL

'Tis good breeding now to be civil to none but players and Exchange women. They are treated by 'em as much above their condition as others are below theirs.

OLD BELLAIR

Out a pize on 'em! Talk no more: the rogues ha' got an ill habit of   125
preferring beauty, no matter where they find it.

LADY WOODVILL

See, your son and my daughter. They have improved their acquaintance since they were within!

OLD BELLAIR

Adod, methinks they have! Let's keep back and observe.

YOUNG BELLAIR [*to* HARRIET]

Now for a look and gestures that may persuade 'em I am saying   130
all the passionate things imaginable.

HARRIET

Your head a little more on one side. Ease yourself on your left leg and play with your right hand.

YOUNG BELLAIR

Thus, is it not?

HARRIET

Now set your right leg firm on the ground, adjust your belt, then   135
look about you.

---

119 *fleering* mocking, jeering
123 *Exchange women* women serving in the shops of the New Exchange

YOUNG BELLAIR

A little exercising will make me perfect.

HARRIET

Smile, and turn to me again very sparkish.

YOUNG BELLAIR

Will you take your turn and be instructed?

HARRIET

With all my heart.   140

YOUNG BELLAIR

At one motion play your fan, roll your eyes, and then settle a kind look upon me.

HARRIET

So.

YOUNG BELLAIR

Now spread your fan, look down upon it, and tell the sticks with a finger.   145

HARRIET

Very modish.

YOUNG BELLAIR

Clap your hand up to your bosom, hold down your gown. Shrug a little, draw up your breasts and let 'em fall again, gently, with a sigh or two, *etc.*

HARRIET

By the good instructions you give, I suspect you for one of those   150
malicious observers who watch people's eyes and from innocent looks make scandalous conclusions.

YOUNG BELLAIR

I know some, indeed, who out of mere love to mischief are as vigilant as jealousy itself, and will give you an account of every glance that passes at a play and i' the Circle.   155

HARRIET

'Twill not be amiss now to seem a little pleasant.

YOUNG BELLAIR

Clap your fan then in both your hands, snatch it to your mouth, smile, and with a lively motion fling your body a little forwards. So,—now spread it, fall back on the sudden, cover your face with it, and break out into a loud laughter.—Take up! Look   160
grave, and fall a-fanning of yourself. Admirably well acted!

HARRIET

I think I am pretty apt at these matters.

49 *etc.* Carnochan regards this as a stage direction, and comments, 'the actors were, evidently, to improvise'.

55 *the Circle* probably the 'Tour' or Ring in Hyde Park, used by the fashionable for riding and walking. Carnochan points out that the reference may possibly be to the assembly at Court (cf. IV.i, 120).

OLD BELLAIR [*to* LADY WOODVILL]
   Adod, I like this well.

LADY WOODVILL
   This promises something.

OLD BELLAIR [*coming forward*]
   Come, there is love i' the case, adod there is, or will be.—What   165
   say you, young lady?

HARRIET
   All in good time, sir. You expect we should fall to and love as
   gamecocks fight, as soon as we are set together. Adod, you're
   unreasonable!

OLD BELLAIR
   Adod, sirrah, I like thy wit well.   170

—   *Enter a* SERVANT

SERVANT
   The coach is at the door, madam.

OLD BELLAIR
   Go, get you and take the air together.

LADY WOODVILL
   Will not you go with us?

OLD BELLAIR
   Out a pize! Adod, I ha' business and cannot. We shall meet at
   night at my sister Townley's.   175

YOUNG BELLAIR (*aside*)
   He's going to Emilia. I overheard him talk of a collation.

                                        Exeunt

Act III, Scene ii
[LADY TOWNLEY'*s house*]

Enter LADY TOWNLEY, EMILIA, *and* MEDLEY

LADY TOWNLEY
   I pity the young lovers we last talked of, though to say truth,
   their conduct has been so indiscreet they deserve to be unfortunate.

MEDLEY
   You have an exact account, from the great lady i' the box down to
   the little orange-wench.   5

---

170 *sirrah* applied to a woman seriously or in jest up to 1711, but almost certainly
     used here to indicate Old Bellair's old-fashioned vulgarity.

EMILIA

You're a living libel, a breathing lampoon. I wonder you are not
torn in pieces.

MEDLEY

What think you of setting up an office of intelligence for these
matters? The project may get money.

LADY TOWNLEY

You would have great dealings with country ladies. 10

MEDLEY

More than Muddiman has with their husbands.

Enter BELLINDA

LADY TOWNLEY

Bellinda, what has been become of you? We have not seen you
here of late with your friend Mrs Loveit.

BELLINDA

Dear creature, I left her but now so sadly afflicted.

LADY TOWNLEY

With her old distemper, jealousy? 15

MEDLEY

Dorimant has played her some new prank.

BELLINDA

Well, that Dorimant is certainly the worst man breathing.

EMILIA

I once thought so.

BELLINDA

And do you not think so still?

EMILIA

No, indeed. 20

BELLINDA

Oh, Jesu!

EMILIA

The town does him a great deal of injury, and I will never believe
what it says of a man I do not know again, for his sake.

6 *libel* . . . *lampoon* libel in the sense of a broadsheet or manuscript poem attacking
a person's character, thus making it almost synonymous with lampoon, and
supporting the pun on Medley being torn to pieces. Libels, which were often
pinned to their victim's door, circulated in manuscript—Sir Roger L'Estrange
complained in 1677 that 'it is notorious that not one in forty libels ever comes to
the press, though by the help of manuscripts they are well-nigh as public'
(quoted, *Poems of Affairs of State*, vol. I (1660–78), ed. G. de F. Lord (New
Haven and London, 1963), p. xxxvii). See also I, 242–3 and note.

11 *Muddiman* Henry Muddiman (1629–92), first editor of the *London Gazette*, but
referred to here for his newsletters, which had great popularity among country
gentlemen.

BELLINDA

You make me wonder.

LADY TOWNLEY

He's a very well-bred man.   2!

BELLINDA

But strangely ill-natured.

EMILIA

Then he's a very witty man.

BELLINDA

But a man of no principles.

MEDLEY

Your man of principles is a very fine thing, indeed!

BELLINDA

To be preferred to men of parts by women who have regard to   3(
their reputation and quiet. Well, were I minded to play the fool,
he should be the last man I'd think of.

MEDLEY

He has been the first in many ladies' favours, though you are so
severe, madam.

LADY TOWNLEY

What he may be for a lover, I know not, but he's a very pleasant   3!
acquaintance, I am sure.

BELLINDA

Had you seen him use Mrs Loveit as I have done, you would
never endure him more.

EMILIA

What, he has quarrelled with her again?

BELLINDA

Upon the slightest occasion. He's jealous of Sir Fopling.   4(

LADY TOWNLEY

She never saw him in her life but yesterday, and that was here.

EMILIA

On my conscience, he's the only man in town that's her aversion.
How horribly out of humour she was all the while he talked to
her!

BELLINDA

And somebody has wickedly told him—   4!

EMILIA

Here he comes.

Enter DORIMANT

MEDLEY

Dorimant, you are luckily come to justify yourself. Here's a
lady—

BELLINDA
—Has a word or two to say to you from a disconsolate person.
DORIMANT
You tender your reputation too much, I know, madam, to   50
whisper with me before this good company.
BELLINDA
To serve Mrs Loveit, I'll make a bold venture.
DORIMANT
Here's Medley, the very spirit of scandal.
BELLINDA
No matter!
EMILIA
'Tis something you are unwilling to hear, Mr Dorimant.   55
LADY TOWNLEY
Tell him, Bellinda, whether he will or no.
BELLINDA (*aloud*)
Mrs Loveit—
DORIMANT
Softly, these are laughers. You do not know 'em.
BELLINDA (*to* DORIMANT, *apart*)
In a word, you've made me hate you, which I thought you never
could have done.   60
DORIMANT
In obeying your commands.
BELLINDA
'Twas a cruel part you played. How could you act it?
DORIMANT
Nothing is cruel to a man who could kill himself to please you.
Remember, five o'clock tomorrow morning.
BELLINDA
I tremble when you name it.   65
DORIMANT
Be sure you come.
BELLINDA
I shan't.
DORIMANT
Swear you will.
BELLINDA
I dare not.
DORIMANT
Swear, I say!   70
BELLINDA
By my life, by all the happiness I hope for—
DORIMANT
You will.

BELLINDA
　I will.
DORIMANT
　Kind.
BELLINDA
　I am glad I've sworn. I vow I think I should ha' failed you else.　75
DORIMANT
　Surprisingly kind! In what temper did you leave Loveit?
BELLINDA
　Her raving was prettily over, and she began to be in a brave way
　of defying you and all your works. Where have you been since
　you went from thence?
DORIMANT
　I looked in at the play.　80
BELLINDA
　I have promised and must return to her again.
DORIMANT
　Persuade her to walk in the Mall this evening.
BELLINDA
　She hates the place and will not come.
DORIMANT
　Do all you can to prevail with her.
BELLINDA
　For what purpose?　85
DORIMANT
　Sir Fopling will be here anon. I'll prepare him to set upon her
　there before me.
BELLINDA
　You persecute her too much. But I'll do all you'll ha' me.
DORIMANT (aloud)
　Tell her plainly, 'tis grown so dull a business I can drudge on no
　longer.　90
EMILIA
　There are afflictions in love, Mr Dorimant.
DORIMANT
　You women make 'em, who are commonly as unreasonable in
　that as you are at play: without the advantage be on your side, a
　man can never quietly give over when he's weary.
MEDLEY
　If you would play without being obliged to complaisance,　95
　Dorimant, you should play in public places.

---

77 *prettily* cleverly, aptly

95 *complaisance* see note to I, 373.

DORIMANT

Ordinaries were a very good thing for that, but gentlemen do not
of late frequent 'em. The deep play is now in private houses.

BELLINDA *offering to steal away*

LADY TOWNLEY

Bellinda, are you leaving us so soon?

BELLINDA

I am to go to the Park with Mrs Loveit, madam. [*Exit* BELLINDA]   100

LADY TOWNLEY

This confidence will go nigh to spoil this young creature.

MEDLEY

'Twill do her good, madam. Young men who are brought up
under practising lawyers prove the abler counsel when they
come to be called to the bar themselves.

DORIMANT

The town has been very favourable to you this afternoon, my   105
Lady Townley. You use to have an *embarras* of chairs and
coaches at your door, an uproar of footmen in your hall, and a
noise of fools above here.

LADY TOWNLEY

Indeed, my house is the general rendezvous and, next to the
playhouse, is the common refuge of all the young idle people.   110

EMILIA

Company is a very good thing, madam, but I wonder you do not
love it a little more chosen.

LADY TOWNLEY

'Tis good to have an universal taste. We should love wit, but for
variety be able to divert ourselves with the extravagancies of
those who want it.   115

MEDLEY

Fools will make you laugh.

EMILIA

For once or twice—but the repetition of their folly after a visit or
two grows tedious and insufferable.

LADY TOWNLEY

You are a little too delicate, Emilia.

---

97 *Ordinaries* eating houses, taverns
101 *confidence* excess of assurance, impudence (or, possibly, intimate relationship)

---

106 *embarras . . . coaches* cf. *embarras de voitures* (Fr.), a congestion of carriages.
Although 'embarras' (i.e. embarrassment) occurs as an uncommon English
word from 1664 into the eighteenth century, Q1's spelling 'ambara's' suggests
that Etherege intended the French word. It is used again by Sir Fopling (l.
165).

Enter a PAGE

PAGE

Sir Fopling Flutter, madam, desires to know if you are to be   120
seen.

LADY TOWNLEY

Here's the freshest fool in town, and one who has not cloyed you
yet.—Page!

PAGE

Madam?

LADY TOWNLEY

Desire him to walk up.   [*Exit* PAGE]   125

DORIMANT

Do not you fall on him, Medley, and snub him. Soothe him up in
his extravagance. He will show the better.

MEDLEY

You know I have a natural indulgence for fools and need not this
caution, sir.

Enter SIR FOPLING, *with his* PAGE *after him*

SIR FOPLING

Page, wait without.   [*Exit* PAGE]   130
([*To*]LADY TOWNLEY) Madam, I kiss your hands. I see yesterday
was nothing of chance; the *belles assemblées* form themselves here
every day. (*To* EMILIA) Lady, your servant.—Dorimant, let me
embrace thee. Without lying, I have not met with any of my
acquaintance who retain so much of Paris as thou dost—the very   135
air thou hadst when the marquise mistook thee i' the Tuileries
and cried, '*Hé, chevalier!*' and then begged thy pardon.

DORIMANT

I would fain wear in fashion as long as I can, sir. 'Tis a thing to be
valued in men as well as baubles.

SIR FOPLING

Thou art a man of wit and understands the town. Prithee, let   140
thee and I be intimate. There is no living without making some
good man the *confident* of our pleasures.

---

132 *belles assemblées* fashionable gatherings
140 *understands* Q1 (understand'st W, V)

---

126 *Soothe . . . up* encourage or humour a person by expressing assent or approval
(1573–1705). *OED* cites this as an example.
136 *the Tuileries* the gardens of the Palais de Tuileries, laid out by Le Nôtre for
Louis XIV, and so called because the palace occupied the site of an old
brick-yard.

DORIMANT

'Tis true—but there is no man so improper for such a business as
I am.

SIR FOPLING

Prithee, why hast thou so modest an opinion of thyself?   145

DORIMANT

Why, first, I could never keep a secret in my life; and then, there
is no charm so infallibly makes me fall in love with a woman as
my knowing a friend loves her. I deal honestly with you.

SIR FOPLING

Thy humour's very gallant, or let me perish. I knew a French
count so like thee.   150

LADY TOWNLEY

Wit, I perceive, has more power over you than beauty, Sir
Fopling, else you would not have let this lady stand so long
neglected.

SIR FOPLING (*to* EMILIA)

A thousand pardons, madam—some civilities due of course
upon the meeting a long absent friend. The *éclat* of so much   155
beauty, I confess, ought to have charmed me sooner.

EMILIA

The *brillant* of so much good language, sir, has much more
power than the little beauty I can boast.

SIR FOPLING

I never saw anything prettier than this high work on your *point
d'Espagne*.   160

EMILIA

'Tis not so rich as *point de Venise*.

SIR FOPLING

Not altogether, but looks cooler, and is more proper for the
season.—Dorimant, is not that Medley?

DORIMANT

The same, sir.

---

154 *madam ... civilities* Q1 (madam. Some civility's Q2–3, CA)
155 *éclat* brilliance
157 *brillant* glitter
159 *high work* raised needlework
159–60 *point d'Espagne* Spanish lace
161 *point de Venise* Venetian lace

---

54 *madam ... of course* 'of course' means customary, natural, and Sir Fopling's
    ellipsis can be paraphrased, 'My rudeness to you was occasioned by the need to
    pay the customary civilities ...' Carnochan's emendation (see textual note)
    gives the sense, 'some civility is naturally due ...', and is a possible reading.

SIR FOPLING [*to* MEDLEY]

Forgive me, sir; in this *embarras* of civilities I could not come to   16.
have you in my arms sooner. You understand an equipage the
best of any man in town, I hear.

MEDLEY

By my own you would not guess it.

SIR FOPLING

There are critics who do not write, sir.

MEDLEY

Our peevish poets will scarce allow it.   17(

SIR FOPLING

Damn 'em, they'll allow no man wit who does not play the fool
like themselves and show it! Have you taken notice of the gallesh
I brought over?

MEDLEY

Oh, yes! 'T has quite another air than the English makes.

SIR FOPLING

'Tis as easily known from an English tumbril as an Inns of Court   17.
man is from one of us.

DORIMANT

Truly there is a *bel air* in galleshes as well as men.

MEDLEY

But there are few so delicate to observe it.

SIR FOPLING

The world is generally very *grossier* here, indeed.

---

165 *embarras* V, CA (Ambara's Q1ᵘ; Ambaras Q1ᶜ; the change may be meant to
     suggest that Sir Fopling mispronounces the French) embarrassment
172 *gallesh* Q1 (*calèche* V)
175 *tumbril* two-wheeled cart which tips to empty its load, especially a dung-cart
175 *Inns of Court man* lawyer
177 *bel air* elegant style
177 *galleshes* Q1 (*calèshes* V)
179 *grossier* vulgar, coarse

---

166 *equipage* presumably in the sense of retinue, train of attendants (*OED*,
     1590–1736), rather than apparel, costume. (Sir Fopling's comment at ll. 172–3
     suggests that he could be thinking of 'equipage' as meaning his carriage and
     attendants, but that appears to be an eighteenth-century usage).
172, 177 *gallesh* var. spelling of 'calash' from Fr. *calèche*: a light carriage with low
     wheels and a removable folding hood or top. Newly introduced from France.
     OED records the first occurrence in 1666, and Dryden's *Marriage-à-la-Mode*
     (1673) has, 'I have been at your Lodgings in my new *Galeche*' (*Dramatic Works*,
     ed. M. Summers (1931–32), vol. 3, 212).
178 *delicate* Dorimant plays on two meanings—1) fastidious, discerning, 2) dainty,
     effeminate (obs.)

LADY TOWNLEY [*to* EMILIA]

He's very fine.   180

EMILIA

Extreme proper!

SIR FOPLING

A slight suit I made to appear in at my first arrival—not worthy your consideration, ladies.

DORIMANT

The pantaloon is very well mounted.

SIR FOPLING

The tassels are new and pretty.   185

MEDLEY

I never saw a coat better cut.

SIR FOPLING

It makes me show long-waisted, and, I think, slender.

DORIMANT

That's the shape our ladies dote on.

MEDLEY

Your breech, though, is a handful too high, in my eye, Sir Fopling.   190

SIR FOPLING

Peace, Medley, I have wished it lower a thousand times, but a pox on 't, 'twill not be!

LADY TOWNLEY

His gloves are well fringed, large, and graceful.

SIR FOPLING

I was always eminent for being *bien ganté*.

EMILIA

He wears nothing but what are originals of the most famous   195
hands in Paris.

SIR FOPLING

You are in the right, madam.

LADY TOWNLEY

The suit?

---

194 *bien ganté* well-gloved

---

184 *pantaloon* usually in plural, 'pantaloons': a kind of breeches in fashion after the
Restoration, hanging wide down to the knees. Evelyn is cited by *OED* as saying
in 1661, '. . . Pantaloons, which are a kind of Hermaphrodite and of neither
sex'. Since Dorimant uses the singular, he may be playing on Pantaloon, the
foolish old man in Italian harlequinade.
184 *mounted* Dorimant appears to be punning: 1) the breeches are well-mounted,
that is, raised up away from the legs, 2) metaphorically, the ridiculous pantaloons are ridden (mounted) by an appropriate fool.

SIR FOPLING
　Barroy.
EMILIA
　The garniture?   200
SIR FOPLING
　Le Gras.
MEDLEY
　The shoes?
SIR FOPLING
　Piccar.
DORIMANT
　The periwig?
SIR FOPLING
　Chedreux.   205
LADY TOWNLEY, EMILIA
　The gloves?
SIR FOPLING
　Orangerie—you know the smell, ladies. —Dorimant, I could
　find in my heart for an amusement to have a gallantry with some
　of our English ladies.
DORIMANT
　'Tis a thing no less necessary to confirm the reputation of your 210
　wit than a duel will be to satisfy the town of your courage.
SIR FOPLING
　Here was a woman yesterday—
DORIMANT
　Mrs Loveit.
SIR FOPLING
　You have named her!
DORIMANT
　You cannot pitch on a better for your purpose.   215
SIR FOPLING
　Prithee, what is she?

199–205 *Barroy . . . Chedreux* of this list of fashionable Parisian merchants I can
　　identify only Chedreux, who gave his name to a kind of wig.
200 *garniture* ornament, trimming of ribbons and jewellery, added to clothing.
　　Strongly connected to its French origins at this date. First example in *OED* is
　　from 1667. J. Lacey's *Sir Hercules Buffoon* (1684) has, 'My French garniture, a
　　pox on 'em, is not yet arrived from Paris' (II.ii).
207 *Orangerie* scent or perfume extracted from the orange-flower. *OED* records
　　this instance as its first occurrence. Essence of orange was a popular scent, and
　　in Dryden's *The Kind Keeper* (1680) Mrs Tricksy tells Limberham, 'I have
　　been looking over the last present of *Orange* Gloves you made me; and
　　methinks I do not like the scent' (III.i). A quart of orange-flower water is
　　included in the effects of a fop in *Tatler*, No. 113. See also note to V.i, 34.

DORIMANT

A person of quality, and one who has a rest of reputation enough
to make the conquest considerable. Besides I hear she likes you
too.

SIR FOPLING

Methoughts she seemed, though, very reserved and uneasy all   220
the time I entertained her.

DORIMANT

Grimace and affectation! You will see her i' the Mall tonight.

SIR FOPLING

Prithee, let thee and I take the air together.

DORIMANT

I am engaged to Medley, but I'll meet you at St James's and give
you some information upon the which you may regulate your   225
proceedings.

SIR FOPLING

All the world will be in the Park tonight. —Ladies, 'twere pity to
keep so much beauty longer within doors and rob the Ring of all
those charms that should adorn it. —Hey, page!

Enter PAGE

See that all my people be ready.   [PAGE] *goes out again*   230
Dorimant, *à revoir*.   [*Exit* SIR FOPLING]

MEDLEY

A fine-mettled coxcomb.

DORIMANT

Brisk and insipid—

MEDLEY

Pert and dull.

EMILIA

However you despise him, gentlemen, I'll lay my life he passes   235
for a wit with many.

---

217 *rest* remainder
229–30 s.d. *Enter . . . again* CA (Q1 and all other texts give as a single sentence after
    l. 229)
231 *à revoir* ed. (a Revoir Q1; *au revoir* V, CA)

---

228 *the Ring* see note to III.i, 155
231 *à revoir* in following Q1 here the text adopts Brian Gibbons's shrewd observa-
    tion that since Dorimant mocks Sir Fopling's usage (l. 246), the knight is
    probably pretending that his is the fashionable pronunciation of the phrase in
    Paris. Or it may be an example of his 'pretty lisp' (I, 327).

DORIMANT

That may very well be. Nature has her cheats, stums a brain, and puts sophisticate dullness often on the tasteless multitude for true wit and good humour. —Medley, come.

MEDLEY

I must go a little way. I will meet you i' the Mall.   24

DORIMANT

I'll walk through the garden thither. (*To the women*) We shall meet anon and bow.

LADY TOWNLEY

Not tonight. We are engaged about a business, the knowledge of which may make you laugh hereafter.

MEDLEY

Your servant, ladies.   24

DORIMANT

À revoir, as Sir Fopling says.

[*Exeunt* MEDLEY *and* DORIMANT]

LADY TOWNLEY

The old man will be here immediately.

EMILIA

Let's expect him i' the garden.

LADY TOWNLEY

Go, you are a rogue!

EMILIA

I can't abide you!   *Exeunt*   25

Act III, Scene iii
The Mall

Enter HARRIET *and* YOUNG BELLAIR, *she pulling him*

HARRIET

Come along!

246 *A revoir* ed. (a Revoir Q1; *au revoir* V, CA)
248 *expect* wait for

---

237 *stum* to renew (wine) by mixing with stum or must and raising a new fermentation (from the Dutch). *OED* gives first occurrence as 1656, and the first figurative use in 1661. Oldham's *Letter from the Country* (1678) has, 'As the poor Drunkard, when Wine stums his brains, /Anointed with that Liquor, thinks he reigns'.

238 *sophisticate* probably in the obsolescent sense, 'adulterated, impure, mixed with some foreign substance'. The last example given by the *OED* is from Maynwaring's *Ancient and Modern Practice of Physick* (1671), 66, 'Yet this cheap sophisticate Medicine . . . will cost you six times as much'. This sense would continue Dorimant's metaphor of adulterated wine passed off upon the 'tasteless multitude'.

YOUNG BELLAIR
  And leave your mother?
HARRIET
  Busy will be sent with a hue and cry after us; but that's no
  matter.
YOUNG BELLAIR
  'Twill look strangely in me.   5
HARRIET
  She'll believe it a freak of mine and never blame your manners.
YOUNG BELLAIR [*pointing*]
  What reverend acquaintance is that she has met?
HARRIET
  A fellow beauty of the last king's time, though by the ruins you
  would hardly guess it.   *Exeunt*

> *Enter* DORIMANT *and crosses the stage*
> *Enter* YOUNG BELLAIR *and* HARRIET

YOUNG BELLAIR
  By this time your mother is in a fine taking.   10
HARRIET
  If your friend Mr Dorimant were but here now, that she might
  find me talking with him!
YOUNG BELLAIR
  She does not know him but dreads him, I hear, of all mankind.
HARRIET
  She concludes if he does but speak to a woman, she's undone—is
  on her knees every day to pray heaven defend me from him.   15
YOUNG BELLAIR
  You do not apprehend him so much as she does?
HARRIET
  I never saw anything in him that was frightful.
YOUNG BELLAIR
  On the contrary, have you not observed something extreme
  delightful in his wit and person?
HARRIET
  He's agreeable and pleasant, I must own, but he does so much   20
  affect being so, he displeases me.
YOUNG BELLAIR
  Lord, madam, all he does and says is so easy and so natural.
HARRIET
  Some men's verses seem so to the unskilful; but labour i' the one
  and affectation in the other to the judicious plainly appear.

6 *freak* whim, capricious humour
10 *taking* excited or impassioned state

YOUNG BELLAIR

I never heard him accused of affectation before.   25

Enter DORIMANT *and stares upon her*

HARRIET

It passes on the easy town, who are favourably pleased in him to call it humour.   [*Exeunt* YOUNG BELLAIR *and* HARRIET]

DORIMANT

'Tis she! It must be she—that lovely hair, that easy shape, those wanton eyes, and all those melting charms about her mouth which Medley spoke of. I'll follow the lottery and put in for a   30 prize with my friend Bellair.

[*Exit* DORIMANT, *repeating*]—
'In love the victors from the vanquished fly;
They fly that wound, and they pursue that die'.

Enter YOUNG BELLAIR *and* HARRIET, *and after them* DORIMANT, *standing at a distance*

YOUNG BELLAIR

Most people prefer Hyde Park to this place.

HARRIET

It has the better reputation, I confess; but I abominate the dull   35 diversions there—the formal bows, the affected smiles, the silly by-words and amorous tweers in passing. Here one meets with a little conversation now and then.

YOUNG BELLAIR

These conversations have been fatal to some of your sex, madam.   40

HARRIET

It may be so. Because some who want temper have been undone

26 *passes on* goes uncensured by
41 *temper* character, self-control

26, 28 *easy* see note to I, 119, and Barnard (op. cit.), p. xxxiii.
28–30 '*Tis* . . . *of* see I, 117–25 and notes.
30 *the lottery* common way of raising money for the government or for individuals.
32–3 *In* . . . *die* final couplet of Waller's 'To a Friend, of the Different Successes of their Loves' (*Poems*, ed. G. Thorn Drury (1901), vol. 1, 103).
34 *Hyde Park* Etherege's form *High Park*, here and at V.ii, 138, is unusual and probably went out of use by the early eighteenth century. Brett-Smith knew of no occurrences outside Etherege, but Conaghan cites Lady Margaret Cavendish's *A Piece of a Play*, 'Madam, are you for a Play? or Court? or *High-Park* to day?' (*Plays* (1668), p. 14).
37 *tweer* var. spelling of 'twire', a glance, leer (obs. slang). *OED* gives this as first occurrence (the last is from 1719), but the verb occurs from 1600, and remained in dialect until the nineteenth century.

by gaming, must others who have it wholly deny themselves the
pleasure of play?

DORIMANT (*coming up gently and bowing to her*)

Trust me, it were unreasonable, madam.

HARRIET

Lord! Who's this?   *She starts and looks grave*   45

YOUNG BELLAIR

Dorimant.

DORIMANT

Is this the woman your father would have you marry?

YOUNG BELLAIR

It is.

DORIMANT

Her name?

YOUNG BELLAIR

Harriet.   50

DORIMANT [*aside*]

I am not mistaken. —She's handsome.

YOUNG BELLAIR

Talk to her; her wit is better than her face. We were wishing for
you but now.

DORIMANT (*to* HARRIET)

Overcast with seriousness o' the sudden! A thousand smiles were
shining in that face but now—I never saw so quick a change of   55
weather.

HARRIET (*aside*)

I feel as great a change within, but he shall never know it.

DORIMANT

You were talking of play, madam. Pray, what may be your stint?

HARRIET

A little harmless discourse in public walks, or at most an
appointment in a box, barefaced, at the playhouse. You are for   60
masks and private meetings, where women engage for all they
are worth, I hear.

DORIMANT

I have been used to deep play, but I can make one at small game
when I like my gamester well.

HARRIET

And be so unconcerned you'll ha' no pleasure in 't.   65

DORIMANT

Where there is a considerable sum to be won, the hope of
drawing people in makes every trifle considerable.

58 *stint* upper limit

HARRIET

The sordidness of men's natures, I know, makes 'em willing to
flatter and comply with the rich, though they are sure never to be
the better for 'em.   70

DORIMANT

'Tis in their power to do us good, and we despair not but at some
time or other they may be willing.

HARRIET

To men who have fared in this town like you, 'twould be a great
mortification to live on hope. Could you keep a Lent for a
mistress?   75

DORIMANT

In expectation of a happy Easter, and though time be very
precious, think forty days well lost to gain your favour.

HARRIET

Mr Bellair! Let us walk. 'Tis time to leave him. Men grow dull
when they begin to be particular.

DORIMANT

You're mistaken. Flattery will not ensue, though I know you're   80
greedy of the praises of the whole Mall.

HARRIET

You do me wrong.

DORIMANT

I do not. As I followed you, I observed how you were pleased
when the fops cried 'She's handsome, very handsome, by God
she is!' and whispered aloud your name—the thousand several   85
forms you put your face into; then, to make yourself more
agreeable, how wantonly you played with your head, flung back
your locks, and looked smilingly over your shoulder at 'em.

HARRIET

I do not go begging the men's, as you do the ladies' good liking,
with a sly softness in your looks and a gentle slowness in your   90
bows as you pass by 'em. As thus, sir—(*Acts him*) Is not this like
you?

Enter LADY WOODVILL *and* BUSY

YOUNG BELLAIR

Your mother, madam!   *Pulls* HARRIET. *She composes herself*

LADY WOODVILL

Ah, my dear child Harriet!

85-6 *name*— ... *into;* CA (name, ... into; Q1; name; ... into; B)

68 *sordidness* low, mean, or mercenary character or motives.

BUSY [aside]

    Now is she so pleased with finding her again, she cannot chide   95
her.

LADY WOODVILL

    Come away!

DORIMANT

    'Tis now but high Mall, madam—the most entertaining time of
all the evening.

HARRIET

    I would fain see that Dorimant, mother, you so cry out of for a   100
monster. He's in the Mall, I hear.

LADY WOODVILL

    Come away, then! The plague is here, and you should dread the
infection.

YOUNG BELLAIR

    You may be misinformed of the gentleman.

LADY WOODVILL

    Oh, no! I hope you do not know him. He is the prince of all the   105
devils in the town—delights in nothing but in rapes and riots.

DORIMANT

    If you did but hear him speak, madam—

LADY WOODVILL

    Oh, he has a tongue, they say, would tempt the angels to a second
fall.

    Enter SIR FOPLING *with his equipage, six footmen and a page*

SIR FOPLING

    Hey, Champagne, Norman, La Rose, La Fleur, La Tour, La   110
Verdure!—Dorimant!—

LADY WOODVILL

    Here, here he is among this rout! He names him!— Come away,
Harriet, come away!

    Exeunt LADY WOODVILL, HARRIET, BUSY, *and* YOUNG BELLAIR

DORIMANT [aside]

    This fool's coming has spoiled all. She's gone, but she has left a
pleasing image of herself behind that wanders in my soul.— It   115
must not settle there.

100 *of* Q1 (V omits)

---

  98 *high Mall* the busiest and most fashionable hour for visiting the Mall.

109 s.d. *equipage* here 'retinue', but see note to III.ii, 166.

110 *Champagne ... Verdure* see note to III.iii, 252–3, which accounts for some of
    these names. On 'champagne' see note to IV.i, 371.

SIR FOPLING
>What reverie is this? Speak, man.

DORIMANT
>   'Snatched from myself, how far behind
>   Already I behold the shore!'

Enter MEDLEY

MEDLEY
>Dorimant, a discovery! I met with Bellair—   120

DORIMANT
>You can tell me no news, sir. I know all.

MEDLEY
>How do you like the daughter?

DORIMANT
>You never came so near truth in your life as you did in her description.

MEDLEY
>What think you of the mother?   12[

DORIMANT
>Whatever I think of her, she thinks very well of me, I find.

MEDLEY
>Did she know you?

DORIMANT
>She did not. Whether she does now or no, I know not. Here was a pleasant scene towards, when in came Sir Fopling, mustering up his equipage, and at the latter end named me and frighted her   13[
>away.

MEDLEY
>Loveit and Bellinda are not far off. I saw 'em alight at St James's.

DORIMANT
>Sir Fopling, hark you, a word or two. (*Whispers*)—Look you do not want assurance.

SIR FOPLING
>I never do on these occasions.   13[

---

129 *towards* imminent

---

117 *reverie* bears the modern meaning, but in Middle English it had meant 'revel-ling, rejoicing', and was readopted from French *rêverie* in the seventeenth century. *OED* records its first instance from 1657, but it retained a strong sense of its French origin into the eighteenth century.

118–19 *Snatched . . . shore* Waller, 'Of Loving at First Sight', ll. 3–4 (*Poems*, ed. G. Thorn Drury (1901), vol. 1, 100).

132 *St James's* Carnochan thinks the reference is to St James's Palace, opposite the Park.

DORIMANT

Walk on, we must not be seen together. Make your advantage of what I have told you. The next turn you will meet the lady.

SIR FOPLING

Hey! Follow me all.   *Exeunt* SIR FOPLING *and his equipage*

DORIMANT

Medley, you shall see good sport anon between Loveit and this Fopling.   140

MEDLEY

I thought there was something toward, by that whisper.

DORIMANT

You know a worthy principle of hers?

MEDLEY

Not to be so much as civil to a man who speaks to her in the presence of him she professes to love.

DORIMANT

I have encouraged Fopling to talk to her tonight.   145

MEDLEY

Now you are here, she will go nigh to beat him.

DORIMANT

In the humour she's in, her love will make her do some very extravagant thing, doubtless.

MEDLEY

What was Bellinda's business with you at my Lady Townley's?

DORIMANT

To get me to meet Loveit here in order to an *éclaircissement*. I   150
made some difficulty of it and have prepared this rencounter to make good my jealousy.

MEDLEY

Here they come.

Enter MRS LOVEIT, BELLINDA, *and* PERT

DORIMANT

I'll meet her and provoke her with a deal of dumb civility in

---

137 *next turn* next circuit of the Mall
150 *éclaircissement* clearing up (of a mystery, misunderstanding)

---

151 *rencounter* chance meeting is the primary meaning, but the word could also
mean a military skirmish, a duel, or a contest in wit or argument (*OED*). Verity
emends to *rencontre* (unnecessarily since Q1's 'rancounter' is a variant spelling
of 'rencounter').

passing by, then turn short and be behind her when Sir Fopling   155
sets upon her—[*Bows to* MRS LOVEIT]
                    'See how unregarded now
                    That piece of beauty passes'.
                                    Exeunt DORIMANT *and* MEDLEY

BELLINDA
How wonderful respectfully he bowed!
PERT
He's always over-mannerly when he has done a mischief.   160
BELLINDA
Methoughts, indeed, at the same time he had a strange, despis-
ing countenance.
PERT
The unlucky look he thinks becomes him.
BELLINDA
I was afraid you would have spoke to him, my dear.
MRS LOVEIT
I would have died first. He shall no more find me the loving fool   165
he has done.
BELLINDA
You love him still!
MRS LOVEIT
No.
PERT
I wish you did not.
MRS LOVEIT
I do not, and I will have you think so!— What made you hale me   170
to this odious place, Bellinda?
BELLINDA
I hate to be hulched up in a coach. Walking is much better.
MRS LOVEIT
Would we could meet Sir Fopling now!
BELLINDA
Lord, would you not avoid him?
MRS LOVEIT
I would make him all the advances that may be.   175
BELLINDA
That would confirm Dorimant's suspicion, my dear.

---

163 *unlucky* mischievous, malicious

157–8 *See ... passes* Suckling, 'Sonnet I', ll. 1–2, which actually begins 'Do'st ...'
    (*Sir John Suckling, The Non-Dramatic Works*, ed. Thomas Clayton (Oxford
    1971), p. 47).
172 *hulched up* doubled up (obs.). *OED* gives this as the only example of the verb
    formed from 'hulch', hunch-backed (1611–1708).

MRS LOVEIT

He is not jealous, but I will make him so, and be revenged a way he little thinks on.

BELLINDA (*aside*)

If she should make him jealous, that may make him fond of her again. I must dissuade her from it.— Lord, my dear, this will   180
certainly make him hate you.

MRS LOVEIT

'Twill make him uneasy, though he does not care for me. I know the effects of jealousy on men of his proud temper.

BELLINDA

'Tis a fantastic remedy: its operations are dangerous and uncertain.   185

MRS LOVEIT

'Tis the strongest cordial we can give to dying love. It often brings it back when there's no sign of life remaining. But I design not so much the reviving his, as my revenge.

Enter SIR FOPLING *and his equipage*

SIR FOPLING

Hey! Bid the coachman send home four of his horses and bring the coach to Whitehall. I'll walk over the Park. [*To* MRS LOVEIT]   190
Madam, the honour of kissing your fair hands is a happiness I missed this afternoon at my Lady Townley's.

MRS LOVEIT

You were very obliging, Sir Fopling, the last time I saw you there.

SIR FOPLING

The preference was due to your wit and beauty. [*To* BELLINDA]   195
Madam, your servant. There never was so sweet an evening.

BELLINDA

'T has drawn all the rabble of the town hither.

SIR FOPLING

'Tis pity there's not an order made that none but the *beau monde* should walk here.

---

186 *cordial* medicine or beverage to stimulate the heart

186–7 *'Tis . . . remaining* cf. Etherege's 'Song' (Tell me no more you love; in vain), ll. 13–16, 'Each smile and kiss which you bestow,/Are like those cordials which we give/To dying men, to make them live,/And languish out an hour in pain' (Thorpe, p. 24). First published 1669.

190 *Whitehall* royal palace, burned down in 1698. It was across St James's Park from the Mall.

MRS LOVEIT

'Twould add much to the beauty of the place. See what a sort of   200
nasty fellows are coming!

Enter four ill-fashioned fellows singing:
    ''Tis not for kisses alone, etc.'

MRS LOVEIT

Foh! Their periwigs are scented with tobacco so strong—

SIR FOPLING

—It overcomes our pulvilio. Methinks I smell the coffee-house
they come from.   205

FIRST MAN

Dorimant's convenient, Madam Loveit.

SECOND MAN

I like the oily buttock with her.

THIRD MAN [*pointing to* SIR FOPLING]

What spruce prig is that?

---

201 s.d. *four* (three V)
208 *spruce prig* fop, coxcomb (slang)

---

200 *sort* either 1) variety, kind, or 2) body (of people), company (obs.). The latter
    meaning persisted into the nineteenth century (*OED* 17c), though Conaghan
    cites E. Fenton (1730), who felt the usage old-fashioned. See following note.
201 s.d. *four* the number is given as 'three' in the Dramatis Personae, and Verity
    emends here to match. Conaghan, noting that 'sort' (l. 200) could mean
    'crowd', argues for the present reading—'The author may have considered the
    theatrical effectiveness of having the "nasty Fellows" outnumber the people of
    fashion on stage'. Since the text of Q1 descends from an authorial manuscript
    (see Note on the Text), the cast list, which unlike the earlier part of Q1
    distinguishes between Young and Old Bellair, must have been prepared after
    the text. Cutting the 'ill-fashioned fellows' from four to three probably reflects
    an economy made for production.
202, 211 *'Tis . . . etc., There's . . . etc.* Lines from the second stanza of an anonymous
    song, 'Tell me no more you love'. For the words and source see Appendix B.
204 *pulvilio* scented powder (from It. 'polviglio'). A new word: *OED* gives its first
    example from Wycherley's *The Country Wife* (1675).
206 *convenient* mistress (obs.). Earliest of *OED*'s three examples. Cf. P. Motteux,
    Rabelais (1708; 1737 ed.), vol. 5, 217, 'Concubines, Convenients, Cracks'.
207 *oily buttock* 'buttock' was slang for a whore. James Dalton in *A Narrative . . .*
    (1728) defines a 'Buttock' as 'One that dispenses her Favours without Advan-
    tage', i.e., free of charge. 'Oily' could mean greasy or smooth in manner,
    'slippery'. Most obviously the bully refers to Bellinda, but Mrs Loveit appar-
    ently knows one of them by sight (ll. 229–30), and the reference is conceivably
    to her.

FIRST MAN

A caravan, lately come from Paris.

SECOND MAN

Peace, they smoke!   *All of them coughing*   210

'There's something else to be done, etc.'

Exeunt singing

Enter DORIMANT *and* MEDLEY

DORIMANT

They're engaged—

MEDLEY

She entertains him as if she liked him.

DORIMANT

Let us go forward, seem earnest in discourse, and show ourselves. Then you shall see how she'll use him.   215

BELLINDA

Yonder's Dorimant, my dear.

MRS LOVEIT

I see him. (*Aside*) He comes insulting, but I will disappoint him
in his expectation. (*To* SIR FOPLING)—I like this pretty, nice
humour of yours, Sir Fopling. [*To* BELLINDA] With what a
loathing eye he looked upon those fellows!   220

SIR FOPLING

I sat near one of 'em at a play today and was almost poisoned with
a pair of cordovan gloves he wears.

MRS LOVEIT

Oh, filthy cordovan! How I hate the smell!

Laughs in a loud, affected way

SIR FOPLING

Did you observe, madam, how their cravats hung loose an inch
from their neck, and what a frightful air it gave 'em?   225

MRS LOVEIT

Oh! I took particular notice of one that is always spruced up with
a deal of dirty, sky-coloured ribbon.

---

210 *smoke* take note, 'twig'

---

209 *caravan* object of plunder (thieves' cant). *OED* gives first example, however,
from Shadwell, *Squire of Alsatia* (1688), and also cites B. E., *Dictionary of the
Canting Crew* (1690), '*Caravan*, a good round Sum of Money about a Man, and
him that is cheated of it'.

211 *There's ... etc.* see note to l. 202 above.

222 *cordovan* a Spanish leather, originally made from tanned and dressed goatskins,
but later from split horse-hides (cf. 'cordwain', *OED*). Q1 spells 'cordivant'.

BELLINDA

That's one of the walking flageolets who haunt the Mall o' nights.

MRS LOVEIT

Oh, I remember him! He has a hollow tooth, enough to spoil the
sweetness of an evening.   230

SIR FOPLING

I have seen the tallest walk the streets with a dainty pair of boxes,
neatly buckled on.

MRS LOVEIT

And a little footboy at his heels, pocket-high, with a flat cap, a
dirty face—

SIR FOPLING

—And a snotty nose.   235

MRS LOVEIT

Oh, odious! There's many of my own sex, with that Holborn
equipage, trig to Gray's Inn Walks, and now and then travel
hither on a Sunday.

MEDLEY [to DORIMANT]

She takes no notice of you.

DORIMANT

Damn her! I am jealous of a counterplot.   240

MRS LOVEIT

Your liveries are the finest, Sir Fopling. Oh, that page! that page
is the prettily'st dressed. They are all Frenchmen?

SIR FOPLING

There's one damned English blockhead among 'em. You may
know him by his mien.

---

229 *He has* ed. (H' has Q1; He's V, B)   237 *trig* Q1 (trip V) dress smartly

---

228 *flageolet* a relation of the recorder with six fingerholes, invented in France. 'The
flageolet was popular in England from about 1666 until it was set aside in favour
of the recorder some fifteen years later' (*Grove's Dictionary*). Pepys played the
flageolet.

229 *He has . . . tooth* Brett-Smith defends his reading, which makes the hollow tooth
a metaphor for the man, by citing Sparkish's calling Lucy in *The Country Wife*
(1675), V.iv, an 'eternal Rotten-tooth'.

231 *boxes* Carnochan suggests, 'wooden overshoes (?)'. The *OED* is of no help, but
the reference is to some unfashionable form of footwear.

233 *flat cap* round cap with a low, flat crown, worn in the sixteenth and seventeenth
centuries by London citizens, especially apprentices.

236–7 *Holborn equipage* unfashionable retinue characteristic of the City. Holborn
was a centre of commerce and business.

237 *Gray's Inn Walks* gardens of Gray's Inn, an Inn of Court in Holborn, notorious
as a place for assignations.

244 *mien* Sir Fopling may be using the French word *mine* (Q1 spells 'Meine'): in
Etherege's earlier plays the word is spelt both 'mine' and 'meen'.

MRS LOVEIT
　　Oh, that's he, that's he! What do you call him?　　　　　　245
SIR FOPLING [*calling* FOOTMAN]
　　Hey!—I know not what to call him.
MRS LOVEIT
　　What's your name?
FOOTMAN
　　John Trott, madam.
SIR FOPLING
　　Oh, insufferable! Trott, Trott, Trott! There's nothing so bar-
　　barous as the names of our English servants. What countryman　　250
　　are you, sirrah?
FOOTMAN
　　Hampshire, sir.
SIR FOPLING
　　Then Hampshire be your name. Hey, Hampshire!
MRS LOVEIT
　　Oh, that sound! That sound becomes the mouth of a man of
　　quality.　　　　　　　　　　　　　　　　　　　　　　　　255
MEDLEY
　　Dorimant, you look a little bashful on the matter.
DORIMANT
　　She dissembles better than I thought she could have done.
MEDLEY
　　You have tempted her with too luscious a bait. She bites at the
　　coxcomb.
DORIMANT
　　She cannot fall from loving me to that?　　　　　　　　　　260

---

250 *countryman* i.e., which country do you come from?
252–3 *Hampshire* Brett-Smith draws attention to Congreve's reference: 'The
　　Ancients us'd to call their Servants by the names of the Countries from whence
　　they came ... The *French* to this Day do the same, and call their Footmen
　　Champagne[,]*le Picard, le Gascon, le Bourgignon*, &c. and Sir *George Etheridge* in
　　his Sir *Fopling Flutter*, the *Hampshire*, &c. speaking to his Valet imitates this
　　Custom' ('Notes on the Third Book of *Ovid's Art of Love*', *Ovid's Art of Love in
　　Three Books ... By Several Eminent Hands* (1709), pp. 253–4).

MEDLEY
> You begin to be jealous in earnest.

DORIMANT
> Of one I do not love?

MEDLEY
> You did love her.

DORIMANT
> The fit has long been over.

MEDLEY
> But I have known men fall into dangerous relapses when they   265
> have found a woman inclining to another.

DORIMANT (*to himself*)
> He guesses the secret of my heart. I am concerned but dare not
> show it, lest Bellinda should mistrust all I have done to gain her.

BELLINDA (*aside*)
> I have watched his look and find no alteration there. Did he love
> her, some signs of jealousy would have appeared.   270

DORIMANT [*to* MRS LOVEIT]
> I hope this happy evening, madam, has reconciled you to the
> scandalous Mall. We shall have you now hankering here again.

MRS LOVEIT
> Sir Fopling, will you walk?

SIR FOPLING
> I am all obedience, madam.

MRS LOVEIT
> Come along then, and let's agree to be malicious on all the   275
> ill-fashioned things we meet.

SIR FOPLING
> We'll make a critique on the whole Mall, madam.

MRS LOVEIT
> Bellinda, you shall engage—

BELLINDA
> To the reserve of our friends, my dear.

MRS LOVEIT
> No! No exceptions.   280

SIR FOPLING
> We'll sacrifice all to our diversion.

---

272 *hankering* 'hanging about'   278 *engage* participate
277 *critique* CA (Critick Q1; *critique* V)   279 *To . . . of* with the exception of

---

277 *critique* probably not the French word (see textual note). *OED*'s first example
is from Addison (1702–21). The normal English spelling was 'critick' (and so
pronounced); it altered to the French spelling during the eighteenth century,
and was given the French pronunciation in the nineteenth.

MRS LOVEIT
  All—all—
SIR FOPLING
  All!
BELLINDA
  All? Then let it be.

Exeunt SIR FOPLING, MRS LOVEIT, BELLINDA, *and* PERT, *laughing*

MEDLEY
  Would you had brought some more of your friends, Dorimant,   285
  to have been witnesses of Sir Fopling's disgrace and your
  triumph!
DORIMANT
  'Twere unreasonable to desire you not to laugh at me, but pray
  do not expose me to the town this day or two.
MEDLEY
  By that time you hope to have regained your credit?   290
DORIMANT
  I know she hates Fopling and only makes use of him in hope to
  work me on again. Had it not been for some powerful considerations which will be removed tomorrow morning, I had
  made her pluck off this mask and show the passion that lies
  panting under.   295

Enter a FOOTMAN

MEDLEY
  Here comes a man from Bellair, with news of your last adven-
  ture.
DORIMANT
  I am glad he sent him. I long to know the consequence of our
  parting.
FOOTMAN
  Sir, my master desires you to come to my Lady Townley's   300
  presently and bring Mr Medley with you. My Lady Woodvill
  and her daughter are there.
MEDLEY
  Then all's well, Dorimant.
FOOTMAN
  They have sent for the fiddles and mean to dance. He bid me tell
  you, sir, the old lady does not know you, and would have you   305
  own yourself to be Mr Courtage. They are all prepared to receive
  you by that name.

301 *presently* immediately

DORIMANT

That foppish admirer of quality, who flatters the very meat at
honourable tables and never offers love to a woman below a
lady-grandmother!   310

MEDLEY

You know the character you are to act, I see.

DORIMANT

This is Harriet's contrivance—wild, witty, lovesome, beautiful,
and young.— Come along, Medley.

MEDLEY

This new woman would well supply the loss of Loveit.

DORIMANT

That business must not end so. Before tomorrow sun is set, I will   315
revenge and clear it.

      And you and Loveit, to her cost, shall find
      I fathom all the depths of womankind.   *Exeunt*

312–13 *wild ... young* Brett-Smith compares with Waller, 'Of the Danger his
    Majesty (Being Prince) Escaped in the Road at Saint Andrews', ll. 13–14: 'Of
    the Fourth Edward was his noble song,/Fierce, goodly, valiant, beautiful, and
    young' (ed. G. Thorn Drury (1901), vol. 1, 1).

Act IV, Scene i
[LADY TOWNLEY's *house*]

The scene opens with the fiddles playing a country dance

Enter DORIMANT [*and*] LADY WOODVILL, YOUNG BELLAIR *and*
MRS HARRIET, OLD BELLAIR *and* EMILIA, MR MEDLEY *and* LADY
TOWNLEY, *as having just ended the dance*

OLD BELLAIR

So, so, so! A smart bout, a very smart bout, adod!

LADY TOWNLEY

How do you like Emilia's dancing, brother?

OLD BELLAIR

Not at all, not at all!

LADY TOWNLEY

You speak not what you think, I am sure.

OLD BELLAIR

No matter for that—go, bid her dance no more. It don't become   5
her, it don't become her. Tell her I say so. (*Aside*) Adod, I love
her.

DORIMANT (*to* LADY WOODVILL)

All people mingle nowadays, madam. And in public places
women of quality have the least respect showed 'em.

LADY WOODVILL

I protest you say the truth, Mr Courtage.   10

DORIMANT

Forms and ceremonies, the only things that uphold quality and
greatness, are now shamefully laid aside and neglected.

LADY WOODVILL

Well, this is not the women's age, let 'em think what they will.
Lewdness is the business now; love was the business in my time.

DORIMANT

The women, indeed, are little beholding to the young men of this   15
age. They're generally only dull admirers of themselves and
make their court to nothing but their periwigs and their
cravats—and would be more concerned for the disordering of
'em, though on a good occasion, than a young maid would be for
the tumbling of her head or handkercher.   20

15 *beholding* Q1 (beholden Q3)
20 *handkercher* Q1 (handkerchief W, V) unusual variant of 'handkerchief' (not in
   OED), meaning here a kerchief for the neck or head

LADY WOODVILL

I protest you hit 'em.

DORIMANT

They are very assiduous to show themselves at court, well-dressed, to the women of quality; but their business is with the stale mistresses of the town, who are prepared to receive their lazy addresses by industrious old lovers who have cast 'em off   25
and made 'em easy.

HARRIET [to MEDLEY]

He fits my mother's humour so well, a little more and she'll dance a kissing dance with him anon.

MEDLEY

Dutifully observed, madam.

DORIMANT

They pretend to be great critics in beauty—by their talk you   30
would think they liked no face—and yet can dote on an ill one if it belong to a laundress or a tailor's daughter. They cry a woman's past her prime at twenty, decayed at four-and-twenty, old and insufferable at thirty.

LADY WOODVILL

Insufferable at thirty! That they are in the wrong, Mr Courtage,   35
at five-and-thirty there are living proofs enough to convince 'em.

DORIMANT

Ay, madam! There's Mrs Setlooks, Mrs Droplip, and my Lady Loud. Show me among all our opening buds a face that promises so much beauty as the remains of theirs.

LADY WOODVILL

The depraved appetite of this vicious age tastes nothing but   40
green fruit and loathes it when 'tis kindly ripened.

DORIMANT

Else so many deserving women, madam, would not be so untimely neglected.

LADY WOODVILL

I protest, Mr Courtage, a dozen such good men as you would be enough to atone for that wicked Dorimant and all the under-   45
debauchees of the town. (HARRIET, EMILIA, YOUNG BELLAIR, MEDLEY [and] LADY TOWNLEY break out into a laughter)—What's the matter there?

41 *kindly* naturally, seasonably

28 *kissing dance* i.e., cushion-dance, a round dance formerly danced at weddings, in which the men and women alternately knelt on a cushion to be kissed. Referred to as 'old' in 1698 (*OED*),

MEDLEY

A pleasant mistake, madam, that a lady has made, occasions a
little laughter.   50

OLD BELLAIR [*to* DORIMANT *and* LADY WOODVILL]

Come, come, you keep 'em idle! They are impatient till the
fiddles play again.

DORIMANT

You are not weary, madam?

LADY WOODVILL

One dance more. I cannot refuse you, Mr Courtage.

They dance. After the dance, OLD BELLAIR *singing and dancing up to*
EMILIA

EMILIA

You are very active, sir.   55

OLD BELLAIR

Adod, sirrah, when I was a young fellow, I could ha' capered up
to my woman's gorget.

DORIMANT [*to* LADY WOODVILL]

You are willing to rest yourself, madam?

LADY TOWNLEY [*to* DORIMANT *and* LADY WOODVILL]

We'll walk into my chamber and sit down.

MEDLEY

Leave us Mr Courtage; he's a dancer, and the young ladies are   60
not weary yet.

LADY WOODVILL

We'll send him out again.

HARRIET

If you do not quickly, I know where to send for Mr Dorimant.

LADY WOODVILL

This girl's head, Mr Courtage, is ever running on that wild
fellow.   65

DORIMANT

'Tis well you have got her a good husband, madam. That will
settle it.

　　　　Exeunt LADY TOWNLEY, LADY WOODVILL, *and* DORIMANT

OLD BELLAIR (*to* EMILIA)

Adod, sweetheart, be advised and do not throw thyself away on a
young idle fellow.

EMILIA

I have no such intention, sir.   70

56-7 *capered . . . gorget* kicked as high as the garment covering my partner's neck
　　　and shoulders.

OLD BELLAIR

Have a little patience! Thou shalt have the man I spake of. Adod, he loves thee and will make a good husband. But no words—

EMILIA

But, sir—

OLD BELLAIR

No answer—out a pize! Peace, and think on 't.

Enter DORIMANT

DORIMANT

Your company is desired within, sir.   7?

OLD BELLAIR

I go, I go! Good Mr Courtage, fare you well. (*To* EMILIA) Go, I'll see you no more!

EMILIA

What have I done, sir?

OLD BELLAIR

You are ugly, you are ugly!—Is she not, Mr Courtage?

EMILIA

Better words, or I shan't abide you!   80

OLD BELLAIR

Out a pize! Adod, what does she say?—Hit her a pat for me there.   *Exit* OLD BELLAIR

MEDLEY [*to* DORIMANT]

You have charms for the whole family.

DORIMANT

You'll spoil all with some unseasonable jest, Medley.

MEDLEY

You see I confine my tongue and am content to be a bare   85 spectator, much contrary to my nature.

EMILIA

Methinks, Mr Dorimant, my Lady Woodvill is a little fond of you.

DORIMANT

Would her daughter were.

MEDLEY

It may be you may find her so. Try her. You have an opportun-   90 ity.

DORIMANT

And I will not lose it. —Bellair, here's a lady has something to say to you.

YOUNG BELLAIR

I wait upon her. —Mr Medley, we have both business with you.

DORIMANT

Get you all together, then. [*He bows to* HARRIET; *she curtsies*] (*To*   95

HARRIET) That demure curtsy is not amiss in jest, but do not
think in earnest it becomes you.

HARRIET

Affectation is catching, I find. From your grave bow I got it.

DORIMANT

Where had you all that scorn and coldness in your look?

HARRIET

From nature, sir—pardon my want of art. I have not learnt those   100
softnesses and languishings which now in faces are so much in
fashion.

DORIMANT

You need 'em not. You have a sweetness of your own, if you
would but calm your frowns and let it settle.

HARRIET

My eyes are wild and wandering like my passions, and cannot yet   105
be tied to rules of charming.

DORIMANT

Women, indeed, have commonly a method of managing those
messengers of love. Now they will look as if they would kill, and
anon they will look as if they were dying. They point and rebate
their glances, the better to invite us.   110

HARRIET

I like this variety well enough, but hate the set face that always
looks as it would say, 'Come love me'—a woman who at plays
makes the *doux yeux* to a whole audience and at home cannot
forbear 'em to her monkey.

DORIMANT

Put on a gentle smile and let me see how well it will become you.   115

HARRIET

I am sorry my face does not please you as it is, but I shall not be
complaisant and change it.

DORIMANT

Though you are obstinate, I know 'tis capable of improvement,
and shall do you justice, madam, if I chance to be at court when
the critics of the circle pass their judgment—for thither you   120
must come.

HARRIET

And expect to be taken in pieces, have all my features examined,

---

109 *point and rebate* sharpen and blunt
113 *makes ... to* make eyes at

---

117 *complaisant* see note to I, 373.
120 *circle* probably 'an assembly surrounding the principal person' (Johnson), as at
Court, at a drawing-room or levee, though the *OED*'s first example is from
1714. More broadly it means a 'set' or coterie.

every motion censured, and on the whole be condemned to be
but pretty—or a beauty of the lowest rate. What think you?

DORIMANT

The women—nay, the very lovers who belong to the drawing   125
room—will maliciously allow you more than that. They always
grant what is apparent, that they may the better be believed
when they name concealed faults they cannot easily be disproved
in.

HARRIET

Beauty runs as great a risk exposed at court as wit does on the   130
stage, where the ugly and the foolish all are free to censure.

DORIMANT (*aside*)

I love her and dare not let her know it. I fear she has an ascendant
o'er me and may revenge the wrongs I have done her sex. (*To her*)
Think of making a party, madam; love will engage.

HARRIET

You make me start! I did not think to have heard of love from   135
you.

DORIMANT

I never knew what 'twas to have a settled ague yet, but now and
then have had irregular fits.

HARRIET

Take heed, sickness after long health is commonly more violent
and dangerous.   140

DORIMANT (*aside*)

I have took the infection from her and feel the disease now
spreading in me. (*To her*) Is the name of love so frightful that you
dare not stand it?

HARRIET

'Twill do little execution out of your mouth on me, I am sure.

---

132 *ascendant* dominance (orig. astrological)
137 *settled ague* chronic fever

125–6 *drawing room* shortened from 'withdrawing-room', it came to mean a room
    for receptions. From 1673 the word could refer to the people gathered in the
    drawing-room, and hence, a levee, or the sovereign's formal reception at which
    ladies were 'presented' at Court.
130 *risk* as Q1's spelling 'risque' suggests, a relatively recent importation from the
    French. *OED*'s first example dates from 1661.
134 *making a party* 'to make one's party good' means to make good one's cause or
    position; 'to take a party' means making a resolution on one side or the other,
    i.e., Harriet should take the side of beauty against 'the ugly and the foolish' (l.
    131), and love will support her. 'Engage' suggests the possibility of a military
    metaphor—'party' meant a small body of troops selected for a particular duty
    (1645–).

DORIMANT

It has been fatal—   145

HARRIET

To some easy women, but we are not all born to one destiny. I
was informed you use to laugh at love, and not make it.

DORIMANT

The time has been, but now I must speak—

HARRIET

If it be on that idle subject, I will put on my serious look, turn my
head carelessly from you, drop my lip, let my eyelids fall and   150
hang half o'er my eyes—thus, while you buzz a speech of an hour
long in my ear and I answer never a word. Why do you not begin?

DORIMANT

That the company may take notice how passionately I make
advances of love and how disdainfully you receive 'em.

HARRIET

When your love's grown strong enough to make you bear being   155
laughed at, I'll give you leave to trouble me with it. Till when,
pray forbear, sir.

Enter SIR FOPLING *and others in masks*

DORIMANT

What's here—masquerades?

HARRIET

I thought that foppery had been left off, and people might have
been in private with a fiddle.   160

DORIMANT

'Tis endeavoured to be kept on foot still by some who find
themselves the more acceptable the less they are known.

YOUNG BELLAIR

This must be Sir Fopling.

MEDLEY

That extraordinary habit shows it.

YOUNG BELLAIR

What are the rest?   165

147 *use* are accustomed to
164 *habit* dress, attire

153–4 *make advances* the word 'advances' begins to be used in this sense from 1668
        according to the *OED*. For the phrase, compare with French, *faire des avances*.
158 *masquerades* Conaghan aptly cites Burnet, 'At this time [1669] the court fell into
        much extravagance in masquerading; both King and queen, and all the court,
        went about masked, and came into houses unknown, and danced. People were
        so disguised, that without being on the secret none could distinguish them'.
        (*History of my Own Time*, ed. O. Airy (1897), Part I, i, 473.)

MEDLEY

A company of French rascals whom he picked up in Paris and has
brought over to be his dancing equipage on these occasions.
Make him own himself; a fool is very troublesome when he
presumes he is incognito.

SIR FOPLING (*to* HARRIET)

Do you know me?   170

HARRIET

Ten to one but I guess at you.

SIR FOPLING

Are you women as fond of a vizard as we men are?

HARRIET

I am very fond of a vizard that covers a face I do not like, sir.

YOUNG BELLAIR

Here are no masks, you see, sir, but those which came with you.
This was intended a private meeting, but because you look like a   175
gentleman, if you will discover yourself and we know you to be
such, you shall be welcome.

SIR FOPLING (*pulling off his mask*)

Dear Bellair!

MEDLEY

Sir Fopling! How came you hither?

SIR FOPLING

Faith, as I was coming late from Whitehall, after the King's   180
couchée, one of my people told me he had heard fiddles at my
Lady Townley's, and—

DORIMANT

You need not say any more, sir.

SIR FOPLING

Dorimant, let me kiss thee.

DORIMANT

Hark you, Sir Fopling—   *Whispers* 185

SIR FOPLING

Enough, enough, Courtage.—[*Looking at* HARRIET] A pretty
kind of young woman that, Medley. I observed her in the Mall,

---

178 s.d. *off* Q3, W, V, B, CA (of Q1)
181 *couchée* ed. (Coucheé Q1; *couchée* V, CA)

---

167 *dancing equipage* see note to III.ii, 166.
180–1 *King's couchée* cf. Fr., *coucher le roi*, the reception preceding the King's going
    to bed. *OED* cites this as first example in English. Contemporary spelling
    varies, reflecting its origin. The word was probably brought over by Charles
    II's Court.

more *éveillée* than our English women commonly are. Prithee,
what is she?

MEDLEY

The most noted coquette in town. Beware of her.   190

SIR FOPLING

Let her be what she will, I know how to take my measures. In
Paris the mode is to flatter the *prude*, laugh at the *faux-prude*,
make serious love to the *demi-prude*, and only rally with the
coquette. Medley, what think you?

DORIMANT

That for all this smattering of the mathematics, you may be out   195
in your judgment at tennis.

SIR FOPLING

What a *coq-à-l' âne* is this? I talk of women, and thou answerest
tennis.

MEDLEY

Mistakes will be, for want of apprehension.

SIR FOPLING

I am very glad of the acquaintance I have with this family.   200

MEDLEY

My lady truly is a good woman.

SIR FOPLING

Ah, Dorimant—Courtage, I would say—would thou hadst
spent the last winter in Paris with me. When thou wert there, La

---

192 *faux-prude* false prude
193 *demi-prude* half prude
193 *with* Q1 (at Q2–3)
197 *coq-à-l'âne* cock and bull story

---

188 *éveillée* wide-awake. Verity cites *Spectator*, No. 45 (21 April 1711), where
     Addison, advising women to stop their 'Sprightliness from degenerating into
     Levity', says, 'the whole Discourse and Behaviour of the *French* is to make the
     Sex more Fantastical, or (as they are pleased to term it,) *more awakened*, than is
     consistent either with Virtue or Discretion'.
191 *to ... measures* to make my plans. From the French idiom, *prendre des mesures*,
     though the first example given by the *OED* is from 1698, indicating that Sir
     Fopling uses the phrase self-consciously.
191–4 *In Paris ... coquette* Sir Fopling echoes contemporary French gallantry. See
     Brett-Smith for a parallel with a poem by Comte de Bussy.

Corneus and Sallyes were the only *habitudes* we had; a comedian
would have been a *bonne fortune*. No stranger ever passed his   205
time so well as I did some months before I came over. I was well
received in a dozen families, where all the women of quality used
to visit. I have intrigues to tell thee more pleasant than ever thou
read'st in a novel.

HARRIET

Write 'em, sir, and oblige us women. Our language wants such   210
little stories.

SIR FOPLING

Writing, madam, 's a mechanic part of wit. A gentleman should
never go beyond a song or a *billet*.

HARRIET

Bussy was a gentleman.

SIR FOPLING

Who, d'Ambois?   215

MEDLEY [*aside*]

Was there ever such a brisk blockhead?

HARRIET

Not d'Ambois, sir, but Rabutin—he who writ the *Loves of
France*.

SIR FOPLING

That may be, madam! Many gentlemen do things that are below

---

208 *to visit* Q1 (to come to visit Q2–3)

---

204 *La Corneus and Sallyes* Verity suggests the fashionable Parisians, Mesdames
Cornuel and Sallé. 'Une certaine madame Sallé, femme d'un maître des comp-
tes' is mentioned in *La France Galante*, often attributed to Comte de Bussy
(see note to IV. i, 217–18) and printed with his *Histoire Amoureuse des Gaulles
(Histoire Amoureuse . . . suivie de la France Galante . . .*, ed. A. Poitevin (Paris,
1857), vol. 2, 355).

204 *habitudes* i.e., acquaintances. *OED* gives this single instance. It may reveal Sir
Fopling's ignorance, or, as Carnochan suggests, come from a memory of the
French idiom, *avoir ses habitudes dans une maison*, to be at home in someone's
house.

204–5 *a comedian . . . fortune* 'The implication is that *even* a comic actor would have
been a "piece of good luck"' (Carnochan). Probably Sir Fopling shows his
ignorance: Madame Cornuel was known for her wit.

215 *d'Ambois* Louis de Clermont d'Amboise, Sieur de Bussy (1549–79), adventurer and murderer, familiar to theatregoers as Chapman's *Bussy d'Ambois*
(1607), which was still performed. Sir Fopling's mistake reveals his French
culture as a sham. He knows only the popular Bussy, and not the fashionable
contemporary writer, Comte de Bussy.

217–18 *Rabutin . . . France* Roger de Rabutin, Comte de Bussy (1618–93), author
of the famous *Histoire Amoureuse des Gaulles* and cousin of Madame de Sévigné,
with whom he corresponded. (See also note to l. 204 above.)

'em. —Damn your authors, Courtage, women are the prettiest 220
things we can fool away our time with.

HARRIET

I hope ye have wearied yourself tonight at court, sir, and will not
think of fooling with anybody here.

SIR FOPLING

I cannot complain of my fortune there, madam. —Dorimant—

DORIMANT

Again! 225

SIR FOPLING

Courtage, a pox on 't! I have something to tell thee. When I had
made my court within, I came out and flung myself upon the mat
under the state i' the outward room, i' the midst of half a dozen
beauties who were withdrawn to jeer among themselves, as they
called it. 230

DORIMANT

Did you know 'em?

SIR FOPLING

Not one of 'em, by heavens, not I! But they were all your friends.

DORIMANT

How are you sure of that?

SIR FOPLING

Why, we laughed at all the town—spared nobody but yourself.
They found me a man for their purpose. 235

DORIMANT

I know you are malicious to your power.

SIR FOPLING

And, faith, I had occasion to show it, for I never saw more
gaping fools at a ball or on a Birthday.

DORIMANT

You learned who the women were?

SIR FOPLING

No matter!—they frequent the drawing room. 240

DORIMANT

And entertain themselves pleasantly at the expense of all the fops
who come there.

---

228 *state* canopy
229 *jeer* V, CA (jeèr Q1; jeér W; the accent may, as Carnochan suggests, indicate an
affected mispronunciation by Sir Fopling)
236 *to your* within your

229 *jeer* Carnochan suggests that the early edd. show Sir Fopling using a pseudo-
French accentuation. But the accenting in Q1 is too eccentric for certainty.
238 *Birthday* celebration of the King's birthday.

SIR FOPLING

That's their business. Faith, I sifted 'em and find they have a sort of wit among them. (*Pinches a tallow candle*)—Ah, filthy!

DORIMANT

Look, he has been pinching the tallow candle.   245

SIR FOPLING

How can you breathe in a room where there's grease frying? Dorimant, thou art intimate with my lady—advise her, for her own sake and the good company that comes hither, to burn wax lights.

HARRIET

What are these masquerades who stand so obsequiously at a   250 distance?

SIR FOPLING

A set of baladines, whom I picked out of the best in France and brought over with a flute douce or two—my servants. They shall entertain you.

HARRIET

I had rather see you dance yourself, Sir Fopling.   255

SIR FOPLING

And I had rather do it—all the company knows it. But, madam—

MEDLEY

Come, come! No excuses, Sir Fopling!

SIR FOPLING

By heavens, Medley—

MEDLEY

Like a woman I find you must be struggled with before one   260 brings you to what you desire.

HARRIET (*aside*)

Can he dance?

EMILIA

And fence and sing too, if you'll believe him.

DORIMANT

He has no more excellence in his heels than in his head. He went

---

243 *sifted* questioned closely, made enquiry of
253 *flute douce* ed. (Flutes deux Q1; Flutes doux CO; *flûtes douces* V; *flute douce* CA; Q1's 'deux' is probably a misreading of 'doux' in copy)
261 *to* W, V, B, CA, CO (omitted Q1–3)

---

252 *baladines* see note to II.i, 140.
253 *flute douce* see note to II.i, 120.

to Paris a plain, bashful English blockhead, and is returned a   265
fine, undertaking French fop.

MEDLEY [to HARRIET]

I cannot prevail.

SIR FOPLING

Do not think it want of complaisance, madam.

HARRIET

You are too well-bred to want that, Sir Fopling. I believe it want
of power.   270

SIR FOPLING

By heavens, and so it is! I have sat up so damned late and drunk
so cursed hard since I came to this lewd town that I am fit for
nothing but low dancing now—a *courante*, a *bourrée*, or a *menuet*.
But St André tells me, if I will but be regular, in one month I
shall rise again. (*Endeavours at a caper*)—Pox on this   275
debauchery!

EMILIA

I have heard your dancing much commended.

SIR FOPLING

It had the good fortune to please in Paris. I was judged to rise
within an inch as high as the Basque in an entry I danced there.

HARRIET [to EMILIA]

I am mightily taken with this fool. Let us sit.—Here's a seat, Sir   280
Fopling.

SIR FOPLING

At your feet, madam. I can be nowhere so much at ease.—By
your leave, gown.   [*Sits*]

HARRIET, EMILIA

Ah, you'll spoil it!

SIR FOPLING

No matter, my clothes are my creatures. I make 'em to make my   285

266 *undertaking* possibly chiding, reproving, a sense recorded by *OED* in 1691, or,
   willing to take in hand (i.e. affirmative and positive where he had once been
   'plain and bashful').
273 *low dancing ... menuet* the three dances are 'low' because they call for no
   'capers'.
274 *St André* a French dancer brought over to perform in Shadwell's *Psyche* (1675)
   and described as 'the most famous Master of *France*' (Preface). He also heads
   the list of dancers in Crowne's *Calisto*, produced at Court in the same year.
279 *the Basque* probably a reference to 'le Basque sauteur', a French dancer whose
   affair with Madame de Berthillac is recounted in *La France Galante* (ed.
   Poitevin, vol. 2, 84–5).
279 *entry* a dance introduced between the parts of an entertainment. A fairly new
   word (from Fr. *entrée* or *entrée de ballet*). *OED*'s earliest example dates from
   1651, 'A masque at Court, where the French King in person danced five
   entries' (Evelyn, *Memoirs* (1857), vol. 1, 276).

court to you ladies.—Hey! *qu'on commence*!   *Dance*
(*To* [JOHN TROTT, *one of the dancers*])—English motions! I was
forced to entertain this fellow, one of my set miscarrying.—Oh,
horrid! Leave your damned manner of dancing and put on the
French air. Have you not a pattern before you?   29(
[*Dances*]—Pretty well! Imitation in time may bring him to
something.

After the dance, enter OLD BELLAIR, LADY WOODVILL, *and* LADY
TOWNLEY

OLD BELLAIR
Hey, adod, what have we here? A mumming?
LADY WOODVILL
Where's my daughter?—Harriet!
DORIMANT
Here, here, madam. I know not but under these disguises there   29:
may be dangerous sparks. I gave the young lady warning.
LADY WOODVILL
Lord! I am so obliged to you Mr Courtage.
HARRIET
Lord! How you admire this man!
LADY WOODVILL
What have you to except against him?
HARRIET
He's a fop.   30(
LADY WOODVILL
He's not a Dorimant, a wild, extravagant fellow of the times.

---

286 *qu'on commence* begin!
286–7 *commence*! . . . *motions*! ed. (Comencé, English motions. Q1^u; Comencé to an
      English Dancer English motions Q1^c; *commence*—to an English dancer
      English motions. V, B, CA (who further adds an s.d. after 'fellow' in l. 288,
      '*pointing to John Trott*'); CO first introduced the emendation
288 *entertain* retain, hire
288 *miscarrying* coming to harm, or behaving badly, or going astray
290 *not a* Q1^c (not had a Q1^u)

286–7 *commence*! . . . *motions*! Conaghan, who first discovered the corrected and
      uncorrected states, gives 'to an English Dancer' as an s.d., and comments,
      'Lack of punctuation in Q1^c suggests that the compositor made the insertion
      without attending to its purpose: *to . . . Dancer* is almost certainly a stage
      direction'. Q1's reading makes possible sense as Sir Fopling's interjection, but
      Conaghan's emendation is preferable.
290 *not a* as Conaghan says, the change in Q1^c 'allows for a demonstration of
      dancing by Sir Fopling'.
301 *wild, extravagant* see Barnard (op. cit.), pp. xxix–xxxiii.

HARRIET

He's a man made up of forms and commonplaces, sucked out of
the remaining lees of the last age.

LADY WOODVILL

He's so good a man that were you not engaged—

LADY TOWNLEY

You'll have but little night to sleep in. 305

LADY WOODVILL

Lord! 'tis perfect day—

DORIMANT (*aside*)

The hour is almost come I appointed Bellinda, and I am not so
foppishly in love here to forget. I am flesh and blood yet.

LADY TOWNLEY

I am very sensible, madam.

LADY WOODVILL

Lord, madam— 310

HARRIET

Look, in what a struggle is my poor mother yonder!

YOUNG BELLAIR

She has much ado to bring out the compliment.

DORIMANT

She strains hard for it.

HARRIET

See, see—her head tottering, her eyes staring, and her underlip
trembling. 315

DORIMANT

Now, now she's in the very convulsions of her civility.
(*Aside*)—'Sdeath, I shall lose Bellinda! I must fright her hence.
She'll be an hour in this fit of good manners else. (*To* LADY
WOODVILL) Do you not know Sir Fopling, madam?

LADY WOODVILL

I have seen that face. Oh heaven!—'tis the same we met in the 320
Mall! How came he here?

DORIMANT

A fiddle in this town is a kind of fop-call. No sooner it strikes up,
but the house is besieged with an army of masquerades straight.

LADY WOODVILL

Lord, I tremble, Mr Courtage! For certain Dorimant is in the
company. 325

DORIMANT

I cannot confidently say he is not. You had best begone; I will
wait upon you. Your daughter is in the hands of Mr Bellair.

302 *forms* see note to I, 110–11.
306 *perfect day* i.e., broad daylight
309 *sensible* aware of (your courtesy)

LADY WOODVILL
    I'll see her before me.—Harriet, come away!
                        [*Exeunt* LADY WOODVILL *and* HARRIET]
YOUNG BELLAIR
    Lights, lights!
LADY TOWNLEY
    Light, down there!   330
OLD BELLAIR
    Adod, it needs not—
                [*Exeunt* LADY TOWNLEY, EMILIA *and* YOUNG BELLAIR]
DORIMANT [*calling to the servants outside*]
    Call my Lady Woodvill's coach to the door, quickly.
                                                [*Exit* DORIMANT]
OLD BELLAIR
    Stay, Mr Medley, let the young fellows do that duty. We will
    drink a glass of wine together. 'Tis good after dancing. [*Looks at*
    SIR FOPLING]—What mumming spark is that?   335
MEDLEY
    He is not to be comprehended in few words.
SIR FOPLING
    Hey, La Tour!
MEDLEY
    Whither away, Sir Fopling?
SIR FOPLING
    I have business with Courtage.
MEDLEY
    He'll but put the ladies into their coach and come up again.   340
OLD BELLAIR
    In the meantime I'll call for a bottle.   [*Exit* OLD BELLAIR]

                        Enter YOUNG BELLAIR

MEDLEY
    Where's Dorimant?
YOUNG BELLAIR
    Stolen home. He has had business waiting for him there all this
    night, I believe, by an impatience I observed in him.
MEDLEY
    Very likely. 'Tis but dissembling drunkenness, railing at his   345
    friends, and the kind soul will embrace the blessing and forget
    the tedious expectation.
SIR FOPLING
    I must speak with him before I sleep.
YOUNG BELLAIR [*to* MEDLEY]
    Emilia and I are resolved on that business.
337 *Tour* V, CA (Towèr Q1)

MEDLEY
  Peace, here's your father.   350

          Enter OLD BELLAIR *and butler with a bottle of wine*

OLD BELLAIR
  The women are all gone to bed.—Fill, boy!—Mr Medley, begin
  a health.
MEDLEY (*whispers*)
  To Emilia.
OLD BELLAIR
  Out a pize! She's a rogue, and I'll not pledge you.
MEDLEY
  I know you will.   355
OLD BELLAIR
  Adod, drink it, then!
SIR FOPLING
  Let us have the new *bachique*.
OLD BELLAIR
  Adod, that is a hard word! What does it mean, sir?
MEDLEY
  A catch or drinking song.
OLD BELLAIR
  Let us have it, then.   360
SIR FOPLING
  Fill the glasses round, and draw up in a body.—Hey, music!

                        They sing

    The pleasures of love and the joys of good wine,
    To perfect our happiness wisely we join.
        We to beauty all day
        Give the sovereign sway   365
    And her favourite nymphs devoutly obey.
    At the plays we are constantly making our court,

55 *will* V, B, CA (well Q1)

---

57 *bachique* drinking song, as Medley explains. *OED* cites this as its single
   example (cf. Fr. *chanson bachique*). Although it occurs as an adjective from 1669
   to 1699, this is probably another example of Sir Fopling's French, not the
   isolated occurrence of an English word.
62–83 *The pleasures … fire* Thorpe, p. 103, records several subsequent printed
   appearances of this song, and notes Etherege's own preference for women over
   heavy drinking; as Dryden said, 'For wine to leave a whore or play,/Was ne'er
   Your Excellence's way' ('Mr Dryden's Letter to Sir George Etherege', ll.
   53–4). Carnochan cites lines from two songs in Shadwell's *Psyche* (1675) which
   deal with the *topoi* of the first two lines of Etherege's song.

And when they are ended, we follow the sport
   To the Mall and the Park,
   Where we love till 'tis dark.   370
   Then sparkling champagne
   Puts an end to their reign:
   It quickly recovers
   Poor languishing lovers,
Makes us frolic and gay, and drowns all our sorrow;   375
But alas, we relapse again on the morrow.
   Let every man stand
   With his glass in his hand,
And briskly discharge at the word of command.
   Here's a health to all those   380
   Whom tonight we depose.
Wine and beauty by turns great souls should inspire;
Present all together—and now, boys, give fire!

               [*They drink*]

OLD BELLAIR
Adod, a pretty business and very merry!
SIR FOPLING
Hark you, Medley, let you and I take the fiddles and go waken   385
Dorimant.
MEDLEY
We shall do him a courtesy, if it be as I guess. For after the
fatigue of this night, he'll quickly have his belly full and be glad
of an occasion to cry, 'Take away, Handy!'
YOUNG BELLAIR
I'll go with you; and there we'll consult about affairs, Medley.   390
OLD BELLAIR
Adod, 'tis six o'clock!
SIR FOPLING
Let's away, then.
OLD BELLAIR
Mr Medley, my sister tells me you are an honest man. And,

---

382 *should* Q1 (shall Q2–3)

---

371 *champagne* a new word (and drink) from the French. First example in *OED* is
from *Hudibras* (1664). The modern technique for making champagne is the
invention of Dom Pérignon, cellarer at the Abbey of Hautvillers from 1668 to
1715, though champagne was available prior to his discoveries.
383 *Present all together* i.e., raise your drinks and aim. The military metaphor runs
through the song's last seven lines.

adod, I love you.—Few words and hearty, that's the way with
old Harry, old Harry.   395

SIR FOPLING [*to his servants*]

Light your flambeaux! Hey!

OLD BELLAIR

What does the man mean?

MEDLEY

'Tis day, Sir Fopling.

SIR FOPLING

No matter; our serenade will look the greater.   *Exeunt omnes*

Act IV, Scene ii

DORIMANT's *lodging; a table, a candle, a toilet, etc.* HANDY *tying up
linen*

Enter DORIMANT *in his gown, and* BELLINDA

DORIMANT

Why will you be gone so soon?

BELLINDA

Why did you stay out so late?

DORIMANT

Call a chair, Handy.   [*Exit* HANDY]
—What makes you tremble so?

BELLINDA

I have a thousand fears about me. Have I not been seen, think   5
you?

DORIMANT

By nobody but myself and trusty Handy.

BELLINDA

Where are all your people?

DORIMANT

I have dispersed 'em on sleeveless errands. What does that sigh
mean?   10

BELLINDA

Can you be so unkind to ask me? Well—(*sighs*)—were it to do
again—

DORIMANT

We should do it, should we not?

BELLINDA

I think we should: the wickeder man you, to make me love so
well. Will you be discreet now?   15

396 *flambeaux* torches, esp. ones made from several thick wicks dipped in wax
9 *sleeveless* trifling

---

399 *serenade* see note to II.i, 115.

DORIMANT

I will.

BELLINDA

You cannot.

DORIMANT

Never doubt it.

BELLINDA

I will not expect it.

DORIMANT

You do me wrong.   20

BELLINDA

You have no more power to keep the secret than I had not to trust
you with it.

DORIMANT

By all the joys I have had, and those you keep in store—

BELLINDA

—You'll do for my sake what you never did before.

DORIMANT

By that truth thou hast spoken, a wife shall sooner betray herself   25
to her husband.

BELLINDA

Yet I had rather you should be false in this than in another thing
you promised me.

DORIMANT

What's that?

BELLINDA

That you would never see Loveit more but in public places—in   30
the Park, at court and plays.

DORIMANT

'Tis not likely a man should be fond of seeing a damned old play
when there is a new one acted.

BELLINDA

I dare not trust your promise.

DORIMANT

You may.   35

BELLINDA

This does not satisfy me. You shall swear you never will see her
more.

DORIMANT

I will, a thousand oaths! By all—

BELLINDA

Hold! You shall not, now I think on 't better.

23-4 *By ... before* Dorimant's speech begins to fall into an Alexandrine, but
  Bellinda 'is quick to interrupt his heroics with her rhyming reply' (Brett-
  Smith).

DORIMANT
I will swear!   40
BELLINDA
I shall grow jealous of the oath and think I owe your truth to that,
not to your love.
DORIMANT
Then, by my love! No other oath I'll swear.

Enter HANDY

HANDY
Here's a chair.
BELLINDA
Let me go.   45
DORIMANT
I cannot.
BELLINDA
Too willingly, I fear.
DORIMANT
Too unkindly feared. When will you promise me again?
BELLINDA
Not this fortnight.
DORIMANT
You will be better than your word.   50
BELLINDA
I think I shall. Will it not make you love me less?
                                                        Fiddles without
(*Starting*) Hark, what fiddles are these?
DORIMANT
Look out, Handy.   *Exit* HANDY *and returns*
HANDY
Mr Medley, Mr Bellair, and Sir Fopling. They are coming up.
DORIMANT
How got they in?   55
HANDY
The door was open for the chair.
BELLINDA
Lord, let me fly!
DORIMANT
Here, here, down the back stairs. I'll see you into your chair.
BELLINDA
No, no! Stay and receive 'em. And be sure you keep your word
and never see Loveit more. Let it be a proof of your kindness.   60
DORIMANT
It shall.—Handy, direct her.—(*Kissing her hand*) Everlasting

love go along with thee.   *Exeunt* BELLINDA *and* HANDY

Enter YOUNG BELLAIR, MEDLEY, *and* SIR FOPLING [*with his page*]

YOUNG BELLAIR
Not abed yet?
MEDLEY
You have had an irregular fit, Dorimant.
DORIMANT
I have.   65
YOUNG BELLAIR
And is it off already?
DORIMANT
Nature has done her part, gentlemen. When she falls kindly to
work, great cures are effected in little time, you know.
SIR FOPLING
We thought there was a wench in the case, by the chair that
waited. Prithee, make us a *confidence*.   70
DORIMANT
Excuse me.
SIR FOPLING
Le sage Dorimant. Was she pretty?
DORIMANT
So pretty she may come to keep her coach and pay parish duties,
if the good humour of the age continue.
MEDLEY
And be of the number of the ladies kept by public-spirited men   75
for the good of the whole town.
SIR FOPLING
Well said, Medley.   SIR FOPLING *dancing by himself*
YOUNG BELLAIR
See Sir Fopling dancing.
DORIMANT
You are practising and have a mind to recover, I see.
SIR FOPLING
Prithee, Dorimant, why hast not thou a glass hung up here? A   80
room is the dullest thing without one!
YOUNG BELLAIR
Here is company to entertain you.

72 *Le sage* judicious, discreet

---

64 *irregular fit* unexpected bout of illness. Presumably Medley overhears Dorimant at IV.i, 138.
73-4 *So . . . continue* 'an instance of Dorimant's discretion. The description could
   hardly apply to Bellinda, who is not mercenary' (Conaghan).

SIR FOPLING

But I mean in case of being alone. In a glass a man may entertain himself—

DORIMANT

The shadow of himself, indeed.   85

SIR FOPLING

—Correct the errors of his motions and his dress.

MEDLEY

I find, Sir Fopling, in your solitude you remember the saying of the wise man, and study yourself.

SIR FOPLING

'Tis the best diversion in our retirements. Dorimant, thou art a pretty fellow and wearest thy clothes well, but I never saw thee   90
have a handsome cravat. Were they made up like mine, they'd give another air to thy face. Prithee, let me send my man to dress thee but one day. By heavens, an Englishman cannot tie a ribbon!

DORIMANT

They are something clumsy-fisted.   95

SIR FOPLING

I have brought over the prettiest fellow that ever spread a toilet. He served some time under Mérille, the greatest *génie* in the world for a *valet de chambre*.

DORIMANT

What, he who formerly belonged to the Duke of Candale?

SIR FOPLING

The same, and got him his immortal reputation.   100

---

97 *Mérille* Mérille had been in service with the Duc de Candale, and was his 'principal confident'. After de Candale's death Mérille was in service with the Duc d'Orléans and by 1673 was his 'premier valet de chambre' (*Correspondance* (1858), vol. 3, 240).

97 *génie* man of genius (cf. Fr. *homme de génie*). *OED* gives only three instances, of which this is the first, between 1676 and 1687. It should probably be regarded as a French word.

98 *valet de chambre* although *OED* records this as English from 1646 onwards, and Handy is so described in the Dramatis Personæ, Sir Fopling looks to the French (as Q1's spelling, 'Valet d'Chambré', may indicate).

99 *Duke of Candale* Louis-Charles Gaston de Nogaret de Foix, Duc de Candale (1627–58), French general. Bussy reports, 'Sa taille étoit admirable. Il s'habilloit bien, et les plus proches tâchoient de l'imiter', but attributed this not to his valet but his mistress: Mlle de la Roche-Posay 'avoit pris tant de soin de le dresser, et lui de plaire cette belle, que l'art avoit passé le nature, et qu'il étoit beaucoup plus honnête homme que mille gens qui avoient plus d'esprit que lui' (*Histoire Amoureuse* ..., ed. Poitevin (1857), vol. 1, 69–70).

DORIMANT

You've a very fine brandenburgh on, Sir Fopling.

SIR FOPLING

It serves to wrap me up, after the fatigue of a ball.

MEDLEY

I see you often in it, with your periwig tied up.

SIR FOPLING

We should not always be in a set dress. 'Tis more *en cavalier* to appear now and then in a *déshabillé*. 105

MEDLEY

Pray, how goes your business with Loveit?

SIR FOPLING

You might have answered yourself in the Mall last night.—Dorimant, did you not see the advances she made me? I have been endeavouring at a song.

DORIMANT

Already? 110

SIR FOPLING

'Tis my *coup d'essai* in English. I would fain have thy opinion of it.

DORIMANT

Let's see it.

SIR FOPLING

Hey, page, give me my song.—Bellair, here. Thou hast a pretty voice, sing it. 115

YOUNG BELLAIR

Sing it yourself, Sir Fopling.

SIR FOPLING

Excuse me.

YOUNG BELLAIR

You learnt to sing in Paris.

104 *en cavalier* jaunty, dashing
105 *déshabillé* V, CA (dissabillé Q1)
111 *coup d'essai* trial shot, first attempt

---

101 *brandenburgh* morning gown (named after the Prussian city famous for its woollen goods). Conaghan cites the epilogue to Lee's *Gloriana* (1676): 'Huge Brandenburgh had so disguis'd each one,/That from your Coachman you could scarce be known'. *OED* cites Etherege's use as its first occurrence, but there is an earlier instance in Wycherley's *The Plain-Dealer* (1677, first acted 1674).
103 *periwig tied up* i.e., to save combing.
105 *in a déshabillé* casually dressed, Q1's spelling, 'dissabilée', appears to be a phonetic rendering of the French. Compare with II.ii, 76 and textual note. The audience may have felt a pun.
108 *advances ... made* see not to IV.i, 153–4.

SIR FOPLING

    I did—of Lambert, the greatest master in the world; but I have
    his own fault, a weak voice, and care not to sing out of a ruelle.   120

DORIMANT

    A ruelle is a pretty cage for a singing fop, indeed.

                            YOUNG BELLAIR *reads the song*

        How charming Phillis is, how fair!
           Ah, that she were as willing
        To ease my wounded heart of care,
           And make her eyes less killing.   125
        I sigh! I sigh! I languish now,
           And love will not let me rest;
        I drive about the Park and bow,
           Still as I meet my dearest.

SIR FOPLING

    Sing it, sing it, man! It goes to a pretty new tune which I am   130
    confident was made by Baptiste.

MEDLEY

    Sing it yourself, Sir Fopling. He does not know the tune.

SIR FOPLING

    I'll venture.   SIR FOPLING *sings*

DORIMANT

    Ay, marry, now 'tis something. I shall not flatter you, Sir
    Fopling: there is not much thought in 't, but 'tis passionate and   135
    well-turned.

129 *Still as* whenever

---

119 *Lambert* Michel Lambert (1610–96), French lutenist and singer. He was made
    master of the royal chamber music by Cardinal Richelieu, and was a popular
    teacher in Louis XIV's Court.

120, 121 *ruelle* 'a bedroom, where ladies of fashion, in the seventeenth and
    eighteenth centuries, esp. in France, held a morning reception of persons of
    distinction; hence, a reception of this kind' (*OED*, which gives this as its first
    example). As Brett-Smith points out, Littré's *Dictionnaire* (1863–72) shows the
    peculiar aptness to Sir Fopling better—'se disait particulièrement des
    chambres à coucher sous Louis XIV, des alcôves de certaines dames de qualité,
    servant de salon de conversation et où régnait souvent le ton précieux'.

122–9 *How ... dearest* Thorpe (p. 104) gives later printings, those from 1707
    onwards having music by Ramonden, though its satirical intent is lost out of
    context in the songbooks.

131 *Baptiste* probably Jean-Baptiste Lully (1632–87), Louis XIV's master of court
    music, composer, and credited with the founding of French opera. Called by
    Pepys (18 June 1666) 'the present great composer'. But, as Conaghan says,
    'Baptist' at this time often refers to Giovanni Battista Draghi (*c*. 1640–*c*. 1710),
    an Italian harpsichordist and composer, who had settled in England after the
    Restoration. He composed the operatic music for Shadwell's adaptation of *The
    Tempest* (1674) as well as for his *Psyche* (1675).

MEDLEY
After the French way.
SIR FOPLING
That I aimed at. Does it not give you a lively image of the thing?
Slap, down goes the glass, and thus we are at it.
DORIMANT
It does indeed. I perceive, Sir Fopling, you'll be the very head of   140
the sparks who are lucky in compositions of this nature.

Enter SIR FOPLING'S FOOTMAN

SIR FOPLING
La Tour, is the bath ready?
FOOTMAN
Yes, sir.
SIR FOPLING
Adieu donc, mes chers.
                    Exit SIR FOPLING [*with* FOOTMAN *and* PAGE]
MEDLEY
When have you your revenge on Loveit, Dorimant?   145
DORIMANT
I will but change my linen and about it.
MEDLEY
The powerful considerations which hindered have been
removed then?
DORIMANT
Most luckily, this morning. You must go along with me; my
reputation lies at stake there.   150
MEDLEY
I am engaged to Bellair.
DORIMANT
What's your business?
MEDLEY
Ma-tri-mony, an't like you.
DORIMANT
It does not, sir.
YOUNG BELLAIR
It may in time, Dorimant. What think you of Mrs Harriet?   155

142 *Tour* V, CA (Tower Q1)
144 *Adieu donc, mes chers* goodbye then, my friends

---

139 *glass* Carnochan suggests 'coach-window', but looking-glass seems more likely
    from the context.
153 *Ma-tri-mony an't like you* i.e., 'Medley mimics tradesmen's speech, in response
    to Dorimant's "business"' (Conaghan).

DORIMANT

What does she think of me?

YOUNG BELLAIR

I am confident she loves you.

DORIMANT

How does it appear?

YOUNG BELLAIR

Why, she's never well but when she's talking of you, but then she
finds all the faults in you she can. She laughs at all who commend   160
you; but then she speaks ill of all who do not.

DORIMANT

Women of her temper betray themselves by their over-cunning.
I had once a growing love with a lady who would always quarrel
with me when I came to see her, and yet was never quiet if I
stayed a day from her.   165

YOUNG BELLAIR

My father is in love with Emilia.

DORIMANT

That is a good warrant for your proceedings. Go on and
prosper—I must to Loveit. Medley, I am sorry you cannot be a
witness.

MEDLEY

Make her meet Sir Fopling again in the same place and use him   170
ill before me.

DORIMANT

That may be brought about, I think.—I'll be at your aunt's anon
and give you joy, Mr Bellair.

YOUNG BELLAIR

You had not best think of Mrs Harriet too much. Without
church security, there's no taking up there.   175

DORIMANT

I may fall into the snare, too. But,
    The wise will find a difference in our fate:
    You wed a woman, I a good estate.   *Exeunt*

---

173 *give you joy* congratulate you
174 *not best* Q1 (best not CA)

---

175 *taking up* hire, buy up wholesale, borrow at interest (extending the metaphor
established in 'church security').

Act IV, Scene iii
[*Outside* MRS LOVEIT'S]

Enter the chair with BELLINDA; *the men set it down and open it.*
BELLINDA *starting*

BELLINDA (*surprised*)
Lord, where am I? In the Mall! Whither have you brought me?
FIRST CHAIRMAN
You gave us no directions, madam.
BELLINDA (*aside*)
The fright I was in made me forget it.
FIRST CHAIRMAN
We use to carry a lady from the squire's hither.
BELLINDA (*aside*)
This is Loveit! I am undone if she sees me.—Quickly, carry me   5
away!
FIRST CHAIRMAN
Whither, an't like your honour?
BELLINDA
Ask no questions!

Enter Mrs Loveit's FOOTMAN

FOOTMAN
Have you seen my lady, madam?
BELLINDA
I am just come to wait upon her.   10
FOOTMAN
She will be glad to see you, madam. She sent me to you this
morning to desire your company, and I was told you went out by
five o'clock.
BELLINDA (*aside*)
More and more unlucky!
FOOTMAN
Will you walk in, madam?   15
BELLINDA
I'll discharge my chair and follow. Tell your mistress I am here.
[*Exit* FOOTMAN]
Take this!([BELLINDA] *gives the* CHAIRMEN *money*)—and if ever
you should be examined, be sure you say you took me up in the
Strand, over against the Exchange—as you will answer it to Mr
Dorimant.

CHAIRMEN
  We will, an't like your honour.   [*Exeunt* CHAIRMEN]   20
BELLINDA
  Now to come off, I must on:
      In confidence and lies some hope is left;
      'Twere hard to be found out in the first theft.   *Exit*

Act V, Scene i
[MRS LOVEIT'S]

Enter MRS LOVEIT *and* PERT, *her woman*

PERT
Well! In my eyes, Sir Fopling is no such despicable person.
MRS LOVEIT
You are an excellent judge.
PERT
He's as handsome a man as Mr Dorimant, and as great a gallant.
MRS LOVEIT
Intolerable! Is 't not enough I submit to his impertinences, but
must I be plagued with yours too?   5
PERT
Indeed, madam—
MRS LOVEIT
'Tis false, mercenary malice—

Enter her FOOTMAN

FOOTMAN
Mrs Bellinda, madam.
MRS LOVEIT
What of her?
FOOTMAN
She's below.   10
MRS LOVEIT
How came she?
FOOTMAN
In a chair—Ambling Harry brought her.
MRS LOVEIT
He bring her! His chair stands near Dorimant's door and always
brings me from thence.—Run and ask him where he took her
up. Go!   [*Exit* FOOTMAN]   15
There is no truth in friendship neither. Women as well as men,
all are false—or all are so to me at least.
PERT
You are jealous of her too?
MRS LOVEIT
You had best tell her I am. 'Twill become the liberty you take of
late. [*Aside*] This fellow's bringing of her, her going out by five 20
o'clock—I know not what to think.

Enter BELLINDA

Bellinda, you are grown an early riser, I hear!

BELLINDA

Do you not wonder, my dear, what made me abroad so soon?

MRS LOVEIT

You do not use to be so.

BELLINDA

The country gentlewomen I told you of—Lord, they have the 25
oddest diversions!—would never let me rest till I promised to go
with them to the markets this morning to eat fruit and buy
nosegays.

MRS LOVEIT

Are they so fond of a filthy nosegay?

BELLINDA

They complain of the stinks of the town and are never well but 30
when they have their noses in one.

MRS LOVEIT

There are essences and sweet waters.

BELLINDA

Oh, they cry out upon perfumes, they are unwholesome. One of
'em was falling into a fit with the smell of these nerolii.

MRS LOVEIT

Methinks, in complaisance you should have had a nosegay too. 35

BELLINDA

Do you think, my dear, I could be so loathsome to trick myself
up with carnations and stock-gillyflowers? I begged their pardon
and told them I never wore anything but orange-flowers and
tuberose. That which made me willing to go was a strange desire
I had to eat some fresh nectarines. 40

MRS LOVEIT

And had you any?

34 *nerolii* presumably the plural of 'neroli', which normally meant the essential oil
distilled from the flowers of the bitter orange and used for scenting gloves.
(Named after the Italian princess to whom its discovery is attributed.) Here it
seems to refer to the gloves worn by Bellinda (see l. 38). For the popularity of
essence of orange, see note to III.ii, 207.

35 *complaisance* see note to I, 373.

37 *stock-gillyflower* white stock (*matthiola incana*). So-called both because of its
clove-like smell and because it blooms in July.

39 *tuberose* liliaceous flower, with creamy white, funnel-shaped, fragrant flowers
and a tuberous root. Like the orange-flower this was an exotic having only
recently reached England (Evelyn mentions it in 1664 and the *London Gazette*,
No. 2654/4 (1691), reports, 'There are lately brought from Italy . . . Onions of
Tubereuse'). In the language of flowers, tuberose signifies dangerous
pleasures.

BELLINDA
The best I ever tasted.

MRS LOVEIT
Whence came you now?

BELLINDA
From their lodgings, where I crowded out of a coach and took a
chair to come and see you, my dear.   45

MRS LOVEIT
Whither did you send for that chair?

BELLINDA
'Twas going by empty.

MRS LOVEIT
Where do these country gentlewomen lodge, I pray?

BELLINDA
In the Strand, over against the Exchange.

PERT
That place is never without a nest of 'em. They are always, as one   50
goes by, fleering in balconies or staring out of windows.

Enter FOOTMAN

MRS LOVEIT (*to the* FOOTMAN)
Come hither.   *Whispers*

BELLINDA (*aside*)
This fellow by her order has been questioning the chairmen. I
threatened 'em with the name of Dorimant. If they should have
told truth, I am lost forever.   55

MRS LOVEIT
In the Strand, said you?

FOOTMAN
Yes, madam, over against the Exchange.   [*Exit* FOOTMAN]

MRS LOVEIT
She's innocent, and I am much to blame.

BELLINDA (*aside*)
I am so frightened my countenance will betray me.

MRS LOVEIT
Bellinda, what makes you look so pale?   60

BELLINDA
Want of my usual rest and jolting up and down so long in an
odious hackney.

FOOTMAN *returns*

51 *fleering* jeering

48–51 *Where . . . windows* see note to I, 54.

FOOTMAN
Madam, Mr Dorimant. [*Exit* FOOTMAN]

MRS LOVEIT
What makes him here?

BELLINDA (*aside*)
Then I am betrayed indeed. He has broke his word, and I love a 65
man that does not care for me.

MRS LOVEIT
Lord!—you faint, Bellinda.

BELLINDA
I think I shall—such an oppression here on the sudden.

PERT
She has eaten too much fruit, I warrant you.

MRS LOVEIT
Not unlikely. 70

PERT
'Tis that lies heavy on her stomach.

MRS LOVEIT
Have her into my chamber, give her some surfeit-water, and let
her lie down a little.

PERT
Come, madam. I was a strange devourer of fruit when I was
young—so ravenous. 75

Exeunt BELLINDA *and* PERT, *leading her off*

MRS LOVEIT
Oh, that my love would be but calm awhile, that I might receive
this man with all the scorn and indignation he deserves!

Enter DORIMANT

DORIMANT
Now for a touch of Sir Fopling to begin with.—Hey, page! Give
positive order that none of my people stir. Let the *canaille* wait,
as they should do.—Since noise and nonsense have such 80
powerful charms,
'I, that I may successful prove,
Transform myself to what you love'.

---

64 *What . . . here* What's brought him here?
72 *surfeit-water* medicinal drink made by diffusion or distillation
74 *strange* exceptional
79 *canaille* riff-raff

82–3 *I . . . love* Waller, 'To the Mutable Fair', ll. 5–6 (*Poems*, ed. G. Thorn Drury
(1901), vol. 1, 106). Dorimant changes the first word from 'And' to 'I'.

MRS LOVEIT

If that would do, you need not change from what you are—you
can be vain and loud enough.   85

DORIMANT

But not with so good a grace as Sir Fopling.—'Hey, Hampshire!'—Oh, that sound! That sound becomes the mouth of a
man of quality.

MRS LOVEIT

Is there a thing so hateful as a senseless mimic?

DORIMANT

He's a great grievance, indeed, to all who—like yourself,   90
madam—love to play the fool in quiet.

MRS LOVEIT

A ridiculous animal, who has more of the ape than the ape has of
the man in him.

DORIMANT

I have as mean an opinion of a sheer mimic as yourself; yet were
he all ape, I should prefer him to the gay, the giddy, brisk,   95
insipid, noisy fool you dote on.

MRS LOVEIT

Those noisy fools, however you despise 'em, have good qualities
which weigh more (or ought, at least) with us women than all the
pernicious wit you have to boast of.

DORIMANT

That I may hereafter have a just value for their merit, pray do me   100
the favour to name 'em.

MRS LOVEIT

You'll despise 'em as the dull effects of ignorance and vanity, yet
I care not if I mention some. First, they really admire us, while
you at best but flatter us well.

DORIMANT

Take heed!—fools can dissemble too.   105

MRS LOVEIT

They may—but not so artificially as you. There is no fear they
should deceive us. Then, they are assiduous, sir. They are ever
offering us their service and always waiting on our will.

DORIMANT

You owe that to their excessive idleness. They know not how to
entertain themselves at home, and find so little welcome abroad,   110
they are fain to fly to you who countenance 'em, as a refuge
against the solitude they would be otherwise condemned to.

MRS LOVEIT

Their conversation, too, diverts us better.

DORIMANT

Playing with your fan, smelling to your gloves, commending

your hair, and taking notice how 'tis cut and shaded after the new 115
way—

MRS LOVEIT

Were it sillier than you can make it, you must allow 'tis pleasanter
to laugh at others than to be laughed at ourselves, though never
so wittily. Then, though they want skill to flatter us, they flatter
themselves so well, they save us the labour. We need not take 120
that care and pains to satisfy 'em of our love, which we so often
lose on you.

DORIMANT

They commonly, indeed, believe too well of themselves, and
always better of you than you deserve.

MRS LOVEIT

You are in the right: they have an implicit faith in us, which 125
keeps 'em from prying narrowly into our secrets, and saves us the
vexatious trouble of clearing doubts which your subtle and
causeless jealousies every moment raise.

DORIMANT

There is an inbred falsehood in women which inclines 'em still to
them whom they may most easily deceive. 130

MRS LOVEIT

The man who loves above his quality does not suffer more from
the insolent impertinence of his mistress than the woman who
loves above her understanding does from the arrogant presump-
tions of her friend.

DORIMANT

You mistake the use of fools: they are designed for properties 135
and not for friends. You have an indifferent stock of reputation
left yet. Lose it all like a frank gamester on the square. 'Twill
then be time enough to turn rook and cheat it up again on a good,
substantial bubble.

135 *properties* mere instruments, tools, cat's-paws
136 *indifferent* tolerable
138 *rook* cheat, swindler (especially in gaming)

137 *on the square* face to face, openly. The modern idiom makes sense here, and was
in use from 1611, but the phrase may have been a term in gaming. The sense,
'without deceit, fraud, or trickery' occurs from 1667–68 onwards, and is
frequently used of gaming. Wheadle, the gamester in *Love in a Tub*, says that he
could stay within the law if he could give up gaming—'Could I but leave this
Ordinary [notorious for late-night gaming], this Square . . .' (I.ii). Brett-Smith
is unable to explain this, but taking the two passages together the 'square' may
refer to the gaming-table or board.
139 *bubble* a dupe or gull, esp. in gaming. A Restoration word. The use of the verb
by Wheadle in *Love in a Tub* (1664), II.iii, precedes the first instance in *OED*,
and suggests that it began as gaming slang.

MRS LOVEIT

The old and the ill-favoured are only fit for properties, indeed,   140
but young and handsome fools have met with kinder fortunes.

DORIMANT

They have, to the shame of your sex be it spoken. 'Twas this, the
thought of this, made me by a timely jealousy endeavour to
prevent the good fortune you are providing for Sir Fopling. But
against a woman's frailty all our care is vain.   145

MRS LOVEIT

Had I not with a dear experience bought the knowledge of your
falsehood, you might have fooled me yet. This is not the first
jealousy you have feigned to make a quarrel with me, and get a
week to throw away on some such unknown, inconsiderable slut
as you have been lately lurking with at plays.   150

DORIMANT

Women, when they would break off with a man, never want the
address to turn the fault on him.

MRS LOVEIT

You take a pride of late in using of me ill, that the town may know
the power you have over me, which now (as unreasonably as
yourself) expects that I, do me all the injuries you can, must love   155
you still.

DORIMANT

I am so far from expecting that you should, I begin to think you
never did love me.

MRS LOVEIT

Would the memory of it were so wholly worn out in me that I did
doubt it too. What made you come to disturb my growing quiet?   160

DORIMANT

To give you joy of your growing infamy.

MRS LOVEIT

Insupportable! Insulting devil! This from you, the only author
of my shame! This from another had been but justice, but from
you, 'tis a hellish and inhuman outrage. What have I done?

DORIMANT

A thing that puts you below my scorn and makes my anger as   165
ridiculous as you have made my love.

MRS LOVEIT

I walked last night with Sir Fopling.

DORIMANT

You did, madam; and you talked and laughed aloud, 'Ha, ha,
ha'. Oh, that laugh! That laugh becomes the confidence of a
woman of quality.   170

MRS LOVEIT

You, who have more pleasure in the ruin of a woman's reputation

than in the endearments of her love, reproach me not with
yourself—and I defy you to name the man can lay a blemish on
my fame.

DORIMANT

To be seen publicly so transported with the vain follies of that   175
notorious fop, to me is an infamy below the sin of prostitution
with another man.

MRS LOVEIT

Rail on! I am satisfied in the justice of what I did: you had
provoked me to it.

DORIMANT

What I did was the effect of a passion whose extravagancies you   180
have been willing to forgive.

MRS LOVEIT

And what I did was the effect of a passion you may forgive if you
think fit.

DORIMANT

Are you so indifferent grown?

MRS LOVEIT

I am.   185

DORIMANT

Nay, then 'tis time to part. I'll send you back your letters you
have so often asked for. [*Looks in his pockets*] I have two or three
of 'em about me.

MRS LOVEIT

Give 'em me.

DORIMANT

You snatch as if you thought I would not. [*Gives her the*   190
letters]—There. And may the perjuries in 'em be mine if e'er I
see you more.   *Offers to go: she catches him*

MRS LOVEIT

Stay!

DORIMANT

I will not.

MRS LOVEIT

You shall!   195

DORIMANT

What have you to say?

MRS LOVEIT

I cannot speak it yet.

DORIMANT

Something more in commendation of the fool. Death, I want
patience! Let me go.

MRS LOVEIT

I cannot. (*Aside*) I can sooner part with the limbs that hold   200 him.—I hate that nauseous fool, you know I do.

DORIMANT

Was it the scandal you were fond of, then?

MRS LOVEIT

You had raised my anger equal to my love, a thing you ne'er
could do before; and in revenge I did—I know not what I did.
Would you would not think on't any more.   205

DORIMANT

Should I be willing to forget it, I shall be daily minded of it.
'Twill be a commonplace for all the town to laugh at me, and
Medley, when he is rhetorically drunk, will ever be declaiming
on it in my ears.

MRS LOVEIT

'Twill be believed a jealous spite! Come, forget it.   210

DORIMANT

Let me consult my reputation; you are too careless of it. (*Pauses*)
You shall meet Sir Fopling in the Mall again tonight.

MRS LOVEIT

What mean you?

DORIMANT

I have thought on it, and you must. 'Tis necessary to justify my
love to the world. You can handle a coxcomb as he deserves when   215
you are not out of humour, madam.

MRS LOVEIT

Public satisfaction for the wrong I have done you! This is some
new device to make me more ridiculous.

DORIMANT

Hear me.

MRS LOVEIT

I will not.   220

DORIMANT

You will be persuaded.

MRS LOVEIT

Never!

DORIMANT

Are you so obstinate?

MRS LOVEIT

Are you so base?

DORIMANT

You will not satisfy my love?   225

MRS LOVEIT

I would die to satisfy that; but I will not, to save you from a
thousand racks, do a shameless thing to please your vanity.

DORIMANT

Farewell, false woman!

MRS LOVEIT
Do! Go!

DORIMANT
You will call me back again.   230

MRS LOVEIT
Exquisite fiend! I knew you came but to torment me.

Enter BELLINDA *and* PERT

DORIMANT (*surprised*)
Bellinda here!

BELLINDA (*aside*)
He starts and looks pale. The sight of me has touched his guilty
soul.

PERT
'Twas but a qualm, as I said, a little indigestion. The surfeit-   235
water did it, madam, mixed with a little mirabilis.

DORIMANT [*aside*]
I am confounded, and cannot guess how she came hither.

MRS LOVEIT
'Tis your fortune, Bellinda, ever to be here when I am abused by
this prodigy of ill nature.

BELLINDA
I am amazed to find him here. How has he the face to come near   240
you?

DORIMANT (*aside*)
Here is fine work towards! I never was at such a loss before.

BELLINDA
One who makes a public profession of breach of faith and
ingratitude—I loathe the sight of him.

DORIMANT [*aside*]
There is no remedy. I must submit to their tongues now and   245
some other time bring myself off as well as I can.

BELLINDA
Other men are wicked, but then they have some sense of shame.
He is never well but when he triumphs—nay, glories—to a
woman's face in his villainies.

MRS LOVEIT
You are in the right, Bellinda; but methinks your kindness for   250
me makes you concern yourself too much with him.

236 *mirabilis* aqua mirabilis, a medicinal drink—'The wonderful water, prepared
of cloves, galangols, cubebs, mace, cardomums, nutmegs, ginger, and spirits of
wine, digested twenty-four hours' (Johnson).
248 *glories* Hobbes, *Leviathan* . . . (1651) defines 'glory' as '*Joy*, arising from imagination of a mans own power and ability, is that exultation of the mind which is
called GLORYING . . .' (pp. 26–7).

BELLINDA

It does indeed, my dear. His barbarous carriage to you yesterday
made me hope you ne'er would see him more, and the very next
day to find him here again provokes me strangely. But because I
know you love him, I have done.   255

DORIMANT

You have reproached me handsomely, and I deserve it for
coming hither, but—

PERT

You must expect it, sir! All women will hate you for my lady's
sake.

DORIMANT [aside]

Nay, if she begins too, 'tis time to fly. I shall be scolded to death, 260
else. (Aside to Bellinda) I am to blame in some circumstances, I
confess; but as to the main, I am not so guilty as you imagine.
[Aloud] I shall seek a more convenient time to clear myself.

MRS LOVEIT

Do it now! What impediments are here?

DORIMANT

I want time, and you want temper.   265

MRS LOVEIT

These are weak pretences!

DORIMANT

You were never more mistaken in your life—and so farewell.

                                            DORIMANT flings off

MRS LOVEIT

Call a footman, Pert. Quickly! I will have him dogged.

PERT

I wish you would not, for my quiet and your own.

MRS LOVEIT

I'll find out the infamous causes of all our quarrels, pluck her 270
mask off, and expose her bare-faced to the world!

                                                    [Exit PERT]

BELLINDA (aside)

Let me but escape this time, I'll never venture more.

MRS LOVEIT

Bellinda, you shall go with me.

BELLINDA

I have such a heaviness hangs on me with what I did this
morning, I would fain go home and sleep, my dear.   275

MRS LOVEIT

Death and eternal darkness! I shall never sleep again. Raging

252 *carriage* behaviour
274 *heaviness* torpor, dullness

fevers seize the world and make mankind as restless all as I am!

> *Exit* MRS LOVEIT

BELLINDA

I knew him false and helped to make him so. Was not her ruin enough to fright me from the danger? It should have been, but love can take no warning.   280

> *Exit* BELLINDA

Act V, Scene ii
LADY TOWNLEY'*s house*

Enter MEDLEY, YOUNG BELLAIR, LADY TOWNLEY, EMILIA, *and* [SMIRK, *a*] *chaplain*

MEDLEY

Bear up, Bellair, and do not let us see that repentance in thine we daily do in married faces.

LADY TOWNLEY

This wedding will strangely surprise my brother when he knows it.

MEDLEY

Your nephew ought to conceal it for a time, madam. Since   5
marriage has lost its good name, prudent men seldom expose their own reputations till 'tis convenient to justify their wives'.

OLD BELLAIR (*without*)

Where are you all there? Out, adod, will nobody hear?

LADY TOWNLEY

My brother! Quickly, Mr Smirk, into this closet. You must not be seen yet.   [SMIRK] *goes into the closet*   10

Enter OLD BELLAIR *and* LADY TOWNLEY'*s* PAGE

OLD BELLAIR [*to* PAGE]

Desire Mr Fourbe to walk into the lower parlour. I will be with him presently.   [*Exit* PAGE]
(*To* YOUNG BELLAIR) Where have you been, sir, you could not wait on me today?

YOUNG BELLAIR

About a business.   15

OLD BELLAIR

Are you so good at business? Adod, I have a business too you shall dispatch out of hand, sir.—Send for a parson, sister. My Lady Woodvill and her daughter are coming.

---

9 *closet* small inner room for privacy

11 *Mr Fourbe* see note to II.i, 37.

LADY TOWNLEY
What need you huddle up things thus?

OLD BELLAIR
Out a pize! Youth is apt to play the fool, and 'tis not good it   20
should be in their power.

LADY TOWNLEY
You need not fear your son.

OLD BELLAIR
He has been idling this morning, and adod, I do not like him. (*To*
EMILIA)—How dost thou do, sweetheart?

EMILIA
You are very severe, sir. Married in such haste!   25

OLD BELLAIR
Go to, thou'rt a rogue, and I will talk with thee anon. Here's my
Lady Woodvill come.

Enter LADY WOODVILL, HARRIET, *and* BUSY

Welcome, madam. Mr Fourbe's below with the writings.

LADY WOODVILL
Let us down and make an end, then.

OLD BELLAIR
Sister, show the way. (*To* YOUNG BELLAIR, *who is talking to*   30
HARRIET)—Harry, your business lies not there yet!—Excuse
him till we have done, lady, and then, adod, he shall be for
thee.—Mr Medley, we must trouble you to be a witness.

MEDLEY
I luckily came for that purpose, sir.

Exeunt OLD BELLAIR, MEDLEY, YOUNG BELLAIR, LADY TOWNLEY,
and LADY WOODVILL

BUSY [*to* HARRIET]
What will you do, madam?   35

HARRIET
Be carried back and mewed up in the country again, run away
here—anything rather than be married to a man I do not care
for.—Dear Emilia, do thou advise me.

EMILIA
Mr Bellair is engaged, you know.

HARRIET
I do, but know not what the fear of losing an estate may fright   40
him to.

26 *Go to* 'Come along!'
26 *to* V, CA (too Q1)
28 *writings* i.e., the legal documents for the marriage settlement
36 *mewed up* shut up, cooped up

EMILIA

In the desperate condition you are in, you should consult with some judicious man. What think you of Mr Dorimant?

HARRIET

I do not think of him at all.

BUSY [*aside*]

She thinks of nothing else, I am sure.   45

EMILIA

How fond your mother was of Mr Courtage.

HARRIET

Because I contrived the mistake to make a little mirth, you believe I like the man.

EMILIA

Mr Bellair believes you love him.

HARRIET

Men are seldom in the right when they guess at a woman's mind.   50
Would she whom he loves loved him no better!

BUSY (*aside*)

That's e'en well enough, on all conscience.

EMILIA

Mr Dorimant has a great deal of wit.

HARRIET

And takes a great deal of pains to show it.

EMILIA

He's extremely well-fashioned.   55

HARRIET

Affectedly grave, or ridiculously wild and apish.

BUSY

You defend him still against your mother.

HARRIET

I would not, were he justly rallied; but I cannot hear anyone undeservedly railed at.

EMILIA

Has your woman learnt the song you were so taken with?   60

HARRIET

I was fond of a new thing. 'Tis dull at second hearing.

EMILIA

Mr Dorimant made it.

BUSY

She knows it, madam, and has made me sing it at least a dozen times this morning.

HARRIET

Thy tongue is as impertinent as thy fingers.   65

56 *wild and apish* for 'wild' see Barnard (op. cit.), pp. xxix–xxxi. 'Apish' meant
   either ape-like, or foolishly imitative like an ape.

EMILIA [*to* BUSY]
You have provoked her.

BUSY
'Tis but singing the song and I shall appease her.

EMILIA
Prithee, do.

HARRIET
She has a voice will grate your ears worse than a catcall, and
dresses so ill she's scarce fit to trick up a yeoman's daughter on a   70
holiday.

BUSY *sings*
Song, by Sir C. S.

As Amoret with Phillis sat
  One evening on the plain,
And saw the charming Strephon wait
  To tell the nymph his pain,   75

The threat'ning danger to remove,
  She whispered in her ear,
'Ah, Phillis, if you would not love,
  This shepherd do not hear:

None ever had so strange an art,   80
  His passion to convey
Into a list'ning virgin's heart
  And steal her soul away.

Fly, fly betimes, for fear you give
  Occasion for your fate'.   85
'In vain', said she, 'in vain I strive.
  Alas, 'tis now too late'.

---

84 *betimes* in good time

---

69 *catcall* a kind of whistle. On 7 March 1660 Pepys went to Pope's Head Alley and
'bought a catcall there, it cost me two groats'. Certainly it was used later in the
century and in the eighteenth-century theatre to demonstrate an audience's
disapproval. See Leo Hughes, *The Drama's Patrons* (Austin and London,
1971), pp. 35–43.

71 s.d. *Sir C.S.* almost certainly by Sir Car Scroope who wrote the prologue,
rather than Sir Charles Sedley to whom it was attributed in 1722. Brett-Smith
supplies the lines from an elegy by Comtesse de la Suze in the *Recueil des Pièces
Gallantes* which Scroope imitated. It was an unusually popular song, and
appears in several manuscripts, musical broadsides, and songbooks (Thorpe,
p. 144).

Enter DORIMANT

DORIMANT

'Music so softens and disarms the mind—'

HARRIET

'That not one arrow does resistance find'.

DORIMANT

Let us make use of the lucky minute, then.   90

HARRIET (*aside, turning from* DORIMANT)

My love springs with my blood into my face. I dare not look upon
him yet.

DORIMANT

What have we here—the picture of a celebrated beauty giving
audience in public to a declared lover?

HARRIET

Play the dying fop and make the piece complete, sir.   95

DORIMANT

What think you if the hint were well improved—the whole
mystery of making love pleasantly designed and wrought in a suit
of hangings?

HARRIET

'Twere needless to execute fools in effigy who suffer daily in
their own persons.   100

DORIMANT (*to* EMILIA, *aside*)

Mistress Bride, for such I know this happy day has made you—

EMILIA

Defer the formal joy you are to give me, and mind your business
with her. (*Aloud*)—Here are dreadful preparations, Mr Dorimant—writings sealing, and a parson sent for.

DORIMANT

To marry this lady?   105

BUSY

Condemned she is; and what will become of her I know not,
without you generously engage in a rescue.

DORIMANT

In this sad condition, madam, I can do no less than offer you my
service.

93 *a celebrated* B, CA, CO (celebrated Q1; Brett-Smith believes 'a' was accidentally omitted and notes the parallelism with 'a declared lover' in l. 94)
97–8 *suit of hangings* set of tapestry wall-hangings
101 *Mistress* ed. (Mrs. Q1)

88–9 *Music . . . find* Waller, 'Of my Lady Isabella, Playing on the Lute', ll. 11–12
(*Poems*, ed. G. Thorn Drury (1901), vol. 1, 90), but with 'one' substituted for
'an'.

HARRIET

    The obligation is not great; you are the common sanctuary for all 110
young women who run from their relations.

DORIMANT

    I have always my arms open to receive the distressed. But I will
open my heart and receive you where none yet did ever enter.
You have filled it with a secret, might I but let you know it—

HARRIET

    Do not speak it if you would have me believe it. Your tongue is so 115
famed for falsehood, 'twill do the truth an injury.

                                        Turns away her head

DORIMANT

    Turn not away, then, but look on me and guess it.

HARRIET

    Did you not tell me there was no credit to be given to faces—that
women nowadays have their passions as much at will as they have
their complexions, and put on joy and sadness, scorn and kind- 120
ness, with the same ease they do their paint and patches? Are
they the only counterfeits?

DORIMANT

    You wrong your own while you suspect my eyes. By all the hope
I have in you, the inimitable colour in your cheeks is not more
free from art than are the sighs I offer. 125

HARRIET

    In men who have been long hardened in sin, we have reason to
mistrust the first signs of repentance.

DORIMANT

    The prospect of such a heaven will make me persevere and give
you marks that are infallible.

HARRIET

    What are those? 130

DORIMANT

    I will renounce all the joys I have in friendship and wine,
sacrifice to you all the interest I have in other women—

HARRIET

    Hold! Though I wish you devout, I would not have you turn
fanatic. Could you neglect these a while and make a journey into
the country? 135

DORIMANT

    To be with you, I could live there and never send one thought to
London.

HARRIET

    Whate'er you say, I know all beyond Hyde Park's a desert to you,
and that no gallantry can draw you farther.

DORIMANT

That has been the utmost limit of my love; but now my passion   140
knows no bounds, and there's no measure to be taken of what I'll
do for you from anything I ever did before.

HARRIET

When I hear you talk thus in Hampshire, I shall begin to think
there may be some little truth enlarged upon.

DORIMANT

Is this all? Will you not promise me—   145

HARRIET

I hate to promise! What we do then is expected from us and
wants much of the welcome it finds when it surprises.

DORIMANT

May I not hope?

HARRIET

That depends on you and not on me; and 'tis to no purpose to
forbid it.   *Turns to* BUSY 150

BUSY

Faith, madam, now I perceive the gentleman loves you too. E'en
let him know your mind, and torment yourselves no longer.

HARRIET

Dost think I have no sense of modesty?

BUSY

Think, if you lose this, you may never have another opportunity.

HARRIET

May he hate me—a curse that frights me when I speak it!—if   155
ever I do a thing against the rules of decency and honour.

DORIMANT (*to* EMILIA)

I am beholding to you for your good intentions, madam.

EMILIA

I thought the concealing of our marriage from her might have
done you better service.

DORIMANT

Try her again.   160

EMILIA [*to* HARRIET]

What have you resolved, madam? The time draws near.

HARRIET

To be obstinate and protest against this marriage.

Enter LADY TOWNLEY *in haste*

LADY TOWNLEY (*to* EMILIA)

Quickly, quickly, let Mr Smirk out of the closet!

SMIRK *comes out of the closet*

144 *little* Q1ᶜ (*omitted* Q1ᵘ, W, V)

HARRIET

A parson! [*To* DORIMANT]—Had you laid him in here?

DORIMANT

I knew nothing of him.   165

HARRIET

Should it appear you did, your opinion of my easiness may cost
you dear.

Enter OLD BELLAIR, YOUNG BELLAIR, MEDLEY, *and* LADY WOODVILL

OLD BELLAIR

Out a pize, the canonical hour is almost past! Sister, is the man of
God come?

LADY TOWNLEY [*indicating* SMIRK]

He waits your leisure.   170

OLD BELLAIR [*to* SMIRK]

By your favour, sir—Adod, a pretty spruce fellow! What may we
call him?

LADY TOWNLEY

Mr Smirk—my Lady Biggot's chaplain.

OLD BELLAIR

A wise woman, adod she is! The man will serve for the flesh as
well as the spirit.—Please you, sir, to commission a young   175
couple to go to bed together a God's name?—Harry!

YOUNG BELLAIR

Here, sir.

OLD BELLAIR

Out a pize! Without your mistress in your hand?

SMIRK

Is this the gentleman?

OLD BELLAIR

Yes, sir.   180

SMIRK

Are you not mistaken, sir?

OLD BELLAIR

Adod, I think not, sir!

SMIRK

Sure you are, sir.

OLD BELLAIR

You look as if you would forbid the banns, Mr Smirk. I hope you
have no pretension to the lady!   185

---

176 *a* Q1 (i' V)

166 *easiness* see note to I, 119.
168 *canonical hour* the hours in which marriage could take place legally (8–12 a.m.).

SMIRK
  Wish him joy, sir! I have done him the good office today already.
OLD BELLAIR
  Out a pize! What do I hear?
LADY TOWNLEY
  Never storm, brother. The truth is out.
OLD BELLAIR
  How say you, sir? Is this your wedding day?
YOUNG BELLAIR
  It is, sir.   190
OLD BELLAIR
  And, adod, it shall be mine too. (*To* EMILIA) Give me thy hand,
  sweetheart. [*She refuses*] What dost thou mean? Give me thy
  hand, I say!   EMILIA *kneels, and* YOUNG BELLAIR
LADY TOWNLEY
  Come, come, give her your blessing. This is the woman your son
  loved and is married to.   195
OLD BELLAIR
  Ha! Cheated! Cozened! And by your contrivance, sister!
LADY TOWNLEY
  What would you do with her? She's a rogue, and you can't abide
  her.
MEDLEY
  Shall I hit her a pat for you, sir?
OLD BELLAIR
  Adod, you are all rogues, and I never will forgive you.   200
                                     [*Flings away, as if to exit*]
LADY TOWNLEY
  Whither? Whither away?
MEDLEY
  Let him go and cool awhile.
LADY WOODVILL (*to* DORIMANT)
  Here's a business broke out now, Mr Courtage. I am made a fine
  fool of.
DORIMANT
  You see the old gentleman knew nothing of it.   205
LADY WOODVILL
  I find he did not. I shall have some trick put upon me, if I stay in
  this wicked town any longer.—Harriet, dear child, where art
  thou? I'll into the country straight.
OLD BELLAIR
  Adod, madam, you shall hear me first—

                Enter MRS LOVEIT *and* BELLINDA

196 *Cozened* defrauded, duped

MRS LOVEIT

Hither my m. n dogged him.   210

BELLINDA

Yonder he sta. ls, my dear.

MRS LOVEIT

I see him, (*aside*) and with him the face that has undone me. Oh,
that I were but where I might throw out the anguish of my heart!
Here it must rage within and break it.

LADY TOWNLEY

Mrs Loveit! A' you afraid to come forward?   215

MRS LOVEIT

I was amazed to see so much company here in a morning. The
occasion sure is extraordinary.

DORIMANT (*aside*)

Loveit and Bellinda! The devil owes me a shame today, and I
think never will h ve done paying it.

MRS LOVEIT

Married! Dear Emilia, how am I transported with the news!   220

HARRIET (*to* DORIMANT)

I little thought Emilia was the woman Mr Bellair was in love
with. I'll chide her for not trusting me with the secret.

DORIMANT

How do you like Mrs Loveit?

HARRIET

She's a famed mistress of yours, I hear.

DORIMANT

She has been, on occasion.   225

OLD BELLAIR (*to* LADY WOODVILL)

Adod, madam, I cannot help it.

LADY WOODVILL

You need make no more apologies, sir.

EMILIA (*to* MRS LOVEIT)

The old gentleman's excusing himself to my Lady Woodvill.

MRS LOVEIT

Ha, ha, ha! I never heard of anything so pleasant.

HARRIET (*to* DORIMANT)

She's extremely overjoyed at something.   230

DORIMANT

At nothing. She is one of those hoiting ladies who gaily fling

224 *mistress* V, CA (Mrs. Q1)
231 *hoiting* involved in riotous and noisy mirth, acting the hoyden

218–19 *The devil . . . it* Carnochan points out that Dorimant varies the proverb, 'the
    devil owed (one) a shame and now has paid it' (Tilley, op. cit., pp. 152–3).

themselves about and force a laugh when their aching hearts are
full of discontent and malice.

MRS LOVEIT

Oh heaven! I was never so near killing myself with laughing.—Mr Dorimant, are you a brideman?   235

LADY WOODVILL

Mr Dorimant! Is this Mr Dorimant, madam?

MRS LOVEIT

If you doubt it, your daughter can resolve you, I suppose.

LADY WOODVILL

I am cheated too, basely cheated!

OLD BELLAIR

Out a pize, what's here? More knavery yet?

LADY WOODVILL

Harriet! On my blessing, come away, I charge you.   240

HARRIET

Dear mother, do but stay and hear me.

LADY WOODVILL

I am betrayed, and thou art undone, I fear.

HARRIET

Do not fear it. I have not, nor never will, do anything against my
duty. Believe me, dear mother, do!

DORIMANT (*to* MRS LOVEIT)

I had trusted you with this secret but that I knew the violence of 245
your nature would ruin my fortune—as now unluckily it has. I
thank you, madam.

MRS LOVEIT

She's an heiress, I know, and very rich.

DORIMANT

To satisfy you, I must give up my interest wholly to my love.
Had you been a reasonable woman, I might have secured 'em   250
both and been happy.

MRS LOVEIT

You might have trusted me with anything of this kind, you know
you might. Why did you go under a wrong name?

DORIMANT

The story is too long to tell you now. Be satisfied; this is the
business, this is the mask has kept me from you.   255

BELLINDA (*aside*)

He's tender of my honour, though he's cruel to my love.

MRS LOVEIT

Was it no idle mistress, then?

DORIMANT

Believe me—a wife, to repair the ruins of my estate that needs
it.

MRS LOVEIT
The knowledge of this makes my grief hang lighter on my soul,
but I shall never more be happy.   260

DORIMANT
Bellinda—

BELLINDA
Do not think of clearing yourself with me. It is impossible. Do all
men break their words thus?

DORIMANT
Th' extravagant words they speak in love. 'Tis as unreasonable to
expect we should perform all we promise then, as do all we   265
threaten when we are angry. When I see you next—

BELLINDA
Take no notice of me, and I shall not hate you.

DORIMANT
How came you to Mrs Loveit?

BELLINDA
By a mistake the chairmen made for want of my giving them
directions.   270

DORIMANT
'Twas a pleasant one. We must meet again.

BELLINDA
Never.

DORIMANT
Never?

BELLINDA
When we do, may I be as infamous as you are false.

LADY TOWNLEY
Men of Mr Dorimant's character always suffer in the general   275
opinion of the world.

MEDLEY
You can make no judgment of a witty man from common fame,
considering the prevailing faction, madam.

OLD BELLAIR
Adod, he's in the right.

---

273 *Never?* V, CA (Never! Q1)

---

278 *prevailing faction* antipathy to the Wits, and the Wits' defensive reaction, is
evident in Dryden's dedication of *The Assignation* (1673) to Sir Charles Sedley,
which speaks of 'the ignorant and ridiculous Descriptions which some Pedants
have given of the Wits (as they are pleas'd to call them) . . . those wretches Paint
leudness, Atheism, Folly, ill-Reasoning, and all manner of Extravagances
amongst us, for want of understanding what we are' (*Dramatic Works*, ed. M.
Summers (1931–32), vol. 3, 276). (Cited by Conaghan.)

MEDLEY

Besides, 'tis a common error among women to believe too well of   280
them they know and too ill of them they don't.

OLD BELLAIR

Adod, he observes well.

LADY TOWNLEY

Believe me, madam, you will find Mr Dorimant as civil a
gentleman as you thought Mr Courtage.

HARRIET

If you would but know him better—   285

LADY WOODVILL

You have a mind to know him better? Come away! You shall
never see him more.

HARRIET

Dear mother, stay!

LADY WOODVILL

I won't be consenting to your ruin.

HARRIET

Were my fortune in your power—   290

LADY WOODVILL

Your person is.

HARRIET

Could I be disobedient, I might take it out of yours and put it
into his.

LADY WOODVILL

'Tis that you would be at! You would marry this Dorimant!

HARRIET

I cannot deny it. I would, and never will marry any other man.   295

LADY WOODVILL

Is this the duty that you promised?

HARRIET

But I will never marry him against your will.

LADY WOODVILL (*aside*)

She knows the way to melt my heart. (*To* HARRIET)—Upon
yourself light your undoing.

MEDLEY (*to* OLD BELLAIR)

Come, sir, you have not the heart any longer to refuse your   300
blessing.

OLD BELLAIR

Adod, I ha' not.—Rise, and God bless you both! Make much of
her, Harry; she deserves thy kindness. (*To* EMILIA) Adod, sirrah,
I did not think it had been in thee.

Enter SIR FOPLING *and his* PAGE

SIR FOPLING

'Tis a damned windy day. Hey, page! Is my periwig right?   305

PAGE

A little out of order, sir.

SIR FOPLING

Pox o' this apartment! It wants an antechamber to adjust one's self in. (*To* MRS LOVEIT)—Madam, I came from your house, and your servants directed me hither.

MRS LOVEIT

I will give order hereafter they shall direct you better.   310

SIR FOPLING

The great satisfaction I had in the Mall last night has given me much disquiet since.

MRS LOVEIT

'Tis likely to give me more than I desire.

SIR FOPLING [*aside*]

What the devil makes her so reserved?—Am I guilty of an indiscretion, madam?   315

MRS LOVEIT

You will be of a great one, if you continue your mistake, sir.

SIR FOPLING

Something puts you out of humour.

MRS LOVEIT

The most foolish, inconsiderable thing that ever did.

SIR FOPLING

Is it in my power?

MRS LOVEIT

To hang or drown it. Do one of 'em, and trouble me no more.   320

SIR FOPLING

So *fière*? *Serviteur*, madam!—Medley, where's Dorimant?

MEDLEY

Methinks the lady has not made you those advances today she did last night, Sir Fopling.

SIR FOPLING

Prithee, do not talk of her.

MEDLEY

She would be a *bonne fortune*.   325

SIR FOPLING

Not to me at present.

MEDLEY

How so?

307–8 *one's self* ed. (ones self Q1; oneself V, CA)
321 *fière* proud, haughty
321 *Serviteur* your servant

SIR FOPLING
    An intrigue now would be but a temptation to me to throw away
    that vigour on one which I mean shall shortly make my court to
    the whole sex in a ballet.   330

MEDLEY
    Wisely considered, Sir Fopling.

SIR FOPLING
    No one woman is worth the loss of a cut in a caper.

MEDLEY
    Not when 'tis so universally designed.

LADY WOODVILL
    Mr Dorimant, everyone has spoke so much in your behalf that I
    can no longer doubt but I was in the wrong.   335

MRS LOVEIT [*to* BELLINDA]
    There's nothing but falsehood and impertinence in this world.
    All men are villains or fools. Take example from my misfor-
    tunes. Bellinda, if thou wouldst be happy, give thyself wholly up
    to goodness.

HARRIET (*to* MRS LOVEIT)
    Mr Dorimant has been your God Almighty long enough. 'Tis   340
    time to think of another.

MRS LOVEIT [*to* BELLINDA]
    Jeered by her! I will lock myself up in my house and never see the
    world again.

HARRIET
    A nunnery is the more fashionable place for such a retreat and
    has been the fatal consequence of many a *belle passion*.   345

MRS LOVEIT [*aside*]
    Hold, heart, till I get home! Should I answer, 'twould make her
    triumph greater.   *Is going out*

DORIMANT
    Your hand, Sir Fopling—

SIR FOPLING
    Shall I wait upon you, madam?

MRS LOVEIT
    Legion of fools, as many devils take thee!   *Exit* MRS LOVEIT   350

MEDLEY
    Dorimant! I pronounce thy reputation clear, and henceforward,

---

337–8 *misfortunes. Bellinda*, Q1 (misfortunes, Bellinda; V, B)
345 *belle passion* violent passion

---

332 *cut* a step in dancing (*OED* gives this as its first example). From the verb 'cut',
    to spring into the air and kick the feet with great rapidity (current from 1603).
350 *Legion* innumerable hosts, with an echo of Mark v. 9, 'My name *is* Legion for we
    are many'. Cf. Epilogue, l. 18.

when I would know anything of woman, I will consult no other oracle.

SIR FOPLING

Stark mad, by all that's handsome!—Dorimant, thou hast engaged me in a pretty business.   355

DORIMANT

I have not leisure now to talk about it.

OLD BELLAIR

Out a pize, what does this man of mode do here again?

LADY TOWNLEY

He'll be an excellent entertainment within, brother, and is luckily come to raise the mirth of the company.

LADY WOODVILL

Madam, I take my leave of you.   360

LADY TOWNLEY

What do you mean, madam?

LADY WOODVILL

To go this afternoon part of my way to Hartley—

OLD BELLAIR

Adod, you shall stay and dine first! Come, we will all be good friends, and you shall give Mr Dorimant leave to wait upon you and your daughter in the country.   365

LADY WOODVILL

If his occasions bring him that way, I have now so good an opinion of him, he shall be welcome.

HARRIET

To a great, rambling, lone house that looks as it were not inhabited, the family's so small. There you'll find my mother, an old lame aunt, and myself, sir, perched up on chairs at a distance   370
in a large parlour, sitting moping like three or four melancholy birds in a spacious volary. Does not this stagger your resolution?

DORIMANT

Not at all, madam. The first time I saw you, you left me with the pangs of love upon me, and this day my soul has quite given up her liberty.   375

HARRIET

This is more dismal than the country.—Emilia, pity me who am going to that sad place. Methinks I hear the hateful noise of rooks

366 *occasions* 1) needs, requirements, 2) affairs, business

---

362 *Hartley* there are a Hartley Wespall, a Hartley Mauditt, and a Hartley Wintney in Hampshire.

372 *volary* a large bird-cage; an aviary. Introduced from the French *volière* in the seventeenth century. *OED* cites first instance from Jonson's *New Inn* (1630), V.i.

already—kaw, kaw, kaw. There's music in the worst cry in
London—'My dill and cucumbers to pickle'.

OLD BELLAIR

Sister, knowing of this matter, I hope you have provided us some   380
good cheer.

LADY TOWNLEY

I have, brother, and the fiddles too.

OLD BELLAIR

Let 'em strike up then. The young lady shall have a dance before
she departs.   *Dance*

(*After the dance*) So now we'll in, and make this an arrant   385
wedding day.

(*To the pit*)

       And if these honest gentlemen rejoice,
       Adod, the boy has made a happy choice.

                           Exeunt omnes

---

379 *My dill ... pickle* Addison, writing on the cries of London street-traders, 'I am
always pleased with that particular Time of the Year which is proper for the
pickling of Dill and Cucumbers; but alas this Cry, like the Song of the
Nightingales, is not heard above two Months' (*The Spectator*, No. 251 (18 Dec.
1711)).

THE EPILOGUE
By Mr Dryden

Most modern wits such monstrous fools have shown,
They seemed not of heav'n's making, but their own.
Those nauseous harlequins in farce may pass,
But there goes more to a substantial ass!
Something of man must be exposed to view,   5
That, gallants, it may more resemble you.
Sir Fopling is a fool so nicely writ,
The ladies would mistake him for a wit,
And when he sings, talks loud, and cocks, would cry:
'I vow, methinks, he's pretty company—   10
So brisk, so gay, so travelled, so refined!'
As he took pains to graft upon his kind,
True fops help nature's work, and go to school
To file and finish God A'mighty's fool.
Yet none Sir Fopling him, or him, can call—   15
He's knight o' the shire and represents ye all.
From each he meets, he culls whate'er he can:
Legion's his name, a people in a man.

6 *it* B, CA (they Q1; Brett-Smith adopts text from Bodleian ms.)
9 *cocks* struts, brags, or crows over
10 *I vow* Q1 (I now B; Aye, now CA; both readings follow ms. text)
11 *refined!'* ed. (refin'd! Q1; refined, CA; V regards l. 11 as the only line cried out by the ladies)
12 *upon . . . kind* upon what nature gave him
12 *kind,* ed. (kind. Q1; kind.' CA)
12–14 Sloane ms. adds an extra couplet after l. 12: 'Labouring to put in more as Mr. Bayes/Thrums in Additions to his ten yeares playes'. Bodleian ms. places the couplet, with slight variants, after l. 14. (Further, see Note on Text)
16 *knight o' the shire* parliamentary representative of a shire (or county)

3 *harlequins* Harlequin is the traditional figure in French and Italian farce.
   Travelling companies from the continent had been well received in England,
   but were disapproved of by Dryden (and later Pope) as a vulgar, 'low' form.
12–14 See textual note. Dryden's additional couplet 'turns the tables on George
   Villiers, Duke of Buckingham, for his satiric portrait of Dryden as Bayes in *The
   Rehearsal*; Buckingham's play was several years in the making before its first
   appearance in 1671 and was often amended afterward' (Carnochan).
18 *Legion* see note to V.ii, 350.

His bulky folly gathers as it goes,
And, rolling o'er you, like a snowball grows.
His various modes from various fathers follow;
One taught the toss, and one the new French wallow.
His sword-knot, this, his cravat, this designed —
And this, the yard-long snake he twirls behind.
From one, the sacred periwig he gained,
Which wind ne'er blew, nor touch of hat profaned;
Another's diving bow he did adore,
Which with a shog casts all the hair before,
Till he with full decorum brings it back
And rises with a water spaniel shake.
As for his songs (the ladies' dear delight),
Those sure he took from most of you who write.
Yet every man is safe from what he feared,
For no one fool is hunted from the herd.

21 *modes* see note to II. ii, 29.
22 *toss* i.e., of the head. *OED* gives as first example of this usage.
22 *wallow* rolling walk or gait. *OED* gives this sole example
24 *snake* long curl or tail attached to a wig. *OED* gives this example, and one from Swift (1728).
26 *nor ... profaned* for the fashion of carrying the hat (to avoid disordering the wig), cf. Dryden's 'Epilogue Spoken at the Opening of the New House', l. 13, 'So may your Hats your Foretops never press ...'
28 *shog* shake, jerk. Cotgrave (1611) gives 'shake, shog, or shocke' as synonyms.
33–4 *Yet ... herd* a conventional claim, but although identifications were quickly made, Dryden's claim is probably correct.

APPENDIX A

DR STAGGINS'S SETTINGS OF DORIMANT'S SONG AND SIR CAR SCROOPE'S SONG

These two settings of Dorimant's song ('When first Amintas charmed my heart') in Act III, Scene i, and Sir Car Scroope's song ('As Amoret with Phillis sat') in Act V, Scene ii, are the nearest contemporary settings known. Dr Nicholas Staggins (1650?–1700) was made master of 'his Majesty's Music' in 1675, but he published few of his compositions.

The nearest contemporary setting of Sir Fopling's song (Act IV, Scene ii) dates from 1707, and is by Ramonden (see Thorpe, pp. 103–104).

Mr Philip Wilby has kindly made these modern realizations from the original printed music. The part for the piano, which would have been improvised at will, has been added by Mr Wilby.

Staggins's setting of Dorimant's song is printed in John Playford's *Choice Ayres and Songs to sing to the Theorbo-Lute, or Bass-Viol: being most of the Newest Ayres and Songs Sung at Court, And at the Publick Theatres. Composed by Several Gentlemen of His Majesty's Music, and Others :.. The Fifth Book* (1684), p. 38. Ramonden's setting, dating from 1707, is also extant. For a record of other printings of the song, and reprintings of Staggins's music, see Thorpe, p. 102.

Staggins's setting of Sir Car Scroope's song is printed in Playford's *Choice Ayres ... The Second Book* (1679), p. 5. It was an unusually popular song. Thorpe (p. 144) records manuscript copies, various printings, and further notes that its popularity continued into the early eighteenth century.

'When First Amintas Charmed My Heart'

VOICE

When first A-min-tas charmed my heart, My

PIANO

GUITAR   Dm   Gm   Asup⁴ 3 Dm Bb

heed-less sheep be- gan to stray; The wolves soon stole the

C7 Am Bb   Gm   A   D   G7   C

great-est part, And all will now be made a prey.

Dm7 G C F   Dm   E Am   Esup⁴ 3 Am

Ah! let not love your thoughts pos-sess, 'Tis

Am   Dm   Gm   D7   G

fa - tal to a shep - herd - ess; The dan - g'-rous pas - sion

A7   Dm Gm   Gm   C   C   F   Cm7 F

you must shun, Or else like me be quite un-done.

G7   A7   Dm Gm   A   Dm   Gm G   Asup4 3   Dm

'As Amoret with Phillis Sat'

As A - mor-et with Phil - lis sat, One

Gm   Gm   Eb Cm   D

even - ing on the plain, And saw the charm-ing

C(m)   Gm Cm D7   Gm   Cm   F7

Stre - phon wait to tell the nymph his pain, The

Bb   F   Eb   F7   Bb

threat'-ning dan-ger to re-move, She whis-pered in her

ear, Ah Phil-lis, if you would not love

This shep-herd do not hear, This shep-herd do not hear.

APPENDIX B

THE BULLIES' SONG

The scraps of the song directed by the bullies at Sir Fopling, Mrs
Loveit, and Bellinda in Act III, Scene iii, 202, 211 have been
identified by W. B. Carnochan as being from an anonymous ballad
in *A New Collection of the Choicest Songs. Now in Esteem in Town or
Court* (1676), sig. B6ˣ. The volume also contains Dorimant's song
('When first Amintas'), mistakenly attributed to Sir Fopling, the
drinking-song from Act IV, Scene i, and Sir Car Scroope's song.
The song sung by the bullies became the basis for a ballad, 'Love
al-a-Mode, or, the Modish Mistris' (Pepys Collection, iii. 102;
Pepysian Library, Magdalene College, Cambridge). The text in *A
New Collection*, which has no musical setting, is as follows:

> Tell me no more you love,
>   Unless you will grant my desire,
> Ev'rything else will prove,
>   But fuel to my fire.
>
> 'Tis not for kisses alone,
>   So long I have made my address,
> There's some thing else to be done,
>   Which you cannot chuse but guess.
>
> 'Tis not a charming smile,
>   That brings me the perfect Joys,
> Nor can you me beguile,
>   With sighs and with languishing eyes:
>
> There is an essence within,
>   Kind Nature hath clear'd the doubt,
> Such bliss can never be sin,
>   And therefore i'le find it out.

The Plain Dealer

———✦uuuuᴌᴌ◉ᴌᴌᴌuuu✦———

WILLIAM WYCHERLEY

Edited by
JAMES L. SMITH

ABBREVIATIONS

Textual

Q1	First quarto of 1677 (Q1a uncorrected, Q1b corrected)
Q2	Second quarto of 1677 (two states, Q2a dated 1677, Q2b dated 1678)
Q3	Third quarto of 1681 (two states, Q3a dated 1677, Q3b dated 1681)
Q4	Fourth quarto of 1686
Q5	Fifth quarto of 1691
Q6	Sixth quarto of 1694 (Q6a uncorrected, Q6b corrected)
Q7	Seventh quarto of 1700
Q8	Eighth quarto of 1709, marked 'The Sixth Edition'
O	London octavo of 1712

Explanatory

B.E.	B.E., *A New Dictionary of the Terms Ancient and Modern of the Canting Crew* (1699)
Blount	Thomas Blount, *A Law-Dictionary* (1670)
Chamberlayne	Edward Chamberlayne, *Angliæ Notitia: or the Present State of England,* 2 vols. (1676)
Dennis	*The Critical Works of John Dennis,* ed. Edward Niles Hooker, 2 vols. (Baltimore, 1939–43)
Pack	Richardson Pack, 'Some memoirs of Mr Wycherley's life', prefixed to Wycherley's *Posthumous Works,* ed. Lewis Theobald (1728)
Phillips	Edward Phillips, *The New World of English Words: or, a General Dictionary* (1658)

THE
PLAIN-DEALER.
A
COMEDY.

As it is Acted at the
Theatre Royal.

Written by Mr WYCHERLEY.

HORAT.

—— *Ridiculum acre*
Fortius & melius magnas plerumque secat res.

Licensed *Jan.* 9. 1676.
ROGER L'ESTRANGE.

LONDON,
Printed by *T.N.* for *James Magnes* and *Rich. Bentley*
in *Russel-Street* in *Covent-garden* near the *Piazza's.*
M.DC.LXXVII.

ridiculum acri
fortius et melius magnas plerumque secat res.

---

acri Q2–8, O (acre Q1)

Motto
Jesting often cuts hard knots more forcefully and effectively than gravity (Horace, *Sat.* I. x. 14–15).

To my Lady B—

Madam,

Though I never had the honour to receive a favour from you,
nay, or be known to you, I take the confidence of an author to
write to you a *billet-doux* dedicatory, which is no new thing,   5
for by most dedications it appears that authors, though they
praise their patrons from top to toe and seem to turn 'em inside out, know 'em as little as sometimes their patrons their
books, though they read 'em out; and if the poetical daubers
did not write the name of the man or woman on top of the   10
picture, 'twere impossible to guess whose it were. But you,
madam, without the help of a poet, have made yourself known
and famous in the world, and because you do not want it are
therefore most worthy of an epistle dedicatory. And this play
claims naturally your protection, since it has lost its reputation   15
with the ladies of stricter lives in the playhouse; and, you
know, when men's endeavours are discountenanced and refused by the nice coy women of honour, they come to you; to
you, the great and noble patroness of rejected and bashful
men, of which number I profess myself to be one, though a   20
poet, a dedicating poet; to you, I say, madam, who have as
discerning a judgment in what's obscene or not as any quick-
sighted civil person of 'em all, and can make as much of a
double-meaning saying as the best of 'em; yet would not, as
some do, make nonsense of a poet's jest rather than not make   25
it bawdy, by which they show they as little value wit in a play
as in a lover, provided they can bring t'other thing about. Their
sense, indeed, lies all one way, and therefore are only for that
in a poet which is moving, as they say. But what do they
mean by that word 'moving'? Well, I must not put 'em to   30
the blush, since I find I can do't. In short, madam, you would
not be one of those who ravish a poet's innocent words, and

---

 1 *Lady B—* Mother Bennett, a celebrated procuress; Pepys describes
   her at work on 22 September 1660
21 *poet* author (frequent in Wycherley)
29 *moving* The innuendo is clarified in Farquhar's *The Beaux' Stratagem*
   (1707); when Dorinda boasts her lover 'spoke the softest moving
   things', Mrs Sullen replies 'Mine had his moving things too' (IV. i).

make 'em guilty of their own naughtiness, as 'tis termed, in
spite of his teeth. Nay, nothing is secure from the power of
their imaginations, no, not their husbands, whom they cuckold 35
with themselves by thinking of other men and so make the
lawful matrimonial embraces adultery, wrong husbands and
poets in thought and word, to keep their own reputations.
But your ladyship's justice, I know, would think a woman's
arraigning and damning a poet for her own obscenity like 40
her crying out a rape, and hanging a man for giving her
pleasure, only that she might be thought not to consent to't;
and so to vindicate her honour forfeits her modesty. But you,
madam, have too much modesty to pretend to't, though you
have as much to say for your modesty as many a nicer she, 45
for you never were seen at this play, no, not the first day;
and 'tis no matter what people's lives have been, they are un-
questionably modest who frequent not this play. For as
Master Bayes says of his, that it is the only touchstone of
men's wit and understanding, mine is, it seems, the only 50
touchstone of women's virtue and modesty. But hold, that
'touchstone' is equivocal, and by the strength of a lady's
imagination may become something that is not civil; but
your ladyship, I know, scorns to misapply a touchstone.
And, madam, though you have not seen this play, I hope 55
like other nice ladies you will the rather read it. Yet, lest the
chambermaid or page should not be trusted, and their indulgence could gain no further admittance for it than to their
ladies' lobbies or outward rooms, take it into your care and
protection, for by your recommendation and procurement it 60
may have the honour to get into their closets; for what they
renounce in public often entertains 'em there, with your help

33 *naughtiness* wickedness, depravity
41 *hanging a man* Rape was a felony punished by death.
45 *nicer she* more fastidious woman
49 *Bayes* the conceited dramatist in Buckingham's *The Rehearsal* (1671);
   he flatters Johnson with 'I know you have wit by the judgement you
   make of this Play; for that's the measure I go by: my Play is my
   Touch-stone' (III. i)
52 *touchstone* perhaps used in a *double entendre* for testicles
56–63 *Yet . . . especially* perhaps borrowed from Montaigne, *Essais*, III.
   v. (ed. M. Rat, 3 vols., Paris, 1952, III, 66): 'Je m'ennuie que mes
   Essais servent les dames de meuble commun seulement, et de meuble
   de sale. Ce chapitre me fera du cabinet'. G. B. Ives translates: 'It
   annoys me that the ladies use my Essays merely as a common piece
   of furniture, furniture for the reception-room. This chapter will make
   me suitable for the boudoir' (2 vols., New York, 1946, II, 1148)

especially. In fine, madam, for these and many other reasons,
you are the fittest patroness or judge of this play, for you show
no partiality to this or that author. For from some many   65
ladies will take a broad jest as cheerfully as from the watermen, and sit at some downright filthy plays, as they call 'em, as
well satisfied and as still as a poet could wish 'em elsewhere.
Therefore it must be the doubtful obscenity of my plays alone
they take exceptions at, because it is too bashful for 'em; and   70
indeed most women hate men for attempting to halves on their
chastity, and bawdy I find, like satire, should be home, not
to have it taken notice of. But, now I mention satire, some
there are who say 'tis the plain dealing of the play, not the
obscenity, 'tis taking off the ladies' masks, not offering at their   75
petticoats, which offends 'em. And generally they are not the
handsomest, or most innocent, who are the most angry at
being discovered:

Nihil est audacius illis
Deprensis: iram atque animos a crimine sumunt.   80

Pardon, madam, the quotation, for a dedication can no more
be without ends of Latin than flattery; and 'tis no matter
whom it is writ to, for an author can as easily, I hope, suppose people to have more understanding and languages than
they have, as well as more virtues. But why the devil should   85
any of the few modest and handsome be alarmed? (For some
there are who as well as any deserve those attributes, yet refrain not from seeing this play, nor think it any addition to
their virtue to set up for it in a playhouse, lest there it should
look too much like acting.) But why, I say, should any at all of   90
the truly virtuous be concerned, if those who are not so are
distinguished from 'em? For by that mask of modesty which
women wear promiscuously in public, they are all alike, and
you can no more know a kept wench from a woman of

---

80 Deprensis ed. (*Deprehensis* Q1–8, 0)
89 *lest there* Q1, 0 (lest Q2–8)

---

63 *In fine* in short, to sum up (frequent in Wycherley)
66–7 *watermen* The Thames boatmen habitually attacked other fares
  with obscene abuse; the joke was to reply in kind.
71 *to halves* by halves, imperfectly
72 *home* searching, trenchant
79–80 *Nihil . . . sumunt* There's no effrontery like that of a woman
  caught in the act; her very guilt inspires her with wrath and insolence
  (Juvenal, *Sat.* vi. 284–5).
89 *set up for* support
93 *promiscuously* indiscriminately

honour by her looks than by her dress. For those who are   95
of quality without honour, if any such there are, they have
their quality to set off their false modesty as well as their false
jewels, and you must no more suspect their countenances for
counterfeit than their pendants, though, as the plain dealer
Montaigne says,   100

> Elles envoyent leur conscience au bordel, et tiennent
> leur contenance en règle.

But those who act as they look ought not to be scandalized
at the reprehension of others' faults, lest they tax themselves
with 'em, and by too delicate and quick an apprehension not   105
only make that obscene which I meant innocent, but that
satire on all which was intended only on those who deserved
it. But, madam, I beg your pardon for this digression to civil
women and ladies of honour, since you and I shall never be
the better for 'em; for a comic poet and a lady of your pro-   110
fession make most of the other sort, and the stage and your
houses, like our plantations, are propagated by the least nice
women; and, as with the ministers of justice, the vices of the
age are our best business. But now I mention public persons,
I can no longer defer doing you the justice of a dedication   115
and telling you your own, who are, of all public-spirited
people, the most necessary, most communicative, most
generous and hospitable. Your house has been the house of
the people, your sleep still disturbed for the public, and when
you arose 'twas that others might lie down, and you waked   120
that others might rest. The good you have done is unspeakable. How many young, unexperienced heirs have you
kept from rash, foolish marriages, and from being jilted for
their lives by the worst sort of jilts, wives? How many unbe-
witched widowers' children have you preserved from the   125
tyranny of stepmothers? How many old dotards from

101 Elles envoyent Q2 (*Els envoy* Q1, 0; *Eles envoyent* Q3–8)

101–2 *Elles . . . règle Essais,* III. v. (ed. cit., III, 65); Wycherley rewrites
Montaigne, making women, not men, the subject; G. B. Ives translates: 'Men send their conscience to the brothel and keep their
demeanour in good order' (ed. cit., II, 1147)
112 *plantations* Statutes entitled some female felons to choose between
transportation and execution.
116 *your own* the plain truth about yourself (usually in a bad sense)
117 *communicative* (1) informative (2) sharing, i.e., fornicating (and perhaps passing on venereal disease)
119 *still* continually
120 *waked* stayed awake, kept watch

cuckoldage, and keeping other men's wenches and children?
How many adulteries and unnatural sins have you prevented?
In fine, you have been a constant scourge to the old lecher,
and often a terror to the young; you have made concupiscence   130
its own punishment, and extinguished lust with lust, like
blowing up of houses to stop the fire.

*Nimirum, propter continentiam incontinentia necessaria
est, incendium ignibus extinguetur.*

There's Latin for you again, madam. I protest to you, as I   135
am an author, I cannot help it. Nay, I can hardly keep myself
from quoting Aristotle and Horace, and talking to you of the
rules of writing (like the French authors), to show you and
my reader I understand 'em in my epistle, lest neither of you
should find it out by the play; and according to the rules of   140
dedications, 'tis no matter whether you understand or no what
I quote or say to you of writing, for an author can as easily
make anyone a judge or critic in an epistle as an hero in his
play. But, madam, that this may prove to the end a true
epistle dedicatory, I'd have you know 'tis not without a design   145
upon you which is in the behalf of the fraternity of
Parnassus: that songs and sonnets may go at your houses and
in your liberties for guineas and half-guineas, and that wit,
at least with you, as of old, may be the price of beauty; and
so you will prove a true encourager of poetry, for love is a   150
better help to it than wine, and poets, like painters, draw
better after the life than by fancy. Nay, in justice, madam,

---

134 extinguetur ed. (*extinguitur* Q1–8, 0)
139 *reader* Q2–8, 0 (readers Q1)

---

132 *blowing . . . fire* During the Fire of 2–6 September 1666, houses at
    risk were pulled down with hooks and blown up with gunpowder to
    make a gap the flames could not leap.
133–4 *Nimirum . . . extinguetur* No doubt it is for the sake of continence
    that incontinence is necessary; no doubt a fire will be extinguished
    by flames.—Tertullian, *De Pudicitia,* I. xvi. (ed. J.-P. Migne, Paris,
    1878, col. 1034; tr. W. P. le Saint, London, 1959, p. 56); Wycherley
    probably read it in Montaigne, *Essais,* III. v. (ed. cit., III, 79), which
    also prints *extinguitur* for *extinguetur*; Q1 sets out the Tertullian as
    verse.
138 *French authors* The 1660 edition of Pierre Corneille's *Théâtre* in-
    cluded three *Discours sur le poème dramatique* and *Examens* to
    individual plays; many of Jean Racine's masterpieces between *Andro-
    maque* (1667) and *Phèdre* (1677) were published with critical pre-
    faces.
148 *liberties* districts outside the city, where most London brothels were
    situated

I think a poet ought to be as free of your houses as of the
playhouses, since he contributes to the support of both and is
as necessary to such as you as a ballad-singer to a pickpurse,   155
in convening the cullies at the theatres, to be picked up and
carried to supper and bed at your houses. And, madam, the
reason of this motion of mine is because poor poets can get
no favour in the tiring-rooms, for they are no keepers, you
know; and folly and money, the old enemies of wit, are   160
even too hard for it on its own dunghill; and for other ladies,
a poet can least go to the price of them. Besides, his wit,
which ought to recommend him to 'em, is as much an obstruc-
tion to his love as to his wealth or preferment, for most
women nowadays apprehend wit in a lover as much as in a   165
husband. They hate a man that knows 'em. They must have a
blind, easy fool whom they can lead by the nose, and, as the
Scythian women of old, must baffle a man and put out his
eyes ere they will lie with him; and then too, like thieves,
when they have plundered and stripped a man, leave him.   170
But if there should be one of an hundred of those ladies
generous enough to give herself to a man that has more wit
than money, all things considered, he would think it cheaper
coming to you for a mistress, though you made him pay his
guinea; as a man in a journey, out of good husbandry, had   175
better pay for what he has in an inn than lie on free cost at a
gentleman's house.

In fine, madam, like a faithful dedicator I hope I have done
myself right in the first place, then you and your profession,

---

155 *a pickpurse* Q8, 0 (the pickpurse Q1–7)

153–4 *free . . . playhouses* Dramatists were often admitted to the
     theatres free.
155 *ballad-singer . . . pickpurse* One draws and diverts the crowd while
     the other robs them.
156 *cullies* gulls dupes (frequent in Wycherley)
159 *tiring-rooms* dressing-rooms
159 *keepers* men who keep mistresses
167 *nose* perhaps used in a *double entendre* for penis
168 *Scythian women* Wycherley here borrows again from Montaigne,
     Essais, III. v. (ed. cit., III, 88), which G. B. Ives translates: 'The
     Scythian women put out the eyes of all their slaves and prisoners of
     war, to make use of them more freely and more secretly' (ed. cit., II,
     1174).
168 *baffle* hoodwink
168–9 *put out his eyes* used with a sidelong reference to blindness caused
     by venereal disease
176 *on free cost* cost-free; tipping the servants would cost a guest more
     than his bill at an inn

which in the wisest and most religious government of the   180
world is honoured with the public allowance, and in those
that are thought the most uncivilized and barbarous is pro-
tected and supported by the ministers of justice. And of you,
madam, I ought to say no more here, for your virtues deserve
a poem rather than an epistle, or a volume entire to give the   185
world your memoirs or life at large, and which (upon the word
of an author that has a mind to make an end of his dedication) I promise to do when I write the annals of our British
love, which shall be dedicated to the ladies concerned if they
will not think them something too obscene too, when your   190
life, compared with many that are thought innocent, I doubt
not may vindicate you and me to the world for the confidence
I have taken in this address to you, which then may be
thought neither impertinent nor immodest. And, whatsoever
your amorous misfortunes have been, none can charge you   195
with that heinous and worst of women's crimes, hypocrisy;
nay, in spite of misfortunes or age, you are the same woman
still, though most of your sex grow Magdalens at fifty and, as
a solid French author has it,

> *Après le plaisir vient la peine,*   200
> *Après la peine, la vertu.*

But sure, an old sinner's continency is much like a gamester's
forswearing play when he has lost all his money, and modesty
is a kind of a youthful dress which, as it makes a young
woman more amiable, makes an old one more nauseous; a   205
bashful old woman is like an hopeful old man, and the
affected chastity of antiquated beauties is rather a reproach
than an honour to 'em, for it shows the men's virtue only,
not theirs. But you, in fine, madam, are no more an hypocrite
than I am when I praise you; therefore I doubt not will be   210
thought even by yours and the play's enemies, the nicest
ladies, to be the fittest patroness for,
                    madam,
                    your ladyship's most obedient,
                    faithful, humble servant, and   215
                    THE PLAIN DEALER.

---

198 *Magdalens* reformed prostitutes, named after Mary of Magdala
    (Luke, viii. 2; usually identified with the 'sinner' of Luke, vii. 37–8)
199 *French author* unidentified
200–1 *Après . . . vertu* After pleasure comes pain, after pain virtue.

THE PERSONS

MANLY, *of an honest, surly, nice humour,*   Mr Hart
supposed first, in the time of the Dutch
war, to have procured the command of
a ship out of honour, not interest, and
choosing a sea life only to avoid the   5
world

FREEMAN, *Manly's lieutenant, a gentle-*   Mr Kynaston
man well educated, but of a broken
fortune, a complier with the age

VERNISH, *Manly's bosom and only friend*   Mr Griffin   10

NOVEL, *a pert, railing coxcomb and an*   Mr Clark
admirer of novelties; makes love to
Olivia

MAJOR OLDFOX, *an old, impertinent fop,*   Mr Cartwright
given to scribbling; makes love to the   15
Widow Blackacre

MY LORD PLAUSIBLE, *a ceremonious,*   Mr Haines
supple, commending coxcomb, in love
with Olivia

JERRY BLACKACRE, *a true raw squire,*   Mr Charlton   20
under age and his mother's govern-
ment, bred to the law

[SERJEANT PLODDON
[QUAINT
[BLUNDER
[PETULANT   } *lawyers*]   25
[BUTTONGOWN
[SPLITCAUSE

1 *nice humour* strict temperament
2–3 *Dutch war* probably the third Anglo-Dutch war of 1672–74; Captain
    Wycherley served in the second campaign
10 VERNISH i.e., varnish, 'a specious gloss or outward show; a pretence'
    (*OED*)
14 OLDFOX 'a subtil old Fellow; also an old broad Sword' (*B.E.*)
17 PLAUSIBLE 'smooth, specious, Taking' (*B.E.*)
23 PLODDON cf. '*Plodder*, a Porer in Records, Writings or Books, a dull
    Drudge' (*B.E.*)
28 SPLITCAUSE cf. '*Splitter-of-Causes,* a Lawyer' (*B.E.*)

OLIVIA, *Manly's mistress*	*Mrs Marshall*	
FIDELIA, *in love with Manly, and followed him to sea in man's clothes*	*Mrs Boutell*	30
ELIZA, *cousin to Olivia*	*Mrs Knepp*	
LETTICE, *Olivia's woman*	*Mrs Knight*	
THE WIDOW BLACKACRE, *a petulant litigious widow, always in law, and mother to Squire Jerry*	*Mrs Corey*	35

LAWYERS, KNIGHTS OF THE POST, BAILIFFS, AN ALDERMAN, A BOOKSELLER'S PRENTICE, A FOOTBOY [*to Olivia*], SAILORS, WAITERS, [A CONSTABLE] *and* ATTENDANTS

The scene: *London*   40

---

30 FIDELIA sincerity, trust, faithfulness (from Latin *fidelis*)
34 BLACKACRE arbitrary name for a parcel of land, used in stating hypothetical law cases
37 KNIGHTS OF THE POST professional false witnesses, 'Irish Evidence' (*B.E.*); they admit perjury, forgery, and fraud in V. ii. 389–92.

PROLOGUE

Spoken by the Plain Dealer

I the Plain Dealer am to act today,
And my rough part begins before the play.
First, you who scribble, yet hate all that write,
And keep each other company in spite,
As rivals in your common mistress, fame,   5
And with faint praises one another damn;
'Tis a good play, we know, you can't forgive,
But grudge yourselves the pleasure you receive:
Our scribbler therefore bluntly bid me say
He would not have the wits pleased here today.   10
Next you, the fine, loud gentlemen o'th' pit
Who damn all plays, yet if y'ave any wit
'Tis but what here you sponge, and daily get;
Poets, like friends to whom you are in debt,
You hate; and so rooks laugh, to see undone   15
Those pushing gamesters whom they live upon.
Well, you are sparks, and still will be i'th' fashion:
Rail then at plays, to hide your obligation.
Now, you shrewd judges who the boxes sway,   ⎫
Leading the ladies' hearts and sense astray,   ⎬   20
And, for their sakes, see all, and hear no play: ⎭
Correct your cravats, foretops, lock behind,
The dress and breeding of the play ne'er mind;
Plain dealing is, you'll say, quite out of fashion;
You'll hate it here, as in a dedication.   25
And your fair neighbours in a limning poet
No more than in a painter will allow it.
Pictures too like, the ladies will not please,
They must be drawn too here like goddesses;

Prologue addressing the critics (3) and fops (11) in the pit, then Society
    escorts (19) in the boxes; the citizens and footmen in the galleries
    are ignored
13 *sponge* steal (from the dramatists)
15 *rooks* sharpers, swindlers (frequent in Wycherley)
22 *foretops* real or false locks decorating the forehead
26 *limning poet* author of character sketches

You, as at Lely's too, would truncheon wield,   30
And look like heroes in a painted field.
But the coarse dauber of the coming scenes
To follow life and nature only means;
Displays you as you are: makes his fine woman
A mercenary jilt, and true to no man;   35
His men of wit and pleasure of the age
Are as dull rogues as ever cumbered stage;
He draws a friend only to custom just,
And makes him naturally break his trust.
I, only, act a part like none of you,   40
And yet, you'll say, it is a fool's part too:
An honest man who like you never winks
At faults, but unlike you speaks what he thinks;
The only fool who ne'er found patron yet,
For truth is now a fault as well as wit.   45
And where else but on stages do we see
Truth pleasing, or rewarded honesty?
Which our bold poet does this day in me.
If not to th' honest, be to th' prosp'rous kind:
Some friends at court let the Plain Dealer find.   50

---

30 *Lely* Peter Lely (1618–80), the fashionable portrait-painter of celebrated beauties like the Duchess of Cleveland (at Hampton Court)
   and heroic generals like Sir George Ayscue, complete with truncheon
   (at Greenwich); an engraving of his portrait of Wycherley is repro-
   duced as the Frontispiece
30 *truncheon* baton carried as symbol of military command
38 *just* faithful, true

THE PLAIN DEALER

Act I, Scene i

CAPTAIN MANLY's *Lodging*
Enter CAPTAIN MANLY, *surlily, and my* LORD PLAUSIBLE
following him, and two SAILORS *behind*

MANLY

Tell not me, my good Lord Plausible, of your decorums,
supercilious forms, and slavish ceremonies; your little tricks
which you, the spaniels of the world, do daily over and over
for and to one another, not out of love or duty, but your
servile fear.   5

LORD PLAUSIBLE

Nay, i'faith, i'faith, you are too passionate, and I must
humbly beg your pardon and leave to tell you they are the
arts and rules the prudent of the world walk by.

MANLY

Let 'em. But I'll have no leading-strings; I can walk alone.
I hate a harness, and will not tag on in a faction, kissing my   10
leader behind, that another slave may do the like to me.

LORD PLAUSIBLE

What, will you be singular then, like nobody? follow, love,
and esteem nobody?

MANLY

Rather than be general, like you: follow everybody, court
and kiss everybody, though perhaps at the same time you   15
hate everybody.

LORD PLAUSIBLE

Why, seriously, with your pardon, my dear friend—

MANLY

With your pardon, my no friend, I will not, as you do,
whisper my hatred or my scorn, call a man fool or knave by
signs or mouths over his shoulder, whilst you have him in   20
your arms; for such as you, like common whores and pickpockets, are only dangerous to those you embrace.

10 *tag* ed. (tug Q1–8, 0)
12 *follow, love* ed. (follow Love Q1–8, 0)

---

9 *leading-strings* reins to guide children learning to walk

LORD PLAUSIBLE

Such as I? Heavens defend me! Upon my honour—

MANLY

Upon your title, my lord, if you'd have me believe you.

LORD PLAUSIBLE

Well then, as I am a person of honour, I never attempted to   25
abuse or lessen any person in my life.

MANLY

What, you were afraid?

LORD PLAUSIBLE

No, but seriously, I hate to do a rude thing; no, faith, I speak
well of all mankind.

MANLY

I thought so; but know, that speaking well of all mankind is   30
the worst kind of detraction, for it takes away the reputation
of the few good men in the world by making all alike. Now
I speak ill of most men because they deserve it, I that can
do a rude thing rather than an unjust thing.

LORD PLAUSIBLE

Well, tell not me, my dear friend, what people deserve; I   35
ne'er mind that. I, like an author in a dedication, never speak
well of a man for his sake, but my own; I will not disparage
any man to disparage myself, for to speak ill of people
behind their backs is not like a person of honour, and, truly,
to speak ill of 'em to their faces is not like a complaisant   40
person. But if I did say or do an ill thing to anybody, it
should be sure to be behind their backs, out of pure good
manners.

MANLY

Very well; but I, that am an unmannerly sea-fellow, if I ever
speak well of people, which is very seldom indeed, it should   45
be sure to be behind their backs; and if I would say or do ill
to any, it should be to their faces. I would justle a proud,
strutting, over-looking coxcomb at the head of his sycophants, rather than put out my tongue at him when he were
past me; would frown in the arrogant, big, dull face of an   50
overgrown knave of business, rather than vent my spleen
against him when his back were turned; would give fawning
slaves the lie whilst they embrace or commend me; cowards,
whilst they brag; call a rascal by no other title though his

48 *over-looking* disdainful
50–1 *an overgrown . . . business* a pompous, unscrupulous man of
affairs

father had left him a duke's; laugh at fools aloud before their 55
mistresses; and must desire people to leave me, when their
visits grow at last as troublesome as they were at first
impertinent.

LORD PLAUSIBLE
I would not have my visits troublesome.

MANLY
The only way to be sure not to have 'em troublesome is to 60
make 'em when people are not at home, for your visits, like
other good turns, are most obliging when made or done to
a man in his absence. A pox! Why should anyone, because
he has nothing to do, go and disturb another man's business?

LORD PLAUSIBLE
I beg your pardon, my dear friend. What, you have business? 65

MANLY
If you have any, I would not detain your lordship.

LORD PLAUSIBLE
Detain me, dear sir! I can never have enough of your
company.

MANLY
I'm afraid I should be tiresome. I know not what you think.

LORD PLAUSIBLE
Well, dear sir, I see you would have me gone. 70

MANLY *(Aside)*
But I see you won't.

LORD PLAUSIBLE
Your most faithful—

MANLY
God be w'ye, my lord.

LORD PLAUSIBLE
Your most humble—

MANLY
Farewell. 75

LORD PLAUSIBLE
And eternally—

MANLY
And eternally ceremony. *(Aside)* Then the devil take thee
eternally.

LORD PLAUSIBLE
You shall use no ceremony, by my life.

MANLY
I do not intend it. 80

---

73 *God be w'ye* God be with you, not yet contracted to *Good-bye*

LORD PLAUSIBLE
  Why do you stir, then?
MANLY
  Only to see you out of doors, that I may shut 'em against
  more welcomes.
LORD PLAUSIBLE
  Nay, faith, that shan't pass upon your most faithful, humble
  servant.   85
MANLY (*Aside*)
  Nor this any more upon me.
LORD PLAUSIBLE
  Well, you are too strong for me.
MANLY (*Aside*)
  I'd sooner be visited by the plague, for that only would keep
  a man from visits and his doors shut.
                        (*Exit, thrusting out my* LORD PLAUSIBLE)

                        Manent SAILORS

1 SAILOR
  Here's a finical fellow, Jack. What a brave fair-weather   90
  captain of a ship he would make!
2 SAILOR
  He, a captain of a ship! It must be when she's in the dock
  then, for he looks like one of those that get the king's commissions for hulls to sell a king's ship, when a brave fellow
  has fought her almost to a longboat.   95
1 SAILOR
  On my conscience then, Jack, that's the reason our bully tar
  sunk our ship: not only that the Dutch might not have her,
  but that the courtiers, who laugh at wooden legs, might not
  make her prize.
2 SAILOR
  A pox of his sinking, Tom; we have made a base, broken,   100
  short voyage of it.
1 SAILOR
  Ay, your brisk dealers in honour always make quick returns
  with their ship to the dock and their men to the hospitals.

  84 *pass upon* impose upon, gain credit with
  90 *finical* over-fastidious
  93–4 *commissions for hulls* Charles II gave friends the rights to sell
      dismantled ships; Pepys received one while Secretary of the Navy
      Board.
  95 *longboat* where a ship's crew under attack would make a last stand
      before escaping

'Tis, let me see, just a month since we set out of the river,
and the wind was almost as cross to us as the Dutch.   105

2 SAILOR

Well, I forgive him sinking my own poor truck, if he would
but have given me time and leave to have saved black Kate
of Wapping's small venture.

1 SAILOR

Faith, I forgive him, since, as the purser told me, he sunk
the value of five or six thousand pound of his own with   110
which he was to settle himself somewhere in the Indies; for
our merry lieutenant was to succeed him in his commission
for the ship back, for he was resolved never to return again
for England.

2 SAILOR

So it seemed, by his fighting.   · 115

1 SAILOR

No, but he was aweary of this side of the world here, they
say.

2 SAILOR

Ay, or else he would not have bid so fair for a passage into
t'other.

1 SAILOR

Jack, thou think'st thyself in the forecastle, thou'rt so wag- 120
gish. But I tell you then, he had a mind to go live and bask
himself on the sunny side of the globe.

2 SAILOR

What, out of any discontent? For he's always as dogged as
an old tarpaulin when hindered of a voyage by a young
pantaloon captain.   125

1 SAILOR

'Tis true, I never saw him pleased but in the fight; and then
he looked like one of us coming from the pay-table, with a

---

106 *truck* goods for trading
108 *Wapping* seamen's hamlet on the Thames below the Tower
111 *Indies* Manly's ship fell to the Dutch while acting as convoy to an
     East India merchantman probably bound for Java, Sumatra, or
     Bombay.
113 *back* i.e., on the home voyage
123 *dogged* ill-tempered, morose (frequent in Wycherley)
125 *pantaloon captain* Commissions given to unfledged 'gentlemen'
     captains (in fashionable pantaloon breeches) were resented by dis-
     placed 'tarpaulings of Wapping and Blackwall, from whence the
     good commanders of old were all used to be chosen' (Pepys, quoted
     in David Ogg, *England in the Reign of Charles II*, 2 vols. (Oxford,
     1956), I.)

new lining to our hats under our arms.

2 SAILOR

A pox! He's like the Bay of Biscay, rough and angry let the
wind blow where 'twill.   130

1 SAILOR

Nay, there's no more dealing with him than with the land in
a storm; no near!

2 SAILOR

'Tis a hurry-durry blade. Dost thou remember, after we had
tugged hard the old, leaky longboat to save his life, when I
welcomed him ashore, he gave me a box on the ear and   135
called me fawning water-dog?

Enter MANLY *and* FREEMAN

1 SAILOR

Hold thy peace, Jack, and stand by; the foul weather's
coming.

MANLY

You rascals! dogs! how could this tame thing get through
you?   140

1 SAILOR

Faith, to tell your honour the truth, we were at hob in the
hall, and whilst my brother and I were quarrelling about a
cast he slunk by us.

2 SAILOR

He's a sneaking fellow, I warrant for't.

MANLY

Have more care for the future, you slaves. Go, and with   145
drawn cutlasses stand at the stair-foot and keep all that ask
for me from coming up; suppose you were guarding the
scuttle to the powder-room; let none enter here, at your and
their peril.

1 SAILOR

No, for the danger would be the same: you would blow   150
them and us up if we should.

2 SAILOR

Must no one come to you, sir?

128 *lining to our hats* 'in steps another of the *Tarpauling Fraternity*,
with his Hat under his Arm, half full of Money' (Ned Ward, *The
London Spy*, ed. Ralph Straus (1924), p. 332)
132 *no near* 'a command to the helmsman to come no closer to the
wind' (*OED*); here=look out! Perhaps he hears Manly returning.
133 *hurry-durry blade* boisterous fellow
141 *hob* quoits, probably played here with coins for rings and an improvised target or 'hob'

MANLY

No man, sir.

1 SAILOR

No man, sir; but a woman then, an't like your honour—

MANLY

No woman neither, you impertinent dog. Would you be 155
pimping? A sea-pimp is the strangest monster she has.

2 SAILOR

Indeed, an't like your honour, 'twill be hard for us to deny
a woman anything, since we are so newly come on shore.

1 SAILOR

We'll let no old woman come up, though it were our trusting
landlady at Wapping. 160

MANLY

Would you be witty, you brandy casks you? You become a
jest as ill as you do a horse. Begone, you dogs! I hear a noise
on the stairs. *(Exeunt SAILORS)*

FREEMAN

Faith, I am sorry you would let the fop go; I intended to
have had some sport with him. 165

MANLY

Sport with him! A pox, then why did you not stay? You
should have enjoyed your coxcomb and had him to yourself,
for me.

FREEMAN

No, I should not have cared for him without you neither,
for the pleasure which fops afford is like that of drinking, 170
only good when 'tis shared; and a fool, like a bottle, which
would make you merry in company, will make you dull
alone. But how the devil could you turn a man of his quality
down stairs? You use a lord with very little ceremony, it
seems. 175

MANLY

A lord! What, thou art one of those who esteem men only
by the marks and value fortune has set upon 'em, and never
consider intrinsic worth. But counterfeit honour will not be
current with me; I weigh the man, not his title; 'tis not the
king's stamp can make the metal better or heavier. Your lord 180
is a leaden shilling, which you may bend every way, and
debases the stamp he bears instead of being raised by't.—
Here again, you slaves?

Enter SAILORS

1 SAILOR

Only to receive farther instructions, an't like your honour.
What if a man should bring you money, should we turn him   185
back?

MANLY

All men, I say. Must I be pestered with you too? You dogs,
away.

2 SAILOR

Nay, I know one man your honour would not have us hinder
coming to you, I'm sure.   190

MANLY

Who's that? Speak quickly, slaves.

2 SAILOR

Why, a man that should bring you a challenge, for though
you refuse money, I'm sure you love fighting too well to
refuse that.

MANLY

Rogue! rascal! dog!   *(Kicks the* SAILORS *out)*   195

FREEMAN

Nay, let the poor rogues have their forecastle jests; they
cannot help 'em in a fight, scarce when a ship's sinking.

MANLY

Damn their untimely jests. A servant's jest is more sauciness
than his counsel.

FREEMAN

But what, will you see nobody? Not your friends?   200

MANLY

Friends? I have but one, and he, I hear, is not in town; nay,
can have but one friend, for a true heart admits but of one
friendship as of one love. But in having that friend I have a
thousand, for he has the courage of men in despair, yet the
diffidency and caution of cowards, the secrecy of the revenge-   205
ful and the constancy of martyrs: one fit to advise, to keep
a secret, to fight and die for his friend. Such I think him, for
I have trusted him with my mistress in my absence, and the
trust of beauty is sure the greatest we can show.

FREEMAN

Well, but all your good thoughts are not for him alone, I   210
hope. Pray, what d'ye think of me for a friend?

MANLY

Of thee! Why, thou art a latitudinarian in friendship, that is,

212 *latitudinarian* a liberal churchman 'that is no Slave to Rubrick,
Canons, Liturgy, or Oath of Canonical Obedience' (*B.E.*); Manly
suggests Freeman has so many friends the term is meaningless

no friend; thou dost side with all mankind, but wilt suffer for
none. Thou art indeed like your Lord Plausible, the pink of
courtesy, therefore hast no friendship; for ceremony and   215
great professing renders friendship as much suspected as it
does religion.

FREEMAN

And no professing, no ceremony at all in friendship were as
unnatural and as undecent as in religion; and there is hardly
such a thing as an honest hypocrite, who professes himself   220
to be worse than he is, unless it be yourself; for though I
could never get you to say you were my friend, I know
you'll prove so.

MANLY

I must confess I am so much your friend I would not deceive
you; therefore must tell you, not only because my heart is   225
taken up but according to your rules of friendship, I cannot
be your friend.

FREEMAN

Why, pray?

MANLY

Because he that is, you'll say, a true friend to a man is a
friend to all his friends. But you must pardon me; I cannot   230
wish well to pimps, flatterers, detractors, and cowards, stiff,
nodding knaves and supple, pliant, kissing fools. Now, all
these I have seen you use like the dearest friends in the world.

FREEMAN

Ha ha ha! What, you observed me, I warrant, in the galleries at Whitehall, doing the business of the place? Pshaw!   235
Court professions, like court promises, go for nothing, man.
But, faith, could you think I was a friend to all those I
hugged, kissed, flattered, bowed to? Ha ha—

MANLY

You told 'em so, and swore it too; I heard you.

FREEMAN

Ay, but when their backs were turned did I not tell you they   240
were rogues, villains, rascals, whom I despised and hated?

---

216 *professing* avowal, declaration
226 *taken up* i.e., by Vernish, 'for a true heart admits but of one friend-
    ship' (202–3)
235 *Whitehall* The picture galleries of the royal palace at Whitehall
    were the setting for its largest social gatherings; on 6 February
    1685 Evelyn records 'unexpressable luxury, & prophanesse, gaming,
    & all dissolution' there.

MANLY

Very fine! But what reason had I to believe you spoke your
heart to me, since you professed deceiving so many?

FREEMAN

Why, don't you know, good captain, that telling truth is a
quality as prejudicial to a man that would thrive in the world   245
as square play to a cheat or true love to a whore? Would
you have a man speak truth to his ruin? You are severer
than the law, which requires no man to swear against himself. You would have me speak truth against myself, I
warrant, and tell my promising friend, the courtier, he has   250
a bad memory?

MANLY

Yes.

FREEMAN

And so make him remember to forget my business. And I
should tell the great lawyer too that he takes oftener fees to
hold his tongue, than to speak?   255

MANLY

No doubt on't.

FREEMAN

Ay, and have him hang or ruin me, when he should come to
be a judge and I before him. And you would have me tell
the new officer, who bought his employment lately, that he
is a coward?   260

MANLY

Ay.

FREEMAN

And so get myself cashiered, not him, he having the better
friends though I the better sword. And I should tell the
scribbler of honour that heraldry were a prettier and fitter
study for so fine a gentleman than poetry?   265

MANLY

Certainly.

FREEMAN

And so find myself mauled in his next hired lampoon. And
you would have me tell the holy lady too she lies with her
chaplain?

MANLY

No doubt on't.   270

246 *square* honest
264 *scribbler of honour* titled author

FREEMAN

And so draw the clergy upon my back, and want a good
table to dine at sometimes. And by the same reason too I
should tell you that the world thinks you a madman, a
brutal, and have you cut my throat, or worse, hate me. What
other good success of all my plain dealing could I have, than   275
what I've mentioned?

MANLY

Why, first, your promising courtier would keep his word out
of fear of more reproaches, or at least would give you no
more vain hopes; your lawyer would serve you more faithfully, for he, having no honour but his interest, is truest still   280
to him he knows suspects him; the new officer would provoke
thee to make him a coward and so be cashiered, that thou,
or some other honest fellow who had more courage than
money, might get his place; the noble sonneteer would
trouble thee no more with his madrigals; the praying lady   285
would leave off railing at wenching before thee, and not turn
away her chamber-maid for her own known frailty with thee;
and I, instead of hating thee, should love thee for thy plain
dealing; and in lieu of being mortified am proud that the
world and I think not well of one another.   290

FREEMAN

Well, doctors differ. You are for plain dealing, I find; but
against your particular notions I have the practice of the
whole world. Observe but any morning what people do when
they get together on the Exchange, in Westminster Hall, or
the galleries in Whitehall.   295

MANLY

I must confess, there they seem to rehearse Bayes's grand
dance: here you see a bishop bowing low to a gaudy atheist;

274   *brutal* a noun=a brutal person
275   *good success* prosperous result
286–7   *turn away* dismiss
294–5   *Exchange . . . Whitehall* rendezvous for merchants at the Royal
           Exchange in Cornhill (or fashionable shoppers if the New Ex-
           change in the Strand is meant), lawyers at Westminster Hall, and
           courtiers at Whitehall
296   *rehearse* repeat, with a punning reference to Buckingham's play
296–7   *Bayes's grand dance* In Buckingham's *The Rehearsal* (1671), two
           Kings of Brentford descend from the clouds and '*Dance a grand
           Dance*'; the dramatist Bayes comments: 'This, now, is an ancient
           Dance . . . deriv'd, with a little alteration, to the Inns of Court'
           (V.i).
297   *gaudy* showy, flashy

a judge to a door-keeper; a great lord to a fishmonger, or a
scrivener with a jack-chain about his neck; a lawyer to a
serjeant at arms; a velvet physician to a threadbare chemist;   300
and a supple gentleman-usher to a surly beef-eater; and so
tread round in a preposterous huddle of ceremony to each
other, whilst they can hardly hold their solemn false countenances.

FREEMAN

Well, they understand the world.   305

MANLY

Which I do not, I confess.

FREEMAN

But sir, pray believe the friendship I promise you real, whatsoever I have professed to others. Try me, at least.

MANLY

Why, what would you do for me?

FREEMAN

I would fight for you.   310

MANLY

That you would do for your own honour. But what else?

FREEMAN

I would lend you money, if I had it.

MANLY

To borrow more of me another time. That were but putting
your money to interest; a usurer would be as good a friend.
But what other piece of friendship?   315

FREEMAN

I would speak well of you to your enemies.

MANLY

To encourage others to be your friends by a show of gratitude. But what else?

FREEMAN

Nay, I would not hear you ill spoken of behind your back
by my friend.   320

MANLY

Nay, then thou'rt a friend indeed; but it were unreasonable

299 *jack-chain* decorative chain with each link a double loop of un-
   welded wire
300 *serjeant at arms* Parliamentary officer empowered to arrest offenders,
   etc.
300 *chemist* alchemist
301 *gentleman-usher* gentleman attending upon someone of superior rank
301 *beef-eater* 'a well-fed menial' (*OED*)

to expect it from thee as the world goes now, when new
friends, like new mistresses, are got by disparaging old ones.

Enter FIDELIA [*in man's clothes*]

But here comes another will say as much at least.—Dost
not thou love me devilishly too, my little volunteer, as well   325
as he or any man can?

FIDELIA

Better than any man can love you, my dear captain.

MANLY [*To* FREEMAN]

Look you there, I told you so.

FIDELIA

As well as you do truth or honour, sir; as well.

MANLY

Nay, good young gentleman, enough, for shame! Thou hast   330
been a page, by thy flattering and lying, to one of those
praying ladies who love flattery so well they are jealous of it,
and wert turned away for saying the same things to the old
housekeeper for sweetmeats as you did to your lady; for thou
flatterest everything and everybody alike.   335

FIDELIA

You, dear sir, should not suspect the truth of what I say of
you, though to you. Fame, the old liar, is believed when she
speaks wonders of you; you cannot be flattered, sir; your
merit is unspeakable.

MANLY

Hold, hold, sir, or I shall suspect worse of you: that you   340
have been a cushion-bearer to some state hypocrite, and
turned away by the chaplains for out-flattering their probation sermons for a benefice.

FIDELIA

Suspect me for anything, sir, but the want of love, faith, and
duty to you, the bravest, worthiest of mankind. Believe me, I   345
could die for you, sir.

MANLY

Nay, there you lie, sir. Did I not see thee more afraid in the
fight than the chaplain of the ship, or the purser that bought
his place?

FIDELIA

Can he be said to be afraid that ventures to sea with you?   350

342–3 *probation sermons* preached to demonstrate a candidate's fitness
     for church preferment

MANLY

Fie, fie, no more! I shall hate thy flattery worse than thy
cowardice, nay, than thy bragging.

FIDELIA

Well, I own then I was afraid, mightily afraid; yet for you I
would be afraid again, an hundred times afraid. Dying is
ceasing to be afraid, and that I could do sure for you; and   355
you'll believe me one day.   *(Weeps)*

FREEMAN

Poor youth! Believe his eyes, if not his tongue; he seems to
speak truth with them.

MANLY

What, does he cry? A pox on't, a maudlin flatterer is as
nauseously troublesome as a maudlin drunkard.—No more,   360
you little milksop; do not cry. I'll never make thee afraid
again; for of all men, if I had occasion, thou shouldst not be
my second; and when I go to sea again, thou shalt venture
thy life no more with me.

FIDELIA

Why, will you leave me behind then? *(Aside)* If you would   365
preserve my life, I'm sure you should not.

MANLY

Leave thee behind? Ay, ay; thou art a hopeful youth for the
shore only. Here thou wilt live to be cherished by fortune
and the great ones, for thou may'st easily come to out-flatter
a dull poet, out-lie a coffee-house or gazette writer, out-   370
swear a knight of the post, out-watch a pimp, out-fawn a
rook, out-promise a lover, out-rail a wit, and out-brag a sea
captain. All this thou canst do because thou'rt a coward, a
thing I hate; therefore thou'lt do better with the world than
with me, and these are the good courses you must take in the   375
world. There's good advice, at least, at parting; go, and be
happy with't.

FIDELIA

Parting, sir? O, let me not hear that dismal word!

MANLY

If my words frighten thee, be gone the sooner; for, to be
plain with thee, cowardice and I cannot dwell together.   380

---

367 *hopeful* promising
370 *coffee-house . . . writer* Foreign news was received and translated
　　at the coffee-houses before appearing in the *London Gazette* and
　　other news-sheets.
371 *knight of the post* see 'The Persons'

FIDELIA

And cruelty and courage never dwelt together sure, sir. Do not turn me off to shame and misery, for I am helpless and friendless.

MANLY

Friendless! There are half a score friends for thee then; *(Offers her gold)* I leave myself no more. They'll help thee a   385
little. Be gone, go! I must be cruel to thee, if thou call'st it so, out of pity.

FIDELIA

If you would be cruelly pitiful, sir, let it be with your sword, not gold.   *(Exit)*

Enter FIRST SAILOR

1 SAILOR

We have, with much ado, turned away two gentlemen who   390
told us forty times over their names were Master Novel and Major Oldfox.

MANLY

Well, to your post again.   *(Exit* SAILOR*)*
But how come those puppies coupled always together?

FREEMAN

O, the coxcombs keep each other company to show each   395
other, as Novel calls it, or, as Oldfox says, like two knives to whet one another.

MANLY

And set other people's teeth an edge.

Enter SECOND SAILOR

2 SAILOR

Here is a woman, an't like your honour, scolds and bustles with us to come in, as much as a seaman's widow at the   400
Navy Office. Her name is Mistress Blackacre.

MANLY

That fiend too!

389 *not* Q1, 0 (and not Q2–8)

---

381 *sure* securely, confidently
398 *an edge* on edge
399 *bustles* scuffles, struggles
400 *seaman's widow* entitled to a lump sum payment of between £2 and £10, which the Navy Office did not always pay
401 *Navy Office* at Crutched Friars, near Tower Hill; it dealt with all Admiralty business

FREEMAN

The Widow Blackacre, is it not? That litigious she-petti-
fogger, who is at law and difference with all the world! But
I wish I could make her agree with me in the church; they　405
say she has fifteen hundred pounds a year jointure, and the
care of her son—that is, the destruction of his estate.

MANLY

Her lawyers, attorneys, and solicitors have fifteen hundred
pound a year, whilst she is contented to be poor to make
other people so, for she is as vexatious as her father was, the　410
great attorney, nay, as a dozen Norfolk attorneys, and as
implacable an adversary as a wife suing for alimony or a
parson for his tithes; and she loves an Easter term, or any
term, not as other country ladies do, to come up to be fine,
cuckold their husbands, and take their pleasure; for she has　415
no pleasure but in vexing others, and is usually clothed and
daggled like a bawd in disguise, pursued through alleys by
serjeants. When she is in town she lodges in one of the Inns
of Chancery, where she breeds her son and is herself his
tutoress in law-French; and for her country abode, though　420
she has no estate there, she chooses Norfolk. But bid her
come in, with a pox to her.　　　　　　　*(Exit* SAILOR)
She is Olivia's kinswoman, and may make me amends for
her visit by some discourse of that dear woman.

403–4 *pettifogger* dishonest promoter of petty lawsuits
411 *Norfolk attorneys* so numerous and so mischievous their ranks were
　　thinned by statute in 1455
413 *Easter term* 'which beginneth always the seventeenth day after
　　Easter, and lasteth 27 days' (Chamberlayne, II, 129); the others are
　　Trinity, Michaelmas, and Hilary
414 *come up* i.e., to London
417 *daggled* spattered with mud
417 *in disguise* tipsy (?)
418 *serjeants* Court officers empowered to arrest offenders, summon
　　witnesses, etc.
418–19 *Inns of Chancery* eight student residences attached to the Inns of
　　Court, with some accommodation available to outsiders
419 *breeds* educates
420 *law-French* 'the corrupt variety of Norman French used in English
　　law-books' (*OED*)
421 *Norfolk* 'where men are said to *study Law as following the Plough-
　　tail* [and] some would perswade us, that they will *enter an action
　　for their neighbour's horse but looking over their hedge*' (Thomas
　　Fuller, *A History of the Worthies of England*, ed. J. Nichols (1811),
　　II, 125–6)

Enter WIDOW BLACKACRE *with a mantle and a green bag, and several papers in the other hand,* JERRY BLACKACRE *her son, in a gown, laden with green bags, following her*

WIDOW

I never had so much to-do with a judge's door-keeper as   425
with yours, but—

MANLY

But the incomparable Olivia, how does she since I went?

WIDOW

Since you went, my suit—

MANLY

Olivia, I say, is she well?

WIDOW

My suit, if you had not returned—   430

MANLY

Damn your suit! How does your cousin Olivia?

WIDOW

My suit, I say, had been quite lost; but now—

MANLY

But now, where is Olivia? In town? For—

WIDOW

For tomorrow we are to have a hearing.

MANLY

Would you'd let me have a hearing today!   435

WIDOW

But why won't you hear me?

MANLY

I am no judge and you talk of nothing but suits; but, pray
tell me, when did you see Olivia?

WIDOW

I am no visitor but a woman of business; or, if I ever visit,
'tis only the Chancery Lane ladies, ladies towards the law, 440
and not any of your lazy, good-for-nothing flirts who cannot
read law-French, though a gallant writ it. But, as I was
telling you, my suit—

MANLY

Damn these impertinent, vexatious people of business, of all
sexes! They are still troubling the world with the tedious   445

424 s.d. *green bag* in which barristers and lawyers carried documents
   and papers; cf. 'Green-bag, a Lawyer' (*B E.*)
425 *to-do* fuss
440 *Chancery Lane* running from Fleet Street to Holborn, and inhabited
   largely by lawyers, whose families perhaps make up the 'ladies towards (i.e., interested in) the law'   445 *still* always

recitals of their lawsuits, and one can no more stop their mouths than a wit's when he talks of himself, or an intelligencer's when he talks of other people.

WIDOW

And a pox of all vexatious, impertinent lovers! They are still perplexing the world with the tedious narrations of their 450 love-suits and discourses of their mistresses. You are as troublesome to a poor widow of business as a young coxcombly rithming lover.

MANLY

And thou art as troublesome to me as a rook to a losing gamester, or a young putter of cases to his mistress and 455 sempstress, who has love in her head for another.

WIDOW

Nay, since you talk of putting of cases and will not hear me speak, hear our Jerry a little; let him put our case to you, for the trial's tomorrow, and since you are my chief witness, I would have your memory refreshed and your judgment 460 informed, that you may not give your evidence improperly. Speak out, child.

JERRY

Yes, forsooth. Hem hem! John-a-Stiles—

MANLY

You may talk, young lawyer, but I shall no more mind you than a hungry judge does a cause after the clock has struck 465 one.

FREEMAN

Nay, you'll find him as peevish too.

WIDOW

No matter.—Jerry, go on.—[To FREEMAN] Do you observe it then, sir, for I think I have seen you in a gown once. Lord, I could hear our Jerry put cases all day long! Mark him, sir. 470

---

453 *rithming* Q1–3 (riming Q4–7; rhiming Q8, 0)

447–8 *intelligencer* (1) informer (2) newsmonger; both meanings are appropriate here
453 *rithming* At this period *rithme, rhythm,* and *rime* (in this sense) were merely spelling variants for, and pronounced the same as, the modern *rhyme.*
455 *putter of cases* law student
463 *John-a-Stiles* John (who dwells) at the stile; an arbitrary name for one of the parties in a legal suit, like the modern John Doe
465–6 *struck one* 'And Wretches hang that Jury-men may Dine' (Pope, *The Rape of the Lock* (1714), III, 22)

JERRY

> John-a-Stiles—no. There are first Fitz, Pere, and Ayle—no,
> no: Ayle, Pere, and Fitz. Ayle is seised in fee of Blackacre,
> John-a-Stiles disseises Ayle, Ayle makes claim, and the dis-
> seisor dies; then the Ayle—no, the Fitz—

WIDOW

> No; the Pere, sirrah.   475

JERRY

> O, the Pere! Ay, the Pere, sir, and the Fitz—no, the Ayle—
> no, the Pere and the Fitz, sir, and—

MANLY

> Damn Pere, Mere, and Fitz, sir!

WIDOW

> No, you are out, child.—Hear me, captain, then. There are
> Ayle, Pere, and Fitz; Ayle is seised in fee of Blackacre, and   480
> being so seised, John-a-Stiles disseises the Ayle, Ayle makes
> claim, and the disseisor dies; and then the Pere re-enters—
> *(to* JERRY) the Pere, sirrah, the Pere—and the Fitz enters upon
> the Pere, and the Ayle brings his writ of disseisin in the *post,*
> and the Pere brings his writ of disseisin in the *per,* and—   485

MANLY

> Canst thou hear this stuff, Freeman? I could as soon suffer
> a whole noise of flatterers at a great man's levee in a morn-
> ing; but thou hast servile complacency enough to listen to a

---

485 *per* Q2 (Pere Q1, Q3–8, 0)

471 *Fitz, Pere, and Ayle* Son, Father, and Grandfather, law-French
names used like John-a-Stiles. The case which follows bristles with
problems for a student of law. In outline, Ayle has possession of a
piece of land, Stiles dispossesses him (perhaps on behalf of Pere,
who later *re*-enters), Ayle begins proceedings to recover the land,
Stiles dies (and Ayle's case now collapses if he is suing in a personal action of Ejectment), Pere obtains possession (as abator if a
new claimant, or as Stiles' heir, which is possible despite the implied
relationship between Grandfather and Father if Stiles were, say,
Pere's deceased mother's brother), Fitz ousts Pere, and both Ayle
and Pere sue Fitz for recovery of the land, Ayle by writ of entry
sur disseisin in the *post* (alleging more than two steps between dispossessor and defendant, though he should sue in the *per* and *cui,*
since he alleges Fitz only got entry through Pere who got it
through Stiles who dispossessed Ayle), and Pere by writ of entry in
the *per* (though it should be *in le quibus,* since he alleges Fitz is
the original dispossessor, but that would spoil the pun on *per* and
Pere, which is presumably Wycherley's main point).
479 *out* in error
487 *noise* band, company (usually of musicians)

quibbling statesman in disgrace, nay, and be beforehand with
him in laughing at his dull no-jest. But I—   490
                              (*Offering to go out*)
WIDOW

Nay, sir, hold!—Where's the subpœna, Jerry?—I must serve
you, sir. You are required by this to give your testimony—
MANLY

I'll be forsworn, to be revenged on thee.
                        (*Exit* MANLY, *throwing away the subpœna*)
WIDOW

Get you gone, for a lawless companion!—Come, Jerry. I had
almost forgot we were to meet at the master's at three; let   495
us mind our business still, child.
JERRY

Ay, forsooth, e'en so let's.
FREEMAN

Nay madam, now I would beg you to hear me a little, a little
of my business.
WIDOW

I have business of my own calls me away, sir.   500
FREEMAN

My business would prove yours too, dear madam.
WIDOW

Yours would be some sweet business, I warrant. What, 'tis
no Westminster Hall business? Would you have my advice?
FREEMAN

No faith, 'tis a little Westminster Abbey business. I would
have your consent.   505
WIDOW

O fie fie sir, to me such discourse, before my dear minor
there!
JERRY

Ay ay mother, he would be taking livery and seisin of your
jointure by digging the turf. [*Aside*] But I'll watch your
waters, bully, i'fac.—Come away, mother.   510
                              (*Exit* JERRY, *haling away his mother*)

---

489 *quibbling* punning
508 *livery and seisin* i.e., livery of seisin, delivery of possession of lands,
    a common law ceremony where 'the Vendor takes . . . a clod of
    Earth upon a twig or bough, which he delivers to the Vendee, in
    the name of Possession' (Blount); if Freeman takes the livery, the
    Widow digs the turf, but Jerry's inaccuracy makes possible the
    double entendre
509–10 *watch your waters* keep a sharp eye on you (slang)
510 *i'fac* in faith

Manet FREEMAN. *Enter to him* FIDELIA

FIDELIA

Dear sir, you have pity; beget but some in our captain for me.

FREEMAN

Where is he?

FIDELIA

Within, swearing as much as he did in the great storm, and cursing you, and sometimes sinks into calms and sighs, and   515
talks of his Olivia.

FREEMAN

He would never trust me to see her; is she handsome?

FIDELIA

No, if you'll take my word; but I am not a proper judge.

FREEMAN

What is she?

FIDELIA

A gentlewoman, I suppose, but of as mean a fortune as   520
beauty; but her relations would not suffer her to go with him to the Indies, and his aversion to this side of the world, together with the late opportunity of commanding the convoy, would not let him stay here longer, though to enjoy her.   525

FREEMAN

He loves her mightily then?

FIDELIA

Yes, so well, that the remainder of his fortune (I hear about five or six thousand pounds) he has left her, in case he had died by the way or before she could prevail with her friends to follow him, which he expected she should do; and has left   530
behind him his great bosom friend to be her convoy to him.

FREEMAN

What charms has she for him, if she be not handsome?

FIDELIA

He fancies her, I suppose, the only woman of truth and sincerity in the world.

FREEMAN

No common beauty, I confess.   535

FIDELIA

Or else sure he would not have trusted her with so great a

529 *by the way* on the journey

share of his fortune in his absence: I suppose, since his late
loss, all he has.

FREEMAN

Why, has he left it in her own custody?

FIDELIA

I am told so. 540

FREEMAN

Then he has showed love to her indeed in leaving her, like an
old husband that dies as soon as he has made his wife a good
jointure. But I'll go in to him and speak for you, and know
more from him of his Olivia. (*Exit*)

Manet FIDELIA, *sola*

FIDELIA

His Olivia, indeed, his happy Olivia! 545
Yet she was left behind, when I was with him;
But she was ne'er out of his mind or heart.
She has told him she loved him; I have showed it,
And durst not tell him so till I had done,
Under this habit, such convincing acts 550
Of loving friendship for him, that through it
He first might find out both my sex and love;
And, when I'd had him from his fair Olivia
And this bright world of artful beauties here,
Might then have hoped he would have looked on me 555
Amongst the sooty Indians; and I could,
To choose, there live his wife, where wives are forced
To live no longer when their husbands die;
Nay, what's yet worse, to share 'em whilst they live
With many rival wives. But here he comes, 560
And I must yet keep out of his sight, not
To lose it for ever. (*Exit*)

Enter MANLY *and* FREEMAN

557 *To choose* By choice, If I had my choice
557–60 *there* . . . *wives* cf. Montaigne, *Essais,* II. xxix (ed. cit., II, 428):
  'C'est bien autre chose des femmes Indiennes: . . . estant leur
  coustume, aux marys d'avoir plusieurs femmes, et à la plus chere
  d'elles de se tuer après son mary'; G. B. Ives translates: 'It is quite
  another thing with the Indian women; . . . it being customary with
  them for the husband to have many wives, and for the one who is
  dearest to kill herself when her husband dies' (ed. cit., II, 954)
562 s.d. (*Exit*) Restoration dramatists did not follow the Elizabethan
  practice of beginning a new scene every time the stage is momen-
  tarily cleared.

FREEMAN

But, pray, what strange charms has she that could make you
love?

MANLY

Strange charms indeed! She has beauty enough to call in   565
question her wit or virtue, and her form would make a
starved hermit a ravisher; yet her virtue and conduct would
preserve her from the subtle lust of a pampered prelate. She
is so perfect a beauty that art could not better it, nor affectation deform it; yet all this is nothing. Her tongue as well as   570
face ne'er knew artifice, nor ever did her words or looks
contradict her heart. She is all truth, and hates the lying,
masking, daubing world as I do, for which I love her and for
which I think she dislikes not me. For she has often shut out
of her conversation, for mine, the gaudy fluttering parrots of   575
the town, apes and echoes of men only, and refused their
commonplace, pert chat, flattery, and submissions, to be
entertained with my sullen bluntness and honest love. And,
last of all, swore to me, since her parents would not suffer
her to go with me, she would stay behind for no other man,   580
but follow me without their leave, if not to be obtained.
Which oath—

FREEMAN

Did you think she would keep?

MANLY

Yes; for she is not, I tell you, like other women, but can keep
her promise, though she has sworn to keep it. But, that she   585
might the better keep it, I left her the value of five or six
thousand pound, for women's wants are generally their most
importunate solicitors to love or marriage.

FREEMAN

And money summons lovers more than beauty, and aug-
ments but their importunity and their number, so makes it   590
the harder for a woman to deny 'em. For my part, I am for
the French maxim: if you would have your female subjects
loyal, keep 'em poor. But, in short, that your mistress may
not marry, you have given her a portion.

MANLY

She had given me her heart first, and I am satisfied with the   595
security. I can never doubt her truth and constancy.

573 *daubing* painting
575 *conversation* company
577 *submissions* 'acts of deference or homage' (*OED*)
592 *French maxim* unidentified

FREEMAN

It seems you do, since you are fain to bribe it with money. But how come you to be so diffident of the man that says he loves you, and not doubt the woman that says it?

MANLY

I should, I confess, doubt the love of any other woman but 600 her, as I do the friendship of any other man but him I have trusted; but I have such proofs of their faith as cannot deceive me.

FREEMAN

Cannot!

MANLY

Not but I know that generally no man can be a great enemy 605 but under the name of friend; and if you are a cuckold, it is your friend only that makes you so, for your enemy is not admitted to your house; if you are cheated in your fortune, 'tis your friend that does it, for your enemy is not made your trustee; if your honour or good name be injured, 'tis 610 your friend that does it still, because your enemy is not believed against you. Therefore I rather choose to go where honest, downright barbarity is professed; where men devour one another like generous, hungry lions and tigers, not like crocodiles; where they think the devil white, of our com- 615 plexion, and I am already so far an Indian. But if your weak faith doubts this miracle of a woman, come along with me and believe, and thou wilt find her so handsome that thou, who art so much my friend, wilt have a mind to lie with her, and so will not fail to discover what her faith and thine is to 620 me.

When we're in love, the great adversity,
Our friends and mistresses at once we try.   [*Exeunt*]

Finis actus primi

614 *generous* noble, magnanimous
615 *crocodiles* hypocrites; crocodiles were thought to weep while devour-
        ing men
615 *they think the devil white* while Europeans think him black;
        Manly agrees: in England, the devil is a hypocrite in a white mask
623 s.d. [*Exeunt*] At this period, an empty stage indicated the end of an
        act; no curtain fell; after the interval, the scenery was changed in
        full view of the audience to the next location.

Act II, Scene i

OLIVIA's *Lodging*

Enter OLIVIA, ELIZA, LETTICE

OLIVIA

Ah, cousin, what a world 'tis we live in! I am so weary of it.

ELIZA

Truly, cousin, I can find no fault with it, but that we cannot
always live in't; for I can never be weary of it.

OLIVIA

O hideous! You cannot be in earnest, sure, when you say
you like the filthy world.   5

ELIZA

You cannot be in earnest, sure, when you say you dislike it.

OLIVIA

You are a very censorious creature, I find.

ELIZA

I must confess I think we women as often discover where we
love by railing, as men when they lie by their swearing; and
the world is but a constant keeping gallant, whom we fail not   10
to quarrel with when anything crosses us, yet cannot part
with't for our hearts.

LETTICE

A gallant indeed, madam, whom ladies first make jealous and
then quarrel with it for being so; for if by her indiscretion a
lady be talked of for a man, she cries presently ' 'Tis a cen-   15
sorious world'; if by her vanity the intrigue be found out, ' 'Tis
a prying, malicious world'; if by her over-fondness the gallant
proves unconstant, ' 'Tis a false world'; and if by her niggard-
liness the chamber-maid tells, ' 'Tis a perfidious world'—but
that, I'm sure, your ladyship cannot say of the world yet, as   20
bad as 'tis.

OLIVIA

But I may say ' 'Tis a very impertinent world'. Hold your
peace.—And, cousin, if the world be a gallant, 'tis such an
one as is my aversion. Pray name it no more.

---

8 *discover* reveal
10 *keeping gallant* lover who maintains his mistress
15 *talked of for a man* linked in gossip with some particular man

ELIZA

But is it possible the world, which has such variety of charms   25
for other women, can have none for you? Let's see. First,
what d'ye think of dressing and fine clothes?

OLIVIA

Dressing? Fie fie, 'tis my aversion. [*To* LETTICE] But come
hither, you dowdy; methinks you might have opened this
tour better. O hideous! I cannot suffer it! D'ye see how it   30
sits?

ELIZA

Well enough, cousin, if dressing be your aversion.

OLIVIA

'Tis so; and for variety of rich clothes, they are more my
aversion.

LETTICE

Ay, 'tis because your ladyship wears 'em too long; for indeed   35
a gown, like a gallant, grows one's aversion by having too
much of it.

OLIVIA

Insatiable creature! I'll be sworn I have had this not above
three days, cousin, and within this month have made some
six more.   40

ELIZA

Then your aversion to 'em is not altogether so great.

OLIVIA

Alas! 'Tis for my woman only I wear 'em, cousin.

LETTICE

If it be for me only, madam, pray do not wear 'em.

ELIZA

But what d'ye think of visits, balls—

OLIVIA

O, I detest 'em.   45

ELIZA

Of plays?

OLIVIA

I abominate 'em. Filthy, obscene, hideous things!

---

29 *dowdy* a noun
30 *tour* artificial curls worn on the forehead
39 *made* i.e., had made; on 1 May 1669 Pepys writes 'the stuff suit I
   made the last year'

ELIZA

What say you to masquerading in the winter, and Hyde Park
in the summer?

OLIVIA

Insipid pleasures I taste not.   50

ELIZA

Nay, if you are for more solid pleasure, what think you of a
rich young husband?

OLIVIA

O horrid! Marriage! What a pleasure you have found out!
I nauseate it of all things.

LETTICE

But what does your ladyship think then of a liberal, hand-   55
some young lover?

OLIVIA

A handsome young fellow, you impudent? Be gone, out of
my sight! Name a handsome young fellow to me! Foh, a
hideous, handsome young fellow I abominate.   (*Spits*)

ELIZA

Indeed! But let's see; will nothing please you? What d'ye   60
think of the court?

OLIVIA

How? The court, the court, cousin! My aversion, my aversion, my aversion of all aversions.

ELIZA

How? The court! Where—

OLIVIA

Where sincerity is a quality as out of fashion and as   65
unprosperous as bashfulness. I could not laugh at a quibble,
though it were a fat privy counsellor's; nor praise a lord's
ill verses, though I were myself the subject; nor an old lady's
young looks, though I were her woman; nor sit to a vain
young simile-maker, though he flattered me. In short, I could   70
not gloat upon a man when he comes into a room, and laugh

---

48 *Hyde Park* 'the promenade of London . . . the rendez-vous of
   magnificence and beauty: every one, therefore, who had either
   sparkling eyes, or a splendid equipage, constantly repaired thither'
   (Anthony Hamilton, *Memoirs of the Count de Grammont* (1926),
   p. 171)
55 *liberal* (1) generous (2) licentious
59 s.d. (*Spits*) to avert a threatened evil; Dryden's Friar Dominic does
   so in *The Spanish Fryar* (1680), when hypocritically disclaiming his
   interest in 'a sweet young girl' (IV. i)
70 *simile-maker* portrait-painter
71 *gloat* 'cast amorous or admiring glances' (*OED*)

at him when he goes out. I cannot rail at the absent to flatter
the standers-by; I—

ELIZA

Well, but railing now is so common that 'tis no more malice,
but the fashion; and the absent think they are no more the 75
worse for being railed at than the present think they're the
better for being flattered; and for the court—

OLIVIA

Nay, do not defend the court, for you'll make me rail at it,
like a trusting citizen's widow.

ELIZA

Or like a Holborn lady, who could not get into the last ball 80
or was out of countenance in the drawing-room the last
Sunday of her appearance there. For none rail at the court
but those who cannot get into it or else who are ridiculous
when they are there; and I shall suspect you were laughed at
when you were last there or would be a maid of honour. 85

OLIVIA

I, a maid of honour! To be a maid of honour were yet of all
things my aversion.

ELIZA

In what sense am I to understand you? But, in fine, by the
word 'aversion' I'm sure you dissemble, for I never knew
woman yet that used it who did not. Come, our tongues belie 90
our hearts more than our pocket-glasses do our faces; but
methinks we ought to leave off dissembling, since 'tis grown
of no use to us; for all wise observers understand us nowadays as they do dreams, almanacs, and Dutch gazettes, by
the contrary; and a man no more believes a woman when 95
she says she has an aversion for him, than when she says
she'll cry out.

OLIVIA

O filthy, hideous! Peace, cousin, or your discourse will be
my aversion; and you may believe me.

76 *they're* Q2b–8, 0 (they are Q1–2a)

---

79 *trusting citizen* credit-giving tradesman, presumably ruined by bad
debts
80 *Holborn* a main highway into the city, running from Tottenham
Court Road to Newgate; an unfashionable address
81 *the drawing-room* The King and Queen held large receptions in
their withdrawing-rooms at Whitehall; Evelyn saw 'innumerable'
visitors 'of the first sort' there on 2 May 1671.
85 *maid of honour* unmarried lady attending upon the Queen
94 *Dutch gazettes* especially unreliable, since they reported matters
from a viewpoint hostile to England

ELIZA

Yes, for if anything be a woman's aversion, 'tis plain dealing   100
from another woman; and perhaps that's your quarrel to the
world, for that will talk, as your woman says.

OLIVIA

Talk not of me, sure; for what men do I converse with, what
visits do I admit?

Enter BOY

BOY

Here's the gentleman to wait upon you, madam.   105

OLIVIA

On me! You little, unthinking fop, d'ye know what you say?

BOY

Yes, madam; 'tis the gentleman that comes every day to you,
who—

OLIVIA

Hold your peace, you heedless little animal, and get you
gone.   *(Exit* BOY*)*   110
This country boy, cousin, takes my dancing-master, tailor, or
the spruce milliner for visitors.

LETTICE

No, madam; 'tis Master Novel, I'm sure, by his talking so
loud. I know his voice too, madam.

OLIVIA

You know nothing, you buffle-headed, stupid creature, you;   115
you would make my cousin believe I receive visits. But if it
be Master—what did you call him?

LETTICE

Master Novel, madam; he that—

OLIVIA

Hold your peace, I'll hear no more of him. But if it be your
Master—(I can't think of his name again), I suppose he has   120
followed my cousin hither.

ELIZA

No, cousin, I will not rob you of the honour of the visit; 'tis
to you, cousin, for I know him not.

OLIVIA

Nor did I ever hear of him before, upon my honour, cousin.
Besides, han't I told you that visits and the business of visits,   125
flattery and detraction, are my aversion? D'ye think then I

112 *milliner* man selling cutlery, haberdashery, and fancy goods
115 *buffle-headed* dim-witted

would admit such a coxcomb as he is, who rather than not
rail, will rail at the dead, whom none speak ill of; and rather
than not flatter, will flatter the poets of the age, whom none
will flatter; who affects novelty as much as the fashion, and　　130
is as fantastical as changeable, and as well known as the
fashion; who likes nothing but what is new, nay, would
choose to have his friend or his title a new one. In fine, he is
my aversion.

ELIZA

I find you do know him, cousin; at least, have heard of him.　　135

OLIVIA

Yes, now I remember, I have heard of him.

ELIZA

Well; but since he is such a coxcomb, for heaven's sake let
him not come up.—Tell him, Mistress Lettice, your lady is
not within.

OLIVIA

No, Lettice, tell him my cousin is here, and that he may come　　140
up;—for, notwithstanding I detest the sight of him, you may
like his conversation; and though I would use him scurvily,
I will not be rude to you in my own lodging. Since he has
followed you hither, let him come up, I say.

ELIZA

Very fine! Pray let him go to the devil, I say, for me; I know　　145
him not, nor desire it.—Send him away, Mistress
Lettice.

OLIVIA

Upon my word, she shan't. I must disobey your commands
to comply with your desires.—Call him up, Lettice.

ELIZA

Nay, I'll swear she shall not stir on that errand.　　　　　　150

(Holds LETTICE)

OLIVIA

Well then, I'll call him myself for you, since you will have
it so. *(Calls out at the door)* Master Novel, sir, sir!

Enter NOVEL

NOVEL

Madam, I beg your pardon; perhaps you were busy. I did
not think you had company with you.

---

131 *fantastical* (1) capricious in opinion (2) foppish in dress
145 *for me* as far as I'm concerned
152 s.d. *door* i.e., one of the permanent doors in the proscenium arch

ELIZA *(Aside)*
Yet he comes to me, cousin!   155

OLIVIA
Chairs there!   [*Exit* LETTICE]

[*Enter* SERVANTS, *who place chairs and withdraw.*] *They sit*

NOVEL
Well, but madam, d'ye know whence I come now?

OLIVIA
From some melancholy place, I warrant, sir, since they have
lost your good company.

ELIZA
So.   160

NOVEL
From a place where they have treated me at dinner with so
much civility and kindness, a pox on 'em, that I could
hardly get away to you, dear madam.

OLIVIA
You have a way with you so new and obliging, sir.

ELIZA *(Apart to* OLIVIA)
You hate flattery, cousin!   165

NOVEL
Nay, faith, madam, d'ye think my way new? Then you are
obliging, madam. I must confess I hate imitation, to do
anything like other people; all that know me do me the
honour to say I am an original, faith. But as I was saying,
madam, I have been treated today with all the ceremony and   170
kindness imaginable at my Lady Autumn's; but the nauseous
old woman at the upper end of her table—

OLIVIA
Revives the old Grecian custom of serving in a death's head
with their banquets.

NOVEL
Ha ha! Fine, just, i'faith; nay, and new. 'Tis like eating with   175

---

156 s.d. [*Exit* LETTICE] Unless her re-entry at 675 is an error, she must
exit sometime before; here is her best opportunity.
173 *serving in a death's head* This is not a Greek custom; Herodotus
says the Egyptians paraded a dummy corpse at their feasts, as a
memento mori (II. 78), but Wycherley probably found it in Montaigne, *Essais*, I, xx (ed. cit., I, 91): 'les Egyptiens, après leurs
festins, faisoient presenter aux assistans une grand'image de la mort
par un qui leur crioit: "Boy et t'esjouy, car, mort, tu seras tel"'.
174 *banquets* sweetmeats, fruit, and wine served as dessert

the ghost in *The Libertine*; she would frighten a man from
her dinner with her hollow invitations, and spoil one's
stomach—

OLIVIA

To meat or women. I detest her hollow, cherry cheeks. She
looks like an old coach new painted, affecting an unseemly   180
smugness whilst she is ready to drop in pieces.

ELIZA *(Apart to* OLIVIA)

You hate detraction I see, cousin!

NOVEL

But the silly old fury, whilst she affects to look like a woman
of this age, talks—

OLIVIA

Like one of the last, and as passionately as an old courtier   185
who has outlived his office.

NOVEL

Yes, madam; but pray let me give you her character. Then
she never counts her age by the years, but—

OLIVIA

By the masques she has lived to see.

NOVEL

Nay then, madam, I see you think a little harmless railing   190
too great a pleasure for any but yourself, and therefore I've
done.

OLIVIA

Nay, faith, you shall tell me who you had there at dinner.

NOVEL

If you would hear me, madam.

OLIVIA

Most patiently. Speak, sir.   195

NOVEL

Then we had her daughter—

OLIVIA

Ay, her daughter, the very disgrace to good clothes, which
she always wears but to heighten her deformity, not mend it;
for she is still most splendidly, gallantly, ugly, and looks like
an ill piece of daubing in a rich frame.   200

---

176 *The Libertine* Novel's memory of Shadwell's play (1675) is blurred;
 only Don John's man is frightened when the statue of his master's
 victim comes to dinner in Act IV, though both refuse to drink a
 glass of blood when the ghost returns hospitality in Act V.
181 *smugness* smartness

NOVEL

So! But have you done with her, madam? And can you spare her to me a little now?

OLIVIA

Ay ay, sir.

NOVEL

Then she is like—

OLIVIA

She is, you'd say, like a city bride: the greater fortune, but   205
not the greater beauty, for her dress.

NOVEL

Well. Yet have you done, madam? Then she—

OLIVIA

Then she bestows as unfortunately on her face all the graces
in fashion, as the languishing eye, the hanging or pouting lip;
but as the fool is never more provoking than when he aims   210
at wit, the ill-favoured of our sex are never more nauseous
than when they would be beauties, adding to their natural
deformity the artificial ugliness of affectation.

ELIZA

So, cousin, I find one may have a collection of all one's
acquaintances' pictures as well at your house as at Master   215
Lely's, only the difference is there we find 'em much hand-
somer than they are and like, here much uglier and like; and
you are the first of the profession of picture-drawing I ever
knew without flattery.

OLIVIA

I draw after the life; do nobody wrong, cousin.   220

ELIZA

No, you hate flattery and detraction!

OLIVIA

But, Master Novel, who had you besides at dinner?

NOVEL

Nay, the devil take me if I tell you, unless you will allow
me the privilege of railing in my turn. But, now I think on't,
the women ought to be your province, as the men are mine;   225
and you must know we had him whom—

OLIVIA

Him, whom—

205-6 city . . . dress another attack on merchants with more money than taste
216 Lely see Prologue 30; Lely was knighted on 11 January 1679/80

NOVEL

What? Invading me already? And giving the character
before you know the man?

ELIZA

No, that is not fair, though it be usual.   230

OLIVIA

I beg your pardon, Master Novel; pray go on.

NOVEL

Then, I say, we had that familiar coxcomb, who is at home
wheresoe'er he comes.

OLIVIA

Ay, that fool—

NOVEL

Nay then, madam, your servant. I'm gone. Taking a fool out   235
of one's mouth is worse than taking the bread out of one's
mouth.

OLIVIA

I've done. Your pardon, Master Novel; pray proceed.

NOVEL

I say, the rogue, that he may be the only wit in company,
will let nobody else talk, and—   240

OLIVIA

Ay, those fops who love to talk all themselves are of all
things my aversion.

NOVEL

Then you'll let me speak, madam, sure. The rogue, I say, will
force his jest upon you, and I hate a jest that's forced upon
a man as much as a glass.   245

ELIZA

Why, I hope, sir, he does not expect a man of your temper-
ance in jesting should do him reason?

NOVEL

What, interruption from this side too! I must then—
        (*Offers to rise.* OLIVIA *holds him*)

OLIVIA

No, sir.—You must know, cousin, that fop he means, though
he talks only to be commended, will not give you leave to   250
do't.

NOVEL

But, madam—

---

247 *do him reason* keep pace with him in drinking
248 s.d. *Offers* Attempts

OLIVIA
He a wit! Hang him, he's only an adopter of straggling jests
and fatherless lampoons, by the credit of which he eats at
good tables and so, like the barren beggar-woman, lives by   255
borrowed children.

NOVEL
Madam—

OLIVIA
And never was author of anything but his news; but that is
still all his own.

NOVEL
Madam, pray—   260

OLIVIA
An eternal babbler, and makes no more use of his ears than
a man that sits at a play by his mistress or in fop-corner.
He's, in fine, a base, detracting fellow, and is my aversion.—
But who else prithee, Master Novel, was there with you?
Nay, you shan't stir.   265

NOVEL
I beg your pardon, madam; I cannot stay in any place where
I'm not allowed a little Christian liberty of railing.

OLIVIA
Nay, prithee, Master Novel, stay; and though you should rail
at me, I would hear you with patience. Prithee, who else was
there with you?   270

NOVEL
Your servant, madam.

OLIVIA
Nay, prithee tell us, Master Novel, prithee do.

NOVEL
We had nobody else.

OLIVIA
Nay, faith, I know you had. Come, my Lord Plausible was
there too, who is, cousin, a—   275

ELIZA
You need not tell me what he is, cousin, for I know him to
be a civil, good-natured, harmless gentleman, that speaks well
of all the world, and is always in good humour, and—

---

262 *fop-corner* the foremost benches of the pit, where wits-about-town
congregated; Otway's *Friendship in Fashion* (1678) refers to 'ev'ry
trim amorous twiring Fop of the Corner, that comes thither to make
a noise, hear no Play, and show himself' (V. 520–2)
271 *Your servant, madam* a polite way of expressing disagreement

OLIVIA

Hold, cousin, hold! I hate detraction, but I must tell you,
cousin, his civility is cowardice, his good nature want of wit,   280
and has neither courage or sense to rail; and for his being
always in humour, 'tis because he is never dissatisfied with
himself. In fine, he is my aversion, and I never admit his
visits beyond my hall.

NOVEL

No, he visit you! Damn him, cringing, grinning rogue! If I   285
should see him coming up to you, I would make bold to
kick him down again.—Ha!

Enter my LORD PLAUSIBLE

My dear lord, your most humble servant.
                    (*Rises and salutes* PLAUSIBLE *and kisses him*)

ELIZA (*Aside*)

So! I find kissing and railing succeed each other with the
angry men as well as with the angry women; and their   290
quarrels are like love-quarrels, since absence is the only cause
of them, for as soon as the man appears again, they are over.

LORD PLAUSIBLE

Your most faithful, humble servant, generous Master Novel;
—and, madam, I am your eternal slave and kiss your fair
hands, which I had done sooner, according to your com-   295
mands, but—

OLIVIA

No excuses, my lord.

ELIZA (*Apart* [*to* OLIVIA])

What, you sent for him then, cousin?

NOVEL (*Aside*)

Ha! invited!

OLIVIA

I know you must divide yourself, for your good company is   300
too general a good to be engrossed by any particular friend.

LORD PLAUSIBLE

O Lord, madam, my company! Your most obliged, faithful,
humble servant. But I could have brought you good company
indeed, for I parted at your door with two of the worthiest,
bravest men—   305

OLIVIA

Who were they, my lord?

288 s.d. *kisses him* 'Lord, what a filthy trick these men have got of kiss-
    ing one another' (Etherege, *The Man of Mode* (1676), I. 69–70)
294–5 *kiss your fair hands* a polite greeting, not necessarily acted upon

NOVEL
Who do you call the worthiest, bravest men, pray?

LORD PLAUSIBLE
O the wisest, bravest gentlemen! Men of such honour and
virtue! Of such good qualities! Ah!

ELIZA *(Aside)*
This is a coxcomb that speaks ill of all people a different 310
way, and libels everybody with dull praise, and commonly
in the wrong place; so makes his panegyrics abusive lampoons.

OLIVIA
But pray let me know who they were.

LORD PLAUSIBLE
Ah! Such patterns of heroic virtue! Such— 315

NOVEL
Well, but who the devil were they?

LORD PLAUSIBLE
The honour of our nation, the glory of our age! Ah, I could
dwell a twelvemonth on their praise, which indeed I might
spare by telling their names: Sir John Current and Sir
Richard Court-Title. 320

NOVEL
Court-Title! Ha ha!

OLIVIA
And Sir John Current! Why will you keep such a wretch
company, my lord?

LORD PLAUSIBLE
Oh, madam, seriously, you are a little too severe, for he is a
man of unquestioned reputation in everything. 325

OLIVIA
Yes, because he endeavours only with the women to pass for
a man of courage, and with the bullies for a wit, with the
wits for a man of business, and with the men of business for
a favourite at court, and at court for good city security.

NOVEL
And for Sir Richard, he— 330

LORD PLAUSIBLE
He loves your choice, picked company, persons that—

OLIVIA
He loves a lord indeed, but—

NOVEL
Pray, dear madam, let me have but a bold stroke or two at
his picture. He loves a lord, as you say, though—

OLIVIA

Though he borrowed his money and ne'er paid him again. 335

NOVEL

And would bespeak a place three days before at the back-
end of a lord's coach to Hyde Park.

LORD PLAUSIBLE

Nay, i'faith, i'faith, you are both too severe.

OLIVIA

Then to show yet more his passion for quality, he makes
love to that fulsome coach-load of honour, my Lady Goodly, 340
for he is always at her lodging.

LORD PLAUSIBLE

Because it is the conventicle gallant, the meeting-house of all
the fair ladies and glorious, superfine beauties of the town.

NOVEL

Very fine ladies! There's first—

OLIVIA

Her honour, as fat as an hostess. 345

LORD PLAUSIBLE

She is something plump indeed, a goodly, comely, graceful
person.

NOVEL

Then there's my Lady Frances—what d'ye call 'er?—as
ugly—

OLIVIA

As a citizen's lawfully begotten daughter. 350

LORD PLAUSIBLE

She has wit in abundance, and the handsomest heel, elbow,
and tip of an ear you ever saw.

NOVEL

Heel and elbow! Ha ha! And there's my Lady Betty, you
know—

OLIVIA

As sluttish and slatternly as an Irishwoman bred in France. 355

LORD PLAUSIBLE

Ah, all she has hangs with a loose air, indeed, and becoming
negligence.

ELIZA

You see all faults with lover's eyes, I find, my lord.

---

342 *meeting-house* Plausible's non-conformist imagery casts doubt upon
the social cachet of Lady Goodly's polished assembly or 'conventicle gallant'.

LORD PLAUSIBLE

Ah, madam, your most obliged, faithful, humble servant to command.—But you can say nothing, sure, against the super- 360
fine Mistress—

OLIVIA

I know who you mean. She is as censorious and detracting a jade as a superannuated sinner.

LORD PLAUSIBLE

She has a smart way of raillery, 'tis confessed.

NOVEL

And then, for Mistress Grideline—   365

LORD PLAUSIBLE

She, I'm sure, is—

OLIVIA

One that never spoke ill of anybody, 'tis confessed; for she is as silent in conversation as a country lover, and no better company than a clock or a weather-glass; for if she sounds, 'tis but once an hour, to put you in mind of the time of day 370
or tell you 'twill be cold or hot, rain or snow.

LORD PLAUSIBLE

Ah, poor creature! She's extremely good and modest.

NOVEL

And for Mistress Bridlechin, she's—

OLIVIA

As proud as a churchman's wife.

LORD PLAUSIBLE

She's a woman of great spirit and honour, and will not make 375
herself cheap, 'tis true.

NOVEL

Then Mistress Hoyden, that calls all people by their sur-
names, and is—

OLIVIA

As familiar a duck—

NOVEL

As an actress in the tiring-room. There I was once before- 380
hand with you, madam.

---

371 *or tell* Q2–8 (or to tell Q1, 0)

---

365 *Grideline* greyish pink; perhaps chosen here to suggest an unhealthy
    complexion, like Sheridan's Miss Sallow in *The School for Scandal*
    (1777, II. ii)
377 *Hoyden* type name for a 'boisterous noisy girl, a romp' (*OED*)
380 *tiring-room* dressing-room, where actresses often entertained gallants

LORD PLAUSIBLE
  Mistress Hoyden! A poor, affable, good-natured soul! But
  the divine Mistress Trifle comes thither too; sure, her beauty,
  virtue, and conduct you can say nothing to.

OLIVIA
  No?   385

NOVEL
  No?—Pray let me speak, madam.

OLIVIA
  First, can anyone be called beautiful that squints?

LORD PLAUSIBLE
  Her eyes languish a little, I own.

NOVEL
  Languish! Ha ha!

OLIVIA
  Languish! Then, for her conduct, she was seen at *The*   390
  Country Wife after the first day. There's for you, my lord.

LORD PLAUSIBLE
  But, madam, she was not seen to use her fan all the play
  long, turn aside her head, or by a conscious blush discover
  more guilt than modesty.

OLIVIA
  Very fine! Then you think a woman modest that sees the   395
  hideous *Country Wife* without blushing or publishing her
  detestation of it? D'ye hear him, cousin?

ELIZA
  Yes, and am, I must confess, something of his opinion, and
  think that as an over-captious fool at a play, by endeavouring
  to show the author's want of wit, exposes his own to more   400
  censure, so may a lady call her own modesty in question by
  publicly cavilling with the poet's; for all those grimaces of
  honour and artificial modesty disparage a woman's real
  virtue as much as the use of white and red does the natural
  complexion, and you must use very, very little if you would   405
  have it thought your own.

399 *over-captious* Q2–8 (over-conscious Q1, 0)

---

384 *conduct* discretion
391 *the first day* The first recorded performance of Wycherley's comedy
     was given at Drury Lane on 12 January 1675; later audiences knew
     the play's reputation for obscenity in advance.
393 *conscious* knowing
404 *white and red* cosmetics for the face and cheeks

OLIVIA

Then you would have a woman of honour with passive looks, ears, and tongue undergo all the hideous obscenity she hears at nasty plays?

ELIZA

Truly, I think a woman betrays her want of modesty by 410 showing it publicly in a playhouse, as much as a man does his want of courage by a quarrel there, for the truly modest and stout say least and are least exceptious, especially in public.

OLIVIA

O hideous! Cousin, this cannot be your opinion; but you are 415 one of those who have the confidence to pardon the filthy play.

ELIZA

Why, what is there of ill in't, say you?

OLIVIA

O fie fie fie, would you put me to the blush anew, call all the blood into my face again? But to satisfy you then; first, the 420 clandestine obscenity in the very name of Horner.

ELIZA

Truly, 'tis so hidden I cannot find it out, I confess.

OLIVIA

O horrid! Does it not give you the rank conception or image of a goat, a town-bull, or a satyr? Nay, what is yet a filthier image than all the rest, that of an eunuch?   425

ELIZA

What then? I can think of a goat, a bull, or satyr without any hurt.

OLIVIA

Ay; but cousin, one cannot stop there.

ELIZA

I can, cousin.

OLIVIA

O no, for when you have those filthy creatures in your head 430 once, the next thing you think is what they do; as their defiling of honest men's beds and couches, rapes upon sleep-

---

409 *nasty* indecent
413 *exceptious* captious, easily offended
421 *Horner* i.e., cuckold-maker; by feigning impotence, Horner gains ready access to eager wives without sullying their reputations or arousing their husbands' jealousy
424 *town-bull* a bull communally owned by the cow-keepers of a village; hence 'one that rides all the Women he meets' (*B.E.*)

ing and waking country virgins under hedges and on haycocks; nay farther—

ELIZA

Nay, no farther, cousin; we have enough of your comment   435
on the play, which will make me more ashamed than the
play itself.

OLIVIA

O, believe me, 'tis a filthy play; and you may take my word
for a filthy play as soon as another's. But the filthiest thing
in that play, or any other play, is—   440

ELIZA

Pray keep it to yourself, if it be so.

OLIVIA

No, faith, you shall know it; I'm resolved to make you out
of love with the play. I say the lewdest, filthiest thing is his
china; nay, I will never forgive the beastly author his china.
He has quite taken away the reputation of poor china itself,   445
and sullied the most innocent and pretty furniture of a lady's
chamber, insomuch that I was fain to break all my defiled
vessels. You see I have none left; nor you, I hope.

ELIZA

You'll pardon me; I cannot think the worse of my china for
that of the playhouse.   450

OLIVIA

Why, you will not keep any now, sure! 'Tis now as unfit an
ornament for a lady's chamber as the pictures that come
from Italy and other hot countries, as appears by their nudities, which I always cover or scratch out, wheresoe'er I find
'em. But china! Out upon't, filthy china, nasty, debauched   455
china!

ELIZA

All this will not put me out of conceit with china nor the
play, which is acted today, or another of the same beastly
author's, as you call him, which I'll go see.   [Going]

433–4 haycocks conical heaps of hay in the field
444 china Horner and Lady Fidget retire on pretence of his giving her a
    piece of china; when she emerges later with a roll-wagon, Mistress
    Squeamish demands china too, but Horner confesses he has 'none
    left now' (IV. iii, 187)
446 furniture ornaments
452–3 pictures . . . Italy pornographic drawings after Giulio Romano's
    illustrations to Aretino's Sonnetti lussoriosi
457 put me out of conceit make me dissatisfied

OLIVIA

You will not, sure! Nay, you shan't venture your reputation   460
by going, and mine by leaving me alone with two men here.
(Pulls her back) Nay, you'll disoblige me for ever if—

ELIZA

I stay.—Your servant.   *(Exit* ELIZA*)*

OLIVIA

Well.—But my lord, though you justify everybody, you
cannot in earnest uphold so beastly a writer, whose ink is so   465
smutty, as one may say.

LORD PLAUSIBLE

Faith, I dare swear the poor man did not think to disoblige
the ladies by any amorous, soft, passionate, luscious saying
in his play.

OLIVIA

Foy, my lord.—But what think you, Master Novel, of the   470
play, though I know you are a friend to all that are new?

NOVEL

Faith, madam, I must confess the new plays would not be the
worse for my advice, but I could never get the silly rogues,
the poets, to mind what I say. But I'll tell you what counsel
I gave the surly fool you speak of.   475

OLIVIA

What was't?

NOVEL

Faith, to put his play into rithme; for rithme, you know,
often makes mystical nonsense pass with the critics for wit,
and a double-meaning saying with the ladies for soft, tender,
and moving passion. But now I talk of passion, I saw your   480
old lover this morning—Captain—   *(Whispers)*

Enter CAPTAIN MANLY, FREEMAN, *and* FIDELIA *standing behind*

OLIVIA

Whom? Nay, you need not whisper.

MANLY

We are luckily got hither unobserved.—How! In a close
conversation with these supple rascals, the outcasts of sempstresses' shops!   485

468 *luscious* lascivious
470 *Foy* Faith (from French *foi*)
477 *rithme* rhyme (see I. 453); the fitness of rhyme for serious plays was
    keenly debated at this time, most memorably in Dryden's *Of
    Dramatic Poesy* (1668), but only Novel could suggest using rhyme
    for a contemporary comedy like *The Country Wife*

FREEMAN

Faith, pardon her, captain, that, since she could no longer be
entertained with your manly bluntness and honest love, she
takes up with the pert chat and commonplace flattery of
these fluttering parrots of the town, apes and echoes of men
only.   490

MANLY

Do not you, sir, play the echo too, mock me, dally with my
own words, and show yourself as impertinent as they are.

FREEMAN

Nay, captain—

FIDELIA

Nay, lieutenant, do not excuse her; methinks she looks very
kindly upon 'em both, and seems to be pleased with what   495
that fool there says to her.

MANLY

You lie, sir; and hold your peace, that I may not be provoked
to give you a worse reply.

OLIVIA

Manly returned, d'ye say? And is he safe?

NOVEL

My lord saw him too. Hark you, my lord.   500
                              (*Whispers to* PLAUSIBLE)

MANLY (*Aside*)

She yet seems concerned for my safety, and perhaps they are
admitted now here but for their news of me; for intelligence
indeed is the common passport of nauseous fools when they
go their round of good tables and houses.

OLIVIA

I heard of his fighting only, without particulars, and confess 505
I always loved his brutal courage, because it made me hope
it might rid me of his more brutal love.

MANLY (*Apart*)

What's that?

OLIVIA

But is he at last returned, d'ye say, unhurt?

NOVEL

Ay, faith, without doing his business; for the rogue has been 510

486–90 *Faith . . . only* Freeman recalls, almost accurately, Manly's
    speech at I. 574–8.
502 *intelligence* information, news
510 *doing his business* ruining or killing himself

these two years pretending to a wooden leg, which he would
take from fortune as kindly as the staff of a marshal of
France, and rather read his name in a gazette—

OLIVIA

Than in the entail of a good estate.

MANLY *(Aside)*

So!   515

NOVEL

I have an ambition, I must confess, of losing my heart before
such a fair enemy as yourself, madam; but that silly rogues
should be ambitious of losing their arms, and—

OLIVIA

Looking like a pair of compasses.

NOVEL

But he has no use of his arms but to set 'em on kimbow, for   520
he never pulls off his hat, at least not to me, I'm sure; for
you must know, madam, he has a fanatical hatred to good
company. He can't abide me.

LORD PLAUSIBLE

O, be not so severe to him as to say he hates good company,
for I assure you he has a great respect, esteem, and kindness   525
for me.

MANLY [*Aside*]

That kind, civil rogue has spoken yet ten thousand times
worse of me than t'other.

OLIVIA

Well, if he be returned, Master Novel, then shall I be pestered again with his boisterous sea-love, have my alcove smell 530
like a cabin, my chamber perfumed with his tarpaulin
brandenburgh, and hear volleys of brandy sighs, enough to
make a fog in one's room. Foh, I hate a lover that smells like
Thames Street!

---

511 *pretending* aspiring
512–13 *marshal of France* 'a Title only, without either pension or com-
    mand' (*OED*, citing Botero's *The World*, tr. R. Johnson (1630), p.
    157)
513 *gazette* The *London Gazette* published special supplements giving
    news of battles during the Dutch wars.
520 *on kimbow* a-kimbo
532 *brandenburgh* a long loose overcoat reaching to the calf; 'it serves
    to wrap me up, after the Fatigue of a Ball' (Etherege, *The Man of
    Mode* (1676), IV. ii, 110–11)
534 *Thames Street* running along the north bank of the river from Black-
    friars to the Tower; it contained Billingsgate fish market

MANLY
(Aside) I can bear no longer, and need her no more. [*To* 535
OLIVIA] But since you have these two pulvilio boxes, these
essence bottles, this pair of musk-cats here, I hope I may
venture to come yet nearer you.

OLIVIA
Overheard us, then?

NOVEL *(Aside)*
I hope he heard me not. 540

LORD PLAUSIBLE
Most noble and heroic captain, your most obliged, faithful,
humble servant.

NOVEL
Dear tar, thy humble servant.

MANLY
Away!—Madam.
        (Thrusts NOVEL *and* PLAUSIBLE *on each side)*

OLIVIA
Nay, I think I have fitted you for listening. 545

MANLY
You have fitted me for believing you could not be fickle
though you were young, could not dissemble love though
'twas your interest, nor be vain though you were handsome,
nor break your promise though to a parting lover, nor abuse
your best friend though you had wit; but I take not your 550
contempt of me worse than your esteem or civility for these
things here, though you know 'em.

NOVEL
Things!

LORD PLAUSIBLE
Let the captain rally a little.

MANLY
Yes, things! *(Coming up to* NOVEL*)* Canst thou be angry, 555
thou thing?

NOVEL
No, since my lord says you speak in raillery; for though

---

544 s.d. *(Thrusts . . . side)* Q1 prints this after Olivia's next speech, so it
    could apply to her or Manly.
548 *be* Q4–8, 0 (be in Q1–3)

---

535 *bear* intransitive
536 *pulvilio* perfumed powder for dressing wigs
537 *musk-cats* animals secreting musk, the basis of many perfumes
545 *fitted you* paid you back

your sea-raillery be something rough, yet I confess we use
one another to as bad every day at Locket's, and never
quarrel for the matter.   560

LORD PLAUSIBLE

Nay, noble captain, be not angry with him. A word with you,
I beseech you.   (*Whispers to* MANLY)

OLIVIA (*Aside*)

Well, we women, like the rest of the cheats of the world,
when our cullies or creditors have found us out and will or
can trust no longer, pay debts and satisfy obligations with a   565
quarrel, the kindest present a man can make to his mistress,
when he can make no more presents; for oftentimes in love,
as at cards, we are forced to play foul only to give over the
game, and use our lovers like the cards: when we can get no
more by 'em, throw 'em up in a pet upon the first dispute.   570

MANLY

My lord, all that you have made me know by your whispering, which I knew not before, is that you have a stinking
breath. There's a secret for your secret.

LORD PLAUSIBLE

Pshaw, pshaw!

MANLY

But madam, tell me, pray, [*Indicating* NOVEL] what was't   575
about this spark could take you? Was it the merit of his
fashionable impudence, the briskness of his noise, the wit of
his laugh, his judgment or fancy in his garniture? Or was it
a well-trimmed glove, or the scent of it that charmed you?

NOVEL

Very well, sir.—'Gad, these sea-captains make nothing of   580
dressing.—But let me tell you, sir, a man by his dress, as
much as by anything, shows his wit and judgment; nay, and
his courage too.

FREEMAN

How his courage, Master Novel?

NOVEL

Why, for example, by red breeches, tucked-up hair or peruke,   585
a greasy broad belt, and nowadays a short sword.

558 *use* accustom
559 *Locket's* an expensive eating-house near Charing Cross
578 *garniture* ribbons and jewels used as trimmings to a suit
579 *glove* often trimmed with ribbons, gold braid, lace, or fur, and
       scented with jasmine, tuberose, cordivant, orangery, or frangipan
585-6 *red . . . sword* the unofficial uniform of a swaggering officer

MANLY

Thy courage will appear more by thy belt than thy sword, I
dare swear.—Then, madam, [*Indicating* PLAUSIBLE] for this
gentle piece of courtesy, this man of tame honour, what
could you find in him? Was it his languishing, affected tone,   590
his mannerly look, his second-hand flattery, the refuse of the
playhouse tiring-rooms? Or his slavish obsequiousness, in
watching at the door of your box at the playhouse for your
hand to your chair? Or his janty way of playing with your
fan? Or was it the gunpowder spot on his hand, or the jewel   595
in his ear, that purchased your heart?

OLIVIA

Good jealous captain, no more of your—

LORD PLAUSIBLE

No, let him go on, madam, for perhaps he may make you
laugh; and I would contribute to your pleasure any way.

MANLY

Gentle rogue!   600

OLIVIA

No, noble captain, you cannot, sure, think anything could
take me more than that heroic title of yours, captain; for
you know we women love honour inordinately.

NOVEL

Ha ha! Faith, she is with thee, bully, for thy raillery.

MANLY (*Aside to* NOVEL)

Faith, so shall I be with you, no bully, for your grinning.   605

OLIVIA

Then, that noble lion-like mien of yours, that soldier-like
weather-beaten complexion, and that manly roughness of
your voice, how can they otherwise than charm us women,
who hate effeminacy!

NOVEL

Ha ha! Faith, I can't hold from laughing.   610

MANLY (*Aside to* NOVEL)

Nor shall I from kicking anon.

---

592 *tiring-rooms* dressing-rooms
594 *hand to your chair* Plausible escorts Olivia to her sedan after the
    play.
594 *janty* well-bred, genteel, elegant
595 *gunpowder spot* a blue beauty spot tattooed into the skin with gun-
    powder; Wycherley's *Miscellany Poems* (1704) include verses '*Upon
    the* Gun-powder Spot *on a* LADY'S Hand'

OLIVIA

And then, that captain-like carelessness in your dress, but
especially your scarf; 'twas just such another, only a little
higher tied, made me in love with my tailor as he passed by
my window the last training day; for we women adore a   615
martial man, and you have nothing wanting to make you
more one, or more agreeable, but a wooden leg.

LORD PLAUSIBLE

Nay, i'faith, there your ladyship was a wag; and it was fine,
just, and well rallied.

NOVEL

Ay ay, madam, with you ladies too martial men must needs   620
be very killing.

MANLY

Peace, you Bartholomew Fair buffoons!—and be not you
vain that these laugh on your side, for they will laugh at
their own dull jests. But no more of 'em, for I will only
suffer now this lady to be witty and merry.   625

OLIVIA

You would not have your panegyric interrupted. I go on
then to your humour. Is there anything more agreeable than
the pretty sullenness of that? Than the greatness of your
courage, which most of all appears in your spirit of contra-
diction, for you dare give all mankind the lie; and your   630
opinion is your only mistress, for you renounce that too
when it becomes another man's.

NOVEL

Ha ha! I cannot hold; I must laugh at thee, tar, faith!

LORD PLAUSIBLE

And i'faith, dear captain, I beg your pardon and leave to
laugh at you too, though I protest I mean you no hurt; but   635
when a lady rallies, a stander-by must be complaisant and
do her reason in laughing. Ha ha!

---

613 *scarf* sash worn round the waist or across the chest to indicate mili-
    tary rank; the *London Gazette* no. 2445 (15–18 April 1689) has:
    'Lost . . . an Officers Scarf, with four Fringes of Gold round the
    Wast, set on crimson silk, a very deep fringe at each end'
615 *training day* legally appointed times for drilling the part-time
    soldiers of a train band; Olivia's insult is doubly galling, since ladies'
    tailors were traditionally thought effeminate
622 *Bartholomew Fair* the great cloth fair held annually at Smithfield
    from 24 August to 7 September; in 1668 Pepys saw there puppets,
    acrobats, rope-dancers, and an educated horse
637 *reason* justice

MANLY

Why, you impudent, pitiful wretches, you presume, sure,
upon your effeminacy to urge me, for you are in all things
so like women that you may think it in me a kind of   640
cowardice to beat you.

OLIVIA

No hectoring, good captain.

MANLY

Or perhaps you think this lady's presence secures you. But
have a care; she has talked herself out of all the respect I
had for her, and by using me ill before you has given me a   645
privilege of using you so before her. But if you would
preserve your respect to her, and not be beaten before her,
go, be gone immediately.

NOVEL

Be gone! What?

LORD PLAUSIBLE

Nay, worthy, noble, generous captain.   650

MANLY

Be gone, I say.

NOVEL

Be gone again! To us, be gone!

MANLY

No chattering, baboons; instantly be gone, or—

> (MANLY *puts 'em out of the room;* NOVEL *struts,*
> PLAUSIBLE *cringes*)

NOVEL

Well, madam, we'll go make the cards ready in your bedchamber; sure, you will not stay long with him.   655

(Exeunt PLAUSIBLE [*and*] NOVEL*)*

OLIVIA

Turn hither your rage, good Captain Swagger-huff, and be
saucy with your mistress, like a true captain; but be civil to
your rivals and betters, and do not threaten anything but me
here, no, not so much as my windows; nor do not think
yourself in the lodgings of one of your suburb mistresses   660
beyond the Tower.

642 *hectoring* blustering, cf. '*Hector,* a Vaporing, Swaggering Coward'
  (*B.E.*)
647 *your respect to her* your self-respect before her (?)
654-5 *bedchamber* often used for entertaining at this period
657 *saucy* insolent
660-1 *suburb mistresses beyond the Tower* like 2 SAILOR's Blake Kate of
  Wapping (I, 107–8); Otway's *The Poet's Complaint of his Muse*
  (1680) mentions 'a worn-out Suburb-Trull' (327) and 'a *Wapping*
  Drab, or *Shoreditch* Quean' (367)

MANLY

Do not give me cause to think so, for those less infamous
women part with their lovers, just as you did from me, with
unforced vows of constancy and floods of willing tears, but
the same winds bear away their lovers and their vows; and   665
for their grief, if the credulous, unexpected fools return,
they find new comforters, fresh cullies, such as I found here.
The mercenary love of those women too suffers shipwreck
with their gallants' fortunes; now you have heard chance has
used me scurvily, therefore you do too. Well, persevere in   670
your ingratitude, falsehood, and disdain; have constancy in
something, and I promise you to be as just to your real
scorn as I was to your feigned love, and henceforward will
despise, contemn, hate, loathe, and detest you, most faithfully.   675

Enter LETTICE

OLIVIA

Get the ombre cards ready in the next room, Lettice, and—
                    (*Whispers to* LETTICE [*who then goes out*])

FREEMAN

Bravely resolved, captain.

FIDELIA

And you'll be sure to keep your word, I hope, sir.

MANLY

I hope so too.

FIDELIA

Do you but hope it, sir? If you are not as good as your   680
word, 'twill be the first time you ever bragged, sure.

MANLY

She has restored my reason with my heart.

FREEMAN

But now you talk of restoring, captain, there are other things
which, next to one's heart, one would not part with: I mean
your jewels and money, which it seems she has, sir.   685

MANLY

What's that to you, sir?

---

668 *suffers* Q2–8, 0 (suffer Q1)

675 s.d. *Enter* LETTICE presumably summoned by Olivia during the cli-
      max of Manly's tirade—and what could be more heartless?
676 *ombre* a fashionable game for three players, using only forty cards;
      Lettice must remove the eights, nines, and tens

FREEMAN

Pardon me; whatsoever is yours, I have a share in't, I'm
sure, which I will not lose for asking, though you may be
too generous or too angry now to do't yourself.

FIDELIA

Nay, then I'll make bold to make my claim too.   690

(Both going towards OLIVIA)

MANLY

Hold, you impertinent, officious fops! *(Aside)* How have I
been deceived!

FREEMAN

Madam, there are certain appurtenances to a lover's heart,
called jewels, which always go along with it.

FIDELIA

And which, with lovers, have no value in themselves, but   695
from the heart they come with. Our captain's, madam, it
seems you scorn to keep, and much more will those worthless things without it, I am confident.

OLIVIA

A gentleman so well made as you are may be confident; us
easy women could not deny you anything you ask, if 'twere   700
for yourself, but since 'tis for another, I beg your leave to
give him my answer. *(Aside)* An agreeable young fellow,
this, and would not be my aversion! [*Aloud*]—Captain,
your young friend here has a very persuading face, I confess; yet you might have asked me yourself for those trifles   705
you left with me, which—*(Aside to* MANLY*)* hark you a little,
for I dare trust you with the secret; you are a man of so
much honour, I'm sure. I say, then, not expecting your
return, or hoping ever to see you again, I have delivered
your jewels to—   710

MANLY

Whom?

OLIVIA

My husband.

MANLY

Your husband!

OLIVIA

Ay, my husband; for, since you could leave me, I am lately
and privately married to one who is a man of so much   715
honour and experience in the world that I dare not ask him
for your jewels again, to restore 'em to you, lest he should
conclude you never would have parted with 'em to me on
any other score but the exchange of my honour, which

rather than you'd let me lose, you'd lose, I'm sure, yourself   720
those trifles of yours.

MANLY

Triumphant impudence! But married too!

OLIVIA

O, speak not so loud; my servants know it not. I am married; there's no resisting one's destiny or love, you know.

MANLY

Why, did you love him too?   725

OLIVIA

Most passionately; nay, love him now, though I have married him, and he me; which mutual love I hope you are too
good, too generous, a man to disturb by any future claim or
visits to me. 'Tis true, he is now absent in the country, but
returns shortly; therefore I beg of you, for your own ease   730
and quiet and my honour, you will never see me more.

MANLY

I wish I never had seen you.

OLIVIA

But if you should ever have anything to say to me hereafter, let that young gentleman there be your messenger.

MANLY

You would be kinder to him. I find he should be welcome.   735

OLIVIA

Alas, his youth would keep my husband from suspicions and
his visits from scandal; for we women may have pity for
such as he, but no love. And I already think you do not well
to spirit him away to sea, and the sea is already but too rich
with the spoils of the shore.   740

MANLY *(Aside)*

True perfect woman! If I could say anything more injurious
to her now, I would; for I could out-rail a bilked whore or
a kicked coward. But, now I think on't, that were rather to
discover my love than hatred; and I must not talk, for
something I must do.   745

OLIVIA

(Aside) I think I have given him enough of me now, never to
be troubled with him again.

Enter LETTICE

[*Aloud*] Well, Lettice, are the cards and all ready within? I
come then.—Captain, I beg your pardon. You will not make
one at ombre?   750

742 *bilked* cheated

MANLY

No, madam; but I'll wish you a little good luck before you go.

OLIVIA

No, if you would have me thrive, curse me; for that you'll do heartily, I suppose.

MANLY

Then, if you will have it so, may all the curses light upon   755
you women ought to fear and you deserve! First, may the
curse of loving play attend your sordid covetousness, and
fortune cheat you by trusting to her as you have cheated
me; the curse of pride, or a good reputation, fall on your
lust; the curse of affectation on your beauty; the curse of   760
your husband's company on your pleasures, and the curse of
your gallant's disappointments in his absence; and the curse
of scorn, jealousy, or despair on your love; and then the
curse of loving on!

OLIVIA

And to requite all your curses, I will only return you your   765
last; may the curse of loving me still fall upon your proud,
hard heart, that could be so cruel to me in these horrid
curses! But heaven forgive you!   (*Exit* OLIVIA)

MANLY

Hell and the devil reward thee!

FREEMAN

Well, you see now mistresses, like friends, are lost by letting   770
'em handle your money; and most women are such kind of
witches, who can have no power over a man unless you give
'em money; but when once they have got any from you,
they never leave you till they have all. Therefore I never dare
give a woman a farthing.   775

MANLY

Well, there is yet this comfort: by losing one's money with
one's mistress, a man is out of danger of getting another, of
being made prize again by love, who, like a pirate, takes you
by spreading false colours, but when once you have run your
ship aground, the treacherous picaroon loofs, so by your   780
ruin you save yourself from slavery at least.

Enter BOY

762 *your gallant's disappointments* i.e., your lover's incapacity to satisfy
    you
779 *spreading false colours* flying unauthorized flags
780 *picaroon* privateer
780 *loofs* luffs, sails near the wind

BOY

Mistress Lettice, here's Madam Blackacre come to wait upon her honour.   [*Exeunt* LETTICE *and* BOY]

MANLY

D'ye hear that? Let us be gone before she comes; for henceforward I'll avoid the whole damned sex for ever, and   785
woman as a sinking ship.   (*Exeunt* MANLY *and* FIDELIA)

FREEMAN

And I'll stay, to revenge on her your quarrel to the sex, for out of love to her jointure and hatred to business I would marry her, to make an end of her thousand suits and my thousand engagements, to the comfort of two unfortunate   790
sorts of people: my plaintiffs and her defendants, my creditors and her adversaries.

Enter WIDOW BLACKACRE, *led in by* MAJOR OLDFOX, *and*
JERRY BLACKACRE *following, laden with green bags*

WIDOW

'Tis an arrant sea-ruffian, but I am glad I met with him at last, to serve him again, major, for the last service was not good in law.—Boy, duck, Jerry, where is my paper of memo-   795
randums? Give me, child. So. Where is my cousin Olivia now, my kind relation?

FREEMAN

Here is one that would be your kind relation, madam.

WIDOW

What mean you, sir?

FREEMAN

Why, faith, to be short, to marry you, widow.   800

WIDOW

Is not this the wild, rude person we saw at Captain Manly's?

JERRY

Ay, forsooth, an't please.

WIDOW

What would you? What are you? Marry me!

FREEMAN

Ay, faith, for I am a younger brother and you are a widow.

WIDOW

You are an impertinent person, and go about your business.   805

---

790 *engagements* legal obligations, here to his creditors
794 *last service* see I. 493
804 *younger brother* i.e., without an inheritance, and so usually reduced
to the church, the army, or a rich marriage

FREEMAN

  I have none, but to marry thee, widow.

WIDOW

  But I have other business, I'd have you to know.

FREEMAN

  But you have no business a-nights, widow, and I'll make you
pleasanter business than any you have. For a-nights, I assure
you, I am a man of great business; for the business—   810

WIDOW

  Go; I'm sure you're an idle fellow.

FREEMAN

  Try me but, widow, and employ me as you find my abilities
and industry.

OLDFOX

  Pray be civil to the lady, Master—; she's a person of quality,
a person that is no person—   815

FREEMAN

  Yes, but she's a person that is a widow. Be you mannerly to
her, because you are to pretend only to be her squire, to
arm her to her lawyer's chambers; but I will be impudent
and bawdy, for she must love and marry me.

WIDOW

  Marry come up, you saucy, familiar Jack! You think with   820
us widows 'tis no more than up and ride. Gad forgive me,
nowadays every idle, young, hectoring, roaring companion,
with a pair of turned red breeches and a broad back, thinks
to carry away any widow of the best degree; but I'd have
you to know, sir, all widows are not got, like places at court,   825
by impudence and importunity only.

OLDFOX

  No, no, soft, soft; you are a young man and not fit—

FREEMAN

  For a widow? Yes, sure, old man, the fitter.

OLDFOX

  Go to, go to; if others had not laid in their claims before
you—   830

FREEMAN

  Not you, I hope.

---

812 *Try me but* Only try me
817 *pretend* claim, presume
818 *arm her* walk arm in arm with her
823 *turned* i.e., remade inside out, for economy's sake
824 *carry away* win

OLDFOX

Why not I, sir? Sure, I am a much more proportionable
match for her than you, sir; I, who am an elder brother, of
a comfortable fortune, and of equal years with her.

WIDOW

How's that? You unmannerly person, I'd have you to know   835
I was born but in *ann' undec' Caroli prim'*.

OLDFOX

Your pardon, lady, your pardon; be not offended with your
very servant.—But I say, sir, you are a beggarly younger
brother, twenty years younger than her, without any land or
stock but your great stock of impudence. Therefore what   840
pretension can you have to her?

FREEMAN

You have made it for me. First, because I am a younger
brother.

[OLDFOX]

Why, is that a sufficient plea to a relict? How appears it,
sir? By what foolish custom?   845

FREEMAN

By custom time out of mind only. Then, sir, because I have
nothing to keep me after her death, I am the likelier to take
care of her life. And for my being twenty years younger
than her and having a sufficient stock of impudence, I leave
it to her whether they will be valid exceptions to me in her   850
widow's law or equity.

OLDFOX

Well, she has been so long in Chancery that I'll stand to her
equity and decree between us. (*Aside to the* WIDOW) Come,
lady, pray snap up this young snap at first, or we shall be
troubled with him. Give him a city widow's answer: that is,   855
with all the ill breeding imaginable. Come, madam.

---

843 s.p. [OLDFOX] ed. (WIDOW Q1–8, 0)

---

836 *ann' undec' Caroli prim'* Law Latin, in the form used for dating
       statutes, for the eleventh year of Charles I's reign: 1636
838 *very servant* true and professed admirer
851 *law or equity* i.e., whether the widow judges by the strict letter of
       the law, or by general principles of justice
852 *Chancery* the chief court of equity
852 *stand to* obey, be bound by
853 *decree* the judgment of an equity court
854 *snap up this young snap* speak sharply to this young fellow
854 *at first* at once, immediately

WIDOW

Well then, to make an end of this foolish wooing, for
nothing interrupts business more. First, for you, major—

OLDFOX

You declare in my favour then?

FREEMAN

What, direct the court? *(To* JERRY*)* Come, young lawyer,   860
thou shalt be a counsel for me.

JERRY

Gad, I shall betray your cause then, as well as an older
lawyer, never stir.

WIDOW

First, I say, for you, major, my walking hospital of an
ancient foundation, thou bag of mummy, that wouldst fall   865
asunder if 'twere not for thy cerecloths—

OLDFOX

How, lady?

FREEMAN

Ha ha—

JERRY

Hey, brave mother! Use all suitors thus, for my sake.

WIDOW

Thou withered, hobbling, distorted cripple; nay, thou art a   870
cripple all over. Wouldst thou make me the staff of thy age,
the crutch of thy decrepidness? Me—

FREEMAN

Well said, widow! Faith, thou wouldst make a man love
thee now without dissembling.

WIDOW

Thou senseless, impertinent, quibbling, drivelling, feeble,   875
paralytic, impotent, fumbling, frigid nicompoop!

JERRY

Hey, brave mother, for calling of names, i'fac!

WIDOW

Wouldst thou make a caudle-maker, a nurse of me? Can't
you be bed-rid without a bedfellow? Won't your swanskins,

---

863 *never stir* never fear (literally, may I never stir if I don't)
876 *fumbling* cf. '*Fumbler*, an unperforming Husband, one that is in-
    sufficient, a weak Brother' (*B.E.*)
878 *caudle* an invalid's drink of spiced wine, sugar, and warm, thin
    gruel
879 *swanskins* fine flannel of extraordinary whiteness

furs, flannels, and the scorched trencher keep you warm   880
there? Would you have me your Scotch warming-pan, with
a pox to you? Me—

OLDFOX

O heavens!

FREEMAN

I told you I should be thought the fitter man, major.

JERRY

Ay, you old fobus, and you would have been my guardian,   885
would you? To have taken care of my estate, that half of 't
should never come to me, by letting long leases at peppercorn rents?

WIDOW

If I would have married an old man, 'tis well known I might
have married an earl, nay, what's more, a judge, and been   890
covered the winter nights with the lambskins, which I prefer
to the ermines of nobles. And dost thou think I would wrong
my poor minor there for you?

FREEMAN

Your minor is a chopping minor, God bless him.

(Strokes JERRY *on the head)*

OLDFOX

Your minor may be a major of horse or foot for his big-   895
ness; and it seems you will have the cheating of your minor
to yourself.

WIDOW

Pray sir, bear witness. Cheat my minor! I'll bring my action
of the case for the slander.

FREEMAN

Nay, I would bear false witness for thee now, widow, since   900

---

880 *scorched trencher* heated platter, usually of metal or earthenware,
  used as a warming-pan
881 *Scotch warming-pan* 'a chambermaid who lay in the bed a while to
  warm it for the intending occupant' (*OED*); hence, a wench
885 *fobus* fool (?), swindler (? cf. '*Fob*, a cheat, trick' (*B.E.*))
887–8 *peppercorn rents* nominal rents of a peppercorn a year, demanded
  to make a free land lease good in law
891 *lambskins* used to line the robes of judges, who were known as
  'Lamb-skin-men' (*B.E.*)
894 *chopping* strapping, healthy
898–9 *action of the case* 'Action upon the Case . . . is a general Action
  given for redress of wrongs done to any Man without force, and
  by Law not especially provided for' (Blount); such wrongs include
  slander

you have done me justice and have thought me the fitter
man for you.

WIDOW

Fair and softly, sir; 'tis my minor's case more than my own.
And I must do him justice now on you.

FREEMAN

How?   905

OLDFOX

So then.

WIDOW

You are first, I warrant, some renegado from the inns of
court and the law, and thou'lt come to suffer for't by the
law: that is, be hanged.

JERRY [*To the* WIDOW]

Not about your neck, forsooth, I hope.   910

FREEMAN

But, madam—

OLDFOX

Hear the court.

WIDOW

Thou art some debauched, drunken, lewd, hectoring, gaming
companion, and want'st some widow's old gold to nick upon;
but I thank you, sir, that's for my lawyers.   915

FREEMAN

Faith, we should ne'er quarrel about that, for guineas would
serve my turn. But, widow—

WIDOW

Thou art a foul-mouthed boaster of thy lust, a mere bragga-
docio of thy strength for wine and women, and wilt belie
thyself more than thou dost women, and art every way a   920
base deceiver of women; and would deceive me too, would
you?

FREEMAN

Nay, faith, widow, this is judging without seeing the evidence.

WIDOW

I say you are a worn-out whore-master at five and twenty
both in body and fortune, and cannot be trusted by the   925

---

905 *How?* an interjection, like the modern 'What?'
907 *renegado* deserter
914 *nick upon* gamble with
916 *guineas* i.e., new gold, first minted in 1663; Pepys found them 'very
     convenient, and of easy disposal' (29 October 1666)

common wenches of the town lest you should not pay 'em,
nor by the wives of the town lest you should pay 'em; so
you want women, and would have me your bawd to procure
'em for you.

FREEMAN

Faith, if you had any good acquaintance, widow, 'twould 930
be civilly done of thee, for I am just come from sea.—

WIDOW

I mean, you would have me keep you that you might turn
keeper, for poor widows are only used like bawds by you:
you go to church with us but to get other women to lie with.
In fine, you are a cheating, chousing spendthrift, and having 935
sold your own annuity, would waste my jointure.

JERRY

And make havoc of our estate personal, and all our old gilt
plate. I should soon be picking up all our mortgaged apostle
spoons, bowls, and beakers out of most of the ale-houses
betwixt 'Hercules' Pillars' and 'The Boatswain' in Wapping; 940
nay, and you'd be scouring amongst my trees, and make 'em
knock down one another like routed, reeling watchmen at
midnight. Would you so, bully?

FREEMAN

Nay, prithee, widow, hear me.

WIDOW

No, sir. I'd have you to know, thou pitiful, paltry, lath- 945
backed fellow, if I would have married a young man, 'tis
well known I could have had any young heir in Norfolk,

926–7 *pay . . . pay* (1) remunerate (2) satisfy (3) requite with just
    deserts; thus whores think him penniless or impotent, wives potent
    and diseased
933 *keeper* a man who keeps mistresses
935 *chousing* swindling
938 *picking up* buying back(?)
938–9 *apostle spoons* 'Old-fashioned silver spoons, the handles of which
    end in figures of the Apostles. They were the usual present of
    sponsors at baptisms.' (*OED*)
940 *Hercules . . . Wapping* i.e., the entire length of London, from the
    east end at Wapping (where 'The Boatswain' has not been identified)
    to 'Hercules' Pillars' at Hyde Park Corner, then at the westernmost
    edge of the city
941 *scouring* rampaging; the scourers were disorderly gangs who roamed
    London by night, breaking windows, molesting wayfarers, and
    knocking down watchmen. Jerry fears his timber would be felled
    and sold.

nay, the hopefull'st young man this day at the King's Bench
bar; I, that am a relict and executrix of known plentiful
assets and parts, who understand myself and the law. And   950
would you have me under covert-baron again? No, sir, no
covert-baron for me.

FREEMAN

But, dear widow, hear me. I value you only, not your
jointure.

WIDOW

Nay, sir, hold there. I know your love to a widow is covet-   955
ousness of her jointure. And a widow a little stricken in
years with a good jointure is like an old mansion house in a
good purchase: never valued, but take one, take t'other; and
perhaps when you are in possession you'd neglect it, let it
drop to the ground, for want of necessary repairs or expenses   960
upon't.

FREEMAN

No, widow, one would be sure to keep all tight when one is
to forfeit one's lease by dilapidation.

WIDOW

Fie fie, I neglect my business with this foolish discourse of
love.—Jerry, child, let me see the list of the jury. I'm sure   965
my cousin Olivia has some relations amongst 'em. But where
is she?

FREEMAN

Nay, widow, but hear me one word only.

WIDOW

Nay, sir, no more, pray. I will no more harken again to your
foolish love-motions than to offers of arbitration.   970

                    (*Exeunt* WIDOW *and* JERRY)

FREEMAN

Well, I'll follow thee yet; for he that has a pretension at
court, or to a widow, must never give over for a little ill
usage.

OLDFOX

Therefore I'll get her by assiduity, patience, and long suffer-

---

948 *hopefull'st* most promising
948 *King's Bench* 'the supreme court of common law in the kingdom'
     (*OED*)
950 *parts* possessions
951 *under covert-baron* under the protection of her lord—law-French
     term for a married woman
957–8 *in a good purchase* i.e., as part of an estate bought on favourable
     terms

ings, which you will not undergo; for you idle young fellows   975
leave off love when it comes to be business, and industry
gets more women than love.

FREEMAN

Ay, industry, the fool's and old man's merit; but I'll be
industrious too and make a business on't, and get her by law,
wrangling, and contests, and not by sufferings. And, because   980
you are no dangerous rival, I'll give thee counsel, major.

> If you litigious widow e'er would gain,
> Sigh not to her, but by the law complain;
> To her, as to a bawd, defendant sue
> With statutes, and make justice pimp for you.   985

(Exeunt)

Finis actus secundi

Act III, Scene i

Westminster Hall

Enter MANLY *and* FREEMAN, *two* SAILORS *behind*

MANLY

I hate this place, worse than a man that has inherited a
Chancery suit. I wish I were well out on't again.

FREEMAN

Why, you need not be afraid of this place, for a man without money needs no more fear a crowd of lawyers than a
crowd of pickpockets.   5

Westminster Hall begun 1097, rebuilt 1399, and housing from 1224
to 1882 the law courts of England: Common Pleas at the lower
end, and at the upper the King's Bench on the right and Chancery
on the left; Equity and the Exchequer shared an adjacent chamber.
At this period, the hall was lined with stalls selling books, law
stationery, haberdashery, and toys.
s.d. *two* SAILORS Tom and Jack, Manly's attendants from Act I;
Jack is addressed at 490, and another 'of your salt-water sharks'
(447), presumably Tom, robs Jerry off-stage between 405 and 428. No
early editions describe their movements, but all difficulties disappear
if we assume that normally they follow Manly throughout.
2 *Chancery suit* 'of eternal continuance, as thousands have found true
by woeful experience' (Tom Brown, *Amusements*, ed. A. L. Hay-
ward (1927), p. 38)

Graverlot Del. C. Mosley Invent. Sculp.

MANLY

This, the reverend of the law would have thought the palace
or residence of justice; but, if it be, she lives here with the
state of a Turkish emperor, rarely seen; and besieged rather
than defended by her numerous black guard here.

FREEMAN

Methinks 'tis like one of their own halls in Christmas time,   10
whither from all parts fools bring their money to try by the
dice (not the worst judges) whether it shall be their own or
no; but after a tedious fretting and wrangling they drop
away all their money on both sides, and, finding neither the
better at last, go emptily and lovingly away together to the   15
tavern, joining their curses against the young lawyers' box,
that sweeps all like the old ones.

MANLY

Spoken like a revelling Christmas lawyer.

FREEMAN

Yes, I was one, I confess, but was fain to leave the law out
of conscience and fall to making false musters; rather chose   20
to cheat the king than his subjects, plunder rather than take
fees.

MANLY

Well, a plague and a purse-famine light on the law, and that

6 *the reverend . . . thought* either 'those who respect the law would
    suppose' or 'respected lawyers would like us to think'
9 *black guard* a triple pun: (1) the Emperor's swarthy attendants (2)
    black-robed lawyers (3) a gang of street urchins who lived on their
    wits and tongues, like the lawyers: '*We . . . are the* City Black-Guard
    *. . . give us a Penny or a Half-penny amongst us, and you shall
    hear any of us . . . say the* Lords-Prayer *backwards. Swear the* Com-
    pass *round; give a new Curse to every step in the* Monument, *call a*
    Whore *as many proper Names as a* Peer *has Titles*' (Ned Ward, *The
    London Spy*, ed. Ralph Straus (1924), pp. 36-7)
10 *Christmas time* At the Inns of Court, gambling was permitted and
    legal between Christmas and Twelfth Night.
13-14 *drop away* lose
16 *young lawyers' box* i.e., the house 'bank': 'what the Dicers allow
    out of each winning to the Butlers Box, usually amounts to about
    50 *l.* a day and night, wherewith, a small Contribution from each
    Student, are the great charges of the whole *Christmas* defrayed'
    (Chamberlayne, II, 230-1)
17 *the old ones* i.e., the old lawyers' cash-box; in gambling and litiga-
    tion, the contestants both lose, and only the lawyers' boxes gain
20 *false musters* Army officers were paid subsistence for each man on
    their muster-roll; sometimes they entered false names and pocketed
    the cash, like Plume in Farquhar's *The Recruiting Officer* (1706,
    I. i).

female limb of it who dragged me hither today! But prithee,
go see if in that crowd of daggled gowns there *(Pointing to a*   25
crowd of lawyers at the end of the stage), thou canst find her.
                                        (Exit FREEMAN*)*

Manet MANLY

How hard it is to be an hypocrite!
At least to me, who am but newly so.
I thought it once a kind of knavery,
Nay, cowardice, to hide one's faults; but now   30
The common frailty, love, becomes my shame.
He must not know I love th'ungrateful still,
Lest he contemn me more than she; for I,
It seems, can undergo a woman's scorn
But not a man's—   35

Enter to him FIDELIA

FIDELIA
Sir, good sir, generous captain.
MANLY
Prithee, kind impertinence, leave me. Why should'st thou
follow me, flatter my generosity now, since thou know'st I
have no money left? If I had it, I'd give it thee to buy my
quiet.   40
FIDELIA
I never followed yet, sir, reward or fame, but you alone; nor
do I now beg anything but leave to share your miseries. You
should not be a niggard of 'em, since, methinks, you have
enough to spare. Let me follow you now because you hate
me, as you have often said.   45
MANLY
I ever hated a coward's company, I must confess.
FIDELIA
Let me follow you till I am none, then, for you, I'm sure,
will through such worlds of dangers that I shall be inured to
'em; nay, I shall be afraid of your anger more than danger,
and so turn valiant out of fear. Dear captain, do not cast me   50

25 *daggled* spattered with mud
25-6 s.d. (*Pointing . . . stage*) probably in the wings, though Raymond
     Williams supposes them painted on the back scene (*Drama in Per-*
     formance (1954, rev. 1968), p. 85)

off till you have tried me once more; do not, do not go to
sea again without me.

MANLY

Thou to sea! To court, thou fool. Remember the advice I
gave thee: thou art a handsome spaniel, and canst fawn
naturally. Go, busk about, and run thyself into the next   55
great man's lobby. First fawn upon the slaves without, and
then run into the lady's bedchamber; thou may'st be admitted
at last to tumble her bed. Go, seek, I say, and lose me, for I
am not able to keep thee. I have not bread for myself.

FIDELIA

Therefore I will not go, because then I may help and serve   60
you.

MANLY

Thou!

FIDELIA

I warrant you, sir; for at worst I could beg or steal for you.

MANLY

Nay, more bragging! Dost thou not know there's venturing
your life in stealing? Go, prithee, away. Thou art as hard to   65
shake off as that flattering, effeminating mischief, love.

FIDELIA

Love, did you name? Why, you are not so miserable as to be
yet in love, sure?

MANLY

No, no; prithee away, be gone, or—. *(Aside)* I had almost
discovered my love and shame. Well, if I had? That thing   70
could not think the worse of me.—Or if he did?—No.—
Yes, he shall know it—he shall—but then I must never leave
him, for they are such secrets that make parasites and pimps
lords of their masters; for any slavery or tyranny is easier
than love's.—[*To* FIDELIA] Come hither. Since thou art so   75
forward to serve me, hast thou but resolution enough to
endure the torture of a secret? For such, to some, is insupportable.

FIDELIA

I would keep it as safe as if your dear, precious life
depended on't.   80

71 *if he* Q1–2, 0 (if I Q3–8)

55 *busk about* cruise around
64–5 *venturing . . . stealing* Robbery and great larceny, 'when the things
    stollen exceed the value of 12 pence', were felonies punishable by
    death (Phillips).

MANLY

Damn your dearness. It concerns more than my life—my honour.

FIDELIA

Doubt it not, sir.

MANLY

And do not discover it by too much fear of discovering it;
but have a great care you let not Freeman find it out.　85

FIDELIA

I warrant you, sir. I am already all joy with the hopes of
your commands, and shall be all wings in the execution of
'em; speak quickly, sir.

MANLY

You said you would beg for me.

FIDELIA

I did, sir.　　　　　　　　　　　　　　　　　　　90

MANLY

Then you shall beg for me.

FIDELIA

With all my heart, sir.

MANLY

That is, pimp for me.

FIDELIA

How, sir!

MANLY

D'ye start? Think'st thou, thou could'st do me any other　95
service? Come, no dissembling honour. I know you can do it
handsomely; thou wert made for't. You have lost your time
with me at sea; you must recover it.

FIDELIA

Do not, sir, beget yourself more reasons for your aversion
to me, and make my obedience to you a fault. I am the　100
unfittest in the world to do you such a service.

MANLY

Your cunning arguing against it shows but how fit you are
for it. No more dissembling. Here, I say, you must go use it
for me to Olivia.

FIDELIA

To her, sir?　　　　　　　　　　　　　　　　　105

---

88 *quickly, sir* Q1–2, 0 (quickly Q3–8)

---

97 *lost* wasted

MANLY

Go flatter, lie, kneel, promise, anything to get her for me. I
cannot live unless I have her. Didst thou not say thou
wouldst do anything to save my life? And she said you had
a persuading face.

FIDELIA

But did not you say, sir, your honour was dearer to you   110
than your life? And would you have me contribute to the
loss of that, and carry love from you to the most infamous,
most false, and—

MANLY *(Sighs, aside)*

And most beautiful!

FIDELIA

—most ungrateful woman that ever lived? For sure she must   115
be so that could desert you so soon, use you so basely, and
so lately too. Do not, do not forget it, sir, and think—

MANLY

No, I will not forget it, but think of revenge. I will lie with
her out of revenge. Go, be gone, and prevail for me, or never
see me more.   120

FIDELIA

You scorned her last night.

MANLY

I know not what I did last night; I dissembled last night.

FIDELIA

Heavens!

MANLY

Be gone, I say, and bring me love or compliance back, or
hopes at least, or I'll never see thy face again, by—   125

FIDELIA

O do not swear, sir; first hear me.

MANLY

I am impatient; away, you'll find me here till twelve.

(Turns away)

FIDELIA

Sir—

MANLY

Not one word, no insinuating argument more, or soothing
persuasion; you'll have need of all your rhetoric with her.   130

121 *last night* Eliza's departure for the play in II. 463 suggests that
   Manly's interview with Olivia took place during the late afternoon.

Go, strive to alter her, not me; be gone.
   (Exit MANLY *at the end of the stage* [*followed by* SAILORS])

       Manet FIDELIA

FIDELIA

Should I discover to him now my sex,
And lay before him his strange cruelty,
'Twould but incense it more.—No, 'tis not time.
For his love must I then betray my own?   135
Were ever love or chance, till now, severe?
Or shifting woman posed with such a task?
Forced to beg that which kills her, if obtained,
And give away her lover not to lose him!   *(Exit* FIDELIA)

Enter WIDOW BLACKACRE *in the middle of half a dozen lawyers,*
whispered to by a fellow in black; JERRY BLACKACRE *following*
the crowd [*which includes* SERJEANT PLODDON, QUAINT, BLUNDER,
and PETULANT]

WIDOW

Offer me a reference, you saucy companion, you! D'ye know   140
who you speak to? Art thou a solicitor in Chancery, and
offer a reference? A pretty fellow!—Master Serjeant
Ploddon, here's a fellow has the impudence to offer me a
reference.

SERJEANT PLODDON

Who's that has the impudence to offer a reference within   145
these walls?

WIDOW

Nay, for a splitter of causes to do't!

SERJEANT PLODDON

No, madam; to a lady learned in the law, as you are, the
offer of a reference were to impose upon you.

WIDOW

No no, never fear me for a reference, Master Serjeant. But   150
come, have you not forgot your brief? Are you sure you
shan't make the mistake of—hark you. *(Whispers)* Go, then,

137 *shifting* evasive, deceitful
140 *reference* i.e., to settle out of court by submitting a controversial
    Chancery suit to the Master in Ordinary for arbitration, which
    would rob the Widow of her fun
147 *splitter of causes* lawyer who subdivided a suit, pleaded each part
    separately and so earned multiple fees; the Widow retains a Master
    Splitcause in her Chancery suit at 272

go to your Court of Common Pleas, and say one thing
over and over again. You do it so naturally you'll never be
suspected for protracting time.   155

SERJEANT PLODDON

Come, I know the course of the court, and your business.

                                    (*Exit* SERJEANT PLODDON)

WIDOW

Let's see, Jerry, where are my minutes?—Come, Master
Quaint, pray go talk a great deal for me in Chancery; let
your words be easy and your sense hard; my cause requires
it. Branch it bravely, and deck my cause with flowers that the   160
snake may lie hidden. Go, go, and be sure you remember the
decree of my Lord Chancellor *tricesimo quart'* of the Queen.

QUAINT

I will, as I see cause, extenuate or examplify matter of fact,
baffle truth with impudence, answer exceptions with questions, though never so impertinent; for reasons give 'em   165
words, for law and equity tropes and figures; and so relax
and enervate the sinews of their argument with the oil of my
eloquence. But when my lungs can reason no longer, and
not being able to say anything more for our cause, say everything of our adversary, whose reputation, though never so   170
clear and evident in the eye of the world, yet with sharp
invectives—

WIDOW

Alias, Billingsgate.

---

163 *examplify* Q1, 0 (amplify Q2–8)

153 *Common Pleas* 'so called, because there are debated the usual
    Pleas between Subject and Subject . . . None but Sergeants at Law
    may plead in this Court' (Chamberlayne, II, 100)
158 *Chancery* 'the Court of Equity & Conscience, moderating the
    severity of other Courts that are more strictly tied to the rigour of
    the Law' (Phillips); 'the less it is perplexed with the quirks of
    Lawyers the more it is guided by Conscience' (Chamberlayne,
    II, 120–1)
160 *Branch it bravely* Decorate it handsomely (with rhetorical ornament)
162 *tricesimo . . . Queen* the thirty-fourth year of Elizabeth I's reign:
    1591
163 *extenuate or examplify* diminish or enlarge
163 *matter of fact* legal term used to distinguish verifiable fact from
    inference or opinion
164 *baffle* confuse, deceive
165 *impertinent* irrelevant or trivial
173 *Billingsgate* 'Scolding, ill Language, foul Words' (*B.E.*), common at
    the fish market in Thames Street

QUAINT

—with poignant and sour invectives, I say, I will deface,
wipe out, and obliterate his fair reputation, even as a record   175
with the juice of lemons; and tell such a story (for the truth
on't is, all that we can do for our client in Chancery is
telling a story), a fine story, a long story, such a story—

WIDOW

Go, save thy breath for the cause; talk at the bar, Master
Quaint. You are so copiously fluent you can weary anyone's   180
ears sooner than your own tongue. Go, weary our adversary's
counsel and the court. Go, thou art a fine-spoken person.
Adad, I shall make thy wife jealous of me, if you can but
court the court into a decree for us. Go, get you gone, and
remember—*(Whispers)*   *(Exit* QUAINT*)*   185
Come, Master Blunder, pray bawl soundly for me at the
King's Bench. Bluster, sputter, question, cavil; but be sure
your argument be intricate enough to confound the court,
and then you do my business. Talk what you will, but be
sure your tongue never stand still, for your own noise will   190
secure your sense from censure. 'Tis like coughing or hem-
ming when one has got the belly-ache, which stifles the
unmannerly noise. Go, dear rogue, and succeed; and I'll
invite thee ere it be long to more soused venison.

BLUNDER

I'll warrant you, after your verdict your judgment shall not   195
be arrested upon if's and and's.   [*Exit* BLUNDER]

WIDOW

Come, Master Petulant, let me give you some new instructions for our cause in the Exchequer. Are the Barons sat?

PETULANT

Yes, no; may be they are, may be they are not. What know
I? What care I?   200

---

184 *gone, and* Q1, 0 (gone, Q2–8)

---

174 *poignant* sharp, severe
183 *Adad* 'an expletive of asseveration or emphasis' (*OED*)
194 *soused* pickled
196 *arrested* i.e., brought to a halt on grounds of error; all proceedings
     are then set aside and an acquittal given
198 *Exchequer* 'Here are tryed all Causes which belong to the Kings
     Treasury or Revenue, as touching Accounts, Disbursements, Cus-
     toms, and all Fines imposed upon any Man' (Chamberlayne, II, 106)
198 *Barons* judges of the Court of Exchequer, 'and they are called
     Barons, because *Barons* of the Realm were wont to be employed
     in that Office' (Blount)

WIDOW

Heyday! I wish you would but snap up the counsel on t'other side anon at the bar as much, and have a little more patience with me, that I might instruct you a little better.

PETULANT

You instruct me! What is my brief for, mistress?

WIDOW

Ay, but you seldom read your brief but at the bar, if you do 205 it then.

PETULANT

Perhaps I do, perhaps I don't, and perhaps 'tis time enough. Pray hold yourself contented, mistress.

WIDOW

Nay, if you go there too, I will not be contented, sir. Though you, I see, will lose my cause for want of speaking, I won't. 210 You shall hear me, and shall be instructed. Let's see your brief.

PETULANT

Send your solicitor to me. Instructed by a woman! I'd have you to know, I do not wear a bar-gown—

WIDOW

By a woman! And I'd have you to know I am no common 215 woman, but a woman conversant in the laws of the land as well as yourself, though I have no bar-gown.

PETULANT

Go to, go to, mistress. You are impertinent, and there's your brief for you. Instruct me!   *(Flings her breviate at her)*

WIDOW

Impertinent to me, you saucy Jack, you! You return my 220 breviate, but where's my fee? You'll be sure to keep that, and scan that so well that if there chance to be but a brass half-crown in't, one's sure to hear on't again. Would you would but look on your breviate half so narrowly! But pray give me my fee too, as well as my brief. 225

PETULANT

Mistress, that's without precedent. When did a counsel ever return his fee, pray? And you are impertinent and ignorant to demand it.

209 *go there* come to that
213 *solicitor* Barristers take their instructions from a client's solicitors, not from a client direct.
219 s.d. *breviate* lawyer's brief
222–3 *brass half-crown* a counterfeit; half-crowns were silver

WIDOW

Impertinent again and ignorant, to me! Gadsbodikins, you
puny upstart in the law, to use me so! you green bag carrier,   230
you murderer of unfortunate causes; the clerk's ink is scarce
off of your fingers, you that newly come from lamp-blacking
the judge's shoes and are not fit to wipe mine; you call me
impertinent and ignorant! I would give thee a cuff on the
ear, sitting the courts, if I were ignorant. Marry gep, if it   235
had not been for me, thou hadst been yet but a hearing
counsel at the bar.   (*Exit* PETULANT)

   Enter MASTER BUTTONGOWN, *crossing the stage in haste*

Master Buttongown, Master Buttongown, whither so fast?
What, won't you stay till we are heard?

BUTTONGOWN

I cannot, Mistress Blackacre, I must be at the council; my   240
lord's cause stays there for me.

WIDOW

And mine suffers here.

BUTTONGOWN

I cannot help it.

WIDOW

I'm undone.

BUTTONGOWN

What's that to me?   245

WIDOW

Consider the five pound fee, if not my cause. That was something to you.

BUTTONGOWN

Away, away; pray be not so troublesome, mistress; I must
be gone.

WIDOW

Nay, but consider a little: I am your old client, my lord but   250
a new one; or let him be what he will, he will hardly be a
better client to you than myself. I hope you believe I shall be

---

229 *Gadsbodikins* (By) God's (=Christ's) dear body
230 *green bag carrier* see I. 424 note
235 *sitting the courts* The punishment 'For striking in *Westminster-Hall*
     whilst the Courts of Justice are sitting, is imprisonment during life,
     and forfeiture of all [the offender's] Estate' (Chamberlayne, I, 46).
235 *Marry gep* (=By Mary Gipcy=By St Mary of Egypt) 'An exclama-
     tion of asseveration, surprise, indignation, etc.' (*OED*)
236–7 *hearing counsel* barrister without a brief, who attends the courts
     but remains silent

in law as long as I live; therefore am no despicable client.
Well, but go to your lord; I know you expect he should make
you a judge one day, but I hope his promise to you will   255
prove a true lord's promise. But, that he might be sure to
fail you, I wish you had his bond for't.

BUTTONGOWN

But what? Will you yet be thus impertinent, mistress?

                                                [*Going*]

WIDOW

Nay, I beseech you, sir, stay, if it be but to tell me my lord's
case. Come, in short.   260

BUTTONGOWN

Nay then—   (*Exit* BUTTONGOWN)

WIDOW

Well, Jerry, observe, child, and lay it up for hereafter: these
are those lawyers who by being in all causes are in none;
therefore, if you would have 'em for you, let your adversary
see 'em, for he may chance to depend upon 'em, and so in   265
being against thee they'll be for thee.

JERRY

Ay, mother; they put me in mind of the unconscionable
wooers of widows, who undertake briskly their matrimonial
business for their money, but when they have got it once,
let who s' will drudge for them. Therefore have a care of   270
'em, forsooth. There's advice for your advice.

WIDOW

Well said, boy.—Come, Master Splitcause, pray go see
when my cause in Chancery comes on, and go speak with
Master Quillet in the King's Bench and Master Quirk in the
Common Pleas, and see how our matters go there.   275

Enter MAJOR OLDFOX

OLDFOX

Lady, a good and propitious morning to you, and may all
your causes go as well as if I myself were judge of 'em.

WIDOW

Sir, excuse me; I am busy, and cannot answer compliments

268–9 *matrimonial business* sexual intercourse
274 *Quillet . . . Quirk* type names for a verbal subtlety or evasion
274 *King's Bench* 'where the King was wont to sit in his own person'
    (Phillips); 'in this Court are handled the Pleas of the Crown, all
    things that concern loss of life, or Member of any Subject . . . all
    Treasons, Felonies, breach of Peace, Oppression, Mis-government'
    (Chamberlayne, II, 96)

in Westminster Hall.—Go, Master Splitcause, and come to
me again to that bookseller's; there I'll stay for you, that you   280
may be sure to find me.

OLDFOX

No, sir, come to the other bookseller's.—I'll attend your
ladyship thither.   *(Exit* SPLITCAUSE*)*

WIDOW

Why to the other?

OLDFOX

Because he is my bookseller, lady.   285

WIDOW

What, to sell you lozenges for your catarrh or medicines for
your corns? What else can a major deal with a bookseller
for?

OLDFOX

Lady, he prints for me.

WIDOW

Why, are you an author?   290

OLDFOX

Of some few essays; deign you, lady, to peruse 'em. *(Aside)*
She is a woman of parts, and I must win her by showing
mine.

The BOOKSELLER'S *BOY [comes forward]*

BOY

Will you see Culpeper, mistress? *Aristotle's Problems? The
Complete Midwife?*   295

WIDOW

No; let's see Dalton, Hughes, Sheppard, Wingate.

BOY

We have no law books.

294-5 *Culpeper . . . Midwife* popular medical guides: Nicholas Culpeper's famous herbal, *The English Physitian* (1652), reached seven
editions by 1669, the spurious *Problemes of Aristotle with other
Philosophers and Phisitions* (1595) was reprinted in 1670, and T.C.'s
The Compleat Midwifes Practice (1656) reached a third edition in
1663; as the Boy is not precise in his offer, other titles may be
intended

296 *Dalton . . . Wingate* legal authors: the seventh edition of Michael
Dalton's *The Countrey Iustice* (1618) appeared in 1666; William
Hughes's most recent book was *Quæries, or choice cæses for moots*
(1675), and William Sheppard's *A Grand Abridgment of the Common and Statute Law* (1675); Edmund Wingate's *The Exact Constable* (?1660) reached its fourth edition in 1676; again, other
titles by these prolific authors may be intended

WIDOW

No? You are a pretty bookseller, then.

OLDFOX

Come, have you e'er a one of my essays left?

BOY

Yes, sir; we have enough, and shall always have 'em.   300

OLDFOX

How so?

BOY

Why, they are good, steady, lasting ware.

OLDFOX

Nay, I hope they will live; let's see.—Be pleased, madam, to
peruse the poor endeavours of my pen; for I have a pen,
though I say it, that—   *(Gives her a book)*   305

JERRY

Pray let me see *St George for Christendom*, or *The Seven
Champions of England*.

WIDOW

No no; give him *The Young Clerk's Guide.*—What, we shall
have you read yourself into a humour of rambling, and
fighting, and studying military discipline and wearing red   310
breeches!

OLDFOX

Nay, if you talk of military discipline, show him my *Treatise
of the Art Military*.

WIDOW

Hold; I would as willingly he should read a play.

JERRY

O pray, forsooth, mother, let me have a play.   315

WIDOW

No, sirrah; there are young students of the law enough
spoiled already by plays. They would make you in love with
your laundress, or, what's worse, some queen of the stage

---

304 *for I have a pen*, Q1, 0 (*omitted* Q2–8)

306–7 *St George . . . England* Amusingly, Jerry confuses the popular
old ballad *St George for England* (which Monsieur recommends as
whore's reading in Act V of *The Gentleman Dancing-Master*) with
Richard Johnson's evergreen prose romance *The most famous History of the Seauen Champions of Christendome* (1596), which
reached its seventh edition in 1670.
308 *The Young Clerk's Guide* by Sir Richard Hutton (1650); the
fourteenth edition appeared in 1673
310–11 *red breeches* see II. 585–6 note

that was a laundress, and so turn keeper before you are of
age.   320

Several crossing the stage

But stay, Jerry, is not that Master What-d'ye-call-him that
goes there, he that offered to sell me a suit in Chancery for
five hundred pound, for a hundred down and only paying the
clerk's fees?

JERRY

Ay, forsooth; 'tis he.   325

WIDOW

Then stay here, and have a care of the bags whilst I follow
him. Have a care of the bags, I say.

JERRY

And do you have a care, forsooth, of the statute against
champerty, I say.   *(Exit* WIDOW*)*

Enter FREEMAN *to them*

FREEMAN

(Aside) So, there's a limb of my widow, which was wont to   330
be inseparable from her; she can't be far. *[Aloud]* How now,
my pretty son-in-law that shall be, where's my widow?

JERRY

My mother, but not your widow, will be forthcoming
presently.

FREEMAN

Your servant, major. What, are you buying furniture for a   335
little sleeping closet, which you miscall a study? For you do
only by your books as by your wenches: bind 'em up neatly
and make 'em fine, for other people to use 'em; and your
bookseller is properly your upholster, for he furnishes your
room rather than your head.   340

OLDFOX

Well, well, good sea-lieutenant, study you your compass;
that's more than your head can deal with. *(Aside)* I will go
find out the widow, to keep her out of his sight, or he'll
board her whilst I am treating a peace.   *(Exit* OLDFOX*)*

Manent FREEMAN, JERRY[, BOY]

319 *keeper* one who keeps a mistress
329 *champerty* legal term for an illegal bargain where an outsider con-
     tributed to the costs of a suit in exchange for a share of the spoils
     if it succeeded
335 *furniture* furnishings, ornaments, like Olivia's china in II. 446
339 *upholster* a dealer in small items of furniture (the modern *up-
     holsterer* is more limited in application)
344 *treating* negotiating, arranging terms for

JERRY [*To* BOY]

Nay, prithee, friend, now let me have but *The Seven Champions*; you shall trust me no longer than till my mother's Master Splitcause comes, for I hope he'll lend me wherewithal to pay for't.

FREEMAN

Lend thee! Here, I'll pay him. Do you want money, squire? I'm sorry a man of your estate should want money.   350

JERRY

Nay, my mother will ne'er let me be at age; and till then, she says—

FREEMAN

At age! Why, you are at age already to have spent an estate, man; there are younger than you have kept their women these three years, have had half a dozen claps, and lost as   355 many thousand pounds at play.

JERRY

Ay, they are happy sparks! Nay, I know some of my schoolfellows who, when we were at school, were two years younger than me, but now, I know not how, are grown men before me, and go where they will and look to themselves; but my   360 curmudgeonly mother won't allow me wherewithal to be a man of myself with.

FREEMAN

Why, there 'tis; I knew your mother was in the fault. Ask but your schoolfellows what they did to be men of themselves.   365

JERRY

Why, I know they went to law with their mothers, for they say there's no good to be done upon a widow mother till one goes to law with her; but mine is as plaguey a lawyer as any's of our Inn. Then would she marry too, and cut down my trees. Now I should hate, man, to have my father's wife   370 kissed and slapped and t'other thing too (you know what I mean) by another man; and our trees are the purest, tall, even, shady twigs, by my fa—

---

355 *these* Q1, 0 (this Q2–8)

355 *claps* attacks of gonorrhœa
360 *look to* take care of
361-2 *a man of myself* my own master
366 *went to law with* sought legal redress from
372 *purest* finest (an adjective popular with the unsophisticated, like Margery in *The Country Wife* (1675, III. i, 10))

FREEMAN

Come, squire, let your mother and your trees fall as she
pleases, rather than wear this gown and carry green bags all   375
thy life and be pointed at for a Tony. But you shall be able
to deal with her yet the common way: thou shalt make false
love to some lawyer's daughter, whose father, upon the
hopes of thy marrying her, shall lend thee money and law to
preserve thy estate and trees; and thy mother is so ugly   380
nobody will have her, if she cannot cut down thy trees.

JERRY

Nay, if I had but anybody to stand by me, I am as stomachful as another.

FREEMAN

That will I; I'll not see any hopeful young gentleman abused.

BOY *(Aside)*

By any but yourself.   385

JERRY

The truth on't is, mine's as arrant a widow mother to her
poor child as any's in England. She won't so much as let one
have sixpence in one's pocket to see a motion, or the dancing
of the ropes, or—

FREEMAN

Come, you shan't want money; there's gold for you.   390

JERRY

O Lord, sir, two guineas! D'ye lend me this? Is there no trick
in't? Well, sir, I'll give you my bond for security.

FREEMAN

No no, thou hast given me thy face for security; anybody
would swear thou dost not look like a cheat. You shall have
what you will of me, and if your mother will not be kinder   395
to you, come to me, who will.

JERRY

(Aside) By my fa— he's a curious fine gentleman! [*Aloud*]
But will you stand by one?

FREEMAN

If you can be resolute.

JERRY

Can be resolved! Gad, if she gives me but a cross word, I'll   400
leave her tonight and come to you. But now I have got

376 *Tony* 'a silly Fellow, or Ninny' (*B.E.*)
382–3 *stomachful* courageous
388–9 *motion . . . ropes* puppet shows and tightrope walkers, both
    popular entertainments at Bartholomew Fair (see II. 622 note)

money, I'll go to Jack of All Trades at t'other end of the
Hall, and buy the neatest, purest things—

FREEMAN [*Aside*]

And I'll follow the great boy, and my blow at his mother:
steal away the calf, and the cow will follow you.   405

    (*Exit* JERRY, *followed by* FREEMAN[; *the* BOOKSELLER'S BOY
retires])

Enter, on the other side, MANLY [*followed by* SECOND SAILOR],
WIDOW BLACKACRE, *and* OLDFOX

MANLY

Damn your cause! Can't you lose it without me?—which
you are like enough to do, if it be, as you say, an honest
one. I will suffer no longer for't.

WIDOW

Nay, captain, I tell you, you are my prime witness; and the
cause is just now coming on, Master Splitcause tells me.   410
Lord, methinks you should take a pleasure in walking here,
as half you see now do, for they have no business here, I
assure you.

MANLY

Yes, but I'll assure you, then, their business is to persecute
me. But d'ye think I'll stay any longer, to have a rogue,   415
because he knows my name, pluck me aside and whisper a
news-book secret to me with a stinking breath? A second
come piping angry from the court, and sputter in my face
his tedious complaints against it? A third law-coxcomb,
because he saw me once at a reader's dinner, come and put   420
me a long law case, to make a discovery of his indefatigable
dullness and my wearied patience? A fourth, a most barbarous civil rogue, who will keep a man half an hour in the
crowd with a bowed body and a hat off, acting the reformed
sign of the Salutation Tavern, to hear his bountiful profes- 425

---

402 *Jack of All Trades* apparently the name of a stall selling toys
404 *blow at* plot against (?)
417 *news-book secret* A secret that's published is no secret at all.
420 *reader's dinner* banquet given by a distinguished lecturer in law at
    one of the Inns of Court: 'During the Readings, which heretofore
    was three Weeks and three Days . . . the Reader keeps a Constant
    and Sumptuous Feasting, Inviting the Chief Nobles, Judges, Bishops,
    Great Officers of the Kingdom, and sometimes the King himself'
    (Thomas Delaune, *Angliæ Metropolis* (1690), p. 170)
425 *Salutation Tavern* Pepys visited a tavern of this name in Billingsgate
    on 5 March, 1659/60, but there were several others; the sign, re-
    formed under the Commonwealth, showed two men bowing politely,
    instead of the Angel Gabriel saluting Mary.

sions of service and friendship, whilst he cares not if I were
damned and I am wishing him hanged out of my way? I'd
as soon run the gauntlet as walk t'other turn.

Enter to them JERRY BLACKACRE *without his bags, but laden with
trinkets, which he endeavours to hide from his mother, and
followed at a distance by* FREEMAN

WIDOW
O, are you come, sir? But where have you been, you ass?
And how come you thus laden?   430

JERRY
Look here, forsooth, mother; now here's a duck, here's a
boar-cat, and here's an owl. (*Making a noise with catcalls,
and other suchlike instruments*)

WIDOW
Yes, there is an owl, sir.

OLDFOX
He's an ungracious bird, indeed.

WIDOW
But go, thou trangam, and carry back those trangams, which   435
thou hast stolen or purloined; for nobody would trust a
minor in Westminster Hall, sure.

JERRY
Hold yourself contented, forsooth; I have these commodities
by a fair bargain and sale, and there stands my witness and
creditor.   440

WIDOW
How's that!—What, sir, d'ye think to get the mother by
giving the child a rattle?—But where are my bags, my writings, you rascal?

JERRY (*Aside*)
O law! Where are they indeed?

WIDOW
How, sirrah? Speak, come—   445

MANLY (*Apart to him*)
You can tell her, Freeman, I suppose?

FREEMAN (*Apart to him*)
'Tis true, I made one of your salt-water sharks steal 'em

428 s.d. *trinkets* cheap toys
432 *boar-cat* tom-cat
432 s.d. *catcalls* whistles or squeakers which make funny noises
435 *trangam* (1) pseudo-legal term for anything contemptible (2) toy

whilst he was eagerly choosing his commodities, as he calls
'em, in order to my design upon his mother.

WIDOW

Won't you speak? Where were you, I say, you son of a—an   450
unfortunate woman?—O, major, I'm undone. They are all
that concern my estate, my jointure, my husband's deed of
gift, my evidences for all my suits now depending! What will
become of them?

FREEMAN

(Aside) I'm glad to hear this. [*Aloud*] They'll be safe, I   455
warrant you, madam.

WIDOW

O where, where? Come, you villain, along with me, and show
me where.   *(Exeunt* WIDOW, JERRY, OLDFOX*)*

Manent MANLY, FREEMAN [, SAILOR]

MANLY

Thou hast taken the right way to get a widow, by making
her great boy rebel; for when nothing will make a widow   460
marry, she'll do't to cross her children. But canst thou in
earnest marry this harpy, this volume of shrivelled blurred
parchments and law, this attorney's desk?

FREEMAN

Ay ay, I'll marry and live honestly—that is, give my creditors,
not her, due benevolence: pay my debts.   465

MANLY

Thy creditors, you see, are not so barbarous as to put thee
in prison, and wilt thou commit thyself to a noisome dun-
geon for thy life, which is the only satisfaction thou canst
give thy creditors by this match?

FREEMAN

Why, is not she rich?   470

MANLY

Ay, but he that marries a widow for her money will find
himself as much mistaken as the widow that marries a young
fellow for due benevolence, as you call it.

FREEMAN

Why, d'ye think I shan't deserve wages? I'll drudge faithfully.   475

MANLY

I tell thee again, he that is the slave in the mine has the least
propriety in the ore. You may dig and dig, but if thou

449 *in order to* for the sake of, to bring about

wouldst have her money, rather get to be her trustee than
her husband; for a true widow will make over her estate to
anybody, and cheat herself, rather than be cheated by her   480
children or a second husband.

Enter to them JERRY, *running in a fright*

JERRY

O law! I'm undone, I'm undone! My mother will kill me.—
You said you'd stand by one.

FREEMAN

So I will, my brave squire, I warrant thee.

JERRY

Ay, but I dare not stay till she comes; for she's as furious,   485
now she has lost her writings, as a bitch when she has lost
her puppies.

MANLY

The comparison's handsome!

JERRY

O, she's here!

Enter WIDOW BLACKACRE *and* OLDFOX

FREEMAN (*To the* SAILOR)

Take him, Jack, and make haste with him to your master's   490
lodging; and be sure you keep him up till I come.

(*Exeunt* JERRY *and* SAILOR)

WIDOW

O my dear writings! Where's this heathen rogue, my minor?

FREEMAN

Gone to drown or hang himself.

WIDOW

No, I know him too well; he'll ne'er be *felo de se* that way,
but he may go and choose a guardian of his own head and   495
so be *felo de ses biens*, for he has not yet chosen one.

491 *up* upstairs (and so out of sight from pursuers in the street)
494 *felo de se* 'Is he that commits Felony by murdring himself'
       (Blount); he is denied Christian burial, and forfeits his goods to the
       Crown
495 *choose a guardian* 'A Son at the age of 14, may chuse his Guardian,
       may claim his Land, . . . may consent to Marriage, may, by Will,
       dispose of Goods and Chattels' (Chamberlayne, I, 297).
495 *of his own head* as he pleases, of his own choice
496 *felo de ses biens* literally 'a felon with regard to his goods': a
       pseudo-legal term coined by the Widow, who fears Jerry will
       appoint a guardian who will mismanage the goods entrusted to him

FREEMAN *(Aside)*
  Say you so? And he shan't want one.

WIDOW
  But now I think on't, 'tis you, sir, have put this cheat upon
  me; for there is a saying, 'take hold of a maid by her smock
  and a widow by her writings, and they cannot get from you'.   500
  But I'll play fast and loose with you yet, if there be law, and
  my minor and writings are not forthcoming, I'll bring my
  action of detinue or trover. But first, I'll try to find out this
  guardianless, graceless villain. Will you jog, major?

MANLY
  If you have lost your evidence, I hope your causes cannot   505
  go on, and I may be gone?

WIDOW
  O no, stay but a making-water while, as one may say, and
  I'll be with you again.   *(Exeunt* WIDOW *and* OLDFOX*)*

                Manent MANLY, FREEMAN

FREEMAN
  Well, sure, I am the first man that ever began a love intrigue
  in Westminster Hall.   510

MANLY
  No, sure; for the love to a widow generally begins here, and
  as the widow's cause goes against the heir or executors, the
  jointure rivals commence their suit to the widow.

FREEMAN
  Well, but how, pray, have you passed your time here since
  I was forced to leave you alone? You have had a great deal   515
  of patience.

MANLY
  Is this a place to be alone or have patience in? But I have
  had patience indeed, for I have drawn upon me, since I came,
  but three quarrels and two lawsuits.

497 *want* lack
499 *a saying* not known
501–2 *and my* if my
503 *detinue* 'a Writ that lieth against him who having goods or chattels
     delivered him to keep, refuseth to deliver them again' (Phillips)
503 *trover* 'an action against him who having found another mans goods,
     refuseth to deliver them upon demand' (Phillips); the Widow sus-
     pects Jerry of collusion (*detinue*) or negligence (*trover*), but as
     Freeman stole the bags, neither action is appropriate here
507 *a making-water while* so Shadwell's boorish country gentleman has
     'not so much as a pissing while' in Act IV of *The Sullen Lovers*
     (1668)

FREEMAN

Nay, faith, you are too curst to be let loose in the world; 520
you should be tied up again in your sea-kennel, called a ship.
But how could you quarrel here?

MANLY

How could I refrain? A lawyer talked peremptorily and
saucily to me, and as good as gave me the lie.

FREEMAN

They do it so often to one another at the bar, that they make 525
no bones on't elsewhere.

MANLY

However, I gave him a cuff on the ear; whereupon he jogs
two men whose backs were turned to us, for they were reading at a bookseller's, to witness I struck him, sitting the
courts; which office they so readily promised that I called 530
'em rascals and knights of the post. One of 'em presently
calls two other absent witnesses, who were coming towards
us at a distance; whilst the other, with a whisper, desires to
know my name, that he might have satisfaction by way of
challenge as t'other by way of writ, but if it were not rather 535
to direct his brother's writ than his own challenge. There,
you see, is one of my quarrels and two of my lawsuits.

FREEMAN

So; and the other two?

MANLY

For advising a poet to leave off writing and turn lawyer,
because he is dull and impudent, and says or writes nothing 540
now but by precedent.

FREEMAN

And the third quarrel?

MANLY

For giving more sincere advice to a handsome, well-dressed
young fellow, who asked it too, not to marry a wench that
he loved and I had lain with. 545

FREEMAN

Nay, if you will be giving your sincere advice to lovers and
poets, you will not fail of quarrels.

---

520 *curst* cantankerous, quarrelsome
531 *knights of the post* see 'The Persons'
531 *presently* immediately
535 *if it were not* i.e., it was surely
547 *fail* keep clear

MANLY

Or if I stay in this place, for I see more quarrels crowding
upon me. Let's be gone and avoid 'em.

Enter NOVEL *at a distance, coming towards them*

A plague on him, that sneer is ominous to us. He is coming   550
upon us, and we shall not be rid of him.

NOVEL

Dear bully, don't look so grum upon me; you told me just
now you had forgiven me a little harmless raillery upon
wooden legs last night.

MANLY

Yes yes; pray be gone, I am talking of business.   555

NOVEL

Can't I hear it? I love thee and will be faithful, and always—

MANLY

Impertinent! 'Tis business that concerns Freeman only.

NOVEL

Well, I love Freeman too, and would not divulge his secret.
Prithee speak, prithee, I must—

MANLY

Prithee let me be rid of thee; I must be rid of thee.   560

NOVEL

Faith, thou canst hardly, I love thee so. Come, I must know
the business.

MANLY

(Aside) So, I have it now. *[Aloud]* Why, if you needs will
know it, he has a quarrel and his adversary bids him bring
two friends with him; now I am one, and we are thinking   565
who we shall have for a third.

Several crossing the stage

NOVEL

A pox, there goes a fellow owes me an hundred pound, and
goes out of town tomorrow. I'll speak with him, and come
to you presently.   *(Exit* NOVEL*)*

MANLY

No, but you won't.   570

FREEMAN

You are dextrously rid of him.

Enter OLDFOX

552 *grum* morose, surly (adj.)
554 *last night* see 121 note

MANLY

To what purpose, since here comes another as impertinent? I know by his grin he is bound hither.

OLDFOX

Your servant, worthy, noble captain. Well, I have left the widow, because she carried me from your company; for, 575 faith, captain, I must needs tell thee, thou art the only officer in England, who was not an Edgehill officer, that I care for.

MANLY

I'm sorry for't.

OLDFOX

Why, wouldst thou have me love them?

MANLY

Anybody, rather than me.   580

OLDFOX

What, you are modest, I see; therefore, too, I love thee.

MANLY

No, I am not modest, but love to brag myself and can't patiently hear you fight over the last civil war. Therefore, go look out the fellow I saw just now here, that walks with his stockings and his sword out at heels, and let him tell you the 585 history of that scar on his cheek, to give you occasion to show yours, got in the field at Bloomsbury, not that of Edgehill. Go to him, poor fellow; he is fasting and has not yet the happiness this morning to stink of brandy and tobacco. Go, give him some to hear you; I am busy.   590

OLDFOX

Well, egad, I love thee now, boy, for thy surliness; thou art no tame captain, I see, that will suffer—

MANLY

An old fox.

OLDFOX

All that shan't make me angry; I consider thou art peevish, and fretting at some ill success at law. Prithee, tell me what 595 ill luck you have met with here.

---

586 *scar on his cheek* 'Scars in the face commonly give a man a certain fierce and martial air, which sets him off to advantage' (Anthony Hamilton, *Memoirs of the Count de Grammont* (1926), p. 165).

587 *Bloomsbury* The open fields to the north of Southampton House, where Russell Square now stands, were favourite duelling grounds.

587-8 *Edgehill* in Warwickshire, site of the first major battle of the Civil War, 23 October 1642; to judge from 616, Oldfox fought on Cromwell's side

595 *ill success* unfavourable outcome

MANLY

You.

OLDFOX

Do I look like the picture of ill luck? Gadsnouns, I love
thee more and more; and shall I tell thee what made me love
thee first?   600

MANLY

Do; that I may be rid of that damned quality and thee.

OLDFOX

'Twas thy wearing that broadsword there.

MANLY

Here, Freeman, let's change. I'll never wear it more.

OLDFOX

How! You won't, sure. Prithee, don't look like one of our
holiday captains nowadays, with a bodkin by your side, your   605
martinet rogues.

MANLY

(Aside) O, then there's hopes. [Aloud] What, d'ye find fault
with martinet? Let me tell you, sir, 'tis the best exercise in
the world, the most ready, most easy, most graceful exercise
that ever was used, and the most—   610

OLDFOX

Nay nay, sir, no more, sir, your servant; if you praise
martinet once, I have done with you, sir. Martinet!
Martinet!   (Exit OLDFOX)

FREEMAN

Nay, you have made him leave you as willingly as ever he
did an enemy, for he was truly for the king and parliament: 615
for the parliament in their list, and for the king in cheating
'em of their pay, and never hurting the king's party in the
field.

Enter a LAWYER *towards them*

MANLY

A pox, this way! Here's a lawyer I know threatening us with
another greeting.   620

598 *Gadsnouns* (By) God's (=Christ's) wounds
602 *broadsword* a short, old-fashioned sword; Oldfox's approval is not
    surprising in view of his name
606 *martinet* the system of arms drill invented by General Jean Martinet,
    a contemporary French drill-master and rigid disciplinarian; Captain
    Wycherley was obliged to learn the exercise during the winter of
    1673–4, when quartered with the fleet at Yarmouth on the Isle of
    Wight during the third Anglo-Dutch war
616 *list* pay-roll

LAWYER

Sir, sir, your very servant. I was afraid you had forgotten
me.

MANLY

I was not afraid you had forgotten me.

LAWYER

No, sir; we lawyers have pretty good memories.

MANLY

You ought to have, by your wits.   625

LAWYER

O, you are a merry gentleman, sir; I remember you were
merry when I was last in your company.

MANLY

I was never merry in thy company, Master Lawyer, sure.

LAWYER

Why, I'm sure you joked upon me and shammed me all night
long.   630

MANLY

Shammed! Prithee, what barbarous law term is that?

LAWYER

Shamming? Why, don't you know that? 'Tis all our way of
wit, sir.

MANLY

I am glad I do not know it, then. Shamming!—What does he
mean by't, Freeman?   635

FREEMAN

Shamming is telling you an insipid, dull lie with a dull face,
which the sly wag the author only laughs at himself; and
making himself believe 'tis a good jest, puts the sham only
upon himself.

MANLY

So your lawyer's jest, I find, like his practice, has more   640
knavery than wit in't. I should make the worst shammer in
England. I must always deal ingenuously; as I will with you,
Master Lawyer, and advise you to be seen rather with
attorneys and solicitors than such fellows as I am; they will
credit your practice more.   645

LAWYER

No, sir; your company's an honour to me.

642 *ingenuously* Q6–7 (ingeniously Q1–5, 8, 0)

629 *shammed me* hoaxed me, 'sent me up'; cf. IV. ii, 24
645 *credit ... more* do more credit to

MANLY

No, faith, go thy ways. There goes an attorney; leave me for
him. Let it be never said a lawyer's civility did him hurt.

LAWYER

No, worthy, honoured sir; I'll not leave you for any attorney,
sure.   650

MANLY

Unless he had a fee in his hand.

LAWYER

Have you any business here, sir? Try me. I'd serve you
sooner than any attorney breathing.

MANLY

Business? *(Aside)* So, I have thought of a sure way. [*Aloud*]
Yes, faith, I have a little business.   655

LAWYER

Have you so, sir? In what court, sir? What is't, sir? Tell me
but how I may serve you, and I'll do't, sir, and take it for
as great an honour—

MANLY

Faith, 'tis for a poor orphan of a sea officer of mine, that
has no money; but if it could be followed *in forma pauperis*,   660
and when the legacy's recovered—

LAWYER

Forma pauperis, sir?

MANLY

Ay, sir.

Several crossing the stage

LAWYER

Master Bumblecase, Master Bumblecase, a word with you.
[*To* MANLY] Sir, I beg your pardon at present; I have a little   665
business—

MANLY

Which is not *in forma pauperis*.   *(Exit* LAWYER*)*

FREEMAN

So, you have now found a way to be rid of people without
quarrelling.

Enter ALDERMAN

---

647 *thy ways* Q2–8 (this way Q1, 0)

---

660 *in forma pauperis* 'Is when any Man, who hath just cause of Sute in
  Chancery, and . . . is not worth Five pounds, . . . shall have Council,
  and Clerks assigned him, without paying Fees' (Blount)

MANLY

But here's a city rogue will stick as hard upon us as if I   670
owed him money.

ALDERMAN

Captain, noble sir, I am yours heartily, d'ye see. Why should
you avoid your old friends?

MANLY

And why should you follow me? I owe you nothing.

ALDERMAN

Out of my hearty respects to you, for there is not a man in   675
England—

MANLY

Thou wouldst save from hanging with the expense of a
shilling only.

ALDERMAN

Nay, nay; but captain, you are like enough to tell me—

MANLY

Truth, which you won't care to hear; therefore you had   680
better go talk with somebody else.

ALDERMAN

No; I know nobody can inform me better of some young wit
or spendthrift, that has a good dipped seat and estate in
Middlesex, Hertfordshire, Essex, or Kent; any of these would
serve my turn. Now, if you knew of such an one, and would   685
but help—

MANLY

You to finish his ruin.

ALDERMAN

I'faith, you should have a snip—

MANLY

Of your nose! You thirty in the hundred rascal, would you
make me your squire setter, you bawd for manors?   690

(Takes him by the nose)

ALDERMAN

O!

FREEMAN

Hold, or here will be your third lawsuit.

683 *dipped seat* mortgaged estate
688 *snip* share, cut
689 *thirty in the hundred rascal* money-lender charging 30 per cent
      interest
690 *setter* a spy who informs thieves of suitable victims
690 *bawd* pimp

ALDERMAN

Gadsprecious, you hectoring person you, are you wild? I
meant you no hurt, sir; I begin to think, as things go, land
security best, and have, for a convenient mortgage, some ten,   695
fifteen, or twenty thousand pound by me.

MANLY

Then go lay it out upon an hospital and take a mortgage of
heaven, according to your city custom, for you think by
laying out a little money to hook in that too hereafter; do,
I say, and keep the poor you've made by taking forfeitures,   700
that heaven may not take yours.

ALDERMAN

No, to keep the cripples you make this war; this war spoils
our trade.

MANLY

Damn your trade; 'tis the better for't.

ALDERMAN

What, will you speak against our trade?   705

MANLY

And dare you speak against the war, our trade?

ALDERMAN

(Aside) Well, he may be a convoy of ships I am concerned in.
[Aloud] Come, captain, I will have a fair correspondency
with you, say what you will.

MANLY

Then prithee be gone.   710

ALDERMAN

No, faith; prithee, captain, let's go drink a dish of laced
coffee, and talk of the times. Come, I'll treat you; nay, you
shall go, for I have no business here.

MANLY

But I have.

ALDERMAN

To pick up a man to give thee a dinner? Come, I'll do thy   715
business for thee.

MANLY

Faith, now I think on't, so you may as well as any man; for

693 *Gadsprecious* (By) God's (=Christ's) precious (?blood)
693 *hectoring* bullying, domineering
697 *hospital* alms-house
707 *convoy* see I. 111 note
708 *have a fair correspondency* be on friendly terms
711–12 *laced coffee* 'Sugar'd' (*B.E.*) coffee

'tis to pick up a man to be bound with me to one who
expects city security, for—

ALDERMAN

Nay, then your servant, captain; business must be done.   720

MANLY

Ay, if it can; but hark you, alderman, without you—

ALDERMAN

Business, sir, I say, must be done;

Several crossing the stage

and there's an officer of the Treasury I have an affair with—
                                               (Exit ALDERMAN*)*

MANLY

You see now what the mighty friendship of the world is;
what all ceremony, embraces, and plentiful professions come   725
to. You are no more to believe a professing friend than a
threatening enemy; and as no man hurts you that tells you
he'll do you a mischief, no man, you see, is your servant
who says he is so. Why the devil, then, should a man be
troubled with the flattery of knaves, if he be not a fool or   730
cully; or with the fondness of fools, if he be not a knave or
cheat?

FREEMAN

Only for his pleasure; for there is some in laughing at fools
and disappointing knaves.

MANLY

That's a pleasure, I think, would cost you too dear, as well   735
as marrying your widow to disappoint her; but, for my part,
I have no pleasure by 'em but in despising 'em wheresoe'er I
meet 'em, and then the pleasure of hoping so to be rid of
'em. But now my comfort is, I am not worth a shilling in the
world, which all the world shall know; and then I'm sure I   740
shall have none of 'em come near me.

FREEMAN

A very pretty comfort, which I think you pay too dear for.
But is the twenty pound gone since the morning?

MANLY

To my boat's crew. Would you have the poor, honest, brave
fellows want?   745

FREEMAN

Rather than you or I.

725 *professions* promises, declarations
731 *fondness* silliness

MANLY

Why, art thou without money, thou who art a friend to
everybody?

FREEMAN

I ventured my last stake upon the squire, to nick him of his
mother, and cannot help you to a dinner, unless you will go   750
dine with my lord—

MANLY

No no; the ordinary is too dear for me where flattery must
pay for my dinner. I am no herald, or poet.

FREEMAN

We'll go then to the bishop's—

MANLY

There you must flatter the old philosophy. I cannot renounce   755
my reason for a dinner.

FREEMAN

Why, then let's go to your alderman's.

MANLY

Hang him, rogue! That were not to dine, for he makes you
drunk with lees of sack before dinner to take away your
stomach; and there you must call usury and extortion God's   760
blessings, or the honest turning of the penny; hear him brag
of the leather breeches in which he trotted first to town, and
make a greater noise with his money in his parlour than his
cashiers do in his counting-house, without hopes of borrowing
a shilling.   765

FREEMAN

Ay, a pox on't; 'tis like dining with the great gamesters, and
when they fall to their common dessert, see the heaps of
gold drawn on all hands, without going to twelve. Let us go
to my Lady Goodly's.

749 *nick him of* win him from
752-3 *the ordinary . . . dinner* i.e., I cannot afford my lord's table, which
    is like a public eating-house or *ordinary*, except that you pay with
    flattery instead of cash
753 *herald, or poet* two sycophants who fawn upon the nobility
755-6 *renounce my reason* The bishop's views are opposed to the
    fashionable new rationalism of Hobbes.
760 *stomach* appetite
767 *common dessert* i.e., their last course is gambling
768 *going to twelve* joining in with an equal share; cf. Shamwell in
    Shadwell's *The Squire of Alsatia* (1688): 'You Rogue, *Cheatly* . . .
    you will go to twelve with the Squire: If you do, I will have my
    snack' (V. i)
769 *Lady Goodly* here given a different character from that of II.
    340-7.

MANLY

There, to flatter her looks, you must mistake her grand- 770
children for her own, praise her cook that she may rail at
him, and feed her dogs, not yourself.

FREEMAN

What d'ye think of eating with your lawyer, then?

MANLY

Eat with him! Damn him; to hear him employ his barbarous
eloquence in a reading upon the two and thirty good bits in 775
a shoulder of veal, and be forced yourself to praise the cold
bribe pie that stinks, and drink law-French wine as rough and
harsh as his law-French. A pox on him, I'd rather dine in the
Temple Rounds or Walks with the knights without noses, or
the knights of the post, who are honester fellows and better 780
company. But let us home, and try our fortune; for I'll stay
no longer here for your damned widow.

FREEMAN

Well, let us go home then; for I must go for my damned
widow, and look after my new damned charge. Three or four
hundred years ago, a man might have dined in this Hall. 785

MANLY

But now the lawyer only here is fed,
And, bully-like, by quarrels gets his bread. *(Exeunt)*

Finis actus tertii

775 *reading* lecture
775–6 *the two . . . veal* from the proverb 'In a shoulder of *veal* there
   are twenty and two good bits'; in *A Collection of English Proverbs*
   (1678), John Ray explains that 'This is a piece of country wit. They
   mean by it, There are twenty (others say forty) bits in a shoulder of
   veal, and but two good ones' (p. 83)
779 *knights without noses* weather-beaten effigies of crusader knights in
   the Round of the Temple Church, where lawyers walked with
   clients and false witnesses plied for hire
785 *dined . . . Hall* where 'all the Kings of *England* since the Conquest
   . . . have . . . kept their Feasts, of Coronation especially; and other
   solemn Feasts, as at *Christmas*, and such like, most commonly'
   (John Stow, *A survey of . . . London,* ed. John Strype (1720), VI, 47);
   the last coronation breakfast here was that of George IV

Act IV, Scene i

MANLY's *Lodging*

Enter MANLY *and* FIDELIA

MANLY

Well, there's success in thy face. Hast thou prevailed, say?

FIDELIA

As I could wish, sir.

MANLY

So; I told thee what thou wert fit for, and thou wouldst not
believe me. Come, thank me for bringing thee acquainted
with thy genius. Well, thou hast mollified her heart for me?   5

FIDELIA

No, sir, not so; but what's better.

MANLY

How! What's better?

FIDELIA

I shall harden your heart against her.

MANLY

Have a care, sir; my heart is too much in earnest to be
fooled with, and my desire at height and needs no delays to   10
incite it. What, you are too good a pimp already, and know
how to endear pleasure by withholding it? But leave off your
page's bawdy-house tricks, sir, and tell me, will she be kind?

FIDELIA

Kinder than you could wish, sir.

MANLY

So, then. Well, prithee, what said she?   15

FIDELIA

She said—

MANLY

What? Thou'rt so tedious; speak comfort to me. What?

FIDELIA

That, of all things, you were her aversion.

MANLY

How!

---

18 *were* Q1 (are Q2–8, 0)

5 *genius* special ability
14 *Kinder* Fidelia puns on *kind* (1) benevolent (2) true to her own
nature, i.e., lecherous

FIDELIA

That she would sooner take a bedfellow out of an hospital,   20
and diseases, into her arms than you.

MANLY

What?

FIDELIA

That she would rather trust her honour with a dissolute,
debauched hector; nay, worse, with a finical, baffled coward,
all over loathsome with affectation of the fine gentleman.   25

MANLY

What's all this you say?

FIDELIA

Nay, that my offers of your love to her were more offensive
than when parents woo their virgin daughters to the enjoyment of riches only, and that you were in all circumstances
as nauseous to her as a husband on compulsion.   30

MANLY

Hold; I understand you not.

FIDELIA (Aside)

So, 'twill work, I see.

MANLY

Did not you tell me—

FIDELIA

She called you ten thousand ruffians.

MANLY

Hold, I say.   35

FIDELIA

Brutes—

MANLY

Hold.

FIDELIA

Sea monsters—

MANLY

Damn your intelligence! Hear me a little now.

FIDELIA

Nay, surly coward she called you too.   40

MANLY

Won't you hold yet? Hold, or—

FIDELIA

Nay, sir, pardon me; I could not but tell you she had the

24 *hector* 'a Vaporing, Swaggering Coward' (*B.E.*)
24 *finical, baffled* over-nice, disgraced
39 *intelligence* information, news

baseness, the injustice, to call you coward, sir; coward,
coward, sir.

MANLY

Not yet?   45

FIDELIA

I've done. Coward, sir.

MANLY

Did not you say she was kinder than I could wish her?

FIDELIA

Yes, sir.

MANLY

How then?—O, I understand you now. At first she appeared
in rage and disdain, the truest sign of a coming woman; but   50
at last you prevailed, it seems; did you not?

FIDELIA

Yes, sir.

MANLY

So then, let's know that only. Come, prithee, without delays.
I'll kiss thee for that news beforehand.

FIDELIA *(Aside)*

So; the kiss, I'm sure, is welcome to me, whatsoe'er the news   55
will be to you.

MANLY

Come, speak, my dear volunteer.

FIDELIA *(Aside)*

How welcome were that kind word too, if it were not for
another woman's sake!

MANLY

What, won't you speak? You prevailed for me at last, you   60
say?

FIDELIA

No, sir.

MANLY

No more of your fooling, sir; it will not agree with my
impatience or temper.

FIDELIA

Then, not to fool you, sir, I spoke to her for you, but pre-   65
vailed for myself. She would not hear me when I spoke in
your behalf, but bid me say what I would in my own, though
she gave me no occasion, she was so coming, and so was

---

50 *coming* eager
54 *I'll kiss thee* see II. 288 note; Farquhar repeats this situation when
   Plume kisses 'Jack Wilful' in IV. i of *The Recruiting Officer* (1706)

kinder, sir, than you could wish; which I was only afraid to
let you know without some warning.   70

MANLY

How's this? Young man, you are of a lying age; but I must
hear you out, and if—

FIDELIA

I would not abuse you, and cannot wrong her by any report
of her, she is so wicked.

MANLY

How, wicked! Had she the impudence, at the second sight   75
of you only—

FIDELIA

Impudence, sir? O, she has impudence enough to put a court
out of countenance and debauch a stews.

MANLY

Why, what said she?

FIDELIA

Her tongue, I confess, was silent; but her speaking eyes   80
gloated such things, more immodest and lascivious than
ravishers can act or women under a confinement think.

MANLY

I know there are whose eyes reflect more obscenity than the
glasses in alcoves, but there are others too who use a little
art with their looks to make 'em seem more beautiful, not   85
more loving; which vain young fellows like you are apt to
interpret in their own favour and to the lady's wrong.

FIDELIA

Seldom, sir; pray, have you a care of gloating eyes; for he
that loves to gaze upon 'em will find at last a thousand fools
and cuckolds in 'em, instead of cupids.   90

MANLY

Very well, sir; but what, you had only eye-kindness from
Olivia?

FIDELIA

I tell you again, sir, no woman sticks there. Eye-promises of
love they only keep; nay, they are contracts which make you
sure of 'em. In short, sir, she, seeing me with shame and   95

84 *others too* Q1, 0 (others Q2–8)

---

78 *stews* brothel
81 *gloated such things* made amorous promises (see II. 71; 'such things'
   is perhaps a cognate object)
82 *under a confinement* in child-bed (not cited in *OED* before 1774)
84 *glasses in alcoves* bedroom mirrors

amazement dumb, unactive, and resistless, threw her twisting
arms about my neck and smothered me with a thousand
tasteless kisses; believe me, sir, they were so to me.

MANLY

Why did you not avoid 'em, then?

FIDELIA

I fenced with her eager arms as you did with the grapples of   100
the enemy's fire-ship, and nothing but cutting 'em off could
have freed me.

MANLY

Damned, damned woman, that could be so false and infamous! And damned, damned heart of mine, that cannot
yet be false, though so infamous! What easy, tame, suffering,   105
trampled things does that little god of talking cowards make
of us! But—

FIDELIA *(Aside)*

So! It works, I find, as I expected.

MANLY

But she was false to me before; she told me so herself, and
yet I could not quite believe it; but she was, so that her second   110
falseness is a favour to me, not an injury, in revenging me
upon the man that wronged me first of her love. Her love!
A whore's, a witch's love!—But what, did she not kiss well,
sir? I'm sure I thought her lips—but I must not think of 'em
more; but yet they are such I could still kiss, grow to—and   115
then tear off with my teeth, grind 'em into mammocks, and
spit 'em into her cuckold's face.

FIDELIA *(Aside)*

Poor man, how uneasy he is! I have hardly the heart to give
him so much pain, though withal I give him a cure, and to
myself new life.   120

MANLY

But what, her kisses sure could not but warm you into desire
at last, or a compliance with hers at least?

FIDELIA

Nay more, I confess—

---

 98 *tasteless* insipid
101 *fire-ship* (1) a burning ship, set adrift amongst others to destroy
    them, hence (2) 'a Pockey Whore' (*B.E.*), a pardonable overstate-
    ment by Fidelia
115 *still kiss* go on kissing
116 *mammocks* shreds, little torn pieces

MANLY

What more? Speak.

FIDELIA

All you could fear had passed between us, if I could have   125
been made to wrong you, sir, in that nature.

MANLY

Could have been made? You lie; you did.

FIDELIA

Indeed, sir, 'twas impossible for me; besides, we were interrupted by a visit. But, I confess, she would not let me stir
till I promised to return to her again within this hour, as   130
soon as it should be dark, by which time she would dispose
of her visit and her servants and herself for my reception;
which I was fain to promise, to get from her.

MANLY

Ha!

FIDELIA

But if ever I go near her again, may you, sir, think me as   135
false to you as she is; hate and renounce me, as you ought to
do her and, I hope, will do now.

MANLY

Well, but now I think on't, you shall keep your word with
your lady. What, a young fellow, and fail the first, nay, so
tempting an assignation!   140

FIDELIA

How, sir?

MANLY

I say you shall go to her when 'tis dark, and shall not disappoint her.

FIDELIA

I, sir! I should disappoint her more by going, for—

MANLY

How so?   145

FIDELIA

Her impudence and injustice to you will make me disappoint
her love, loathe her.

MANLY

Come, you have my leave; and if you disgust her, I'll go with
you and act love, whilst you shall talk it only.

FIDELIA

You, sir! Nay, then I'll never go near her. You act love, sir!   150

133 *fain* obliged, under the circumstances
148 *disgust* dislike

You must but act it indeed, after all I have said to you.
Think of your honour, sir. Love—

MANLY

Well, call it revenge, and that is honourable. I'll be revenged
on her; and thou shalt be my second.

FIDELIA

Not in a base action, sir, when you are your own enemy. O,   155
go not near her, sir; for heaven's sake, for your own, think
not of it!

MANLY

How concerned you are! I thought I should catch you. What,
you are my rival at last and are in love with her yourself;
and have spoken ill of her out of your love to her, not me;   160
and therefore would not have me go to her!

FIDELIA

Heaven witness for me, 'tis because I love you only I would
not have you go to her.

MANLY

Come, come, the more I think on't, the more I'm satisfied
you do love her. Those kisses, young man, I knew were   165
irresistible; 'tis certain.

FIDELIA

There is nothing certain in the world, sir, but my truth and
your courage.

MANLY

Your servant, sir. Besides, false and ungrateful as she has
been to me, and though I may believe her hatred to me great   170
as you report it, yet I cannot think you are so soon and at
that rate beloved by her, though you may endeavour it.

FIDELIA

Nay, if that be all and you doubt it still, sir, I will conduct
you to her and, unseen, your ears shall judge of her falseness and my truth to you, if that will satisfy you.   175

MANLY

Yes, there is some satisfaction in being quite out of doubt,
because 'tis that alone withholds us from the pleasure of
revenge.

FIDELIA

Revenge! What revenge can you have, sir? Disdain is best
revenged by scorn, and faithless love by loving another and   180

---

169 *Your servant, sir* i.e., I disagree, sir; see II. 271 note

making her happy with the other's losings; which, if I might
advise—

Enter FREEMAN

MANLY

Not a word more.

FREEMAN

What, are you talking of love yet, captain? I thought you
had done with't.   185

MANLY

Why, what did you hear me say?

FREEMAN

Something imperfectly of love, I think.

MANLY

I was only wondering why fools, rascals, and desertless
wretches should still have the better of men of merit with all
women, as much as with their own common mistress, fortune. 190

FREEMAN

Because most women, like fortune, are blind, seem to do all
things in jest, and take pleasure in extravagant actions; their
love deserves neither thanks or blame, for they cannot help
it; 'tis all sympathy. Therefore the noisy, the finical, the
talkative, the cowardly and effeminate have the better of the 195
brave, the reasonable, and man of honour, for they have no
more reason in their love or kindness than fortune herself.

MANLY

Yes, they have their reason. First, honour in a man they
fear too much to love, and sense in a lover upbraids their
want of it; and they hate anything that disturbs their admira- 200
tion of themselves. But they are of that vain number who
had rather show their false generosity in giving away pro-
fusely to worthless flatterers than in paying just debts; and,
in short, all women, like fortune, as you say, and rewards,
are lost by too much meriting.   205

FIDELIA

All women, sir? Sure, there are some who have no other
quarrel to a lover's merit but that it begets their despair of
him.

MANLY

Thou art young enough to be credulous, but we—

Enter FIRST SAILOR

194 *finical* over-fastidious

1 SAILOR

Here are now below the scolding, daggled gentlewoman and   210
that Major Old—Old—fop, I think you call him.

FREEMAN

Oldfox. Prithee, bid 'em come up—with your leave, captain,
for now I can talk with her upon the square, if I shall not
disturb you.   [*Exit* SAILOR]

MANLY

No, for I'll be gone. Come, volunteer.   215

FREEMAN

Nay, pray stay; the scene between us will not be so tedious
to you as you think. Besides, you shall see how I have rigged
my squire out with the remains of my shipwrecked ward-
robe; he is under your sea valet-de-chambre's hands, and by
this time dressed, and will be worth your seeing. Stay, and   220
I'll fetch my fool.

MANLY

No; you know I cannot easily laugh. Besides, my volunteer
and I have business abroad.

    (*Exeunt* MANLY, FIDELIA *on one side,* FREEMAN *on t'other*)

        Enter MAJOR OLDFOX *and* WIDOW BLACKACRE

WIDOW

What, nobody here! Did not the fellow say he was within?

OLDFOX

Yes, lady; and he may be perhaps a little busy at present; but   225
if you think the time long till he comes, (*Unfolding papers*)
I'll read you here some of the fruits of my leisure, the over-
flowings of my fancy and pen. (*Aside*) To value me right, she
must know my parts. [*Aloud*] Come—

WIDOW

No no, I have reading work enough of my own in my bag,   230
I thank you.

OLDFOX

Ay, law, madam; but here is a poem in blank verse, which
I think a handsome declaration of one's passion.

WIDOW

O, if you talk of declarations, I'll show you one of the

210 *daggled* spattered with mud
213 *upon the square* openly, directly (since Jerry is now under his con-
    trol)
223 s.d. *Enter* . . . BLACKACRE With two permanent doors on each side
    of the forestage, there is no risk of an unwanted meeting here.
234 *declarations* papers 'shewing in writing the grief of the Demandant
    or Plaintife against the Tenent or Defendant' (Phillips)

prettiest penned things, which I mended too myself, you must   235
know.

OLDFOX

Nay, lady, if you have used yourself so much to the reading
of harsh law that you hate smooth poetry, here is a character
for you of—

WIDOW

A character! Nay, then I'll show you my bill in chancery   240
here, that gives you such a character of my adversary, makes
him as black—

OLDFOX

Pshaw; away, away, lady. But if you think the character too
long, here is an epigram, not above twenty lines, upon a cruel
lady who decreed her servant should hang himself to demon-   245
strate his passion.

WIDOW

Decreed! If you talk of decreeing, I have such a decree here,
drawn by the finest clerk—

OLDFOX

O lady, lady, all interruption and no sense between us, as if
we were lawyers at the bar! But I had forgot, Apollo and   250
Littleton never lodge in a head together. If you hate verses,
I'll give you a cast of my politics in prose. 'Tis a letter to a
friend in the country, which is now the way of all such
sober, solid persons as myself, when they have a mind to
publish their disgust to the times; though perhaps, between   255
you and I, they have no friend in the country. And sure a
politic, serious person may as well have a feigned friend in
the country to write to, as well as an idle poet a feigned

---

237 *used* accustomed
238 *character* short prose portrait, usually satiric, of a well-known type:
     miser, hypocrite, choleric man, etc.
245 *servant* professed lover
245–6 *hang . . . passion* an unwitting *double entendre*: hanging gave a
     man an erection
247 *decree* the judgment of an equity court, as in II. 853
250–1 *Apollo and Littleton* i.e., poetry and law; Sir Thomas Littleton's
     Tenures (1481), translated from law-French into English in 1525, and
     with the commentary by Sir Edward Coke added in 1628, had been
     reprinted as recently as 1671.
252 *cast* specimen
255 *disgust* aversion
256 *you and I* common usage at this period; cf. 'Let you and I tickle
     him' (*The Country Wife* (1675), IV. iii, 79)

mistress to write to. And so here's my *Letter to a Friend* (or
no friend) *in the Country, concerning the late conjuncture of*   260
affairs in relation to Coffee-houses; or, the Coffee-man's Case.

WIDOW

Nay, if your letter have a case in't, 'tis something; but first
I'll read you a letter of mine to a friend in the country,
called a letter of attorney.

Enter to them FREEMAN *and* JERRY BLACKACRE *in an old*
gaudy suit and red breeches of Freeman's

OLDFOX (*Aside*)

What, interruption still? O the plague of interruption, worse   265
to an author than the plague of critics!

WIDOW

What's this I see, Jerry Blackacre my minor in red breeches!
—What, hast thou left the modest, seemly garb of gown and
cap for this? And have I lost all my good Inns of Chancery
breeding upon thee, then? And thou wilt go a-breeding   270
thyself from our Inn of Chancery and Westminster Hall, at
coffee-houses and ordinaries, playhouses, tennis courts, and
bawdy-houses?

JERRY

Ay ay, what then? Perhaps I will; but what's that to you?
Here's my guardian and tutor now, forsooth, that I am out   275
of your huckster's hands.

---

259 *here's* Q2–8, 0 (here is Q1)

259–61 *Letter . . . Case* Supposedly, one of many pamphlets attacking
the royal proclamation of 29 December 1675/6 to suppress coffee-
houses as 'places where the disaffected met, and spread scandalous
reports concerning the conduct of His Majesty and His Ministers'
(B. Lillywhite, *London Coffee Houses* (1963), p. 18); the public
outcry was so great it was never put into effect.
264 *letter of attorney* formal document whereby 'any friend made choice
of for that purpose, is appointed to do a lawful act in anothers
stead' (Phillips)
264 s.d. *suit* here, matching coat and waistcoat
269 *Inns of Chancery* see I. 418–19 note
272 *ordinaries* public eating-houses, often used for gambling; the other
locations are also rakish haunts; cf. Vincent to Ranger in Wycherley's *Love in a Wood* (1671): 'I was going to look you out, between
the Scenes at the Play-House, the Coffee-house, Tennis-Court, or
Gifford's', a notorious brothel (IV. iii)
275–6 *out . . . hands* free from your disastrous usage; cf. 'In Huckster's
Hands, at a desperate Pass, or Condition, or in a fair way to be
Lost' (*B.E.*)

WIDOW

How? Thou hast not chosen him for thy guardian yet?

JERRY

No, but he has chosen me for his charge, and that's all one;
and I'll do anything he'll have me, and go all the world over
with him, to ordinaries and bawdy-houses, or anywhere else.   280

WIDOW

To ordinaries and bawdy-houses! Have a care, minor; thou
wilt enfeeble there thy estate and body. Do not go to
ordinaries and bawdy-houses, good Jerry.

JERRY

Why, how come you to know any ill by bawdy-houses? You
never had any hurt by 'em, had you, forsooth? Pray hold   285
yourself contented; if I do go where money and wenches are
to be had, you may thank yourself, for you used me so
unnaturally you would never let me have a penny to go
abroad with, nor so much as come near the garret where
your maidens lay; nay, you would not so much as let me play   290
at hot cockles with 'em, nor have any recreation with 'em,
though one should have kissed you behind, you were so
unnatural a mother, so you were.

FREEMAN

Ay, a very unnatural mother, faith, squire.

WIDOW

But, Jerry, consider thou art yet but a minor; however, if   295
thou wilt go home with me again and be a good child, thou
shalt see—

FREEMAN

Madam, I must have a better care of my heir under age than
so; I would sooner trust him alone with a stale waiting-
woman and a parson, than with his widow mother and her   300
lover or lawyer.

WIDOW

Why, thou villain, part mother and minor! Rob me of my
child and my writings! But thou shalt find there's law, and

278 *all one* the same thing
290 *maidens* maid-servants
291 *hot cockles* a childish game where one player lies face downwards
and tries to guess who hits his back
292 *kissed you behind* followed you meekly (?); cf. I. 10–11
299 *stale* i.e., past her prime

as in the case of ravishment of guard: Westminster the
Second.   305

OLDFOX

Young gentleman, squire, pray be ruled by your mother and
your friends.

JERRY

Yes, I'll be ruled by my friends, therefore not by my mother,
so I won't. I'll choose him for my guardian till I am of age,
nay, maybe for as long as I live.   310

WIDOW

Wilt thou so, thou wretch? And when thou'rt of age, thou
wilt sign, seal, and deliver too, wilt thou?

JERRY

Yes, marry will I, if you go there too.

WIDOW

O do not squeeze wax, son; rather go to ordinaries and
bawdy-houses than squeeze wax. If thou dost that, farewell   315
the goodly manor of Blackacre, with all its woods, underwoods, and appurtenances whatever. O, O!   (*Weeps*)

FREEMAN

Come, madam; in short, you see I am resolved to have a
share in the estate, yours or your son's; if I cannot get you,
I'll keep him, who is less coy, you find; but if you would   320
have your son again, you must take me too. Peace or war?
Love or law? You see my hostage is in my hand; I'm in
possession.

WIDOW

Nay, if one of us must be ruined, e'en let it be him. By my
body, a good one! Did you ever know yet a widow marry   325

304–5 *Westminster the Second* Chapter 35 of the statute known as Westminster 2 (1285) provided legal remedy against the abduction of a
ward (ravishment de gard)
313 *go there* come to that (also at 343 and 351)
314 *squeeze wax* set seal to a document (and so be permanently bound
by it)
316–17 *underwoods* stretches of brushwood, etc. growing beneath tall
timber
317 *appurtenances* things belonging to something more principal, 'as
Hamlets to a cheif Mannor, Common of Pasture, Turbary, Piscary,
and such like' (Blount)
322 *in my hand* led by my will
325 *a good one* ironic comment on an improbable statement, cf. 'That's
a good one' in *The Country Wife* (1675, III. ii, 204); *OED* notes
'that's a good 'un' as 'early 19th-century slang'

or not marry for the sake of her child? I'd have you to
know, sir, I shall be hard enough for you both yet, without
marrying you, if Jerry won't be ruled by me.—What say
you, booby, will you be ruled? Speak.

JERRY

Let one alone, can't you?   330

WIDOW

Wilt thou choose him for guardian whom I refuse for
husband?

JERRY

Ay, to choose, I thank you.

WIDOW

And are all my hopes frustrated? Shall I never hear thee put
cases again to John the butler, or our vicar? Never see thee   335
amble the circuit with the judges, and hear thee, in our town
hall, louder than the crier?

JERRY

No, for I have taken my leave of lawyering and pettifogging.

WIDOW

Pettifogging! Thou profane villain, hast thou so? Pettifogging! Then you shall take your leave of me and your   340
estate too; thou shalt be an alien to me and it forever.
Pettifogging!

JERRY

O, but if you go there too, mother, we have the deeds and
settlements, I thank you. Would you cheat me of my estate,
i'fac?   345

WIDOW

No no, I will not cheat your little brother Bob; for thou
wert not born in wedlock.

FREEMAN

How's that?

JERRY

How? What quirk has she got in her head now?

WIDOW

I say thou canst not, shalt not inherit the Blackacre's estate.   350

JERRY

Why? Why, forsooth? What d'ye mean, if you go there too?

WIDOW

Thou art but my base child, and according to the law canst

351 *too* Q2–8, 0 (to Q1)

352 *base* illegitimate

not inherit it; nay, thou art not so much as bastard eigne.

JERRY

What, what? Am I then the son of a whore, mother?

WIDOW

The law says—   355

FREEMAN

Madam, we know what the law says; but have a care what
you say. Do not let your passion to ruin your son ruin your
reputation.

WIDOW

Hang reputation, sir! Am not I a widow, have no husband,
nor intend to have any? Nor would you, I suppose, now   360
have me for a wife. So I think now I'm revenged on my son
and you, without marrying, as I told you.

FREEMAN

But consider, madam.

JERRY

What, have you no shame left in you, mother?

WIDOW *(Aside, to* OLDFOX)

Wonder not at it, major; 'tis often the poor pressed widow's   365
case, to give up her honour to save her jointure, and seem to
be a light woman rather than marry; as some young men,
they say, pretend to have the filthy disease, and lose credit
with most women to avoid the importunities of some.

FREEMAN

But one word with you, madam.   370

WIDOW

No no, sir.—Come, major, let us make haste now to the
Prerogative Court.

OLDFOX

But, lady, if what you say be true, will you stigmatize your
reputation on record? And if it be not true, how will you
prove it?   375

WIDOW

Pshaw! I can prove anything; and for my reputation, know,
major, a wise woman will no more value her reputation in
disinheriting a rebellious son of a good estate, than she would
in getting him, to inherit an estate.

                                        (Exeunt WIDOW *and* OLDFOX)

353 *bastard eigne* bastard son of parents who later marry and have a
      legitimate son
372 *Prerogative Court* an archbishop's court which 'sits upon Inheri-
      tances fallen either by the Intestate, or by Will and Testament'
      (Phillips)

FREEMAN

Madam!—We must not let her go so, squire.   380

JERRY

Nay, the devil can't stop her though, if she has a mind to't.
But come, bully guardian, we'll go and advise with three
attorneys, two proctors, two solicitors, and a shrewd man of
Whitefriars, neither attorney, proctor, or solicitor, but as pure
a pimp to the law as any of 'em; and sure all they will be   385
hard enough for her, for I fear, bully guardian, you are too
good a joker to have any law in your head.

FREEMAN

Thou'rt in the right on't, squire; I understand no law,
especially that against bastards, since I'm sure the custom is
against that law, and more people get estates by being so   390
than lose 'em.   *(Exeunt)*

[Act IV, Scene ii]

The scene changes to OLIVIA'*s Lodging*

Enter LORD PLAUSIBLE, *and* BOY *with a candle*

LORD PLAUSIBLE

Little gentleman, your most obedient, faithful, humble
servant. Where, I beseech you, is that divine person, your
noble lady?

BOY

Gone out, my lord; but commanded me to give you this
letter.   *(Gives him a letter)*   5

Enter to him NOVEL

383 *attorneys . . . solicitors* Proctors managed their clients' causes in
     courts of civil or canon law, attorneys and solicitors in courts of
     common law and chancery.
384 *Whitefriars* site of a dissolved convent near Fleet Street, which re-
     tained until 1697 privilege of sanctuary, and consequently harboured
     many criminals and their aides
     s.d. *scene changes* i.e., the wings and back scene slide away on
     shutters to reveal others depicting Olivia's rooms, in all full view
     of the audience
     s.d. *with a candle* to suggest that the scene is played by its light,
     though the theatre remained fully illuminated throughout the per-
     formance; when the candle is removed (102), the characters are left
     'in the dark' (107) until Vernish re-enters '*with a light*' (354); the
     same convention is employed in V, iii

LORD PLAUSIBLE *(Aside)*

Which he must not observe.   *(Puts it up)*

NOVEL

Hey, boy, where is thy lady?

BOY

Gone out, sir; but I must beg a word with you.

> *(Gives him a letter, and exit)*

NOVEL

For me? So. *(Puts up the letter)*—Servant, servant, my lord.
You see the lady knew of your coming, for she is gone out. 10

LORD PLAUSIBLE

Sir, I humbly beseech you not to censure the lady's good
breeding; she has reason to use more liberty with me than
with any other man.

NOVEL

How, viscount, how?

LORD PLAUSIBLE

Nay, I humbly beseech you, be not in choler; where there is 15
most love, there may be most freedom.

NOVEL

Nay, then 'tis time to come to an *éclaircissement* with you,
and to tell you, you must think no more of this lady's love.

LORD PLAUSIBLE

Why, under correction, dear sir?

NOVEL

There are reasons, reasons, viscount.   20

LORD PLAUSIBLE

What, I beseech you, noble sir?

NOVEL

Prithee, prithee, be not impertinent, my lord; some of you
lords are such conceited, well-assured, impertinent rogues.

LORD PLAUSIBLE

And you noble wits are so full of shamming and drolling
one knows not where to have you, seriously.   25

NOVEL

Well, you shall find me in bed with this lady one of these
days.

17 *éclaircissement* explanation (also at 33); the word is affected by
   Melantha in Dryden's *Marriage à la Mode* (1671, V. i) and the fop
   Sparkish in *The Country Wife* (1675, III. ii, 285)
24 *shamming* hoaxing; see III. 629–39
26 *in bed with this lady* On the wedding night, bride and groom were
   put to bed by their friends, who awakened them next morning with
   a sack-posset; Plausible pretends to misunderstand Novel here.

LORD PLAUSIBLE
Nay, I beseech you, spare the lady's honour; for hers and mine will be all one shortly.

NOVEL
Prithee, my lord, be not an ass. Dost thou think to get her from me? I have had such good encouragements—   30

LORD PLAUSIBLE
I have not been thought unworthy of 'em.

NOVEL
What, not like mine! Come to an *éclaircissement*, as I said.

LORD PLAUSIBLE
Why, seriously then, she has told me viscountess sounded prettily.   35

NOVEL
And me, that Novel was a name she would sooner change hers for than for any title in England.

LORD PLAUSIBLE
She has commended the softness and respectfulness of my behaviour.

NOVEL
She has praised the briskness of my raillery of all things,   40
man.

LORD PLAUSIBLE
The sleepiness of my eyes she liked.

NOVEL
Sleepiness! Dullness, dullness. But the fierceness of mine she adored.

LORD PLAUSIBLE
The brightness of my hair she liked.   45

NOVEL
The brightness! No, the greasiness, I warrant. But the blackness and lustre of mine she admires.

LORD PLAUSIBLE
The gentleness of my smile.

NOVEL
The subtlety of my leer.

LORD PLAUSIBLE
The clearness of my complexion.   50

NOVEL
The redness of my lips.

LORD PLAUSIBLE
The whiteness of my teeth.

31 *such good* Q2–8 (such Q1, 0)

NOVEL

My janty way of picking them.

LORD PLAUSIBLE

The sweetness of my breath.

NOVEL

Ha ha! Nay, then she abused you, 'tis plain; for you know   55
what Manly said, The sweetness of your pulvilio she might
mean, but for your breath! Ha ha ha! Your breath is such,
man, that nothing but tobacco can perfume, and your complexion nothing could mend but the smallpox.

LORD PLAUSIBLE

Well, sir, you may please to be merry; but, to put you out of   60
all doubt, sir, she has received some jewels from me of value.

NOVEL

And presents from me, besides what I presented her jantily,
by way of ombre, of three or four hundred pound value,
which I'm sure are the earnest pence for our love bargain.

LORD PLAUSIBLE

Nay then, sir, with your favour, and to make an end of all   65
your hopes, look you there, sir, she has writ to me—

NOVEL

How! How! Well, well, and so she has to me; look you
there—   ([*They*] *deliver to each other their letters*)

LORD PLAUSIBLE

What's here!

NOVEL

How's this? (*Reads out*) 'My dear lord, You'll excuse me for   70
breaking my word with you, since 'twas to oblige, not offend
you, for I am only gone abroad but to disappoint Novel and
meet you in the drawing-room, where I expect you with as
much impatience as when I used to suffer Novel's visits, the
most impertinent fop that ever affected the name of a wit,   75
therefore not capable, I hope, to give you jealousy; for, for
your sake alone, you saw I renounced an old lover, and will
do all the world. Burn the letter, but lay up the kindness of
it in your heart, with your Olivia'.—Very fine! But pray let's
see mine.   80

---

53 *janty* well-bred, genteel, elegant
56 *what Manly said* in II. 571–3
56 *pulvilio* perfumed powder for dressing wigs
64 *earnest pence* a small sum paid as deposit to secure a bargain
73 *drawing-room* at Whitehall; see II. 81 note

LORD PLAUSIBLE

I understand it not; but sure she cannot think so of me.

NOVEL

(Reads the other letter) Hum! Ha!—'meet—for your sake'
—umh!—'quitted an old lover—world—burn—in your
heart, with your Olivia'.—Just the same, the names only
altered.   85

LORD PLAUSIBLE

Surely there must be some mistake, or somebody has abused
her and us.

NOVEL

Yes, you are abused, no doubt on't, my lord; but I'll to
Whitehall and see.

LORD PLAUSIBLE

And I, where I shall find you are abused.   90

NOVEL

Where, if it be so, for our comfort we cannot fail of meeting
with fellow-sufferers enough; for, as Freeman said of another,
she stands in the drawing-room like the glass, ready for all
comers to set their gallantry by her, and, like the glass too,
lets no man go from her unsatisfied with himself.   95

(Exeunt ambo)

Enter OLIVIA *and* BOY

OLIVIA

Both here, and just gone?

BOY

Yes, madam.

OLIVIA

But are you sure neither saw you deliver the other a letter?

BOY

Yes yes, madam, I am very sure.

OLIVIA

Go then to the Old Exchange, to Westminster, Holborn,   100
and all the other places I told you of; I shall not need you
these two hours. Be gone, and take the candle with you; and
be sure you leave word again below, I am gone out to all
that ask.

84 *Just the same* not quite, since 'quitted' is substituted for 'renounced'
100 *Old . . . Holborn* i.e., all over town, from Westminster at its south-
    west boundary to Holborn in the north and the Royal Exchange in
    Cornhill, deep in the city

BOY

Yes, madam.   *(Exit)*   105

OLIVIA

And my new lover will not ask, I'm sure. He has his lesson,
and cannot miss me here, though in the dark, which I have
purposely designed as a remedy against my blushing gallant's modesty; for young lovers, like game cocks, are made
bolder by being kept without light.   110

Enter her husband VERNISH, *as from a journey*

VERNISH

Where is she? Darkness everywhere!

OLIVIA *(Softly)*

What, come before your time? My soul! My life! Your
haste has augmented your kindness, and let me thank you for
it thus, and thus—*(Embracing and kissing him)*. And though,
my soul, the little time since you left me has seemed an age   115
to my impatience, sure it is yet but seven—

VERNISH

How! Who's that you expected after seven?

OLIVIA *(Aside)*

Ha! My husband returned! And have I been throwing away
so many kind kisses on my husband, and wronged my lover
already?   120

VERNISH

Speak, I say, who was't you expected after seven?

OLIVIA

(Aside) What shall I say? O! [*Aloud*] Why, 'tis but seven
days, is it, dearest, since you went out of town? And I
expected you not so soon.

VERNISH

No, sure, 'tis but five days since I left you.   125

OLIVIA

Pardon my impatience, dearest; I thought 'em seven at least.

VERNISH

Nay, then—

---

118 s.d. *(Aside)* Q2–8 *(omitted* Q1, 0)

---

109 *game cocks* cocks trained for fighting; since game (=amorous play)
    and cock (=penis) are well-established *double entendres*, it is likely
    that *game cock* itself, first recorded by *OED* in this passage, is also
    equivocal
111 s.d. *(Softly)* placed between 111 and 112 in Q1; Olivia's mistake is
    more plausible if Vernish speaks softly, but since she speaks softly
    to Fidelia at 177, she probably does so here as well

OLIVIA

But, my life, you shall never stay half so long from me again;
you shan't indeed, by this kiss, you shan't.

VERNISH

No no; but why alone in the dark?   130

OLIVIA

Blame not my melancholy in your absence. But, my soul,
since you went, I have strange news to tell you: Manly is
returned.

VERNISH

Manly returned! Fortune forbid!

OLIVIA

Met with the Dutch in the Channel, fought, sunk his ship   135
and all he carried with him. He was here with me yesterday.

VERNISH

And did you own our marriage to him?

OLIVIA

I told him I was married, to put an end to his love and my
trouble; but to whom is yet a secret kept from him and all
the world. And I have used him so scurvily his great spirit   140
will ne'er return to reason it farther with me; I have sent him
to sea again, I warrant.

VERNISH

'Twas bravely done. And sure he will now hate the shore
more than ever, after so great a disappointment. Be you sure
only to keep awhile our great secret till he be gone. In the   145
mean time, I'll lead the easy, honest fool by the nose, as I
used to do; and whilst he stays, rail with him at thee, and
when he's gone, laugh with thee at him. But have you his
cabinet of jewels safe? Part not with a seed pearl to him to
keep him from starving.   150

OLIVIA

Nor from hanging.

VERNISH

He cannot recover 'em and, I think, will scorn to beg 'em
again.

OLIVIA

But, my life, have you taken the thousand guineas he left in
my name out of the goldsmith's hands?   155

VERNISH

Ay ay, they are removed to another goldsmith's.

152 *recover 'em* obtain possession of them by legal process
155 *goldsmith* who doubled as banker at this period; we learn at 409 he
    is also an alderman

OLIVIA

> Ay, but, my soul, you had best have a care he find not where
> the money is; for his present wants, as I'm informed, are
> such as will make him inquisitive enough.

VERNISH

> You say true, and he knows the man too; but I'll remove it   160
> tomorrow.

OLIVIA

> Tomorrow! O do not stay till tomorrow; go tonight,
> immediately.

VERNISH

> Now I think on't, you advise well, and I will go presently.

OLIVIA

> Presently? Instantly! I will not let you stay a jot.   165

VERNISH

> I will then, though I return not home till twelve.

OLIVIA

> Nay, though not till morning, with all my heart. Go, dearest;
> I am impatient till you are gone.   *(Thrusts him out)*
> So, I have at once now brought about those two grateful
> businesses which all prudent women do together, secured   170
> money and pleasure; and now all interruptions of the last
> are removed. Go husband, and come up friend; just the
> buckets in the well: the absence of one brings the other; but
> I hope, like them too, they will not meet in the way, justle,
> and clash together.   175

Enter FIDELIA, *and* MANLY *treading softly and staying behind
at some distance*

> So, are you come? [*Aside*] But not the husband-bucket, I
> hope, again. *(Softly)* Who's there? My dearest?

FIDELIA

> My life—

OLIVIA

> Right, right. Where are thy lips? Here, take the dumb and
> best welcomes, kisses and embraces; 'tis not a time for idle   180
> words. In a duel of love, as in others, parleying shows
> basely. Come, we are alone, and now the word is only satis-
> faction, and defend not thyself.

MANLY *(Aside)*

> How's this? Wuh, she makes love like a devil in a play; and

169 *grateful* welcome, agreeable
172 *friend* lover

in this darkness, which conceals her angel's face, if I were   185
apt to be afraid, I should think her a devil.

OLIVIA

What, you traverse ground, young gentleman.

> (FIDELIA *avoiding her*)

FIDELIA

I take breath only.

MANLY *(Aside)*

Good heavens! How was I deceived!

OLIVIA

Nay, you are a coward; what, are you afraid of the fierce-   190
ness of my love?

FIDELIA

Yes, madam, lest its violence might presage its change; and
I must needs be afraid you would leave me quickly, who
could desert so brave a gentleman as Manly.

OLIVIA

O, name not his name! For in a time of stolen joys, as this   195
is, the filthy name of husband were not a more allaying
sound.

MANLY *(Aside)*

There's some comfort yet.

FIDELIA

But did you not love him?

OLIVIA

Never. How could you think it?   200

FIDELIA

Because he thought it, who is a man of that sense, nice
discerning, and diffidency, that I should think it hard to
deceive him.

OLIVIA

No; he that distrusts most the world trusts most to himself,
and is but the more easily deceived because he thinks he can't   205
be deceived. His cunning is like the coward's sword, by which
he is oftener worsted than defended.

FIDELIA

Yet, sure, you used no common art to deceive him.

OLIVIA

I knew he loved his own singular moroseness so well as to
dote upon any copy of it; wherefore I feigned an hatred to   210
the world too, that he might love me in earnest. But if it had
been hard to deceive him, I'm sure 'twere much harder to

---

187 *traverse ground* move from side to side (like a fencer or pugilist)

love him. A dogged, ill-mannered—

FIDELIA *(Aside, to* MANLY*)*

D'ye hear her, sir? Pray hear her.

OLIVIA

Surly, untractable, snarling brute! He! A masty dog were as   215
fit a thing to make a gallant of.

MANLY *(Aside)*

Ay, a goat or monkey were fitter for thee.

FIDELIA

I must confess, for my part, though my rival, I cannot but
say he has a manly handsomeness in's face and mien.

OLIVIA

So has a Saracen in the sign.   220

FIDELIA

Is proper, and well made.

OLIVIA

As a drayman.

FIDELIA

Has wit.

OLIVIA

He rails at all mankind.

FIDELIA

And undoubted courage.   225

OLIVIA

Like the hangman's, can murder a man when his hands are
tied. He has cruelty indeed, which is no more courage than
his railing is wit.

MANLY *(Aside)*

Thus women, and men like women, are too hard for us when
they think we do not hear 'em; and reputation, like other   230
mistresses, is never true to a man in his absence.

FIDELIA

He is—

OLIVIA

Prithee, no more of him. I thought I had satisfied you
enough before that he could never be a rival for you to
apprehend, and you need not be more assured of my aversion   235

---

215 *masty dog* mastiff
220 *a Saracen in the sign* 'When our Country-men came home from
     fighting with the *Saracens,* and were beaten by them, they pictured
     them with huge, big, terrible Faces (as you still see the Sign of
     the *Saracen*'s-head is)' (John Selden, *Table-Talk* (1689), p. 58); there
     was a coaching inn of this name at Snow Hill, Newgate
221 *proper* handsome

to him but by the last testimony of my love to you, which I
am ready to give you. Come, my soul, this way—

(Pulls FIDELIA)

FIDELIA

But, madam, what could make you dissemble love to him,
when 'twas so hard a thing for you, and flatter his love to
you?   240

OLIVIA

That which makes all the world flatter and dissemble: 'twas
his money. I had a real passion for that. Yet I loved not that
so well as for it to take him, for as soon as I had his money,
I hastened his departure; like a wife who, when she has made
the most of a dying husband's breath, pulls away the pillow.   245

MANLY *(Aside)*

Damned money! Its master's potent rival still, and like a
saucy pimp corrupts itself the mistress it procures for us.

OLIVIA

But I did not think with you, my life, to pass my time in
talking. Come hither, come; yet stay, till I have locked a
door in the other room that may chance to let us in some   250
interruption, which reciting poets or losing gamesters fear
not more than I at this time do.   *(Exit* OLIVIA)

FIDELIA

Well, I hope you are now satisfied, sir, and will be gone to
think of your revenge.

MANLY

No, I am not satisfied, and must stay to be revenged.   255

FIDELIA

How, sir? You'll use no violence to her, I hope, and forfeit
your own life to take away hers? That were no revenge.

MANLY

No no, you need not fear; my revenge shall only be upon her
honour, not her life.

FIDELIA

How, sir? Her honour? O heavens! Consider, sir. she has no   260
honour. D'ye call that revenge? Can you think of such a
thing? But reflect, sir, how she hates and loathes you.

MANLY

Yes, so much she hates me, that it would be a revenge

---

246 s.d. (*Aside*) Q6–7 (*omitted* Q1–5, 8, 0)
250 *may* Q2–8, 0 (might Q1)

244–5 *wife . . . pillow* cf. *Love in a Wood* (1671); 'she is as arrant a Jilt,
    as ever pull'd pillow from under husband's head' (II. i)

sufficient to make her accessary to my pleasure, and then let
her know it.   265

FIDELIA

No, sir, no; to be revenged on her now, were to disappoint
her. Pray, sir, let us be gone.   *(Pulls* MANLY*)*

MANLY

Hold off. What, you are my rival then; and therefore you
shall stay and keep the door for me, whilst I go in for you.
But when I'm gone, if you dare to stir off from this very   270
board, or breathe the least murmuring accent, I'll cut her
throat first; and if you love her, you will not venture her life.
Nay, then I'll cut your throat too; and I know you love your
own life at least.

FIDELIA

But sir, good sir.   275

MANLY

Not a word more, lest I begin my revenge on her by killing
you.

FIDELIA

But are you sure 'tis revenge that makes you do this? How
can it be?

MANLY

Whist!   280

FIDELIA

'Tis a strange revenge indeed.

MANLY

If you make me stay, I shall keep my word and begin with
you. No more.   *(Exit* MANLY, *at the same door* OLIVIA *went)*

Manet FIDELIA

FIDELIA

O heavens, is there not punishment enough
In loving well, if you will have't a crime,   285
But you must add fresh torments daily to't,
And punish us like peevish rivals still
Because we fain would find a heaven here?
But did there never any love like me,
That, untried tortures, you must find me out?   290
Others, at worst, you force to kill themselves,
But I must be self-murd'ress of my love,
Yet will not grant me power to end my life,

---

269 *go in for you* perhaps with a sexual *double entendre*
287 *peevish* foolish (?)

My cruel life; for when a lover's hopes
Are dead and gone, life is unmerciful.   295

(Sits down and weeps)

Enter MANLY *to her*

MANLY

[*Aside*] I have thought better on't. I must not discover myself
now; I am without witnesses. For if I barely should publish
it, she would deny it with as much impudence as she would
act it again with this young fellow here. [*Aloud*] Where are
you?   300

FIDELIA

Here. O—now I suppose we may be gone.

MANLY

I will, but not you. You must stay and act the second part
of a lover; that is, talk kindness to her.

FIDELIA

Not I, sir.

MANLY

No disputing, sir, you must; 'tis necessary to my design of   305
coming again tomorrow night.

FIDELIA

What, can you come again then hither?

MANLY

Yes, and you must make the appointment, and an apology
for your leaving her so soon; for I have said not a word to
her, but have kept your counsel, as I expect you should do   310
mine. Do this faithfully, and I promise you here, you shall
run my fortune still and we will never part as long as we
live; but if you do not do it, expect not to live.

FIDELIA

'Tis hard, sir, but such a consideration will make it easier.
You won't forget your promise, sir?   315

MANLY

No, by heavens. But I hear her coming.   *(Exit)*

Enter OLIVIA *to* FIDELIA

295 s.d. *Enter* MANLY During Fidelia's soliloquy he has lain with Olivia
but not revealed his identity.
297 *barely* baldly, without corroboration
310 *counsel* secret
312 *run my fortune still* share my lot always

OLIVIA

Where is my life? Run from me already! You do not love
me, dearest; nay, you are angry with me, for you would not
so much as speak a kind word to me within. What was the
reason?   320

FIDELIA

I was transported too much.

OLIVIA

That's kind; but come, my soul, what make you here? Let us
go in again; we may be surprised in this room, 'tis so near
the stairs.

FIDELIA

No, we shall hear the better here, if anybody should come   325
up.

OLIVIA

Nay, I assure you, we shall be secure enough within. Come,
come—

FIDELIA

I am sick, and troubled with a sudden dizziness; cannot stir
yet.   330

OLIVIA

Come, I have spirits within.

FIDELIA

O!—Don't you hear a noise, madam?

OLIVIA

No no, there is none. Come, come.   *(Pulls her)*

FIDELIA

Indeed there is; and I love you so much I must have a care
of your honour, if you won't, and go, but to come to you   335
tomorrow night, if you please.

OLIVIA

With all my soul. But you must not go yet. Come, prithee.

FIDELIA

O!—I am now sicker, and am afraid of one of my fits.

OLIVIA

What fits?

FIDELIA

Of the falling sickness; and I lie generally an hour in a   340
trance. Therefore pray consider your honour for the sake of
my love, and let me go that I may return to you often.

OLIVIA

But will you be sure, then, to come tomorrow night?

340 *the falling sickness* epilepsy

FIDELIA
  Yes.
OLIVIA
  Swear.   345
FIDELIA
  By our past kindness.
OLIVIA
  Well, go your ways then, if you will, you naughty creature
  you.   *(Exit* FIDELIA*)*
  These young lovers, with their fears and modesty, make
  themselves as bad as old ones to us; and I apprehend their   350
  bashfulness more than their tattling.

                      FIDELIA *returns*

FIDELIA
  O madam, we're undone! There was a gentleman upon the
  stairs, coming up with a candle, which made me retire. Look
  you, here he comes!

            Enter VERNISH *and his* MAN *with a light*

OLIVIA
  How! My husband! O, undone indeed! This way.   *(Exit)*   355
VERNISH
  Ha! You shall not scape me so, sir.   *(Stops* FIDELIA*)*
FIDELIA *(Aside)*
  O heavens, more fears, plagues, and torments yet in store!
VERNISH
  Come, sir, I guess what your business was here, but this must
  be your business now. Draw.   *(Draws)*
FIDELIA
  Sir—   360
VERNISH
  No expostulations; I shall not care to hear of't. Draw.
FIDELIA
  Good sir!
VERNISH
  How, you rascal! Not courage to draw, yet durst do me the
  greatest injury in the world? Thy cowardice shall not save
  thy life.   *(Offers to run at* FIDELIA*)*   365
FIDELIA
  O hold, sir, and send but your servant down, and I'll satisfy
  you, sir, I could not injure you as you imagine.

356 *scape* Q1 (escape Q2–8, 0)

VERNISH

Leave the light and be gone.   *(Exit* SERVANT*)*

Now quickly, sir, what you've to say, or—

FIDELIA

I am a woman, sir, a very unfortunate woman.   370

VERNISH

How! A very handsome woman, I'm sure then. *(Pulls off her
peruke and feels her breasts)* Here are witnesses of't too, I
confess. *(Aside)* Well, I'm glad to find the tables turned,
my wife in more danger of cuckolding than I was.

FIDELIA

Now, sir, I hope you are so much a man of honour as to let   375
me go, now I have satisfied you, sir.

VERNISH

When you have satisfied me, madam, I will.

FIDELIA

I hope, sir, you are too much a gentleman to urge those
secrets from a woman which concern her honour. You may
guess my misfortune to be love by my disguise, but a pair of   380
breeches could not wrong you, sir.

VERNISH

I may believe love has changed your outside, which could
not wrong me; but why did my wife run away?

FIDELIA

I know not, sir; perhaps because she would not be forced
to discover me to you, or to guide me from your suspicions   385
that you might not discover me yourself; which ungentleman-
like curiosity I hope you will cease to have, and let me go.

VERNISH

Well, madam, if I must not know who you are, 'twill suffice
for me only to know certainly what you are, which you must
not deny me. Come, there is a bed within, the proper rack   390
for lovers; and if you are a woman, there you can keep no
secrets; you'll tell me there all unasked. Come.   *(Pulls her)*

FIDELIA

O! What d'ye mean? Help, O—

VERNISH

I'll show you; but 'tis in vain to cry out. No one dares help
you, for I am lord here.   395

FIDELIA

Tyrant here! But if you are master of this house, which I
have taken for a sanctuary, do not violate it yourself.

VERNISH

No, I'll preserve you here and nothing shall hurt you, and

will be as true to you as your disguise; but you must trust
me then. Come, come.   400

FIDELIA

O O! Rather than you shall drag me to a death so horrid
and so shameful, I'll die here a thousand deaths. But you do
not look like a ravisher, sir.

VERNISH

Nor you like one would put me to't, but if you will—

FIDELIA

O O! Help, help—   405

Enter SERVANT

VERNISH

You saucy rascal, how durst you come in when you heard
a woman squeak? That should have been your cue to shut
the door.

SERVANT

I come, sir, to let you know the alderman, coming home
immediately after you were at his house, has sent his cashier 410
with the money, according to your note.

VERNISH

Damn his money! Money never came to any, sure, unseason-
ably till now. Bid him stay.

SERVANT

He says he cannot a moment.

VERNISH

Receive it you, then.   415

SERVANT

He says he must have your receipt for it. He is in haste, for
I hear him coming up, sir.

VERNISH

Damn him. Help me in here then with this dishonourer of
my family.

FIDELIA

O! O!   420

SERVANT

You say she is a woman, sir.

VERNISH

No matter, sir. Must you prate?

FIDELIA

O heavens, is there— *(They thrust her in and lock the door)*

407 *shut* lock
422 *Must you prate?* probably addressed to Fidelia

VERNISH

Stay there, my prisoner. You have a short reprieve.

> I'll fetch the gold, and that she can't resist;   425
> For with a full hand 'tis we ravish best.   *(Exeunt)*

Finis actus quarti

Act V, Scene i

ELIZA's *Lodging*

Enter OLIVIA *and* ELIZA

OLIVIA

Ah, cousin, nothing troubles me but that I have given the malicious world its revenge and reason now, to talk as freely of me as I used to do of it.

ELIZA

Faith, then, let not that trouble you; for to be plain, cousin, the world cannot talk worse of you than it did before.   5

OLIVIA

How, cousin! I'd have you to know, before this *faux pas*, this trip of mine, the world could not talk of me.

ELIZA

Only that you mind other people's actions so much that you take no care of your own, but to hide 'em; that, like a thief, because you know yourself most guilty, you impeach your   10
fellow criminals first to clear yourself.

OLIVIA

O wicked world!

ELIZA

That you pretend an aversion to all mankind in public, only that their wives and mistresses may not be jealous, and hinder you of their conversation in private.   15

OLIVIA

Base world!

ELIZA

That abroad you fasten quarrels upon innocent men for talking of you, only to bring 'em to ask you pardon at home, and to become dear friends with 'em, who were hardly your acquaintance before.   20

19 *'em* Q1 (them Q2–8, O)

OLIVIA
Abominable world!

ELIZA
That you condemn the obscenity of modern plays, only that
you may not be censured for never missing the most obscene
of the old ones.

OLIVIA
Damned world!   25

ELIZA
That you deface the nudities of pictures and little statues
only because they are not real.

OLIVIA
O fie fie fie; hideous, hideous, cousin! The obscenity of their
censures makes me blush.

ELIZA
The truth of 'em, the naughty world would say now.   30

Enter LETTICE *hastily*

LETTICE
O madam, here is that gentleman coming up who now you
say is my master.

OLIVIA
O cousin, whither shall I run? Protect me, or—
                    (OLIVIA *runs away and stands at a distance*)

Enter VERNISH

VERNISH
Nay nay, come—

OLIVIA
O sir, forgive me.   35

VERNISH
Yes yes, I can forgive you being alone in the dark with a
woman in man's clothes; but have a care of a man in
woman's clothes.

OLIVIA *(Aside)*
What does he mean? He dissembles, only to get me into his
power. Or has my dear friend made him believe he was a   40
woman? My husband may be deceived by him, but I'm sure
I was not.

VERNISH
Come, come, you need not have lain out of your house for

26–7 borrowed from Célimène in Molière's *Le Misanthrope*: 'Elle fait
    des tableaux couvrir les nudités,/Mais elle a de l'amour pour les
    réalités' (943–4); Olivia echoes the same couplet at II. 452–4

this; but perhaps you were afraid, when I was warm with
suspicions, you must have discovered who she was; and   45
prithee, may I not know it?

OLIVIA

She was—*(Aside)* I hope he has been deceived; and since my
lover has played the card, I must not renounce.

VERNISH

Come, what's the matter with thee? If I must not know who
she is, I'm satisfied without. Come hither.   50

OLIVIA

Sure you do know her; she has told you herself, I suppose.

VERNISH

No; I might have known her better, but that I was interrupted by the goldsmith you know, and was forced to lock
her into your chamber to keep her from his sight; but when
I returned I found she was got away by tying the window   55
curtains to the balcony, by which she slid down into the
street. For, you must know, I jested with her and made her
believe I'd ravish her, which she apprehended, it seems, in
earnest.

OLIVIA

Then she got from you?   60

VERNISH

Yes.

OLIVIA

And is quite gone?

VERNISH

Yes.

OLIVIA

I'm glad on't—otherwise you had ravished her, sir? But how
dar'st you go so far as to make her believe you would ravish   65
her? Let me understand that, sir. What! There's guilt in your
face; you blush too; nay, then you did ravish her, you did,
you base fellow. What, ravish a woman in the first month of
our marriage! 'Tis a double injury to me, thou base, ungrateful man. Wrong my bed already, villain! I could tear out   70
those false eyes, barbarous, unworthy wretch.

ELIZA

So, so—

---

48 *renounce* fail to follow suit; in ombre, 'If you renounce you are to
   double the Stake' (Charles Cotton, *The Compleat Gamester* (1674),
   p. 102)
64 *I'm glad on't* perhaps an aside

VERNISH
> Prithee hear, my dear.

OLIVIA
> I will never hear you, my plague, my torment.

VERNISH
> I swear—prithee, hear me.   75

OLIVIA
> I have heard already too many of your false oaths and vows,
> especially your last in the church. O wicked man! And
> wretched woman that I was! I wish I had then sunk down
> into a grave, rather than to have given you my hand, to be
> led to your loathsome bed. O, O—   *(Seems to weep)*   80

VERNISH
> So, very fine! Just a marriage quarrel! which, though it
> generally begins by the wife's fault, yet in the conclusion it
> becomes the husband's; and whosoever offends at first, he
> only is sure to ask pardon at last. My dear—

OLIVIA
> My devil!   85

VERNISH
> Come, prithee be appeased and go home; I have bespoken
> our supper betimes, for I could not eat till I found you. Go,
> I'll give you all kind of satisfactions, and one which uses
> to be a reconciling one: two hundred of those guineas I
> received last night, to do what you will with.   90

OLIVIA
> What, would you pay me for being your bawd?

VERNISH
> Nay, prithee no more; go, and I'll thoroughly satisfy you
> when I come home; and then, too, we will have a fit of
> laughter at Manly, whom I am going to find at 'The Cock' in
> Bow Street, where, I hear, he dined. Go, dearest, go home.   95

ELIZA *(Aside)*
> A very pretty turn indeed, this!

VERNISH
> Now, cousin, since by my wife I have that honour and
> privilege of calling you so, I have something to beg of you

---

92 *thoroughly* Q1 (throughly Q2–8, 0)

---

81 *Just a marriage quarrel* A proper marriage quarrel
94–5 *'The Cock' in Bow Street* Oxford Kate's, a tavern notorious for
    Sedley's nude debauch (see Pepys, 1 July 1663); Wycherley enter-
    tained here when lodging in Bow Street

too; which is, not to take notice of our marriage to any
whatever yet awhile, for some reasons very important to me;   100
and next, that you will do my wife the honour to go home
with her, and me the favour to use that power you have
with her in our reconcilement.

ELIZA

That, I dare promise, sir, will be no hard matter. Your
servant.   *(Exit* VERNISH)   105
—Well, cousin, this I confess was reasonable hypocrisy; you
were the better for't.

OLIVIA

What hypocrisy?

ELIZA

Why, this last deceit of your husband was lawful, since in
your own defence.   110

OLIVIA

What deceit? I'd have you to know I never deceived my
husband.

ELIZA

You do not understand me, sure; I say, this was an honest
come-off, and a good one. But 'twas a sign your gallant had
had enough of your conversation, since he could so dex-   115
trously cheat your husband in passing for a woman.

OLIVIA

What d'ye mean, once more, with my gallant and passing for
a woman?

ELIZA

What do you mean? You see your husband took him for a
woman.   120

OLIVIA

Whom?

ELIZA

Heyday! Why, the man he found you with, for whom last
night you were so much afraid, and who you told me—

OLIVIA

Lord, you rave, sure!

ELIZA

Why, did not you tell me last night—   125

OLIVIA

I know not what I might tell you last night, in a fright.

  99 *take notice of* mention
114 *come-off* evasion
115 *conversation* (1) society (2) sexual intimacy; Eliza suggests Olivia
     has reduced her gallant to temporary impotence

ELIZA

Ay, what was that fright for? For a woman? Besides, were
you not afraid to see your husband just now? I warrant, only
for having been found with a woman! Nay, did you not just
now too own your false step, or trip, as you called it?   130
Which was with a woman too! Fie, this fooling is so insipid,
'tis offensive.

OLIVIA

And fooling with my honour will be more offensive. Did
you not hear my husband say he found me with a woman in
man's clothes? And d'ye think he does not know a man from   135
a woman?

ELIZA

Not so well, I'm sure, as you do; therefore I'd rather take
your word.

OLIVIA

What, you grow scurrilous and are, I find, more censorious
than the world! I must have a care of you, I see.   140

ELIZA

No, you need not fear yet; I'll keep your secret.

OLIVIA

My secret! I'd have you to know I have no need of confidents, though you value yourself upon being a good one.

ELIZA

O admirable confidence! You show more in denying your
wickedness than other people in glorying in't.   145

OLIVIA

Confidence, to me! To me, such language! Nay, then I'll
never see your face again. *(Aside)* I'll quarrel with her, that
people may never believe I was in her power, but take for
malice all the truth she may speak against me. [*Aloud*]
Lettice, where are you? Let us be gone from this censorious, 150
ill woman.

ELIZA

(Aside) Nay, thou shalt stay a little, to damn thyself quite.
[*Aloud*] One word first, pray, madam. Can you swear that
whom your husband found you with—

OLIVIA

Swear! Ay, that whosoever 'twas that stole up, unknown,   155
into my room when 'twas dark, I know not whether man or
woman, by heavens, by all that's good, or may I never more
have joys here or in the other world! Nay, may I eternally—

144 *confidence* impudence (with a pun on 'confidents')

ELIZA

Be damned. So so, you are damned enough already by your
oaths, and I enough confirmed; and now you may please to   160
be gone. Yet take this advice with you: in this plain-dealing
age, to leave off forswearing yourself. For when people
hardly think the better of a woman for her real modesty,
why should you put that great constraint upon yourself to
feign it?   165

OLIVIA

O hideous, hideous advice! Let us go out of the hearing of
it. She will spoil us, Lettice.

(*Exeunt* OLIVIA *and* LETTICE *at one door,* ELIZA *at t'other*)

[Act V, Scene ii]

The scene changes to 'The Cock' in Bow Street
A table, [*chair,*] *and bottles* [*set*]

MANLY *and* FIDELIA [*discovered*]

MANLY

How! Saved her honour by making her husband believe you
were a woman! 'Twas well, but hard enough to do, sure.

FIDELIA

We were interrupted before he could contradict me.

MANLY

But can't you tell me, d'ye say, what kind of man he was?

FIDELIA

I was so frightened, I confess, I can give no other account   5
of him but that he was pretty tall, round faced, and one I'm
sure I ne'er had seen before.

MANLY

But she, you say, made you swear to return tonight?

FIDELIA

But I have since sworn never to go near her again; for the
husband would murder me, or worse, if he caught me again.   10

MANLY

No, I'll go with you and defend you tonight, and then I'll
swear, too, never to go near her again.

FIDELIA

Nay, indeed, sir, I will not go, to be accessary to your death
too. Besides, what should you go again, sir, for?

167 *spoil* destroy, ruin

MANLY

No disputing or advice, sir; you have reason to know I am   15
unalterable. Go, therefore, presently, and write her a note to
enquire if her assignation with you holds, and if not to be at
her own house, where else; and be importunate to gain admittance to her tonight. Let your messenger, ere he deliver your
letter, enquire first if her husband be gone out. Go, 'tis now   20
almost six of the clock; I expect you back here before seven,
with leave to see her then. Go, do this dextrously, and expect
the performance of my last night's promise never to part with
you.

FIDELIA

Ay, sir, but will you be sure to remember that?   25

MANLY

Did I ever break my word? Go, no more replies or doubts.

(Exit FIDELIA*)*

Enter FREEMAN *to* MANLY

Where hast thou been?

FREEMAN

In the next room, with my Lord Plausible and Novel.

MANLY

Ay, we came hither because 'twas a private house, but with
thee indeed no house can be private, for thou hast that   30
pretty quality of the familiar fops of the town, who in an
eating-house always keep company with all people in't but
those they came with.

FREEMAN

I went into their room but to keep them, and my own fool
the squire, out of your room. But you shall be peevish now,   35
because you have no money. But why the devil won't you
write to those we were speaking of? Since your modesty, or
your spirit, will not suffer you to speak to 'em, to lend you
money, why won't you try 'em at last that way?

MANLY

Because I know 'em already, and can bear want better than   40
denials, nay, than obligations.

FREEMAN

Deny you! They cannot. All of 'em have been your intimate
friends.

MANLY

No, they have been people only I have obliged particularly.

29 *private house* inn with some rooms available for private parties

FREEMAN

Very well; therefore you ought to go to 'em the rather, sure.   45

MANLY

No no; those you have obliged most, most certainly avoid
you when you can oblige 'em no longer; and they take your
visits like so many duns. Friends, like mistresses, are avoided
for obligations past.

FREEMAN

Pshaw! But most of 'em are your relations, men of great   50
fortune and honour.

MANLY

Yes, but relations have so much honour as to think poverty
taints the blood, and disown their wanting kindred; believing,
I suppose, that as riches at first makes a gentleman, the want
of 'em degrades him. But, damn 'em, now I am poor I'll   55
anticipate their contempt and disown them.

FREEMAN

But you have many a female acquaintance whom you have
been liberal to, who may have a heart to refund to you a
little, if you would ask it. They are not all Olivias.

MANLY

Damn thee! How could'st thou think of such a thing? I   60
would as soon rob my footman of his wages. Besides, 'twere
in vain too; for a wench is like a box in an ordinary, receives
all people's money easily, but there's no getting, nay, shaking
any out again, and he that fills it is surest never to keep the
key.   65

FREEMAN

Well, but noble captain, would you make me believe that
you who know half the town, have so many friends, and
have obliged so many, can't borrow fifty or an hundred
pound?

MANLY

Why, noble lieutenant, you who know all the town, and call   70
all you know friends, methinks should not wonder at it,
since you find ingratitude too; for how many lords' families,

---

55 *I am* Q2–8, 0 (I'm Q1)
64 *surest* Q1b, 2–8 (sure Q1a, 0)

---

45 *the rather* sooner, more readily
62 *a box in an ordinary* i.e., the 'bank' at a public eating-house used
   for gambling: 'Rooks can do little harm in the day time at an
   Ordinary, being forc'd to play upon the *Square,* although now and
   then they make an advantage, when the *Box-keeper goes with*
   [them]' (Charles Cotton, *The Compleat Gamester* (1674), p. 5)

though descended from blacksmiths or tinkers, hast thou
called great and illustrious? how many ill tables called good
eating? how many noisy coxcombs wits? how many pert,   75
cocking cowards stout? how many tawdry, affected rogues
well-dressed? how many perukes admired? and how many
ill verses applauded? and yet canst not borrow a shilling.
Dost thou expect I, who always spoke truth, should?

FREEMAN

Nay, now you think you have paid me; but hark you,   80
captain, I have heard of a thing called grinning honour, but
never of starving honour.

MANLY

Well, but it has been the fate of some brave men; and if they
won't give me a ship again, I can go starve anywhere with
a musket on my shoulder.   85

FREEMAN

Give you a ship! Why, you will not solicit it.

MANLY

If I have not solicited it by my services, I know no other way.

FREEMAN

Your servant, sir. Nay, then I'm satisfied, I must solicit my
widow the closer, and run the desperate fortune of matrimony on shore.   *(Exit)*   90

Enter to MANLY, VERNISH

MANLY

How! Nay, here is a friend indeed, and he that has him in
his arms can know no wants.   *(Embraces* VERNISH*)*

VERNISH

Dear sir! And he that is in your arms is secure from all fears
whatever. Nay, our nation is secure by your defeat at sea,
and the Dutch that fought against you have proved enemies   95
to themselves only, in bringing you back to us.

---

74 *called good* Q6–7 (call good Q1–5, 8, 0)
76 *cocking* Q1b, 2–8 (coaching Q1a, 0)

---

76 *cocking* setting the hat with a flourish; hence, strutting, swaggering
76 *stout* brave
81 *grinning honour* Falstaff's comment on the dead Sir Walter Blunt in
   1 Henry IV, V. iii, 59; Freeman suggests that Manly's integrity will
   prove as fatal
88 *Your servant, sir* Freeman disagrees with Manly, and withdraws
   from the discussion; see II. 271 note.
88 *satisfied* convinced
89 *run the desperate fortune* risk the dangerous undertaking

MANLY

    Fie fie, this from a friend! And yet from any other 'twere
unsufferable. I thought I should never have taken anything
ill from you.

VERNISH

    A friend's privilege is to speak his mind, though it be taken   100
ill.

MANLY

    But your tongue need not tell me you think too well of me;
I have found it from your heart, which spoke in actions, your
unalterable heart. But Olivia is false, my friend, which I
suppose is no news to you.   105

VERNISH *(Aside)*

    He's in the right on't.

MANLY

    But could'st thou not keep her true to me?

VERNISH

    Not for my heart, sir.

MANLY

    But could you not perceive it at all before I went? Could she
so deceive us both?   110

VERNISH

    I must confess, the first time I knew it was three days after
your departure, when she received the money you had left
in Lombard Street in her name; and her tears did not hinder
her, it seems, from counting that. You would trust her with
all, like a true, generous lover!   115

MANLY

    And she, like a mean, jilting—

VERNISH

    Traitorous—

MANLY

    Base—

VERNISH

    Damned—

MANLY

    Covetous—   120

VERNISH

    Mercenary whore—*(Aside)* I can hardly hold from laughing.

---

113 *Lombard Street* in the heart of the city; many bankers traded here,
    including Pepys's Master Backwell (29 May 1662) who, like Vernish's
    associate in IV. ii, 155, 409, was also a goldsmith and an alderman

MANLY
Ay, a mercenary whore indeed, for she made me pay her
before I lay with her.

VERNISH
How!—Why, have you lain with her?

MANLY
Ay ay.   125

VERNISH
Nay, she deserves you should report it at least, though you
have not.

MANLY
Report it! By heaven, 'tis true.

VERNISH
How! Sure not.

MANLY
I do not use to lie, nor you to doubt me.   130

VERNISH
When?

MANLY
Last night, about seven or eight of the clock.

VERNISH
Ha! *(Aside)* Now I remember, I thought she spake as if she
expected some other, rather than me. A confounded whore
indeed!   135

MANLY
But what, thou wonderest at it! Nay, you seem to be angry
too.

VERNISH
I cannot but be enraged against her, for her usage of you.
Damned, infamous, common jade!

MANLY
Nay, her cuckold, who first cuckolded me in my money, shall   140
not laugh all himself; we will do him reason, shan't we?

VERNISH
Ay ay.

MANLY
But thou dost not, for so great a friend, take pleasure enough
in your friend's revenge, methinks.

VERNISH
Yes yes; I'm glad to know it, since you have lain with her.   145

MANLY
Thou canst not tell me who that rascal, her cuckold, is?

141 *do him reason* give him what he deserves

VERNISH

No.

MANLY

She would keep it from you, I suppose.

VERNISH

Yes, yes.

MANLY

Thou wouldst laugh if thou knewest but all the circum- 150
stances of my having her. Come, I'll tell thee.

VERNISH

Damn her! I care not to hear any more of her.

MANLY

Faith, thou shalt. You must know—

Enter FREEMAN *backwards, endeavouring to keep out* NOVEL,
LORD PLAUSIBLE, JERRY, *and* OLDFOX, *who all press in upon him*

FREEMAN

I tell you, he has a wench with him and would be private.

MANLY

Damn 'em! A man can't open a bottle in these eating-houses, 155
but presently you have these impudent, intruding, buzzing
flies and insects in your glass.—Well, I'll tell thee all anon.
In the mean time, prithee go to her, but not from me, and
try if you can get her to lend me but an hundred pound of
my money, to supply my present wants; for I suppose there 160
is no recovering any of it by law.

VERNISH

Not any; think not of it. Nor by this way neither.

MANLY

Go, try, at least.

VERNISH

I'll go, but I can satisfy you beforehand 'twill be to no
purpose. You'll no more find a refunding wench— 165

MANLY

Than a refunding lawyer; indeed their fees alike scarce ever
return. However, try her, put it to her.

VERNISH

Ay ay, I'll try her, put it to her home, with a vengeance.

(Exit VERNISH)

Manent caeteri

156 *presently* at once

NOVEL

Nay, you shall be our judge, Manly.—Come, major, I'll
speak it to your teeth. If people provoke me to say bitter   170
things to their faces, they must take what follows; though,
like my Lord Plausible, I'd rather do't civilly behind their
backs.

MANLY

Nay, thou art a dangerous rogue, I've heard, behind a man's
back.   175

LORD PLAUSIBLE

You wrong him sure, noble captain; he would do a man no
more harm behind his back than to his face.

FREEMAN

I am of my lord's mind.

MANLY

Yes, a fool, like a coward, is the more to be feared behind
a man's back, more than a witty man; for as a coward is   180
more bloody than a brave man, a fool is more malicious than
a man of wit.

NOVEL

A fool, tar, a fool! Nay, thou art a brave sea-judge of wit!
A fool! Prithee, when did you ever find me want something
to say, as you do often?   185

MANLY

Nay, I confess thou art always talking, roaring, or making a
noise; that I'll say for thee.

NOVEL

Well, and is talking a sign of a fool?

MANLY

Yes, always talking, especially too if it be loud and fast, is
the sign of a fool.   190

NOVEL

Pshaw! Talking is like fencing, the quicker the better; run
'em down, run 'em down, no matter for parrying, push on
still, sa, sa, sa! no matter whether you argue in form, push in
guard, or no.

MANLY

Or hit, or no. I think thou always talk'st without thinking,   195
Novel.

170 *to your teeth* face to face, in direct confrontation
186 *roaring* roistering, behaving riotously
192 *push on* press forward
193 *sa, sa, sa* a hunting cry, used here for a fencer's attacking advance
193–4 *push in guard* attack from a defensive position

NOVEL

Ay ay, studied play's the worse, to follow the allegory, as the
old pedant says.

OLDFOX

A young fop!

MANLY

I ever thought the man of most wit had been like him of   200
most money, who has no vanity in showing it everywhere,
whilst the beggarly pusher of his fortune has all he has about
him still, only to show.

NOVEL

Well, sir, and makes a very pretty show in the world, let me
tell you; nay, a better than your close hunks. A pox, give me   205
ready money in play. What care I for a man's reputation?
What are we the better for your substantial, thrifty cur-
mudgeon in wit, sir?

LORD PLAUSIBLE

Thou art a profuse young rogue, indeed.

NOVEL

So much for talking, which I think I have proved a mark of   210
wit; and so is railing, roaring, and making a noise, for railing
is satire, you know, and roaring and making a noise, humour.

Enter to them FIDELIA, *taking* MANLY *aside and showing him
a paper*

FIDELIA

The hour is betwixt seven and eight exactly. 'Tis now half an
hour after six.

MANLY

Well, go then to the Piazza and wait for me; as soon as it is   215
quite dark, I'll be with you. I must stay here yet awhile for
my friend.   *(Exit* FIDELIA*)*
But is railing satire, Novel?

197 *studied play* premeditated sword-play
197 *follow the allegory* continue the metaphor
198 *old pedant* unidentified
202 *pusher* promoter
205 *hunks* 'a covetous Creature, a miserable Wretch' (*B.E.*)
213 *betwixt . . . exactly* i.e., 'half an hour after seven precisely' (329)
215 *the Piazza* 'On the North and East Sides [of Covent Garden] are
    Rows of very good and large Houses, called the *Piazzo's,* sustained
    by Stone Pillars, to support the Buildings. Under which are Walks,
    broad and convenient, paved with Freestone' (John Stow, *A survey of
    . . . London,* ed. John Strype (1720), VI, 89)

FREEMAN

And roaring and making a noise, humour?

NOVEL

What, won't you confess there's humour in roaring and mak- 220
ing a noise?

FREEMAN

No.

NOVEL

Nor in cutting napkins and hangings?

MANLY

No, sure.

NOVEL

Dull fops! 225

OLDFOX

O rogue, rogue, insipid rogue!—Nay, gentlemen, allow him
those things for wit, for his parts lie only that way.

NOVEL

Peace, old fool! I wonder not at thee; but that young fellows
should be so dull as to say there's no humour in making a
noise and breaking windows! I tell you, there's wit and 230
humour too in both, and a wit is as well known by his frolic
as by his simile.

OLDFOX

Pure rogue! There's your modern wit for you! Wit and
humour in breaking of windows! There's mischief, if you
will, but no wit or humour. 235

NOVEL

Prithee, prithee, peace, old fool. I tell you, where there is
mischief there's wit. Don't we esteem the monkey a wit
amongst beasts, only because he's mischievous? And let me
tell you, as good nature is a sign of a fool, being mischievous
is a sign of wit. 240

OLDFOX

O rogue, rogue! Pretend to be a wit by doing mischief and
railing!

---

223 *cutting . . . hangings* putting a sword through the table linen and
      curtains of an inn or whore's lodging
227 *parts* abilities, talents
230 *breaking windows* another pastime of the roaring boys; in
      Etherege's *The Comical Revenge* (1664) Sir Frederick Frollick
      'committed a general massacre on the glass-windows' of his whore's
      lodging (I. ii); cf. 373–5
237 *monkey* a fashionable pet; Huysmans painted Rochester crowning
      his with a laurel wreath

NOVEL

Why, thou, old fool, hast no other pretence to the name of
a wit but by railing at new plays.

OLDFOX

Thou, by railing at that facetious, noble way of wit, quib-   245
bling.

NOVEL

Thou call'st thy dullness gravity, and thy dozing thinking.

OLDFOX

You, sir, your dullness spleen; and you talk much and say
nothing.

NOVEL

Thou read'st much and understand'st nothing, sir.   250

OLDFOX

You laugh loud and break no jest.

NOVEL

You rail, and nobody hangs himself. And thou hast nothing
of the satyr but in thy face.

OLDFOX

And you have no jest but your face, sir.

NOVEL

Thou art an illiterate pedant.   255

OLDFOX

Thou art a fool with a bad memory.

MANLY

Come, a pox on you both! You have done like wits now; for
you wits, when you quarrel, never give over till you prove
one another fools.

NOVEL

And you fools have never any occasion of laughing at us   260
wits but when we quarrel.—Therefore, let us be friends,
Oldfox.

MANLY

They are such wits as thou art who make the name of a wit
as scandalous as that of bully, and signify a loud-laughing,

245–6 *quibbling* punning
248 *spleen* melancholy, a fashionable malady; 'every heavy wretch, who
has nothing to say, excuses his dulness by complaining of the
spleen' (the *Spectator* no. 53, 1 May 1711)
253 *satyr* Satire was thought to derive from the chorus of lustful goat-
like satyrs in Greek drama; thus Novel attacks simultaneously Oldfox's virility, appearance, and wit.

talking, incorrigible coxcomb, as bully a roaring, hardened 265
coward.

FREEMAN

And would have his noise and laughter pass for wit, as
t'other his huffing and blustering for courage.

Enter VERNISH

MANLY

Gentlemen, with your leave, here is one I would speak with,
and I have nothing to say to you. *(Puts 'em out of the room)* 270

Manent MANLY, VERNISH

VERNISH

I told you 'twas in vain to think of getting money out of her.
She says, if a shilling would do't, she would not save you
from starving or hanging or, what you would think worse,
begging or flattering; and rails so at you, one would not
think you had lain with her.   275

MANLY

O friend, never trust for that matter a woman's railing, for
she is no less a dissembler in her hatred than her love; and
as her fondness of her husband is a sign he's a cuckold, her
railing at another man is a sign she lies with him.

VERNISH *(Aside)*

He's in the right on't; I know not what to trust to.   280

MANLY

But you did not take any notice of it to her, I hope?

VERNISH *(Aside)*

So! Sure he is afraid I should have disproved him by an
enquiry of her; all may be well yet.

MANLY

What hast thou in thy head that makes thee seem so unquiet?

VERNISH

Only this base, impudent woman's falseness; I cannot put her 285
out of my head.

MANLY

O my dear friend, be not you too sensible of my wrongs, for
then I shall feel 'em too with more pain, and think 'em
unsufferable. Damn her, her money, and that ill-natured

265 *hardened* confirmed
268 *huffing* swaggering
281 *take any notice of* mention

whore too, Fortune herself! But if thou would'st ease a little   290
my present trouble, prithee go borrow me somewhere else
some money; I can trouble thee.

VERNISH

You trouble me indeed, most sensibly, when you command
me anything I cannot do. I have lately lost a great deal of
money at play, more than I can yet pay, so that not only my   295
money but my credit too is gone, and know not where to
borrow; but could rob a church for you. *(Aside)* Yet would
rather end your wants by cutting your throat.

MANLY

Nay, then I doubly feel my poverty, since I'm incapable of
supplying thee.   *(Embraces* VERNISH*)*   300

VERNISH

But, methinks, she that granted you the last favour, as they
call it, should not deny you anything.

NOVEL *looks in*

NOVEL

Hey, tarpaulin, have you done?   *(*[NOVEL] *retires again)*

VERNISH

I understand not that point of kindness, I confess.

MANLY

No, thou dost not understand it, and I have not time to let   305
you know all now, for these fools, you see, will interrupt us;
but anon, at supper, we'll laugh at leisure together at Olivia's
cuckold, who took a young fellow, that goes between his wife
and me, for a woman.

VERNISH

Ha!   310

MANLY

Senseless, easy rascal! 'Twas no wonder she chose him for a
husband; but she thought him, I thank her, fitter than me for
that blind, bearing office.

VERNISH *(Aside)*

I could not be deceived in that long woman's hair tied up
behind, nor those infallible proofs, her pouting, swelling   315
breasts; I have handled too many, sure, not to know 'em.

---

303 s.d. After 'done' Q1 prints (NOVEL *looks in, and retires again*).

292–3 *trouble* (1) inconvenience (2) distress; Manly uses the formula of
    a polite request, which Vernish takes up seriously
313 *bearing* suffering, enduring

MANLY

What, you wonder the fellow could be such a blind coxcomb?

VERNISH

Yes, yes—

NOVEL looks in again

NOVEL

Nay, prithee come to us, Manly. Gad, all the fine things one   320
says in their company are lost without thee.

MANLY

Away, fop! I'm busy yet.   *([NOVEL] retires)*
You see we cannot talk here at our ease; besides, I must be
gone immediately, in order to meeting with Olivia again
tonight.   325

VERNISH

Tonight! It cannot be, sure—

MANLY

I had an appointment just now from her.

VERNISH

For what time?

MANLY

At half an hour after seven precisely.

VERNISH

Don't you apprehend the husband?   330

MANLY

He! Snivelling gull! He a thing to be feared! A husband, the
tamest of creatures!

VERNISH *(Aside)*

Very fine!

MANLY

But, prithee, in the mean time, go try to get me some money.
Though thou art too modest to borrow for thyself, thou   335
canst do anything for me, I know. Go, for I must be gone
to Olivia. Go, and meet me here anon.—Freeman, where are
you?   *(Exit MANLY)*

Manet VERNISH

VERNISH

Ay, I'll meet with you, I warrant, but it shall be at Olivia's.
Sure, it cannot be; she denies it so calmly, and with that   340

---

319 s.d. After 'yes—' Q1 prints (NOVEL *looks in again, and retires*).

324 *in order to* for the sake of

honest, modest assurance, it can't be true—and he does not
use to lie—but belying a woman when she won't be kind is
the only lie a brave man will least scruple. But then the
woman in man's clothes, whom he calls a man! Well, but by
her breasts I know her to be a woman. But then again, his   345
appointment from her to meet with him tonight! I am distracted more with doubt than jealousy. Well, I have no
way to disabuse or revenge myself but by going home
immediately, putting on a riding suit, and pretending to my
wife the same business which carried me out of town last   350
requires me again to go post to Oxford tonight. Then, if the
appointment he boasts of be true, it's sure to hold, and I shall
have an opportunity either of clearing her or revenging
myself on both. Perhaps she is his wench of an old date,
and I am his cully, whilst I think him mine, and he has   355
seemed to make his wench rich only that I might take her
off his hands; or if he has but lately lain with her, he must
needs discover by her my treachery to him, which I'm sure
he will revenge with my death, and which I must prevent
with his, if it were only but for fear of his too just   360
reproaches; for I must confess I never had till now any
excuse but that of interest for doing ill to him.

(Exit VERNISH)

Re-enter MANLY *and* FREEMAN

MANLY

Come hither; only, I say, be sure you mistake not the time.
You know the house exactly where Olivia lodges; 'tis just
hard by.   365

FREEMAN

Yes yes.

MANLY

Well then, bring 'em all, I say, thither, and all you know
that may be then in the house; for the more witnesses I have
of her infamy, the greater will be my revenge. And be sure
you come straight up to her chamber, without more ado.   370
Here, take the watch. You see 'tis above a quarter past
seven. Be there in half an hour exactly.

FREEMAN

You need not doubt my diligence or dexterity; I am an old

357 *off* Q2–8, 0 (off of Q1)

351 *post* by post-horses, i.e., speedily
371 *above* after

scourer, and can naturally beat up a wench's quarters that
won't be civil. Shan't we break her windows too? 375

MANLY

No no. Be punctual only. *(Exeunt ambo)*

Enter WIDOW BLACKACRE *and two* KNIGHTS OF THE POST, *a*
WAITER *with wine*

WIDOW

Sweetheart, are you sure the door was shut close, that none
of those roisters saw us come in?

WAITER

Yes, mistress; and you shall have a privater room above
instantly. *(Exit* WAITER) 380

WIDOW

You are safe enough, gentlemen, for I have been private in
this house ere now upon other occasions, when I was something younger. Come, gentlemen; in short, I leave my business
to your care and fidelity; and so, here's to you.

1 KNIGHT

We were ungrateful rogues if we should not be honest to 385
you, for we have had a great deal of your money.

WIDOW

And you have done me many a good job for't; and so, here's
to you again.

2 KNIGHT

Why, we have been perjured but six times for you.

1 KNIGHT

Forged but four deeds, with your husband's last deed of gift. 390

2 KNIGHT

And but three wills.

1 KNIGHT

And counterfeited hands and seals to some six bonds; I
think that's all, brother.

WIDOW

Ay, that's all, gentlemen; and so, here's to you again.

2 KNIGHT

Nay, 'twould do one's heart good to be forsworn for you; 395
you have a conscience in your ways, and pay us well.

1 KNIGHT

You are in the right on't, brother; one would be damned for
her with all one's heart.

374 *scourer* roisterer
374 *beat . . . quarters* raid a whore's lodging

2 KNIGHT

But there are rogues who make us forsworn for 'em, and
when we come to be paid, they'll be forsworn too, and not   400
pay us our wages, which they promised with oaths sufficient.

1 KNIGHT

Ay, a great lawyer that shall be nameless bilked me too.

WIDOW

That was hard, methinks, that a lawyer should use gentlemen
witnesses no better.

2 KNIGHT

A lawyer! D'ye wonder a lawyer should do't? I was bilked   405
by a reverend divine, that preaches twice on Sundays and
prays half an hour still before dinner.

WIDOW

How! A conscientious divine, and not pay people for damning themselves! Sure then, for all his talking, he does not
believe damnation. But come, to our business. Pray be sure   410
to imitate exactly the flourish at the end of this name.

(Pulls out a deed or two)

1 KNIGHT

O he's the best in England at untangling a flourish, madam.

WIDOW

And let not the seal be a jot bigger. Observe well the dash
too, at the end of this name.

2 KNIGHT

I warrant you, madam.   415

WIDOW

Well, these and many other shifts poor widows are put to
sometimes; for everybody would be riding a widow, as they
say, and breaking into her jointure. They think marrying a
widow an easy business, like leaping the hedge where another
has gone over before; a widow is a mere gap, a gap with   420
them.

Enter to them MAJOR OLDFOX *with two* WAITERS.
The KNIGHTS OF THE POST *huddle up the writings*

What, he here! Go then, go, my hearts, you have your
instructions.   *(Exeunt* KNIGHTS OF THE POST*)*

OLDFOX

Come, madam, to be plain with you, I'll be fobbed off no
longer. *(Aside)* I'll bind her and gag her, but she shall hear   425

---

402 *bilked* cheated
421 s.d. *huddle up* hide (in a heap)

me. [*To the* WAITERS] Look you, friends, there's the money
I promised you; and now do what you promised me. Here
are my garters, and here's a gag. [*To* WIDOW BLACKACRE]
You shall be acquainted with my parts, lady, you shall.

WIDOW

Acquainted with your parts! A rape, a rape! What, will you   430
ravish me?

    (*The* WAITERS *tie her to the chair and gag her, and exeunt*)

OLDFOX

Yes, lady, I will ravish you; but it shall be through the ear,
lady, the ear only, with my well-penned acrostics.

Enter to them FREEMAN, JERRY BLACKACRE, *three* BAILIFFS, *a*
CONSTABLE *and his* ASSISTANTS, *with the two* KNIGHTS OF THE
POST [*as prisoners*]

What, shall I never read my things undisturbed again?

JERRY

O law! My mother bound hand and foot, and gaping as if   435
she rose before her time today!

FREEMAN

What means this, Oldfox? [*To* WIDOW BLACKACRE] But I'll
release you from him; you shall be no man's prisoner but
mine.—Bailiffs, execute your writ.   (FREEMAN *unties her*)

OLDFOX [*Aside*]

Nay, then I'll be gone, for fear of being bail and paying her   440
debts without being her husband.   (*Exit* OLDFOX)

1 BAILIFF [*To* WIDOW BLACKACRE]

We arrest you in the King's name at the suit of Master
Freeman, guardian to Jeremiah Blackacre, esquire, in an
action of ten thousand pounds.

WIDOW

How! How! In a choke-bail action! What, and the pen and   445
ink gentlemen taken too!—Have you confessed, you rogues?

1 KNIGHT

We needed not to confess, for the bailiffs dogged us hither
to the very door and overheard all that you and we said.

WIDOW

Undone, undone then! No man was ever too hard for me till

428 *garters* long ribbons worn at the knee for display: 'I was set upon
    by a great dogg, who got hold of my garters' (Pepys, 11 May 1663)
429 *parts* abilities, talents, which the Widow takes in a sexual sense
435 *gaping* staring wildly
445 *choke-bail action* one where such large sums or serious offences are
    involved that bail is not allowed

now.—O Jerry, child, wilt thou vex again the womb that bore   450
thee?

JERRY

Ay, for bearing me before wedlock, as you say. But I'll teach
you to call a Blackacre a bastard, though you were never so
much my mother.

WIDOW

(Aside) Well, I'm undone. Not one trick left? No law-meuse   455
imaginable? [*To* FREEMAN] Cruel sir, a word with you, I pray.

FREEMAN

In vain, madam; for you have no other way to release yourself but by the bonds of matrimony.

WIDOW

How, sir, how! That were but to sue out an *habeas corpus*
for a removal from one prison to another. Matrimony!   460

FREEMAN

Well, bailiffs, away with her.

WIDOW

O stay, sir; can you be so cruel as to bring me under covert-
baron again, and put it out of my power to sue in my own
name? Matrimony to a woman is worse than excommunica-
tion, in depriving her of the benefit of the law, and I would   465
rather be deprived of life. But hark you, sir; I am contented
you should hold and enjoy my person by lease or patent, but
not by the spiritual patent called a licence; that is, to have
the privileges of a husband without the dominion; that is,
durante beneplacito: in consideration of which I will, out of   470
my jointure, secure you an annuity of three hundred pounds
a year and pay your debts; and that's all you younger
brothers desire to marry a widow for, I'm sure.

FREEMAN

Well, widow, if—

JERRY

What! I hope, bully guardian, you are not making agree-   475
ments without me?

---

464 *woman is* Q4–8, 0 (woman, Q1–3)

---

455 *law-meuse* loophole in the law
462–3 *under covert-baron* see II. 951 note; wives 'are wholly . . . at the
Will and Disposition of the Husband . . . The Wife can make no
Contract without her Husbands consent, and in Law-Matters *Sine
viro respondere non potest*' (Chamberlayne, I, 291)
470 *durante beneplacito* during good pleasure, i.e., as long as one pleases;
a legal phrase more usually applied to the tenure of judges in e.g.
the Common Pleas.

FREEMAN

No no. First, widow, you must say no more that he is the
son of a whore; have a care of that. And then he must have
a settled exhibition of forty pounds a year, and a nag of
assizes, kept by you, but not upon the common; and have   480
free ingress, egress, and regress to and from your maids'
garret.

WIDOW

Well, I can grant all that too.

JERRY

Ay ay, fair words butter no cabbage; but, guardian, make
her sign, sign and seal; for otherwise, if you knew her as well   485
as I, you would not trust her word for a farthing.

FREEMAN

I warrant thee, squire.—Well, widow, since thou art so
generous, I will be generous too; and if you'll secure me four
hundred pound a year but during your life, and pay my
debts, not above a thousand pound, I'll bate you your person   490
to dispose of as you please.

WIDOW

Have a care, sir; a settlement without a consideration is void
in the law. You must do something for't.

FREEMAN

Prithee, then let the settlement on me be called alimony, and
the consideration our separation. Come; my lawyer, with   495
writings ready drawn, is within, and in haste. Come.

WIDOW

But what, no other kind of consideration, Master Freeman?
Well, a widow, I see, is a kind of a *sine cure*, by custom of
which the unconscionable incumbent enjoys the profits without any duty, but does that still elsewhere. *(Exeunt omnes)*   500

---

493 *in the* Q2–8 (in Q1, 0)

---

479 *settled exhibition* fixed allowance
479–80 *of assizes* of guaranteed quality
480 *not upon the common* since the grass is greener in a private field
  than in pastures available to all
481 *ingress . . . regress* entry, exit, and re-entry (legal terms)
484 *fair . . . cabbage* cf. 'Fair words butter no parsnips' (Tilley, W791)
490 *bate you your person* i.e., make no sexual demands on you
496 *in haste* so is Freeman, who promised Manly at 373 to be at
  Olivia's with a gang of witnesses in half an hour

[Act V, Scene iii]

The scene changes to OLIVIA's *Lodging*
Enter OLIVIA *with a candle in her hand*

OLIVIA

So, I am now prepared once more for my timorous young
lover's reception. My husband is gone; and go thou out too,
thou next interrupter of love. *(Puts out the candle)* Kind
darkness, that frees us lovers from scandal and bashfulness,
from the censure of our gallants and the world! So, are you   5
there?

Enter to OLIVIA, FIDELIA, *followed softly by* MANLY

Come, my dear punctual lover; there is not such another in
the world. Thou hast beauty and youth to please a wife,
address and wit to amuse and fool a husband; nay, thou
hast all things to be wished in a lover, but your fits. I hope,   10
my dear, you won't have one tonight; and that you may not,
I'll lock the door, though there be no need of it but to lock
out your fits, for my husband is just gone out of town again.
Come, where are you?   *(Goes to the door and locks it)*

MANLY *(Aside)*

Well, thou hast impudence enough to give me fits too and   15
make revenge itself impotent, hinder me from making thee
yet more infamous, if it can be.

OLIVIA

Come, come, my soul, come.

FIDELIA

Presently, my dear; we have time enough, sure.

OLIVIA

How! Time enough! True lovers can no more think they   20
ever have time enough than love enough. You shall stay with
me all night; but that is but a lover's moment. Come.

FIDELIA

But won't you let me give you and myself the satisfaction of
telling you how I abused your husband last night?

OLIVIA

Not when you can give me and yourself too the satisfaction   25
of abusing him again tonight. Come.

9 *amuse* deceive

FIDELIA

Let me but tell you how your husband—

OLIVIA

O name not his or Manly's more loathsome name, if you
love me! I forbid 'em last night; and you know I mentioned
my husband but once, and he came. No talking, pray; 'twas   30
ominous to us. *(A noise at the door)* You make me fancy a
noise at the door already, but I'm resolved not to be interrupted. Where are you? Come; for rather than lose my dear
expectation now, though my husband were at the door, and
the bloody ruffian Manly here in the room with all his awful   35
insolence, I would give myself to this dear hand, to be led
away to heavens of joys which none but thou canst give.
(The noise at the door increases) But what's this noise at the
door? So, I told you what talking would come to. Ha!
(OLIVIA listens at the door) O heavens, my husband's voice!   40

MANLY *(Aside)*

Freeman is come too soon.

OLIVIA

O 'tis he! Then here's the happiest minute lost that ever
bashful boy or trifling woman fooled away! I'm undone! My
husband's reconcilement too was false as my joy, all delusion.
But come this way; here's a back door.   *(Exit, and returns)*   45
The officious jade has locked us in, instead of locking others
out. But let us then escape your way, by the balcony; and
whilst you pull down the curtains I'll fetch from my closet
what next will best secure our escape. I have left my key in
the door, and 'twill not suddenly be broke open.   *(Exit)*   50
(A noise as it were people forcing the door)

MANLY

Stir not; yet fear nothing.

FIDELIA

Nothing but your life, sir.

MANLY

We shall now know this happy man she calls husband.

OLIVIA *re-enters*

OLIVIA

O, where are you? What, idle with fear? Come, I'll tie the
curtains, if you will hold. Here, take this cabinet and purse,   55
for it is thine if we escape. *(MANLY takes from her the cabinet
and purse)* Therefore let us make haste.   *(Exit OLIVIA)*

42 *here's* Q2–6, 8, 0 (here is Q1; her's Q7)

MANLY

'Tis mine indeed now again, and it shall never escape more
from me, to you at least.

The door broken open, enter VERNISH *alone, with a dark-
lantern and a sword, running at* MANLY, *who draws, puts by the
thrust and defends himself, whilst* FIDELIA *runs at* VERNISH
behind

VERNISH *(With a low voice)*

So, there I'm right, sure—   60

MANLY *(Softly)*

Sword and dark-lantern, villain, are some odds, but—

VERNISH *(With a low voice)*

Odds! I'm sure I find more odds than I expected. What, has
my insatiable two seconds at once? But—

Whilst they fight, OLIVIA *re-enters, tying two curtains together*

OLIVIA

Where are you now?—What, is he entered then, and are they
fighting?—O do not kill one that can make no defence!   65
*(*MANLY *throws* VERNISH *down and disarms him)* How! But
I think he has the better on't. Here's his scarf; 'tis he.—So,
keep him down still. I hope thou hast no hurt, my dearest?
                                    (Embracing MANLY*)*

Enter to them FREEMAN, LORD PLAUSIBLE, NOVEL, JERRY
BLACKACRE, *and the* WIDOW BLACKACRE, *lighted in by the
two* SAILORS *with torches*

Ha! What? Manly!—And have I been thus concerned for
him, embracing him? And has he his jewels again too? What   70
means this? O 'tis too sure, as well as my shame, which I'll
go hide for ever.   *(Offers to go out;* MANLY *stops her)*

MANLY

No, my dearest; after so much kindness as has passed
between us, I cannot part with you yet.—Freeman, let
nobody stir out of the room; for notwithstanding your lights,   75

---

59 s.d. *dark-lantern* one shuttered to direct the light, thus blinding an
   onlooker
67 *his scarf* Perhaps Olivia kneels to identify Vernish by his sash; if
   she feels Manly's, it must resemble one usually worn by Fidelia (see
   II. 613 note).
72 s.d. *Offers* Attempts

we are yet in the dark till this gentleman please to turn his
face. *(Pulls* VERNISH *by the sleeve)* How! Vernish! Art thou
the happy man then? Thou! Thoú! Speak, I say; but thy
guilty silence tells me all. Well, I shall not upbraid thee, for
my wonder is striking me as dumb as thy shame has made   80
thee.—But, what? My little volunteer, hurt and fainting!

FIDELIA

My wound, sir, is but a slight one in my arm; 'tis only my
fear of your danger, sir, not yet well over.

MANLY

But what's here? More strange things! *(Observing* FIDELIA'*s
hair untied behind, and without a peruke, which she lost in
the scuffle)* What means this long woman's hair? and face,   85
now all of it appears, too beautiful for a man, which I still
thought womanish indeed! What, you have not deceived me
too, my little volunteer?

OLIVIA *(Aside)*

Me she has, I'm sure.

MANLY

Speak.   90

Enter ELIZA *and* LETTICE

ELIZA

What, cousin, I am brought hither by your woman, I suppose,
to be a witness of the second vindication of your honour?

OLIVIA

Insulting is not generous. You might spare me; I have you.

ELIZA

Have a care, cousin. You'll confess anon too much, and I
would not have your secrets.   95

MANLY *(To* FIDELIA)

Come, your blushes answer me sufficiently, and you have
been my volunteer in love.

FIDELIA

I must confess I needed no compulsion to follow you all the
world over, which I attempted in this habit, partly out of
shame to own my love to you, and fear of a greater shame,   100
your refusal of it; for I knew of your engagement to this
lady, and the constancy of your nature, which nothing could
have altered but herself.

MANLY

Dear madam, I desired you to bring me out of confusion,
and you have given me more. I know not what to speak to   105
you, or how to look upon you. The sense of my rough, hard,

and ill usage of you, though chiefly your own fault, gives me
more pain now 'tis over than you had when you suffered it;
and if my heart, the refusal of such a woman *(Pointing to*
OLIVIA*)*, were not a sacrifice to profane your love, and a   110
greater wrong to you than ever yet I did you, I would beg
of you to receive it, though you used it as she had done; for
though it deserved not from her the treatment she gave it, it
does from you.

FIDELIA

Then it has had punishment sufficient from her already, and   115
needs no more from me; and, I must confess, I would not be
the only cause of making you break your last night's oath to
me, of never parting with me, if you do not forget or
repent it.

MANLY

Then take for ever my heart, and this with it *(Gives her the*   120
cabinet), for 'twas given to you before, and my heart was
before your due. I only beg leave to dispose of these few.
—Here, madam, I never yet left my wench unpaid.
         (Takes some of the jewels and offers 'em to OLIVIA; *she*
              strikes 'em down; PLAUSIBLE *and* NOVEL *take 'em up)*

OLIVIA

So it seems, by giving her the cabinet.

LORD PLAUSIBLE

These pendants appertain to your most faithful, humble   125
servant.

NOVEL

And this locket is mine; my earnest for love, which she never
paid, therefore my own again.

WIDOW

By what law, sir, pray?—Cousin Olivia, a word. What, do
they make a seizure on your goods and chattels, *vi et armis*?   130
Make your demand, I say, and bring your trover, bring your
trover. I'll follow the law for you.

OLIVIA

And I my revenge.   *(Exit* OLIVIA*)*

MANLY

(To VERNISH*)* But 'tis, my friend, in your consideration most
that I would have returned part of your wife's portion, for   135

127 *earnest* initial payment (cf. 'earnest pence' IV. ii, 64 note)
130 *vi et armis* with force and weapons, i.e., by force of arms; a legal
    phrase often used in complaints of assault
131 *trover* strictly, 'an action against him who having found another
    mans goods, refuseth to deliver them upon demand' (Phillips)

'twere hard to take all from thee, since thou hast paid so
dear for't in being such a rascal. Yet thy wife is a fortune
without a portion, and thou art a man of that extraordinary
merit in villainy the world and fortune can never desert thee,
though I do; therefore be not melancholy. Fare you well,   140
sir.   *(Exit* VERNISH *doggedly)*
Now, madam *(Turning to* FIDELIA*)*, I beg your pardon for
lessening the present I made you; but my heart can never be
lessened. This, I confess, was too small for you before, for
you deserve the Indian world, and I would now go thither   145
out of covetousness for your sake only.

FIDELIA

Your heart, sir, is a present of that value I can never make
any return to't. *(Pulling* MANLY *from the company)* But I can
give you back such a present as this, which I got by the loss
of my father, a gentleman of the north of no mean extrac-   150
tion, whose only child I was; therefore left me in the present
possession of two thousand pounds a year, which I left, with
multitudes of pretenders, to follow you, sir, having in several
public places seen you, and observed your actions throughly,
with admiration, when you were too much in love to take   155
notice of mine, which yet was but too visible. The name of
my family is Grey, my other Fidelia. The rest of my story
you shall know when I have fewer auditors.

MANLY

Nay, now, madam, you have taken from me all power of
making you any compliment on my part; for I was going to   160
tell you that for your sake only I would quit the unknown
pleasure of a retirement, and rather stay in this ill world of
ours still, though odious to me, than give you more frights
again at sea, and make again too great a venture there in
you alone. But if I should tell you now all this, and that your 165
virtue (since greater than I thought any was in the world)
had now reconciled me to't, my friend here would say 'tis
your estate that has made me friends with the world.

FREEMAN

I must confess I should, for I think most of our quarrels to
the world are just such as we have to a handsome woman: 170
only because we cannot enjoy her as we would do.

MANLY

Nay, if thou art a plain dealer too, give me thy hand, for now

153 *pretenders* suitors
154 *throughly* thoroughly

I'll say I am thy friend indeed; and for your two sakes,
though I have been so lately deceived in friends of both sexes,

> I will believe there are now in the world   175
> Good-natured friends who are not prostitutes,
> And handsome women worthy to be friends.
> Yet, for my sake, let no one e'er confide
> In tears or oaths, in love or friend untried.

(Exeunt omnes)

FINIS

EPILOGUE

Spoken by the WIDOW BLACKACRE

To you, the judges learned in stage laws,
Our poet now, by me, submits his cause;
For with young judges, such as most of you,
The men by women best their business do:
And truth on't is, if you did not sit here   5
To keep for us a term throughout the year,
We could not live by'r tongues; nay, but for you,
Our chamber-practice would be little too.
And 'tis not only the stage practiser
Who by your meeting gets her living here;   10
For as in Hall of Westminster
Sleek sempstress vents amidst the courts her ware,
So, while we bawl and you in judgment sit,
The visor-mask sells linen too i'th' pit.
O many of your friends, besides us here,   15
Do live by putting off their several ware.
Here's daily done the great affair o'th' nation;
Let love and us then ne'er have long vacation.
But hold; like other pleaders, I have done
Not my poor client's business, but my own.   20
Spare me a word then, now, for him. First know,
Squires of the long robe, he does humbly show
He has a just right in abusing you,
Because he is a brother-Templar too;

8 *chamber-practice double entendre* referring to the work of a cham-
ber-council, who does not plead in court
11 *Hall of Westminster* where Ned Ward saw sempstresses 'pleating
Turn-overs and *Ruffles* for the *Young Students,* and Coaxing them
with their *Amorous Looks, Obliging Cant,* and *Inviting Gestures,* to
give so Extravagant a Price for what they Buy, that they may now
and then afford to fling them a Nights Lodging into the Bargain'
(*The London Spy,* ed. Ralph Straus (1924), p. 191)
12 *vents* sells
14 *visor-mask* the identifying disguise of a whore plying for custom in
the pit
16 *putting off* selling, with a suggestion of fraud
24 *brother-Templar* Wycherley was admitted to the Inner Temple on
10 November 1659.

331

For at the bar you rally one another,   25
And 'fool' and 'knave' is swallowed from a brother;
If not the poet here, the Templar spare,
And maul him when you catch him at the bar.
From you, our common modish censurers,
Your favour, not your judgment, 'tis he fears;   30
Of all loves begs you then to rail, find fault,
For plays, like women, by the world are thought,
When you speak kindly of 'em, very naught.

26 *And 'fool'* Q1, 0 (Nay, fool Q2–8)

Love for Love

WILLIAM CONGREVE

Edited by

M. M. KELSALL

ABBREVIATIONS

Q1	First Quarto of 1695.
Q2	Second edition of 1695.
Q3	Third edition of 1697.
Q4	Fourth edition of 1704.
W1	Congreve's *Works* of 1710.
W2	Congreve's *Works* of 1719.
Davis	Herbert Davis, ed., *Complete Plays* (Chicago, 1967).
Summers	Montague Summers, ed., *The Complete Works of William Congreve* (1923).

LOVE for LOVE:

A

COMEDY.

Acted at the

THEATRE in *Little Lincolns-Inn Fields,*

B Y

His Majesty's Servants.

Written by Mr. *CONGREVE.*

Nudus agris, nudus nummis paternis,
Infanire parat certa ratione modoque. Hor.

L O N D O N:

Printed for *Jacob Tonson,* at the *Judge's-Head,* near the
Inner-Temple-Gate in *Fleetstreet.* 1695.

Motto. Horace II *Sat.* iii 184 and 271 (reading *paret* not *parat*):
stripped of his lands and paternal wealth he prepares to go mad
by regular system and method

To the Right Honourable Charles Earl of Dorset and
Middlesex, Lord Chamberlain of His Majesty's Household,
and Knight of the Most Noble Order of the Garter, &c.

MY LORD,

A young poet is liable to the same vanity and indiscretion   5
with a young lover; and the great man that smiles upon one,
and the fine woman that looks kindly upon t'other, are each of
'em in danger of having the favour published with the first
opportunity.

But there may be a different motive, which will a little   10
distinguish the offenders. For though one should have a vanity
in ruining another's reputation, yet the other may only have an
ambition to advance his own. And I beg leave, my Lord, that I
may plead the latter, both as the cause and excuse of this
dedication.   15

Whoever is king, is also the father of his country; and as
nobody can dispute your Lordship's monarchy in poetry, so all
that are concerned ought to acknowledge your universal
patronage: and it is only presuming on the privilege of a loyal
subject that I have ventured to make this my address of thanks   20
to your Lordship; which, at the same time, includes a prayer
for your protection.

I am not ignorant of the common form of poetical dedications, which are generally made up of panegyrics, where the
authors endeavour to distinguish their patrons, by the shining   25
characters they give them, above other men. But that, my Lord,
is not my business at this time, nor is your Lordship *now* to be
distinguished. I am contented with the honour I do myself in
this epistle, without the vanity of attempting to add to, or
explain, your Lordship's character.   30

I confess it is not without some struggling that I behave
myself in this case as I ought: for it is very hard to be pleased
with a subject, and yet forbear it. But I choose rather to follow
Pliny's precept than his example, when in his panegyric to the
Emperor Trajan, he says,   35

6 *that smiles* (who smiles Ww)   7 *that looks* (who looks Ww)
7 *are each of* (are both of Ww)

1–2 *Charles . . . Middlesex*. (1638–1706). As Lord Chamberlain he was
  instrumental in the licensing of the Lincoln's Inn Theatre which
  opened with this play. He was a patron of Dryden and many others.

Nec minus considerabo quid aures ejus pati possint,
  Quam quid virtutibus debeatur.

I hope I may be excused the pedantry of a quotation when it
is so justly applied. Here are some lines in the print (and which
your Lordship read before this play was acted) that were   40
omitted on the stage; and particularly one whole scene in the
third act, which not only helps the design forward with less
precipitation, but also heightens the ridiculous character of
Foresight, which indeed seems to be maimed without it. But I
found myself in great danger of a long play, and was glad to   45
help it where I could. Though notwithstanding my care, and
the kind reception it had from the town, I could heartily wish
it yet shorter: but the number of different characters represented in it would have been too much crowded in less room.

This reflection on prolixity (a fault for which scarce any one   50
beauty will atone) warns me not to be tedious now and detain
your Lordship any longer with the trifles of,

> MY LORD,
> Your Lordship's
>   Most Obedient   55
>   and Most Humble
>   Servant,
> WILL. CONGREVE

36–7 *Nec minus . . . debeatur* I will consider what he can tolerate to
  hear no less than what is due to his virtues
58 *WILL* (William Ww)

41–2 *scene in the third act.* Probably III. xi (in the edition of 1710).

A
PROLOGUE
FOR

The opening of the new Play-House, proposed to be spoken by
Mrs. Bracegirdle in man's clothes.

Sent from an unknown hand.

Custom, which everywhere bears mighty sway,
Brings me to act the orator today:
But women, you will say, are ill at speeches—
'Tis true, and therefore I appear in breeches:
Not for example to you City-wives;   5
That by prescription's settled for your lives.
Was it for gain the husband first consented?
O yes, their gains are mightily augmented:
Making horns with her hands over her head
And yet, methinks, it must have cost some strife:
A passive husband, and an active wife!   10
'Tis awkward, very awkward, by my life.
But to my speech—assemblies of all nations
Still are supposed to open with orations:
Mine shall begin, to show our obligations.
To you, our benefactors, lowly bowing,   15
Whose favours have prevented our undoing;
A long Egyptian bondage we endured,
Till freedom by your justice we procured:
Our taskmasters were grown such very Jews,
We must at length have played in wooden shoes,   20
Had not your bounty taught us to refuse.
Freedom's of English growth, I think, alone;
What for lost English freedom can atone?
A free-born player loathes to be compelled;
Our rulers tyrannized, and we rebelled.   25
Freedom! the wise man's wish, the poor man's wealth;
Which you, and I, and most of us enjoy by stealth;
The soul of pleasure, and the sweet of life,
The woman's charter, widow, maid, or wife,
This they'd have cancelled, and thence grew the strife.   30
But you perhaps would have me here confess
How we obtained the favour—can't you guess?

Prologue this prologue is om. in Ww

338

Why then I'll tell you (for I hate a lie),
By brib'ry, arrant brib'ry, let me die:
I was their agent, but by Jove I swear   35
No honourable member had a share,
Though young and able members bid me fair:
I chose a wiser way to make you willing,
Which has not cost the house a single shilling;
Now you suspect at least I went a-billing.   40
You see I'm young, and to that air of youth,
Some will add beauty, and a little truth;
These pow'rful charms, improved by pow'rful arts,
Prevailed to captivate your opening hearts.
Thus furnished, I preferred my poor petition,   45
And bribed ye to commiserate our condition:
I laughed, and sighed, and sung, and leered upon ye;
With roguish loving looks, and that way won ye:
The young men kissed me, and the old I kissed,
And luringly I led them as I list.   50
The ladies in mere pity took our parts,
Pity's the darling passion of their hearts.
Thus bribing, or thus bribed, fear no disgraces:
For thus you may take bribes, and keep your places.

PROLOGUE

Spoken at the opening of the New House,
By Mr. Betterton

The husbandman in vain renews his toil,
To cultivate each year a hungry soil;
And fondly hopes for rich and generous fruit,
When what should feed the tree, devours the root:
Th'unladen boughs, he sees, bode certain dearth, 5
Unless transplanted to more kindly earth.
So, the poor husbands of the stage, who found
Their labours lost upon the ungrateful ground,
This last and only remedy have proved;
And hope new fruit from ancient stocks removed. 10
Well may they hope, when you so kindly aid,
And plant a soil which you so rich have made.
As Nature gave the world to man's first age,
So from your bounty we receive this stage;
The freedom man was born to, you've restored, 15
And to our world such plenty you afford,
It seems like Eden, fruitful of its own accord.
But since in Paradise frail flesh gave way,
And when but two were made, both went astray;
Forbear your wonder, and the fault forgive, 20
If in our larger family we grieve
One falling Adam, and one tempted Eve;
We who remain would gratefully repay
What our endeavours can, and bring this day,
The first-fruit offering of a virgin play. 25
We hope there's something that may please each taste,
And though of homely fare we make the feast,
Yet you will find variety at least.
There's humour, which for cheerful friends we got,
And for the thinking party there's a plot. 30
We've something too, to gratify ill nature
(If there be any here) and that is Satire—

8 *upon the* (upon Ww)
12 *And plant* (plant Ww)

---

22 *Adam . . . Eve.* Joseph Williams and Susanna Mountfort, both of
whom had seceded from Lincoln's Inn Fields to the 'taskmasters' of
the rival company.

Though Satire scarce dares grin, 'tis grown so mild;
Or only shows its teeth, as if it smiled.
As asses thistles, poets mumble wit,   35
And dare not bite, for fear of being bit.
They hold their pens, as swords are held by fools,
And are afraid to use their own edge-tools.
Since the *Plain Dealer*'s scenes of manly rage,
Not one has dared to lash this crying age.   40
This time the poet owns the bold essay,
Yet hopes there's no ill manners in his play:
And he declares by me, he has designed
Affront to none, but frankly speaks his mind.
And should th'ensuing scenes not chance to hit,   45
He offers but this one excuse: 'twas writ
Before your late encouragement of wit.

35 *mumble* chew with toothless gums, see V. 131.
39 *Plain Dealer's . . . rage.* Wycherley's play (1676). The misanthropic
hero is called Manly. Congreve is paying lip-service to the 17th-
century belief that satire should lash vice (as Wycherley and Juvenal
had done), but his manner is closer to the polite ridicule of Horace.
Times were changing.

[Dramatis Personae]

Men

SIR SAMPSON LEGEND, *father to Valentine and Ben*   *Mr. Underhill*

VALENTINE, *fallen under his father's displeasure by his expensive way of living, in love with Angelica*   *Mr. Betterton*

SCANDAL, *his friend, a free speaker*   *Mr. Smith*

TATTLE, *a half-witted beau, vain of his amours, yet valuing himself for secrecy*   *Mr. Bowman*

BEN, *Sir Sampson's younger son, half home-bred, and half sea-bred, designed to marry Miss Prue*   *Mr. Dogget*

FORESIGHT, *an illiterate old fellow, peevish and positive, superstitious, and pretending to understand astrology, palmistry, physiognomy, omens, dreams, etc., uncle to Angelica*   *Mr. Sandford*

JEREMY, *servant to Valentine*   *Mr. Bowen*

TRAPLAND, *a scrivener*   *Mr. Triffusis*

BUCKRAM, *a lawyer*   *Mr. Freeman*

Women

ANGELICA, *niece to Foresight, of a considerable fortune in her own hands*   *Mrs. Bracegirdle*

MRS. FORESIGHT, *second wife to Foresight*   *Mrs. Bowman*

MRS. FRAIL, *sister to Mrs. Foresight, a woman of the town*   *Mrs. Barry*

MISS PRUE, *daughter to Foresight by a former wife, a silly, awkward, country girl*   *Mrs. Ayliff*

NURSE *to Miss [Prue]*   *Mrs. Leigh*

JENNY, *maid to Angelica*   *Mrs. Lawson*

A STEWARD, OFFICERS, SAILORS, AND SEVERAL SERVANTS

[The Scene: *in London*]

2 *Men* ed. (Men by Q1)
18 *Women* ed. (Women by Q1)
27 *maid to Angelica* (om. Ww)

LOVE FOR LOVE

[Act I, Scene i]

VALENTINE *in his chamber, reading.* JEREMY *waiting. Several
books upon the table*

VALENTINE
Jeremy.
JEREMY
Sir.
VALENTINE
Here, take away. I'll walk a turn and digest what I have read.
JEREMY (*Aside, and taking away the books*)
You'll grow devilish fat upon this paper diet.
VALENTINE
And d'ye hear, go you to breakfast. There's a page doubled   5
down in Epictetus that is a feast for an emperor.
JEREMY
Was Epictetus a real cook, or did he only write receipts?
VALENTINE
Read, read, sirrah, and refine your appetite; learn to live
upon instruction; feast your mind, and mortify your flesh;
read, and take your nourishment in at your eyes; shut up   10
your mouth, and chew the cud of understanding. So
Epictetus advises.
JEREMY
O Lord! I have heard much of him when I waited upon a
gentleman at Cambridge. Pray, what was that Epictetus?
VALENTINE
A very rich man—not worth a groat.   15
JEREMY
Humph, and so he has made a very fine feast, where there is
nothing to be eaten.
VALENTINE
Yes.
JEREMY
Sir, you're a gentleman, and probably understand this fine
feeding; but if you please, I had rather be at board-wages.   20
Does your Epictetus, or your Seneca here, or any of these

7 *receipts* recipes

343

poor rich rogues, teach you how to pay your debts without
money? Will they shut up the mouths of your creditors?
Will Plato be bail for you? Or Diogenes, because he understands confinement and lived in a tub, go to prison for you?   25
S'life, sir, what do you mean, to mew yourself up here with
three or four musty books in commendation of starving and
poverty?

VALENTINE

Why, sirrah, I have no money, you know it; and therefore
resolve to rail at all that have: and in that I but follow the   30
examples of the wisest and wittiest men in all ages, these
poets and philosophers whom you naturally hate, for just
such another reason: because they abound in sense, and you
are a fool.

JEREMY

Aye, sir, I am a fool, I know it; and yet, heaven help me,   35
I'm poor enough to be a wit. But I was always a fool when I
told you what your expenses would bring you to; your
coaches and your liveries; your treats and your balls; your
being in love with a lady that did not care a farthing for you
in your prosperity; and keeping company with wits that   40
cared for nothing but your prosperity; and now when you
are poor, hate you as much as they do one another.

VALENTINE

Well, and now I am poor, I have an opportunity to be
revenged on 'em all; I'll pursue Angelica with more love
than ever, and appear more notoriously her admirer in this   45
restraint, than when I openly rivalled the rich fops that
made court to her; so shall my poverty be a mortification to
her pride and, perhaps, make her compassionate that love
which has principally reduced me to this lowness of fortune.
And for the wits, I'm sure I'm in a condition to be even   50
with them.

JEREMY

Nay, your condition is pretty even with theirs, that's the
truth on't.

VALENTINE

I'll take some of their trade out of their hands.

31–2 *men in all ages, these poets and* (om. Ww)
48 *that love* (the love Q3, 4, Ww)
50 *I'm sure I'm* (I'm sure I am Ww)

JEREMY

Now heaven of mercy continue the tax upon paper; you 55
don't mean to write!

VALENTINE

Yes, I do; I'll write a play.

JEREMY

Hem! Sir, if you please to give me a small certificate of three
lines—only to certify those whom it may concern: that the
bearer hereof, Jeremy Fetch by name, has for the space of 60
seven years truly and faithfully served Valentine Legend
Esq.; and that he is not now turned away for any misde-
meanour; but does voluntarily dismiss his master from any
future authority over him—

VALENTINE

No, sirrah, you shall live with me still. 65

JEREMY

Sir, it's impossible—I may die with you, starve with you, or
be damned with your works; but to live even three days, the
life of a play, I no more expect it than to be canonized for a
Muse after my decease.

VALENTINE

You are witty, you rogue! I shall want your help. I'll have 70
you learn to make couplets, to tag the ends of acts, d'ye
hear, get the maids to Crambo in an evening, and learn the
knack of rhyming. You may arrive at the height of a song,
sent by an unknown hand, or a chocolate-house lampoon.

JEREMY

But, sir, is this the way to recover your father's favour? 75
Why, Sir Sampson will be irreconcilable. If your younger
brother should come from sea, he'd never look upon you
again. You're undone, sir; you're ruined; you won't have a
friend left in the world if you turn poet. Ah, pox confound
that Will's Coffee-House; it has ruined more young men 80
than the Royal Oak Lottery. Nothing thrives that belongs
to't. The man of the house would have been an alderman by
this time with half the trade if he had set up in the City.
For my part, I never sit at the door that I don't get double

---

72 *Crambo* capping verses

67–8 *three days . . . play.* The third night's proceeds were for the author's
'benefit'.
80 *Will's Coffee-House.* The resort of Congreve himself and other leading
literary figures.

the stomach that I do at a horse race. The air upon Banstead   85
Downs is nothing to it for a whetter; yet I never see it, but
the Spirit of Famine appears to me; sometimes like a decayed
porter, worn out with pimping and carrying *billet-doux* and
songs; not like other porters for hire, but for the jest's sake;
now like a thin chairman, melted down to half his proportion   90
with carrying a poet upon tick to visit some great fortune;
and his fare to be paid him like the wages of sin, either at the
day of marriage, or the day of death.

VALENTINE
Very well, sir; can you proceed?

JEREMY
Sometimes like a bilked bookseller, with a meagre terrified   95
countenance, that looks as if he had written for himself, or
were resolved to turn author and bring the rest of his
brethren into the same condition. And lastly, in the form of
a worn-out punk, with verses in her hand, which her vanity
had preferred to settlements, without a whole tatter to her   100
tail, but as ragged as one of the Muses; or as if she were
carrying her linen to the paper-mill, to be converted into
folio books, of warning to all young maids not to prefer
poetry to good sense; or lying in the arms of a needy wit,
before the embraces of a wealthy fool.   105

[Act I, Scene ii]

Enter SCANDAL

SCANDAL
What, Jeremy holding forth?

VALENTINE
The rogue has (with all the wit he could muster up) been
declaiming against wit.

SCANDAL
Aye? Why then I'm afraid Jeremy has wit; for wherever it
is, it's always contriving its own ruin.   110

JEREMY
Why, so I have been telling my master, sir. Mr. Scandal, for
heaven's sake, sir, try if you can dissuade him from turning
poet.

SCANDAL
Poet! He shall turn soldier first, and rather depend upon the

85-6 *Banstead Downs* a racecourse near Epsom
95 *bilked* cheated
99 *punk* prostitute

outside of his head than the lining. Why, what the devil, has 115
not your poverty made you enemies enough? Must you
needs show your wit to get more?

JEREMY

Aye, more indeed; for who cares for anybody that has more
wit than himself?

SCANDAL

Jeremy speaks like an oracle. Don't you see how worthless 120
great men, and dull rich rogues, avoid a witty man of small
fortune? Why, he looks like a writ of enquiry into their titles
and estates; and seems commissioned by heaven to seize the
better half.

VALENTINE

Therefore I would rail in my writings and be revenged. 125

SCANDAL

Rail? At whom? The whole world? Impotent and vain!
Who would die a martyr to sense in a country where the
religion is folly? You may stand at bay for awhile; but when
the full cry is against you, you won't have fair play for your
life. If you can't be fairly run down by the hounds, you will 130
be treacherously shot by the huntsmen. No, turn pimp,
flatterer, quack, lawyer, parson, be chaplain to an atheist, or
stallion to an old woman, anything but poet; a modern poet
is worse, more servile, timorous, and fawning, than any I
have named; without you could retrieve the ancient honours 135
of the name, recall the stage of Athens, and be allowed the
force of open honest satire.

VALENTINE

You are as inveterate against our poets as if your character
had been lately exposed upon the stage. Nay, I am not
violently bent upon the trade. (*One knocks*) Jeremy, see 140
who's there.   *Exit* JEREMY
But tell me what you would have me do? What do the world
say of me, and my forced confinement?

SCANDAL

The world behaves itself as it used to do on such occasions;
some pity you, and condemn your father; others excuse him, 145
and blame you; only the ladies are merciful and wish you
well, since love and pleasurable expense have been your
greatest faults.

129 *you won't* (you shan't Ww)
141 s.d. *Exit* JEREMY (JEREMY *goes to the door* Ww)
142 *What do* (What does Ww)   144 *used* (uses Ww)

Enter JEREMY

VALENTINE
How now?

JEREMY
Nothing new, sir; I have despatched some half a dozen duns   150
with as much dexterity as a hungry judge does causes at
dinner time.

VALENTINE
What answer have you given 'em?

SCANDAL
Patience, I suppose, the old receipt.

JEREMY
No, faith, sir; I have put 'em off so long with patience and   155
forbearance and other fair words, that I was forced now to
tell 'em in plain downright English—

VALENTINE
What?

JEREMY
That they should be paid.

VALENTINE
When?   160

JEREMY
Tomorrow.

VALENTINE
And how the devil do you mean to keep your word?

JEREMY
Keep it? Not at all; it has been so very much stretched that
I reckon it will break of course by tomorrow, and nobody be
surprised at the matter. (*Knocking*) Again! Sir, if you don't   165
like my negotiation, will you be pleased to answer these
yourself?

VALENTINE
See who they are.   *Exit* JEREMY

[Act I, Scene iii]

VALENTINE
By this, Scandal, you may see what it is to be great; Secre-
taries of State, Presidents of the Council, and generals of an   170
army lead just such a life as I do, have just such crowds of
visitants in a morning, all soliciting of past promises; which
are but a civiller sort of duns, that lay claim to voluntary
debts.

148 s.d. *Enter* JEREMY (om. Ww)
150 *duns* creditors, or their agents, demanding payment

SCANDAL

And you, like a true great man, having engaged their   175
attendance, and promised more than ever you intend to
perform, are more perplexed to find evasions than you would
be to invent the honest means of keeping your word, and
gratifying your creditors.

VALENTINE

Scandal, learn to spare your friends, and do not provoke   180
your enemies; this liberty of your tongue will one day bring
a confinement on your body, my friend.

[Act I, Scene iv]

Enter JEREMY

JEREMY

O, sir, there's Trapland the scrivener, with two suspicious
fellows like lawful pads, that would knock a man down with
pocket-tipstaves—and there's your father's steward, and   185
the nurse with one of your children from Twitnam.

VALENTINE

Pox on her, could she find no other time to fling my sins in
my face? Here, give her this (*Gives money*) and bid her
trouble me no more. [*To* SCANDAL] A thoughtless two-
handed whore, she knows my condition well enough and   190
might have overlaid the child a fortnight ago if she had had
any forecast in her.

SCANDAL

What, is it bouncing Margery and my godson?

JEREMY

Yes, sir.

SCANDAL

My blessing to the boy, with this token (*Gives money*) of my   195
love. And, d'ye hear, bid Margery put more flocks in her
bed, shift twice a week, and not work so hard, that she may
not smell so vigorously.—I shall take the air shortly.

---

176 *intend* (intended Ww)
183 *scrivener* one who 'supplied those who wanted to raise money on security'
   (O.E.D.)
184 *lawful pads* not thieves (footpads) but bailiffs or constables
185 *tipstaves* metal-headed bludgeons
186 *Twitnam* Twickenham
191 *overlaid* smothered
193 *and my* (with my Ww)

VALENTINE

Scandal, don't spoil my boy's milk! [*To* JEREMY] Bid
Trapland come in.   *Exit* JEREMY   200
If I can give that Cerberus a sop, I shall be at rest for one
day.

[Act I, Scene v]

Enter TRAPLAND *and* JEREMY

VALENTINE

O Mr. Trapland! My old friend! Welcome. Jeremy, a chair
quickly; a bottle of sack and a toast—fly—a chair first.

TRAPLAND

A good morning to you, Mr. Valentine, and to you, Mr.   205
Scandal.

SCANDAL

The morning's a very good morning, if you don't spoil it.

VALENTINE

Come sit you down, you know his way.

TRAPLAND (*Sits*)

There is a debt, Mr. Valentine, of 1500 pounds of pretty
long standing—   210

VALENTINE

I cannot talk about business with a thirsty palate.—Sirrah,
the sack.

TRAPLAND

And I desire to know what course you have taken for the
payment?

VALENTINE

Faith and troth, I am heartily glad to see you, my service to   215
you. [*To* JEREMY] Fill, fill, to honest Mr. Trapland, fuller.

TRAPLAND

Hold, sweetheart. This is not to our business—my service to
you, Mr. Scandal. (*Drinks*) I have forborne as long—

VALENTINE

T'other glass, and then we'll talk. Fill, Jeremy.

TRAPLAND

No more, in truth.—I have forborne, I say—   220

VALENTINE [*To* JEREMY]

Sirrah, fill when I bid you.—And how does your handsome
daughter? Come, a good husband to her!   *Drinks*

TRAPLAND

Thank you.—I have been out of this money—

204 *sack* sherry

VALENTINE
Drink first. Scandal, why do you not drink?   *They drink*

TRAPLAND
And in short, I can be put off no longer.   225

VALENTINE
I was much obliged to you for your supply: it did me signal
service in my necessity. But you delight in doing good.—
Scandal, drink to me, my friend Trapland's health. An
honester man lives not, nor one more ready to serve his
friend in distress, though I say it to his face. Come, fill each   230
man his glass.

SCANDAL
What, I know Trapland has been a whoremaster and loves a
wench still. You never knew a whoremaster that was not an
honest fellow.

TRAPLAND
Fie, Mr. Scandal, you never knew—   235

SCANDAL
What don't I know?—I know the buxom black widow in the
Poultry—800 pounds a year jointure, and 20,000 pounds in
money. Ahah, old Trap!

VALENTINE
Say you so, i'faith! Come, we'll remember the widow;
I know whereabouts you are: come, to the widow!   240

TRAPLAND
No more indeed.

VALENTINE
What, the widow's health; give it him—off with it! (*They
drink*) A lovely girl, i'faith, black sparkling eyes, soft pouting
ruby lips! Better sealing there than a bond for a million,
hah!   245

TRAPLAND
No, no, there's no such thing; we'd better mind our
business—you're a wag.

VALENTINE
No, faith, we'll mind the widow's business. Fill again.
Pretty round heaving breasts, a Barbary shape, and a jut with
her bum would stir an anchorite; and the prettiest foot! O,   250
if a man could but fasten his eyes to her feet, as they steal

236–7 *the Poultry* a street at the business end of London, east of
    Cheapside
237 *jointure* property settled on a woman at marriage to be enjoyed
    after her husband's death
249 *Barbary* Moorish; graceful in shape like an Arab steed

in and out, and play at Bo-peep under her petticoats, ah,
Mr. Trapland?

TRAPLAND

Verily, give me a glass—you're a wag—and here's to the
widow.   *Drinks* 255

SCANDAL

He begins to chuckle; ply him close, or he'll relapse into a
dun.

[Act I, Scene vi]

Enter OFFICER

OFFICER

By your leave, gentlemen—Mr. Trapland, if we must do our
office, tell us. We have half a dozen gentlemen to arrest in
Pall Mall and Covent Garden; and if we don't make haste 260
the chairmen will be abroad and block up the chocolate-
houses, and then our labour's lost.

TRAPLAND

Udso, that's true. Mr. Valentine, I love mirth, but business
must be done. Are you ready to—

JEREMY

Sir, your father's steward says he comes to make proposals 265
concerning your debts.

VALENTINE

Bid him come in. Mr. Trapland, send away your officer, you
shall have an answer presently.

TRAPLAND

Mr. Snap, stay within call.   *Exit* OFFICER

[Act I, Scene vii]

Enter STEWARD *and whispers* VALENTINE

SCANDAL

Here's a dog now, a traitor in his wine. [*To* TRAPLAND] 270
Sirrah, refund the sack: Jeremy, fetch him some warm water,
or I'll rip up his stomach and go the shortest way to his
conscience.

TRAPLAND

Mr. Scandal, you are uncivil; I did not value your sack;
but you cannot expect it again when I have drank it.   275

269 s.d. *Enter* STEWARD *and whispers* (*Enter* STEWARD *who whispers* Ww)
275 *drank* (drunk Ww)

SCANDAL

And how do you expect to have your money again when a
gentleman has spent it?

VALENTINE [*To* STEWARD]

You need say no more, I understand the conditions; they are
very hard, but my necessity is very pressing: I agree to 'em.
Take Mr. Trapland with you, and let him draw the writing.   280
Mr. Trapland, you know this man; he shall satisfy you.

TRAPLAND

Sincerely, I am loath to be thus pressing, but my necessity—

VALENTINE

No apology, good Mr. Scrivener; you shall be paid.

TRAPLAND

I hope you forgive me, my business requires—

                Exeunt STEWARD, TRAPLAND *and* JEREMY

[Act I, Scene viii]

SCANDAL

He begs pardon like a hangman at an execution.   285

VALENTINE

But I have got a reprieve.

SCANDAL

I am surprised; what, does your father relent?

VALENTINE

No; he has sent me the hardest conditions in the world: you
have heard of a booby brother of mine that was sent to sea
three years ago? This brother, my father hears, is landed;   290
whereupon he very affectionately sends me word, if I will
make a deed of conveyance of my right to his estate after his
death to my younger brother, he will immediately furnish
me with four thousand pound to pay my debts, and make
my fortune. This was once proposed before, and I refused it;   295
but the present impatience of my creditors for their money,
and my own impatience of confinement and absence from
Angelica, force me to consent.

SCANDAL

A very desperate demonstration of your love to Angelica;
and I think she has never given you any assurance of hers.   300

VALENTINE

You know her temper; she never gave me any great reason
either for hope or despair.

SCANDAL

Women of her airy temper, as they seldom think before they

act, so they rarely give us any light to guess at what they
mean: but you have little reason to believe that a woman of   305
this age, who has had an indifference for you in your prosperity, will fall in love with your ill fortune; besides,
Angelica has a great fortune of her own; and great fortunes
either expect another great fortune, or a fool.

[Act I, Scene ix]

Enter JEREMY

JEREMY
More misfortunes, sir.   310
VALENTINE
What, another dun?
JEREMY
No, sir, but Mr. Tattle is come to wait upon you.
VALENTINE
Well, I can't help it,—you must bring him up; he knows I
don't go abroad.   *Exit* JEREMY

[Act I, Scene x]

SCANDAL
Pox on him, I'll be gone.   315
VALENTINE
No, prithee stay: Tattle and you should never be asunder;
you are light and shadow, and show one another; he is per-
fectly thy reverse both in humour and understanding; and
as you set up for defamation, he is a mender of reputations.
SCANDAL
A mender of reputations! Aye, just as he is a keeper of   320
secrets, another virtue that he sets up for in the same manner.
For the rogue will speak aloud in the posture of a whisper;
and deny a woman's name, while he gives you the marks of
her person. He will forswear receiving a letter from her, and
at the same time show you her hand upon the superscription; 325
and yet perhaps he has counterfeited the hand too; and
sworn to a truth, but he hopes not to be believed; and
refuses the reputation of a lady's favour, as a doctor says, no,
to a bishopric, only that it may be granted him. In short, he
is a public professor of secrecy, and makes proclamation   330
that he holds private intelligence.—He's here.

325 *upon the* (in the Ww)

[Act I, Scene xi]

Enter TATTLE

TATTLE

Valentine, good morrow; Scandal, I am yours—that is, when
you speak well of me.

SCANDAL

That is, when I am yours; for while I am my own, or
anybody's else, that will never happen.　　　335

TATTLE

How inhuman!

VALENTINE

Why, Tattle, you need not be much concerned at anything
that he says: for to converse with Scandal is to play at Losing
Loadum; you must lose a good name to him before you can
win it for yourself.　　　340

TATTLE

But how barbarous that is, and how unfortunate for him,
that the world shall think the better of any person for his
calumniation! I thank heaven, it has always been a part of
my character to handle the reputation of others very
tenderly.　　　345

SCANDAL

Aye, such rotten reputations as you have to deal with are to
be handled tenderly indeed.

TATTLE

Nay, but why rotten? Why should you say rotten, when you
know not the persons of whom you speak? How cruel that is!

SCANDAL

Not know 'em? Why, thou never hadst to do with anybody　　　350
that did not stink to all the town.

TATTLE

Ha, ha, ha! Nay, now you make a jest of it indeed. For there
is nothing more known than that nobody knows anything of
that nature of me: as I hope to be saved, Valentine, I never
exposed a woman since I knew what woman was.　　　355

VALENTINE

And yet you have conversed with several.

338–9 *Losing Loadum* a card game in which the aim was to lose tricks
344 *reputation* (reputations Ww)
345 *tenderly* (tenderly indeed Ww)

TATTLE

    To be free with you, I have—I don't care if I own that. Nay,
more (I'm going to say a bold word now), I never could
meddle with a woman that had to do with anybody else.

SCANDAL

    How!   360

VALENTINE

    Nay, faith, I'm apt to believe him.—Except her husband,
Tattle.

TATTLE

    O that—

SCANDAL

    What think you of that noble commoner, Mrs. Drab?

TATTLE

    Pooh, I know Madam Drab has made her brags in three or   365
four places that I said this and that, and writ to her, and did
I know not what—but, upon my reputation, she did me
wrong.—Well, well, that was malice, but I know the bottom
of it. She was bribed to that by one that we all know—a man,
too—only to bring me into disgrace with a certain woman   370
of quality—

SCANDAL

    Whom we all know.

TATTLE

    No matter for that.—Yes, yes, everybody knows, no doubt
on't, everybody knows my secrets. But I soon satisfied the
lady of my innocence; for I told her—madam, says I, there   375
are some persons who make it their business to tell stories,
and say this and that of one and t'other, and everything in
the world; and, says I, if your Grace—

SCANDAL

    Grace!

TATTLE

    O Lord, what have I said? My unlucky tongue!   380

VALENTINE

    Ha, ha, ha!

SCANDAL

    Why Tattle, thou hast more impudence than one can in
reason expect: I shall have an esteem for thee. Well, and ha,
ha, ha! well, go on, and what did you say to her Grace?

VALENTINE

    I confess this is something extraordinary.   385

369 *one that we* (one we Ww)

TATTLE

Not a word, as I hope to be saved, an arrant *lapsus linguae*—come, let's talk of something else.

VALENTINE

Well, but how did you acquit yourself?

TATTLE

Pooh, pooh, nothing at all, I only rallied with you.—A woman of ordinary rank was a little jealous of me, and I told   390 her something or other, faith—I know not what—come, let's talk of something else.   *Hums a song*

SCANDAL

Hang him, let him alone; he has a mind we should inquire.

TATTLE

Valentine, I supped last night with your mistress, and her uncle old Foresight. I think your father lies at Foresight's?   395

VALENTINE

Yes.

TATTLE

Upon my soul, Angelica's a fine woman—and so is Mrs. Foresight, and her sister Mrs. Frail.

SCANDAL

Yes, Mrs. Frail is a very fine woman; we all know her.

TATTLE

O, that is not fair.   400

SCANDAL

What?

TATTLE

To tell.

SCANDAL

To tell what? Why, what do you know of Mrs. Frail?

TATTLE

Who, I? Upon honour I don't know whether she be man or woman but by the smoothness of her chin and roundness of   405 her lips.

SCANDAL

No!

TATTLE

No.

SCANDAL

She says otherwise.

TATTLE

Impossible!   410

386 *lapsus linguae* slip of the tongue.   406 *lips* (hips Ww)

SCANDAL

Yes, faith. Ask Valentine else.

TATTLE

Why then, as I hope to be saved, I believe a woman only
obliges a man to secrecy that she may have the pleasure of
telling herself.

SCANDAL

No doubt on't. Well, but has she done you wrong, or no?   415
You have had her? Ha?

TATTLE

Though I have more honour than to tell first, I have more
manners than to contradict what a lady has declared.

SCANDAL

Well, you own it?

TATTLE

I am strangely surprised! Yes, yes, I can't deny it, if she   420
taxes me with it.

SCANDAL

She'll be here by and by; she sees Valentine every morning.

TATTLE

How!

VALENTINE

She does me the favour—I mean of a visit sometimes. I did
not think she had granted more to anybody.   425

SCANDAL

Nor I, faith—but Tattle does not use to belie a lady; it is
contrary to his character.—How one may be deceived in a
woman, Valentine!

TATTLE

Nay, what do you mean, gentlemen?

SCANDAL

I'm resolved I'll ask her.   430

TATTLE

O barbarous! Why did you not tell me—

SCANDAL

No, you told us.

TATTLE

And bid me ask Valentine?

VALENTINE

What did I say? I hope you won't bring me to confess an
answer, when you never asked me the question.   435

TATTLE

But, gentlemen, this is the most inhuman proceeding—

VALENTINE

Nay, if you have known Scandal thus long, and cannot avoid such a palpable decoy as this was, the ladies have a fine time whose reputations are in your keeping.

[Act I, Scene xii]

Enter JEREMY

JEREMY

Sir, Mrs. Frail has sent to know if you are stirring.   440

VALENTINE

Show her up when she comes.   *Exit* JEREMY

[Act I, Scene xiii]

TATTLE

I'll be gone.

VALENTINE

You'll meet her.

TATTLE

Have you not a back way?

VALENTINE

If there were, you have more discretion than to give Scandal   445
such an advantage; why, your running away will prove all
that he can tell her.

TATTLE

Scandal, you will not be so ungenerous.—O, I shall lose my
reputation of secrecy forever! I shall never be received but
upon public days, and my visits will never be admitted be-   450
yond a drawing room: I shall never see a bedchamber again,
never be locked in a closet, nor run behind a screen, or under
a table; never be distinguished among the waiting-women by
the name of trusty Mr. Tattle more.—You will not be so
cruel!   455

VALENTINE

Scandal, have pity on him; he'll yield to any conditions.

TATTLE

Any, any terms.

SCANDAL

Come then, sacrifice half a dozen women of good reputation
to me presently. Come, where are you familiar?—And see
that they are women of quality, too, the first quality.   460

444 *Have you* (Is there Ww)
459 *you* Ww (your Qq)

TATTLE

'Tis very hard. Won't a baronet's lady pass?

SCANDAL

No, nothing under a Right Honourable.

TATTLE

O inhuman! You don't expect their names?

SCANDAL

No, their titles shall serve.

TATTLE

Alas, that's the same thing. Pray spare me their titles; I'll   465
describe their persons.

SCANDAL

Well, begin then; but take notice, if you are so ill a painter
that I cannot know the person by your picture of her, you
must be condemned, like other bad painters, to write the
name at the bottom.   470

TATTLE

Well, first then—

[Act I, Scene xiv]

Enter MRS. FRAIL

TATTLE

O unfortunate! She's come already. Will you have patience
till another time—I'll double the number.

SCANDAL

Well, on that condition. Take heed you don't fail me.

MRS. FRAIL

Hey day! I shall get a fine reputation by coming to see   475
fellows in a morning. Scandal, you devil, are you here too?
O, Mr. Tattle, everything is safe with you we know.

SCANDAL

Tattle!

TATTLE

Mum.—O, madam, you do me too much honour.

VALENTINE

Well, Lady Galloper, how does Angelica?   480

MRS. FRAIL

Angelica? Manners!

VALENTINE

What, you will allow an absent lover—

475 *Hey day* (om. Ww)

MRS. FRAIL
> No, I'll allow a lover present with his mistress to be particu-
> lar, but otherwise I think his passion ought to give place to
> his manners.   485

VALENTINE
> But what if he have more passion than manners?

MRS. FRAIL
> Then let him marry and reform.

VALENTINE
> Marriage indeed may qualify the fury of his passion, but it
> very rarely mends a man's manners.

MRS. FRAIL
> You are the most mistaken in the world; there is no creature   490
> perfectly civil but a husband. For in a little time he grows
> only rude to his wife, and that is the highest good breeding,
> for it begets his civility to other people. Well, I'll tell you
> news; but I suppose you hear your brother Benjamin is
> landed. And my brother Foresight's daughter is come out of   495
> the country. I assure you, there's a match talked of by the
> old people. Well, if he be but as great a sea-beast as she
> is a land-monster, we shall have a most amphibious breed.
> The progeny will be all otters; he has been bred at sea, and
> she has never been out of the country.   500

VALENTINE
> Pox take 'em, their conjunction bodes no good I'm sure.

MRS. FRAIL
> Now you talk of conjunction, my brother Foresight has cast
> both their nativities, and prognosticates an admiral and an
> eminent justice of the peace to be the issue-male of their
> two bodies. 'Tis the most superstitious old fool! He would   505
> have persuaded me that this was an unlucky day and would
> not let me come abroad: but I invented a dream and sent
> him to Artimedorus for interpretation, and so stole out to
> see you. Well, and what will you give me now? Come, I
> must have something.   510

---

486 *he have* (he has Ww)
501 *bodes no* Q1–2 (bodes me no Q3, 4, Ww)
502 *conjunction* the apparent proximity of two heavenly bodies; their
    sharing the same longitude
502 *has* (hast Q1 uncorr. cited by Davis)

---

508 *Artimedorus*. Soothsayer and interpreter of dreams (2nd century A.D.).

VALENTINE

Step into the next room—and I'll give you something.

SCANDAL

Aye, we'll all give you something.

MRS. FRAIL

Well, what will you all give me?

VALENTINE

Mine's a secret.

MRS. FRAIL

I thought you would give me something that would be a   515
trouble to you to keep.

VALENTINE

And Scandal shall give you a good name.

MRS. FRAIL

That's more than he has for himself. And what will you give
me, Mr. Tattle?

TATTLE

I? My soul, madam.   520

MRS. FRAIL

Pooh, no, I thank you, I have enough to do to take care of my
own. Well; but I'll come and see you one of these mornings:
I hear you have a great many pictures.

TATTLE

I have a pretty good collection at your service, some
originals.   525

SCANDAL

Hang him, he has nothing but the *Seasons* and the *Twelve
Caesars*, paltry copies; and the *Five Senses*, as ill represented
as they are in himself; and he himself is the only original
you will see there.

MRS. FRAIL

Aye, but I hear he has a closet of beauties.   530

SCANDAL

Yes, all that have done him favours, if you will believe him.

MRS. FRAIL

Aye, let me see those, Mr. Tattle.

TATTLE

O, madam, those are sacred to love and contemplation. No
man but the painter and myself was ever blest with the sight.

526-7 *Seasons*. Prints of the paintings of Pierre Breughel le Jeune (Davis). The
    Twelve Caesars adorn the walls in Hogarth's *Rake's Progress*, III (Summers),
    and are ascribed to Titian.

MRS. FRAIL

Well, but a woman—　　　　　　　　　　　　　　535

TATTLE

Nor woman, till she consented to have her picture there too
—for then she is obliged to keep the secret.

SCANDAL

No, no; come to me if you would see pictures.

MRS. FRAIL

You?

SCANDAL

Yes, faith, I can show you your own picture and most of　540
your acquaintance to the life, and as like as at Kneller's.

MRS. FRAIL

O lying creature—Valentine, does not he lie? I can't believe
a word he says.

VALENTINE

No, indeed, he speaks truth now: for as Tattle has pictures
of all that have granted him favours, he has the pictures of　545
all that have refused him; if satires, descriptions, characters
and lampoons are pictures.

SCANDAL

Yes, mine are most in black and white. And yet there are
some set out in their true colours, both men and women. I
can show you pride, folly, affectation, wantonness, incon-　550
stancy, covetousness, dissimulation, malice and ignorance,
all in one piece. Then I can show you lying, foppery, vanity,
cowardice, bragging, lechery, impotence and ugliness in
another piece; and yet one of these is a celebrated beauty
and t'other a professed beau. I have paintings too, some　555
pleasant enough.

MRS. FRAIL

Come, let's hear 'em.

SCANDAL

Why, I have a beau in a bagnio, cupping for a complexion,
and sweating for a shape.

MRS. FRAIL

So.　　　　　　　　　　　　　　　　　　　　560

537 *she is* (she's Ww)
538 *you would* (you'd Ww)
558 *bagnio* bathing house
558 *cupping* being bled

---

541 *Kneller's.* Sir Godfrey Kneller (1646–1723), the fashionable and
prolific portrait painter. He painted the Kit-Cat Club portraits.

SCANDAL

Then I have a lady burning of brandy in a cellar with a
hackney-coachman.

MRS. FRAIL

O devil! Well, but that story is not true.

SCANDAL

I have some hieroglyphics too; I have a lawyer with a
hundred hands, two heads, and but one face; a divine with   565
two faces, and one head; and I have a soldier with his brains
in his belly, and his heart where his head should be.

MRS. FRAIL

And no head?

SCANDAL

No head.

MRS. FRAIL

Pooh, this is all invention. Have you ne'er a poet?   570

SCANDAL

Yes, I have a poet weighing words and selling praise for
praise, and a critic picking his pocket. I have another large
piece too, representing a school, where there are huge-
proportioned critics, with long wigs, laced coats, Steinkirk
cravats, and terrible faces; with cat-calls in their hands, and   575
hornbooks about their necks. I have many more of this kind,
very well painted, as you shall see.

MRS. FRAIL

Well, I'll come, if it be only to disprove you.

[Act I, Scene xv]

Enter JEREMY

JEREMY

Sir, here's the steward again from your father.

VALENTINE

I'll come to him.—Will you give me leave? I'll wait on you   580
again presently.

561 *burning of brandy* (burning brandy Ww)
574–5 *Steinkirk cravats* a carelessly tied neckcloth (as worn by French
        officers at the battle of Steinkirk, 1692)
575 *cat-calls* squeaking instruments used at the theatre to express
        disapproval
576 *hornbooks* first books for children consisting of a leaf of paper
        protected by a leaf of transparent horn
578 *be only to* (be but to Ww)

MRS. FRAIL

No, I'll be gone. Come, who squires me to the Exchange? I
must call my sister Foresight there.

SCANDAL

I will; I have a mind to your sister.

MRS. FRAIL

Civil! 585

TATTLE

I will; because I have a tender for your ladyship.

MRS. FRAIL

That's somewhat the better reason, to my opinion.

SCANDAL

Well, if Tattle entertains you, I have the better opportunity
to engage your sister.

VALENTINE

Tell Angelica I am about making hard conditions to come 590
abroad and be at liberty to see her.

SCANDAL

I'll give an account of you, and your proceedings. If indiscretion be a sign of love, you are the most a lover of anybody
that I know: you fancy that parting with your estate will help
you to your mistress. In my mind he is a thoughtless 595
adventurer,

Who hopes to purchase wealth, by selling land;

Or win a mistress, with a losing hand. *Exeunt*

[Act II, Scene i]

A room in FORESIGHT'S *house*

[Enter] FORESIGHT *and* SERVANT

FORESIGHT

Hey day! What, are all the women of my family abroad? Is
not my wife come home? Nor my sister, nor my daughter?

SERVANT

No, sir.

FORESIGHT

Mercy on us, what can be the meaning of it? Sure the moon
is in all her fortitudes. Is my niece Angelica at home? 5

586 *tender* (tendre W2)
590 *making* (to make Q4)
   4-5 *moon . . . fortitudes* the inconstant moon exerts her greatest
       power

SERVANT

Yes, sir.

FORESIGHT

I believe you lie, sir.

SERVANT

Sir?

FORESIGHT

I say you lie, sir. It is impossible that anything should be
as I would have it; for I was born, sir, when the Crab was   10
ascending, and all my affairs go backward.

SERVANT

I can't tell indeed, sir.

FORESIGHT

No, I know you can't, sir: but I can tell, sir, and foretell, sir.

[Act II, Scene ii]

Enter NURSE

FORESIGHT

Nurse, where's your young mistress?

NURSE

Wee'st heart, I know not; they're none of 'em come home   15
yet: poor child, I warrant she's fond o'seeing the town—
marry, pray heaven they ha' given her any dinner.—Good
lack-a-day, ha, ha, ha, O strange; I'll vow and swear now, ha,
ha, ha, marry, and did you ever see the like!

FORESIGHT

Why, how now, what's the matter?   20

NURSE

Pray heaven send your worship good luck, marry and amen
with all my heart, for you have put on one stocking with
the wrong side outward.

FORESIGHT

Ha, how? Faith and troth, I'm glad of it! and so I have! That
may be good luck in troth, in troth it may, very good luck: 25
nay, I have had some omens; I got out of bed backwards
too this morning, without premeditation; pretty good that
too; but then I stumbled coming down stairs, and met a
weasel; bad omens those: some bad, some good, our lives
are chequered, mirth and sorrow, want and plenty, night   30
and day, make up our time, but in troth I am pleased at my

13 *tell, sir, and* (*tell and* Ww)
15 *Wee'st* Woe is the

stocking; very well pleased at my stocking.—O, here's my
niece!

Enter ANGELICA

[*To* SERVANT] Sirrah, go tell Sir Sampson Legend I'll wait
on him if he's at leisure.—'Tis now three o'clock, a very   35
good hour for business; Mercury governs this hour.

Exit SERVANT

[Act II, Scene iii]

ANGELICA

Is not it a good hour for pleasure, too? Uncle, pray lend me
your coach; mine's out of order.

FORESIGHT

What, would you be gadding too? Sure all females are mad
today. It is of evil portent and bodes mischief to the master   40
of a family. I remember an old prophecy written by
Messehalah the Arabian, and thus translated by a reverend
Buckinghamshire bard.

>   When housewives all the house forsake,
>   And leave good man to brew and bake,   45
>   Withouten guile, then be it said,
>   That house doth stond upon its head;
>   And when the head is set in grond,
>   Ne marl, if it be fruitful fond.

Fruitful, the head fruitful, that bodes horns; the fruit of the   50
head is horns.—Dear niece, stay at home—for by the head of
the house is meant the husband; the prophecy needs no
explanation.

ANGELICA

Well, but I can neither make you a cuckold, uncle, by going
abroad; nor secure you from being one, by staying at home.   55

36 *Mercury* the god of merchandise and eloquence
48–9 *grond . . . fond* ground . . . found
49 *Ne marl* no wonder

---

42 *Messehalah.* Called by William Lilly, *England's Propheticall Merline*
(1644) 'a learned Arabian'. Congreve possessed a copy of Lilly (see
John C. Hodges, ed., *The Library of William Congreve*, New York;
New York Public Library, 1955, item no. 359) and drew most of the
names of his astrologers thence. See III.435 *n.*
43 *Buckinghamshire bard.* John Mason (d.1694). He was a millenarian.

FORESIGHT

Yes, yes; while there's one woman left, the prophecy is not
in full force.

ANGELICA

But my inclinations are in force; I have a mind to go abroad;
and if you won't lend me your coach, I'll take a hackney or
a chair and leave you to erect a scheme and find who's in   60
conjunction with your wife. Why don't you keep her at
home, if you're jealous when she's abroad? You know my
aunt is a little retrograde (as you call it) in her nature. Uncle,
I'm afraid you are not lord of the ascendant, ha, ha, ha!

FORESIGHT

Well, Jill-flirt, you are very pert, and always ridiculing that   65
celestial science.

ANGELICA

Nay, uncle, don't be angry. If you are, I'll reap up all your
false prophecies, ridiculous dreams and idle divinations.
I'll swear you are a nuisance to the neighbourhood. What a
bustle did you keep against the last invisible eclipse, laying   70
in provision, as 'twere for a siege? What a world of fire and
candle, matches and tinderboxes did you purchase! One
would have thought we were ever after to live underground,
or at least making a voyage to Greenland to inhabit there all
the dark season.   75

FORESIGHT

Why, you malapert slut—

ANGELICA

Will you lend me your coach, or I'll go on—nay, I'll declare
how your prophesied Popery was coming, only because the
butler had mislaid some of the apostle's spoons and thought
they were lost. Away went religion and spoon-meat together.   80
Indeed, uncle, I'll indict you for a wizard.

60 *erèct a scheme* calculate by astrology
62 *jealous when* (jealous of her when Ww)
70 *did* (hid Q1 uncorr. cited by Davis)
76 *malapert* saucy
79 *apostle's spoons* (apostle spoons Ww)
80 *spoon-meat* broth, soft food given to infants

58 *inclinations . . . force*, a play on inclination in its astronomical sense.
   She also puns on 'retrograde' (astrologically: moving westward relative
   to the fixed stars) and 'ascendant' (astrologically: referring to the
   easternmost star rising at one's birth which was supposed to exert a
   commanding influence over one's life), here a jibe at Foresight's
   impotence.

FORESIGHT

How, hussy! was there ever such a provoking minx?

NURSE

O merciful father, how she talks!

ANGELICA

Yes, I can make oath of your unlawful midnight practices;
you and the old nurse there—   85

NURSE

Marry, heaven defend! I at midnight practices—O Lord,
what's here to do? I in unlawful doings with my master's
worship! Why, did you ever hear the like now?—Sir, did
ever I do anything of your midnight concerns—but warm
your bed, and tuck you up, and set the candle, and your   90
tobacco-box, and your urinal by you, and now and then rub
the soles of your feet?—O Lord, I!

ANGELICA

Yes, I saw you together, through the keyhole of the closet,
one night, like Saul and the Witch of Endor, turning the
sieve and shears, and pricking your thumbs, to write poor   95
innocent servants' names in blood, about a little nutmeg-
grater, which she had forgot in the caudle-cup. Nay, I know
something worse, if I would speak of it—

FORESIGHT

I defy you, hussy! But I'll remember this, I'll be revenged on
you, cockatrice; I'll hamper you.—You have your fortune in   100
your own hands, but I'll find a way to make your lover, your
prodigal spendthrift gallant, Valentine, pay for all, I will.

ANGELICA

Will you? I care not, but all shall out then.—Look to it,
nurse; I can bring witness that you have a great unnatural
teat under your left arm, and he another; and that you   105
suckle a young devil in the shape of a tabby-cat by turns; I
can.

NURSE

A teat, a teat, I an unnatural teat! O the false slanderous
thing! Feel, feel here, if I have anything but like another

97 *caudle-cup* 'thin gruel, mixed with wine or ale, sweetened and spiced' (O.E.D.)
100 *cockatrice* a serpent, hatched from a cock's egg, which killed by its glance.
103 *to it* (to't Ww)

___

94 *Witch of Endor.* See I *Samuel* xxviii.
95 *sieve and shears.* A means of divination in which the sieve was held
between the extended points of the shears.

Christian (*Crying*) or any teats but two that han't given suck 110
this thirty years.

FORESIGHT

I will have patience, since it is the will of the stars I should be
thus tormented. This is the effect of the malicious conjunc-
tions and oppositions in the third house of my nativity;
there the curse of kindred was foretold.—But I will have my 115
doors locked up—I'll punish you, not a man shall enter my
house.

ANGELICA

Do, uncle, lock 'em up quickly before my aunt come home.
You'll have a letter for alimony tomorrow morning. But let
me be gone first, and then let no mankind come near the 120
house, but converse with spirits and the celestial signs, the
Bull, and the Ram, and the Goat. Bless me! There are a great
many horned beasts among the twelve signs, uncle. But
cuckolds go to heaven.

FORESIGHT

But there's but one Virgin among the twelve signs, spitfire, 125
but one Virgin.

ANGELICA

Nor there had not been that one, if she had had to do with
anything but astrologers, uncle. That makes my aunt go
abroad.

FORESIGHT

How? How? Is that the reason? Come, you know something; 130
tell me, and I'll forgive you; do, good niece. Come, you shall
have my coach and horses, faith and troth you shall. Does
my wife complain? Come, I know women tell one another.
She is young and sanguine, has a wanton hazel eye, and was
born under Gemini, which may incline her to society; she 135
has a mole upon her lip, with a moist palm, and an open
liberality on the mount of Venus.

ANGELICA

Ha, ha, ha!

FORESIGHT

Do you laugh? Well, gentlewoman, I'll—but come, be a good
girl, don't perplex your poor uncle, tell me—won't you 140
speak? Odd, I'll—

110–11 *or any teats . . . years* (om. Ww)
114· *oppositions* the situation of heavenly bodies 180° apart
114 *third house* the third division of the Zodiac relates to brethren

136–7 *a mole . . . Venus.* These were all signs of sensuality.

[Act II, Scene iv]

Enter SERVANT

SERVANT

Sir Sampson is coming down to wait upon you.

ANGELICA

Goodbye, uncle. [*To* SERVANT] Call me a chair. I'll find out
my aunt, and tell her she must not come home.

Exit ANGELICA *and* SERVANT

FORESIGHT

I'm so perplexed and vexed, I am not fit to receive him; I   145
shall scarce recover myself before the hour be past. Go,
nurse, tell Sir Sampson I'm ready to wait on him.

NURSE

Yes, sir.   *Exit* NURSE

FORESIGHT

Well—why if I was born to be a cuckold, there's no more to
be said—   150

[Act II, Scene v]

Enter SIR SAMPSON LEGEND *with a paper*

SIR SAMPSON

Nor no more to be done, old boy; that's plain—Here 'tis, I
have it in my hand, old Ptolemy; I'll make the ungracious
prodigal know who begat him; I will, old Nostrodamus.
What, I warrant my son thought nothing belonged to a father
but forgiveness and affection; no authority, no correction,   155
no arbitrary power; nothing to be done, but for him to
offend, and me to pardon. I warrant you, if he danced till
doomsday, he thought I was to pay the piper. Well, but here
it is under black and white, *signatum*, *sigillatum*, and
deliberatum; that as soon as my son Benjamin is arrived, he 160
is to make over to him his right of inheritance. Where's my
daughter that is to be?—Hah! old Merlin! Body o'me, I'm
so glad I'm revenged on this undutiful rogue.

150 *said*— (said— he's here already. Ww)
159–60 *signatum . . . deliberatum* signed, sealed, decided

***

153 *Nostrodamus*. (1503–66) Physician to Charles IX. He published a
   book of rhymed prophecies called *Centuries*.
162 *Merlin*. Alluding to Merlin's feats of divination, and perhaps to the
   assistance he gave in the marriage of Uther and Igraine (from which
   Arthur was born).

FORESIGHT

Odso, let me see; let me see the paper.—Aye, faith and troth, here 'tis, if it will but hold. I wish things were done and the 165
conveyance made. When was this signed, what hour? Odso, you should have consulted me for the time. Well, but we'll make haste—

SIR SAMPSON

Haste, aye, aye; haste enough. My son Ben will be in town tonight. I have ordered my lawyer to draw up writings of 170
settlement and jointure. All shall be done tonight. No matter for the time; prithee, brother Foresight, leave superstition. Pox o'th' time; there's no time but the time present, there's no more to be said of what's past, and all that is to come will happen. If the sun shine by day and the stars 175
by night, why, we shall know one another's faces without the help of a candle, and that's all the stars are good for.

FORESIGHT

How, how? Sir Sampson, that all? Give me leave to contradict you, and tell you, you are ignorant.

SIR SAMPSON

I tell you I am wise; and *sapiens dominabitur astris*; there's 180
Latin for you to prove it, and an argument to confound your Ephemeris. Ignorant! I tell you, I have travelled, old Fircu, and know the globe. I have seen the Antipodes, where the sun rises at midnight, and sets at noonday.

FORESIGHT

But I tell you, I have travelled, and travelled in the celestial 185
spheres, know the signs and the planets, and their houses; can judge of motions direct and retrograde, of sextiles, quadrates, trines and oppositions, fiery trigons and aquatical trigons; know whether life shall be long or short, happy or unhappy, whether diseases are curable or incurable, 190
if journeys shall be prosperous, undertakings successful, or goods stolen recovered, I know—

---

180 *sapiens dominabitur astris* the wise man will be superior to the stars. The
  tag was attributed to Ptolemy (Davis).
182 *Ephemeris* almanac
182 *Fircu* familiar spirit?
187-8 *sextiles . . . oppositions* the aspect of two planets as seen from
  earth distant from each other by a sixth, a quarter, a third or half
  the circle of the Zodiac
188-9 *fiery trigons and aquatical trigons* a trigon is the conjunction of
  three signs of the Zodiac; the fiery trigon: Aries, Leo, Sagittarius;
  the aquatical: Cancer, Scorpio, Pisces

SIR SAMPSON

I know the length of the Emperor of China's foot, have
kissed the Great Mogul's slipper, and rid a-hunting upon
an elephant with the Cham of Tartary. Body o'me, I have   195
made a cuckold of a king, and the present Majesty of
Bantam is the issue of these loins.

FORESIGHT

I know when travellers lie or speak truth, when they don't
know it themselves.

SIR SAMPSON

I have known an astrologer made a cuckold in the twinkling   200
of a star, and seen a conjurer that could not keep the devil
out of his wife's circle.

FORESIGHT (*Aside*)

What, does he twit me with my wife too? I must be better
informed of this.—Do you mean my wife, Sir Sampson?
Though you made a cuckold of the King of Bantam, yet by   205
the body of the sun—

SIR SAMPSON

By the horns of the moon, you would say, Brother Capricorn.

FORESIGHT

Capricorn in your teeth, thou modern Mandeville; Ferdi-
nand Mendez Pinto was but a type of thee, thou liar of the
first magnitude. Take back your paper of inheritance; send   210
your son to sea again. I'll wed my daughter to an Egyptian
mummy, ere she shall incorporate with a contemner of
sciences and a defamer of virtue.

SIR SAMPSON

Body o'me, I have gone too far; I must not provoke honest
Albumazar.—An Egyptian mummy is an illustrious creature,   215
my trusty hieroglyphic, and may have significations of
futurity about him; odsbud, I would my son were an
Egyptian mummy for thy sake. What, thou art not angry

197 *Bantam* in Java
202 *wife's* Ww (wives Qq)
207 *Capricorn* the goat, i.e. cuckold

208-9 *Mandeville . . . Pinto.* Sir John Mandeville was the supposed author of the
      famous Travels (mid-14th century); Pinto (?1509-85) was a Portuguese traveller
      in the far east.
215   *Albumazar.* A 9th-century Arabian astronomer and astrologer. Thomas
      Tomkis' play *Albumazar* (1615), an adaptation from the Italian, had
      been revived in 1668.

for a jest, my good Haly? I reverence the sun, moon and
stars with all my heart. What, I'll make thee a present of a   220
mummy: now I think on't, body o'me, I have a shoulder of
an Egyptian king that I purloined from one of the pyramids,
powdered with hieroglyphics; thou shalt have it sent home
to thy house, and make an entertainment for all the philomaths and students in physic and astrology in and about   225
London.

FORESIGHT

But what do you know of my wife, Sir Sampson?

SIR SAMPSON

Thy wife is a constellation of virtues; she's the moon, and
thou art the man in the moon: nay, she is more illustrious
than the moon, for she has her chastity without her   230
inconstancy. 'S'bud, I was but in jest.

[Act II, Scene vi]

Enter JEREMY

SIR SAMPSON

How now, who sent for you? Ha! what would you have?

FORESIGHT

Nay, if you were but in jest.—Who's that fellow? I don't like
his physiognomy.

SIR SAMPSON

My son, sir? What son, sir? My son Benjamin, hoh?   235

JEREMY

No, sir, Mr. Valentine, my master. 'Tis the first time he has
been abroad since his confinement, and he comes to pay his
duty to you.

SIR SAMPSON

Well, sir.

---

223 *sent home* (brought home Ww)
224-5 *philomaths* lovers of learning in mathematics (and astrology).

---

219 *Haly*. Referred to by Lilly as Hally Rodboan, and mentioned in
Tomkis' *Albumazar*. Cited as an authority in predicting the weather in W.
Ramsey, *Astrologie Restored* (1660) (Davis).

[Act II, Scene vii]

Enter VALENTINE

JEREMY

He is here, sir. 240

VALENTINE

Your blessing, sir.

SIR SAMPSON

You've had it already, sir: I think I sent it you today in a
bill of four thousand pound. A great deal of money, brother
Foresight.

FORESIGHT

Aye, indeed, Sir Sampson, a great deal of money for a young 245
man; I wonder what he can do with it!

SIR SAMPSON

Body o'me, so do I.—Hark ye, Valentine, if there is too
much, refund the superfluity; do'st hear, boy?

VALENTINE

Superfluity, sir; it will scarce pay my debts. I hope you will
have more indulgence than to oblige me to those hard 250
conditions which my necessity signed to.

SIR SAMPSON

Sir, how; I beseech you, what were you pleased to intimate
concerning indulgence?

VALENTINE

Why, sir, that you would not go to the extremity of the
conditions, but release me at least from some part. 255

SIR SAMPSON

O, sir, I understand you,—that's all, ha?

VALENTINE

Yes, sir, all that I presume to ask.—But what you, out of
fatherly fondness, will be pleased to add, shall be doubly
welcome.

SIR SAMPSON

No doubt of it, sweet sir, but your filial piety and my 260
fatherly fondness would fit like two tallies.—Here's a rogue,
brother Foresight, makes a bargain under hand and seal in
the morning, and would be released from it in the afternoon.
—Here's a rogue, dog, here's conscience and honesty; this is
your wit now, this is the morality of your wits! You are a wit, 265
and have been a beau, and may be a—why, sirrah, is it not
here under hand and seal? Can you deny it?

247 *is too* (be too Ww)

VALENTINE
Sir, I don't deny it.

SIR SAMPSON
Sirrah, you'll be hanged; I shall live to see you go up
Holborn Hill.—Has he not a rogue's face? Speak brother, 270
you understand physiognomy; a hanging look to me; of all
my boys the most unlike me; a has a damned Tyburn face,
without the benefit o'the clergy.

FORESIGHT
Hum, truly I don't care to discourage a young man; he has a
violent death in his face, but I hope no danger of hanging. 275

VALENTINE
Sir, is this usage for your son? For that old weather-headed
fool, I know how to laugh at him; but you, sir—

SIR SAMPSON
You, sir; and you, sir! Why, who are you, sir?

VALENTINE
Your son, sir.

SIR SAMPSON
That's more than I know, sir, and I believe not. 280

VALENTINE
Faith, I hope not.

SIR SAMPSON
What, would you have your mother a whore! Did you ever
hear the like! Did you ever hear the like! Body o'me—

VALENTINE
I would have an excuse for your barbarity and unnatural
usage. 285

SIR SAMPSON
Excuse! Impudence! Why, sirrah, mayn't I do what I
please? Are not you my slave? Did not I beget you? And
might not I have chosen whether I would have begot you or
no? Ouns, who are you? Whence came you? What brought
you into the world? How came you here, sir? Here, to stand 290
here, upon those two legs, and look erect with that audacious
face, hah? Answer me that? Did you come a volunteer into
the world? Or did I beat up for you with the lawful
authority of a parent, and press you to the service?

VALENTINE
I know no more why I came, than you do why you called 295

272 *a has* (he has Q2–4, Ww)
293–4 *beat up for you . . . and* (om. Ww)

270 *Holborn Hill.* On the way from Newgate prison to Tyburn gallows.

me. But here I am, and if you don't mean to provide for me,
I desire you would leave me as you found me.

SIR SAMPSON

With all my heart: come, uncase, strip, and go naked out of
the world as you came into't.

VALENTINE

My clothes are soon put off; but you must also deprive me of   300
reason, thought, passions, inclinations, affections, appetites,
senses, and the huge train of attendants that you begot along
with me.

SIR SAMPSON

Body o'me, what a many-headed monster have I propagated!

VALENTINE

I am of myself, a plain easy simple creature, and to be kept   305
at small expense; but the retinue that you gave me are
craving and invincible; they are so many devils that you
have raised, and will have employment.

SIR SAMPSON

Ouns, what had I to do to get children? Can't a private man
be born without all these followers? Why, nothing under   310
an emperor should be born with appetites. Why, at this rate
a fellow that has but a groat in his pocket may have a stomach
capable of a ten-shilling ordinary.

JEREMY

Nay, that's as clear as the sun; I'll make oath of it before any
justice in Middlesex.   315

SIR SAMPSON

Here's a cormorant too.—'S'heart, this fellow was not born
with you? I did not beget him, did I?

JEREMY

By the provision that's made for me, you might have begot
me too: nay, and to tell your worship another truth, I
believe you did, for I find I was born with those same   320
whoreson appetites too, that my master speaks of.

SIR SAMPSON

Why, look you there now. I'll maintain it, that by the rule of
right reason, this fellow ought to have been born without a
palate. 'S'heart, what should he do with a distinguishing
taste? I warrant now he'd rather eat a pheasant than a piece   325
of poor John; and smell, now, why I warrant he can smell,

300 *deprive* (divest Ww)
313 *ordinary* eating house
316 *cormorant* glutton (the voracious seabird)
326 *poor John* dried or salted fish

and loves perfumes above a stink. Why, there's it, and
music—don't you love music, scoundrel?

JEREMY

Yes, I have a reasonable good ear, sir, as to jigs and country
dances, and the like; I don't much matter your solos or   330
sonatas; they give me the spleen.

SIR SAMPSON

The spleen, ha, ha, ha!—a pox confound you, solos and
sonatas? Ouns, whose son are you? How were you engen-
dered, muckworm?

JEREMY

I am, by my father, the son of a chairman; my mother sold   335
oysters in winter and cucumbers in summer; and I came
upstairs into the world, for I was born in a cellar.

FORESIGHT

By your looks, you should go upstairs out of the world too,
friend.

SIR SAMPSON

And if this rogue were anatomized now, and dissected, he   340
has his vessels of digestion and concoction, and so forth, large
enough for the inside of a cardinal, this son of a cucumber.
These things are unaccountable and unreasonable. Body
o'me, why was not I a bear, that my cubs might have lived
upon sucking their paws? Nature has been provident only to   345
bears and spiders; the one has its nutriment in his own
hands, and t'other spins his habitation out of his entrails.

VALENTINE

Fortune was provident enough to supply all the necessities
of my nature, if I had my right of inheritance.

SIR SAMPSON

Again! Ouns, han't you four thousand pound? If I had it   350
again, I would not give thee a groat. What, wouldst thou
have me turn pelican and feed thee out of my own vitals?
'S'heart, live by your wits. You were always fond of the wits,
now let's see if you have wit enough to keep yourself. Your
brother will be in town tonight, or tomorrow morning, and   355
then look you perform covenants, and so your friend and
servant.—Come, brother Foresight.

Exeunt SIR SAMPSON *and* FORESIGHT

347 *his entrails* (his own entrails Ww)

[Act II, Scene viii]

JEREMY

I told you what your visit would come to.

VALENTINE

'Tis as much as I expected. I did not come to see him: I came
to Angelica; but since she was gone abroad, it was easily   360
turned another way, and at least looked well on my side.—
What's here? Mrs. Foresight and Mrs. Frail; they are
earnest. I'll avoid 'em. Come this way, and go and inquire
when Angelica will return.   [*Exeunt*]

[Act II, Scene ix]

Enter MRS. FORESIGHT *and* MRS. FRAIL

MRS. FRAIL

What have you to do to watch me? S'life, I'll do what I   365
please.

MRS. FORESIGHT

You will?

MRS. FRAIL

Yes, marry will I. A great piece of business to go to Covent
Garden Square in a hackney-coach and take a turn with
one's friend.   370

MRS. FORESIGHT

Nay, two or three turns, I'll take my oath.

MRS. FRAIL

Well, what if I took twenty? I warrant if you had been there,
it had been only innocent recreation. Lord, where's the
comfort of this life, if we can't have the happiness of
conversing where we like?   375

MRS. FORESIGHT

But can't you converse at home? I own it, I think there's no
happiness like conversing with an agreeable man; I don't
quarrel at that, nor I don't think but your conversation was
very innocent; but the place is public, and to be seen with a
man in a hackney-coach is scandalous: what if anybody else   380
should have seen you alight as I did? How can anybody be
happy, while they're in perpetual fear of being seen and
censured? Besides, it would not only reflect upon you,
sister, but me.

MRS. FRAIL

Pooh, here's a clutter. Why should it reflect upon you? I   385

don't doubt but you have thought yourself happy in a
hackney-coach before now. If I had gone to Knightsbridge,
or to Chelsea, or to Spring-Garden, or Barn-Elms with a
man alone, something might have been said.

MRS. FORESIGHT

Why, was I ever in any of these places? What do you mean,   390
sister?

MRS. FRAIL

Was I? What do you mean?

MRS. FORESIGHT

You have been at a worse place.

MRS. FRAIL

I at a worse place, and with a man!

MRS. FORESIGHT

I suppose you would not go alone to the *World's-End*?   395

MRS. FRAIL

The world's end! What, do you mean to banter me?

MRS. FORESIGHT

Poor innocent! You don't know that there's a place called
the *World's-End*? I'll swear you can keep your countenance
purely; you'd make an admirable player.

MRS. FRAIL

I'll swear you have a great deal of impudence, and in my   400
mind too much for the stage.

MRS. FORESIGHT

Very well, that will appear who has most. You never were
at the *World's-End*?

MRS. FRAIL

No.

MRS. FORESIGHT

You deny it positively to my face?   405

MRS. FRAIL

Your face, what's your face?

MRS. FORESIGHT

No matter for that; it's as good a face as yours.

MRS. FRAIL

Not by a dozen years' wearing.—But I do deny it positively
to your face then.

390 *these* (those Ww)
400 *impudence* (confidence Ww)

---

395 *World's-End.* In Chelsea. All the places referred to were resorts of
doubtful character.

MRS. FORESIGHT

I'll allow you now to find fault with my face; for I'll swear   410
your impudence has put me out of countenance: but look you
here now—where did you lose this gold bodkin?—O, sister,
sister!

MRS. FRAIL

My bodkin!

MRS. FORESIGHT

Nay, 'tis yours, look at it.   415

MRS. FRAIL

Well, if you go to that, where did you find this bodkin? O,
sister, sister! Sister every way.

MRS. FORESIGHT (*Aside*)

O devil on't, that I could not discover her without betraying
myself.

MRS. FRAIL

I have heard gentlemen say, sister, that one should take great   420
care when one makes a thrust in fencing, not to lie open
one's self.

MRS. FORESIGHT

It's very true, sister: well, since all's out, and as you say,
since we are both wounded, let us do that is often done in
duels, take care of one another, and grow better friends than   425
before.

MRS. FRAIL

With all my heart. Ours are but slight flesh wounds, and if
we keep 'em from air, not at all dangerous: well, give me
your hand in token of sisterly secrecy and affection.

MRS. FORESIGHT

Here 'tis with all my heart.   430

MRS. FRAIL

Well, as an earnest of friendship and confidence, I'll acquaint
you with a design that I have: to tell truth and speak openly
one to another, I'm afraid the world have observed us more
than we have observed one another. You have a rich husband
and are provided for; I am at a loss and have no great stock   435
either of fortune or reputation, and therefore must look
sharply about me. Sir Sampson has a son that is expected
tonight, and by the account I have heard of his education,
can be no conjurer; the estate, you know, is to be made
over to him: now if I could wheedle him, sister, ha? You   440
understand me?

412 *bodkin* ornamental pin
424 *that* (what Ww)

MRS. FORESIGHT

I do; and will help you to the utmost of my power. And I
can tell you one thing that falls out luckily enough: my
awkward daughter-in-law, who you know is designed for his
wife, is grown fond of Mr. Tattle; now if we can improve that,   445
and make her have an aversion for the booby, it may go a
great way towards his liking of you. Here they come together;
and let us contrive some way or other to leave 'em together.

[Act II, Scene x]

Enter TATTLE *and* MISS PRUE

MISS PRUE

Mother, mother, mother, look you here.

MRS. FORESIGHT

Fie, fie, miss, how you bawl. Besides, I have told you, you   450
must not call me mother.

MISS PRUE

What must I call you then? Are not you my father's wife?

MRS. FORESIGHT

Madam; you must say, madam. By my soul, I shall fancy
myself old indeed, to have this great girl call me mother.
Well, but, miss, what are you so overjoyed at?   455

MISS PRUE

Look you here, madam, then, what Mr. Tattle has given me.
Look you here, cousin, here's a snuff-box; nay, there's snuff
in't;— here, will you have any?—O good! How sweet it is.—
Mr. Tattle is all over sweet, his peruke is sweet, and his
gloves are sweet, and his handkerchief is sweet, pure sweet,   460
sweeter than roses.—Smell him, mother, madam, I mean.
He gave me this ring for a kiss.

TATTLE

O fie, miss, you must not kiss and tell.

MISS PRUE

Yes; I may tell my mother.—And he says he'll give me
something to make me smell so.—O, pray lend me your   465
handkerchief. Smell, cousin.—He says he'll give me something that will make my smocks smell this way. Is not it

444 *daughter-in-law* step-daughter
444 *for* (to be Ww)
447 *liking of you* (liking you Ww)
452 *Are not you* (Are you not Q3, 4, Ww)
459 *peruke* an artificial cap of hair

pure? It's better than lavender, mun. I'm resolved I won't
let nurse put any more lavender among my smocks, ha,
cousin?　　　　　　　　　　　　　　　　　　　　　　　　　470

MRS. FRAIL

Fie, miss; amongst your linen, you must say. You must never
say smock.

MISS PRUE

Why, it is not bawdy, is it, cousin?

TATTLE

O, madam, you are too severe upon miss; you must not find
fault with her pretty simplicity, it becomes her strangely.—　475
Pretty miss, don't let 'em persuade you out of your
innocency.

MRS. FORESIGHT

O, damn you, toad! I wish you don't persuade her out of her
innocency.

TATTLE

Who, I, madam? O Lord, how can your ladyship have such a　480
thought? Sure, you don't know me?

MRS. FRAIL

Ah devil, sly devil.—He's as close, sister, as a confessor. He
thinks we don't observe him.

MRS. FORESIGHT

A cunning cur; how soon he could find out a fresh harmless
creature; and left us, sister, presently.　　　　　　　　485

TATTLE

Upon reputation—

MRS. FORESIGHT

They're all so, sister, these men. They love to have the
spoiling of a young thing; they are as fond of it, as of being
first in the fashion, or of seeing a new play the first day. I
warrant it would break Mr. Tattle's heart to think that　490
anybody else should be beforehand with him.

TATTLE

O Lord, I swear I would not for the world—

MRS. FRAIL

O hang you; who'll believe you? You'd be hanged before
you'd confess. We know you.—She's very pretty! Lord,
what pure red and white! She looks so wholesome; ne'er　495
stir, I don't know, but I fancy, if I were a man—

MISS PRUE

How you love to jeer one, cousin.

MRS. FORESIGHT

Harkee, sister, by my soul, the girl is spoiled already. D'ye

think she'll ever endure a great lubberly tarpaulin? Gad, I
warrant you, she won't let him come near her after Mr.   500
Tattle.

MRS. FRAIL

O'my soul, I'm afraid not. Eh! filthy creature, that smells
all of pitch and tar!—Devil take you, you confounded toad,
why did you see her before she was married?

MRS. FORESIGHT

Nay, why did we let him? My husband will hang us. He'll   505
think we brought 'em acquainted.

MRS. FRAIL

Come, faith, let us be gone. If my brother Foresight should
find us with them, he'd think so, sure enough.

MRS. FORESIGHT

So he would. But then, leaving 'em together is as bad. And
he's such a sly devil, he'll never miss an opportunity.   510

MRS. FRAIL

I don't care; I won't be seen in't.

MRS. FORESIGHT

Well, if you should, Mr. Tattle, you'll have a world to
answer for. Remember I wash my hands of it; I'm
thoroughly innocent.

Exeunt MRS. FORESIGHT *and* MRS. FRAIL

[Act II, Scene xi]

MISS PRUE

What makes 'em go away, Mr. Tattle? What do they mean?   515
Do you know?

TATTLE

Yes, my dear, I think I can guess. But hang me if I know the
reason of it.

MISS PRUE

Come, must not we go too?

TATTLE

No, no, they don't mean that.   520

MISS PRUE

No! What then? What shall you and I do together?

TATTLE

I must make love to you, pretty miss; will you let me make
love to you?

MISS PRUE

Yes, if you please.

TATTLE (*Aside*)

Frank, egad, at least. What a pox does Mrs. Foresight mean 525
by this civility? Is it to make a fool of me? Or does she leave
us together out of good morality, and do as she would be
done by? Gad, I'll understand it so.

MISS PRUE

Well, and how will you make love to me? Come, I long to
have you begin. Must I make love too? You must tell me 530
how.

TATTLE

You must let me speak miss, you must not speak first; I must
ask you questions, and you must answer.

MISS PRUE

What, is it like the catechism? Come then, ask me.

TATTLE

D'ye think you can love me? 535

MISS PRUE

Yes.

TATTLE

Pooh, pox, you must not say yes already; I shan't care a
farthing for you then in a twinkling.

MISS PRUE

What must I say then?

TATTLE

Why, you must say no, or you believe not, or you can't tell. 540

MISS PRUE

Why, must I tell a lie then?

TATTLE

Yes, if you would be well-bred. All well-bred persons lie.
Besides, you are a woman; you must never speak what you
think; your words must contradict your thoughts; but your
actions may contradict your words. So, when I ask you if you 545
can love me, you must say no, but you must love me too. If
I tell you you are handsome, you must deny it, and say I
flatter you. But you must think yourself more charming than
I speak you, and like me for the beauty which I say you have
as much as if I had it myself. If I ask you to kiss me, you 550
must be angry, but you must not refuse me. If I ask you for
more, you must be more angry, but more complying; and as
soon as ever I make you say you'll cry out, you must be sure
to hold your tongue.

542 *you would* (you'd Ww)

MISS PRUE

O Lord, I swear this is pure. I like it better than our old- 555
fashioned country way of speaking one's mind; and must
not you lie too?

TATTLE

Hum—yes—but you must believe I speak truth.

MISS PRUE

O Gemini! Well, I always had a great mind to tell lies, but
they frighted me, and said it was a sin. 560

TATTLE

Well, my pretty creature; will you make me happy by giving
me a kiss?

MISS PRUE

No, indeed; I'm angry at you.   *Runs and kisses him*

TATTLE

Hold, hold, that's pretty well, but you should not have given
it me, but have suffered me to take it. 565

MISS PRUE

Well, we'll do it again.

TATTLE

With all my heart. Now then, my little angel.   *Kisses her*

MISS PRUE

Pish.

TATTLE

That's right. Again, my charmer.   *Kisses again*

MISS PRUE

O fie, nay, now I can't abide you. 570

TATTLE

Admirable! That was as well as if you had been born and
bred in Covent Garden all the days of your life; and won't
you show me, pretty miss, where your bedchamber is?

MISS PRUE

No, indeed won't I: but I'll run there, and hide myself from
you behind the curtains. 575

TATTLE

I'll follow you.

MISS PRUE

Ah, but I'll hold the door with both hands, and be angry;
and you shall push me down before you come in.

TATTLE

No, I'll come in first, and push you down afterwards.

555 *pure* excellent.
565 *to take* (to have taken Ww)
572 *all . . . life* (om. Ww)

MISS PRUE

Will you? Then I'll be more angry, and more complying.   580

TATTLE

Then I'll make you cry out.

MISS PRUE

O, but you shan't, for I'll hold my tongue.

TATTLE

O my dear, apt scholar.

MISS PRUE

Well, now I'll run and make more haste than you.

Exit MISS PRUE

TATTLE

You shall not fly so fast, as I'll pursue.   *Exit after her*   585

[Act III, Scene i]

NURSE

Miss, miss, Miss Prue. Mercy on me, marry and amen: why, what's become of the child? Why miss, Miss Foresight! Sure she has not locked herself up in her chamber and gone to sleep, or to prayers. Miss, miss! I hear her. Come to your father, child; open the door. Open the door, miss. I hear   5
you cry husht. O Lord, who's there? (*Peeps*) What's here to do? O the Father! A man with her! Why, miss I say, God's my life, here's fine doings towards—O Lord, we're all undone. O you young harlotry. (*Knocks*) Od's my life, won't you open the door? I'll come in the back way.   *Exit*   10

[Act III, Scene ii]

TATTLE *and* MISS PRUE *at the door*

MISS PRUE

O Lord, she's coming, and she'll tell my father. What shall I do now?

TATTLE

Pox take her; if she had stayed two minutes longer, I should have wished for her coming.

MISS PRUE

O dear, what shall I say? Tell me, Mr. Tattle, tell me a lie.   15

TATTLE

There's no occasion for a lie; I could never tell a lie to no

3 *has not* (has Ww)
10 s.d. *at the door* (om. Ww)

purpose. But since we have done nothing, we must say nothing, I think. I hear her. I'll leave you together, and come off as you can.   *Thrusts her in, and shuts the door*

[Act III, Scene iii]

Enter VALENTINE, SCANDAL, *and* ANGELICA

ANGELICA
You can't accuse me of inconstancy; I never told you that I   20
loved you.
VALENTINE
But I can accuse you of uncertainty, for not telling me
whether you did or no.
ANGELICA
You mistake indifference for uncertainty; I never had
concern enough to ask myself the question.   25
SCANDAL
Nor good nature enough to answer him that did ask you;
I'll say that for you, madam.
ANGELICA
What, are you setting up for good nature?
SCANDAL
Only for the affectation of it, as the women do for ill nature.
ANGELICA
Persuade your friend that it is all affectation.   30
VALENTINE
I shall receive no benefit from the opinion: for I know no
effectual difference between continued affectation and
reality.
TATTLE (*Coming up. Aside to* SCANDAL)
Scandal, are you in private discourse, anything of secrecy?
SCANDAL
Yes, but I dare trust you; we were talking of Angelica's love   35
for Valentine. You won't speak of it?
TATTLE
No, no, not a syllable. I know that's a secret, for it's
whispered everywhere.
SCANDAL
Ha, ha, ha.

23 *or no* (or not Ww)
31 s.p. VALENTINE (ANGELICA W1, SCANDAL W2)
36 *for Valentine* (to Valentine Ww)

ANGELICA
What is, Mr. Tattle? I heard you say something was   40
whispered everywhere.

SCANDAL
Your love of Valentine.

ANGELICA
How!

TATTLE
No, madam, his love for your ladyship. Gad take me, I beg
your pardon, for I never heard a word of your ladyship's   45
passion till this instant.

ANGELICA
My passion! And who told you of my passion, pray, sir?

SCANDAL
Why, is the devil in you? Did not I tell it you for a secret?

TATTLE
Gadso; but I thought she might have been trusted with her
own affairs.   50

SCANDAL
Is that your discretion? Trust a woman with herself?

TATTLE
You say true, I beg your pardon; I'll bring all off.—It was
impossible, madam, for me to imagine that a person of your
ladyship's wit and gallantry could have so long received the
passionate addresses of the accomplished Valentine, and yet   55
remain insensible; therefore, you will pardon me if from a
just weight of his merit, with your ladyship's good judgment,
I formed the balance of a reciprocal affection.

VALENTINE
O the devil, what damned costive poet has given thee this
lesson of fustian to get by rote?   60

ANGELICA
I dare swear you wrong him; it is his own. And Mr. Tattle
only judges of the success of others from the effects of his
own merit. For certainly Mr. Tattle was never denied
anything in his life.

TATTLE
O Lord! yes indeed, madam, several times.   65

ANGELICA
I swear I don't think 'tis possible

TATTLE
Yes, I vow and swear I have: Lord, madam, I'm the most

59 *costive* constipated; slow in his mental processes

unfortunate man in the world, and the most cruelly used by
the ladies.

ANGELICA

Nay, now you're ungrateful.   70

TATTLE

No, I hope not. 'Tis as much ingratitude to own some
favours, as to conceal others.

VALENTINE

There, now it's out.

ANGELICA

I don't understand you now. I thought you had never asked
anything, but what a lady might modestly grant, and you   75
confess.

SCANDAL

So, faith, your business is done here; now you may go brag
somewhere else.

TATTLE

Brag! O heavens! Why, did I name anybody?

ANGELICA

No; I suppose that is not in your power; but you would if   80
you could, no doubt on't.

TATTLE

Not in my power, madam! What, does your ladyship mean,
that I have no woman's reputation in my power?

SCANDAL (*Aside*)

Ouns, why you won't own it, will you?

TATTLE

Faith, madam, you're in the right; no more I have, as I hope 85
to be saved; I never had it in my power to say anything to a
lady's prejudice in my life. For as I was telling you, madam,
I have been the most unsuccessful creature living in things
of that nature, and never had the good fortune to be trusted
once with a lady's secret, not once.   90

ANGELICA

No?

VALENTINE

Not once, I dare answer for him.

SCANDAL

And I'll answer for him; for I'm sure if he had, he would
have told me. I find, madam, you don't know Mr. Tattle.

TATTLE

No indeed, madam, you don't know me at all I find: for sure   95
my intimate friends would have known—

ANGELICA

Then it seems you would have told, if you had been trusted.

TATTLE

O pox, Scandal, that was too far put.—Never have told
particulars, madam. Perhaps I might have talked as of a
third person, or have introduced an amour of my own in   100
conversation by way of novel; but never have explained
particulars.

ANGELICA

But whence comes the reputation of Mr. Tattle's secrecy, if
he was never trusted?

SCANDAL

Why thence it arises—the thing is proverbially spoken, but   105
may be applied to him—as if we should say in general terms,
he only is secret who never was trusted: a satirical proverb
upon our sex. There's another upon yours: as she is chaste
who was never asked the question. That's all.

VALENTINE

A couple of very civil proverbs, truly: 'tis hard to tell   110
whether the lady or Mr. Tattle be the more obliged to you.
For you found her virtue upon the backwardness of the men,
and his secrecy, upon the mistrust of the women.

TATTLE

Gad, it's very true, madam; I think we are obliged to acquit
ourselves. And for my part—but your ladyship is to speak   115
first—

ANGELICA

Am I? Well, I freely confess I have resisted a great deal of
temptation.

TATTLE

And I, gad, I have given some temptation that has not been
resisted.   120

VALENTINE

Good.

ANGELICA

I cite Valentine here, to declare to the court how fruitless
he has found his endeavours, and to confess all his solicitations and my denials.

VALENTINE

I am ready to plead, not guilty for you; and guilty for myself. 125

SCANDAL

So, why this is fair, here's demonstration with a witness.

TATTLE

Well, my witnesses are not present. But I confess I have had

favours from persons—but as the favours are numberless, so
the persons are nameless.

SCANDAL

Pooh, pox, this proves nothing.   130

TATTLE

No? I can show letters, lockets, pictures, and rings, and if
there be occasion for witnesses, I can summon the maids at
the chocolate-houses, all the porters of Pall Mall and
Covent Garden, the doorkeepers at the playhouse, the
drawers at Locket's, Pontack's, the Rummer, Spring-   135
Garden; my own landlady and *valet de chambre;* all who shall
make oath that I receive more letters than the secretary's
office; and that I have more vizor-masks to inquire for me
than ever went to see the hermaphrodite or the naked
prince. And it is notorious that in a country church, once, an 140
inquiry being made who I was, it was answered, I was the
famous Tattle, who had ruined so many women.

VALENTINE

It was there, I suppose, you got the nickname of the Great
Turk.

TATTLE

True; I was called Turk-Tattle all over the parish. The   145
next Sunday all the old women kept their daughters at
home, and the parson had not half his congregation. He
would have brought me into the spiritual court, but I was
revenged upon him, for he had a handsome daughter whom
I initiated into the science. But I repented it afterwards, for 150
it was talked of in town—and a lady of quality that shall be
nameless, in a raging fit of jealousy, came down in her coach
and six horses, and exposed herself upon my account; gad,
I was sorry for it with all my heart.—You know whom I
mean—you know where we raffled—   155

SCANDAL

Mum, Tattle,

VALENTINE

S'death, are not you ashamed?

130 *pox* (om. Ww)
133 *porters of* (porters at Ww)
135 *drawers* tapsters; barmen

139–40 *hermaphrodite . . . naked prince.* Popular shows of the day. The
'Prince' was the son of a 'King Moangis' (Summers).

155 *raffled.* I do not understand the allusion. Were they raffling for women
(or the reputation of having slept with them?).

ANGELICA

    O barbarous! I never heard so insolent a piece of vanity. Fie,
Mr. Tattle, I'll swear I could not have believed it. Is this
your secrecy? 160

TATTLE

    Gadso, the heat of my story carried me beyond my discre-
tion, as the heat of the lady's passion hurried her beyond her
reputation. But I hope you don't know whom I mean, for
there were a great many ladies raffled.—Pox on't, now
could I bite off my tongue. 165

SCANDAL

    No, don't; for then you'll tell us no more. (*Goes to the
door*) Come, I'll recommend a song to you upon the hint of
my two proverbs, and I see one in the next room that will
sing it.

TATTLE

    For heaven's sake, if you do guess, say nothing. Gad, I'm 170
very unfortunate.

            Re-enter SCANDAL, *with one to sing*

SCANDAL

    Pray sing the first song in the last new play.

                  SONG
          Set by Mr. John Eccles
A nymph and a swain to Apollo once prayed;
The swain had been jilted, the nymph been betrayed;
Their intent was to try if his oracle knew 175
E'er a nymph that was chaste, or a swain that was true.

Apollo was mute, and had like t'have been posed,
But sagely at length he this secret disclosed:
He alone won't betray in whom none will confide,
And the nymph may be chaste that has never been tried. 180

           [Act III, Scene iv]

    Enter SIR SAMPSON, MRS. FRAIL, MISS PRUE, *and* SERVANT

SIR SAMPSON

    Is Ben come? Odso, my son Ben come? Odd, I'm glad on't.

---

166 *don't* Q3, 4, Ww (doubt on't Q1, 2)
177 *posed* puzzled

---

172 *Eccles.* (d.1735) He wrote the music for more than 40 plays, including
    The Way of the World.

Where is he? I long to see him. Now, Mrs. Frail, you shall
see my son Ben. Body o'me, he's the hopes of my family. I
han't seen him these three years. I warrant he's grown.
Call him in; bid him make haste. I'm ready to cry for joy.   185
                                        Exit SERVANT

MRS. FRAIL
Now, miss, you shall see your husband.

MISS PRUE (*Aside to* MRS. FRAIL)
Pish, he shall be none of my husband.

MRS. FRAIL
Hush. Well, he shan't, leave that to me.—I'll beckon Mr.
Tattle to us.

ANGELICA
Won't you stay and see your brother?   190

VALENTINE
We are the twin stars and cannot shine in one sphere: when
he rises I must set. Besides, if I should stay, I don't know
but my father in good nature may press one to the immediate
signing the deed of conveyance of my estate, and I'll defer it
so long as I can. Well, you'll come to a resolution.   195

ANGELICA
I can't. Resolution must come to me, or I shall never have
one.

SCANDAL
Come Valentine, I'll go with you; I've something in my
head to communicate to you.

                             Exit VALENTINE *and* SCANDAL

[Act III, Scene v]

SIR SAMPSON
What, is my son Valentine gone? What, is he sneaked off and   200
would not see his brother? There's an unnatural whelp!
There's an ill-natured dog! What, were you here too,
madam, and could not keep him! Could neither love, nor
duty, nor natural affection oblige him? Odsbud, madam,
have no more to say to him; he is not worth your considera-   205
tion. The rogue has not a dram of generous love about him:
all interest, all interest; he's an undone scoundrel, and

193 *one* Q1, 2 (me Q3, 4, Ww)

---

191 *twin stars*. Castor and Pollux. They were allowed by Zeus to dwell in
  Heaven on alternate days.

courts your estate: body o'me, he does not care a doit for
your person.

ANGELICA

I'm pretty even with him, Sir Sampson, for if ever I could   210
have liked anything in him, it should have been his estate
too. But since that's gone, the bait's off, and the naked
hook appears.

SIR SAMPSON

Odsbud, well spoken, and you are a wiser woman than I
thought you were; for most young women nowadays are to   215
be tempted with a naked hook.

ANGELICA

If I marry, Sir Sampson, I'm for a good estate with any
man, and for any man with a good estate; therefore, if I
were obliged to make a choice, I declare I'd rather have you
than your son.   220

SIR SAMPSON

Faith and troth, you're a wise woman, and I'm glad to hear
you say so; I was afraid you were in love with the reprobate.
Odd, I was sorry for you with all my heart. Hang him, mon-
grel! Cast him off; you shall see the rogue show himself and
make love to some desponding Cadua of fourscore for   225
sustenance. Odd, I love to see a young spendthrift forced to
cling to an old woman for support, like ivy round a dead oak.
Faith, I do; I love to see 'em hug and cotton together, like
down upon a thistle.

[Act III, Scene vi]

Enter BEN LEGEND *and* SERVANT

BEN

Where's father?   230

SERVANT

There, sir, his back's toward you.

SIR SAMPSON

My son Ben! Bless thee, my dear boy; body o'me, thou art
heartily welcome.

BEN

Thank you, father, and I'm glad to see you.

208 *doit* a Dutch coin worth almost nothing
225 *Cadua* an obscure word, a windfall?
231 *toward* (towards W2)

SIR SAMPSON

    Odsbud, and I'm glad to see thee. Kiss me, boy; kiss me; 235
again and again, dear Ben.   *Kisses him*

BEN

    So, so, enough, father.—Mess, I'd rather kiss these gentle-
women.

SIR SAMPSON

    And so thou shalt.—Mrs. Angelica, my son Ben.

BEN

    Forsooth an you please. (*Salutes her*) Nay, mistress, I'm not 240
for dropping anchor here; about ship, i'faith. (*Kisses* MRS.
FRAIL) Nay, and you too, my little cockboat—so. (*Kisses*
MISS PRUE)

TATTLE

    Sir, you're welcome ashore.

BEN

    Thank you, thank you, friend.

SIR SAMPSON

    Thou has been many a weary league, Ben, since I saw thee. 245

BEN

    Ey, ey, been! Been far enough, an that be all.—Well, father,
and how do all at home? How does brother Dick, and brother
Val?

SIR SAMPSON

    Dick, body o'me, Dick has been dead these two years; I writ
you word when you were at Leghorn.   250

BEN

    Mess, and that's true; marry, I had forgot. Dick's dead, as
you say—well, and how? I have a many questions to ask
you. Well, you ben't married again, father, be you?

SIR SAMPSON

    No, I intend you shall marry, Ben; I would not marry for
thy sake.   255

BEN

    Nay, what does that signify? An you marry again—why then,
I'll go to sea again, so there's one for t'other, an that be all.
Pray don't let me be your hindrance; e'en marry, a God's
name, an the wind sit that way. As for my part, mayhap I
have no mind to marry.   260

MRS. FRAIL

    That would be pity, such a handsome young gentleman.

240 *an you* (if you Ww)
251 *and that's* (that's Ww)

BEN

Handsome! he, he, he, nay, forsooth, an you be for joking,
I'll joke with you, for I love my jest, an the ship were sinking, as we sayn at sea. But I'll tell you why I don't much
stand towards matrimony. I love to roam about from port   265
to port, and from land to land: I could never abide to be
port-bound, as we call it. Now a man that is married has, as
it were, d'ye see, his feet in the bilboes, and mayhap
mayn't get 'em out again when he would.

SIR SAMPSON

Ben's a wag.   270

BEN

A man that is married, d'ye see, is no more like another
man, than a galley slave is like one of us free sailors; he is
chained to an oar all his life, and mayhap forced to tug a
leaky vessel into the bargain.

SIR SAMPSON

A very wag, Ben's a very wag; only a little rough, he wants   275
a little polishing.

MRS. FRAIL

Not at all; I like his humour mightily, it's plain and honest.
I should like such a humour in a husband extremely.

BEN

Sayn you so, forsooth? Marry, and I should like such a
handsome gentlewoman for a bedfellow hugely. How say   280
you, mistress, would you like going to sea? Mess, you're a
tight vessel and well rigged, and you were but as well
manned.

MRS. FRAIL

I should not doubt that, if you were master of me.

BEN

But I'll tell you one thing, an you come to sea in a high   285
wind, or that lady [*To* ANGELICA], you mayn't carry so much
sail o'your head—top and top-gallant, by the mess.

MRS. FRAIL

No, why so?

BEN

Why an you do, you may run the risk to be overset, and then
you'll carry your keels above water, he, he, he.   290

268 *bilboes* fetters
287 *top and top-gallant* the sail set above the main mast and the sail
    above that

ANGELICA

I swear, Mr. Benjamin is the veriest wag in nature; an
absolute sea-wit.

SIR SAMPSON

Nay, Ben has parts, but as I told you before, they want a
little polishing: you must not take anything ill, madam.

BEN

No, I hope the gentlewoman is not angry; I mean all in good   295
part: for if I give a jest, I'll take a jest. And so forsooth you
may be as free with me.

ANGELICA

I thank you, sir, I am not at all offended; but methinks,
Sir Sampson, you should leave him alone with his mistress.
Mr. Tattle, we must not hinder lovers.   300

TATTLE (*Aside to* MISS PRUE)

Well, miss, I have your promise.

SIR SAMPSON

Body o'me, madam, you say true. Look you Ben; this is
your mistress. Come miss, you must not be shamefaced;
we'll leave you together.

MISS PRUE

I can't abide to be left alone. Mayn't my cousin stay with   305
me?

SIR SAMPSON

No, no. Come, let's away.

BEN

Look you father, mayhap the young woman mayn't take a
liking to me.

SIR SAMPSON

I warrant thee, boy. Come, come, we'll be gone; I'll   310
venture that.

Exeunt all but BEN *and* MISS PRUE

[Act III, Scene vii]

BEN

Come mistress, will you please to sit down, for an you stand
astern a that'n, we shall never grapple together. Come, I'll
haul a chair; there, an you please to sit, I'll sit by you.

MISS PRUE

You need not sit so near one; if you have anything to say, I   315
can hear you farther off, I an't deaf.

313 *astern a that'n* she has turned her back on him

BEN

Why, that's true, as you say, nor I an't dumb; I can be
heard as far as another. I'll heave off to please you. (*Sits
farther off*) An we were a league asunder, I'd undertake to
hold discourse with you, an 'twere not a main high wind   320
indeed, and full in my teeth. Look you forsooth, I am, as it
were, bound for the land of matrimony; 'tis a voyage, d'ye
see, that was none of my seeking. I was commanded by
father, and if you like of it, mayhap I may steer into your
harbour. How say you, mistress? The short of the thing is   325
this, that if you like me, and I like you, we may chance to
swing in a hammock together.

MISS PRUE

I don't know what to say to you, nor I don't care to speak
with you at all.

BEN

No, I'm sorry for that. But pray, why are you so scornful?   330

MISS PRUE

As long as one must not speak one's mind, one had better not
speak at all, I think, and truly I won't tell a lie for the
matter.

BEN

Nay, you say true in that; it's but a folly to lie: for to speak
one thing and to think just the contrary way is, as it were,   335
to look one way, and to row another. Now, for my part,
d'ye see, I'm for carrying things above board, I'm not for
keeping anything under hatches; so that if you ben't as
willing as I, say so, a God's name, there's no harm done;
mayhap you may be shamefaced; some maidens, tho'f they   340
love a man well enough, yet they don't care to tell'n so
to's face. If that's the case, why, silence gives consent.

MISS PRUE

But I'm sure it is not so, for I'll speak sooner than you
should believe that; and I'll speak truth, though one
should always tell a lie to a man; and I don't care, let my   345
father do what he will; I'm too big to be whipped, so I'll
tell you plainly, I don't like you, nor love you at all, nor
never will, that's more. So there's your answer for you, and
don't trouble me no more, you ugly thing.

BEN

Look you, young woman, you may learn to give good words,   350
however. I spoke you fair, d'ye see, and civil. As for your

325–6 *is this, that* (is, that Ww)

love or your liking, I don't value it of a rope's end; and
mayhap I like you as little as you do me: what I said was in
obedience to father; gad, I fear a whipping no more than you
do. But I tell you one thing, if you should give such language   355
at sea, you'd have a cat-o'-nine-tails laid cross your shoulders. Flesh! who are you? You heard t'other handsome
young woman speak civilly to me of her own accord. Whatever you think of yourself, gad, I don't think you are any
more to compare to her, than a can of small beer to a bowl   360
of punch.

MISS PRUE

Well, and there's a handsome gentleman, and a fine gentleman, and a sweet gentleman, that was here that loves me, and
I love him; and if he sees you speak to me any more, he'll
thrash your jacket for you, he will, you great sea-calf.   365

BEN

What, do you mean that fair-weather spark that was here just
now? Will he thrash my jacket? Let'n—let'n. But an he
comes near me, mayhap I may giv'n a salt eel for's supper,
for all that. What does father mean to leave me alone as
soon as I come home with such a dirty dowdy? Sea-calf?   370
I an't calf enough to lick your chalked face, you cheese-curd
you. Marry thee! Ouns, I'll marry a Lapland witch as soon,
and live upon selling of contrary winds and wrecked vessels.

MISS PRUE

I won't be called names, nor I won't be abused thus, so I
won't. If I were a man, (*Cries*) you durst not talk at this   375
rate. No, you durst not, you stinking tar-barrel.

[Act III, Scene viii]

Enter MRS. FORESIGHT, *and* MRS. FRAIL

MRS. FORESIGHT

They have quarrelled just as we could wish.

BEN

Tar-barrel? Let your sweetheart there call me so, if he'll take
your part, your Tom Essence, and I'll say something to him;
gad, I'll lace his musk-doublet for him, I'll make him stink;   380

368 *salt eel* rope's end (a thrashing)
373 *selling of* (selling Ww)
379 *Tom Essence* a comedy by Thomas Rawlins (1676)

he shall smell more like a weasel than a civet cat afore I ha'
done with 'en.

MRS. FORESIGHT

Bless me, what's the matter? Miss—what, does she cry?—
Mr. Benjamin, what have you done to her?

BEN

Let her cry: the more she cries, the less she'll—She has been   385
gathering foul weather in her mouth, and now it rains out
at her eyes.

MRS. FORESIGHT

Come miss, come along with me, and tell me, poor child.

MRS. FRAIL

Lord, what shall we do? There's my brother Foresight and
Sir Sampson coming. Sister, do you take miss down into   390
the parlour, and I'll carry Mr. Benjamin into my chamber,
for they must not know that they are fallen out. Come sir,
will you venture yourself with me?   *Looks kindly on him*

BEN

Venture, mess, and that I will, though 'twere to sea in a
storm.   *Exeunt*   395

[Act III, Scene ix]

Enter SIR SAMPSON *and* FORESIGHT

SIR SAMPSON

I left 'em together here. What, are they gone? Ben's a brisk
boy: he has got her into a corner, father's own son! faith,
he'll tousle her, and mousle her: the rogue's sharp set,
coming from sea. If he should not stay for saying grace, old
Foresight, but fall to without the help of a parson, ha? Odd,   400
if he should, I could not be angry with him; 'twould be
but like me, a chip of the old block. Ha! thou'rt melancholy,
old prognostication; as melancholy as if thou hadst spilt the
salt or pared thy nails of a Sunday. Come cheer up, look
about thee. Look up, old stargazer. Now is he poring upon   405
the ground for a crooked pin, or an old horse-nail, with the
head towards him.

381 *civet cat* African and Asiatic animal from which the perfume
civet was obtained
393 s.d. *Looks* (Looking Ww)
402 *melancholy* (melancholic Ww)
403 *melancholy* (melancholic Ww)
404 *of a* (on a Ww)

FORESIGHT
  Sir Sampson, we'll have the wedding tomorrow morning.
SIR SAMPSON
  With all my heart.
FORESIGHT
  At ten o'clock, punctually at ten.   410
SIR SAMPSON
  To a minute, to a second; thou shall set thy watch, and the
  bridegroom shall observe its motions; they shall be married
  to a minute, go to bed to a minute; and when the alarm
  strikes, they shall keep time like the figures of St. Dunstan's
  clock, and *consummatum est* shall ring all over the parish.   415

[Act III, Scene x]

Enter SCANDAL

SCANDAL
  Sir Sampson, sad news.
FORESIGHT
  Bless us!
SIR SAMPSON
  Why, what's the matter?
SCANDAL
  Can't you guess at what ought to afflict you and him, and all
  of us, more than anything else?   420
SIR SAMPSON
  Body o'me, I don't know any universal grievance, but a new
  tax and the loss of the Canary Fleet; without Popery should
  be landed in the west, or the French fleet were at anchor at
  Blackwall.
SCANDAL
  No. Undoubtedly Mr. Foresight knew all this, and might   425
  have prevented it.
FORESIGHT
  'Tis no earthquake!
SCANDAL
  No, not yet; nor whirlwind. But we don't know what it may
  come to. But it has had a consequence already that touches
  us all.   430

---

415 *consummatum est* blasphemous i) it is finished ii) the marriage
    is consummated   422 *and* (or Ww)
422 *Canary Fleet* England was at war with France
422 *without* (unless Ww)

SIR SAMPSON

Why, body o'me, out with't.

SCANDAL

Something has appeared to your son Valentine. He's gone to
bed upon't, and very ill. He speaks little, yet says he has a
world to say; asks for his father and the wise Foresight;
talks of Raymond Lully, and the ghost of Lilly. He has   435
secrets to impart, I suppose, to you two. I can get nothing
out of him but sighs. He desires he may see you in the
morning, but would not be disturbed tonight, because he has
some business to do in a dream.

SIR SAMPSON

Hoity toity! What have I to do with his dreams or his   440
divination? Body o'me, this is a trick to defer signing the
conveyance. I warrant the devil will tell him in a dream
that he must not part with his estate: but I'll bring him a
parson to tell him that the devil's a liar. Or if that won't
do, I'll bring a lawyer that shall out-lie the devil. And so I'll   445
try whether my blackguard or his shall get the better of the
day.   *Exit*

[Act III, Scene xi]

SCANDAL

Alas, Mr. Foresight, I'm afraid all is not right. You are a
wise man, and a conscientious man; a searcher into obscurity
and futurity; and if you commit an error, it is with a great   450
deal of consideration, and discretion, and caution.

FORESIGHT

Ah, good Mr. Scandal—

SCANDAL

Nay, nay, 'tis manifest; I do not flatter you. But Sir
Sampson is hasty, very hasty; I'm afraid he is not scrupulous
enough, Mr. Foresight. He has been wicked, and heaven   455
grant he may mean well in his affair with you—but my mind
misgives me, these things cannot be wholly insignificant.
You are wise, and should not be overreached, methinks you
should not—

433 *yet says* (yet he says Ww)

---

435 *Lully* (?1235-1315) The mystic and missionary.

435 *Lilly.* (1602–81) Among the most famous of 17th-century English
astrologers. He published an annual almanac, and was consulted by the
Court. He predicted the Great Fire and Plague of London.

FORESIGHT

Alas, Mr. Scandal, *humanum est errare*. 460

SCANDAL

You say true, man will err; mere man will err—but you are something more. There have been wise men; but they were such as you: men who consulted the stars and were observers of omens. Solomon was wise, but how?—by his judgment in astrology. So says Pineda in his third book and eighth 465 chapter.

FORESIGHT

You are learned, Mr. Scandal!

SCANDAL

A trifler, but a lover of art—and the wise men of the east owed their instruction to a star, which is rightly observed by Gregory the Great in favour of astrology! And Albertus 470 Magnus makes it the most valuable science, because, says he, it teaches us to consider the causation of causes, in the causes of things.

FORESIGHT

I protest I honour you, Mr. Scandal. I did not think you had been read in these matters. Few young men are inclined— 475

SCANDAL

I thank my stars that have inclined me. But I fear this marriage and making over this estate, this transferring of a rightful inheritance, will bring judgments upon us. I prophesy it, and I would not have the fate of Cassandra, not to be believed. Valentine is disturbed; what can be the 480 cause of that? And Sir Sampson is hurried on by an unusual violence. I fear he does not act wholly from himself; methinks he does not look as he used to.

FORESIGHT

He was always of an impetuous nature. But as to this marriage, I have consulted the science, and all appearances 485 are prosperous.

468 *of art* (of the art Q4)
485 *science* (stars Q3, 4, Ww)

---

465 *Pineda.* (1557–1637) Spanish Jesuit and commentator on Solomon (Summers verifies the references).

470 *Gregory.* Pope 590–604, one of the four greater Doctors of the Western Church. Probably best known now for despatching St. Augustine to convert the English.

470–71 *Albertus Magnus.* (*c.*1200–80) Scholastic philosopher and polymath. He was the teacher of St. Thomas Aquinas.

SCANDAL

Come, come, Mr. Foresight, let not the prospect of worldly
lucre carry you beyond your judgment, nor against your
conscience. You are not satisfied that you act justly.

FORESIGHT

How!   490

SCANDAL

You are not satisfied, I say. I am loath to discourage you,
but it is palpable that you are not satisfied.

FORESIGHT

How does it appear, Mr. Scandal? I think I am very well
satisfied.

SCANDAL

Either you suffer yourself to deceive yourself, or you do   495
not know yourself.

FORESIGHT

Pray explain yourself.

SCANDAL

Do you sleep well o'nights?

FORESIGHT

Very well.

SCANDAL

Are you certain? You do not look so.   500

FORESIGHT

I am in health, I think.

SCANDAL

So was Valentine this morning, and looked just so.

FORESIGHT

How! Am I altered any way! I don't perceive it.

SCANDAL

That may be, but your beard is longer than it was two hours
ago.   505

FORESIGHT

Indeed! Bless me.

[Act III, Scene xii]

Enter MRS. FORESIGHT

MRS. FORESIGHT

Husband, will you go to bed? It's ten o'clock. Mr. Scandal,
your servant.

SCANDAL

Pox on her, she has interrupted my design. But I must work
her into the project.—You keep early hours, madam.   510

MRS. FORESIGHT

Mr. Foresight is punctual; we sit up after him.

FORESIGHT

My dear, pray lend me your glass, your little looking glass.

SCANDAL

Pray lend it him, madam. I'll tell you the reason. (*She gives him the glass*; SCANDAL *and she whisper*) My passion for you is grown so violent—that I am no longer master of myself. I 515 was interrupted in the morning, when you had charity enough to give me your attention, and I had hopes of finding another opportunity of explaining myself to you, but was disappointed all this day; and the uneasiness that has attended me ever since brings me now hither at this 520 unseasonable hour.

MRS. FORESIGHT

Was there ever such impudence, to make love to me before my husband's face? I'll swear I'll tell him.

SCANDAL

Do, I'll die a martyr, rather than disclaim my passion. But come a little farther this way, and I'll tell you what project I 525 had to get him out of the way, that I might have an opportunity of waiting upon you.   *Whisper*

FORESIGHT (*Looking in the glass*)

I do not see any revolution here. Methinks I look with a serene and benign aspect—pale, a little pale—but the roses of these cheeks have been gathered many years. Ha! I do 530 not like that sudden flushing—gone already! Hem, hem, hem! faintish. My heart is pretty good—yet it beats; and my pulses, ha!—I have none—mercy on me! Hum—yes, here they are. Gallop, gallop, gallop, gallop, gallop, gallop, hey! Whither will they hurry me? Now they're gone again. And 535 now I'm faint again; and pale again, and hem! and my hem!—breath, hem!—grows short; hem! hem! he, he, hem!

SCANDAL

It takes; pursue it in the name of love and pleasure.

MRS. FORESIGHT

How do you do, Mr. Foresight?

FORESIGHT

Hum, not so well as I thought I was. Lend me your hand. 540

SCANDAL

Look you there now. Your lady says your sleep has been unquiet of late.

FORESIGHT

Very likely.

MRS. FORESIGHT

O, mighty restless, but I was afraid to tell him so. He has
been subject to talking and starting. 545

SCANDAL

And did not use to be so.

MRS. FORESIGHT

Never, never; till within these three nights; I cannot say
that he has once broken my rest since we have been married.

FORESIGHT

I will go to bed.

SCANDAL

Do so, Mr. Foresight, and say your prayers. He looks 550
better then he did.

MRS. FORESIGHT

Nurse, nurse! *Calls*

FORESIGHT

Do you think so, Mr. Scandal?

SCANDAL

Yes, yes, I hope this will be gone by morning, taking it in
time. 555

FORESIGHT

I hope so.

[Act III, Scene xiii]

Enter NURSE

MRS. FORESIGHT

Nurse, your master is not well; put him to bed.

SCANDAL

I hope you will be able to see Valentine in the morning.
You had best take a little diacodium and cowslip water,
and lie upon your back; maybe you may dream. 560

FORESIGHT

I thank you, Mr. Scandal, I will.—Nurse, let me have a
watch-light, and lay the *Crumbs of Comfort* by me.

NURSE

Yes, sir.

554 *taking* (take W2)
559 *diacodium* syrup of poppies

---

562 *Crumbs of Comfort* (1623) by Michael Sparke. A popular work of
devotion.

FORESIGHT

And—hem, hem! I am very faint.

SCANDAL

No, no, you look much better.   565

FORESIGHT

Do I? [*To* NURSE] And d'ye hear—bring me, let me see—
within a quarter of twelve—hem—he—hem!—just upon
the turning of the tide, bring me the urinal; and I hope
neither the lord of my ascendant nor the moon will be
combust; and then I may do well.   570

SCANDAL

I hope so. Leave that to me; I will erect a scheme; and I
hope I shall find both Sol and Venus in the sixth house.

FORESIGHT

I thank you, Mr. Scandal. Indeed, that would be a great
comfort to me. Hem, hem! Good night.   *Exit*

[Act III, Scene xiv]

SCANDAL

Good night, good Mr. Foresight; and I hope Mars and   575
Venus will be in conjunction—while your wife and I are
together.

MRS. FORESIGHT

Well; and what use do you hope to make of this project?
You don't think that you are ever like to succeed in your
design upon me?   580

SCANDAL

Yes, faith I do; I have a better opinion both of you and
myself than to despair.

MRS. FORESIGHT

Did you ever hear such a toad? Harkee devil; do you think
any woman honest?

SCANDAL

Yes, several, very honest; they'll cheat a little at cards,   585
sometimes, but that's nothing.

MRS. FORESIGHT

Pshaw! but virtuous, I mean.

SCANDAL

Yes, faith, I believe some women are virtuous too; but 'tis

570 *combust* close to the sun, thus having their influence destroyed

---

572 *sixth house*. Virgo—perhaps another thrust at Foresight's impotence
    (his wife is still a virgin).

as I believe some men are valiant, through fear. For why
should a man court danger, or a woman shun pleasure? 590

MRS. FORESIGHT

O monstrous! What are conscience and honour?

SCANDAL

Why, honour is a public enemy, and conscience a domestic
thief; and he that would secure his pleasure must pay a
tribute to one, and go halves with the t'other. As for
honour, that you have secured, for you have purchased a 595
perpetual opportunity for pleasure.

MRS. FORESIGHT

An opportunity for pleasure!

SCANDAL

Aye, your husband. A husband is an opportunity for
pleasure, so you have taken care of honour, and 'tis the
least I can do to take care of conscience. 600

MRS. FORESIGHT

And so you think we are free for one another?

SCANDAL

Yes, faith, I think so; I love to speak my mind.

MRS. FORESIGHT

Why then, I'll speak my mind. Now, as to this affair between
you and me. Here you make love to me; why, I'll confess
it does not displease me. Your person is well enough, and 605
your understanding is not amiss.

SCANDAL

I have no great opinion of myself; yet I think I'm neither
deformed, nor a fool.

MRS. FORESIGHT

But you have a villainous character; you are a libertine in
speech as well as practice. 610

SCANDAL

Come, I know what you would say. You think it more
dangerous to be seen in conversation with me, than to allow
some other men the last favour. You mistake; the liberty
I take in talking is purely affected for the service of your
sex. He that first cries out stop thief, is often he that has 615
stolen the treasure. I am a juggler that acts by confederacy;
and if you please, we'll put a trick upon the world.

MRS. FORESIGHT

Aye; but you are such a universal juggler—that I'm afraid
you have a great many confederates.

594 *with the t'other* (with t'other Q3, 4, Ww)
607 *yet I* (but I Ww)

SCANDAL

Faith, I'm sound. 620

MRS. FORESIGHT

O fie—I'll swear you're impudent.

SCANDAL

I'll swear you're handsome.

MRS. FORESIGHT

Pish, you'd tell me so, though you did not think so.

SCANDAL

And you'd think so, though I should not tell you so: and now
I think we know one another pretty well. 625

MRS. FORESIGHT

O Lord, who's here?

[Act III, Scene xv]

Enter MRS. FRAIL *and* BEN

BEN

Mess, I love to speak my mind. Father has nothing to do
with me. Nay, I can't say that neither; he has something to
do with me. But what does that signify? If so be that I
ben't minded to be steered by him, 'tis as tho'f he should 630
strive against wind and tide.

MRS. FRAIL

Aye, but, my dear, we must keep it secret, till the estate be
settled; for you know, marrying without an estate is like
sailing in a ship without ballast.

BEN

He, he, he; why, that's true; just so, for all the world it is 635
indeed, as like as two cable ropes.

MRS. FRAIL

And though I have a good portion, you know one would not
venture all in one bottom.

BEN

Why, that's true again; for mayhap one bottom may spring a
leak. You have hit it indeed; mess, you've nicked the 640
channel.

MRS. FRAIL

Well, but if you should forsake me after all, you'd break
my heart.

BEN

Break your heart? I'd rather the *Marigold* should break her

620 *sound* free from venereal disease
621 *you're* (your Q1 uncorr. cited by Davis)

cable in a storm, as well as I love her. Flesh, you don't 645
think I'm false-hearted like a landman? A sailor will be
honest, tho'f mayhap he has never a penny of money in his
pocket. Mayhap I may not have so fair a face as a citizen or a
courtier; but for all that, I've as good blood in my veins, and
a heart as sound as a biscuit.   650

MRS. FRAIL

And will you love me always?

BEN

Nay, an I love once, I'll stick like pitch; I'll tell you that.
Come, I'll sing you a song of a sailor.

MRS. FRAIL

Hold, there's my sister; I'll call her to hear it.

MRS. FORESIGHT [*To* SCANDAL]

Well, I won't go to bed to my husband tonight, because I'll 655
retire to my own chamber and think of what you have said.

SCANDAL

Well, you'll give me leave to wait upon you to your chamber
door, and leave you my last instructions.

MRS. FORESIGHT

Hold, here's my sister coming toward us.

MRS. FRAIL

If it won't interrupt you, I'll entertain you with a song.   660

BEN

The song was made upon one of our ship's crew's wife; our
boatswain made the song; mayhap you may know her, sir.
Before she was married, she was called buxom Joan of
Deptford.

SCANDAL

I have heard of her.   665

                                                   BEN *sings*

BALLAD
Set by Mr. John Eccles
A soldier and a sailor,
A tinker, and a tailor,
Had once a doubtful strife, sir,
To make a maid a wife, sir,
Whose name was buxom Joan.   670
For now the time was ended,
When she no more intended,
To lick her lips at men, sir,

659 *toward* (towards Ww)
663 *was married* (married W2)

And gnaw the sheets in vain, sir,
And lie o'nights alone.   675

2.

The soldier swore like thunder,
He loved her more than plunder;
And showed her many a scar, sir,
That he had brought from far, sir,
With fighting for her sake.   680
The tailor thought to please her,
With off'ring her his measure.
The tinker too with mettle,
Said he could mend her kettle,
And stop up ev'ry leak.   685

3.

But while these three were prating,
The sailor slyly waiting,
Thought if it came about, sir,
That they should all fall out, sir:
He then might play his part.   690
And just e'en as he meant, sir,
To loggerheads they went, sir,
And then he let fly at her,
A shot 'twixt wind and water,
That won this fair maid's heart.   695

BEN

If some of our crew that came to see me are not gone, you
shall see that we sailors can dance sometimes as well as other
folks. (*Whistles*) I warrant that brings 'em, an they be
within hearing.

Enter SEAMEN

O, here they be—and fiddles along with 'em. Come my lads,   700
let's have a round, and I'll make one.   *Dance*
We're merry folk, we sailors; we han't much to care for. Thus
we live at sea: eat biscuit, and drink flip, put on a clean shirt
once a quarter, come home and lie with our landladies once
a year, get rid of a little money; and then put off with the 705
next fair wind. How d'ye like us?

MRS. FRAIL

O, you are the happiest, merriest men alive.

682 *measure* i) his yard ii) penis
703 *flip* a hot drink of sweetened beer and spirits

MRS. FORESIGHT

    We're beholding to Mr. Benjamin for this entertainment.
I believe it's late.

BEN

    Why, forsooth, an you think so, you had best go to bed. For   710
my part, I mean to toss a can, and remember my sweetheart,
afore I turn in; mayhap I may dream of her.

MRS. FORESIGHT

    Mr. Scandal, you had best go to bed and dream too.

SCANDAL

    Why, faith, I have a good lively imagination, and can dream
as much to the purpose as another, if I set about it: but   715
dreaming is the poor retreat of a lazy, hopeless, and imper-
fect lover; 'tis the last glimpse of love to worn-out sinners,
and the faint dawning of a bliss to wishing girls and growing
boys.

        There's nought but willing, waking love, that can   720
        Make blest the ripened maid, and finished man.

                                  Exeunt

[Act IV, Scene i]

VALENTINE'S *Lodging*

Enter SCANDAL *and* JEREMY

SCANDAL

    Well, is your master ready? Does he look madly, and talk
madly?

JEREMY

    Yes, sir; you need make no great doubt of that; he that was
so near turning poet yesterday morning can't be much to
seek in playing the madman today.   5

SCANDAL

    Would he have Angelica acquainted with the reason of his
design?

JEREMY

    No, sir, not yet. He has a mind to try whether his playing
the madman won't make her play the fool, and fall in love
with him; or at least own that she has loved him all this while   10
and concealed it.

SCANDAL

    I saw her take coach just now with her maid, and think I
heard her bid the coachman drive hither.

708 *beholding* (beholden Ww)

JEREMY

Like enough, sir, for I told her maid this morning my master
was run stark mad only for love of her mistress. I hear a   15
coach stop; if it should be she, sir, I believe he would not
see her till he hears how she takes it.

SCANDAL

Well, I'll try her.—'Tis she, here she comes.

[Act IV, Scene ii]

Enter ANGELICA *with* JENNY

ANGELICA

Mr. Scandal, I suppose you don't think it a novelty to see a
woman visit a man at his own lodgings in a morning?   20

SCANDAL

Not upon a kind occasion, madam. But when a lady comes
tyrannically to insult a ruined lover, and make manifest
the cruel triumphs of her beauty, the barbarity of it
something surprises me.

ANGELICA

I don't like raillery from a serious face. Pray tell me what   25
is the matter?

JEREMY

No strange matter, madam; my master's mad, that's all. I
suppose your ladyship has thought him so a great while.

ANGELICA

How d'ye mean, mad?

JEREMY

Why, faith, madam, he's mad for want of his wits, just as   30
he was for want of money; his head is e'en as light as his
pockets, and anybody that has a mind to a bad bargain can't
do better than to beg him for his estate.

ANGELICA

If you speak truth, your endeavouring at wit is very
unseasonable—   35

SCANDAL (*Aside*)

She's concerned, and loves him.

ANGELICA

Mr. Scandal, you can't think me guilty of so much inhuman-
ity as not to be concerned for a man I must own myself
obliged to—pray tell me truth.

31 *was for* (was poor for Q3, 4, Ww)
39 *tell me truth* (tell me the truth W2)

SCANDAL

　Faith, madam, I wish telling a lie would mend the matter.　　40
But this is no new effect of an unsuccessful passion.

ANGELICA (*Aside*)

　I know not what to think. Yet I should be vexed to have a
trick put upon me.—May I not see him?

SCANDAL

　I'm afraid the physician is not willing you should see him
yet.— Jeremy, go in and inquire.　　　　　　　　*Exit* JEREMY　　45

[Act IV, Scene iii]

ANGELICA (*Aside*)

　Ha! I saw him wink and smile. I fancy 'tis a trick! I'll
try.—I would disguise to all the world a failing, which I
must own to you. I fear my happiness depends upon the
recovery of Valentine. Therefore I conjure you, as you are
his friend, and as you have compassion upon one fearful of　　50
affliction, to tell me what I am to hope for.—I cannot
speak.—But you may tell me; tell me, for you know what
I would ask.

SCANDAL (*Aside*)

　So, this is pretty plain.—Be not too much concerned,
madam; I hope his condition is not desperate: an acknow-　　55
ledgment of love from you, perhaps, may work a cure, as the
fear of your aversion occasioned his distemper.

ANGELICA (*Aside*)

　Say you so; nay, then I'm convinced: and if I don't play
trick for trick, may I never taste the pleasure of revenge.—
Acknowledgment of love! I find you have mistaken my　　60
compassion, and think me guilty of a weakness I am a
stranger to. But I have too much sincerity to deceive you, and
too much charity to suffer him to be deluded with vain
hopes. Good nature and humanity oblige me to be concerned
for him; but to love is neither in my power nor inclination;　　65
and if he can't be cured without I suck the poison from his
wounds, I'm afraid he won't recover his senses till I lose
mine.

SCANDAL

　Hey, brave woman, i'faith—won't you see him then, if he
desire it?　　　　　　　　　　　　　　　　　　　　70

---

52 *tell me; tell me, for* (tell me, for W2)

ANGELICA

What signify a madman's desires? Besides, 'twould make me uneasy. If I don't see him, perhaps my concern for him may lessen. If I forget him, 'tis no more than he has done by himself; and now the surprise is over, methinks I am not half so sorry for him as I was.   75

SCANDAL

So, faith, good nature works apace; you were confessing just now an obligation to his love.

ANGELICA

But I have considered that passions are unreasonable and involuntary; if he loves, he can't help it; and if I don't love, I can't help it; no more than he can help his being a man, or   80 I my being a woman; or no more than I can help my want of inclination to stay longer here.—Come, Jenny.

Exit ANGELICA *and* JENNY

[Act IV, Scene iv]

SCANDAL

Humph! An admirable composition, faith, this same womankind.

Enter JEREMY

JEREMY

What, is she gone, sir?   85

SCANDAL

Gone! Why, she was never here, nor anywhere else; nor I don't know her if I see her, nor you neither.

JEREMY

Good lack! What's the matter now? Are any more of us to be mad? Why, sir, my master longs to see her, and is almost mad in good earnest with the joyful news of her being here.   90

SCANDAL

We are all under a mistake. Ask no questions, for I can't resolve you; but I'll inform your master. In the meantime, if our project succeed no better with his father than it does with his mistress, he may descend from his exaltation of madness into the road of common sense, and be content only to be   95 made a fool with other reasonable people. I hear Sir Sampson. You know your cue; I'll to your master.   *Exit*

75 *sorry for him as* (sorry as Q3, 4, Ww)

[Act IV, Scene v]

Enter SIR SAMPSON LEGEND *with* [BUCKRAM] *a lawyer*

SIR SAMPSON

D'ye see, Mr. Buckram, here's the paper signed with his own hand.

BUCKRAM

Good, sir. And the conveyance is ready drawn in this box, if   100
he be ready to sign and seal.

SIR SAMPSON

Ready, body o'me, he must be ready; his sham sickness shan't excuse him.—O, here's his scoundrel. Sirrah, where's your master?

JEREMY

Ah, sir, he's quite gone.   105

SIR SAMPSON

Gone! What, he is not dead?

JEREMY

No, sir, not dead.

SIR SAMPSON

What, is he gone out of town, run away, ha! Has he tricked me? Speak, varlet.

JEREMY

No, no, sir; he's safe enough, sir, an he were but as sound,   110
poor gentleman. He is indeed here, sir, and not here, sir.

SIR SAMPSON

Hey day, rascal, do you banter me? Sirrah, d'ye banter me? Speak, sirrah, where is he, for I will find him.

JEREMY

Would you could, sir, for he has lost himself. Indeed, sir, I have almost broke my heart about him.—I can't refrain   115
tears when I think of him, sir; I'm as melancholy for him as a passing-bell, sir, or a horse in a pound.

SIR SAMPSON

A pox confound your similitudes, sir. Speak to be under-stood, and tell me in plain terms what the matter is with him, or I'll crack your fool's skull.   120

JEREMY

Ah, you've hit it, sir; that's the matter with him, sir; his skull's cracked, poor gentleman; he's stark mad, sir.

SIR SAMPSON

Mad!

BUCKRAM
>   What, is he *non compos*?

JEREMY
>   Quite *non compos*, sir.   125

BUCKRAM
>   Why, then all's obliterated, Sir Sampson. If he be *non compos
>   mentis*, his act and deed will be of no effect; it is not good in
>   law.

SIR SAMPSON
>   Ouns, I won't believe it; let me see him, sir.—Mad! I'll
>   make him find his senses.   130

JEREMY
>   Mr. Scandal is with him, sir; I'll knock at the door.
>   *Goes to the scene, which opens and discovers* VALENTINE *upon
>   a couch disorderly dressed,* SCANDAL *by him*

[Act IV, Scene vi]

SIR SAMPSON
>   How now, what's here to do?

VALENTINE (*Starting*)
>   Ha! Who's that?

SCANDAL
>   For heaven's sake, softly, sir, and gently; don't provoke him.

VALENTINE
>   Answer me; who is that? and that?   135

SIR SAMPSON
>   Gads bobs, does he not know me? Is he mischievous? I'll
>   speak gently.—Val, Val, dost thou not know me, boy? Not
>   know thy own father, Val! I am thy own father, and this is
>   honest Brief Buckram the lawyer.

VALENTINE
>   It may be so—I did not know you.—The world is full.—   140
>   There are people that we do know, and people that we do not
>   know; and yet the sun shines upon all alike. There are
>   fathers that have many children, and there are children that
>   have many fathers.—'Tis strange! But I am Truth, and come
>   to give the world the lie.   145

SIR SAMPSON
>   Body o'me, I know not what to say to him.

VALENTINE
>   Why does that lawyer wear black? Does he carry his con-

138-9 *this is honest* (this honest W2)

science withoutside?—Lawyer, what are thou? Dost thou
know me?

BUCKRAM

O Lord, what must I say?—Yes, sir.   150

VALENTINE

Thou liest, for I am Truth. 'Tis hard I cannot get a livelihood amongst you. I have been sworn out of Westminster
Hall the first day of every term. Let me see—no matter how
long. But I'll tell you one thing; it's a question that would
puzzle an arithmetician if you should ask him: whether the   155
Bible saves more souls in Westminster Abbey, or damns
more in Westminster Hall. For my part, I am Truth, and
can't tell; I have very few acquaintance.

SIR SAMPSON

Body o'me, he talks sensibly in his madness.—Has he no
intervals?   160

JEREMY

Very short, sir.

BUCKRAM

Sir, I can do you no service while he's in this condition;
here's your paper, sir. He may do me a mischief if I stay.
The conveyance is ready, sir, if he recover his senses. *Exit*

[Act IV, Scene vii]

SIR SAMPSON

Hold, hold, don't you go yet.   165

SCANDAL

You'd better let him go, sir, and send for him if there be
occasion, for I fancy his presence provokes him more.

VALENTINE

Is the lawyer gone? 'Tis well. Then we may drink about
without going together by the ears. Heigh ho! What o'clock
is't? My father here! Your blessing, sir?   170

SIR SAMPSON

He recovers.—Bless thee, Val. How dost thou do, boy?

VALENTINE

Thank you, sir, pretty well. I have been a little out of
order. Won't you please to sit, sir?

SIR SAMPSON

Aye, boy. Come, thou shalt sit down by me.

VALENTINE

Sir, 'tis my duty to wait.   175

152–3 *Westminster Hall* the principal law court

SIR SAMPSON

No, no, come, come, sit you down, honest Val. How dost
thou do? Let me feel thy pulse. O, pretty well now, Val.
Body' o'me, I was sorry to see thee indisposed; but I'm
glad thou'rt better, honest Val.

VALENTINE

I thank you, sir.   180

SCANDAL (*Aside*)

Miracle! The monster grows loving.

SIR SAMPSON

Let me feel thy hand again, Val. It does not shake. I believe
thou canst write, Val: ha, boy? Thou canst write thy name,
Val? (*In a whisper to* JEREMY) Jeremy, step and overtake Mr.
Buckram; bid him make haste back with the conveyance—   185
quick—quick.   *Exit* JEREMY

[Act IV, Scene viii]

SCANDAL (*Aside*)

That ever I should suspect such a heathen of any remorse!

SIR SAMPSON

Dost thou know this paper, Val? I know thou'rt honest and
wilt perform articles.

> *Shows him the paper, but holds it out of his reach*

VALENTINE

Pray let me see it, sir. You hold it so far off that I can't tell   190
whether I know it or no.

SIR SAMPSON

See it, boy? Aye, aye, why thou dost see it. 'Tis thy own
hand, Val. Why, let me see, I can read it as plain as can be:
look you here, (*Reads*) *The condition of this obligation*—
Look you, as plain as can be, so it begins, and then at the   195
bottom, *As witness my hand*, VALENTINE LEGEND, in great
letters. Why, 'tis as plain as the nose in one's face; what, are
my eyes better than thine? I believe I can read it farther off
yet—let me see.

> *Stretches his arm as far as he can*

VALENTINE

Will you please to let me hold it, sir?   200

SIR SAMPSON

Let thee hold it, sayst thou? Aye, with all my heart. What
matter is it who holds it? What need anybody hold it? I'll

176 *sit you* (sit thee Ww)
193 *Val* (Vally Ww)

put it up in my pocket, Val, and then nobody need hold it.
(*Puts the paper in his pocket*) There Val: it's safe enough,
boy. But thou shalt have it as soon as thou has set thy hand　205
to another paper, little Val.

[Act IV, Scene ix]

Re-enter JEREMY *with* BUCKRAM

VALENTINE

What, is my bad genius here again! O no, 'tis the lawyer
with an itching palm, and he's come to be scratched. My
nails are nót long enough. Let me have a pair of red-hot
tongs quickly, quickly, and you shall see me act St.　210
Dunstan, and lead the devil by the nose.

BUCKRAM

O Lord, let me be gone; I'll not venture myself with a
madman.　　　　　　　　　　　　　　　　*Exit* BUCKRAM

[Act IV, Scene x]

VALENTINE

Ha, ha, ha, you need not run so fast; honesty will not overtake you. Ha, ha, ha, the rogue found me out to be *in forma*　215
pauperis presently.

SIR SAMPSON

Ouns! What a vexation is here! I know not what to do, or
say, nor which way to go.

VALENTINE

Who's that, that's out of his way?—I am Truth, and can
set him right. Harkee, friend, the straight road is the worst　220
way you can go. He that follows his nose always will very
often be led into a stink. *Probatum est.* But what are you for?
Religion or politics? There's a couple of topics for you, no
more like one another than oil and vinegar; and yet those
two beaten together by a state-cook make sauce for the　225
whole nation.

SIR SAMPSON

What the devil had I to do ever to beget sons? Why did I
ever marry?

VALENTINE

Because thou wert a monster, old boy: the two greatest

215-6 *in forma pauperis.* legally not liable for costs because of poverty.

monsters in the world are a man and a woman. What's thy   230
opinion?

SIR SAMPSON

Why, my opinion is, that those two monsters joined together
make yet a greater, that's a man and his wife.

VALENTINE

Aha! Old truepenny, sayst thou so? Thou hast nicked it.
But it's wonderful strange, Jeremy.   235

JEREMY

What is, sir?

VALENTINE

That grey hairs should cover a green head—and I make a
fool of my father.
        Enter FORESIGHT, MRS. FORESIGHT *and* MRS. FRAIL
What's here? *Erra pater*? Or a bearded sybil? If Prophecy
comes, Truth must give place.   *Exit with* JEREMY   240

[Act IV, Scene xi]

FORESIGHT

What says he? What, did he prophesy? Ha, Sir Sampson,
bless us! How are we?

SIR SAMPSON

Are we? A pox o' your prognostication. Why, we are fools
as we use to be. Ouns, that you could not foresee that the
moon would predominate, and my son be mad. Where's   245
your oppositions, your trines, and your quadrates? What did
your Cardan and your Ptolemy tell you? Your Messahalah
and your Longomontanus, your harmony of chiromancy
with astrology. Ah! pox on't, that I that know the world, and
men and manners, that don't believe a syllable in the sky   250
and stars, and sun and almanacs, and trash, should be
directed by a dreamer, an omen-hunter, and defer business
in expectation of a lucky hour, when, body o'me, there
never was a lucky hour after the first opportunity.
                                        Exit SIR SAMPSON

234 *truepenny* trusty fellow
239 *Erra pater* a fabulous astrologer, author of a 16th century almanac.
244 *use to be* (us'd to be W2)   248 *chiromancy* palmistry.

247 *Cardan.* Jerome Cardan (1501–76) Italian mathematician, physician
    and astrologer.
248 *Longomontanus* (1562–1647), a Danish astronomer. Both he and Cardan
    combined an interest in mathematics with astrological calculation.

[Act IV, Scene xii]

FORESIGHT

Ah, Sir Sampson, heaven help your head. This is none of　255
your lucky hour; *nemo omnibus horis sapit*. What, is he gone,
and in contempt of science! Ill stars and unconverted
ignorance attend him.

SCANDAL

You must excuse his passion, Mr. Foresight, for he has been
heartily vexed. His son is *non compos mentis*, and thereby　260
incapable of making any conveyance in law; so that all his
measures are disappointed.

FORESIGHT

Ha! say you so?

MRS. FRAIL (*Aside to* MRS. FORESIGHT)

What, has my sea-lover lost his anchor of hope then?

MRS. FORESIGHT

O, sister, what will you do with him?　　　　265

MRS. FRAIL

Do with him? Send him to sea again in the next foul weather.
He's used to an inconstant element, and won't be surprised
to see the tide turned.

FORESIGHT (*Considers*)

Wherein was I mistaken, not to foresee this?

SCANDAL (*Aside to* MRS. FORESIGHT)

Madam, you and I can tell him something else that he did　270
not foresee, and more particularly relating to his own
fortune.

MRS. FORESIGHT

What do you mean? I don't understand you.

SCANDAL

Hush, softly—the pleasures of last night, my dear, too
considerable to be forgot so soon.　　　　275

MRS. FORESIGHT

Last night! And what would your impudence infer from last
night? Last night was like the night before, I think.

SCANDAL

S'death, do you make no difference between me and your
husband?

MRS. FORESIGHT

Not much. He's superstitious, and you are mad, in my　280
opinion.

256 *nemo . . . sapit* no one is wise all the time, Pliny, *Nat. Hist.* VII, xl.
257 *unconverted* (unconvertible Ww)

SCANDAL

You make me mad. You are not serious. Pray recollect yourself.

MRS. FORESIGHT

O yes, now I remember. You were very impertinent and impudent, and would have come to bed to me.   285

SCANDAL

And did not?

MRS. FORESIGHT

Did not! With that face can you ask the question?

SCANDAL [*Aside*]

This I have heard of before, but never believed. I have been told she had that admirable quality of forgetting to a man's face in the morning that she had lain with him all night,   290
and denying favours with more impudence than she could grant 'em.—Madam, I'm your humble servant and honour you.—You look pretty well, Mr. Foresight. How did you rest last night?

FORESIGHT

Truly, Mr. Scandal, I was so taken up with broken dreams   295
and distracted visions that I remember little.

SCANDAL

'Twas a very forgetting night. But would you not talk with Valentine? Perhaps you may understand him; I'm apt to believe there is something mysterious in his discourses, and sometimes rather think him inspired than mad.   300

FORESIGHT

You speak with singular good judgment, Mr. Scandal, truly. I am inclining to your Turkish opinion in this matter, and do reverence a man whom the vulgar think mad. Let us go in to him.

MRS. FRAIL

Sister, do you stay with them; I'll find out my lover and   305
give him his discharge, and come to you. O'my conscience, here he comes.

          Exeunt FORESIGHT, MRS. FORESIGHT, *and* SCANDAL

287 *that face* (what face W2)
291 *denying favours* (denying that she had done favours Ww)
303–4 *in to him* (to him Ww)

[Act IV, Scene xiii]

Enter BEN

BEN

All mad, I think. Flesh, I believe all the calentures of the sea
are come ashore, for my part.

MRS. FRAIL

Mr. Benjamin in choler!   310

BEN

No, I'm pleased well enough, now I have found you. Mess,
I've had such a hurricane upon your account yonder.

MRS FRAIL

My account! Pray, what's the matter?

BEN

Why, father came and found me squabbling with yon
chitty-faced thing, as he would have me marry; so he asked   315
what was the matter. He asked in a surly sort of a way. (It
seems brother Val is gone mad, and so that put'n into a
passion; but what did I know that, what's that to me?) So he
asked in a surly sort of manner, and gad I answered'n as surlily.
What tho'f he be my father, I an't bound prentice to 'en: so   320
faith, I told'n in plain terms, if I were minded to marry, I'd
marry to please myself, not him; and for the young woman
that he provided for me, I thought it more fitting for her to
learn her sampler, and make dirt-pies, than to look after a
husband; for my part I was none of her man. I had another   325
voyage to make, let him take it as he will.

MRS. FRAIL

So then you intend to go to sea again?

BEN

Nay, nay, my mind run upon you, but I would not tell him so
much. So he said he'd make my heart ache, and if so be that
he could get a woman to his mind, he'd marry himself. Gad,   330
says I, an you play the fool and marry at these years, there's
more danger of your head's aching than my heart. He was
woundy angry when I gav'n that wipe. He hadn't a word to
say, and so I left'n and the green girl together. Mayhap the
bee may bite and he'll marry her himself, with all my heart.   335

---

308 *calentures* fevers contracted by sailors in hot climates
315 *chitty-faced* baby-faced
324 *sampler* ornamental embroidery

MRS. FRAIL

And were you this undutiful and graceless wretch to your father?

BEN

Then why was he graceless first? If I am undutiful and graceless, why did he beget me so? I did not get myself.

MRS. FRAIL

O impiety! How have I been mistaken! What an inhuman 340 merciless creature have I set my heart upon? O, I am happy to have discovered the shelves and quicksands that lurk beneath that faithless smiling face.

BEN

Hey toss! What's the matter now? Why, you ben't angry, be you? 345

MRS. FRAIL

O, see me no more, for thou wert born amongst rocks, suckled by whales, cradled in a tempest, and whistled to by winds; and thou art come forth with fins and scales, and three rows of teeth, a most outrageous fish of prey.

BEN

O Lord, O Lord, she's mad, poor young woman! Love has 350 turned her senses, her brain is quite overset. Well-a-day, how shall I do to set her to rights?

MRS. FRAIL

No, no, I am not mad, monster; I am wise enough to find you out. Hadst thou the impudence to aspire at being a husband with that stubborn and disobedient temper? You that know 355 not how to submit to a father, presume to have a sufficient stock of duty to undergo a wife? I should have been finely fobbed indeed, very finely fobbed.

BEN

Harkee forsooth; if so be that you are in your right senses, d'ye see, for aught as I perceive I'm like to be finely fobbed 360 —if I have got anger here upon your account, and you are tacked about already. What d'ye mean, after all your fair speeches, and stroking my cheeks, and kissing and hugging, what, would you sheer off so? Would you, and leave me aground? 365

MRS. FRAIL

No, I'll leave you adrift, and go which way you will.

BEN

What, are you false-hearted then?

358 *fobbed* cheated

MRS. FRAIL
Only the wind's changed.

BEN
More shame for you—the wind's changed? It's an ill wind
blows nobody good. Mayhap I have good riddance on you,   370
if these be your tricks. What d'ye mean all this while, to make
a fool of me?

MRS. FRAIL
Any fool but a husband.

BEN
Husband! Gad, I would not be your husband, if you would
have me, now I know your mind, tho'f you had your weight   375
in gold and jewels and tho'f I loved you never so well.

MRS. FRAIL
Why, canst thou love, porpoise?

BEN
No matter what I can do. Don't call names—I don't love you
so well as to bear that, whatever I did. I'm glad you show
yourself, mistress. Let them marry you as don't know you.   380
Gad, I know you too well, by sad experience; I believe he
that marries you will go to sea in a hen-pecked frigate. I
believe that, young woman—and mayhap may come to an
anchor at Cuckold's Point; so there's a dash for you, take it
as you will. Mayhap you may holla after me when I won't   385
come to.   *Exit*

MRS. FRAIL
Ha, ha, ha, no doubt on't.—(*Sings*) *My true love is gone to
sea*—

[Act IV, Scene xiv]

Enter MRS. FORESIGHT

MRS. FRAIL
O, sister, had you come a minute sooner, you would have seen
the resolution of a lover. Honest Tar and I are parted; and   390
with the same indifference that we met. O'my life, I am half
vexed at the insensibility of a brute that I despised.

MRS. FORESIGHT
What then, he bore it most heroically?

370 *have good* (have a good Ww)
371 *d'ye* (did you Ww)
384 *Cuckold's Point* on the Thames at Rotherhithe

MRS. FRAIL

Most tyrannically, for you see he has got the start of me; and
I, the poor forsaken maid, am left complaining on the shore.   395
But I'll tell you a hint that he has given me: Sir Sampson is
enraged, and talks desperately of committing matrimony
himself. If he has a mind to throw himself away, he can't do
it more effectually than upon me, if we could bring it about.

MRS. FORESIGHT

O, hang him, old fox, he's too cunning; besides, he hates both   400
you and me. But I have a project in my head for you, and I
have gone a good way towards it. I have almost made a
bargain with Jeremy, Valentine's man, to sell his master to
us.

MRS. FRAIL

Sell him, how?   405

MRS. FORESIGHT

Valentine raves upon Angelica, and took me for her, and
Jeremy says will take anybody for her that he imposes on
him. Now I have promised him mountains, if in one of his
mad fits he will bring you to him in her stead, and get you
married together, and put to bed together; and after con-   410
summation, girl, there's no revoking. And if he should
recover his senses, he'll be glad at least to make you a good
settlement.—Here they come. Stand aside a little, and tell me
how you like the design.

[Act IV, Scene xv]

Enter VALENTINE, SCANDAL, FORESIGHT, *and* JEREMY

SCANDAL (*To* JEREMY)

And have you given your master a hint of their plot upon   415
him?

JEREMY

Yes, sir. He says he'll favour it, and mistake her for Angelica.

SCANDAL

It may make sport.

FORESIGHT

Mercy on us!

VALENTINE

Husht, interrupt me not—I'll whisper prediction to thee, and   420
thou shalt prophesy. I am Truth, and can teach thy tongue

418 *make sport* (make us sport Ww)

a new trick. I have told thee what's past, now I tell what's
to come. Dost thou know what will happen tomorrow?
Answer me not, for I will tell thee. Tomorrow knaves will
thrive through craft, and fools through fortune; and honesty   425
will go as it did, frost-nipped in a summer suit. Ask me
questions concerning tomorrow.

SCANDAL

Ask him, Mr. Foresight.

FORESIGHT

Pray, what will be done at court?

VALENTINE

Scandal will tell you; I am Truth, I never come there.   430

FORESIGHT

In the city?

VALENTINE

O, prayers will be said in empty churches at the usual hours.
Yet you will see such zealous faces behind counters as if
religion were to be sold in every shop. O, things will go
methodically in the city; the clocks will strike twelve at   435
noon, and the horned herd buzz in the Exchange at two.
Wives and husbands will drive distinct trades, and care and
pleasure separately occupy the family. Coffee-houses will be
full of smoke and stratagem, and the cropt prentice, that
sweeps his master's shop in the morning, may ten to one,   440
dirty his sheets before night. But there are two things that
you will see very strange; which are wanton wives, with
their legs at liberty, and tame cuckolds, with chains about
their necks. But hold, I must examine you before I go
further; you look suspiciously. Are you a husband?   445

FORESIGHT

I am married.

VALENTINE

Poor creature! Is your wife of Covent Garden parish?

FORESIGHT

No, St. Martin's-in-the-Fields.

VALENTINE

Alas, poor man; his eyes are sunk, and his hands shrivelled;
his legs dwindled, and his back bowed. Pray, pray, for a   450

---

422 *I tell* (I'll tell you Ww)
437 *Wives and husbands* (Husbands and wives W2)

---

447 *Covent Garden parish.* Covent Garden was notorious as a centre of
dissipation. Valentine suggests that Foresight's wife is a whore.

metamorphosis. Change thy shape, and shake off age; get
thee Medea's kettle, and be boiled anew; come forth with
labouring callous hands, a chine of steel, and Atlas' shoulders. Let Taliacotius trim the calves of twenty chairmen,
and make thee pedestals to stand erect upon and look matri-   455
mony in the face. Ha, ha, ha! That a man should have a
stomach to a wedding supper, when the pigeons ought
rather to be laid to his feet, ha, ha, ha.

FORESIGHT
His frenzy is very high now, Mr. Scandal.

SCANDAL
I believe it is a spring tide.   460

FORESIGHT
Very likely truly; you understand these matters. Mr.
Scandal, I shall be very glad to confer with you about these
things which he has uttered. His sayings are very mysterious
and hieroglyphical.

VALENTINE
O, why would Angelica be absent from my eyes so long?   465

JEREMY
She's here, sir.

MRS. FORESIGHT
Now, sister.

MRS. FRAIL
O Lord, what must I say?

SCANDAL
Humour him, madam, by all means.

VALENTINE
Where is she? O, I see her. She comes, like riches, health,   470
and liberty at once, to a despairing, starving, and abandoned
wretch. O welcome, welcome.

MRS. FRAIL
How d'ye, sir? Can I serve you?

---

453 *chine* spine

452 *Medea's kettle.* The cauldron in which the Colchian witch Medea
    prepared the magic herbs with which she restored youth to Jason's
    father, Aeson.
454 *Taliacotius.* (1545–99) Bolognese surgeon famous for his experiments
    in skin grafting.
457–8 *pigeons . . . feet.* A restorative for the dying, see Pepys' *Diary*, 19
    October 1663, 'The Queen . . . . was so ill as to be shaved and pidgeons
    put to her feet, and to have the extreme unction given her by the
    priests'.

VALENTINE

Harkee, I have a secret to tell you—Endymion and the moon
shall meet us upon Mount Latmos, and we'll be married in   475
the dead of night—but say not a word. Hymen shall put his
torch into a dark lanthorn, that it may be secret; and Juno
shall give her peacock poppy-water, that he may fold his
ogling tail, and Argos's hundred eyes be shut, ha? Nobody
shall know but Jeremy.   480

MRS. FRAIL

No, no, we'll keep it secret; it shall be done presently.

VALENTINE

The sooner the better.—Jeremy, come hither—closer—
that none may overhear us. Jeremy, I can tell you news:
Angelica is turned nun, and I am turning friar, and yet we'll
marry one another in spite of the Pope. Get me a cowl and   485
beads that I may play my part, for she'll meet me two hours
hence in black and white, and a long veil to cover the project,
and we won't see one another's faces till we have done
something to be ashamed of; and then we'll blush once for
all.   490

[Act IV, Scene xvi]

Enter TATTLE *and* ANGELICA

JEREMY

I'll take care, and—

VALENTINE

Whisper.

ANGELICA

Nay, Mr. Tattle, if you make love to me, you spoil my
design, for I intended to make you my confidant.

TATTLE

But, madam, to throw away your person, such a person!   495
and such a fortune, on a madman!

ANGELICA

I never loved him till he was mad; but don't tell anybody so.

494 *intended* (intend Q3, 4, Ww)

---

474 *Endymion.* The shepherd with whom the moon fell in love as he slept
on Mount Latmos.
476-9 *Hymen . . . shut.* We shall be married in secret. Juno was protec-
tress of marriage. Argos was the hundred-eyed watchman she employed
to keep Jupiter from his mistress Io, but Mercury killed him. His eyes
were then placed in the peacock's tail.

SCANDAL

How's this! Tattle making love to Angelica!

TATTLE

Tell, madam! Alas, you don't know me. I have much ado to
tell your ladyship how long I have been in love with you,   500
but encouraged by the impossibility of Valentine's making
any more addresses to you, I have ventured to declare the
very inmost passion of my heart. O, madam, look upon us
both. There you see the ruins of a poor decayed creature,
here, a complete and lively figure, with youth and health,   505
and all his five senses in perfection, madam, and to all this,
the most passionate lover—

ANGELICA

O, fie for shame, hold your tongue; a passionate lover, and
five senses in perfection! When you are as mad as Valentine,
I'll believe you love me, and the maddest shall take me.   510

VALENTINE

It is enough. Ha! Who's here?

MRS. FRAIL (*To* JEREMY)

O Lord, her coming will spoil all.

JEREMY

No, no, madam, he won't know her. If he should, I can
persuade him.

VALENTINE

Scandal, who are all these? Foreigners? If they are, I'll tell   515
you what I think. (*Whispers*) Get away all the company but
Angelica, that I may discover my design to her.

SCANDAL

I will. I have discovered something of Tattle, that is of a
piece with Mrs. Frail. He courts Angelica, if we could contrive to couple 'em together. Harkee.   *Whispers*   520

MRS. FORESIGHT

He won't know you, cousin; he knows nobody.

FORESIGHT

But he knows more than anybody. O, niece, he knows things
past and to come, and all the profound secrets of time.

TATTLE

Look you, Mr. Foresight, it is not my way to make many
words of matters, and so I shan't say much, but in short,   525
d'ye see, I will hold you a hundred pound now that I
know more secrets than he.

---

505 *complete and lively* (complete, lively W2)
515 *are all these?* (are these? Q3, 4, Ww)

FORESIGHT

How! I cannot read that knowledge in your face, Mr. Tattle.
Pray, what do you know?

TATTLE

Why d'ye think I'll tell you, sir! Read it in my face? No, sir,   530
'tis written in my heart. And safer there, sir, than letters
writ in juice of lemon, for no fire can fetch it out. I am no
blab, sir.

VALENTINE (*To* SCANDAL)

Acquaint Jeremy with it; he may easily bring it about. They
are welcome, and I'll tell 'em so myself.—What, do you look   535
strange upon me? Then I must be plain. (*Coming up to them*)
I am Truth, and hate an old acquaintance with a new face.

SCANDAL *goes aside with* JEREMY

TATTLE

Do you know me, Valentine?

VALENTINE

You? Who are you? No, I hope not.

TATTLE

I am Jack Tattle, your friend.   540

VALENTINE

My friend, what to do? I am no married man, and thou canst
not lie with my wife; I am very poor, and thou canst not
borrow money of me; then what employment have I for a
friend?

TATTLE

Hah! A good open speaker, and not to be trusted with a   545
secret.

ANGELICA

Do you know me, Valentine?

VALENTINE

O, very well.

ANGELICA

Who am I?

VALENTINE

You're a woman, one to whom heaven gave beauty when it   550
grafted roses on a briar. You are the reflection of heaven in a
pond, and he that leaps at you is sunk. You are all white, a
sheet of lovely spotless paper, when you first are born; but
you are to be scrawled and blotted by every goose's quill. I
know you; for I loved a woman, and loved her so long that   555
I found out a strange thing: I found out what a woman was
good for.

TATTLE

Aye, prithee, what's that?

VALENTINE

Why, to keep a secret.

TATTLE

O Lord!   560

VALENTINE

O exceeding good to keep a secret: for though she should
tell, yet she is not to be believed.

TATTLE

Hah! good again, faith.

VALENTINE

I would have music. Sing me the song that I like.

SONG

Set by Mr. Finger

I tell thee, Charmion, could I time retrieve,   565
And could again begin to love and live,
To you I should my earliest off'ring give;
    I know my eyes would lead my heart to you,
    And I should all my vows and oaths renew,
    But to be plain, I never would be true.   570

For by our weak and weary truth, I find,
Love hates to centre in a point assigned,
But runs with joy the circle of the mind.
    Then never let us chain what should be free,
    But for relief of either sex agree,   575
    Since women love to change, and so do we.

VALENTINE (*Walks musing*)

No more, for I am melancholy.

JEREMY (*To* SCANDAL)

I'll do't, sir.

SCANDAL

Mr. Foresight, we had best leave him. He may grow outrageous and do mischief.   580

FORESIGHT

I will be directed by you.

JEREMY (*To* MRS. FRAIL)

You'll meet, madam, I'll take care everything shall be ready.

---

564 *Finger.* Godfrey Finger (fl. 1685-1717), a Moravian composer. He wrote a score
    for Congreve's *The Mourning Bride*.

MRS. FRAIL

Thou shalt do what thou wilt, have what thou wilt; in short, I will deny thee nothing.

TATTLE (*To* ANGELICA)

Madam, shall I wait upon you?   585

ANGELICA

No, I'll stay with him; Mr. Scandal will protect me. Aunt, Mr. Tattle desires you would give him leave to wait on you.

TATTLE [*Aside*]

Pox on't, there's no coming off, now she has said that.— Madam, will you do me the honour?

MRS. FORESIGHT

Mr. Tattle might have used less ceremony.   590

> *Exeunt* FORESIGHT, MRS. FORESIGHT, TATTLE, MRS. FRAIL

[Act IV, Scene xvii]

SCANDAL

Jeremy, follow Tattle.   *Exit* JEREMY

ANGELICA

Mr. Scandal, I only stay till my maid comes, and because I had a mind to be rid of Mr. Tattle.

SCANDAL

Madam, I am very glad that I overheard a better reason, which you gave to Mr. Tattle; for his impertinence forced   595 you to acknowledge a kindness for Valentine, which you denied to all his sufferings and my solicitations. So I'll leave him to make use of the discovery, and your ladyship to the free confession of your inclinations.

ANGELICA

O heavens! You won't leave me alone with a madman?   600

SCANDAL

No, madam; I only leave a madman to his remedy.

> *Exit* SCANDAL

[Act IV, Scene xviii]

VALENTINE

Madam, you need not be very much afraid, for I fancy I begin to come to myself.

ANGELICA (*Aside*)

Aye, but if I don't fit you, I'll be hanged.

---

583 *have what thou wilt* (om. Ww)   604 *fit* punish, trick

VALENTINE

You see what disguises love makes us put on. Gods have   605
been in counterfeited shapes for the same reason, and the
divine part of me, my mind, has worn this mask of madness,
and this motley livery, only as the slave of love, and menial
creature of your beauty.

ANGELICA

Mercy on me, how he talks! Poor Valentine!   610

VALENTINE

Nay, faith, now let us understand one another, hypocrisy
apart. The comedy draws toward an end, and let us think of
leaving acting and be ourselves; and since you have loved
me, you must own I have at length deserved you should
confess it.   615

ANGELICA (*Sighs*)

I would I had loved you, for heaven knows I pity you; and
could I have foreseen the sad effects, I would have striven;
but that's too late.

VALENTINE

What sad effects? What's too late? My seeming madness has
deceived my father, and procured me time to think of means   620
to reconcile me to him and preserve the right of my inheritance to his estate, which otherwise by articles I must this
morning have resigned: and this I had informed you of
today, but you were gone before I knew you had been here.

ANGELICA

How! I thought your love of me had caused this transport   625
in your soul, which, it seems, you only counterfeited for
mercenary ends and sordid interest.

VALENTINE

Nay, now you do me wrong; for if any interest was considered, it was yours, since I thought I wanted more than
love to make me worthy of you.   630

ANGELICA

Then you thought me mercenary.—But how am I deluded
by this interval of sense, to reason with a madman?

VALENTINE

O, 'tis barbarous to misunderstand me longer.

617 *sad effects* (bad effects Q3, 4, Ww)
626–7 *for mercenary* (for by, mercenary Q1, 2; for by mercenary
    Q3, 4, W1)

[Act IV, Scene xix]

Enter JEREMY

ANGELICA

O, here's a reasonable creature.—Sure he will not have the
impudence to persevere.—Come, Jeremy, acknowledge   635
your trick, and confess your master's madness counterfeit.

JEREMY

Counterfeit, madam! I'll maintain him to be as absolutely
and substantially mad as any freeholder in Bethlehem; nay,
he's as mad as any projector, fanatic, chemist, lover, or poet
in Europe.   640

VALENTINE

Sirrah, you lie; I am not mad.

ANGELICA

Ha, ha, ha, you see he denies it.

JEREMY

O Lord, madam, did you ever know any madman mad
enough to own it?

VALENTINE

Sot, can't you apprehend?   645

ANGELICA

Why, he talked very sensibly just now.

JEREMY

Yes, madam, he has intervals: but you see he begins to look
wild again now.

VALENTINE

Why, you thick-skulled rascal, I tell you the farce is done,
and I will be mad no longer.   *Beats him*   650

ANGELICA

Ha, ha, ha, is he mad, or no, Jeremy?

JEREMY

Partly, I think, for he does not know his mind two hours.
I'm sure I left him just now in a humour to be mad, and I
think I have not found him very quiet at this present.
(*One knocks*) Who's there?   655

VALENTINE

Go see, you sot.—I'm very glad that I can move your mirth,
though not your compassion.   *Exit* JEREMY

638 *Bethlehem* St. Mary of Bethlehem the lunatic asylum (Bedlam)
652 *his mind* (his own mind Ww)
653 *a humour* (the humour Ww)
657 s.d. *Exit* JEREMY (om. Ww)

ANGELICA
  I did not think you had apprehension enough to be exceptious: but madmen show themselves most by overpretending
  to a sound understanding, as drunken men do by over-acting   660
  sobriety. I was half inclining to believe you, till I accidentally
  touched upon your tender part; but now you have restored
  me to my former opinion and compassion.

                    Enter JEREMY

JEREMY
  Sir, your father has sent to know if you are any better yet.
  Will you please to be mad, sir, or how?   665

VALENTINE
  Stupidity! You know the penalty of all I'm worth must pay
  for the confession of my senses; I'm mad, and will be mad to
  everybody but this lady.

JEREMY
  So, just the very backside of Truth. But lying is a figure in
  speech that interlards the greatest part of my conversation. 670
  —Madam, your ladyship's woman.   *Goes to the door*

                 [Act IV, Scene xx]

                    Enter JENNY

ANGELICA
  Well, have you been there? Come hither.

JENNY
  Yes, madam. (*Aside to* ANGELICA) Sir Sampson will wait
  upon you presently.

VALENTINE
  You are not leaving me in this uncertainty?   675

ANGELICA
  Would anything but a madman complain of uncertainty?
  Uncertainty and expectation are the joys of life. Security is
  an insipid thing, and the overtaking and possessing of a wish
  discovers the folly of the chase. Never let us know one
  another better; for the pleasure of a masquerade is done   680
  when we come to show faces. But I'll tell you two things
  before I leave you: I am not the fool you take me for; and
  you are mad and don't know it.
                    Exeunt ANGELICA *and* JENNY

663 s.d. *Enter* JEREMY (om. Ww)
681 *show faces* (show our faces Ww)

[Act IV, Scene xxi]

VALENTINE
From a riddle you can expect nothing but a riddle. There's
my instruction, and the moral of my lesson.   685

Re-enter JEREMY

JEREMY
What, is the lady gone again, sir? I hope you understood one
another before she went?

VALENTINE
Understood! She is harder to be understood than a piece of
Egyptian antiquity, or an Irish manuscript; you may pore
till you spoil your eyes, and not improve your knowledge.   690

JEREMY
I have heard 'em say, sir, they read hard Hebrew books
backwards; maybe you begin to read at the wrong end.

VALENTINE
They say so of a witch's prayer, and dreams and Dutch
almanacs are to be understood by contraries. But there's
regularity and method in that; she is a medal without a   695
reverse or inscription, for indifference has both sides alike.
Yet while she does not seem to hate me, I will pursue her,
and know her if it be possible, in spite of the opinion of
my satirical friend, Scandal, who says
    That women are like tricks by sleight of hand,   700
    Which, to admire, we should not understand.

Exeunt

[Act V, Scene i]

A room in FORESIGHT'S *house*
Enter ANGELICA *and* JENNY

ANGELICA
Where is Sir Sampson? Did you not tell me he would be
here before me?

JENNY
He's at the great glass in the dining room, madam, setting his
cravat and wig.

ANGELICA
How! I'm glad on't. If he has a mind I should like him, it's   5
a sign he likes me; and that's more than half my design.

1 s.d. *room* (Rome Q1, 2)

JENNY
    I hear him, madam.
ANGELICA
    Leave me, and, d'ye hear, if Valentine should come, or send,
    I am not to be spoken with.   *Exit* JENNY

[Act V, Scene ii]

Enter SIR SAMPSON

SIR SAMPSON
    I have not been honoured with the commands of a fair lady   10
    a great while—odd, madam, you have revived me—not
    since I was five and thirty.
ANGELICA
    Why, you have no great reason to complain, Sir Sampson;
    that is not long ago.
SIR SAMPSON
    Zooks, but it is, madam, a very great while; to a man that   15
    admires a fine woman as much as I do.
ANGELICA
    You're an absolute courtier, Sir Sampson.
SIR SAMPSON
    Not at all, madam; odsbud, you wrong me: I am not so old,
    neither, to be a bare courtier, only a man of words. Odd, I
    have warm blood about me yet; I can serve a lady any way.   20
    Come, come, let me tell you, you women think a man old too
    soon, faith and troth you do. Come, don't despise fifty; odd,
    fifty, in a hale constitution, is no such contemptible age.
ANGELICA
    Fifty a contemptible age! Not at all, a very fashionable age I
    think. I assure you I know very considerable beaux that set a   25
    good face upon fifty. Fifty! I have seen fifty in a side box, by
    candle-light, out-blossom five and twenty.
SIR SAMPSON
    O pox, outsides, outsides, a pize take 'em, mere outsides.
    Hang your side-box beaux; no, I'm none of those, none of
    your forced trees, that pretend to blossom in the fall, and   30
    bud when they should bring forth fruit. I am of a long-lived
    race, and inherit vigour; none of my family married till

20 *I can* (and can Q3, 4, Ww)
28 *O pox* (om. Ww)
32 *family* (ancestors Ww)

fifty, yet they begot sons and daughters till fourscore. I am
of your patriarchs, I, a branch of one of your antediluvian
families, fellows that the flood could not wash away. Well,   35
madam, what are your commands? Has any young rogue
affronted you, and shall I cut his throat? or—

ANGELICA

No, Sir Sampson, I have no quarrel upon my hands; I have
more occasion for your conduct than your courage at this
time. To tell you the truth, I'm weary of living single, and   40
want a husband.

SIR SAMPSON

Odsbud, and 'tis pity you should. (*Aside*) Odd, would she
would like me; then I should hamper my young rogues; odd,
would she would; faith and troth, she's devilish handsome.
—Madam, you deserve a good husband, and 'twere pity you   45
should be thrown away upon any of these young idle rogues
about the town. Odd, there's ne'er a young fellow worth
hanging—that is a very young fellow. Pize on 'em, they never
think beforehand of anything; and if they commit matrimony, 'tis as they commit murder, out of a frolic; and are   50
ready to hang themselves, or to be hanged by the law, the
next morning. Odso, have a care, madam.

ANGELICA

Therefore I ask your advice, Sir Sampson: I have fortune
enough to make any man easy that I can like; if there were
such a thing as a young, agreeable man, with a reasonable   55
stock of good nature and sense—for I would neither have an
absolute wit, nor a fool.

SIR SAMPSON

Odd, you are hard to please, madam; to find a young fellow
that is neither a wit in his own eye, nor a fool in the eye of
the world, is a very hard task. But, faith and troth, you speak   60
very discreetly, for I hate both a wit and a fool.

ANGELICA

She that marries a fool, Sir Sampson, commits the reputation of her honesty or understanding to the censure of the
world; and she that marries a very witty man submits both to
the severity and insolent conduct of her husband. I should   65
like a man of wit for a lover, because I would have such an

---

45 *'twere pity* ('twere a pity Q4)
48 *that is* (that's Q2)
62–4 *commits . . . to the censure of the world* (forfeits Ww)
64 *submits both* (is a slave Ww)

one in my power; but I would no more be his wife than his
enemy; for his malice is not a more terrible consequence of
his aversion, than his jealousy is of his love.

SIR SAMPSON

None of old Foresight's sibyls ever uttered such a truth.   70
Odsbud, you have won my heart; I hate a wit—I had a son
that was spoiled among 'em; a good, hopeful lad, till he
learned to be a wit—and might have risen in the state. But,
a pox on't, his wit run him out of his money, and now his
poverty has run him out of his wits.   75

ANGELICA

Sir Sampson, as your friend, I must tell you, you are very
much abused in that matter; he's no more mad than you are.

SIR SAMPSON

How, madam! Would I could prove it.

ANGELICA

I can tell you how that may be done.—But it is a thing that
would make me appear to be too much concerned in your   80
affairs.

SIR SAMPSON (*Aside*)

Odsbud, I believe she likes me.—Ah, madam, all my affairs
are scarce worthy to be laid at your feet; and I wish, madam,
they stood in a better posture, that I might make a more
becoming offer to a lady of your incomparable beauty and   85
merit. If I had Peru in one hand and Mexico in t'other, and
the Eastern Empire under my feet, it would make me only a
more glorious victim to be offered at the shrine of your
beauty.

ANGELICA

Bless me, Sir Sampson, what's the matter?   90

SIR SAMPSON

Odd, madam, I love you, and if you would take my advice in
a husband—

ANGELICA

Hold, hold, Sir Sampson. I asked your advice for a husband,
and you are giving me your consent. I was indeed thinking
to propose something like it in a jest, to satisfy you about   95
Valentine: for if a match were seemingly carried on between
you and me, it would oblige him to throw off his disguise of
madness in apprehension of losing me, for you know he has
long pretended a passion for me.

84 *stood* (were Ww)
95 *a jest* (jest Q3, 4, Ww)

SIR SAMPSON

Gadzooks, a most ingenious contrivance—if we were to go   100
through with it. But why must the match only be seemingly
carried on? Odd, let it be a real contract.

ANGELICA

O fie, Sir Sampson, what would the world say?

SIR SAMPSON

Say, they would say, you were a wise woman, and I a happy
man. Odd, madam, I'll love you as long as I live, and leave   105
you a good jointure when I die.

ANGELICA

Aye, but that is not in your power, Sir Sampson; for when
Valentine confesses himself in his senses, he must make over
his inheritance to his younger brother.

SIR SAMPSON

Odd, you're cunning, a wary baggage! Faith and troth, I like   110
you the better. But, I warrant you, I have a proviso in the
obligation in favour of myself. Body o'me, I have a trick to
turn the settlement upon the issue male of our two bodies
begotten. Odsbud, let us find children, and I'll find an
estate.   115

ANGELICA

Will you? Well, do you find the estate, and leave the t'other
to me—

SIR SAMPSON

O rogue! But I'll trust you. And will you consent? Is it a
match then?

ANGELICA

Let me consult my lawyer concerning this obligation; and if I   120
find what you propose practicable, I'll give you my answer.

SIR SAMPSON

With all my heart. Come in with me, and I'll lend you the
bond. You shall consult your lawyer, and I'll consult a
parson. Odzooks, I'm a young man; odzooks, I'm a young
man, and I'll make it appear—Odd, you're devilish hand-   125
some; faith and troth, you're very handsome, and I'm very
young, and very lusty. Odsbud, hussy, you know how to
choose, and so do I. Odd, I think we are very well met. Give
me your hand; odd, let me kiss it; 'tis as warm and as soft—
as what?—odd, as t'other hand—give me t'other hand, and   130
I'll mumble 'em, and kiss 'em till they melt in my mouth.

ANGELICA

Hold, Sir Sampson, you're profuse of your vigour before

116 *the t'other* (the other W2)

your time: you'll spend your estate before you come to it.

SIR SAMPSON

No, no, only give you a rent-roll of my possessions—ah
baggage!—I warrant you, for little Sampson. Odd, Samp-   135
son's a very good name for an able fellow: your Sampsons
were strong dogs from the beginning.

ANGELICA

Have a care, and don't over-act your part. If you remember,
the strongest Sampson of your name pulled an old house
over his head at last.   140

SIR SAMPSON

Say you so, hussy? Come, let's go then. Odd, I long to be
pulling down too, come away. Odso, here's somebody
coming.   *Exeunt*

[Act V, Scene iii]

Enter TATTLE *and* JEREMY

TATTLE

Is not that she, gone out just now?

JEREMY

Aye, sir, she's just going to the place of appointment. Ah,   145
sir, if you are not very faithful and close in this business,
you'll certainly be the death of a person that has a most
extraordinary passion for your honour's service.

TATTLE

Aye, who's that?

JEREMY

Even my unworthy self, sir. Sir, I have had an appetite to be   150
fed with your commands a great while; and now, sir, my
former master having much troubled the fountain of his
understanding, it is a very plausible occasion for me to
quench my thirst at the spring of your bounty. I thought I
could not recommend myself better to you, sir, than by the   155
delivery of a great beauty and fortune into your arms, whom
I have heard you sigh for.

TATTLE

I'll make thy fortune; say no more. Thou art a pretty fellow,
and canst carry a message to a lady in a pretty soft kind of
phrase, and with a good persuading accent.   160

139 *the strongest . . . name* (Sampson, the strongest of the name Ww)
139 *old house* 'entailed cuckoldom' upon himself, Aphra Behn, *The Lucky Chance*,
    V.vii
142 *pulling down* (pulling Ww)

JEREMY

Sir, I have the seeds of rhetoric and oratory in my head—I
have been at Cambridge.

TATTLE

Aye, 'tis well enough for a servant to be bred at an university,
but the education is a little too pedantic for a gentleman. I
hope you are secret in your nature, private, close, ha?   165

JEREMY

O, sir, for that, sir, 'tis my chief talent; I'm as secret as the
head of Nilus.

TATTLE

Aye? Who's he, though? A Privy Counsellor?

JEREMY (*Aside*)

O ignorance!—A cunning Egyptian, sir, that with his arms
would overrun the country, yet nobody could ever find out   170
his headquarters.

TATTLE

Close dog! A good whoremaster, I warrant him.—The time
draws nigh, Jeremy. Angelica will be veiled like a nun, and I
must be hooded like a friar, ha, Jeremy?

JEREMY

Aye, sir, hooded like a hawk, to seize at first sight upon the   175
quarry. It is the whim of my master's madness to be so
dressed; and she is so in love with him, she'll comply with
anything to please him. Poor lady, I'm sure she'll have
reason to pray for me, when she finds what a happy exchange
she has made between a madman and so accomplished a   180
gentleman.

TATTLE

Aye, faith, so she will, Jeremy: you're a good friend to her,
poor creature. I swear I do it hardly so much in consideration of myself, as compassion to her.

JEREMY

'Tis an act of charity, sir, to save a fine woman with 30,000   185
pound from throwing herself away.

TATTLE

So 'tis, faith. I might have saved several others in my time;
but, egad, I could never find in my heart to marry anybody
before.

JEREMY

Well, sir, I'll go and tell her my master's coming; and meet   190

---

167 *head of Nilus.* The source of the Nile was not determined until the
mid-19th century.

you in half a quarter of an hour, with your disguise, at your
own lodgings. You must talk a little madly; she won't
distinguish the tone of your voice.

TATTLE

No, no, let me alone for a counterfeit; I'll be ready for you.

[Act V, Scene iv]

Enter MISS PRUE

MISS PRUE

O, Mr. Tattle, are you here! I'm glad I have found you; I   195
have been looking up and down for you like anything, till
I'm as tired as anything in the world.

TATTLE (*Aside*)

O pox, how shall I get rid of this foolish girl?

MISS PRUE

O, I have pure news; I can tell you pure news. I must not
marry the seaman now; my father says so. Why won't you be   200
my husband? You say you love me, and you won't be my
husband. And I know you may be my husband now if you
please.

TATTLE

O fie, miss; who told you so, child?

MISS PRUE

Why, my father. I told him that you loved me.   205

TATTLE

O fie, miss, why did you do so? And who told you so, child?

MISS PRUE

Who? Why, you did; did not you?

TATTLE

O pox, that was yesterday, miss; that was a great while ago,
child. I have been asleep since; slept a whole night, and did
not so much as dream of the matter.   210

MISS PRUE

Pshaw. O, but I dreamt that it was so, though.

TATTLE

Aye, but your father will tell you that dreams come by contraries, child. O fie; what, we must not love one another now;
pshaw, that would be a foolish thing indeed. Fie, fie, you're a
woman now, and must think of a new man every morning,   215
and forget him every night. No, no, to marry is to be a child
again, and play with the same rattle always. O fie, marrying
is a paw thing.

218 *paw* obscene

MISS PRUE

Well, but don't you love me as well as you did last night, then? 220

TATTLE

No, no, child, you would not have me.

MISS PRUE

No? Yes, but I would, though.

TATTLE

Pshaw, but I tell you, you would not. You forget you're a woman and don't know your own mind.

MISS PRUE

But here's my father, and he knows my mind. 225

[Act V, Scene v]

Enter FORESIGHT

FORESIGHT

O, Mr. Tattle, your servant. You are a close man, but methinks your love to my daughter was a secret I might have been trusted with—or had you a mind to try if I could discover it by my art. Hum, ha! I think there is something in your physiognomy that has a resemblance of her; and the 230 girl is like me.

TATTLE

And so you would infer that you and I are alike. (*Aside*) What does the old prig mean? I'll banter him, and laugh at him, and leave him.—I fancy you have a wrong notion of faces. 235

FORESIGHT

How? What? A wrong notion! How so?

TATTLE

In the way of art. I have some taking features, not obvious to vulgar eyes, that are indications of a sudden turn of good fortune in the lottery of wives, and promise a great beauty and great fortune reserved alone for me, by a private intrigue 240 of destiny, kept secret from the piercing eye of perspicuity, from all astrologers and the stars themselves.

FORESIGHT

How! I will make it appear that what you say is impossible.

TATTLE

Sir, I beg your pardon; I'm in haste—

FORESIGHT

For what? 245

239 *promise a* (promise of Q2–4)

TATTLE

To be married, sir, married.

FORESIGHT

Aye, but pray take me along with you, sir—

TATTLE

No, sir; 'tis to be done privately. I never make confidants.

FORESIGHT

Well; but my consent, I mean. You won't marry my
daughter without my consent?   250

TATTLE

Who, I, sir? I'm an absolute stranger to you and your
daughter, sir.

FORESIGHT

Hey day! What time of the moon is this?

TATTLE

Very true, sir, and desire to continue so. I have no more love
for your daughter than I have likeness of you; and I have a   255
secret in my heart, which you would be glad to know, and
shan't know; and yet you shall know it too, and be sorry for't
afterwards. I'd have you to know, sir, that I am as knowing
as the stars, and as secret as the night. And I'm going to be
married just now, yet did not know of it half an hour ago;   260
and the lady stays for me, and does not know of it yet. There's
a mystery for you.—I know you love to untie difficulties. Or
if you can't solve this, stay here a quarter of an hour, and I'll
come and explain it to you.   *Exit*

[Act V, Scene vi]

MISS PRUE

O, father, why will you let him go? Won't you make him be   265
my husband?

FORESIGHT

Mercy on us, what do these lunacies portend? Alas! he's
mad, child, stark wild.

MISS PRUE

What, and must not I have e'er a husband then? What, must
I go to bed to nurse again, and be a child as long as she's an   270
old woman? Indeed, but I won't: for now my mind is set
upon a man, I will have a man some way or other. O!
methinks I'm sick when I think of a man; and if I can't have
one, I would go to sleep all my life, for when I'm awake, it

265 *him be* (him to be Q3, 4, Ww)

makes me wish and long, and I don't know for what—and 275
I'd rather be always asleeping, than sick with thinking.

FORESIGHT

O fearful! I think the girl's influenced too.—Hussy, you
shall have a rod.

MISS PRUE

A fiddle of a rod, I'll have a husband; and if you won't get
me one, I'll get one for myself: I'll marry our Robin, the 280
butler. He says he loves me, and he's a handsome man, and
shall be my husband. I warrant he'll be my husband and
thank me too, for he told me so.

[Act V, Scene vii]

Enter SCANDAL, MRS. FORESIGHT, *and* NURSE

FORESIGHT

Did he so—I'll dispatch him for't presently. Rogue!— O,
nurse, come hither. 285

NURSE

What is your worship's pleasure?

FORESIGHT

Here, take your young mistress, and lock her up presently,
till further orders from me. Not a word, hussy; do what I
bid you; no reply, away. And bid Robin make ready to give
an account of his plate and linen; d'ye hear, be gone when 290
I bid you.

Exeunt NURSE *and* MISS PRUE

MRS. FORESIGHT

What's the matter, husband?

FORESIGHT

'Tis not convenient to tell you now.—Mr. Scandal, heaven
keep us all in our senses; I fear there is a contagious frenzy
abroad. How does Valentine? 295

SCANDAL

O, I hope he will do well again. I have a message from him to
your niece Angelica.

FORESIGHT

I think she has not returned since she went abroad with Sir
Sampson.

276 *always asleeping* (always asleep Q3, 4, Ww)
291 s.d. *Exeunt* NURSE *and* MISS PRUE (om. Ww, but add at the end of
the scene; Nurse, why are you not gone?)

[Act V, Scene viii]

Enter BEN

MRS. FORESIGHT

Here's Mr. Benjamin, he can tell us if his father be come 300
home.

BEN

Who, father? Aye he's come home with a vengeance.

MRS. FORESIGHT

Why, what's the matter.

BEN

Matter! Why, he's mad.

FORESIGHT

Mercy on us, I was afraid of this. 305

BEN

And there's the handsome young woman, she, as they say,
brother Val went mad for; she's mad too, I think.

FORESIGHT

O my poor niece, my poor niece, is she gone too? Well, I
shall run mad next.

MRS. FORESIGHT

Well, but how mad? How d'ye mean? 310

BEN

Nay, I'll give you leave to guess. I'll undertake to make a
voyage to Antigua; no, hold, I mayn't say so neither—but
I'll sail as far as Leghorn and back again, before you shall
guess at the matter, and do nothing else; mess, you may take
in all the points of the compass, and not hit right. 315

MRS. FORESIGHT

Your experiment will take up a little too much time.

BEN

Why then, I'll tell you: there's a new wedding upon the
stocks, and they two are a-going to be married to rights.

SCANDAL

Who?

BEN

Why, father and—the young woman. I can't hit of her name. 320

SCANDAL

Angelica?

BEN

Aye, the same.

312 *no, hold, I* (no, I W2)

MRS. FORESIGHT
  Sir Sampson and Angelica, impossible!
BEN
  That may be, but I'm sure it is as I tell you.
SCANDAL
  S'death, it's a jest. I can't believe it.   325
BEN
  Look you, friend, it's nothing to me whether you believe it or
  no. What I say is true; d'ye see, they are married, or just
  going to be married, I know not which.
FORESIGHT
  Well, but they are not mad, that is, not lunatic?
BEN
  I don't know what you may call madness, but she's mad for a   330
  husband, and he's horn-mad, I think, or they'd ne'er make
  a match together.—Here they come.

[Act V, Scene ix]

Enter SIR SAMPSON, ANGELICA, *with* BUCKRAM

SIR SAMPSON
  Where is this old soothsayer, this uncle of mine elect? Aha,
  old Foresight, uncle Foresight, wish me joy, uncle Foresight,
  double joy, both as uncle and astrologer; here's a conjunction   335
  that was not foretold in all your Ephemeris. The brightest
  star in the blue firmament—is shot from above, in a jelly of
  love, and so forth; and I'm lord of the ascendant. Odd,
  you're an old fellow, Foresight, uncle I mean, a very old
  fellow, uncle Foresight; and yet you shall live to dance at my   340
  wedding; faith and troth, you shall. Odd, we'll have the
  music of the spheres for thee, old Lilly, that we will, and
  thou shalt lead up a dance in *via lactea*.
FORESIGHT
  I'm thunderstruck! You are not married to my niece?
SIR SAMPSON
  Not absolutely married, uncle, but very near it; within a kiss   345
  of the matter, as you see.   *Kisses* ANGELICA

343 *via lactea* the Milky Way

336–8 *brightest star . . . jelly of love.* The star is Venus, the jelly Dryden's,
    from *Tyrannic Love* IV. i: 'And drop from above/In a jelly of love!'
    The play had been revived at the Theatre Royal 1694.

ANGELICA

    'Tis very true indeed, uncle; I hope you'll be my father, and give me.

SIR SAMPSON

    That he shall, or I'll burn his globes. Body o'me, he shall be thy father, I'll make him thy father, and thou shalt make   350 me a father, and I'll make thee a mother, and we'll beget sons and daughters enough to put the weekly bills out of countenance.

SCANDAL

    Death and hell! Where's Valentine?   *Exit* SCANDAL

[Act V, Scene x]

MRS. FORESIGHT

    This is so surprising—   355

SIR SAMPSON

    How! What does my aunt say? Surprising, aunt? Not at all, for a young couple to make a match in winter. Not at all— it's a plot to undermine cold weather, and destroy that usurper of a bed called a warming pan.

MRS. FORESIGHT

    I'm glad to hear you have so much fire in you, Sir Sampson.   360

BEN

    Mess, I fear his fire's little better than tinder; mayhap it will only serve to light up a match for somebody else. The young woman's a handsome young woman, I can't deny it; but, father, if I might be your pilot in this case, you should not marry her. It's just the same thing as if so be you should sail   365 so far as the Straits without provision.

SIR SAMPSON

    Who gave you authority to speak, sirrah? To your element, fish; be mute, fish, and to sea; rule your helm, sirrah, don't direct me.

BEN

    Well, well, take you care of your own helm, or you mayn't   370 keep your own vessel steady.

SIR SAMPSON

    Why, you impudent tarpaulin! Sirrah, do you bring your forecastle jests upon your father? But I shall be even with you: I won't give you a groat. Mr. Buckram, is the convey-

366 *Straits* of Gibraltar
370 *own* (new Q3, 4, Ww)

ance so worded that nothing can possibly descend to this 375
scoundrel? I would not so much as have him have the prospect of an estate, though there were no way to come to it, but
by the Northeast Passage.

BUCKRAM

Sir, it is drawn according to your directions; there is not the
least cranny of the law unstopt. 380

BEN

Lawyer, I believe there's many a cranny and leak unstopt in
your conscience. If so be that one had a pump to your bosom,
I believe we should discover a foul hold. They say a witch
will sail in a sieve, but I believe the devil would not venture
aboard o'your conscience. And that's for you. 385

SIR SAMPSON

Hold your tongue, sirrah. How now, who's there?

[Act V, Scene xi]

Enter TATTLE *and* MRS. FRAIL

MRS. FRAIL

O, sister, the most unlucky accident!

MRS. FORESIGHT

What's the matter?

TATTLE

O, the two most unfortunate poor creatures in the world we
are. 390

FORESIGHT

Bless us! How so?

MRS. FRAIL

Ah, Mr. Tattle and I, poor Mr. Tattle and I are—I can't
speak it out.

TATTLE

Nor I—but poor Mrs. Frail and I are—

MRS. FRAIL

Married. 395

MRS. FORESIGHT

Married! How?

TATTLE

Suddenly—before we knew where we were—that villain
Jeremy, by the help of disguises, tricked us into one another.

378 *Northeast Passage* the impossible route north of Russia to the east
386 *there?* (here? Ww)
387 *sister* (sir Q4)
394 *but poor* (poor Ww)

FORESIGHT

Why, you told me just now you went hence in haste to be
married.   400

ANGELICA

But I believe Mr. Tattle meant the favour to me; I thank
him.

TATTLE

I did; as I hope to be saved, madam, my intentions were
good. But this is the most cruel thing, to marry one does
not know how, nor why, nor wherefore. The devil take me if   405
ever I was so much concerned at anything in my life.

ANGELICA

'Tis very unhappy, if you don't care for one another.

TATTLE

The least in the world—that is for my part; I speak for
myself. Gad, I never had the least thought of serious kindness; I never liked anybody less in my life. Poor woman!   410
Gad, I'm sorry for her too, for I have no reason to hate her
neither; but I believe I shall lead her a damned sort of life.

MRS. FORESIGHT (*Aside to* MRS. FRAIL)

He's better than no husband at all, though he's a coxcomb.

MRS. FRAIL (*To her*)

Aye, aye, it's well it's no worse.—Nay, for my part I always
despised Mr. Tattle of all things; nothing but his being my   415
husband could have made me like him less.

TATTLE

Look you there, I thought as much. Pox on't, I wish we could
keep it secret. Why, I don't believe any of this company
would speak of it.

MRS. FRAIL

But, my dear, that's impossible; the parson and that rogue   420
Jeremy will publish it.

TATTLE

Aye, my dear; so they will, as you say.

ANGELICA

O, you'll agree very well in a little time; custom will make it
easy to you.

TATTLE

Easy! Pox on't, I don't believe I shall sleep tonight.   425

SIR SAMPSON

Sleep, quotha! No! Why you would not sleep o'your wedding night? I'm an older fellow than you, and don't mean to
sleep.

BEN

Why, there's another match now, as tho'f a couple of
privateers were looking for a prize, and should fall foul of   430
one another. I'm sorry for the young man with all my heart.
Look you, friend, if I may advise you, when she's going—
for that you must expect, I have experience of her—when
she's going, let her go. For no matrimony is tough enough to
hold her, and if she can't drag her anchor along with her,   435
she'll break her cable, I can tell you that. Who's here? The
madman?

[Scene the Last]

Enter VALENTINE *dressed,* SCANDAL, *and* JEREMY

VALENTINE

No, here's the fool; and if occasion be, I'll give it under my
hand.

SIR SAMPSON

How now?   440

VALENTINE

Sir, I'm come to acknowledge my errors, and ask your
pardon.

SIR SAMPSON

What, have you found your senses at last then? In good
time, sir.

VALENTINE

You were abused, sir; I never was distracted.   445

FORESIGHT

How! Not mad! Mr. Scandal?

SCANDAL

No really, sir; I'm his witness; it was all counterfeit.

VALENTINE

I thought I had reasons. But it was a poor contrivance; the
effect has shown it such.

SIR SAMPSON

Contrivance, what, to cheat me? To cheat your father!   450
Sirrah, could you hope to prosper?

VALENTINE

Indeed, I thought, sir, when the father endeavoured to undo
the son, it was a reasonable return of nature.

SIR SAMPSON

Very good, sir.—Mr. Buckram, are you ready?—Come, sir,
will you sign and seal?   455

VALENTINE
If you please, sir; but first I would ask this lady one question.

SIR SAMPSON
Sir, you must ask my leave first. That lady, no, sir; you shall ask that lady no questions, till you have asked her blessing, sir; that lady is to be my wife.

VALENTINE
I have heard as much, sir; but I would have it from her own   460
mouth.

SIR SAMPSON
That's as much as to say I lie, sir, and you don't believe what I say.

VALENTINE
Pardon me, sir. But I reflect that I very lately counterfeited madness; I don't know but the frolic may go round.   465

SIR SAMPSON
Come, chuck, satisfy him, answer him.—Come, come, Mr. Buckram, the pen and ink.

BUCKRAM
Here it is, sir, with the deed; all is ready.

VALENTINE *goes to* ANGELICA

ANGELICA
'Tis true, you have a great while pretended love to me; nay, what if you were sincere? Still you must pardon me, if I   470
think my own inclinations have a better right to dispose of my person, than yours.

SIR SAMPSON
Are you answered now, sir?

VALENTINE
Yes, sir.

SIR SAMPSON
Where's your plot, sir, and your contrivance now, sir? Will   475
you sign, sir? Come, will you sign and seal?

VALENTINE
With all my heart, sir.

SCANDAL
S'death, you are not mad, indeed, to ruin yourself?

VALENTINE
I have been disappointed of my only hope; and he that loses hope may part with anything. I never valued fortune, but as it   480

457 *my leave* (me leave Q3, 4, Ww)
466 *Come, come, Mr.* (Come, Mr. W2)

was subservient to my pleasure; and my only pleasure was to
please this lady. I have made many vain attempts, and find
at last that nothing but my ruin can effect it: which, for that
reason, I will sign to—give me the paper.

ANGELICA (*Aside*)

Generous Valentine!   485

BUCKRAM

Here is the deed, sir.

VALENTINE

But where is the bond by which I am obliged to sign this?

BUCKRAM

Sir Sampson, you have it.

ANGELICA

No, I have it; and I'll use it as I would everything that is an
enemy to Valentine.   *Tears the paper* 490

SIR SAMPSON

How now!

VALENTINE

Ha!

ANGELICA (*To* VALENTINE)

Had I the world to give you, it could not make me worthy of
so generous and faithful a passion: here's my hand, my heart
was always yours, and struggled very hard to make this   495
utmost trial of your virtue.

VALENTINE

Between pleasure and amazement, I am lost—but on my
knees I take the blessing.

SIR SAMPSON

Ouns, what is the meaning of this?

BEN

Mess, here's the wind changed again. Father, you and I may 500
make a voyage together now.

ANGELICA

Well, Sir Sampson, since I have played you a trick, I'll advise
you how you may avoid such another. Learn to be a good
father, or you'll never get a second wife. I always loved your
son, and hated your unforgiving nature. I was resolved to   505
try him to the utmost; I have tried you too, and know you
both. You have not more faults than he has virtues; and 'tis
hardly more pleasure to me that I can make him and myself
happy, than that I can punish you.

VALENTINE

If my happiness could receive addition, this kind surprise   510
would make it double.

SIR SAMPSON
Ouns, you're a crocodile.

FORESIGHT
Really, Sir Sampson, this is a sudden eclipse—

SIR SAMPSON
You're an illiterate fool, and I'm another, and the stars are
liars; and if I had breath enough, I'd curse them and you,   515
myself, and everybody. Ouns, cullied, bubbled, jilted,
woman-bobbed at last.—I have not patience.
                                        Exit SIR SAMPSON

TATTLE
If the gentleman is in this disorder for want of a wife, I can
spare him mine. (*To* JEREMY) O, are you there, sir? I'm
indebted to you for my happiness.   520

JEREMY
Sir, I ask you ten thousand pardons, 'twas an arrant mistake.
You see, sir, my master was never mad, nor anything like it.
Then how could it be otherwise?

VALENTINE
Tattle, I thank you, you would have interposed between
me and heaven; but Providence laid purgatory in your way.   525
You have but justice.

SCANDAL
I hear the fiddles that Sir Sampson provided for his own
wedding; methinks 'tis pity they should not be employed
when the match is so much mended. Valentine, though it be
morning, we may have a dance.   530

VALENTINE
Anything, my friend, everything that looks like joy and
transport.

SCANDAL
Call 'em, Jeremy.

ANGELICA
I have done dissembling now, Valentine; and if that coldness
which I have always worn before you should turn to an   535
extreme fondness, you must not suspect it.

VALENTINE
I'll prevent that suspicion, for I intend to dote on at that

514 *illiterate fool* (illiterate old fool Ww)
514–17 *and the stars . . . patience* (om. Ww)
516 *cullied . . . jilted* deceived
517 s.d. *Exit* SIR SAMPSON (om. Ww)
518 *this disorder* (disorder Ww)
537–8 *on . . . rate* (to that immoderate degree Ww)

immoderate rate that your fondness shall never distinguish itself enough to be taken notice of. If ever you seem to love too much, it must be only when I can't love enough.   540

ANGELICA

Have a care of large promises; you know you are apt to run more in debt than you are able to pay.

VALENTINE

Therefore I yield my body as your prisoner, and make your best on't.

SCANDAL

The music stays for you.   545

Dance

Well, madam, you have done exemplary justice in punishing an inhuman father, and rewarding a faithful lover; but there is a third good work which I, in particular, must thank you for: I was an infidel to your sex, and you have converted me. For now I am convinced that all women are not like fortune,   550 blind in bestowing favours, either on those who do not merit, or who do not want 'em.

ANGELICA

'Tis an unreasonable accusation that you lay upon our sex: you tax us with injustice, only to cover your own want of merit. You would all have the reward of love, but few have   555 the constancy to stay till it becomes your due. Men are generally hypocrites and infidels; they pretend to worship, but have neither zeal nor faith. How few, like Valentine, would persevere even unto martyrdom, and sacrifice their interest to their constancy! In admiring me, you misplace   560 the novelty.

> The miracle today is that we find
> A lover true: not that a woman's kind.

Exeunt Omnes

541 *large promises* (promises Q3, 4, Ww)
542 *able to pay* (able pay Q1)
559 *unto* (to Ww)

EPILOGUE

Spoken at the opening of the New House,
by Mrs. Bracegirdle

Sure Providence at first designed this place
To be the player's refuge in distress;
For still in every storm they all run hither,
As to a shed that shields 'em from the weather.
But thinking of this change which last befell us,   5
It's like what I have heard our poets tell us:
For when behind our scenes their suits are pleading,
To help their love, sometimes they show their reading;
And wanting ready cash to pay for hearts,
They top their learning on us, and their parts.   10
Once of philosophers they told us stories,
Whom, as I think they called—Py—Pythagories,
I'm sure 'tis some such Latin name they give 'em,
And we, who know no better, must believe 'em.
Now to these men (say they) such souls were given,   15
That after death ne'er went to hell, nor heaven,
But lived, I know not how, in beasts; and then,
When many years were past, in men again.
Methinks we players resemble such a soul,
That does from bodies, we from houses stroll.   20
Thus Aristotle's soul, of old that was,
May now be damned to animate an ass;
Or in this very house, for aught we know,
Is doing painful penance in some beau;
And this our audience, which did once resort   25
To shining theatres to see our sport,
Now find us tossed into a tennis court.
These walls but t'other day were filled with noise
Of roaring gamesters, and your Damme Boys.
Then bounding balls and racquets they encompassed,   30
And now they're filled with jests, and flights, and bombast!
I vow I don't much like this transmigration,
Strolling from place to place, by circulation.

25 *this* (thus Ww)

---

27 *tennis court*. The new Lincoln's Inn Theatre was in a converted tennis
court.

Grant heaven, we don't return to our first station.
I know not what these think, but for my part,   35
I can't reflect without an aching heart,
How we should end in our original, a cart.
But we can't fear, since you're so good to save us,
That you have only set us up, to leave us.
Thus from the past, we hope for future grace;   40
I beg it—
And some here know I have a begging face.
Then pray continue this your kind behaviour,
For a clear stage won't do, without your favour.

---

37 *cart.* i) The cart on which plays were first performed, and possibly
   ii) the cart which conveyed criminals to be hanged.

The Provoked Wife

━━━∾∿∿∿∿◯∿∿∿∿∾━━━

JOHN VANBRUGH

Edited by
JAMES L. SMITH

ABBREVIATIONS

The Provoked Wife
Dobrée   Bonamy Dobrée and GeoffreyWebb, ed., *The Complete Works of Sir John Vanbrugh*, 4 vols. (1927–28).
P   Collected edition of Vanbrugh's *Plays*, 1719.
Q1   First quarto of 1697.
Q2   Second quarto of 1698.
Q3   Third quarto of 1709.
Zimansky Curt A. Zimansky, ed., *The Provoked Wife* (1969).

Appendix A
D   Dublin edition of 1743.
L   London edition of Vanbrugh's *Plays*, 1759.

Appendix B
L   London edition of Vanbrugh's *Plays*, 1776.
SM   *A Scotch Medley*, undated broadside.

THE
Provok'd Wife:
A
COMEDY,

As it is Acted at the

𝕹𝖊𝖜 𝕿𝖍𝖊𝖆𝖙𝖗𝖊,

IN

Little Lincolns-Inn-Fields.

By the Author of a New Comedy call'd the *Relapse*, or *Virtue in Danger.*

LONDON,

Printed by *J. O.* for *R. Wellington*, at the Lute in St. *Paul's* Church Yard, and *Sam. Briscoe* in *Covent-Garden* 1697.

DRAMATIS PERSONAE

CONSTANT	*Mr Verbruggen*	
HEARTFREE	*Mr Hudson*	
SIR JOHN BRUTE	*Mr Betterton*	
TREBLE, *a singing master*	*Mr Bowman*	
RASOR, *valet de chambre to Sir John Brute*	*Mr Bowen*	5
JUSTICE OF THE PEACE	*Mr Bright*	
LORD RAKE } *companions to Sir John*		
COLONEL BULLY } *Brute*		
CONSTABLE *and* WATCH		
[JO, *a porter*		10
TAILOR		
PAGE *at* 'The Blue Posts'		
FOOTMEN, SERVANTS, *and* DRINKING COMPANIONS *to Lord Rake*]		

LADY BRUTE	*Mrs Barry*	
BELLINDA, *her niece*	*Mrs Bracegirdle*	15
LADY FANCYFULL	*Mrs Bowman*	
MADAMOISELLE	*Mrs Willis*	
CORNET *and* PIPE, *servants to Lady Fancyfull*		
[LOVEWELL, *waiting woman to Lady Brute*]		

17 MADAMOISELLE so spelt in all English editions before 1743

---

19 *waiting woman* A servant who fetches needlework (III.i.14) is more
likely to be a maid than a valet.

PROLOGUE

to *The Provoked Wife*, spoke by Mistress Bracegirdle

Since 'tis the intent and business of the stage,
To copy out the follies of the age;
To hold to every man a faithful glass,
And show him of what species he's an ass;
I hope the next that teaches in the school,   5
Will show our author he's a scribbling fool.
And that the satire may be sure to bite,
Kind heaven, inspire some venomed priest to write,
And grant some ugly lady may indite.
For I would have him lashed, by heavens! I would,   10
Till his presumption swam away in blood.
Three plays at once proclaims a face of brass,
No matter what they are; that's not the case;
To write three plays, e'en that's to be an ass.
But what I least forgive, he knows it too,   15
For to his cost he lately has known you.
Experience shows, to many a writer's smart,
You hold a court where mercy ne'er had part;
So much of the old serpent's sting you have,
You love to damn, as heaven delights to save.   20
In foreign parts, let a bold volunteer
For public good upon the stage appear,
He meets ten thousand smiles to dissipate his fear.
All tickle on th'adventuring young beginner,
And only scourge th'incorrigible sinner;   25
They touch indeed his faults, but with a hand
So gentle, that his merit still may stand;
Kindly they buoy the follies of his pen,
That he may shun 'em when he writes again.

24 *th'* Q1 (the Q2–3, P)

---

8 *venomed priest* prophetic; Jeremy Collier attacked Vanbrugh in *A Short
   View of the Immorality and Profaneness of the English Stage* (1698)
12 *Three . . . once* Preceding *The Provoked Wife* were *The Relapse* and *I
   Aesop*, acted in November and December 1696, respectively. Vanbrugh
   does not count *II Aesop*, a theatrical squib in three scenes, acted in
   March 1697.
16 *I Aesop* was coolly received.

But 'tis not so in this good-natured town;   30
All's one, an ox, a poet, or a crown:
Old England's play was always knocking down.

THE PROVOKED WIFE

Act I, Scene i

SIR JOHN BRUTE'S *House*
Enter SIR JOHN, *solus*

[SIR JOHN]
What cloying meat is love—when matrimony's the sauce to
it! Two years' marriage has debauched my five senses.
Everything I see, everything I hear, everything I feel, everything I smell, and everything I taste—methinks has wife
in't. No boy was ever so weary of his tutor, no girl of her   5
bib, no nun of doing penance, nor old maid of being chaste,
as I am of being married. Sure, there's a secret curse entailed upon the very name of wife. My lady is a young lady,
a fine lady, a witty lady, a virtuous lady—and yet I hate her.
There is but one thing on earth I loathe beyond her; that's   10
fighting. Would my courage come up but to a fourth part of
my ill nature, I'd stand buff to her relations and thrust her
out of doors. But marriage has sunk me down to such an
ebb of resolution, I dare not draw my sword, though even to
get rid of my wife. But here she comes.   15

Enter LADY BRUTE

LADY BRUTE
Do you dine at home today, Sir John?
SIR JOHN
Why, do you expect I should tell you what I don't know
myself?
LADY BRUTE
I thought there was no harm in asking you.
SIR JOHN
If thinking wrong were an excuse for impertinence, women   20
might be justified in most things they say or do.
LADY BRUTE
I'm sorry I have said anything to displease you.

6 *nor* Q1–3 (or P)
12 *stand buff to* stand firm against
22 *I have* Q1–2 (I've Q3, P)

469

SIR JOHN
> Sorrow for things past is of as little importance to me, as my
> dining at home or abroad ought to be to you.

LADY BRUTE
> My enquiry was only that I might have provided what you   25
> liked.

SIR JOHN
> Six to four you had been in the wrong there again; for what
> I liked yesterday I don't like today, and what I like today 'tis
> odds I mayn't like tomorrow.

LADY BRUTE
> But if I had asked you what you liked?   30

SIR JOHN
> Why, then there would have been more asking about it than
> the thing was worth.

LADY BRUTE
> I wish I did but know how I might please you.

SIR JOHN
> Ay, but that sort of knowledge is not a wife's talent.

LADY BRUTE
> Whate'er my talent is, I'm sure my will has ever been to   35
> make you easy.

SIR JOHN
> If women were to have their wills, the world would be finely
> governed!

LADY BRUTE
> What reason have I given you to use me as you do of late? It
> once was otherwise; you married me for love.   40

SIR JOHN
> And you me for money; so you have your reward, and I have
> mine.

LADY BRUTE
> What is it that disturbs you?

SIR JOHN
> A parson.

LADY BRUTE
> Why, what has he done to you?   45

SIR JOHN
> He has married me.   (*Exit* SIR JOHN)

LADY BRUTE (*Sola*)
> The devil's in the fellow, I think!—I was told before I

---

31 *have been* Q1–3 (be P)
32 *was* Q1–3 (is P)
47 s.p. LADY BRUTE (*Sola*) Q2–3, P (*Enter Lady* Brute, *sola* Q1)

married him that thus 'twould be. But I thought I had
charms enough to govern him, and that where there was an
estate a woman must needs be happy; so my vanity has   50
deceived me, and my ambition has made me uneasy. But
some comfort still; if one would be revenged of him, these
are good times; a woman may have a gallant and a separate
maintenance too. —The surly puppy!—Yet he's a fool for't,
for hitherto he has been no monster. But who knows how   55
far he may provoke me? I never loved him, yet I have been
ever true to him; and that, in spite of all the attacks of art
and nature upon a poor weak woman's heart in favour of
a tempting lover. Methinks so noble a defence as I have
made should be rewarded with a better usage.—Or who can   60
tell?—Perhaps a good part of what I suffer from my husband
may be a judgment upon me for my cruelty to my lover.—
Lord, with what pleasure could I indulge that thought,
were there but a possibility of finding arguments to make it
good!—And how do I know but there may? Let me see.—   65
What opposes? My matrimonial vow.—Why, what did I
vow? I think I promised to be true to my husband. Well;
and he promised to be kind to me. But he han't kept his
word.—Why then, I'm absolved from mine. Ay, that seems
clear to me. The argument's good between the king and the   70
people, why not between the husband and the wife?—Oh,
but that condition was not expressed.—No matter; 'twas
understood. Well, by all I see, if I argue the matter a little
longer with myself, I shan't find so many bugbears in the
way as I thought I should. Lord, what fine notions of   75
virtue do we women take up upon the credit of old foolish
philosophers! Virtue's its own reward, virtue's this, virtue's
that—virtue's an ass, and a gallant's worth forty on't.

Enter BELLINDA

Good morrow, dear cousin.

BELLINDA

Good morrow, madam; you look pleased this morning.   80

LADY BRUTE

I am so.

55 *monster* cuckold

53–4 *gallant ... too* An adulteress legally separated from her husband's
    'bed and board' was entitled to alimony, but could not marry her
    gàllant.

70–1 *The ... people* Lady Brute recalls the social contract realized in the
    constitutional settlements of 1689; if James II violates his coronation
    vows, the people are absolved from their oath of allegiance.

BELLINDA
With what, pray?

LADY BRUTE
With my husband.

BELLINDA
Drown husbands! for yours is a provoking fellow. As he
went out just now, I prayed him to tell me what time of day   85
'twas; and he asked me if I took him for the church clock,
that was obliged to tell all the parish.

LADY BRUTE
He has been saying some good obliging things to me too. In
short, Bellinda, he has used me so barbarously of late that I
could almost resolve to play the downright wife—and   90
cuckold him.

BELLINDA
That would be downright indeed.

LADY BRUTE
Why, after all, there's more to be said for't than you'd
imagine, child. I know, according to the strict statute law of
religion, I should do wrong; but if there were a Court of   95
Chancery in heaven, I'm sure I should cast him.

BELLINDA
If there were a House of Lords you might.

LADY BRUTE
In either I should infallibly carry my cause. Why, he is the
first aggressor. Not I.

BELLINDA
Ay, but you know, we must return good for evil.   100

LADY BRUTE
That may be a mistake in the translation.—Prithee be of my
opinion, Bellinda, for I'm positive I'm in the right; and if
you'll keep up the prerogative of a woman, you'll likewise
be positive you are in the right, whenever you do anything
you have a mind to. But I shall play the fool and jest on, till 105
I make you begin to think I'm in earnest.

---

96 *cast him* defeat him in an action at law

95–6 *Court of Chancery* an equity court moderating the rigour of the law
      by reference to general principles of justice, and giving relief in cases
      where the common-law courts provide no remedy; it did not usually
      deal with divorce
97 *House of Lords* A complete divorce, leaving both partners free to
      remarry, could be obtained only by passing a private bill through
      Parliament and up to the royal assent; the first such divorce was granted
      in April 1698.

BELLINDA

I shan't take the liberty, madam, to think of anything that
you desire to keep a secret from me.

LADY BRUTE

Alas, my dear, I have no secrets. My heart could never yet
confine my tongue.   110

BELLINDA

Your eyes, you mean; for I am sure I have seen them
gadding, when your tongue has been locked up safe enough.

LADY BRUTE

My eyes gadding! Prithee after who, child?

BELLINDA

Why, after one that thinks you hate him, as much as I know
you love him.   115

LADY BRUTE

Constant, you mean.

BELLINDA

I do so.

LADY BRUTE

Lord, what should put such a thing into your head?

BELLINDA

That which puts things into most people's heads, observation.   120

LADY BRUTE

Why, what have you observed, in the name of wonder?

BELLINDA

I have observed you blush when you meet him, force yourself away from him, and then be out of humour with
everything about you. In a word, never was poor creature
so spurred on by desire, and so reined in with fear!   125

LADY BRUTE

How strong is fancy!

BELLINDA

How weak is woman!

LADY BRUTE

Prithee, niece, have a better opinion of your aunt's inclinations.

BELLINDA

Dear aunt, have a better opinion of your niece's under-   130
standing.

LADY BRUTE

You'll make me angry.

BELLINDA
You'll make me laugh.

LADY BRUTE
Then you are resolved to persist?

BELLINDA
Positively.   135

LADY BRUTE
And all I can say—

BELLINDA
Will signify nothing.

LADY BRUTE
Though I should swear 'twere false—

BELLINDA
I should think it true.

LADY BRUTE
Then let us both forgive (*Kissing her*), for we have both   140
offended: I in making a secret, you in discovering it.

BELLINDA
Good nature may do much; but you have more reason to
forgive one, than I have to pardon t'other.

LADY BRUTE
'Tis true, Bellinda, you have given me so many proofs of
your friendship, that my reserve has been indeed a crime.   145
But that you may more easily forgive me, remember, child,
that when our nature prompts us to a thing our honour and
religion have forbid us, we would (were't possible) conceal,
even from the soul itself, the knowledge of the body's
weakness.   150

BELLINDA
Well, I hope, to make your friend amends, you'll hide
nothing from her for the future, though the body should
still grow weaker and weaker.

LADY BRUTE
No, from this moment I have no more reserve; and for a
proof of my repentance, I own, Bellinda, I'm in danger.   155
Merit and wit assault me from without; nature and love
solicit me within; my husband's barbarous usage piques me
to revenge; and Satan, catching at the fair occasion, throws
in my way that vengeance which, of all vengeance, pleases
women best.   160

BELLINDA
'Tis well Constant don't know the weakness of the forti-
fications; for o'my conscience he'd soon come on to the
assault.

LADY BRUTE

Ay, and I'm afraid carry the town too. But whatever you
may have observed, I have dissembled so well as to keep   165
him ignorant. So you see I'm no coquette, Bellinda; and if
you'll follow my advice you'll never be one neither. 'Tis
true, coquetry is one of the main ingredients in the natural
composition of a woman, and I, as well as others, could be
well enough pleased to see a crowd of young fellows, ogling   170
and glancing and watching all occasions to do forty foolish
officious things; nay, should some of 'em push on, even to
hanging or drowning. Why—faith—if I should let pure
woman alone, I should e'en be but too well pleased with't.

BELLINDA

I'll swear 'twould tickle me strangely.   175

LADY BRUTE

But, after all, 'tis a vicious practice in us, to give the least
encouragement but where we design to come to a conclusion. For 'tis an unreasonable thing, to engage a man in a
disease which we beforehand resolve we never will apply a
cure to.   180

BELLINDA

'Tis true; but then a woman must abandon one of the
supreme blessings of her life. For I am fully convinced, no
man has half that pleasure in possessing a mistress, as a
woman has in jilting a gallant.

LADY BRUTE

The happiest woman then on earth must be our neighbour.   185

BELLINDA

Oh, the impertinent composition! She has vanity and affectation enough to make her a ridiculous original, in spite of all
that art and nature ever furnished to any of her sex before
her.

LADY BRUTE

She concludes all men her captives; and whatever course   190
they take, it serves to confirm her in that opinion.

BELLINDA

If they shun her, she thinks 'tis modesty, and takes it for a
proof of their passion.

167 *you'll follow* Q1–3 (you follow P)
174 *woman* Q1–3 (women P)
186 *impertinent* incongruous, absurd
187 *original* eccentric

LADY BRUTE
And if they are rude to her, 'tis conduct, and done to prevent
town-talk.   195

BELLINDA
When her folly makes 'em laugh, she thinks they are pleased
with her wit.

LADY BRUTE
And when her impertinence makes 'em dull, concludes they
are jealous of her favours.

BELLINDA
All their actions and their words, she takes for granted, aim   200
at her.

LADY BRUTE
And pities all other women, because she thinks they envy
her.

BELLINDA
Pray, out of pity to ourselves, let us find a better subject, for
I am weary of this. Do you think your husband inclined to   205
jealousy?

LADY BRUTE
Oh, no; he does not love me well enough for that. Lord,
how wrong men's maxims are! They are seldom jealous of
their wives, unless they are very fond of 'em; whereas they
ought to consider the women's inclinations, for there   210
depends their fate. Well, men may talk; but they are not so
wise as we—that's certain.

BELLINDA
At least in our affairs.

LADY BRUTE
Nay, I believe we should outdo 'em in the business of the
state, too; for methinks they do and undo, and make but   215
mad work on't.

BELLINDA
Why then don't we get into the intrigues of government as
well as they?

LADY BRUTE
Because we have intrigues of our own that make us more
sport, child. And so let's in and consider of 'em. (*Exeunt*)   220

194 *conduct* discretion
205 *I am* Q1–2 (I'm Q3, P)
210 *women's* Q2–3, P (woman's Q1)
216 *mad* Q1 (bad Q2–3, P)

Act I, Scene ii

A dressing room
Enter LADY FANCYFULL, MADAMOISELLE, *and* CORNET

LADY FANCYFULL
How do I look this morning?
CORNET
Your ladyship looks very ill, truly.
LADY FANCYFULL
Lard, how ill-natured thou art, Cornet, to tell me so, though
the thing should be true. Don't you know that I have
humility enough to be but too easily out of conceit with   5
myself? Hold the glass; I dare swear that will have more
manners than you have.—Madamoiselle, let me have your
opinion too.
MADAMOISELLE
My opinion pe, matam, dat your ladyship never look so well
in your life.   10
LADY FANCYFULL
Well, the French are the prettiest obliging people; they say
the most acceptable, well-mannered things—and never
flatter.
MADAMOISELLE
Your ladyship say great justice inteed.
LADY FANCYFULL
Nay, everything's just in my house but Cornet. The very   15
looking-glass gives her the *démenti*. (*Looking affectedly in the
glass*) But I'm almost afraid it flatters me, it makes me look
so very engaging.
MADAMOISELLE
Inteed, matam, your face pe hansomer den all de looking-
glass in tee world, *croyez-moi*!   20
LADY FANCYFULL
But is it possible my eyes can be so languishing—and so
very full of fire?
MADAMOISELLE
Matam, if de glass was burning-glass, I believe your eyes
set de fire in de house.
LADY FANCYFULL
You may take that night-gown, Madamoiselle.—Get out of   25

16 *démenti* lie
20 *croyez-moi*! believe me!

the room, Cornet! I can't endure you. (*Exit* CORNET) This
wench, methinks, does look so unsufferably ugly.

MADAMOISELLE

Everyting look ugly, matam, dat stand by your latiship.

LADY FANCYFULL

No, really, Madamoiselle—methinks you look mighty
pretty.   30

MADAMOISELLE

Ah, matam! de moon have no *éclat* ven de sun appear.

LADY FANCYFULL

O pretty expression! Have you ever been in love, Madamoiselle?

MADAMOISELLE (*Sighing*)

Oui, matam.

LADY FANCYFULL

And were you beloved again?   35

MADAMOISELLE (*Sighing*)

No, matam.

LADY FANCYFULL

O ye gods! What an unfortunate creature should I be in such
a case! But nature has made me nice for my own defence:
I'm nice, strangely nice, Madamoiselle; I believe were the
merit of whole mankind bestowed upon one single person,   40
I should still think the fellow wanted something to make
it worth my while to take notice of him. And yet I could
love—nay, fondly love—were it possible to have a thing
made on purpose for me: for I'm not cruel, Madamoiselle,
I'm only nice.   45

MADAMOISELLE

Ah, matam, I wish I was fine gentleman for your sake. I do
all de ting in de world to get leetel way into your heart. I
make song, I make verse, I give you de serenade, I give great
many present to Madamoiselle; I no eat, I no sleep, I be
lean, I be mad, I hang myself, I drown myself. *Ah, ma chère* 50
dame, que je vous aimerais!   (*Embracing her*)

LADY FANCYFULL

Well, the French have strange obliging ways with 'em; you
may take those two pair of gloves, Madamoiselle.

---

26 s.d. (*Exit* CORNET) Q1 prints this after Lady Fancyfull's line (*omitted*
Q2-3, P)
31 *éclat* brightness
35 *you beloved* Q2-3, P (you, beloved Q1) Dobrée thinks the pause
intentional
50-1 *Ah . . . aimerais!* Ah, my dear lady, how I would love you!

MADAMOISELLE
Me humbly tanke my sweet lady.

Enter CORNET

CORNET
Madam, here's a letter for your ladyship by the penny-post.   55
                                        [*Exit*]

LADY FANCYFULL
Some new conquest, I'll warrant you. For, without vanity,
I looked extremely clear last night, when I went to the
Park.—Oh, agreeable! Here's a new song made of me. And
ready set, too! Oh, thou welcome thing! (*Kissing it*)—Call
Pipe hither; she shall sing it instantly.   60

Enter PIPE

Here, sing me this new song, Pipe.

SONG
I

[PIPE]   Fly, fly, you happy shepherds, fly,
                   Avoid Philira's charms;
               The rigour of her heart denies
                   The heaven that's in her arms.   65
               Ne'er hope to gaze, and then retire,
                   Nor yielding, to be blest:
               Nature, who formed her eyes of fire,
                   Of ice composed her breast.
II
               Yet, lovely maid, this once believe   70
                   A slave, whose zeal you move;
               The gods, alas, your youth deceive,
                   Their heaven consists in love.
               In spite of all the thanks you owe,
                   You may reproach 'em this: 75
               That where they did their form bestow
                   They have denied their bliss.   [*Exit*]

LADY FANCYFULL
Well, there may be faults, Madamoiselle, but the design is so

57 *clear* of fresh complexion, blooming
73 *Their* Q1, P (The Q2–3)

55 *penny-post* collected and delivered every two hours in town
58 *Park* St James's Park, a fashionable promenade and lovers' rendezvous

very obliging 'twould be a matchless ingratitude in me to
discover 'em.   80

MADAMOISELLE
Ma foi, matam, I tink de gentelman's song tell you de trute.
If you never love, you never be happy.—*Ah, que j'aime
l'amour, moi!*

Enter SERVANT, *with another letter*

SERVANT
Madam, here's another letter for your ladyship.   [*Exit*]

LADY FANCYFULL
'Tis thus I am importuned every morning, Madamoiselle.   85
Pray, how do the French ladies when they are thus
accablées?

MADAMOISELLE
Matam, dey never complain. *Au contraire!* When one Frense
laty have got hundred lover, den she do all she can—to get
hundred more.   90

LADY FANCYFULL
Well, strike me dead, I think they have *le goût bon*! For 'tis an
unutterable pleasure to be adored by all the men and envied
by all the women.—Yet I'll swear I'm concerned at the
torture I give 'em. Lard, why was I formed to make the
whole creation uneasy?—But let me read my letter. (*Reads*)   95
'If you have a mind to hear of your faults, instead of being
praised for your virtues, take the pains to walk in the Green
Walk in St James's with your woman an hour hence.
You'll there meet one who hates you for some things, as he
could love you for others, and therefore is willing to en-   100
deavour your reformation.—If you come to the place I
mention, you'll know who I am; if you don't, you never
shall: so take your choice'.—This is strangely familiar,
Madamoiselle; now have I a provoking fancy to know who
this impudent fellow is.   105

MADAMOISELLE
Den take your scarf and your mask, and go to de rendezvous. De Frense laty do *justement comme ça*.

81 *Ma foi* Upon my soul
82-3 *Ah . . . moi!* Ah, I like love, I do!
87 *accablées* overwhelmed, snowed under
88 *Au contraire!* On the contrary!
91 *le goût bon* good taste
107 *justement comme ça* exactly like that

97-8 *Green Walk* a long avenue of lime trees ending in a knot of elms

LADY FANCYFULL
  Rendezvous! What, rendezvous with a man, Madamoiselle!

MADAMOISELLE
  Eh, pourquoi non?

LADY FANCYFULL
  What, and a man perhaps I never saw in my life!   110

MADAMOISELLE
  Tant mieux; c'est donc quelque chose de nouveau.

LADY FANCYFULL
  Why, how do I know what designs he may have? He may
intend to ravish me, for aught I know.

MADAMOISELLE
  Ravish?—Bagatelle! I would fain see one impudent rogue
ravish Madamoiselle! *Oui, je le voudrais.*   115

LADY FANCUFULL
  Oh, but my reputation, Madamoiselle, my reputation! *Ah,
ma chère réputation!*

MADAMOISELLE
  Matam, *quand on l'a une fois perdue, on n'en est plus embarrassée.*

LADY FANCYFULL
  Fie, Madamoiselle, fie! Reputation is a jewel.   120

MADAMOISELLE
  —*Qui coûte bien cher*, matam.

LADY FANCYFULL
  Why, sure you would not sacrifice your honour to your
pleasure?

MADAMOISELLE
  Je suis philosophe.

LADY FANCYFULL
  Bless me, how you talk! Why, what if honour be a burden, 125
Madamoiselle, must it not be borne?

---

109 *Eh, pourquoi non?* Well, why not?
111 *Tant ... nouveau* All the better; then it will be an entirely new
experience
115 *Oui, je le voudrais* Yes, I would indeed
116–17 *Ah ... réputation!* Ah, my dear reputation!
118–19 *quand ... embarrassée* once you have lost it, you no longer have it
to worry about
121 *cher* ed. (chère Q1–3, P, but *jewel*, i.e. *bijou* or *joyau*, is masculine)
121 *Qui ... cher* And a very expensive one
124 *Je suis philosophe* I am resigned to the inevitable

MADAMOISELLE

*Chacun à sa façon. Quand quelque chose m'incommode, moi, je
m'en défais, vite.*

LADY FANCYFULL

Get you gone, you little naughty Frenchwoman you! I vow
and swear I must turn you out of doors, if you talk thus.   130

MADAMOISELLE

Turn me out of doors! Turn yourself out of doors and go
see what de gentleman have to say to you!—*Tenez.*—(*Giving
her her things hastily*) *Voilà votre écharpe, voilà votre coiffe,
voilà votre masque, voilà tout!*—(*Calling within*) Hey, Mer-
cure! *Coquin*, call one chair for matam, and one oder for me.   135
Va-t'en vite!—(*Turning to her lady, and helping her on hastily
with her things*) *Allons*, matam; *dépêchez-vous donc. Mon
Dieu, quels scrupules!*

LADY FANCYFULL

Well, for once, Madamoiselle, I'll follow your advice, out
of the intemperate desire I have to know who this ill-bred   140
fellow is. But I have too much *délicatesse* to make a practice
on it.

MADAMOISELLE

*Belle chose vraiment que la délicatesse, lors qu'il s'agit de se
divertir!—Ah, çà!—Vous voilà équipée; partons.—Hé bien!—
qu'avez vous donc?*   145

LADY FANCYFULL

J'ai peur.

MADAMOISELLE

Je n'en ai point, moi.

127–8 *Chacun . . . vite* Each in his own way. When something is a nuisance
to me, I get rid of it, quickly.
132–4 *Tenez . . . tout!* There . . . Here's your scarf, here's your hood, here's
your mask. That's everything!
135 *Coquin* You rascal
136–8 *Va-t'en . . . scrupules!* Go quickly! . . . Come along, matam; make
haste. Heavens, what scruples!
138 *quels* ed. (quelles Q1–3, P)
141 *délicatesse* delicacy
143–7 *Belle . . . moi* 'A fine thing, delicacy, when you are out to enjoy
yourself!—Now then!—You're all dressed up; let's go.—Well, what's
the matter?' 'I'm frightened'. 'I'm not'.

---

135 *Coquin* may be a proper name, for Q1 does not distinguish French
words by italics; but one man can call two sedan-chairs by himself,
particularly when he is named after the Roman god of roads and rascals,
or *coquins*.

LADY FANCYFULL
   I dare not go.

MADAMOISELLE
   Demeurez donc.

LADY FANCYFULL
   Je suis poltronne.   150

MADAMOISELLE
   Tant pis pour vous.

LADY FANCYFULL
   Curiosity's a wicked devil.

MADAMOISELLE
   C'est une charmante sainte.

LADY FANCYFULL
   It ruined our first parents.

MADAMOISELLE
   Elle a bien diverti leurs enfants.   155

LADY FANCYFULL
   L'honneur est contre.

MADAMOISELLE
   Le plaisir est pour.

LADY FANCYFULL
   Must I then go?

MADAMOISELLE
   Must you go?—Must you eat, must you drink, must you
   sleep, must you live? De nature bid you do one; de nature   160
   bid you do t'oder. *Vous me ferez enrager!*

LADY FANCYFULL
   But when reason corrects nature, Madamoiselle?

MADAMOISELLE
   Elle est donc bien insolente; c'est sa soeur aînée.

LADY FANCYFULL
   Do you then prefer your nature to your reason, Madamoiselle?   165

MADAMOISELLE
   Oui-dà!

LADY FANCYFULL
   Pourquoi?

149–51 *Demeurez . . . vous* 'Don't go then'. 'I'm a coward'. 'The more fool
    you'.
153 *C'est . . . sainte* It's a charming saint
155–7 *Elle . . . pour* 'It has given a lot of fun to their children'. 'Honour is
    against it'. 'Pleasure is for it'.
161 *Vous . . . enrager!* You are driving me mad!
163 *Elle . . . aînée* Then she presumes too much; nature is her elder sister
166–7 *Oui-dà! Pourquoi?* 'Yes indeed!' 'Why?'

MADAMOISELLE
Because my nature make me merry, my reason make me sad.
LADY FANCYFULL
Ah, la méchante Française!
MADAMOISELLE
Ah, la belle Anglaise!   ([*Exit,*] *forcing her lady off*)   170

Act II, Scene i

St James's Park
Enter LADY FANCYFULL *and* MADAMOISELLE

LADY FANCYFULL
Well, I vow, Madamoiselle, I'm strangely impatient to
know who this confident fellow is.

Enter HEARTFREE

Look, there's Heartfree. But sure it can't be him; he's a
professed woman-hater. Yet who knows what my wicked
eyes may have done?   5
MADAMOISELLE
Il nous approche, madame.
LADY FANCYFULL
Yes, 'tis he; now will he be most intolerably cavalier, though
he should be in love with me.
HEARTFREE
Madam, I'm your humble servant; I perceive you have more
humility and good nature than I thought you had.   10
LADY FANCYFULL
What you attribute to humility and good nature, sir, may
perhaps be only due to curiosity. I had a mind to know who
'twas had ill manners enough to write that letter.
                                      (*Throwing him his letter*)
HEARTFREE
Well; and now, I hope, you are satisfied.
LADY FANCYFULL
I am so, sir; good-bye to ye.   [*Going*]   15

168 *sad* ed. (mad Q1–3, P)
169–70 *Ah . . . Anglaise!* 'Ah, this wicked Frenchwoman!' 'Ah, this beautiful
    Englishwoman!'
170 s.d. *forcing . . . off* Q1 follows this with 'The End of the first Act'.
  6 *madame* ed. (madam Q1–3, P)
  6 *Il . . . madame* He is approaching us, madam

HEARTFREE

Nay, hold there! though you have done your business, I han't done mine; by your ladyship's leave, we must have one moment's prattle together. Have you a mind to be the prettiest woman about town, or not?—How she stares upon me!—What! this passes for an impertinent question with you now, because you think you are so already.

LADY FANCYFULL

Pray, sir, let me ask you a question in my turn: by what right do you pretend to examine me?

HEARTFREE

By the same right that the strong govern the weak, because I have you in my power; for you cannot get so quickly to your coach but I shall have time enough to make you hear everything I have to say to you.

LADY FANCYFULL

These are strange liberties you take, Mr Heartfree!

HEARTFREE

They are so, madam, but there's no help for it; for know, that I have a design upon you.

LADY FANCYFULL

Upon me, sir!

HEARTFREE

Yes; and one that will turn to your glory and my comfort, if you will but be a little wiser than you use to be.

LADY FANCYFULL

Very well, sir.

HEARTFREE

Let me see.—Your vanity, madam, I take to be about some eight degrees higher than any woman's in the town, let t'other be who she will; and my indifference is naturally about the same pitch. Now, could you find the way to turn this indifference into fire and flames, methinks your vanity ought to be satisfied; and this, perhaps, you might bring about upon pretty reasonable terms.

LADY FANCYFULL

And pray, at what rate would this indifference be bought off, if one should have so depraved an appetite to desire it?

HEARTFREE

Why, madam, to drive a Quaker's bargain and make but one word with you, if I do part with it, you must lay me down—your affectation.

44–5 *Quaker's . . . word* By trading at fixed prices Quakers reduced bargaining to a single word: yea or nay.

LADY FANCYFULL
>My affectation, sir!

HEARTFREE
>Why, I ask you nothing but what you may very well spare.

LADY FANCYFULL
>You grow rude, sir.—Come, Madamoiselle, 'tis high time
>to be gone.   50

MADAMOISELLE
>*Allons, allons, allons!*

HEARTFREE (*Stopping 'em*)
>Nay, you may as well stand still; for hear me you shall,
>walk which way you please.

LADY FANCYFULL
>What mean you, sir?

HEARTFREE
>I mean to tell you, that you are the most ungrateful woman   55
>upon earth.

LADY FANCYFULL
>Ungrateful! To who?

HEARTFREE
>To nature.

LADY FANCYFULL
>Why, what has nature done for me?

HEARTFREE
>What you have undone by art. It made you handsome; it   60
>gave you beauty to a miracle, a shape without a fault, wit
>enough to make 'em relish, and so turned you loose to your
>own discretion; which has made such work with you, that
>you are become the pity of our sex and the jest of your
>own. There is not a feature in your face but you have found   65
>the way to teach it some affected convulsion; your feet,
>your hands, your very fingers' ends, are directed never to
>move without some ridiculous air or other; and your
>language is a suitable trumpet, to draw people's eyes upon
>the raree-show.   70

MADAMOISELLE (*Aside*)
>*Est-ce qu'on fait l'amour en Angleterre comme ça?*

LADY FANCYFULL (*Aside*)
>Now could I cry for madness, but that I know he'd laugh at
>me for it.

51 *Allons, allons, allons!* Come along, come along, let's be off!
52 s.d. *'em* Q1–3 (them P)
71 *Est-ce . . . ça?* Is that how they pay court in England?

---

70 *raree-show* a peep-show hawked round the streets in a box

HEARTFREE

Now do you hate me for telling you the truth, but that's
because you don't believe it is so; for were you once con-   75
vinced of that, you'd reform for your own sake. But 'tis as
hard to persuade a woman to quit anything that makes her
ridiculous, as 'tis to prevail with a poet to see a fault in his
own play.

LADY FANCYFULL

Every circumstance of nice breeding must needs appear   80
ridiculous to one who has so natural an antipathy to good
manners.

HEARTFREE

But suppose I could find the means to convince you that
the whole world is of my opinion? and that those who flatter
and commend you do it to no other intent but to make you   85
persevere in your folly, that they may continue in their
mirth?

LADY FANCYFULL

Sir, though you and all that world you talk of should be so
impertinently officious as to think to persuade me I don't
know how to behave myself, I should still have charity   90
enough for my own understanding to believe myself in the
right, and all you in the wrong.

MADAMOISELLE

Le voilà mort! (*Exeunt* LADY FANCYFULL *and* MADAMOISELLE)

HEARTFREE (*Gazing after her*)

There her single clapper has published the sense of the
whole sex!—Well, this once I have endeavoured to wash   95
the blackamoor white; but henceforward I'll sooner undertake to teach sincerity to a courtier, generosity to an usurer,
honesty to a lawyer, nay, humility to a divine, than discretion to a woman I see has once set her heart upon playing
the fool.   100

Enter CONSTANT

'Morrow, Constant.

CONSTANT

Good morrow, Jack; what are you doing here this morning?

HEARTFREE

Doing! Guess, if thou canst.—Why, I have been endeavouring to persuade my Lady Fancyfull that she's the foolishest
woman about town.   105

93 *Le voilà mort!* That's done for him!
94 *clapper* tongue

CONSTANT

A pretty endeavour, truly!

HEARTFREE

I have told her, in as plain English as I could speak, both
what the town says of her and what I think of her. In short,
I have used her as an absolute king would do Magna Charta.

CONSTANT

And how does she take it?   110

HEARTFREE

As children do pills; bite 'em, but can't swallow 'em.

CONSTANT

But, prithee, what has put it in your head, of all mankind,
to turn reformer?

HEARTFREE

Why, one thing was, the morning hung upon my hands—I
did not know what to do with myself; and another was, that 115
as little as I care for women, I could not see with patience
one that heaven had taken such wondrous pains about, be
so very industrious to make herself the jack-pudding of the
creation.

CONSTANT

Well, now could I almost wish to see my cruel mistress   120
make the selfsame use of what heaven has done for her, that
so I might be cured of a disease that makes me so very
uneasy; for love, love is the devil, Heartfree.

HEARTFREE

And why do you let the devil govern you?

CONSTANT

Because I have more flesh and blood than grace and self-   125
denial. My dear, dear mistress!—'Sdeath! that so genteel a
woman should be a saint, when religion's out of fashion!

HEARTFREE

Nay, she's much in the wrong, truly; but who knows how
far time and good example may prevail?

112 *in* Q1–2 (into Q3, P)
118 *jack-pudding* laughing-stock

---

109 *as ... Charta* i.e., without respect; only constitutional monarchs
    honour charters setting down their people's rights
118 *jack-pudding* Jack Puddings were fairground drolls who 'commit such
    Blunders and Mistakes in every Step they take, and every Word they
    utter, as those who listen to them would be ashamed of' (the *Spectator*,
    no. 47, 24 April 1711).

CONSTANT

Oh, they have played their parts in vain already. 'Tis now   130
two years since that damned fellow her husband invited me
to his wedding; and there was the first time I saw that
charming woman, whom I have loved ever since more than
e'er a martyr did his soul; but she's cold, my friend, still
cold as the northern star.   135

HEARTFREE

So are all women by nature, which makes 'em so willing to
be warmed.

CONSTANT

Oh, don't profane the sex! Prithee think 'em all angels for
her sake, for she's virtuous even to a fault.

HEARTFREE

A lover's head is a good accountable thing truly! He adores   140
his mistress for being virtuous, and yet is very angry with
her because she won't be lewd.

CONSTANT

Well, the only relief I expect in my misery is to see thee
some day or other as deeply engaged as myself, which will
force me to be merry in the midst of all my misfortunes.   145

HEARTFREE

That day will never come, be assured, Ned. Not but that I
can pass a night with a woman, and for the time, perhaps,
make myself as good sport as you can do. Nay, I can court
a woman too, call her nymph, angel, goddess—what you
please. But here's the difference 'twixt you and I: I persuade   150
a woman she's an angel; she persuades you she's one.—
Prithee, let me tell you how I avoid falling in love; that
which serves me for prevention, may chance to serve you
for a cure.

CONSTANT

Well, use the ladies moderately then, and I'll hear you.   155

HEARTFREE

That using 'em moderately undoes us all; but I'll use 'em
justly, and that you ought to be satisfied with.—I always
consider a woman, not as the tailor, the shoemaker, the tire-
woman, the sempstress, and (which is more than all that)
the poet makes her; but I consider her as pure nature has   160

136 *'em* Q1–3 (them P)
138 *'em* Q1–3 (them P)
151 *she* Q1–2 (and she Q3, P)
158–9 *tire-woman* dressmaker
159 *and* (*which* Q3, P) (and which Q1–2)

contrived her, and that more strictly than I should have
done our old grandmother Eve, had I seen her naked in the
garden; for I consider her turned inside out. Her heart well
examined, I find there pride, vanity, covetousness, indiscretion, but above all things—malice: plots eternally   165
a-forging to destroy one another's reputations, and as
honestly to charge the levity of men's tongues with the
scandal; hourly debates how to make poor gentlemen in love
with 'em, with no other intent but to use 'em like dogs
when they have done; a constant desire of doing more   170
mischief, and an everlasting war waged against truth and
good nature.

CONSTANT
Very well, sir; an admirable composition truly!

HEARTFREE
Then for her outside, I consider it merely as an outside;
she has a thin tiffany covering over just such stuff as you and   175
I are made on. As for her motion, her mien, her airs, and all
those tricks, I know they affect you mightily. If you should
see your mistress at a coronation, dragging her peacock's
train with all her state and insolence about her, 'twould
strike you with all the awful thoughts that heaven itself   180
could pretend to from you; whereas I turn the whole matter
into a jest, and suppose her strutting in the selfsame stately
manner, with nothing on but her stays and her under scanty
quilted petticoat.

CONSTANT
Hold thy profane tongue! for I'll hear no more.   185

HEARTFREE
What, you'll love on, then?

CONSTANT
Yes, to eternity.

HEARTFREE
Yet you have no hopes at all?

CONSTANT
None.

HEARTFREE
Nay, the resolution may be discreet enough; perhaps you   190
have found out some new philosophy—that love's like
virtue, its own reward: so you and your mistress will be as
well content at a distance, as others that have less learning
are in coming together.

---

175 *tiffany* a kind of transparent silk
183–4 *under . . . petticoat* a short padded underskirt of coarse cloth

CONSTANT

    No; but if she should prove kind at last, my dear Heartfree! 195
(Embracing him)

HEARTFREE

    Nay, prithee, don't take me for your mistress, for lovers
are very troublesome.

CONSTANT

    Well, who knows what time may do?

HEARTFREE

    —And just now he was sure time could do nothing!

CONSTANT

    Yet not one kind glance in two years is somewhat strange. 200

HEARTFREE

    Not strange at all: she don't like you, that's all the business.

CONSTANT

    Prithee don't distract me!

HEARTFREE

    Nay, you are a good handsome young fellow; she might use
you better. Come, will you go see her? Perhaps she may
have changed her mind; there's some hopes as long as she's 205
a woman.

CONSTANT

    Oh, 'tis in vain to visit her! Sometimes to get a sight of her I
visit that beast her husband, but she certainly finds some
pretence to quit the room as soon as I enter.

HEARTFREE

    It's much she don't tell him you have made love to her, too, 210
for that's another good-natured thing usual amongst women,
in which they have several ends. Sometimes 'tis to recommend their virtue, that they may be lewd with the greater
security. Sometimes 'tis to make their husbands fight, in
hopes they may be killed when their affairs require it should 215
be so. But most commonly 'tis to engage two men in a
quarrel, that they may have the credit of being fought for;
and if the lover's killed in the business, they cry 'Poor
fellow! he had ill luck'—and so they go to cards.

CONSTANT

    Thy injuries to women are not to be forgiven. Look to't, if 220
ever thou dost fall into their hands—

HEARTFREE

    They can't use me worse than they do you, that speak well
of 'em.—O ho! here comes the knight.

Enter SIR JOHN BRUTE

Your humble servant, Sir John.

SIR JOHN
　Servant, sir.   225
HEARTFREE
　How does all your family?
SIR JOHN
　Pox o'my family!
CONSTANT
　How does your lady? I han't seen her abroad a good while.
SIR JOHN
　Do! I don't know how she does, not I. She was well enough
　yesterday; I han't been home tonight.   230
CONSTANT
　What, were you out of town?
SIR JOHN
　Out of town! no, I was drinking.
CONSTANT
　You are a true Englishman; don't know your own happiness.
　If I were married to such a woman, I would not be from
　her a night for all the wine in France.   235
SIR JOHN
　Not from her!—Oons! what a time should a man have of
　that!
HEARTFREE
　Why, there's no division, I hope?
SIR JOHN
　No; but there's a conjunction, and that's worse; a pox o'the
　parson!—Why the plague don't you two marry? I fancy I   240
　look like the devil to you.
HEARTFREE
　Why, you don't think you have horns, do you?
SIR JOHN
　No; I believe my wife's religion will keep her honest.
HEARTFREE
　And what will make her keep her religion?
SIR JOHN
　Persecution; and therefore she shall have it.   245
HEARTFREE
　Have a care, knight! women are tender things.
SIR JOHN
　And yet, methinks, 'tis a hard matter to break their hearts.

230 *tonight* last night; apparently a day passes between I.i and I.ii
236 *Oons* a corruption of *God's wounds*
239 *o'the* Q1–2 (of the Q3, P)

———————————————————————————————

239 *conjunction* the concourse of two planets in the same degree of the
　zodiac; in astrology, generally malign

CONSTANT

Fie, fie! You have one of the best wives in the world, and yet you seem the most uneasy husband.

SIR JOHN

Best wives!—The woman's well enough, she has no vice that 250
I know of, but she's a wife, and—Damn a wife! If I were married to a hogshead of claret, matrimony would make me hate it.

HEARTFREE

Why did you marry, then? You were old enough to know your own mind. 255

SIR JOHN

Why did I marry? I married because I had a mind to lie with her, and she would not let me.

HEARTFREE

Why did not you ravish her?

SIR JOHN

Yes! and so have hedged myself into forty quarrels with her relations, besides buying my pardon. But, more than all 260
that, you must know I was afraid of being damned in those days; for I kept sneaking cowardly company, fellows that went to church, said grace to their meat, and had not the least tincture of quality about 'em.

HEARTFREE

But I think you are got into a better gang now. 265

SIR JOHN

Zoons, sir, my Lord Rake and I are hand and glove; I believe we may get our bones broke together tonight.— Have you a mind to share a frolic?

CONSTANT

Not I, truly; my talent lies to softer exercises.

SIR JOHN

What, a down bed and a strumpet? A pox of venery, I say!— 270
Will you come and drink with me this afternoon?

CONSTANT

I can't drink today, but we'll come and sit an hour with you, if you will.

SIR JOHN

Phugh, pox, sit an hour! Why can't you drink?

CONSTANT

Because I'm to see my mistress. 275

SIR JOHN

Who's that?

258 *not you* Q1–2 (you not Q3, P)
265 *are* Q1–3 (have P)

CONSTANT
> Why, do you use to tell?

SIR JOHN
> Yes.

CONSTANT
> So won't I.

SIR JOHN
> Why?   280

CONSTANT
> Because 'tis a secret.

SIR JOHN
> Would my wife knew it; 'twould be no secret long.

CONSTANT
> Why, do you think she can't keep a secret?

SIR JOHN
> No more than she can keep Lent.

HEARTFREE
> Prithee, tell it her to try, Constant.   285

SIR JOHN
> No, prithee don't, that I mayn't be plagued with it.

CONSTANT
> I'll hold you a guinea you don't make her tell it you.

SIR JOHN
> I'll hold you a guinea I do.

CONSTANT
> Which way?

SIR JOHN
> Why, I'll beg her not to tell it me.   290

HEARTFREE
> Nay, if anything does it, that will.

CONSTANT
> But do you think, sir—

SIR JOHN
> Oons, sir, I think a woman and a secret are the two im-
> pertinentest themes in the universe! Therefore pray let's
> hear no more of my wife nor your mistress. Damn 'em both   295
> with all my heart, and everything else that daggles a petti-
> coat, except four generous whores, with Betty Sands at the
> head of 'em, who were drunk with my Lord Rake and I ten
> times in a fortnight.   (*Exit* SIR JOHN)

296 *daggles* trails through the mud

---

297 *Betty Sands* a fashionable prostitute who later sold oranges at Drury
    Lane and died in penury in 1699

CONSTANT

    Here's a dainty fellow for you! and the veriest coward too.   300
But his usage of his wife makes me ready to stab the villain.

HEARTFREE

    Lovers are short-sighted: all their senses run into that of
feeling. This proceeding of his is the only thing on earth
can make your fortune. If anything can prevail with her to
accept of a gallant, 'tis his ill usage of her; for women will do   305
more for revenge than they'll do for the gospel. Prithee,
take heart, I have great hopes for you; and since I can't
bring you quite off of her, I'll endeavour to bring you quite
on; for a whining lover is the damnedest companion upon
earth.   310

CONSTANT

    My dear friend, flatter me a little more with these hopes;
for whilst they prevail I have heaven within me, and could
melt with joy.

HEARTFREE

    Pray, no melting yet: let things go farther first. This after-
noon, perhaps, we shall make some advance. In the mean-   315
while, let's go dine at Locket's, and let hope get you a
stomach.   (*Exeunt*)

Act II, Scene ii

LADY FANCYFULL's *House*
Enter LADY FANCYFULL *and* MADAMOISELLE

LADY FANCYFULL

    Did you ever see anything so importune, Madamoiselle?

MADAMOISELLE

    Inteed, matam, to say de trute, he want leetel good breeding.

LADY FANCYFULL

    Good breeding? He wants to be caned, Madamoiselle. An
insolent fellow!—And yet let me expose my weakness: 'tis
the only man on earth I could resolve to dispense my favours   5
on, were he but a fine gentleman. Well; did men but know

---

308 *bring you . . . off of* rescue you from
308–9 *bring you . . . on* advance your cause
   1 *importune* vexatious
   2 *want* Q1 (wanted Q2–3, P)

---

316 *Locket's* an expensive tavern near Charing Cross, patronized by Lord
    Foppington in *The Relapse* (II.i.229)

how deep an impression a fine gentleman makes in a lady's
heart, they would reduce all their studies to that of good
breeding alone.

Enter CORNET

CORNET
Madam, here's Mr Treble. He has brought home the verses   10
your ladyship made, and gave him to set.
LADY FANCYFULL
Oh, let him come in by all means. [*Exit* CORNET]—Now,
Madamoiselle, am I going to be unspeakably happy.

Enter TREBLE [*and* PIPE]

So, Mr Treble, you have set my little dialogue?
TREBLE
Yes, madam, and I hope your ladyship will be pleased with   15
it.
LADY FANCYFULL
Oh, no doubt on't; for really, Mr Treble, you set all things
to a wonder. But your music is in particular heavenly when
you have my words to clothe in't.
TREBLE
Your words themselves, madam, have so much music in   20
'em, they inspire me.
LADY FANCYFULL
Nay, now you make me blush, Mr Treble; but pray let's
hear what you have done.
TREBLE
You shall, madam.

A SONG TO BE SUNG BETWEEN A MAN AND A WOMAN
[TREBLE] MAN   Ah, lovely nymph, the world's on fire;   25
                Veil, veil those cruel eyes.
[PIPE]   WOMAN The world may then in flames expire,
                And boast that so it dies.
[TREBLE] MAN   But when all mortals are destroyed,
                Who then shall sing your praise?   30
[PIPE]   WOMAN Those who are fit to be employed:
                The gods shall altars raise.

---

13 s.d. [*and* PIPE] Q1 gives Pipe no entry, though she is addressed at 51; if
   she comes on with Treble she can rescue him from singing the duet with
   himself.

TREBLE

How does your ladyship like it, madam?

LADY FANCYFULL

Rapture! Rapture, Mr Treble! I'm all rapture! O wit and
art, what power you have when joined! I must needs tell　35
you the birth of this little dialogue, Mr Treble. Its father
was a dream, and its mother was the moon. I dreamt that
by an unanimous vote I was chosen queen of that pale world;
and that the first time I appeared upon my throne—all my
subjects fell in love with me. Just then I waked, and seeing　40
pen, ink and paper lie idle upon the table, I slid into my
morning-gown, and writ this impromptu.

TREBLE

So I guess the dialogue, madam, is supposed to be between
your majesty and your first minister of state.

LADY FANCYFULL

Just. He as minister advises me to trouble my head about　45
the welfare of my subjects; which I as sovereign find a very
impertinent proposal. But is the town so dull, Mr Treble,
it affords us never another new song?

TREBLE

Madam, I have one in my pocket, came out but yesterday,
if your ladyship pleases to let Mrs Pipe sing it.　50

LADY FANCYFULL

By all means.—Here, Pipe, make what music you can of
this song, here.

SONG

I

[PIPE]　　　Not an angel dwells above,
　　　Half so fair as her I love;
　　　　　Heaven knows how she'll receive me:　55
　　　If she smiles, I'm blest indeed;
　　　If she frowns, I'm quickly freed;
　　　　　Heaven knows, she ne'er can grieve me.

II

　　　None can love her more than I,
　　　Yet she ne'er shall make me die　60
　　　　　If my flame can never warm her.
　　　Lasting beauty I'll adore;
　　　I shall never love her more,
　　　　　Cruelty will so deform her.

35 *you have* Q1–2 (*have you* Q3, P)
42 *impromptu* perhaps a noun
50 *Mrs Pipe* Q1 (Mr Pipe Q2–3, P)
60–1 die. If my flame can never warm her; Q1–3, P

LADY FANCYFULL

Very well.—This is Heartfree's poetry, without question.   65

TREBLE

Won't your ladyship please to sing yourself this morning?

LADY FANCYFULL

O Lord, Mr Treble, my cold is still so barbarous to refuse
me that pleasure. [*Coughs*] He—he—hem.

TREBLE

I'm very sorry for it, madam. Methinks all mankind should
turn physicians for the cure on't.   70

LADY FANCYFULL

Why truly, to give mankind their due, there's few that
know me but have offered their remedy.

TREBLE

They have reason, madam; for I know nobody sings so
near a cherubin as your ladyship.

LADY FANCYFULL

What I do, I owe chiefly to your skill and care, Mr Treble.   75
People do flatter me, indeed, that I have a voice, and a *je ne
sais quoi* in the conduct of it, that will make music of anything. And truly, I begin to believe so, since what happened
t'other night. Would you think it, Mr Treble? Walking
pretty late in the Park (for I often walk late in the Park, Mr   80
Treble), a whim took me to sing 'Chevy Chase', and—would
you believe it?—next morning I had three copies of verses
and six *billets-doux* at my levee upon it.

TREBLE

And without all dispute you deserved as many more, madam.
Are there any further commands for your ladyship's humble   85
servant?

LADY FANCYFULL

Nothing more at this time, Mr Treble. But I shall expect
you here every morning for this month, to sing my little
matter there to me. I'll reward you for your pains.

TREBLE

O Lord, madam—   90

LADY FANCYFULL

Good morrow, sweet Mr Treble.

76–7 *je ne sais quoi* certain something
83 *billets-doux* ed. (billet-doux Q1–3, P) love-letters

79–80 *Walking ... Park* By night St James's Park was given over to
prostitution.
81 *Chevy Chase* the popular old ballad of Douglas and Percy

TREBLE
Your ladyship's most obedient servant.

(*Exit* TREBLE [*with* PIPE])

Enter SERVANT

SERVANT
Will your ladyship please to dine yet?

LADY FANCYFULL
Yes, let 'em serve. (*Exit* SERVANT)—Sure this Heartfree has
bewitched me, Madamoiselle. You can't imagine how oddly   95
he mixed himself in my thoughts during my rapture e'en
now. I vow 'tis a thousand pities he is not more polished;
don't you think so?

MADAMOISELLE
Matam, I tink it so great pity, dat if I was in your ladyship
place, I take him home in my house, I lock him up in my   100
closet, and I never let him go till I teach him everyting dat
fine laty expect from fine gentelman.

LADY FANCYFULL
Why truly, I believe I should soon subdue his brutality; for
without doubt he has a strange *penchant* to grow fond of me,
in spite of his aversion to the sex, else he would ne'er have   105
taken so much pains about me. Lord, how proud would
some poor creatures be of such a conquest! But I, alas, I
don't know how to receive as a favour what I take to be so
infinitely my due. But what shall I do to new-mould him,
Madamoiselle? for till then he's my utter aversion.   110

MADAMOISELLE
Matam, you must laugh at him in all de place dat you meet
him, and turn into de ridicule all he say and all he do.

LADY FANCYFULL
Why truly, satire has been ever of wondrous use to reform
ill manners. Besides, 'tis my particular talent to ridicule
folks. I can be severe, strangely severe, when I will, Mada-   115
moiselle.—Give me the pen and ink—I find myself whimsical—(*Sitting down to write*) I'll write to him.—(*Rising up
again*) Or I'll let it alone, and be severe upon him that way.—
(*Sitting down*) Yet active severity is better than passive.
—(*Rising*) 'Tis as good let alone too, for every lash I give   120
him, perhaps, he'll take for a favour.—(*Sitting*) Yet 'tis a
thousand pities so much satire should be lost.—(*Rising*) But

104 *penchant* inclination
113 *been ever* Q1–2 (ever been Q3, P)
120 *let* Q1–2 (let it Q3, P)

if it should have a wrong effect upon him, 'twould distract
me.—(*Sitting*) Well, I must write though, after all.—
(*Rising*) Or I'll let it alone, which is the same thing.   125
MADAMOISELLE [*Aside*]
    La voilà déterminée!   (*Exeunt*)

Act III, Scene i

    Scene opens. SIR JOHN, LADY BRUTE, *and* BELLINDA [*dis-
covered,*] *rising from the table.* [SERVANTS *in attendance*]

SIR JOHN (*To a servant*)
    Here, take away the things; I expect company. But first
bring me a pipe; I'll smoke.
      [SERVANTS *bring* SIR JOHN *a pipe, &c., clear the table, and
exeunt*]
LADY BRUTE
    Lord, Sir John, I wonder you won't leave that nasty custom.
SIR JOHN
    Prithee, don't be impertinent.
BELLINDA (*To* LADY BRUTE [*aside*])
    I wonder who those are he expects this afternoon?   5
LADY BRUTE
    I'd give the world to know! Perhaps 'tis Constant; he comes
here sometimes. If it does prove him, I'm resolved I'll
share the visit.
BELLINDA
    We'll send for our work and sit here.
LADY BRUTE
    He'll choke us with his tobacco.   10
BELLINDA
    Nothing will choke us when we are doing what we have a
mind to.—Lovewell!

        Enter LOVEWELL

LOVEWELL
    Madam.

126 *La voilà déterminée!* I see she's made up her mind!
126 s.d. (*Exeunt*) Q1 follows this with 'The End of the Second Act'.

    s.d. *Scene opens* i.e., the two halves of the back-scene are drawn apart
on shutters to reveal Sir John's dining room
  12 *Lovewell!* printed after a long space in Q1. As Zimansky suggests,
perhaps a speech prefix for Lady Brute was dropped.

LADY BRUTE
　　Here; bring my cousin's work and mine hither.
　　　　　　　　　(*Exit* LOVEWELL *and re-enters with their work*)

SIR JOHN
　　Why, pox, can't you work somewhere else?   15

LADY BRUTE
　　We shall be careful not to disturb you, sir.
　　　　　　　　　　　　　　　　　[*Exit* LOVEWELL]

BELLINDA
　　Your pipe would make you too thoughtful, uncle, if you
　　were left alone; our prittle-prattle will cure your spleen.

SIR JOHN (*Sitting and smoking*)
　　Will it so, Mrs Pert? Now I believe it will so increase it, I
　　shall take my own house for a paper-mill.   20

LADY BRUTE (*To* BELLINDA, *aside*)
　　Don't let's mind him; let him say what he will.

SIR JOHN (*Aside*)
　　A woman's tongue a cure for the spleen!—Oons! If a man
　　had got the headache, they'd be for applying the same
　　remedy.

LADY BRUTE
　　You have done a great deal, Bellinda, since yesterday.   25

BELLINDA
　　Yes, I have worked very hard; how do you like it?

LADY BRUTE
　　Oh, 'tis the prettiest fringe in the world! Well, cousin, you
　　have the happiest fancy; prithee, advise me about altering
　　my crimson petticoat.

SIR JOHN
　　A pox o'your petticoat! Here's such a prating, a man can't   30
　　digest his own thoughts for you.

LADY BRUTE
　　(*Aside*) Don't answer him.—[*Aloud*] Well, what do you
　　advise me?

BELLINDA
　　Why, really, I would not alter it at all. Methinks 'tis very
　　pretty as it is.   35

LADY BRUTE
　　Ay, that's true; but you know one grows weary of the
　　prettiest things in the world, when one has had 'em long.

15 *Why* ed. (Whu Q1–3, P, perhaps an exclamation)
17 *would* Q1 (will Q2–3, P)

20 *paper-mill* i.e., somewhere very noisy; Dobrée cites Etherege, *Love in a
　　Tub* (I.ii.112): 'Sh'as made more noise then half a dozen Paper-mills'

SIR JOHN
  Yes, I have taught her that.
BELLINDA [*To* LADY BRUTE, *aside*]
  Shall we provoke him a little?
LADY BRUTE
  With all my heart.—[*Aloud*] Bellinda, don't you long to be   40
  married?
BELLINDA
  Why, there are some things in't I could like well enough.
LADY BRUTE
  What do you think you should dislike?
BELLINDA
  My husband, a hundred to one else.
LADY BRUTE
  Oh, ye wicked wretch! Sure you don't speak as you think?   45
BELLINDA
  Yes, I do; especially if he smoked tobacco.
                              (*He looks earnestly at 'em*)
LADY BRUTE
  Why, that many times takes off worse smells.
BELLINDA
  Then he must smell very ill indeed.
LADY BRUTE
  So some men will, to keep their wives from coming near 'em.
BELLINDA
  Then those wives should cuckold 'em at a distance.   50
SIR JOHN
  Oons, get you gone upstairs, you confederating strumpets
  you, or I'll cuckold you with a vengeance!

  *He rises in a fury, throws his pipe at 'em, and drives 'em
  out. As they run off,* CONSTANT *and* HEARTFREE *enter.* LADY
            BRUTE *runs against* CONSTANT

LADY BRUTE
  O Lord, he'll beat us, he'll beat us! Dear, dear Mr Constant,
  save us!   (*Exeunt* [LADY BRUTE *and* BELLINDA])
SIR JOHN
  I'll cuckold you, with a pox!   55
CONSTANT
  Heavens, Sir John! What's the matter?

  42 *in't* Q1 (in it Q2–3, P)
  52 s.d. *He . . . against* CONSTANT Q1 prints this before Sir John's line

SIR JOHN

Sure, if woman had been ready created, the devil, instead
of being kicked down into hell, had been married.

HEARTFREE

Why, what new plague have you found now?

SIR JOHN

Why, these two gentlewomen did but hear me say I expected   60
you here this afternoon; upon which they presently resolved
to take up the room, o'purpose to plague me and my friends.

CONSTANT

Was that all? Why, we should have been glad of their
company.

SIR JOHN

Then I should have been weary of yours, for I can't relish   65
both together. They found fault with my smoking tobacco,
too; and said men stunk. But I have a good mind—to say
something.

CONSTANT

No, nothing against the ladies, pray.

SIR JOHN

Split the ladies! Come, will you sit down?—[*Calling a*   70
SERVANT] Give us some wine, fellow.—You won't smoke?

CONSTANT

No, nor drink neither, at this time; I must ask your pardon.

SIR JOHN

What, this mistress of yours runs in your head! I'll warrant
it's some such squeamish minx as my wife, that's grown so
dainty of late she finds fault even with a dirty shirt.   75

HEARTFREE

That a woman may do, and not be very dainty neither.

SIR JOHN

Pox o'the women! let's drink. Come, you shall take one glass,
though I send for a box of lozenges to sweeten your mouth
after it.

CONSTANT

Nay, if one glass will satisfy you, I'll drink it without putting   80
you to that expense.

SIR JOHN

Why, that's honest.—Fill some wine, sirrah! So.—Here's
to you, gentlemen!—A wife's the devil. To your being both
married!

HEARTFREE

Oh, your most humble servant, sir!   (*They drink*)   85

57 *woman* Q1–2 (women Q3, P)
85 s.d. (*They drink*) Q1 prints this before Heartfree's line

SIR JOHN
 Well, how do you like my wine?

CONSTANT
 'Tis very good indeed.

HEARTFREE
 'Tis admirable.

SIR JOHN
 Then give us t'other glass.

CONSTANT
 No, pray excuse us now. We'll come another time, and then   90
 we won't spare it.

SIR JOHN
 This one glass, and no more. Come, it shall be your mistress's health—and that's a great compliment from me, I
 assure you.

CONSTANT
 And 'tis a very obliging one to me; so give us the glasses.   95

SIR JOHN
 So. Let her live—

HEARTFREE
 And be kind!   ([*They drink.*] SIR JOHN *coughs in the glass*)

CONSTANT
 What's the matter? Does't go the wrong way?

SIR JOHN
 If I had love enough to be jealous, I should take this for an
 ill omen; for I never drank my wife's health in my life, but   100
 I puked in the glass.

CONSTANT
 Oh, she's too virtuous to make a reasonable man jealous.

SIR JOHN
 Pox of her virtue! If I could but catch her adulterating, I
 might be divorced from her by law.

HEARTFREE
 And so pay her a yearly pension, to be a distinguished   105
 cuckold.

Enter SERVANT

[SERVANT]
 Sir, there's my Lord Rake, Colonel Bully, and some other
 gentlemen at 'The Blue Posts', desire your company. [*Exit*]

98 *Does't* Q1 (*Does it* Q2–3, P)

103–6 See note to I.i.53–4.
108 *'The Blue Posts'* a fashionable tavern in the Haymarket, so named from
 the colour of its door jambs; Sir Jolly Jumble dines there in Otway's
 The Soldier's Fortune (I.i.294)

SIR JOHN

Cod's so, we are to consult about playing the devil tonight.

HEARTFREE

Well, we won't hinder business.   110

SIR JOHN

Methinks I don't know how to leave you, though. But for
once I must make bold.—Or look you, maybe the conference
mayn't last long; so if you'll wait here half an hour, or an
hour, if I don't come then—why, then—I won't come at all.

HEARTFREE (*To* CONSTANT, *aside*)

A good modest proposition, truly!   115

CONSTANT

But let's accept on't, however. Who knows what may
happen?

HEARTFREE [*Aloud*]

Well, sir, to show you how fond we are of your company,
we'll expect your return as long as we can.

SIR JOHN

Nay, maybe I mayn't stay at all; but business, you know,   120
must be done. So, your servant.—Or hark you, if you have
a mind to take a frisk with us, I have an interest with my
lord, I can easily introduce you.

CONSTANT

We are much beholding to you, but for my part I'm engaged
another way.   125

SIR JOHN

What? To your mistress, I'll warrant! Prithee leave your
nasty punk to entertain herself with her own lewd thoughts,
and make one with us tonight.

CONSTANT

Sir, 'tis business that is to employ me.

HEARTFREE

And me; and business must be done, you know.   130

SIR JOHN

Ay, women's business, though the world were consumed
for't.   (*Exit* SIR JOHN [*followed by* SERVANT])

CONSTANT

Farewell, beast!—And now, my dear friend, would my

109 *Cod's* a perversion of *God's*
119 *expect* await (also at 292)
124 *beholding* Q1–3 (beholden P)

132 s.d. [*followed by* SERVANT] The servant who poured wine in 82 may have
been silently dismissed already; this is his last chance to get off stage
before the lovers' quartet.

mistress be but as complaisant as some men's wives, who
think it a piece of good breeding to receive the visits of their   135
husband's friends in his absence!

HEARTFREE

Why, for your sake I could forgive her, though she should
be so complaisant to receive something else in his absence.
But what way shall we invent to see her?

CONSTANT

Oh, ne'er hope it! Invention will prove as vain as wishes.   140

Enter LADY BRUTE *and* BELLINDA

HEARTFREE [*To* CONSTANT, *aside*]
What do you think now, friend?

CONSTANT
I think I shall swoon.

HEARTFREE
I'll speak first then, whilst you fetch breath.

LADY BRUTE
We think ourselves obliged, gentlemen, to come and return
you thanks for your knight-errantry. We were just upon   145
being devoured by the fiery dragon.

BELLINDA
Did not his fumes almost knock you down, gentlemen?

HEARTFREE
Truly, ladies, we did undergo some hardships, and should
have done more, if some greater heroes than ourselves hard
by had not diverted him.   150

CONSTANT
Though I am glad of the service you are pleased to say we
have done you, yet I'm sorry we could do it no other way
than by making ourselves privy to what you would perhaps
have kept a secret.

LADY BRUTE
For Sir John's part, I suppose he designed it no secret,   155
since he made so much noise. And for myself, truly I am
not much concerned, since 'tis fallen only into this gentleman's hands and yours; who, I have many reasons to
believe, will neither interpret nor report anything to my
disadvantage.   160

CONSTANT
Your good opinion, madam, was what I feared I never
could have merited.

152 *it* Q1–3 (it in P)

LADY BRUTE

Your fears were vain then, sir; for I am just to everybody.

HEARTFREE

Prithee, Constant, what is't you do to get the ladies' good
opinions, for I'm a novice at it?   165

BELLINDA

Sir, will you give me leave to instruct you?

HEARTFREE

Yes, that I will, with all my soul, madam.

BELLINDA

Why then, you must never be slovenly, never be out of
humour, fare well and cry roast meat, smoke tobacco, nor
drink but when you are a-dry.   170

HEARTFREE

That's hard.

CONSTANT

Nay, if you take his bottle from him, you break his heart,
madam.

BELLINDA

Why, is it possible the gentleman can love drinking?

HEARTFREE

Only by way of antidote.   175

BELLINDA

Against what, pray?

HEARTFREE

Against love, madam.

LADY BRUTE

Are you afraid of being in love, sir?

HEARTFREE

I should, if there were any danger of it.

LADY BRUTE

Pray, why so?   180

HEARTFREE

Because I always had an aversion to being used like a dog.

BELLINDA

Why truly, men in love are seldom used better.

LADY BRUTE

But was you never in love, sir?

HEARTFREE

No, I thank heaven, madam.

BELLINDA

Pray, where got you your learning, then?   185

169 *cry roast meat* advertise your good luck

---

182 Does Bellinda agree with Heartfree or contradict him?

HEARTFREE

From other people's expense.

BELLINDA

That's being a sponger, sir, which is scarce honest; if you'd
buy some experience with your own money, as 'twould be
fairlier got, so 'twould stick longer by you.

Enter FOOTMAN

FOOTMAN

Madam, here's my Lady Fancyfull to wait upon your   190
ladyship.   [*Exit*]

LADY BRUTE

Shield me, kind heaven! What an inundation of impertinence is here coming upon us!

Enter LADY FANCYFULL, *who runs first to* LADY BRUTE,
then to BELLINDA, *kissing 'em*

LADY FANCYFULL

My dear Lady Brute! And sweet Bellinda! Methinks 'tis
an age since I saw you.   195

LADY BRUTE

Yet 'tis but three days; sure you have passed your time very
ill, it seems so long to you.

LADY FANCYFULL

Why really, to confess the truth to you, I am so everlastingly
fatigued with the addresses of unfortunate gentlemen, that
were it not for the extravagancy of the example I should   200
e'en tear out these wicked eyes with my own fingers, to
make both myself and mankind easy.—What think you
on't, Mr Heartfree, for I take you to be my faithful adviser?

HEARTFREE

Why truly, madam—I think every project that is for the
good of mankind ought to be encouraged.   205

LADY FANCYFULL

Then I have your consent, sir?

HEARTFREE

To do whatever you please, madam.

LADY FANCYFULL

You had a much more limited complaisance this morning,
sir.—Would you believe it, ladies? The gentleman has been
so exceeding generous, to tell me of above fifty faults in less   210
time than it was well possible for me to commit two of 'em.

CONSTANT

Why truly, madam, my friend there is apt to be something
familiar with the ladies.

LADY FANCYFULL

He is indeed, sir, but he's wondrous charitable with it; he
has had the goodness to design a reformation, even down   215
to my fingers' ends.—'Twas thus, I think, sir, you would
have had 'em stand. (*Opening her fingers in an awkward
manner*)—My eyes, too, he did not like.—How was't you
would have directed 'em? Thus, I think. (*Staring at him*)—
Then there was something amiss in my gait, too; I don't   220
know well how 'twas, but as I take it he would have had me
walk like him.—Pray, sir, do me the favour to take a turn
or two about the room, that the company may see you.—
He's sullen, ladies, and won't. But, to make short, and give
you as true an idea as I can of the matter, I think 'twas   225
much about this figure in general he would have moulded
me to. (*She walks awkwardly about, staring and looking
ungainly, then changes on a sudden to the extremity of her usual
affectation*) But I was an obstinate woman, and could not
resolve to make myself mistress of his heart by growing as   230
awkward as his fancy.

(*Here* CONSTANT *and* LADY BRUTE *talk together apart*)

HEARTFREE

Just thus women do, when they think we are in love with
'em, or when they are so with us.

LADY FANCYFULL

'Twould, however, be less vanity for me to conclude the
former than you the latter, sir.   235

HEARTFREE

Madam, all I shall presume to conclude is, that if I were in
love, you'd find the means to make me soon weary on't.

LADY FANCYFULL

Not by over-fondness, upon my word, sir. But pray let's
stop here, for you are so much governed by instinct I know
you'll grow brutish at last.   240

BELLINDA

(*Aside*) Now am I sure she's fond of him. I'll try to make
her jealous.—[*Aloud*] Well, for my part, I should be glad
to find somebody would be so free with me, that I might
know my faults and mend 'em.

LADY FANCYFULL

Then pray let me recommend this gentleman to you: I have   245
known him some time and will be surety for him, that upon
a very limited encouragement on your side, you shall find an
extended impudence on his.

216 *you would* Q1–2 (you'ld Q3, you'd P)
241 *am I* Q1 (I am Q2–3, I'm P)

HEARTFREE

I thank you, madam, for your recommendation; but, hating
idleness, I'm unwilling to enter into a place where I believe   250
there would be nothing to do. I was fond of serving your
ladyship, because I knew you'd find me constant employment.

LADY FANCYFULL

I told you he'd be rude, Bellinda.

BELLINDA

Oh, a little bluntness is a sign of honesty, which makes me   255
always ready to pardon it.—So, sir, if you have no other
exceptions to my service but the fear of being idle in't, you
may venture to 'list yourself; I shall find you work, I warrant
you.

HEARTFREE

Upon those terms I engage, madam; and this (with your   260
leave) I take for earnest.   (*Offering to kiss her hand*)

BELLINDA

Hold there, sir! I'm none of your earnest-givers. But if I'm
well served, I give good wages and pay punctually.

(HEARTFREE *and* BELLINDA *seem to continue talking
familiarly*)

LADY FANCYFULL

(*Aside*) I don't like this jesting between 'em. Methinks the
fool begins to look as if he were in earnest—but then he   265
must be a fool indeed.—(*Looking at* BELLINDA *scornfully*)
Lard, what a difference there is between me and her! How
I should despise such a thing, if I were a man! What a nose
she has! What a chin! What a neck!—Then her eyes!—
And the worst kissing lips in the universe!—No, no, he can   270
never like her, that's positive.—Yet I can't suffer 'em
together any longer.—[*Aloud*] Mr Heartfree! Do you know
that you and I must have no quarrel for all this? I can't
forbear being a little severe now and then; but women, you
know, may be allowed anything.   275

HEARTFREE

Up to a certain age, madam.

LADY FANCYFULL

Which I am not yet past, I hope.

257 *in't* Q1–2 (in it Q3, P)
277 *I am* Q1–2 (I'm Q3, P)

261 *for earnest* (1) in all seriousness (2) as a downpayment to secure the
contract (3) as a foretaste of what is to come

HEARTFREE (*Aside*)
　Nor never will, I dare swear.
LADY FANCYFULL (*To* LADY BRUTE)
　Come, madam; will your ladyship be witness to our recon-
　ciliation?　　　　　　　　　　　　　　　　　　　　　　280
LADY BRUTE
　You agree, then, at last?
HEARTFREE (*Slightingly*)
　We forgive.
LADY FANCYFULL (*Aside*)
　That was a cold ill-natured reply.
LADY BRUTE
　Then there's no challenges sent between you?
HEARTFREE
　Not from me, I promise.—(*Aside, to* CONSTANT) But that's　285
　more than I'll do for her, for I know she can as well be
　damned as forbear writing to me.
CONSTANT
　That I believe. But I think we had best be going, lest she
　should suspect something and be malicious.
HEARTFREE
　With all my heart.　　　　　　　　　　　　　　　　　290
CONSTANT [*Aloud*]
　Ladies, we are your humble servants. I see Sir John is quite
　engaged; 'twould be in vain to expect him.—Come, Heart-
　free.　　　　　　　　　　　　　　　　　　　(*Exit*)
HEARTFREE
　Ladies, your servant.—(*To* BELLINDA) I hope, madam, you
　won't forget our bargain; I'm to say what I please to you.　295
BELLINDA
　Liberty of speech entire, sir.　　　　　　(*Exit* HEARTFREE)
LADY FANCYFULL
　(*Aside*) Very pretty, truly.—But how the blockhead went
　out! languishing at her, and not a look toward me! Well;
　churchmen may talk, but miracles are not ceased. For 'tis
　more than natural such a rude fellow as he, and such a little　300
　impertinent as she, should be capable of making a woman
　of my sphere uneasy. But I can bear her sight no longer;
　methinks she's grown ten times uglier than Cornet. I must
　go home, and study revenge.—(*To* LADY BRUTE) Madam,
　your humble servant; I must take my leave.　　　　　305

---

296 s.d. (*Exit* HEARTFREE) Q1 prints this before Bellinda's line
304 *go home* Q1–2 (home Q3, P)

LADY BRUTE
  What, going already, madam?

LADY FANCYFULL
  I must beg you'll excuse me this once, for really I have
  eighteen visits to return this afternoon; so you see I'm
  importuned by the women as well as the men.

BELLINDA (*Aside*)
  And she's quits with 'em both.   310

LADY FANCYFULL (*Going*)
  Nay, you shan't go one step out of the room.

LADY BRUTE
  Indeed, I'll wait upon you down.

LADY FANCYFULL
  No, sweet Lady Brute; you know I swoon at ceremony.

LADY BRUTE
  Pray, give me leave.

LADY FANCYFULL
  You know I won't.   315

LADY BRUTE
  Indeed I must.

LADY FANCYFULL
  Indeed you shan't.

LADY BRUTE
  Indeed I will.

LADY FANCYFULL
  Indeed you shan't.

LADY BRUTE
  Indeed I will.   320

LADY FANCYFULL
  Indeed you shan't. Indeed, indeed, indeed you shan't!
      (*Exit* LADY FANCYFULL *running*. [LADY BRUTE *and*
                                      BELLINDA] *follow*)

Re-enter LADY BRUTE, *sola*

[LADY BRUTE]
  This impertinent woman has put me out of humour for a
  fortnight.—What an agreeable moment has her foolish visit
  interrupted! Lord, how like a torrent love flows into the

310 *she's* Q1, P (she Q2–3)
310 *'em* Q1–2 (them Q3, P)
321 s.d. LADY BRUTE *and* BELLINDA ed. (*They* Q1)

311 s.p. LADY FANCYFULL (*Going*) Q1 prints this as a stage direction, thus
      making 311 a continuation of Bellinda's speech; but she has no reason
      to prevent Lady Fancyfull's departure.

heart when once the sluice of desire is opened! Good gods!   325
What a pleasure there is in doing what we should not do!

Re-enter CONSTANT

Ha! Here again?
CONSTANT
Though the renewing my visit may seem a little irregular,
I hope I shall obtain your pardon for it, madam, when you
know I only left the room lest the lady who was here should   330
have been as malicious in her remarks as she's foolish in her
conduct.
LADY BRUTE
He who has discretion enough to be tender of a woman's
reputation carries a virtue about him may atone for a great
many faults.   335
CONSTANT
If it has a title to atone for any, its pretensions must needs
be strongest where the crime is love. I therefore hope I shall
be forgiven the attempt I have made upon your heart, since
my enterprise has been a secret to all the world but yourself.
LADY BRUTE
Secrecy indeed in sins of this kind is an argument of weight   340
to lessen the punishment; but nothing's a plea for a pardon
entire, without a sincere repentance.
CONSTANT
If sincerity in repentance consist in sorrow for offending, no
cloister ever enclosed so true a penitent as I should be. But I
hope it cannot be reckoned an offence to love, where 'tis a   345
duty to adore.
LADY BRUTE
'Tis an offence, a great one, where it would rob a woman of
all she ought to be adored for—her virtue.
CONSTANT
Virtue?—Virtue, alas, is no more like the thing that's called
so, than 'tis like vice itself. Virtue consists in goodness,   350
honour, gratitude, sincerity and pity; and not in peevish,
snarling, strait-laced chastity. True virtue, wheresoe'er it
moves, still carries an intrinsic worth about it, and is in
every place and in each sex of equal value. So is not continence, you see—that phantom of honour, which men in   355

336 *title* claim
343 *consist* Q1–2 (consists Q3, P)
354–5 *continence* (1) marital chastity (2) virgin abstinence

every age have so condemned they have thrown it amongst
the women to scrabble for.

LADY BRUTE

If it be a thing of so very little value, why do you so earnestly
recommend it to your wives and daughters?

CONSTANT

We recommend it to our wives, madam, because we would   360
keep 'em to ourselves; and to our daughters, because we
would dispose of 'em to others.

LADY BRUTE

'Tis then of some importance, it seems, since you can't
dispose of 'em without it.

CONSTANT

That importance, madam, lies in the humour of the country,   365
not in the nature of the thing.

LADY BRUTE

How do you prove that, sir?

CONSTANT

From the wisdom of a neighbouring nation in a contrary
practice. In monarchies things go by whimsy, but common-
wealths weigh all things in the scale of reason.   370

LADY BRUTE

I hope we are not so very light a people to bring up fashions
without some ground.

CONSTANT

Pray what does your ladyship think of a powdered coat for
deep mourning?

LADY BRUTE

I think, sir, your sophistry has all the effect that you can   375
reasonably expect it should have; it puzzles, but don't
convince.

CONSTANT

I'm sorry for it.

LADY BRUTE

I'm sorry to hear you say so.

CONSTANT

Pray why?   380

LADY BRUTE

Because if you expected more from it, you have a worse
opinion of my understanding than I desire you should have.

357 *scrabble for* struggle or scramble for
364 *'em* Q1–3 (them P)
371 *bring up* introduce and popularize
373 *powdered* minutely decorated

CONSTANT

(*Aside*) I comprehend her: she would have me set a value
upon her chastity, that I may think myself the more obliged
to her when she makes me a present of it.—(*To her*) I beg 385
you will believe I did but rally, madam; I know you judge
too well of right and wrong to be deceived by arguments
like those. I hope you'll have so favourable an opinion of
my understanding, too, to believe the thing called virtue
has worth enough with me to pass for an eternal obligation 390
where'er 'tis sacrificed.

LADY BRUTE

It is, I think, so great a one as nothing can repay.

CONSTANT

Yes; the making the man you love your everlasting debtor.

LADY BRUTE

When debtors once have borrowed all we have to lend, they
are very apt to grow shy of their creditors' company. 395

CONSTANT

That, madam, is only when they are forced to borrow of
usurers, and not of a generous friend. Let us choose our
creditors, and we are seldom so ungrateful to shun 'em.

LADY BRUTE

What think you of Sir John, sir? I was his free choice.

CONSTANT

I think he's married, madam. 400

LADY BRUTE

Does marriage then exclude men from your rule of constancy?

CONSTANT

It does. Constancy's a brave, free, haughty, generous agent,
that cannot buckle to the chains of wedlock. There's a poor
sordid slavery in marriage, that turns the flowing tide of 405
honour and sinks us to the lowest ebb of infamy. 'Tis a
corrupted soil; ill nature, avarice, sloth, cowardice and dirt
are all its product.

LADY BRUTE

Have you no exceptions to this general rule, as well as to
t'other? 410

CONSTANT

Yes; I would (after all) be an exception to it myself, if you
were free in power and will to make me so.

384 *may* Q1–3 (might P)
395 *shy* P (very shy Q1–3, perhaps repeated from *very apt*)
404 *buckle* submit

LADY BRUTE

Compliments are well placed, where 'tis impossible to lay hold on 'em.

CONSTANT

I would to heaven 'twere possible for you to lay hold on 415
mine, that you might see it is no compliment at all. But since you are already disposed on, beyond redemption, to one who does not know the value of the jewel you have put into his hands, I hope you would not think him greatly wronged though it should sometimes be looked on by a 420
friend, who knows how to esteem it as he ought.

LADY BRUTE

If looking on't alone would serve his turn, the wrong perhaps might not be very great.

CONSTANT

Why, what if he should wear it now and then a day, so he gave good security to bring it home again at night? 425

LADY BRUTE

Small security, I fancy, might serve for that. One might venture to take his word.

CONSTANT

Then where's the injury to the owner?

LADY BRUTE

'Tis an injury to him if he think it one. For if happiness be seated in the mind, unhappiness must be so too. 430

CONSTANT

Here I close with you, madam, and draw my conclusive argument from your own position: if the injury lie in the fancy, there needs nothing but secrecy to prevent the wrong.

LADY BRUTE (*Going*)

A surer way to prevent it, is to hear no more arguments in its behalf. 435

CONSTANT (*Following her*)

But, madam—

LADY BRUTE

But, sir, 'tis my turn to be discreet now, and not suffer too long a visit.

CONSTANT (*Catching her hand*)

By heaven, you shall not stir, till you give me hopes that I shall see you again at some more convenient time and place. 440

LADY BRUTE

I give you just hopes enough—(*Breaking from him*) to get

417 *disposed on* Q1–3 (disposed of P)
429 *an injury* Q1–2 (injury Q3, P)

loose from you; and that's all I can afford you at this time.

(*Exit running*)

CONSTANT (*Solus*)

Now, by all that's great and good, she is a charming woman!
In what ecstasy of joy she has left me! For she gave me hope;
did she not say she gave me hope?—Hope? Ay. What hope?   445
—Enough to make me let her go! Why, that's enough in
conscience. Or no matter how 'twas spoke; hope was the
word: it came from her and it was said to me.

Enter HEARTFREE

Ha, Heartfree! Thou hast done me noble service in prattling
to the young gentlewoman without there; come to my arms,   450
thou venerable bawd, and let me squeeze thee (*Embracing
him eagerly*) as a new pair of stays does a fat country girl,
when she's carried to court to stand for a maid of honour.

HEARTFREE

Why, what the devil's all this rapture for?

CONSTANT

Rapture? There's ground for rapture, man; there's hopes,   455
my Heartfree; hopes, my friend!

HEARTFREE

Hopes! of what?

CONSTANT

Why, hopes that my lady and I together (for 'tis more than
one body's work) should make Sir John a cuckold.

HEARTFREE

Prithee, what did she say to thee?   460

CONSTANT

Say? What did she not say! She said that—says she—she
said—Zoons, I don't know what she said, but she looked as
if she said everything I'd have her; and so if thou'lt go to
the tavern, I'll treat thee with anything that gold can buy;
I'll give all my silver amongst the drawers, make a bonfire   465
before the door, say the plenipos have signed the peace,
and the Bank of England's grown honest.   (*Exeunt*)

465-6 *make . . . peace* Negotiations to end the Continental War had begun
   in May 1696; plenipotentiaries left England in March 1697, and the
   Treaty of Ryswick was signed on 10 September; when Matthew Prior
   brought the news to London on 14 September, bonfires were lit in the
   streets. (All dates are Old Style.)

467 *Bank of England* founded in 1694, badly shaken by the currency crisis
   of 1696, and not yet beyond charges of corruption

Act III, Scene ii

Scene opens. LORD RAKE, SIR JOHN, [COLONEL BULLY] *&c.*
[discovered] at a table, drinking

ALL
Huzza!

LORD RAKE
Come, boys, charge again.—So.—Confusion to all order!
Here's liberty of conscience!

ALL
Huzza!

LORD RAKE
I'll sing you a song I made this morning to this purpose.   5

SIR JOHN
'Tis wicked, I hope.

COLONEL BULLY
Don't my lord tell you he made it?

SIR JOHN
Well then, let's ha't.

LORD RAKE (*Sings*)

I

What a pother of late
Have they kept in the state
    About setting our consciences free!   10
A bottle has more
Dispensation in store,
    Than the king and the state can decree.

II

When my head's full of wine,   15
I o'erflow with design,
    And know no penal laws that can curb me.

---

s.d. *Scene opens* as in III.i, to reveal a room in 'The Blue Posts'. As the
text stands, there has been no opportunity to strike the furniture used
in III.i. One solution would be an act-interval before III.ii; another,
to play the end of III.i against a back-scene set well down-stage.
Garrick's promptbook moves the action to Lady Brute's chamber, set
in the first grooves, at III.i.321.

3 *liberty of conscience* granted to dissenters by the Toleration Act of 1689
and the Quaker Act of 1696

13 *Dispensation* the king's power to suspend the law in an individual case,
invoked by James II to give Roman Catholics military office

17 *penal laws* rarely enforced against Roman Catholics in England, but
applied in Ireland after 1695 with great severity

Whate'er I devise
Seems good in my eyes,
    And religion ne'er dares to disturb me.   20

III

No saucy remorse
Intrudes in my course,
    Nor impertinent notions of evil;
So there's claret in store,
In peace I've my whore,   25
    And in peace I jog on to the devil.

ALL (*Sing*) So there's claret, &c.

LORD RAKE (*Repeats*)
    And in peace I jog on to the devil.

Well, how do you like it, gentlemen?

ALL
Oh, admirable!   30

SIR JOHN
I would not give a fig for a song that is not full of sin and
impudence.

LORD RAKE
Then my muse is to your taste. But drink away; the night
steals upon us; we shall want time to be lewd in.—Hey,
page!   35

[*Enter* PAGE]

Sally out, sirrah, and see what's doing in the camp; we'll
beat up their quarters presently.

PAGE
I'll bring your lordship an exact account.   (*Exit* PAGE)

LORD RAKE
Now let the spirit of clary go round! Fill me a brimmer.
Here's to our forlorn hope! Courage, knight; victory attends   40
you!

SIR JOHN
And laurels shall crown me. Drink away and be damned!

LORD RAKE
Again, boys; t'other glass, and damn morality!

SIR JOHN (*Drunk*)
Ay—damn morality—and damn the watch! And let the
constable be married!   45

40 *forlorn hope* storming party

---

37 *beat . . . quarters* visit their lodgings unexpectedly; a military phrase
    used here for a night raid on a bawdy house
39 *clary* brandy flavoured with honey, spices, and clary-flowers

ALL
> Huzza!

Re-enter PAGE

LORD RAKE
> How are the streets inhabited, sirrah?

PAGE
> My lord, it's Sunday night; they are full of drunken citizens.   [*Exit*]

LORD RAKE
> Along then, boys; we shall have a feast.   50

COLONEL BULLY
> Along, noble knight.

SIR JOHN
> Ay—along, Bully; and he that says Sir John Brute is not as drunk and as religious as the drunkenest citizen of 'em all— is a liar, and the son of a whore.

COLONEL BULLY
> Why, that was bravely spoke, and like a free-born English-   55
> man.

SIR JOHN
> What's that to you, sir, whether I am an Englishman or a Frenchman?

COLONEL BULLY
> Zoons, you are not angry, sir?

SIR JOHN
> Zoons, I am angry, sir!—for if I am a free-born Englishman,   60
> what have you to do even to talk of my privileges?

LORD RAKE
> Why prithee, knight, don't quarrel here; leave private animosities to be decided by daylight, let the night be employed against the public enemy.

SIR JOHN
> My lord, I respect you because you are a man of quality.   65
> But I'll make that fellow know, I am within a hair's breadth as absolute by my privileges as the King of France is by his prerogative. He by his prerogative takes money where it is not his due; I by my privilege refuse paying it where I owe it. Liberty and property and Old England, huzza!   70

ALL
> Huzza!   (*Exit* SIR JOHN *reeling, all following him*)

60 *I am a* Q1–2 (I'm a Q3, P)

---

61 *privileges* here, the constitutional rights of a free-born Englishman
68 *prerogative* here, the unrestricted power of an absolute king

Act III, Scene iii

A bedchamber
Enter LADY BRUTE *and* BELLINDA

LADY BRUTE
Sure, it's late, Bellinda; I begin to be sleepy.

BELLINDA
Yes, 'tis near twelve. Will you go to bed?

LADY BRUTE
To bed, my dear? And by that time I'm fallen into a sweet
sleep (or perhaps a sweet dream, which is better and better),
Sir John will come home roaring drunk, and be overjoyed   5
he finds me in a condition to be disturbed.

BELLINDA
Oh, you need not fear him, he's in for all night. The servants
say he's gone to drink with my Lord Rake.

LADY BRUTE
Nay, 'tis not very likely, indeed, such suitable company
should part presently. What hogs men turn, Bellinda, when   10
they grow weary of women!

BELLINDA
And what owls they are whilst they are fond of 'em!

LADY BRUTE
But that we may forgive well enough, because they are so
upon our accounts.

BELLINDA
We ought to do so, indeed; but 'tis a hard matter. For when   15
a man is really in love, he looks so unsufferably silly that
though a woman liked him well enough before, she has then
much ado to endure the sight of him. And this I take to be
the reason why lovers are so generally ill-used.

LADY BRUTE
Well, I own now, I'm well enough pleased to see a man look   20
like an ass for me.

BELLINDA
Ay, I'm pleased he should look like an ass too—that is, I'm
pleased with myself for making him look so.

LADY BRUTE
Nay truly, I think if he'd find some other way to express his
passion, 'twould be more to his advantage.   25

3 *I'm* Q1–3 (I am P)

BELLINDA·
> Yes; for then a woman might like his passion and him too.

LADY BRUTE
> Yet, Bellinda, after all, a woman's life would be but a dull
> business if 'twere not for men—and men that can look like
> asses, too. We should never blame fate for the shortness of
> our days; our time would hang wretchedly upon our hands.   30

BELLINDA
> Why truly, they do help us off with a good share on't. For
> were there no men in the world, o'my conscience I should
> be no longer a-dressing than I'm a-saying my prayers; nay,
> though it were Sunday: for you know that one may go to
> church without stays on.   35

LADY BRUTE
> But don't you think emulation might do something? For
> every woman you see desires to be finer than her neighbour.

BELLINDA
> That's only that the men may like her better than her neigh-
> bour. No; if there were no men, adieu fine petticoats, we
> should be weary of wearing 'em.   40

LADY BRUTE
> And adieu plays, we should be weary of seeing 'em.

BELLINDA
> Adieu Hyde Park, the dust would choke us.

LADY BRUTE
> Adieu St James's, walking would tire us.

BELLINDA
> Adieu London, the smoke would stifle us.

LADY BRUTE
> And adieu going to church, for religion would ne'er prevail 45
> with us.

BOTH
> Ha ha ha ha ha!

BELLINDA
> Our confession is so very hearty, sure we merit absolution.

LADY BRUTE
> Not unless we go through with't, and confess all. So prithee,
> for the ease of our consciences, let's hide nothing.   50

BELLINDA
> Agreed.

34 *know that* Q1–3 (know P)

---

42 *Hyde Park* 'Here People Coach it to take the Air, amidst a Cloud of
Dust, able to Choak a Foot Soldier' (Tom Brown, *Amusements* (1700),
p. 55).

LADY BRUTE

Why then, I confess that I love to sit in the forefront of a
box; for if one sits behind, there's two acts gone perhaps before one's found out. And when I am there, if I perceive
the men whispering and looking upon me, you must know   55
I cannot for my life forbear thinking they talk to my advantage; and that sets a thousand little tickling vanities on foot—

BELLINDA

Just my case for all the world; but go on.

LADY BRUTE

I watch with impatience for the next jest in the play, that
I may laugh and show my white teeth. If the poet has been   60
dull and the jest be long a-coming, I pretend to whisper one
to my friend, and from thence fall into a little short discourse
in which I take occasion to show my face in all humours:
brisk, pleased, serious, melancholy, languishing.—Not that
what we say to one another causes any of these alterations,   65
but—

BELLINDA

Don't trouble yourself to explain; for if I'm not mistaken,
you and I have had some of these necessary dialogues before
now, with the same intention.

LADY BRUTE

Why, I'll swear, Bellinda, some people do give strange   70
agreeable airs to their faces in speaking. Tell me true—did
you never practise in the glass?

BELLINDA

Why, did you?

LADY BRUTE

Yes, faith, many a time.

BELLINDA

And I too, I own it; both how to speak myself, and how to   75
look when others speak. But my glass and I could never yet
agree what face I should make when they come blurt out
with a nasty thing in a play. For all the men presently look
upon the women, that's certain; so laugh we must not,
though our stays burst for't, because that's telling truth and   80
owning we understand the jest; and to look serious is so
dull, when the whole house is a-laughing—

60 *may* Q1–3 (might P)
60 *poet* author
62 *short* Q1 (small Q2–3, P)
77 *blurt* blurting (adv.)
78 *nasty* obscene
78 *presently* immediately

LADY BRUTE

Besides, that looking serious does really betray our knowledge in the matter as much as laughing with the company
would do; for if we did not understand the thing, we should   85
naturally do like other people.

BELLINDA

For my part, I always take that occasion to blow my nose.

LADY BRUTE

You must blow your nose half off then at some plays.

BELLINDA

Why don't some reformer or other beat the poet for't?

LADY BRUTE

Because he is not so sure of our private approbation as of   90
our public thanks. Well, sure, there is not upon earth so
impertinent a thing as women's modesty.

BELLINDA

Yes; men's fantasque, that obliges us to it. If we quit our
modesty, they say we lose our charms; and yet they know
that very modesty is affectation, and rail at our hypocrisy.   95

LADY BRUTE

Thus one would think 'twere a hard matter to please 'em,
niece; yet our kind Mother Nature has given us something
that makes amends for all. Let our weakness be what it will,
mankind will still be weaker; and whilst there is a world, 'tis
woman that will govern it. But prithee, one word of poor   100
Constant before we go to bed, if it be but to furnish matter
for dreams; I dare swear he's talking of me now, or thinking
of me at least, though it be in the middle of his prayers.

BELLINDA

So he ought, I think; for you were pleased to make him a
good round advance today, madam.   105

LADY BRUTE

Why, I have e'en plagued him enough to satisfy any reasonable woman. He has besieged me these two years to no
purpose.

BELLINDA

And if he besieged you two years more, he'd be well enough
paid, so he had the plundering of you at last.   110

---

93 *fantasque* fancy, whim

---

89 Bellinda has not read Blackmore's Preface to *Prince Arthur* (1695) or
James Wright's *Country Conversations* (1694), which argues that 'most
of our New Comedies are become the very Pictures of Immorality'
(p. 4).

LADY BRUTE

That may be; but I'm afraid the town won't be able to hold
out much longer: for to confess the truth to you, Bellinda,
the garrison begins to grow mutinous.

BELLINDA

Then the sooner you capitulate, the better.

LADY BRUTE

Yet, methinks, I would fain stay a little longer, to see you   115
fixed too, that we might start together and see who could
love longest. What think you, if Heartfree should have a
month's mind to you?

BELLINDA

Why, faith, I could almost be in love with him for despising
that foolish affected Lady Fancyfull; but I'm afraid he's   120
too cold ever to warm himself by my fire.

LADY BRUTE

Then he deserves to be froze to death. Would I were a man
for your sake, my dear rogue.   (*Kissing her*)

BELLINDA

You'd wish yourself a woman again for your own, or the
men are mistaken. But if I could make a conquest of this son   125
of Bacchus, and rival his bottle, what should I do with him?
He has no fortune; I can't marry him; and sure you would
not have me commit fornication.

LADY BRUTE

Why, if you did, child, 'twould be but a good friendly part;
if 'twere only to keep me in countenance whilst I commit—   130
you know what.

BELLINDA

Well, if I can't resolve to serve you that way, I may perhaps
some other, as much to your satisfaction. But pray, how
shall we contrive to see these blades again quickly?

LADY BRUTE

We must e'en have recourse to the old way; make 'em an   135
appointment 'twixt jest and earnest. 'Twill look like a frolic,
and that you know's a very good thing to save a woman's
blushes.

BELLINDA

You advise well; but where shall it be?

118 *month's mind* strong inclination
123 *my dear* Q1–3 (dear P)

LADY BRUTE

In Spring Garden. But they shan't know their women till   140
their women pull off their masks; for a surprise is the most
agreeable thing in the world, and I find myself in a very
good humour, ready to do 'em any good turn I can think on.

BELLINDA

Then pray write 'em the necessary billet without farther
delay.   145

LADY BRUTE

Let's go into your chamber, then, and whilst you say your
prayers I'll do it, child.   (*Exeunt*)

Act IV, Scene i

Covent Garden
Enter LORD RAKE, SIR JOHN, [COLONEL BULLY] *&c., with*
swords drawn

LORD RAKE

Is the dog dead?

COLONEL BULLY

No, damn him, I heard him wheeze.

LORD RAKE

How the witch his wife howled!

COLONEL BULLY

Ay, she'll alarm the watch presently.

LORD RAKE

Appear, knight, then; come, you have a good cause to fight   5
for: there's a man murdered.

SIR JOHN

Is there? Then let his ghost be satisfied; for I'll sacrifice a
constable to it presently, and burn his body upon his wooden
chair.

Enter a TAILOR, *with a bundle under his arm*

147 s.d. (*Exeunt*) Q1 follows this with 'The End of the Third Act'.

---

140 *Spring Garden* a pleasure garden in Lambeth laid out with close walks,
     secluded arbours, and an artificial wilderness; the *Spectator* wanted
     'more Nightingales, and fewer Strumpets' (no. 383, 20 May 1712)
     s.d. *Covent Garden* a noble square behind the Strand, bounded by
     Inigo Jones's piazzas, St Paul's Church, and a market for earthenware
     and fruit
  8 *constable* officer of a city ward on oath to 'Arrest all them that make
     Contest, Riot, Debate or Affray . . . and lead them to the House or
     Compter of one of the *Sheriffs*' (Thomas Delaune, *Angliae Metropolis*
     (1690), p. 247)

COLONEL BULLY

How now! What have we got here, a thief?   10

TAILOR

No, an't please you; I'm no thief.

LORD RAKE

That we'll see presently.—Here, let the general examine
him.

SIR JOHN

Ay, ay; let me examine him, and I'll lay a hundred pound I
find him guilty in spite of his teeth—for he looks—like a—   15
sneaking rascal.—Come sirrah, without equivocation or
mental reservation, tell me of what opinion you are and
what calling; for by them—I shall guess at your morals.

TAILOR

An't please you, I'm a dissenting journeyman tailor.

SIR JOHN

Then, sirrah, you love lying by your religion and theft by   20
your trade. And so, that your punishment may be suitable to
your crimes, I'll have you first gagged—and then hanged.

TAILOR

Pray, good worthy gentlemen, don't abuse me; indeed I'm
an honest man, and a good workman, though I say it that
should not say it.   25

SIR JOHN

No words, sirrah, but attend your fate.

LORD RAKE

Let me see what's in that bundle.

TAILOR

An't please you, it's the doctor of the parish's gown.

LORD RAKE

The doctor's gown!—Hark you, knight, you won't stick at
abusing the clergy, will you?   30

SIR JOHN

No, I'm drunk, and I'll abuse anything—but my wife; and
her I name—with reverence.

LORD RAKE

Then you shall wear this gown whilst you charge the watch,
that though the blows fall upon you, the scandal may light
upon the church.   35

SIR JOHN

A generous design, by all the gods!—Give it me.
                              (*Takes the gown and puts it on*)

28 *it's* Q1–3 (it is P)

_____

12 *general* Lord Rake sustains his series of military metaphors.

TAILOR

O dear gentlemen, I shall be quite undone if you take the gown.

SIR JOHN

Retire, sirrah; and since you carry off your skin—go home, and be happy. 40

TAILOR (*Pausing*)

I think I had e'en as good follow the gentleman's friendly advice. For if I dispute any longer, who knows but the whim may take him to case me? These courtiers are fuller of tricks than they are of money; they'll sooner cut a man's throat than pay his bill. (*Exit* TAILOR) 45

SIR JOHN

So, how d'ye like my shapes now?

LORD RAKE

This will do to a miracle; he looks like a bishop going to the holy war.—But to your arms, gentlemen; the enemy appears.

Enter CONSTABLE *and* WATCH

WATCHMAN

Stand! Who goes there? Come before the constable.

SIR JOHN

The constable's a rascal—and you are the son of a whore. 50

WATCHMAN

A good civil answer for a parson, truly!

CONSTABLE

Methinks, sir, a man of your coat might set a better example.

SIR JOHN

Sirrah, I'll make you know—there are men of my coat can set as bad examples—as you can do, you dog you!

(SIR JOHN *strikes the* CONSTABLE. *They knock him down, disarm him and seize him.* LORD RAKE *&c. run away*)

CONSTABLE

So, we have secured the parson, however. 55

SIR JOHN

Blood and blood—and blood!

WATCHMAN

Lord have mercy upon us! How the wicked wretch raves of blood! I'll warrant he has been murdering somebody tonight.

SIR JOHN

Sirrah, there's nothing got by murder but a halter. My talent 60
lies towards drunkenness and simony.

43 *case* skin

WATCHMAN
Why, that now was spoke like a man of parts, neighbours; it's pity he should be so disguised.

SIR JOHN
You lie—I am not disguised; for I am drunk barefaced.

WATCHMAN
Look you there again!—This is a mad parson, Mr Constable; I'll lay a pot of ale upon's head, he's a good preacher.

CONSTABLE
Come, sir; out of respect to your calling I shan't put you into the round-house; but we must secure you in our drawing-room till morning, that you may do no mischief. So, come along.

SIR JOHN
You may put me where you will, sirrah, now you have overcome me. But if I can't do mischief, I'll think of mischief—in spite of your teeth, you dog you! *(Exeunt)*

65

70

Act IV, Scene ii

A bedchamber
Enter HEARTFREE, *solus*

[HEARTFREE]
What the plague ails me? Love? No, I thank you for that, my heart's rock still.—Yet 'tis Bellinda that disturbs me, that's positive.—Well, what of all that? Must I love her for being troublesome? At that rate I might love all the women I meet, egad. But hold!—Though I don't love her for disturbing me, yet she may disturb me because I love her. Ay, that may be, faith! I have dreamt of her, that's certain.—Well, so I have of my mother; therefore what's that to the purpose? —Ay, but Bellinda runs in my mind waking.—And so does many a damned thing that I don't care a farthing for!— Methinks, though, I would fain be talking to her, and yet I have no business.—Well, am I the first man that has had a mind to do an impertinent thing?

5

10

Enter CONSTANT

64 *I am not* Q1–3 (I'm not P)
5 *egad* (I gad Q1) a softened form of *By God* (also at 69)
13 *impertinent* irrelevant or absurd

68 *round-house* an overnight lock-up

CONSTANT

How now, Heartfree? What makes you up and dressed so
soon? I thought none but lovers quarreled with their beds;   15
I expected to have found you snoring, as I used to do.

HEARTFREE

Why faith, friend, 'tis the care I have of your affairs that
makes me so thoughtful; I have been studying all night
how to bring your matter about with Bellinda.

CONSTANT

With Bellinda?   20

HEARTFREE

With my lady, I mean.—And faith, I have mighty hopes
on't. Sure you must be very well satisfied with her behaviour
to you yesterday?

CONSTANT

So well, that nothing but a lover's fears can make me doubt
of success. But what can this sudden change proceed from?   25

HEARTFREE

Why, you saw her husband beat her, did you not?

CONSTANT

That's true; a husband is scarce to be borne upon any terms,
much less when he fights with his wife. Methinks she should
e'en have cuckolded him upon the very spot, to show that
after the battle she was master of the field.   30

HEARTFREE

A council of war of women would infallibly have advised
her to't. But, I confess, so agreeable a woman as Bellinda
deserves a better usage.

CONSTANT

Bellinda again!

HEARTFREE

My lady, I mean. What a pox makes me blunder so today?—   35
(*Aside*) A plague of this treacherous tongue!

CONSTANT

Prithee, look upon me seriously, Heartfree.—Now answer
me directly: is it my lady, or Bellinda, employs your careful
thoughts thus?

HEARTFREE

My lady, or Bellinda?   40

CONSTANT

In love! by this light, in love!

HEARTFREE

In love?

CONSTANT

Nay, ne'er deny it; for thou'lt do it so awkwardly, 'twill but

make the jest sit heavier about thee. My dear friend, I give
thee much joy.   45

HEARTFREE

Why prithee, you won't persuade me to it, will you?

CONSTANT

That she's mistress of your tongue, that's plain; and I know
you are so honest a fellow, your tongue and heart always go
together. But how—but how the devil—? Pha ha ha ha!—

HEARTFREE

Hey-day! Why, sure you don't believe it in earnest?   50

CONSTANT

Yes, I do; because I see you deny it in jest.

HEARTFREE

Nay, but look you, Ned—a—deny in jest—a—Gadzooks!
you know I say—a—when a man denies a thing in jest—a—

CONSTANT

Pha ha ha ha ha!

HEARTFREE

—Nay, then we shall have it. What, because a man stumbles   55
at a word? Did you never make a blunder?

CONSTANT

Yes, for I am in love; I own it.

HEARTFREE

Then, so am I! (*Embracing him*) Now laugh till thy soul's
glutted with mirth!—But, dear Constant, don't tell the
town on't.   60

CONSTANT

Nay then, 'twere almost pity to laugh at thee after so honest
a confession. But tell us a little, Jack; by what new-invented
arms has this mighty stroke been given?

HEARTFREE

E'en by that unaccountable weapon called *je ne sais quoi*; for
everything that can come within the verge of beauty, I have   65
seen it with indifference.

CONSTANT

So in few words, then, the *je ne sais quoi* has been too hard
for the quilted petticoat.

HEARTFREE

Egad, I think the *je ne sais quoi* is in the quilted petticoat; at
least, 'tis certain I ne'er think on't without—a—a *je ne sais*   70
quoi in every part about me.

---

64 *je ne sais quoi* I know not what, i.e., an indefinable attraction or 'certain
something'

CONSTANT

Well; but have all your remedies lost their virtue? have you
turned her inside out yet?

HEARTFREE

I dare not so much as think on't.

CONSTANT

But don't the two years' fatigue I have had discourage you?   75

HEARTFREE

Yes; I dread what I foresee, yet cannot quit the enterprise—
like some soldiers whose courage dwells more in their honour
than their nature: on they go, though the body trembles at
what the soul makes it undertake.

CONSTANT

Nay, if you expect your mistress will use you as your pro-   80
fanations against her sex deserve, you tremble justly. But
how do you intend to proceed, friend?

HEARTFREE

Thou know'st I'm but a novice; be friendly, and advise me.

CONSTANT

Why, look you then; I'd have you—serenade, and a—write
a song—go to church—look like a fool—be very officious—   85
ogle—write—and lead out; and who knows but in a year or
two's time you may be—called a troublesome puppy and
sent about your business.

HEARTFREE

That's hard.

CONSTANT

Yet thus it oft falls out with lovers, sir.   90

HEARTFREE

Pox on me for making one of the number!

CONSTANT

Have a care! Say no saucy things; 'twill but augment your
crime and, if your mistress hears on't, increase your punishment.

HEARTFREE

Prithee, say something then to encourage me; you know I   95
helped you in your distress.

CONSTANT

Why then, to encourage you to perseverance that you may
be thoroughly ill-used for your offences, I'll put you in
mind that even the coyest ladies of 'em all are made up of
desires, as well as we; and though they do hold out a long   100

---

86 *lead out* Lord Foppington in *The Relapse* spends an hour 'leading . . . aut'
the company after the play (II. i. 235-6)

time, they will capitulate at last. For that thundering
engineer, nature, does make such havoc in the town, they
must surrender at long run or perish in their own flames.

Enter a FOOTMAN

[FOOTMAN (*To* CONSTANT)]
  Sir, there's a porter without with a letter; he desires to give
  it into your own hands.   105
CONSTANT
  Call him in.   [*Exit* FOOTMAN]

Enter PORTER

What, Jo! Is it thee?
PORTER
  An't please you, sir, I was ordered to deliver this into your
  own hands, by two well-shaped ladies at the New Exchange.
  I was at your honour's lodgings, and your servants sent me   110
  hither.
CONSTANT
  'Tis well. Are you to carry any answer?
PORTER
  No, my noble master. They gave me my orders and whip!
  they were gone, like a maidenhead at fifteen.
CONSTANT
  Very well; there.   (*Gives him money*) 115
PORTER
  God bless your honour.   (*Exit* PORTER)
CONSTANT
  Now let's see what honest trusty Jo has brought us.—
  (*Reads*) 'If you and your playfellow can spare time from
  your business and devotions, don't fail to be at Spring
  Garden about eight in the evening. You'll find nothing there 120
  but women, so you need bring no other arms than what you
  usually carry about you'.—So, playfellow, here's something
  to stay your stomach till your mistress's dish is ready for
  you.
HEARTFREE
  Some of our old battered acquaintance. I won't go, not I. 125
CONSTANT
  Nay, that you can't avoid. There's honour in the case; 'tis a
  challenge, and I want a second.

113 *whip!* presto!

---

107 *Jo!* To assist Constant's memory, each porter's name was stamped on
    a ticket at his belt.
109 *New Exchange* a fashionable shopping arcade in the Strand

HEARTFREE

I doubt I shall be but a very useless one to you; for I'm so disheartened by this wound Bellinda has given me, I don't think I shall have courage enough to draw my sword.   130

CONSTANT

Oh, if that be all, come along; I'll warrant you find sword enough for such enemies as we have to deal withal.   (*Exeunt*)

Act IV, Scene iii

Enter CONSTABLE *&c., with* SIR JOHN

CONSTABLE

Come along, sir; I thought to have let you slip this morning, because you were a minister; but you are as drunk and as abusive as ever. We'll see what the justice of the peace will say to you.

SIR JOHN

And you shall see what I'll say to the justice of the peace,   5
sirrah.   (*They knock at the door*)

Enter SERVANT

CONSTABLE

Pray acquaint his worship, we have got an unruly parson here. We are unwilling to expose him, but don't know what to do with him.

SERVANT

I'll acquaint my master.   (*Exit* SERVANT)   10

SIR JOHN

You—constable—what damned justice is this?

CONSTABLE

One that will take care of you, I warrant you.

Enter JUSTICE

JUSTICE

Well, Mr Constable, what's the disorder here?

CONSTABLE

An't please your worship—

---

s.d. *Enter* CONSTABLE ... Q1 continues without any break here, but clearly the scene has changed to the Justice's house, or the street outside it.

SIR JOHN
Let me speak, and be damned; I'm a divine, and can unfold   15
mysteries better than you can do.

JUSTICE
Sadness, sadness, a minister so overtaken!—Pray, sir, give
the constable leave to speak, and I'll hear you very patiently;
I assure you, sir, I will.

SIR JOHN
Sir—you are a very civil magistrate. Your most humble   20
servant.

CONSTABLE
An't please your worship, then, he has attempted to beat the
watch tonight, and swore—

SIR JOHN
You lie!

JUSTICE
Hold, pray sir, a little.   25

SIR JOHN
Sir, your very humble servant.

CONSTABLE
Indeed, sir, he came at us without any provocation, called
us whores and rogues, and laid us on with a great quarter-
staff. He was in my Lord Rake's company; they have been
playing the devil tonight.   30

JUSTICE
Hem, hem.—Pray sir, may you be chaplain to my lord?

SIR JOHN
Sir—I presume—I may if I will.

JUSTICE
My meaning, sir, is: are you so?

SIR JOHN
Sir—you mean very well.

JUSTICE
He hem, hem.—Under favour, sir, pray answer me directly.   35

SIR JOHN
Under favour, sir—do you use to answer directly when you
are drunk?

JUSTICE
Good lack, good lack! Here's nothing to be got from him.—
Pray, sir, may I crave your name?

SIR JOHN
Sir—my name's—(*He hiccups*) Hiccup, sir.   40

17 *overtaken* drunk
28 *laid us on* assailed us

JUSTICE

Hiccup? Doctor Hiccup, I have known a great many country
parsons of that name, especially down in the Fens. Pray
where do you live, sir?

SIR JOHN

Here—and there, sir.

JUSTICE

Why, what a strange man is this!—Where do you preach,   45
sir? Have you any cure?

SIR JOHN

Sir—I have—a very good cure—for a clap, at your service.

JUSTICE

Lord have mercy upon us!

SIR JOHN (*Aside*)

This fellow does ask so many impertinent questions, I
believe, egad, 'tis the justice's wife in the justice's clothes.   50

JUSTICE

Mr Constable, I vow and protest I don't know what to do
with him.

CONSTABLE

Truly, he has been but a troublesome guest to us all night.

JUSTICE

I think I had e'en best let him go about his business, for I'm
unwilling to expose him.   55

CONSTABLE

E'en what your worship thinks fit.

SIR JOHN

Sir—not to interrupt, Mr Constable—I have a small favour
to ask.

JUSTICE

Sir, I open both my ears to you.

SIR JOHN

Sir, your very humble servant. I have a little urgent business   60
calls upon me; and therefore I desire the favour of you to
bring matters to a conclusion.

JUSTICE

Sir, if I were sure that business were not to commit more
disorders, I would release you.

SIR JOHN

None—by my priesthood!   65

JUSTICE

Then, Mr Constable, you may discharge him.

---

42 *the Fens* marshy, low-lying districts in Cambridgeshire, Lincolnshire,
and some adjoining counties

SIR JOHN

    Sir, your very humble servant. If you please to accept of a
    bottle—

JUSTICE

    I thank you kindly, sir; but I never drink in a morning.
    Good-bye to ye, sir, good-bye to ye.   70

SIR JOHN

    Good-bye t'ye, good sir. (*Exit* JUSTICE) So.—Now, Mr
    Constable, shall you and I go pick up a whore together?

CONSTABLE

    No, thank you, sir; my wife's enough to satisfy any reason-
    able man.

SIR JOHN

    (*Aside*) He he he he he!—the fool is married, then.—   75
    [*Aloud*] Well, you won't go?

CONSTABLE

    Not I, truly.

SIR JOHN

    Then I'll go by myself; and you and your wife may be
    damned.   (*Exit* SIR JOHN)

CONSTABLE (*Gazing after him*)

    Why, God a mercy, parson!   (*Exeunt*)   80

Act IV, Scene iv

Spring Garden
CONSTANT *and* HEARTFREE *cross the stage*

CONSTANT

    So. I think we are about the time appointed; let us walk up
    this way.

    Exeunt. As they go off, enter LADY FANCYFULL *and*
    MADAMOISELLE, *masked and dogging 'em*

LADY FANCYFULL

    Good. Thus far I have dogged 'em without being discovered.
    'Tis infallibly some intrigue that brings them to Spring
    Garden. How my poor heart is torn and racked with fear   5
    and jealousy! Yet let it be anything but that flirt Bellinda,
    and I'll try to bear it. But if it prove her, all that's woman in
    me shall be employed to destroy her.

                  (*Exeunt after* CONSTANT *and* HEARTFREE)

80 *God a mercy* thank you (ironic)
  2 s.d. *As ... dogging 'em* Q1 prints this immediately before Constant's
    line

Re-enter CONSTANT *and* HEARTFREE, LADY FANCYFULL *and*
MADAMOISELLE *still following at a distance*

CONSTANT
I see no females yet that have anything to say to us. I'm
afraid we are bantered.   10

HEARTFREE
I wish we were, for I'm in no humour to make either them
or myself merry.

CONSTANT
Nay, I'm sure you'll make them merry enough, if I tell 'em
why you are dull. But prithee, why so heavy and sad before
you begin to be ill-used?   15

HEARTFREE
For the same reason, perhaps, that you are so brisk and well
pleased: because both pains and pleasures are generally more
considerable in prospect than when they come to pass.

Enter LADY BRUTE *and* BELLINDA, *masked and poorly*
dressed

CONSTANT
How now, who are these? Not our game, I hope.

HEARTFREE
If they are, we are e'en well enough served, to come hunting   20
here when we had so much better game in chase elsewhere.

LADY FANCYFULL (*To* MADAMOISELLE)
So; those are their ladies, without doubt. But I'm afraid that
doily stuff is not worn for want of better clothes. They are
the very shape and size of Bellinda and her aunt.

MADAMOISELLE
So day be inteed, matam.   25

LADY FANCYFULL
We'll slip into this close arbour, where we may hear all they
say.   (*Exeunt* LADY FANCYFULL *and* MADAMOISELLE)

LADY BRUTE
What, are you afraid of us, gentlemen?

HEARTFREE
Why truly, I think we may, if appearance don't lie.

10 *bantered* (1) cheated, tricked (2) made fun of
20 *hunting* Q1–3 (a hunting P)

18 s.d. *masked* Masks were rarely worn by respectable women at this
   period.
23 *doily stuff* summer-weight woollen cloth, named after Thomas Doyly, a
   London draper specializing in 'such Stuffs as might at once be cheap
   and genteel' (the *Spectator*, no. 283, 24 January 1712)

BELLINDA
  Do you always find women what they appear to be, sir?   30
HEARTFREE
  No, forsooth; but I seldom find 'em better than they appear
  to be.
BELLINDA
  Then the outside's best, you think?
HEARTFREE
  'Tis the honestest.
CONSTANT
  Have a care, Heartfree; you are relapsing again.   35
LADY BRUTE
  Why, does the gentleman use to rail at women?
CONSTANT
  He has done formerly.
BELLINDA
  I suppose he had very good cause for't.—They did not use
  you so well as you thought you deserved, sir.
LADY BRUTE
  They made themselves merry at your expense, sir.   40
BELLINDA
  Laughed when you sighed.
LADY BRUTE
  Slept while you were waking.
BELLINDA
  Had your porter beat.
LADY BRUTE
  And threw your *billets-doux* in the fire.
HEARTFREE
  Hey-day, I shall do more than rail presently.   45
BELLINDA
  Why, you won't beat us, will you?
HEARTFREE
  I don't know but I may.
CONSTANT
  What the devil's coming here? Sir John in a gown?—And
  drunk, i'faith.

                        Enter SIR JOHN

SIR JOHN
  What a pox! Here's Constant, Heartfree—and two whores,   50
  egad!—O you covetous rogues! what, have you never a
  spare punk for your friend? But I'll share with you.
                              (*He seizes both the women*)

  44 *billets-doux* ed. (billet-doux Q1–3, P) love-letters

HEARTFREE
 Why, what the plague have you been doing, knight?

SIR JOHN
 Why, I have been beating the watch, and scandalizing the
 clergy.   55

HEARTFREE
 A very good account, truly.

SIR JOHN
 And what do you think I'll do next?

CONSTANT
 Nay, that no man can guess.

SIR JOHN
 Why, if you'll let me sup with you, I'll treat both your
 strumpets.   60

LADY BRUTE (*Aside*)
 O Lord, we are undone!

HEARTFREE
 No, we can't sup together, because we have some affairs
 elsewhere. But if you'll accept of these two ladies, we'll be so
 complaisant to you to resign our right in 'em.

BELLINDA (*Aside*)
 Lord, what shall we do?   65

SIR JOHN
 Let me see; their clothes are such damned clothes they won't
 pawn for the reckoning.

HEARTFREE
 Sir John, your servant. Rapture attend you!

CONSTANT
 Adieu, ladies; make much of the gentleman.

LADY BRUTE
 Why, sure, you won't leave us in the hands of a drunken   70
 fellow to abuse us?

SIR JOHN
 Who do you call a drunken fellow, you slut you? I'm a man
 of quality; the king has made me a knight.

HEARTFREE
 Ay, ay, you are in good hands! Adieu, adieu!
                                        (HEARTFREE *runs off*)

LADY BRUTE
 The devil's hands! Let me go, or I'll—for heaven's sake,   75
 protect us!
                (*She breaks from him, runs to* CONSTANT, *twitching off her*
                                        mask and clapping it on again)

74 s.d. (HEARTFREE *runs off*) Q1 prints this before Heartfree's line

SIR JOHN
  I'll devil you, you jade you! I'll demolish your ugly face!
CONSTANT
  Hold a little, knight; she swoons.
SIR JOHN
  I'll swoon her!
CONSTANT
  Hey, Heartfree!   80

Re-enter HEARTFREE. BELLINDA *runs to him and shows her
face*

HEARTFREE
  O heavens! My dear creature, stand there a little.
CONSTANT [*To* HEARTFREE, *aside*]
  Pull him off, Jack.
HEARTFREE
  Hold, mighty man; look you, sir, we did but jest with you.
  These are ladies of our acquaintance that we had a mind to
  frighten a little, but now you must leave us.   85
SIR JOHN
  Oons, I won't leave you, not I!
HEARTFREE
  Nay, but you must, though; and therefore make no words
  on't.
SIR JOHN
  Then you are a couple of damned uncivil fellows. And I
  hope your punks will give you sauce to your mutton!   90
                                        (*Exit* SIR JOHN)
LADY BRUTE
  Oh, I shall never come to myself again, I'm so frightened!
CONSTANT
  'Twas a narrow 'scape, indeed.
BELLINDA
  Women must have frolics, you see, whatever they cost 'em.
HEARTFREE
  This might have proved a dear one, though.
LADY BRUTE
  You are the more obliged to us, for the risk we run upon   95
  your accounts.
CONSTANT
  And I hope you'll acknowledge something due to our knight-

90 *sauce* venereal disease (slang)
90 *mutton* prostitute (slang)
93 *must* Q1–3 (must needs P)

errantry, ladies. This is the second time we have delivered
you.

LADY BRUTE
'Tis true; and since we see fate has designed you for our   100
guardians, 'twill make us the more willing to trust ourselves
in your hands. But you must not have the worse opinion of
us for our innocent frolic.

HEARTFREE
Ladies, you may command our opinions in everything that
is to your advantage.   105

BELLINDA
Then, sir, I command you to be of opinion that women are
sometimes better than they appear to be.
                    (LADY BRUTE *and* CONSTANT *talk apart*)

HEARTFREE
Madam, you have made a convert of me in everything. I'm
grown a fool: I could be fond of a woman.

BELLINDA
I thank you, sir, in the name of the whole sex.   110

HEARTFREE
Which sex nothing but yourself could ever have atoned for.

BELLINDA
Now has my vanity a devilish itch, to know in what my merit
consists.

HEARTFREE
In your humility, madam, that keeps you ignorant it consists at all.   115

BELLINDA
One other compliment with that serious face, and I hate you
for ever after.

HEARTFREE
Some women love to be abused; is that it you would be at?

BELLINDA
No, not that neither; but I'd have men talk plainly what's
fit for women to hear, without putting 'em either to a real,   120
or an affected blush.

HEARTFREE
Why then, in as plain terms as I can find to express myself,
I could love you even to—matrimony itself almost, egad.

BELLINDA
Just as Sir John did her ladyship there. What think you?
Don't you believe one month's time might bring you down   125
to the same indifference, only clad in a little better manners,

114–15 *consists* exists

perhaps? Well, you men are unaccountable things; mad till
you have your mistresses, and then stark mad till you are
rid of 'em again. Tell me honestly, is not your patience put
to a much severer trial after possession than before?   130

HEARTFREE

With a great many I must confess it is, to our eternal scandal;
but I—dear creature, do but try me!

BELLINDA

That's the surest way indeed to know, but not the safest.—
(*To* LADY BRUTE) Madam, are not you for taking a turn in the
Great Walk? It's almost dark; nobody will know us.   135

LADY BRUTE

Really, I find myself something idle, Bellinda; besides, I dote
upon this little odd private corner. But don't let my lazy
fancy confine you.

CONSTANT (*Aside*)

So, she would be left alone with me; that's well.

BELLINDA

Well, we'll take one turn and come to you again.—(*To*   140
HEARTFREE) Come, sir; shall we go pry into the secrets of the
garden? Who knows what discoveries we may make!

HEARTFREE

Madam, I'm at your service.

CONSTANT (*To* HEARTFREE, *aside*)

Don't make too much haste back, for—d'ye hear?—I may
be busy.   145

HEARTFREE

Enough.   ([*Exeunt*] BELLINDA *and* HEARTFREE)

LADY BRUTE

Sure you think me scandalously free, Mr Constant. I'm
afraid I shall lose your good opinion of me.

CONSTANT

My good opinion, madam, is like your cruelty, never to be
removed.   150

LADY BRUTE

But if I should remove my cruelty, then there's an end of
your good opinion.

---

146 s.d. [*Exeunt*] ed. (*Exit* Q1–3, P)

134–5 *a turn ... Walk* 'Ladies that have an Inclination to be Private, take
Delight in the Close Walks of *Spring-Gardens*, where both Sexes meet,
and mutually serve one another as Guides to lose their Way' (Tom
Brown, *Amusements* (1700), p. 54).

CONSTANT
> There is not so strict an alliance between 'em, neither. 'Tis
> certain I should love you then better (if that be possible)
> than I do now; and where I love, I always esteem.   155

LADY BRUTE
> Indeed, I doubt you much. Why, suppose you had a wife,
> and she should entertain a gallant?

CONSTANT
> If I gave her just cause, how could I justly condemn her?

LADY BRUTE
> Ah, but you'd differ widely about just causes.

CONSTANT
> But blows can bear no dispute.   160

LADY BRUTE
> Nor ill manners much, truly.

CONSTANT
> Then no woman upon earth has so just a cause as you have.

LADY BRUTE
> Oh, but a faithful wife is a beautiful character.

CONSTANT
> To a deserving husband, I confess it is.

LADY BRUTE
> But can his faults release my duty?   165

CONSTANT
> In equity, without doubt. And where laws dispense with
> equity, equity should dispense with laws.

LADY BRUTE
> Pray, let's leave this dispute; for you men have as much
> witchcraft in your arguments as women have in their eyes.

CONSTANT
> But whilst you attack me with your charms, 'tis but reason-   170
> able I assault you with mine.

LADY BRUTE
> The case is not the same. What mischief we do, we can't
> help, and therefore are to be forgiven.

CONSTANT
> Beauty soon obtains pardon for the pain that it gives, when
> it applies the balm of compassion to the wound; but a fine   175
> face and a hard heart is almost as bad as an ugly face and
> a soft one—both very troublesome to many a poor gentleman.

LADY BRUTE
> Yes, and to many a poor gentlewoman, too, I can assure you.
> But pray, which of 'em is it that most afflicts you?

---

166 *equity* See note to I.i.95–6.

CONSTANT

Your glass and conscience will inform you, madam. But for   180
heaven's sake (for now I must be serious), if pity or if
gratitude can move you (*Taking her hand*), if constancy and
truth have power to tempt you, if love, if adoration can affect
you, give me at least some hopes that time may do what you
perhaps mean never to perform; 'twill ease my sufferings,   185
though not quench my flame.

LADY BRUTE

Your sufferings eased, your flame would soon abate; and
that I would preserve, not quench it, sir.

CONSTANT

Would you preserve it, nourish it with favours; for that's
the food it naturally requires.   190

LADY BRUTE

Yet on that natural food 'twould surfeit soon, should I
resolve to grant all that you would ask.

CONSTANT

And in refusing all, you starve it. Forgive me, therefore,
since my hunger rages, if I at last grow wild and in my
frenzy force at least this from you. (*Kissing her hand*) Or if   195
you'd have my flame soar higher still, then grant me this,
and this, and this, and thousands more. (*Kissing first her
hand, then her neck.—Aside*) For now's the time; she melts
into compassion.

LADY BRUTE

(*Aside*) Poor coward virtue, how it shuns the battle.—   200
[*Aloud*] O heavens! let me go.

CONSTANT

Ay, go, ay. Where shall we go, my charming angel?—Into
this private arbour.—Nay, let's lose no time—moments are
precious.

LADY BRUTE

And lovers wild. Pray let us stop here; at least for this time.   205

CONSTANT

'Tis impossible. He that has power over you can have none
over himself.

LADY BRUTE

Ah, I'm lost!

> As he is forcing her into the arbour, LADY FANCYFULL *and*
> MADAMOISELLE *bolt out upon them, and run over the stage*

192 *all that* Q1–3 (all P)
194 *since . . . rages, if* Q1–3 (if since . . . rages, P)

LADY FANCYFULL
  Fie fie fie fie fie!
MADAMOISELLE
  Fie fie fie fie fie!   210
            [*Exeunt* LADY FANCYFULL *and* MADAMOISELLE]
CONSTANT
  Death and furies! who are these?
LADY BRUTE
  O heavens! I'm out of my wits. If they knew me, I'm ruined.
CONSTANT
  Don't be frightened; ten thousand to one they are strangers
  to you.
LADY BRUTE
  Whatever they are, I won't stay here a moment longer.   215
CONSTANT
  Whither will you go?
LADY BRUTE
  Home, as if the devil were in me. Lord, where's this Bellinda
  now?

                Enter BELLINDA *and* HEARTFREE

  Oh, it's well you are come. I'm so frightened my hair stands
  on end. Let's be gone, for heaven's sake!   220
BELLINDA
  Lord, what's the matter?
LADY BRUTE
  The devil's the matter: we are discovered. Here's a couple
  of women have done the most impertinent thing. Away,
  away, away, away, away!
            (*Exit running* [*with* BELLINDA. *The men follow*])

            Re-enter LADY FANCYFULL *and* MADAMOISELLE

LADY FANCYFULL
  Well, Madamoiselle, 'tis a prodigious thing how women   225
  can suffer filthy fellows to grow so familiar with 'em.
MADAMOISELLE
  Ah, matam, *il n'y a rien de si naturel.*

220 *on end* ed. (an end Q1–3, P, the older form)
227 *il . . . naturel* there's nothing more natural

222–3 *Here's . . . thing* Lady Fancyfull and Madamoiselle, or Lady Brute
and Bellinda?

LADY FANCYFULL

Fie fie fie! But oh, my heart! O jealousy! O torture! I'm
upon the rack. What shall I do? My lover's lost; I ne'er shall
see him mine.—(*Pausing*) But I may be revenged, and that's   230
the same thing. Ah, sweet revenge! Thou welcome thought,
thou healing balsam to my wounded soul! Be but propitious
on this one occasion, I'll place my heaven in thee for all my
life to come.

> To woman, how indulgent nature's kind!   235
> No blast of fortune long disturbs her mind.
> Compliance to her fate supports her still;
> If love won't make her happy—mischief will.   (*Exeunt*)

Act V, Scene i

LADY FANCYFULL'*s House*
Enter LADY FANCYFULL *and* MADAMOISELLE

LADY FANCYFULL

Well, Madamoiselle; did you dog the filthy things?

MADAMOISELLE

O que oui, matam.

LADY FANCYFULL

And where are they?

MADAMOISELLE

Au logis.

LADY FANCYFULL

What, men and all?   5

MADAMOISELLE

Tous ensemble.

LADY FANCYFULL

Oh, confidence! What, carry their fellows to their own
house?

MADAMOISELLE

C'est que le mari n'y est pas.

LADY FANCYFULL

No, so I believe, truly. But he shall be there, and quickly   10
too, if I can find him out. Well, 'tis a prodigious thing, to see
when men and women get together, how they fortify one

---

238 s.d. (*Exeunt*) Q1 follows this with 'The End of the Fourth Act'.
2 *O que oui* Yes indeed
4 *Au logis* At home
6 *Tous ensemble* All of them together
9 *C'est . . . pas* It's because the husband is not there

another in their impudence. But if that drunken fool, her
husband, be to be found in e'er a tavern in town, I'll send him
amongst 'em. I'll spoil their sport!   15

MADAMOISELLE
En vérité, matam, *ce serait dommage*.

LADY FANCYFULL
'Tis in vain to oppose it, Madamoiselle; therefore never go
about it. For I am the steadiest creature in the world—when
I have determined to do mischief. So, come along. (*Exeunt*)

Act V, Scene ii

SIR JOHN BRUTE's *House*
Enter CONSTANT, HEARTFREE, LADY BRUTE, BELLINDA *and*
LOVEWELL

LADY BRUTE
But are you sure you don't mistake, Lovewell?

LOVEWELL
Madam, I saw 'em all go into the tavern together, and my
master was so drunk he could scarce stand.   [*Exit*]

LADY BRUTE
Then, gentlemen, I believe we may venture to let you stay
and play at cards with us an hour or two; for they'll scarce   5
part till morning.

BELLINDA
I think 'tis pity they should ever part.

CONSTANT
The company that's here, madam.

LADY BRUTE
Then, sir, the company that's here must remember to part
itself, in time.   10

CONSTANT
Madam, we don't intend to forfeit your future favours by
an indiscreet usage of this. The moment you give us the
signal, we shan't fail to make our retreat.

LADY BRUTE
Upon those conditions, then, let us sit down to cards.

Enter LOVEWELL

16 *En . . . dommage* In truth, matam, it would be a pity
 7 *pity* Q1–3 (a pity P)
12 *an indiscreet* Q1–2 (indiscreet Q3, P)

[LOVEWELL]

O Lord, madam, here's my master just staggering in upon   15
you! He has been quarrelsome yonder, and they have kicked
him out of the company.   [*Exit*]

LADY BRUTE

Into the closet, gentlemen, for heaven's sake! I'll wheedle
him to bed, if possible.

(CONSTANT *and* HEARTFREE *run into the closet*)

Enter SIR JOHN, *all dirt and bloody*

Ah—ah—he's all over blood!   20

SIR JOHN

What the plague does the woman—squall for? Did you
never see a man in pickle before?

LADY BRUTE

Lord, where have you been?

SIR JOHN

I have been at—cuffs.

LADY BRUTE

I fear that is not all. I hope you are not wounded.   25

SIR JOHN

Sound as a roach, wife.

LADY BRUTE

I'm mighty glad to hear it.

SIR JOHN

You know—I think you lie.

LADY BRUTE

I know you do me wrong to think so, then. For heaven's my
witness, I had rather see my own blood trickle down than   30
yours.

SIR JOHN

Then will I be crucified.

LADY BRUTE

'Tis a hard fate I should not be believed.

SIR JOHN

'Tis a damned atheistical age, wife.

LADY BRUTE

I am sure I have given you a thousand tender proofs, how   35
great my care is of you. Nay, spite of all your cruel thoughts

29 *I know you* Q1–3 (You P)
29 *so, then* Q1–3 (so P)
36 *Nay* Q1–3 (But P)

---

26 proverbial (Tilley, R 143); the roach is a fresh-water fish traditionally
thought incapable of disease

I'll still persist, and at this moment, if I can, persuade you
to lie down and sleep a little.

SIR JOHN

Why—do you think I am drunk—you slut you?

LADY BRUTE

Heaven forbid I should! But I'm afraid you are feverish.   40
Pray let me feel your pulse.

SIR JOHN

Stand off, and be damned.

LADY BRUTE

Why, I see your distemper in your very eyes. You are all on
fire. Pray, go to bed; let me entreat you.

SIR JOHN

—Come kiss me, then.   45

LADY BRUTE (*Kissing him*)

There: now go.—(*Aside*) He stinks like poison.

SIR JOHN

I see it goes damnably against your stomach—and therefore
—kiss me again.

LADY BRUTE

Nay, now you fool me.

SIR JOHN

Do't, I say.   50

LADY BRUTE

(*Aside*) Ah, Lord have mercy upon me!—[*Kissing him*] Well,
there: now will you go?

SIR JOHN

Now, wife, you shall see my gratitude. You give me two
kisses—I'll give you—two hundred. (*Kisses and tumbles her*)

LADY BRUTE

O Lord! Pray, Sir John, be quiet. Heavens, what a pickle   55
am I in!

BELLINDA (*Aside*)

If I were in her pickle, I'd call my gallant out of the closet,
and he should cudgel him soundly.

SIR JOHN

So; now, you being as dirty and as nasty as myself, we may
go pig together. But first I must have a cup of your cold tea,   60
wife.   (*Going to the closet*)

50 *Do't* Q1–2, P(Don't Q3)   59 *nasty* repulsively filthy
60 *pig together* lie together in one bed (slang)

60 *cold tea* prepared in advance for occasional drinking and, to judge from
William Burnaby's *The Reformed Wife* (1700), still so fashionable it
was imitated by tradesmen's wives (II.i.80)

LADY BRUTE

[*Aside*] Oh, I'm ruined!—[*Aloud*] There's none there, my
dear.

SIR JOHN

I'll warrant you I'll find some, my dear.

LADY BRUTE

You can't open the door; the lock's spoiled. I have been   65
turning and turning the key this half-hour to no purpose.
I'll send for the smith tomorrow.

SIR JOHN

There's ne'er a smith in Europe can open a door with more
expedition than I can do.—As for example—pou! (*He bursts
open the door with his foot*)—How now? What the devil have   70
we got here?—Constant!—Heartfree!—and the two whores
again, egad!—This is the worst cold tea—that ever I met
with in my life.

Enter CONSTANT *and* HEARTFREE

LADY BRUTE (*Aside*)

O Lord, what will become of us?

SIR JOHN

Gentlemen—I am your very humble servant—I give you   75
many thanks—I see you take care of my family—I shall do
all I can to return the obligation.

CONSTANT

Sir, how oddly soever this business may appear to you, you
would have no cause to be uneasy if you knew the truth of all
things; your lady is the most virtuous woman in the world,   80
and nothing has passed but an innocent frolic.

HEARTFREE

Nothing else, upon my honour, sir.

SIR JOHN

You are both very civil gentlemen—and my wife, there, is
a very civil gentlewoman; therefore I don't doubt but many
civil things have passed between you. Your very humble   85
servant.

LADY BRUTE (*Aside, to* CONSTANT)

Pray be gone; he's so drunk he can't hurt us tonight, and
tomorrow morning you shall hear from us.

CONSTANT

I'll obey you, madam.—[*Aloud*] Sir, when you are cool
you'll understand reason better; so then I shall take the   90
pains to inform you. If not—I wear a sword, sir, and so good-
bye to you.—Come along, Heartfree.

[*Exeunt* CONSTANT *and* HEARTFREE]

SIR JOHN

Wear a sword, sir? And what of all that, sir?—He comes to
my house, eats my meat, lies with my wife, dishonours my
family, gets a bastard to inherit my estate, and when I ask a   95
civil account of all this—Sir, says he, I wear a sword!—
Wear a sword, sir? Yes sir, says he, I wear a sword!—It may
be a good answer at cross-purposes, but 'tis a damned one
to a man in my whimsical circumstance.—Sir, says he, I
wear a sword!—(*To* LADY BRUTE) And what do you wear   100
now, ha? Tell me. (*Sitting down in a great chair*) What! You
are modest, and can't? Why then, I'll tell you, you slut
you. You wear—an impudent lewd face—a damned
designing heart—and a tail—and a tail full of—
                         (*He falls fast asleep, snoring*)

LADY BRUTE

So; thanks to kind heaven, he's fast for some hours.   105

BELLINDA

'Tis well he is so, that we may have time to lay our story
handsomely; for we must lie like the devil to bring ourselves
off.

LADY BRUTE

What shall we say, Bellinda?

BELLINDA (*Musing*)

I'll tell you: it must all light upon Heartfree and I. We'll   110
say he has courted me some time, but for reasons unknown
to us has ever been very earnest the thing might be kept
from Sir John; that therefore hearing him upon the stairs,
he run into the closet, though against our will, and Constant
with him, to prevent jealousy. And to give this a good im-   115
pudent face of truth (that I may deliver you from the trouble
you are in), I'll e'en (if he pleases) marry him.

LADY BRUTE

I'm beholding to you, cousin; but that would be carrying
the jest a little too far for your own sake. You know he's a
younger brother, and has nothing.   120

BELLINDA

'Tis true; but I like him, and have fortune enough to keep
above extremity. I can't say I would live with him in a cell
upon love and bread and butter; but I had rather have the

104 *tail* pudendum (slang)
118 *beholding* Q1–3 (beholden P)

_____

 98 *cross-purposes* a parlour game in which questions are linked to inappro-
       priate answers, with ludicrous results; it made Pepys 'mighty merry'
       (*Diary*, 26 December 1666)

man I love, and a middle state of life, than that gentleman
in the chair there, and twice your ladyship's splendour.　　125

LADY BRUTE

In truth, niece, you are in the right on't; for I am very
uneasy with my ambition. But perhaps, had I married as
you'll do, I might have been as ill-used.

BELLINDA

Some risk, I do confess, there always is; but if a man has
the least spark either of honour or good nature, he can never　　130
use a woman ill that loves him and makes his fortune both.
Yet I must own to you, some little struggling I still have with
this teasing ambition of ours; for pride, you know, is as
natural to a woman as 'tis to a saint. I can't help being fond
of this rogue; and yet it goes to my heart to think I must　　135
never whisk to Hyde Park with above a pair of horses, have
no coronet upon my coach, nor a page to carry up my train.
But above all, that business of place—. Well, taking place
is a noble prerogative.

LADY BRUTE

Especially after a quarrel.　　140

BELLINDA

Or of a rival. But pray say no more on't, for fear I change my
mind. For o'my conscience, were't not for your affair in the
balance, I should go near to pick up some odious man of
quality yet, and only take poor Heartfree for a gallant.

LADY BRUTE

Then him you must have, however things go?　　145

BELLINDA

Yes.

LADY BRUTE

Why, we may pretend what we will, but 'tis a hard matter
to live without the man we love.

BELLINDA

Especially when we are married to the man we hate. Pray
tell me, do the men of the town ever believe us virtuous,　　150
when they see us do so?

LADY BRUTE

Oh, no; nor indeed hardly, let us do what we will. They
most of 'em think there is no such thing as virtue, considered
in the strictest notions of it; and therefore when you hear
'em say such a one is a woman of reputation, they only　　155
mean she's a woman of discretion. For they consider we have
no more religion than they have, nor so much morality;

138 *place* social precedence

and between you and I, Bellinda, I'm afraid the want of
inclination seldom protects any of us.

BELLINDA

But what think you of the fear of being found out?   160

LADY BRUTE

I think that never kept any woman virtuous long. We are
not such cowards neither. No; let us once pass fifteen, and
we have too good an opinion of our own cunning to believe
the world can penetrate into what we would keep a secret.
And so, in short, we cannot reasonably blame the men for   165
judging of us by themselves.

BELLINDA

But sure we are not so wicked as they are, after all?

LADY BRUTE

We are as wicked, child, but our vice lies another way. Men
have more courage than we, so they commit more bold,
impudent sins. They quarrel, fight, swear, drink, blas-   170
pheme, and the like; whereas we, being cowards, only
backbite, tell lies, cheat at cards, and so forth.—But 'tis late.
Let's end our discourse for tonight, and out of an excess
of charity take a small care of that nasty drunken thing
there.—Do but look at him, Bellinda!   175

BELLINDA

Ah, 'tis a savoury dish.

LADY BRUTE

As savoury as 'tis, I'm cloyed with't. Prithee, call the butler
to take away.

BELLINDA

Call the butler? Call the scavenger!—(*To a servant within*)
Who's there? Call Rasor! Let him take away his master,   180
scour him clean with a little soap and sand, and so put him
to bed.

LADY BRUTE

Come, Bellinda, I'll e'en lie with you tonight; and in the
morning we'll send for our gentlemen to set this matter
even.   185

BELLINDA

With all my heart.

LADY BRUTE (*Making a low curtsy* [*to* SIR JOHN])

Good night, my dear.

---

178 *take* Q1–3 (take it P)   186 *With all* Q2–3, P (Withal Q1)

---

179 *scavenger* officer of a city ward answerable 'that the Ways, Streets, and
Lanes, be cleansed of Dung, and all manner of Filth' (Thomas Delaune,
Angliae Metropolis (1690), p. 248)

BOTH
    Ha ha ha!   (*Exeunt*)

                        Enter RASOR

[RASOR]
    My lady there's a wag—my master there's a cuckold.
    Marriage is a slippery thing; women have depraved appe-   190
    tites. My lady's a wag; I have heard all, I have seen all, I
    understand all—and I'll tell all, for my little Frenchwoman
    loves news dearly. This story'll gain her heart, or nothing
    will.—(*To his master*) Come, sir, your head's too full of fumes
    at present to make room for your jealousy; but I reckon   195
    we shall have rare work with you when your pate's empty.
    Come to your kennel, you cuckoldly drunken sot you!
                            (*Carries him out upon his back*)

                        Act V, Scene iii

                    LADY FANCYFULL's *House*
            Enter LADY FANCYFULL *and* MADAMOISELLE

LADY FANCYFULL
    But why did not you tell me before, Madamoiselle, that
    Rasor and you were fond?
MADAMOISELLE
    De modesty hinder me, matam.
LADY FANCYFULL
    Why truly, modesty does often hinder us from doing things
    we have an extravagant mind to. But does he love you well   5
    enough yet, to do anything you bid him? Do you think to
    oblige you he would speak scandal?
MADAMOISELLE
    Matam, to oblige your ladyship he shall speak blasphemy.
LADY FANCYFULL
    Why then, Madamoiselle, I'll tell you what you shall do.
    You shall engage him to tell his master all that passed at   10
    Spring Garden: I have a mind he should know what a wife
    and a niece he has got.
MADAMOISELLE
    Il le fera, matam.

        Enter a FOOTMAN, *who speaks to* MADAMOISELLE *apart*

    13 *Il le fera* He'll do it

FOOTMAN
    Madamoiselle, yonder's Mr Rasor desires to speak with you.
MADAMOISELLE
    Tell him, I come presently. (*Exit* FOOTMAN)—Rasor be dare,   15
    matam.
LADY FANCYFULL
    That's fortunate. Well, I'll leave you together. And if you
    find him stubborn, Madamoiselle—hark you—don't refuse
    him a few little reasonable liberties to put him into humour.
MADAMOISELLE
    Laissez-moi faire.   ´   (*Exit* LADY FANCYFULL)   20

        RASOR *peeps in, and seeing* LADY FANCYFULL *gone, runs to*
        MADAMOISELLE, *takes her about the neck and kisses her*

    How now, confidence!
RASOR
    How now, modesty!
MADAMOISELLE
    Who make you so familiar, sirrah?
RASOR
    My impudence, hussy.
MADAMOISELLE
    Stand off, rogue-face!   25
RASOR
    Ah, Madamoiselle, great news at our house!
MADAMOISELLE
    Wy, wat be de matter?
RASOR
    The matter? —Why, uptails-all's the matter!
MADAMOISELLE
    Tu te moques de moi.
RASOR
    Now do you long to know the particulars—the time when,   30
    the place where, the manner how. But I won't tell you a
    word more.
MADAMOISELLE
    Nay, den dou kill me, Rasor.
RASOR (*Clapping his hands behind him*)
    Come, kiss me, then.

20 *Laissez-moi faire* Just watch me
29 *Tu . . . moi* You're laughing at me

───────────────────────────────

28 *uptails-all* the name of a card game and an old song, used here as a
    slang term for (1) confusion, high jinks (2) copulation
30–1 *time . . . how* terms which belong to a legal indictment

MADAMOISELLE

    Nay, pridee tell me.   35

RASOR (*Going*)

    Good-bye to ye!

MADAMOISELLE

    Hold, hold! I will kiss dee.   (*Kissing him*)

RASOR

    So; that's civil. Why now, my pretty poll, my goldfinch, my
    little water-wagtail, you must know that—come, kiss me
    again.   40

MADAMOISELLE

    I won't kiss dee no more.

RASOR

    Good-bye to ye!

MADAMOISELLE

    Doucement. (*Kissing him*) Dare; *es-tu content*?

RASOR

    So; now I'll tell thee all. Why the news is, that cuckoldom in
    folio is newly printed, and matrimony in quarto is just going   45
    into the press. Will you buy any books, Madamoiselle?

MADAMOISELLE

    Tu parles comme un libraire; de devil no understand dee.

RASOR

    Why then, that I may make myself intelligible to a waiting-
    woman, I'll speak like a *valet de chambre*. My lady has
    cuckolded my master.   50

MADAMOISELLE

    Bon!

RASOR

    Which we take very ill from her hands, I can tell her that.
    We can't yet prove matter of fact upon her.

MADAMOISELLE

    N'importe.

RASOR

    But we can prove that matter of fact had like to have been   55
    upon her.

38 *poll* ed. (pall Q1) talkative woman (slang)
39 *wagtail* prostitute (slang)
43 *Doucement . . . content?* Wait a minute . . . are you satisfied?
47 *Tu . . . libraire* You're talking like a bookseller
49 *valet de chambre* gentleman's gentleman
51 *Bon!* Good!
54 *N'importe* That doesn't matter

---

53 *matter of fact* another legal term loosely used here to distinguish
verifiable fact from probability or inference

MADAMOISELLE

Oui-dà!

RASOR

For we have such bloody circumstances—

MADAMOISELLE

Sans doute.

RASOR

That any man of parts may draw tickling conclusions from   60
'em.

MADAMOISELLE

Fort bien.

RASOR

We have found a couple of tight, well-built gentlemen
stuffed into her ladyship's closet.

MADAMOISELLE

Le diable!   65

RASOR

And I, in my particular person, have discovered a most
damnable plot how to persuade my poor master that all this
hide-and-seek, this will-in-the-wisp, has no other meaning
than a Christian marriage for sweet Mrs Bellinda.

MADAMOISELLE

Un marriage?—Ah, les drôlesses!   70

RASOR

Don't you interrupt me, hussy; 'tis agreed, I say. And my
innocent lady, to wriggle herself out at the back-door of the
business, turns marriage-bawd to her niece, and resolves to
deliver up her fair body to be tumbled and mumbled by that
young liquorish whipster, Heartfree. Now are you satisfied?   75

MADAMOISELLE

No.

RASOR

Right woman, always gaping for more!

MADAMOISELLE

Dis be all, den, dat dou know?

---

57 *Oui-dà!* To be sure!
59 *Sans doute* I dare say
62 *Fort bien* Very well
65 *Le diable!* The devil you have!
70 *Un . . . drôlesses!* (drôless Q1) A marriage?—Ah, the strumpets!
74 *mumbled* fondled with kisses
75 *liquorish whipster* lecherous swindler

---

70 *drôlesses* The Q1 reading falls between *drôles* (scoundrels) and *drôlesses*
(strumpets); the latter seems more likely.

RASOR
> All! Ay, and a great deal too, I think.

MADAMOISELLE
> Dou be fool, dou know noting. *Écoute, mon pauvre Rasor.* 80
> Dou see des two eyes? Des two eyes have see de devil!

RASOR
> The woman's mad.

MADAMOISELLE
> In Spring Garden, dat rogue Constant meet dy lady—

RASOR
> *Bon!*

MADAMOISELLE
> I'll tell dee no more.   85

RASOR
> Nay, prithee, my swan.

MADAMOISELLE (*Clapping her hands behind her, as he had done
> before*)
> Come, kiss me den.

RASOR
> I won't kiss you, not I.

MADAMOISELLE
> *Adieu!*

RASOR
> Hold! (*Gives her a hearty kiss*)—Now proceed.   90

MADAMOISELLE
> *Ah çà!* I hide myself in one cunning place, where I hear all
> and see all. First, dy drunken master come *mal à propos*; but
> de sot no know his own dear wife, so he leave her to her
> sport. Den de game begin. (*As she speaks,* RASOR *still acts the
> man and she the woman*) De lover say soft ting; de lady look 95
> upon de ground. He take her by de hand; she turn her head
> on oder way. Den he squeez very hard; den she pull—very
> softly. Den he take her in his arm; den she give him leetel
> pat. Den he kiss her *tétons*; den she say—pish! nay, fie!
> Den he tremble; den she—sigh. Den he pull her into de 100
> arbour; den she pinch him.

RASOR
> Ay, but not so hard, you baggage you.

80 *Écoute . . . Rasor* Listen, my dear Rasor
81 *Dou see* Q1–2 (Dou sees Q3, P)
84 *Bon!* Good!
91 *Ah çà!* Well then!
92 *mal à propos* unexpectedly
97 *on* Q2–3, P (one Q1)
99 *tétons* breasts

MADAMOISELLE

Den he grow bold; she grow weak. He tro her down, *il tombe dessus; le diable assiste, il emporte tout.* (RASOR *struggles with her, as if he would throw her down*)—Stand off, sirrah!　　105

RASOR

You have set me afire, you jade you!

MADAMOISELLE

Den go to de river and quench dyself.

RASOR

What an unnatural harlot 'tis!

MADAMOISELLE (*Looking languishingly on him*)

Rasor.

RASOR

Madamoiselle?　　　　　　　　　　　　　　　　110

MADAMOISELLE

Dou no love me?

RASOR

Not love thee?—More than a Frenchman does soup!

MADAMOISELLE

Den dou will refuse noting dat I bid dee?

RASOR

Don't bid me be damned then.

MADAMOISELLE

No; only tell dy master all I have tell dee of dy laty.　　115

RASOR

Why, you little malicious strumpet, you! should you like to be served so?

MADAMOISELLE

Dou dispute den?—*Adieu!*

RASOR

Hold!　But why wilt thou make me be such a rogue, my dear?　　　　　　　　　　　　　　　　　　120

MADAMOISELLE

Voilà un vrai Anglais! Il est amoureux, et cependant il veut raisonner. Va-t'en au diable!

RASOR

Hold once more. In hopes thou'lt give me up thy body, I resign thee up my soul.

103–4 *il ... tout* he falls on top of her; and with the devil's aid, carries all before him

109 s.d. *languishingly* Q1 (languishing Q2–3, P)

111 *me?* P (me Q1–3)

121–2 *Voilà ... diable!* There's a true Englishman! He's in love, and still he wants to argue. To the devil with you!

MADAMOISELLE
> *Bon. Écoute donc*: if dou fail me, I never see dee more; if dou   125
> obey me—(*She takes him about the neck, and gives him a*
> *smacking kiss*) *je m'abandonne à toi!*   (*Exit* MADAMOISELLE)

RASOR (*Licking his lips*)
> Not be a rogue?—*Amor vincit omnia!*   (*Exit* RASOR)

Enter LADY FANCYFULL *and* MADAMOISELLE

LADY FANCYFULL
> Marry, say ye? Will the two things marry?

MADAMOISELLE
> *On le va faire*, matam.   130

LADY FANCYFULL
> Look you, Madamoiselle; in short, I can't bear it. No, I find
> I can't. If once I see 'em abed together, I shall have ten
> thousand thoughts in my head will make me run distracted.
> Therefore run and call Rasor back immediately, for some-
> thing must be done to stop this impertinent wedding. If I   135
> can but defer it four and twenty hours, I'll make such work
> about town with that little pert slut's reputation, he shall
> as soon marry a witch.

MADAMOISELLE (*Aside*)
> *La voilà bien intentionnée!*   (*Exeunt*)

Act V, Scene iv

CONSTANT'*s Lodgings*
Enter CONSTANT *and* HEARTFREE

CONSTANT
> But what dost think will come of this business?

HEARTFREE
> 'Tis easier to think what will not come on't.

CONSTANT
> What's that?

125 *Bon. Écoute donc* Good. Now listen
127 *je . . . toi!* I'm all yours!
128 *Amor vincit omnia!* Love conquers all! (proverbial)
130 *On . . . faire* They are arranging it
136 *but defer it* Q1 (defer it but Q2–3, P)
139 *La . . . intentionnée!* There's fine intentions!

---

132 *see 'em abed together* On the wedding night, it was usual for friends and
relatives of the bride and groom to put them to bed, toss their stockings
for luck, and serve them a sack-posset before withdrawing.

HEARTFREE

A challenge. I know the knight too well for that. His dear
body will always prevail upon his noble soul to be quiet.   5

CONSTANT

But though he dare not challenge me, perhaps he may
venture to challenge his wife.

HEARTFREE

Not if you whisper him in the ear, you won't have him do't;
and there's no other way left that I see. For as drunk as he
was, he'll remember you and I were where we should not   10
be; and I don't think him quite blockhead enough yet to
be persuaded we were got into his wife's closet only to peep
in her prayer-book.

Enter SERVANT, *with a letter*

SERVANT

Sir, here's a letter; a porter brought it.   [*Exit*]

CONSTANT

O ho, here's instructions for us.—(*Reads*) 'The accident that   15
has happened has touched our invention to the quick. We
would fain come off without your help, but find that's impossible. In a word, the whole business must be thrown upon
a matrimonial intrigue between your friend and mine. But if
the parties are not fond enough to go quite through with   20
the matter, 'tis sufficient for our turn they own the design.
We'll find pretences enough to break the match. Adieu'.—
Well, woman for invention! How long would my blockhead
have been a-producing this!—Hey, Heartfree! What, mus-
ing, man? Prithee be cheerful. What say'st thou, friend, to   25
this matrimonial remedy?

HEARTFREE

Why, I say it's worse than the disease.

CONSTANT

Here's a fellow for you! There's beauty and money on her
side, and love up to the ears on his; and yet—

HEARTFREE

And yet, I think I may reasonably be allowed to boggle at   30
marrying the niece, in the very moment that you are a-
debauching the aunt.

CONSTANT

Why truly, there may be something in that. But have not
you a good opinion enough of your own parts, to believe
you could keep a wife to yourself?   35

7 *challenge* bring a charge against
31-2 *a-debauching* Q1-3 (debauching P)

HEARTFREE

I should have, if I had a good opinion enough of hers, to believe she could do as much by me. For to do 'em right, after all, the wife seldom rambles till the husband shows her the way.

CONSTANT

'Tis true; a man of real worth scarce ever is a cuckold but by 40
his own fault. Women are not naturally lewd; there must be something to urge 'em to it. They'll cuckold a churl out of revenge, a fool because they despise him, a beast because they loathe him. But when they make bold with a man they once had a well-grounded value for, 'tis because they first 45
see themselves neglected by him.

HEARTFREE

Nay, were I well assured that I should never grow Sir John, I ne'er should fear Bellinda'd play my lady. But our weakness, thou know'st, my friend, consists in that very change we so impudently throw upon (indeed) a steadier and more 50
generous sex.

CONSTANT

Why faith, we are a little impudent in that matter; that's the truth on't. But this is wonderful, to see you grown so warm an advocate for those (but t'other day) you took so much pains to abuse! 55

HEARTFREE

All revolutions run into extremes: the bigot makes the boldest atheist, and the coyest saint the most extravagant strumpet. But, prithee, advise me in this good and evil, this life and death, this blessing and cursing, that is set before me. Shall I marry—or die a maid? 60

CONSTANT

Why faith, Heartfree, matrimony is like an army going to engage. Love's the forlorn hope, which is soon cut off; the marriage knot is the main body, which may stand buff a long, long time; and repentance is the rear-guard, which rarely gives ground as long as the main battle has a being. 65

HEARTFREE

Conclusion then: you advise me to whore on, as you do.

CONSTANT

That's not concluded yet. For though marriage be a lottery in which there are a wondrous many blanks, yet there is one inestimable lot in which the only heaven on earth is

62 *forlorn hope* vanguard which begins the attack
63 *stand buff* stand firm
65 *main battle* main body of troops

written. Would your kind fate but guide your hand to that,   70
though I were wrapped in all that luxury itself could clothe
me with, I still should envy you.

HEARTFREE
And justly, too; for to be capable of loving one, doubtless
is better than to possess a thousand. But how far that
capacity's in me, alas, I know not.   75

CONSTANT
But you would know?

HEARTFREE
I would so.

CONSTANT
Matrimony will inform you. Come, one flight of resolution
carries you to the land of experience; where, in a very
moderate time, you'll know the capacity of your soul and   80
your body both, or I'm mistaken.   (*Exeunt*)

Act V, Scene v

SIR JOHN BRUTE's *House*
Enter LADY BRUTE *and* BELLINDA

BELLINDA
Well, madam, what answer have you from 'em?

LADY BRUTE
That they'll be here this moment. I fancy 'twill end in a
wedding: I'm sure he's a fool if it don't. Ten thousand
pound, and such a lass as you are, is no contemptible offer to
a younger brother. But are not you under strange agitations?   5
Prithee, how does your pulse beat?

BELLINDA
High and low; I have much ado to be valiant. Sure, it must
feel very strange to go to bed to a man.

LADY BRUTE
Um—it does feel a little odd at first, but it will soon grow
easy to you.   10

Enter CONSTANT *and* HEARTFREE

Good morrow, gentlemen. How have you slept after your
adventure?

HEARTFREE
Some careful thoughts, ladies, on your accounts have kept
us waking.

BELLINDA
And some careful thoughts on your own, I believe, have   15

7 *Sure, it must* P (*omitted* Q1–3)

hindered you from sleeping. Pray, how does this matrimonial
project relish with you?

HEARTFREE

Why faith, e'en as storming towns does with soldiers, where
the hope of delicious plunder banishes the fear of being
knocked on the head.   20

BELLINDA

Is it then possible, after all, that you dare think of downright
lawful wedlock?

HEARTFREE

Madam, you have made me so foolhardy I dare do anything.

BELLINDA

Then, sir, I challenge you; and matrimony's the spot where
I expect you.   25

HEARTFREE

'Tis enough; I'll not fail.—(*Aside*) So, now I am in for
Hobbes's voyage—a great leap in the dark.

LADY BRUTE

Well, gentlemen, this matter being concluded then, have
you got your lessons ready? For Sir John is grown such an
atheist of late, he'll believe nothing upon easy terms.   30

CONSTANT

We'll find ways to extend his faith, madam. But pray, how
do you find him this morning?

LADY BRUTE

Most lamentably morose, chewing the cud after last night's
discovery; of which however he had but a confused notion
e'en now. But I'm afraid his *valet de chambre* has told him   35
all, for they are very busy together at this moment. When
I told him of Bellinda's marriage, I had no other answer but
a grunt; from which you may draw what conclusions you
think fit.—But to your notes, gentlemen; he's here.

19 *hope* ed. (hopes Q1–3, P)   27 *Hobbes's* P (Hobs's Q1–2, Hob's Q3)
35 *his* Q1 (the Q2–3, P)   35 *valet de chambre* man-servant
39 *to your notes* 'i.e. to your parts in the arranged concert' (Dobrée); or
perhaps another reference to the 'lessons' of 29

---

27 *leap . . . dark* 'a hazardous action undertaken in uncertainty as to the
consequences' (*OED*). According to John Watkins, Thomas Hobbes
said death was a leap in the dark (*Characteristic Anecdotes of Men of
Learning and Genius* (1808), p. 276); following Heartfree, Vanbrugh
applies the phrase to his own marriage in a letter dated 1 July 1719
(Dobrée, *Complete Works*, IV, 111).

39 s.d. *and* RASOR All four early editions bring on Rasor here, presumably
on the strength of 36; but he has nothing to overhear until 101, and
would be much better introduced ushering in the disguised Lady
Fancyfull at 92.

Enter SIR JOHN *and* RASOR

CONSTANT
Good morrow, sir.   40
HEARTFREE
Good morrow, Sir John. I'm very sorry my indiscretion
should cause so much disorder in your family.
SIR JOHN
Disorders generally come from indiscretions, sir; 'tis no
strange thing at all.
LADY BRUTE
I hope, my dear, you are satisfied there was no wrong   45
intended you.
SIR JOHN
None, my dove.
BELLINDA
If not, I hope my consent to marry Mr Heartfree will con-
vince you. For as little as I know of amours, sir, I can assure
you one intrigue is enough to bring four people together,   50
without further mischief.
SIR JOHN
And I know, too, that intrigues tend to procreation of more
kinds than one. One intrigue will beget another as soon as
beget a son or a daughter.
CONSTANT
I am very sorry, sir, to see you still seem unsatisfied with a   55
lady whose more than common virtue, I am sure, were she
my wife, should meet a better usage.
SIR JOHN
Sir, if her conduct has put a trick upon her virtue, her
virtue's the bubble, but her husband's the loser.
CONSTANT
Sir, you have received a sufficient answer already to justify   60
both her conduct and mine. You'll pardon me for meddling
in your family affairs; but I perceive I am the man you are
jealous of, and therefore it concerns me.
SIR JOHN
Would it did not concern me, and then I should not care
who it concerned.   65
CONSTANT
Well, sir, if truth and reason won't content you, I know

43 s.p. SIR JOHN ed. (*Constant* Q1–3, P)
52 *tend* Q2–3, P (tends Q1)
58 *put a trick upon* made a fool of
59 *bubble* (1) dupe (2) worthless delusion

but one way more which, if you think fit, you may take.

SIR JOHN

Lord, sir, you are very hasty! If I had been found at prayers
in your wife's closet, I should have allowed you twice as
much time to come to yourself in.   70

CONSTANT

Nay, sir, if time be all you want, we have no quarrel.

(SIR JOHN *muses*)

HEARTFREE [*To* CONSTANT, *aside*]

I told you how the sword would work upon him.

CONSTANT

Let him muse; however, I'll lay fifty pound our foreman
brings us in, not guilty.

SIR JOHN

(*Aside*) 'Tis well—'tis very well! In spite of that young   75
jade's matrimonial intrigue, I am a downright stinking
cuckold.—(*Putting his hand to his forehead*) Here they are.
Boo! Methinks I could butt with a bull.—What the plague
did I marry her for? I knew she did not like me; if she had,
she would have lain with me, for I would have done so   80
because I liked her. But that's past, and I have her.—And
now, what shall I do with her? If I put my horns in my
pocket, she'll grow insolent. If I don't, that goat there, that
stallion, is ready to whip me through the guts. The debate
then is reduced to this: shall I die a hero or live a rascal?— 85
Why, wiser men than I have long since concluded that a
living dog is better than a dead lion.—(*To* CONSTANT *and*
HEARTFREE) Gentlemen, now my wine and my passion are
governable, I must own I have never observed anything in
my wife's course of life to back me in my jealousy of her.   90
But jealousy's a mark of love; so she need not trouble her
head about it, as long as I make no more words on't.

LADY FANCYFULL *enters disguised, and addresses to* BELLINDA
apart

CONSTANT

I am glad to see your reason rule at last. Give me your hand;
I hope you'll look upon me as you are wont.

SIR JOHN

Your humble servant.—(*Aside*) A wheedling son of a whore! 95

HEARTFREE

And that I may be sure you are friends with me too, pray
give me your consent to wed your niece.

71 s.d. (SIR JOHN *muses*) Q1 prints this on the right of Heartfree's line
82 *in* Q1–3 (into P)

SIR JOHN
Sir, you have it with all my heart; damn me if you han't.—
(*Aside*) 'Tis time to get rid of her. A young, pert pimp!
she'll make an incomparable bawd in a little time.   100

Enter a SERVANT, *who gives* HEARTFREE *a letter.*

[*Exit* SERVANT]

BELLINDA
Heartfree your husband, say you? 'Tis impossible.
LADY FANCYFULL
Would to kind heaven it were! But 'tis too true; and in the
world there lives not such a wretch. I'm young; and either
I have been flattered by my friends, as well as glass, or
nature has been kind and generous to me. I had a fortune,   105
too, was greater far than he could ever hope for; but with
my heart I am robbed of all the rest. I'm slighted and I'm
beggared both at once. I have scarce a bare subsistence from
the villain, yet dare complain to none; for he has sworn if
e'er 'tis known I am his wife, he'll murder me. (*Weeping*) 110
BELLINDA
The traitor!
LADY FANCYFULL
I accidentally was told he courted you. Charity soon pre-
vailed upon me to prevent your misery; and, as you see,
I'm still so generous even to him, as not to suffer he should
do a thing for which the law might take away his life.   115
                                                    (*Weeping*)
BELLINDA [*Aside*]
Poor creature, how I pity her! (*They continue talking aside*)
HEARTFREE (*Aside*)
Death and damnation!—Let me read it again.—(*Reads*)
'Though I have a particular reason not to let you know who I
am till I see you, yet you'll easily believe 'tis a faithful
friend that gives you this advice. I have lain with Bellinda'.— 120
Good!—'I have a child by her'—Better and better!—'which
is now at nurse',—Heaven be praised!—'and I think the
foundation laid for another'.—Ha! Old truepenny!—'No
rack could have tortured this story from me; but friendship
has done it. I heard of your design to marry her, and could 125

123 *truepenny* trusty fellow (Zimansky sees an allusion to *Hamlet*, I.v.150,
    161–2)

---

115 *law ... life* English law at this period treated bigamy as a felony
    punishable by death.

not see you abused. Make use of my advice, but keep my
secret till I ask you for't again. Adieu'.

(Exit LADY FANCYFULL*)*

CONSTANT (*To* BELLINDA)

Come, madam; shall we send for the parson? I doubt here's
no business for the lawyer; younger brothers have nothing
to settle but their hearts, and that I believe my friend here   130
has already done, very faithfully.

BELLINDA (*Scornfully*)

Are you sure, sir, there are no old mortgages upon it?

HEARTFREE (*Coldly*)

If you think there are, madam, it mayn't be amiss to defer
the marriage till you are sure they are paid off.

BELLINDA

(*Aside*) How the galled horse kicks!—(*To* HEARTFREE) We'll   135
defer it as long as you please, sir.

HEARTFREE

The more time we take to consider on't, madam, the less
apt we shall be to commit oversights; therefore, if you
please, we'll put it off for just nine months.

BELLINDA

Guilty consciences make men cowards; I don't wonder you   140
want time to resolve.

HEARTFREE

And they make women desperate; I don't wonder you were
so quickly determined.

BELLINDA

What does the fellow mean?

HEARTFREE

What does the lady mean?   145

SIR JOHN

Zoons, what do you both mean?

(HEARTFREE *and* BELLINDA *walk chafing about*)

RASOR (*Aside*)

Here is so much sport going to be spoiled, it makes me ready
to weep again. A pox o'this impertinent Lady Fancyfull and
her plots—and her Frenchwoman too! She's a whimsical,
ill-natured bitch; and when I have got my bones broke in   150
her service, 'tis ten to one but my recompense is a clap.—I
hear 'em tittering without still. Ecod, I'll e'en go lug 'em
both in by the ears and discover the plot, to secure my
pardon.   (*Exit* RASOR)

CONSTANT

Prithee explain, Heartfree.   155

HEARTFREE
A fair deliverance, thank my stars and my friend.

BELLINDA
'Tis well it went no farther. A base fellow!

LADY BRUTE
What can be the meaning of all this?

BELLINDA
What's his meaning, I don't know; but mine is, that if I
had married him—I had had no husband.   160

HEARTFREE
And what's her meaning, I don't know; but mine is, that
if I had married her—I had had wife enough.

SIR JOHN
Your people of wit have got such cramp ways of expressing
themselves, they seldom comprehend one another. Pox take
you both, will you speak that you may be understood?   165

Enter RASOR *in sackcloth, pulling in* LADY FANCYFULL *and*
MADAMOISELLE

RASOR
If they won't, here comes an interpreter.

LADY BRUTE
Heavens! What have we here?

RASOR
A villain—but a repenting villain. Stuff which saints in all
ages have been made of.

ALL
Rasor!   170

LADY BRUTE
What means this sudden metamorphose?

RASOR
Nothing, without my pardon.

LADY BRUTE
What pardon do you want?

RASOR
Imprimis, your ladyship's, for a damnable lie made upon your
spotless virtue and set to the tune of Spring Garden.—(*To*   175
SIR JOHN) Next, at my generous master's feet I bend, for
interrupting his more noble thoughts with phantoms
of disgraceful cuckoldom.—(*To* CONSTANT) Thirdly, I to
this gentleman apply, for making him the hero of my
romance.—(*To* HEARTFREE) Fourthly, your pardon, noble   180

163 *cramp* crabbed, indecipherable

sir, I ask, for clandestinely marrying you without either
bidding of banns, bishop's licence, friends' consent—or your
own knowledge.—(*To* BELLINDA) And lastly, to my good
young lady's clemency I come, for pretending the corn
was sowed in the ground before ever the plough had been　185
in the field.

SIR JOHN (*Aside*)

So that, after all, 'tis a moot point whether I am a cuckold
or not.

BELLINDA

Well sir, upon condition you confess all, I'll pardon you
myself, and try to obtain as much from the rest of the com-　190
pany. But I must know, then, who 'tis has put you upon all
this mischief.

RASOR

Satan and his equipage. Woman tempted me, lust weakened
me, and so the devil overcame me. As fell Adam, so fell I.

BELLINDA

Then pray, Mr Adam, will you make us acquainted with　195
your Eve?

RASOR (*To* MADAMOISELLE)

Unmask, for the honour of France.

ALL

Madamoiselle!

MADAMOISELLE

Me ask ten tousand pardon of all de good company.

SIR JOHN

Why, this mystery thickens instead of clearing up.—(*To*　200
RASOR) You son of a whore you, put us out of our pain.

RASOR

One moment brings sunshine.—(*Showing* MADAMOISELLE)
'Tis true, this is the woman that tempted me.—[*Pointing to*
LADY FANCYFULL] But this is the serpent that tempted the
woman; and if my prayers might be heard, her punishment　205
for so doing should be like the serpent's of old. (*Pulls off*
LADY FANCYFULL'*s mask*) She should lie upon her face all
the days of her life.

ALL

Lady Fancyfull!

BELLINDA

Impertinent!　　　　　　　　　　　　　　　　　　　210

LADY BRUTE

Ridiculous!

ALL

Ha ha ha ha ha!

BELLINDA

I hope your ladyship will give me leave to wish you joy,
since you have owned your marriage yourself.—Mr Heartfree, I vow 'twas strangely wicked in you to think of another   215
wife, when you had one already so charming as her ladyship.

ALL

Ha ha ha ha ha!

LADY FANCYFULL (*Aside*)

Confusion seize 'em, as it seizes me!

MADAMOISELLE [*Aside*]

Que le diable étouffe ce maraud de Rasor!

BELLINDA

Your ladyship seems disordered. A breeding qualm, perhaps?   220
Mr Heartfree, your bottle of Hungary water to your lady!—
Why, madam, he stands as unconcerned as if he were your
husband in earnest.

LADY FANCYFULL

Your mirth's as nauseous as yourself, Bellinda. You think
you triumph o'er a rival now. *Hélas, ma pauvre fille!*   225
Where'er I'm rival there's no cause for mirth. No, my poor
wretch; 'tis from another principle I have acted. I knew that
thing there would make so perverse a husband, and you so
impertinent a wife, that lest your mutual plagues should
make you both run mad, I charitably would have broke the   230
match. He he he he he!

(*Exit laughing affectedly*, MADAMOISELLE *following her*)

MADAMOISELLE

He he he he he!

ALL

Ha ha ha ha ha!

SIR JOHN (*Aside*)

Why, now this woman will be married to somebody too.

BELLINDA

Poor creature, what a passion she's in! But I forgive her.   235

HEARTFREE

Since you have so much goodness for her, I hope you'll
pardon my offence too, madam.

219 *étouffe* ed. (e toute Q1–3, P)
219 *Que . . . Rasor!* May the devil choke that scoundrel Rasor!
221 *Hungary* P (Hungry Q1–3)
225 *o'er* Q1–3 (over P)
225 *Hélas . . . fille!* Alas, my poor girl!

---

221 *Hungary water* a restorative distilled from rosemary flowers, and
'denominated from a Queen of *Hungary*, for whose Use it was first
prepar'd' (Ephraim Chambers, *Cyclopaedia* (1728), I, 263)

BELLINDA

There will be no great difficulty in that, since I am guilty of
an equal fault.

HEARTFREE

Then pardons being passed on all sides, pray let's to church   240
to conclude the day's work.

CONSTANT

But before you go, let me treat you, pray, with a song a new-
married lady made within this week; it may be of use to you
both.

SONG

I

When yielding first to Damon's flame   245
   I sunk into his arms,
He swore he'd ever be the same,
   Then rifled all my charms.
But fond of what he'd long desired,
   Too greedy of his prey,   250
My shepherd's flame, alas, expired
   Before the verge of day.

II

My innocence in lovers' wars
   Reproached his quick defeat;
Confused, ashamed, and bathed in tears,   255
   I mourned his cold retreat.
At length, 'Ah, shepherdess', cried he,
   'Would you my fire renew,
Alas, you must retreat like me;
   I'm lost if you pursue'.   260

HEARTFREE

So, madam; now had the parson but done his business—

BELLINDA

You'd be half weary of your bargain.

HEARTFREE

No, sure, I might dispense with one night's lodging.

BELLINDA

I'm ready to try, sir.

HEARTFREE

Then let's to church.   265
    And if it be our chance to disagree—

BELLINDA

    Take heed—the surly husband's fate you see.

FINIS

249 *he'd* ed. (h'ad Q1–3, P)   263 *dispense with* tolerate

EPILOGUE
By another hand
Spoken by LADY BRUTE *and* BELLINDA

LADY BRUTE
  No epilogue?
BELLINDA   I swear I know of none.
LADY BRUTE
  Lord! How shall we excuse it to the town?
BELLINDA
  Why, we must e'en say something of our own.
LADY BRUTE
  Our own! Ay, that must needs be precious stuff.
BELLINDA
  I'll lay my life, they'll like it well enough.   5
  Come, faith, begin—
LADY BRUTE   Excuse me, after you.
BELLINDA
  Nay, pardon me for that; I know my cue.
LADY BRUTE
  Oh, for the world, I would not have precedence.
BELLINDA
  O Lord!
LADY BRUTE I swear—
BELLINDA   O fie!
LADY BRUTE   I'm all obedience.
  First then, know all, before our doom is fixed,   10
  The third day is for us—
BELLINDA   Nay, and the sixt.
LADY BRUTE
  We speak not from the poet now, nor is it
  His cause—(I want a rhyme)—
BELLINDA   That we solicit.
LADY BRUTE
  Then, sure, you cannot have the hearts to be severe
  And damn us—
BELLINDA   Damn us! Let 'em if they dare.   15

Epilogue Q1 prints this immediately after the Prologue
11 *sixt* Q1 (sixth Q2–3, P)

---

11 The profits of the third, sixth, and ninth performances went to the
dramatist; Vanbrugh has donated his to the actors.

LADY BRUTE
Why, if they should, what punishment remains?

BELLINDA
Eternal exile from behind our scenes.

LADY BRUTE
But if they're kind, that sentence we'll recall;
We can be grateful—

BELLINDA   And have wherewithal.

LADY BRUTE
But at grand treaties hope not to be trusted,   20
Before preliminaries are adjusted.

BELLINDA
You know the time, and we appoint this place;
Where, if you please, we'll meet and sign the peace.

---

17 Despite many prohibitions from the Lord Chamberlain, gallants
frequently went visiting backstage during the performance.

20–3 Another reference to Ryswick, where preliminaries were adjusted
throughout the summer and the peace finally signed in September 1697.

APPENDIX A

THE REVISED SCENES

THESE SCENES, IN which Sir John attacks the law dressed in his wife's gown instead of the parson's, were first published in a Dublin edition of 1743; the title-page reads: 'THE Provok'd Wife: A COMEDY. In which is inserted, an Original SCENE, never before printed'. There were two issues, one printed by Edw. Bate for James Kelburn, the other by S. Powell for George Risk. The first London printing was in an appendix to the play in the first volume of Vanbrugh's *Plays* (1759); most later editions simply substituted them for the original scenes. I have taken as my copy-text the Bodleian Library copy of the Risk issue of the 1743 edition (Vet A4.f.1198), collated against the British Museum copy of 1759 (11771.d.8). As *1759* (L) is not dependent upon *1743* (D), I have thought it worth while to gloss all significant variants.

The new scenes were probably written to remove from the play that strain of clerical satire which had so antagonized Collier and his moralizing friends in the Society for the Reformation of Manners:

> Sir *John Brute* puts on the Habit of a Clergyman, counterfeits himself drunk; quarrels with the *Constable*, and is knock'd down and seiz'd. He rails, swears, curses, is lewd and profane, to all the Heights of Madness and Debauchery: The *Officers* and *Justice* break jests upon him, and make him a sort of Representative of his *Order*. This is rare *Protestant* Diversion, and very much for the Credit of the *Reformation!*[1]

—a charge to which Vanbrugh had replied very smartly in his *Short Vindication* of 1698.

It is not known when these revised scenes were first performed, for during Vanbrugh's lifetime the play was advertised with alterations on three separate occasions. The first was at the Queen's Theatre on 19 January 1706, when Vanbrugh as manager of the theatre was busy trying to fill it by revising his own earlier work. *Squire Trelooby*, which he had originally adapted from Molière in conjunction with Walsh and Congreve, was announced for 28 January 1706 with 'the last Act being entirely new';[2] and Trelooby also parades before the constable and watch dressed as a lady of

[1] Jeremy Collier, *A Short View of the Immorality and Profaneness of the English Stage* (1698), p. 108.
[2] *The London Stage 1660–1800*, ed. W. Van Lennep, E. L. Avery, A. H. Scouten, G. Winchester Stone Jnr, and C. B. Hogan (Carbondale, Illinois, 1960–68), Pt. 2, 115; see also John B. Shipley, 'The authorship of *The Cornish Squire*', *Philological Quarterly*, XLVII (1968), 147.

quality. This parallel with Sir John is strong evidence that the revised scenes were *not* performed at this time, for who would pay to see Trelooby *en travesti* if he had seen Sir John as Lady Brute at the same theatre only ten days before? The 'Alterations' of 1706, like the phrase 'Carefully Revis'd' in the playbills at Lincoln's Inn Fields for 21 December 1715,[3] probably meant no more than the addition of a new song or two, the revision of some outdated topical references to Ryswick and the Bank of England, and the deletion of those 'profane' lines for which Betterton's company had been prosecuted in 1701.[4] There is more convincing evidence for the revival staged at Drury Lane on 11 January 1726. Firstly, the advertisement reads: 'Never Acted there before. Revis'd by the Author'.[5] This is the first time the revisions are directly attributed to Vanbrugh; and Vanbrugh, who was in London in December 1725 and again in March 1726, is not known to have contradicted them. Secondly, they are supported by the independent testimony of Colley Cibber:

> In 1725 we were call'd upon, in a manner that could not be resisted, to revive the *Provok'd Wife*, a Comedy which, while we found our Account in keeping the Stage clear of those loose Liberties it had formerly too justly been charg'd with, we had laid aside for some Years. The Author, Sir *John Vanbrugh*, who was conscious of what it had too much of, was prevail'd upon to substitute a new-written Scene in the Place of one in the fourth Act, where the Wantonness of his Wit and Humour had (originally) made a Rake talk like a Rake in the borrow'd Habit of a Clergyman: To avoid which Offence, he clapt the same Debauchee into the Undress of a Woman of Quality: Now the Character and Profession of a Fine Lady not being so indelibly sacred as that of a Churchman, whatever Follies he expos'd in the Petticoat kept him at least clear of his former Prophaneness, and were now innocently ridiculous to the Spectator.[6]

Cibber played Brute in the Drury Lane revival; his evidence is unambiguous, and he was surely in a position to know the truth. The only difficulty arises from Harper's song (printed in Appendix B), which clearly describes Sir John in his parson's gown. It was published in 1729, and between 15 September 1726 and 16 October 1729 Harper is known to have played Colonel Bully at Drury Lane on at least five separate occasions. Of course, the song may date from 1719–21, when Harper was with Quin at Lincoln's Inn Fields and presumably still playing the Hiccup scenes. But if it dates from

[3] *The London Stage*, Pt. 2, 115 and 381.

[4] See J. W. Krutch, *Comedy and Conscience after the Restoration* (New York, 1924), pp. 169–73.

[5] *The London Stage*, Pt. 2, 850.

[6] Colley Cibber, *An Apology for the Life of Mr Colley Cibber*, ed. R. W. Lowe (1889), II, 233–4.

his later engagement at Drury Lane, as seems more likely, it suggests
that Cibber reverted to the original scenes when the novelty of the
revised ones had been exhausted. Such a change may well date
from 9 November 1727, when the Drury Lane playbills first dropped
'Revis'd by the Author' in favour of 'Written by the late Sir John
Vanbrugh'. [7]

In any event, during the 1730s the new scenes became common
property. Bridgwater played them at Covent Garden on 22 March
1735, and Quin (now at Drury Lane) took them up on 23 April,
advertising 'the Scene in Women's Cloaths' as if it were a novelty.[8]
Garrick revelled in them, revealing an acute observation of

> the many various Airs of the Fair Sex: He is perfectly versed in the
> Exercise of the Fan, the Lips, the Adjustment of the Tucker, and
> even the minutest Conduct of the Finger.[9]

A painting by Zoffany shows him attacking the watch in 'a yellow
satin brocaded dress with a white lining, a green lace shawl and a
lace cap with pink ribbons', and for his last season he wore a ridiculous bonnet decorated with ribbons, feathers, oranges and lemons,
and a bouquet or two of flowers.[10] Most modern Brutes have played
the revised scenes. Mervyn Johns in 1936 and Russell Waters in
1950 both made them 'irresistibly funny', and one critic found
Trevor Martin's portrayal of a 'pathological woman-hater' dressed
up in his wife's clothes 'psychologically revealing as well as extremely funny'.[11] These tributes are well justified. The revised
scenes add a fresh dimension to the role of Sir John Brute, and
afford almost limitless opportunities for the kind of transvestite farce
associated with *Charley's Aunt*. They also have far greater dramatic
relevance than the Hiccup scenes. Sir John's satiric account of the
life of a lady of fashion reflects back upon the empty vanities of
Lady Fancyfull, while his grotesque and implausible impersonation
of Lady Brute keeps the contrasting character of the real Lady
Brute always in our mind. Even in disguise, however, Sir John
retains his own character; his 'Lady Brute' is nothing more than
the feminine version of himself, a gambling lady rake bent like him
upon ruining her marriage by a career of selfish debauchery. Vanbrugh presents her more fully as Lady Arabella Loverule in his
unfinished masterpiece *A Journey to London*; here, she gives depth

[7] *The London Stage*, Pt. 2, 943.
[8] *The London Stage*, Pt. 3, 482.
[9] The *London Chronicle*, 3–5 March 1757, quoted in K. A. Burnim, *David
Garrick, Director* (Pittsburgh, 1961), pp. 183–4.
[10] See Burnim, p. 184; Zoffany's painting is described in R. Mander and J.
Mitchenson, *The Artist and the Theatre* (1955), p. 49.
[11] *The Times*, 6 October 1936; *The Times*, 23 March 1950; the *Observer*,
28 July 1963.

to the farce. For in the ironic interplay between Sir John, Lady Brute, and Sir John's 'Lady Brute' Vanbrugh provides a cool and unexpected commentary upon those matrimonial problems which form the core of his play.

Act IV, Scene i

Covent Garden

Enter LORD RAKE, SIR JOHN, [COLONEL BULLY] *&c., with swords drawn*

LORD RAKE
  Is the dog dead?

COLONEL BULLY
  No, damn him, I heard him wheeze.

LORD RAKE
  How the witch his wife howled!

COLONEL BULLY
  Ay, she'll alarm the watch presently.

LORD RAKE
  Appear, knight, then; come, you have a good cause to fight   5
  for: there's a man murdered.

SIR JOHN
  Is there? Then let his ghost be satisfied; for I'll sacrifice a
  constable to it presently, and burn his body upon his wooden
  chair.

Enter a TAILOR, *with a bundle under his arm*

COLONEL BULLY
  How now! What have we got here, a thief?   10

TAILOR
  No, an't please you; I'm no thief.

LORD RAKE
  That we'll see presently.—Here, let the general examine him.

SIR JOHN
  Ay, ay; let me examine him, and I'll lay a hundred pound I
  find him guilty in spite of his teeth—for he looks—like a—
  sneaking rascal.—Come sirrah, without equivocation or   15
  mental reservation, tell me of what opinion you are and
  what calling; for by them—I shall guess at your morals.

TAILOR
  An't please you, I'm a dissenting journeyman woman's
  tailor.

SIR JOHN
  Then, sirrah, you love lying by your religion and theft by   20

18–19 *woman's tailor* L (tailor D)

your trade. And so, that your punishment may be suitable
to your crimes, I'll have you first gagged—and then hanged.

TAILOR

Pray, good worthy gentlemen, don't abuse me; indeed I'm
an honest man, and a good workman, though I say it that
should not say it.   25

SIR JOHN

No words, sirrah, but attend your fate.

LORD RAKE

Let me see what's in that bundle.

TAILOR

An't please you, it is my lady's short cloak and wrapping-
gown.

SIR JOHN

What lady, you reptile you?   30

TAILOR

My Lady Brute, your honour.

SIR JOHN

My Lady Brute! My wife! The robe of my wife—with
reverence let me approach it! The dear angel is always taking
care of me in danger, and has sent me this suit of armour to
protect me in this day of battle. On they go!   35

ALL

O brave knight!

LORD RAKE

Live Don Quixote the Second!

SIR JOHN

Sancho, my squire, help me on with my armour.

TAILOR

O dear gentlemen, I shall be quite undone if you take the
gown.   40

SIR JOHN

Retire, sirrah; and since you carry off your skin—go home,
and be happy.

TAILOR

I think I'd e'en as good follow the gentleman's advice, for
if I dispute any longer, who knows but the whim may take
'em to case me? These courtiers are fuller of tricks than they   45
are of money; they'll sooner break a man's bones than pay
his bill.   (*Exit*)

28 *it is* D (it's L)
28–9 *wrapping-gown* D (sack L) night-gown
31 *Brute, your* D (Brute, an't please your L)
36 s.p. ALL L (Om. D)
40 *gown* D (sack L)

SIR JOHN
So, how d'ye like my shapes now?

LORD RAKE
To a miracle! He looks like a queen of the Amazons.—But
to your arms, gentlemen! The enemy's upon their march; 50
here's the watch.

SIR JOHN
Oons, if it were Alexander the Great at the head of his army,
I would drive him into a horse-pond.

ALL
Huzza! O brave knight!

Enter WATCHMEN

SIR JOHN
See, here he comes with all his Greeks about him.—Follow 55
me, boys!

1 WATCHMAN
Hey-day! Who have we got here? Stand!

SIR JOHN
Mayhap not!

1 WATCHMAN
What are you all doing here in the street at this time of
night? And who are you, madam, that seem to be at the head 60
of this noble crew?

SIR JOHN
Sirrah, I am Bonduca, Queen of the Welshmen; and with a
leek as long as my pedigree I will destroy your Roman
legion in an instant.—Britons, strike home!

48 *d'ye* L (do you D)
54 s.p. ALL L (Om. D)
54 s.d. L. D prints this after Sir John's next line
55 *Greeks* sharpers, rogues
58 *Mayhap* perhaps
59 *street* D (streets L)
59–60 *of night* D (o'night L)

---

62 *Bonduca* warrior-queen of the Iceni in Fletcher's tragedy *Bonduca*
(1613?), revived with music by Purcell in 1695. 'Britons, strike home'
is sung by the Druids in III.ii of the adaptation:
> To Arms, to Arms: Your Ensigns strait display:
> Now, now, now, set the Battle in Array. . . .
> Britains, *Strike Home: Revenge your Country's Wrongs:*
> *Fight and Record your selves in* Druids *Songs.*
>   (*Bonduca* (1696), p. 22).
63 *leek . . . pedigree* Vanbrugh pokes fun at the Welsh fondness for tracing
pedigrees in *I Aesop*, III.i.42–63.

(They fight off. WATCHMEN *return with* SIR JOHN)

1 WATCHMAN

So! We have got the queen, however. We'll make her pay   65
well for her ransom.—Come, madam, will your majesty
please to walk before the constable?

SIR JOHN

The constable's a rascal! And you are a son of a whore!

1 WATCHMAN

A most princely reply, truly! If this be her royal style, I'll
warrant her maids of honour prattle prettily; but we'll teach   70
you a little of our court dialect before we part with you,
princess.—Away with her to the round-house.

SIR JOHN

Hands off, you ruffians! My honour's dearer to me than
my life! I hope you won't be uncivil.

1 WATCHMAN

Away with her!   75

SIR JOHN

Oh, my honour! my honour!   *(Exeunt)*

Act IV, Scene iii

A Street

Enter CONSTABLE *and* WATCHMEN, *with* SIR JOHN

CONSTABLE

Come, forsooth; come along, if you please! I once in compassion thought to have seen you safe home this morning;
but you have been so rampant and abusive all night, I shall
see what the justice of peace will say to you.

SIR JOHN

And you shall see what I'll say to the justice of peace.   5

(WATCHMAN knocks at the door)

Enter SERVANT

CONSTABLE

Is Mr Justice at home?

SERVANT

Yes.

CONSTABLE

Pray acquaint his worship, we have got an unruly woman

64 s.d. L (*Fights* D)
65 *queen* punning on *quean*, 'a bold, impudent, or ill-behaved woman' (*OED*)
69 *princely* D (*noble* L)   71 *a little* D (*some* L)
76 D; *omitted in* L
  s.d. *A Street* L (Like Q1, D does not begin a new scene here)
5 s.d. L (Watch *knocks, a* Servant *enters* D)

here, and desire to know what he'll please to have done with
her.   10

SERVANT

I'll acquaint my master.   (*Exit*)

SIR JOHN

Hark you, constable, what cuckoldly justice is this?

CONSTABLE

One that will know how to deal with such romps as you are,
I'll warrant you.

Enter JUSTICE

JUSTICE

Well, Mr Constable, what's the matter here?   15

CONSTABLE

An't please your worship, this here comical sort of a gentlewoman has committed great outrages tonight. She has been
frolicking with my Lord Rake and his gang; they attacked
the watch, and I hear there has been a gentleman killed.
I believe 'tis they have done it.   20

SIR JOHN

There may have been murder, for aught I know; and 'tis a
great mercy there has not been a rape too—for this fellow
would have ravished me.

1 WATCHMAN

Ravish! I ravish! O lud, O lud, O lud! I ravish her? Why,
please your honour, I heard Mr Constable say he believed   25
she was little better than a mophrodite.

JUSTICE

Why truly, she does seem to be a little masculine about the
mouth.

1 WATCHMAN

Yes, and about the hands too, an't please your worship. I
did but offer in mere civility to help her up the steps into   30

13 *will know* D (knows L)
13 *romps* boisterous women
15 *what's* D (what is L)
17 *tonight* last night (also at 57)
19 *gentleman* D (man L)
20 *done it* L (done't D)
21 *There* D (Sir, there L)
22 *for this* D (that L)
24 *Ravish! I ravish!* D (Ravish! Ravish! L)
24 *I ravish her?* D (Ravish her! L)
25 *honour* D (worship L)
26 *mophrodite* D (maphrodite L) vulgar corruption of *hermaphrodite*
27 *to be a* D (a L)

our apartment, and with her gripen fist—(SIR JOHN *knocks him down*)—ay, just so, sir.

SIR JOHN
I felled him to the ground like an ox.

JUSTICE
Out upon this boisterous woman! Out upon her!

SIR JOHN
Mr Justice, he would have been uncivil. It was in defence 35
of my honour, and I demand satisfaction.

1 WATCHMAN
I hope your worship will satisfy her honour in Bridewell;
that fist of hers will make an admirable hemp-beater.

SIR JOHN
Sir, I hope you will protect me against that libidinous
rascal; I am a woman of quality, and virtue too, for all I am 40
in a sort of an undress this morning.

JUSTICE
Why, she really has the air of a sort of a woman a little
somethingish out of the common.—Madam, if you expect
I should be favourable to you, I desire I may know who
you are. 45

SIR JOHN
Sir, I am anybody, at your service.

JUSTICE
Lady, I desire to know your name.

SIR JOHN
Sir, my name's Mary.

JUSTICE
Ay, but your surname, madam?

SIR JOHN
Sir, my surname's the very same with my husband's. 50

JUSTICE
A strange woman this!—Who is your husband, pray?

SIR JOHN
Why, Sir John.

JUSTICE
Sir John who?

31 *gripen* L (gippen D) clenched
31–2 s.d. D and L print this at the end of the Watchman's speech
41 *a sort of an* D (an L)
42 *really has* D (has really L)
43 *somethingish* D (something L)
52 *Why, Sir* D (Sir L)

---

37 *Bridewell* a house of correction near Fleet Street, where night-walkers
and other petty offenders were set to hard labour pounding hemp

SIR JOHN
Why, Sir John Brute.

JUSTICE
Is it possible, madam, you can be my Lady Brute?   55

SIR JOHN
That happy woman, sir, am I; only a little in my merriment
tonight.

JUSTICE
I'm concerned for Sir John.

SIR JOHN
Truly, so am I.

JUSTICE
I've heard he's an honest gentleman.   60

SIR JOHN
As ever drank.

JUSTICE
Good lack! Indeed, lady, I am sorry he should have such a
wife.

SIR JOHN
Sir, I am sorry he has any wife at all.

JUSTICE
And so, perhaps, may he.—I doubt you have not given him   65
a very good taste of matrimony.

SIR JOHN
Taste, sir? I have scorned to stint him to a taste; I have given
him a full meal of it.

JUSTICE
Indeed, I believe so!—But pray, fair lady, may he have
given you any occasion for this extraordinary conduct?   70
Does he not use you well?

SIR JOHN
A little upon the rough, sometimes.

JUSTICE
Ay, any man may be out of humour now and then.

SIR JOHN
Sir, I love peace and quiet, and when a woman don't find

54 *Why, Sir* D (Sir L)
58 *I'm* D (I am L)
60 *I've* D (I have L)
62 *I am* D (I'm L)
62 *should have* D (has L)
64 s.p. SIR JOHN L (*Justice* D)
64 *Sir, I* D (I L)
67 *I have scorned* D (Sir, I have scorned L)
72 *upon the rough* harshly

that at home, she's apt sometimes to comfort herself with a   75
few innocent diversions abroad.

JUSTICE

I doubt he uses you but too well. Pray, how does he as to
that weighty thing, money? Does he allow you what's proper
of that?

SIR JOHN

Sir, I have generally enough to pay the reckoning, if this   80
son of a whore the drawer would bring his bill.

JUSTICE

A strange woman this.—Does he spend a reasonable portion
of his time at home, to the comfort of his wife and children?

SIR JOHN

Never gave his wife cause to repine at his being abroad in
his life.   85

JUSTICE

Pray, madam, how may he be in the grand matrimonial
point: is he true to your bed?

SIR JOHN

Chaste?—Oons, this fellow asks so many impertinent
questions, egad, I believe it is the justice's wife in the
justice's clothes.   90

JUSTICE

'Tis a great pity he should have been thus disposed of.—
Pray, madam, and then I have done, what may be your
ladyship's common method of life, if I may presume so far?

SIR JOHN

Why, sir, much like that of a woman of quality.

JUSTICE

Pray how may you generally pass your time, madam? Your   95
morning, for example?

SIR JOHN

Sir, like a woman of quality. I wake about two o'clock in the
afternoon, I stretch, and then—make a sign for my choco-
late. When I have drank three cups, I slide down again upon
my back, with my arms over my head, while two maids put   100

78 *what's* D (what is L)
81 *the drawer* D (of a drawer L)
81 *bring* D (but bring L)
84 *Never* D (He never L)
92 *I have* D (I've L)
94 *much like* D (much L)
98 *and then* D (and L)
100 *two* D (my two L)
100 *put* L (puts D)

on my stockings. Then, hanging upon their shoulders, I am
trailed to my great chair, where I sit, and yawn for my
breakfast. If it don't come presently, I lie down upon my
couch to say my prayers, while my maid reads me the
playbills.   105

JUSTICE

Very well, madam.

SIR JOHN

When the tea is brought in, I drink twelve regular dishes,
with eight slices of bread and butter—and half an hour
after, I send to the cook to know if the dinner is almost ready.

JUSTICE

So, madam.   110

SIR JOHN

By that time my head's half-dressed, I hear my husband
swearing himself into a state of perdition that the meat's all
cold upon the table; to mend which, I come down in an
hour more and have it sent back to the kitchen to be all
dressed over again.   115

JUSTICE

Poor man!

SIR JOHN

When I have dined, and my idle servants are presumptuously
set down at their ease to do so too, I call for my coach, go
to visit fifty dear friends, of whom I hope I never shall find
one at home while I shall live.   120

JUSTICE

So; there's the morning and afternoon pretty well disposed
of.—Pray, madam, how do you pass your evenings?

SIR JOHN

Like a woman of spirit, sir, a great spirit. Give me a box
and dice—seven's the main! Oons, sir, I set you a hundred

111 *head's* D (head is L)
113 *mend* D (amend L)
118–19 *go to visit* D (to go visit L)
119 *never shall* D (shall never L)
124 *set* stake

---

105 *playbills* regularly delivered to the town houses of wealthy patrons of
the theatre
111 *head's half-dressed* The lofty head-dresses affected by ladies of fashion,
which took several hours to erect, are ridiculed in the *Spectator*, no. 98,
22 June 1711.
124 *seven's the main* In the game of hazard, the 'main' is a number between
five and nine called by the caster before the dice are thrown; the odds
against casting seven on any particular throw are five to one.

pounds! Why, do you think women are married now-a-days   125
to sit at home and mend napkins? Sir, we have nobler ways
of passing time.

JUSTICE
Mercy upon us, Mr Constable, what will this age come to?

CONSTABLE
What will it come to, indeed, if such women as these are
not set in the stocks?   130

SIR JOHN
I have a little urgent business calls upon me; and therefore
I desire the favour of you to bring matters to a conclusion.

JUSTICE
Madam, if I were sure that business were not to commit
more disorders, I would release you.

SIR JOHN
None—by my virtue!   135

JUSTICE
Then, Mr Constable, you may discharge her.

SIR JOHN
Sir, your very humble servant. If you please to accept of a
bottle—

JUSTICE
I thank you kindly, madam; but I never drink in a morning.
Good-bye, madam, good-bye to ye.   140

SIR JOHN
Good-bye t'ye, good sir. (*Exit* JUSTICE) So.—Now, Mr
Constable, shall you and I go pick up a whore together?

CONSTABLE
No, thank you, madam; my wife's enough to satisfy any
reasonable man.

SIR JOHN
(*Aside*) He he he he he! The fool is married then.—[*Aloud*]   145
Well, you won't go?

CONSTABLE
Not I, truly.

SIR JOHN
Then I'll go by myself; and you and your wife may be
damned.   (*Exit* SIR JOHN)

CONSTABLE (*Gazing after him*)
Why, God a mercy, my lady!   (*Exeunt*)   150

125 *pounds* D (pound L)
131 *I have* D (Sir, I have L)
150 s.d. *him* D (her L)
150 *my lady* D (lady L)

APPENDIX B

TWO ADDITIONAL SONGS

I

Vanbrugh's songs for the play were soon replaced by others on the stage, and as Treble and Pipe withdrew from the cast lists new singers arrived to provide music at different places in the text. Mrs Willis, who played Madamoiselle, sang the 'Ballad of Sally' at Lincoln's Inn Fields on 20 April 1719, and on 19 March 1726 the same theatre announced 'new Songs proper to the Play, compos'd and sung by Leveridge and Legare'.[1] Since Colonel Bully has only seven lines, his role was an obvious one for a singer who could also act. John Beard, for whom Handel wrote some of his finest tenor parts, played it on 8 January 1742 at Drury Lane, where his predecessor John Harper probably sang the following ditty some time between 15 September 1726 and 16 October 1729. (The problems involved here are discussed in the introduction to Appendix A.) There is no obvious place for this song in Vanbrugh's text, but it would go well at the end of IV.i, when Bully could make a cautious reappearance as the watch go off.

The song was printed in *The Musical Miscellany; Being a Collection of Choice Songs, Set to the Violin and Flute, By the most Eminent Masters* (1729), I, 66–8, which also prints the tenor line. My copytext is the Bodleian Library copy (Douce M.601).[2]

TIPPLING JOHN
Sung by Mr Harper, in *The Provoked Wife*

> As tippling John was jogging on,
>   Upon the riot night,
> With tottering pace and fiery face,
>   Suspicious of high flight,
> The guards who took him, by his look,   5
>   For some chief firebrand,
> Asked whence he came, what was his name,
>   'Who are you? Stand, friend, stand!'

[1] *The London Stage 1660–1800*, ed. W. Van Lennep, E. L. Avery, A. H. Scouten, G. Winchester Stone Jnr, and C. B. Hogan (Carbondale, Illinois, 1960–68), Pt. 2, 536 and 859.
[2] I owe my knowledge of this song to Frank M. Patterson, 'The revised scenes of *The Provok'd Wife*,' *English Language Notes*, IV (1966–67), 19–23, which raises matters discussed in the introduction to Appendix A.

    'I'm going home, from meeting come'.
        'Ay', says one, 'that's the case;   10
    Some meeting he has burnt, you see,
        The flame's still in his face'.
    John thought 'twas time to purge the crime,
        And said 'twas his intent   15
    For to assuage his thirsty rage;
        That meeting 'twas he meant.

    'Come, friend, be plain; you trifle in vain',
        Says one, 'pray let us know,
    That we may find how you're inclined,
        Are you high church or low?'   20
    John said to that, 'I'll tell you what,
        To end debates and strife,
    All I can say, this is the way
        I steer my course of life:

    I ne'er to Bow, nor Burgess go,   25
        To steeple-house nor hall;
    The brisk bar-bell best suits my zeal
        With "Gentlemen, d'ye call?"
    Now judge, am I low church or high,
        From tavern or the steeple,   30
    Whose merry toll exalts the soul
        And makes us high-flown people'.

    The guards came on and looked at John
        With countenance most pleasant;
    By whisper round they all soon found   35
        He was no dangerous peasant.
    So while John stood the best he could,
        Expecting their decision,
    'Pox on't!' says one, 'let him be gone,
        He's of our own religion'.   40

  9 *meeting* (1) private party (2) nonconformist gathering
11 *burnt* fired with zeal
25 *Bow* probably St Mary-le-Bow, Cheapside
25 *Burgess* town hall (not in *OED*)
26 *steeple-house* term used by Quakers for *church*
32 *high-flown* (1) intoxicated (2) extremist for church authority
38 *Expecting* awaiting

II

This Scottish medley, which seems to have two distinct choruses
and is sometimes printed without the second stanza, marks that
moment in the stage history of *The Provoked Wife* when Colonel
Bully's success as a singer enabled him to steal even the tavern
scene from Lord Rake. It was first printed in the 1776 edition of
the play, immediately after 'What a pother of late' with the comment:
'Instead of this song by Lord *Rake*, the following by Colonel *Bully*
is now sung at the Theatre'. This probably refers to the performances
that season at Drury Lane, where a contemporary witness shows it
brought the house down on 30 April 1776,

> Being the last time of Garrick's appearing in character of Sir John
> Brute. When the Song Encor'd Mr Garrick said Come Col. give
> us that Song again for two very good Reasons, the first because
> your friends desire it—and Secondly because I believe I shall never
> be in such good company again.[3]

I have taken as my copy-text the Bodleian Library copy of *1776*
(Vet A5.e.4335), collated against the British Museum copy of the
text in an undated broadside entitled 'A Scotch Medley. *Introduced
in The Provok'd Wife*' (11621.i.11). The broadside (SM) generally
makes better sense of the dialect than *1776* (L).

SONG by COLONEL BULLY

We're gaily yet, and we're gaily yet,
  And we's no very fou, but we're gaily yet.
Then sit ye awhile, and tipple a bit,
  For we's no very fou, but we're gaily yet.

There was a lad, and they cau'd him Dicky,   5
He gae me a kiss, and I bit his lippy,
Then under my apron he showed me a trick.
And we's no very fou, but we're gaily yet.
  And we're gaily yet, *&c.*

There were three lads and they were clad,   10
There were three lasses and them they had.
Three trees in the orchard are newly sprung,

2 *we's* L (we're SM)
2 *no* SM (not L)
2 *fou* drunk
10 *clad* dressed up
11 *them they* L (they them SM)

---

[3] *The London Stage*, Pt. 4, 1972–3.

And we's a' git geer enough, we're but young.
  And we're gaily yet, &c.

    Then up wi't Ailie, Ailie, up wi't Ailie, now;   **15**
    Then up wi't Ailie, quo' cummer, we's get roaring fou.

And one was kissed in the barn,
  Another was kissed on the green,
And t'other behind the pease-stack
  Till the mow flew up to her eyen,   **20**
    Then up wi't Ailie, Ailie, &c.

Now fie, John Thompson, run,
  Gin ever you ran in your life;
De'il get ye, but hie, my dear Jack,
  There's a mon got to bed with your wife.   **25**
    Then up wi't Ailie, &c.

Then away John Thompson ran,
  And egad, he ran with speed,
But before he had run his length,
  The false loon had done the deed.   **30**
    Then up wi't Ailie, &c.

13 *a' git geer* L (a' get geer SM) have got apparel (?)
14 Not in SM
15 *wi't* SM (went L) with it
16 *quo' cummer* SM (quo' Crumma L) said the girl
16 *get* SM (got a L)
19 *And t'other* L (The third SM)
20 *mow* heap of peas
22 *run* L (rin SM)
23 *you ran* SM (ye run L)
24 *ye* L (you SM)
24 *hie* ed. (*hye* L, hey SM) hurry
25 *mon* L (man SM)
25 *to bed* L (a-bed SM)
28 *egad* L (I trow SM)
31 *Then up wi't* (went) *Ailie* L (We're gaily yet SM)

The Recruiting Officer

GEORGE FARQUHAR

Edited by
JOHN ROSS

ABBREVIATIONS

Archer   Archer, William, ed., *George Farquhar* [*Best Plays*], London, new edition, 1949

Ashton   Ashton, John, *Social Life in the Age of Queen Anne*, London, 1883 (facsimile edition, Detroit, Michigan, 1968)

Ewald   Ewald, Alexander Charles, ed., *The Dramatic Works of George Farquhar*, 2 vols., London, 1892

Hunt   Hunt, Leigh, ed., *The Dramatic Works of Wycherley, Congreve, Vanbrugh and Farquhar*, London, 1840

James   James, Eugene Nelson, *The Development of George Farquhar as a Comic Dramatist*, The Hague, 1972

Jeffares   Jeffares, A. Norman, ed., *The Recruiting Officer* (Fountainwell Drama Texts), Edinburgh, 1972

The London Stage   W. Van Lennep, E. L. Avery, A. H. Scouten, G. W. Stone and C. B. Hogan, edd., *The London Stage, 1660–1800*, 11 vols., Carbondale, Illinois, 1965–68

N.T.   National Theatre production, 1963

Nicoll   Nicoll, Allardyce, *A History of English Drama 1660–1900*, 6 vols., Vol. II, *Early Eighteenth Century Drama*, 3rd edition, Cambridge, 1955

Q   early editions

Q1   first edition, 1706

Q2   second edition, 1706

Rothstein   Rothstein, Eric, *George Farquhar*, New York, 1967

Shugrue   Shugrue, Michael, ed., *The Recruiting Officer* (Regents Restoration Drama Series), London, 1966

Stonehill   Stonehill, Charles, ed., *The Complete Works of George Farquhar*, 2 vols., Bloomsbury, 1930

Strauss   Strauss, Louis B., ed., *A Discourse upon Comedy, The Recruiting Officer and The Beaux' Stratagem* (Belles-Lettres Series), Boston [1914]

Tynan   Tynan, Kenneth, ed., '*The Recruiting Officer*': *The National Theatre Production*, London, 1965

THE
Recruiting Officer.
A
COMEDY.

As it is Acted at the

THEATRE ROYAL

IN

DRURY-LANE,

By Her MAJESTY's Servants.

Written by Mr. FARQUHAR.

—— *Captique Æolis, donisque coacti.*
Virg. Lib. II. Æneid.

LONDON:

Printed for BERNARD LINTOTT at the *Cross Keys* next
Nando's Coffee-House near *Temple-Bar.*

Price 1 s. 6 d.

Æolis properly, *dolis* (so corrected, Q1 errata)

Captique dolis, donisque coacti. 'Captured with tricks and brought together with (or, urged on by) gifts', adapted from Virgil's *Æneid*, II, 196: *captique dolis lacrimisque coactis*, 'captured with tricks and forced tears'. Rothstein (p. 133) perceives an ingenious reversal of the situation of the fall of Troy. Since England must avoid like consequences of 'foolish trust and disarmament', Kite's stratagems to enlist defenders receive some degree of justification. On another plane, 'the heroic comparison between beleaguered Troy and beleaguered Tummas Appletree is so grotesque as to indicate Farquhar's limited sympathy for the victims of recruitment'.

EPISTLE DEDICATORY
To All Friends Round the Wrekin

My Lords and Gentlemen,

Instead of the mercenary expectations that attend addresses
of this nature, I humbly beg, that this may be received as an
acknowledgment for the favours you have already conferred.
I have transgressed the rules of dedication in offering you   5
anything in that style without first asking your leave; but the
entertainment I found in Shropshire commands me to be
grateful, and that's all I intend.

'Twas my good fortune to be ordered some time ago into the
place which is made the scene of this comedy; I was a perfect   10
stranger to everything in Salop, but its character of loyalty, the
number of its inhabitants, the alacrity of the gentlemen in
recruiting the army, with their generous and hospitable
reception of strangers.

This character I found so amply verified in every particular,   15
that you made recruiting, which is the greatest fatigue upon
earth to others, to be the greatest pleasure in the world to me.

The kingdom cannot show better bodies of men, better
inclinations for the service, more generosity, more good understanding, nor more politeness, than is to be found at the foot of   20
the Wrekin.

Some little turns of humour that I met with almost within

0.–1, 21, 65 *Wrekin* Q1 errata (Rekin Q1) a dominating, isolated hill,
   1,335 feet high, about ten miles to the east of Shrewsbury
7 *entertainment* reception, treatment
11 *Salop* Shropshire

1–8 Authors customarily dedicated their works to wealthy individuals,
   first asking their permission, in hope of a gift of guineas, and, maybe,
   longer-term patronage. Farquhar affects to believe that dedications, like
   plays, should conform to classical 'rules'.

the shade of that famous hill gave the rise to this comedy; and
people were apprehensive, that, by the example of some others,
I would make the town merry at the expense of the country   25
gentlemen. But they forgot that I was to write a comedy, not a
libel; and that whilst I held to nature, no person of any
character in your country could suffer by being exposed. I have
drawn the justice and the clown in their *puris naturalibus*: the
one an apprehensive, sturdy, brave blockhead; and the other a   30
worthy, honest, generous gentleman, hearty in his country's
cause, and of as good an understanding as I could give him,
which I must confess is far short of his own.

I humbly beg leave to interline a word or two of the adventures of *The Recruiting Officer* upon the stage. Mr Rich, who   35
commands the company for which those recruits were raised,
has desired me to acquit him before the world of a charge
which he thinks lies heavy upon him for acting this play on
Mr Durfey's third night.

Be it known unto all men by these presents, that it was my   40
act and deed, or rather Mr Durfey's; for he *would* play his third
night against the first of mine. He brought down a huge flight
of frightful birds upon me, when, heaven knows, I had not a
feathered fowl in my play except one single Kite; but I

---

23 *rise* origin
28 *country* county
29 *puris naturalibus* natural state
34 *interline* interpolate
40 *these presents* these words, the present document (legal)

23–33 Farquhar here signals 'a major shift in attitude, away from the
   traditional contempt for the squirearchy' (Loftis, p. 72), found in
   nearly all Restoration comedy, and exemplified in Congreve's portrayal
   of Sir Wilfull Witwoud, who is made to come from Shropshire, near
   Shrewsbury, in *The Way of the World* (1700).
35 *Mr Rich.* Christopher Rich (d. 1714), patentee and manager of the
   Theatre Royal, Drury Lane, between 1688 and 1709, notoriously auto-
   cratic towards his actors.
39 *Mr Durfey's third night.* Thomas Durfey's first author's-benefit performance for his comic opera, *Wonders in the Sun; or, The Kingdom of
   the Birds*, which had opened at the rival theatre, the Queen's in the
   Haymarket, on Friday 5 April. Dramatists' incomes largely depended
   on the profits of benefit performances, and the clash left him with a
   sadly thin audience. His opera closed after five nights, earning less than
   half its production costs. Farquhar's first night was 8 April.
42–3 *huge . . . birds.* Durfey's cast included many strange birds, represented by elaborately costumed actors, or painted figures.

presently made Plume a bird, because of his name, and Brazen   45
another, because of the feather in his hat; and with these three
I engaged his whole empire, which I think was as great a *wonder*
as any *in the sun*.

But to answer his complaints more gravely, the season was
far advanced; the officers that made the greatest figures in my   50
play were all commanded to their posts abroad, and waited only
for a wind, which might possibly turn in less time than a day;
and I know none of Mr Durfey's birds that had posts abroad
but his woodcocks, and their season is over; so that he might
put off a day with less prejudice than the *Recruiting Officer*   55
could, who has this farther to say for himself, that he was
posted before the other spoke, and could not with credit recede
from his station.

These and some other rubs this comedy met with before it
appeared. But on the other hand, it had powerful helps to set it   60
forward: the Duke of Ormonde encouraged the author, and the
Earl of Orrery approved the play. My recruits were reviewed
by my general and my colonel, and could not fail to pass
muster, and still to add to my success, they were raised among
my friends round the Wrekin.   65

This Health has the advantage over our other celebrated

---

57 *posted* (a) appointed to his command, or place of duty; (b) adver-
     tised, by sticking play-bills on posts
59 *rubs* hindrances, difficulties
63–4 *pass muster* undergo review without censure; succeed
66 *This Health* i.e., the toast of 'good health'

49–50 *the season was far advanced*. (a) The campaigning season in Flanders
     began in spring: 'the Battle of Ramillies was fought just six weeks after
     the first night of the play' (Archer); (b) the theatrical season ran till
     July, but contained limited provision for new works.
54 *woodcocks*. The only migrants among Durfey's birds: 'their season' for
     migrating south is October–November, returning in April–May; cf.
     The Twin Rivals, II (Stonehill, I, 304); fig., fools.
61 *the Duke of Ormonde*. James Butler (1665–1745), 2nd Duke, appointed
     Lord-Lieutenant of Ireland in 1703, and in 1702, General of the Horse.
     He had approved Farquhar's lieutenancy, and gave him kind words, but
     neither financial help nor further promotion.
61–2 *the Earl of Orrery*. Charles Boyle (1676–1731), 4th Earl, who in 1704
     gave Farquhar a commission as lieutenant of grenadiers in his new
     regiment. He was himself author of a manners-comedy, *As You Find It*
     (1703).

toasts, never to grow worse for the wearing; 'tis a lasting
beauty, old without age and common without scandal. That
you may live long to set it cheerfully round, and to enjoy the
abundant pleasures of your fair and plentiful country, is the   70
hearty wish of,

My Lords and Gentlemen,
Your most obliged,
and most obedient servant,
Geo. Farquhar.   75

67 *toasts* ladies nominated as persons to whom the company is to
   drink (cf. *Tatler*, Nos 24, 31)

THE PROLOGUE

In ancient times, when Helen's fatal charms
Roused the contending universe to arms,
The Grecian council happily deputes
The sly Ulysses forth – to raise recruits.
The artful captain found, without delay,   5
Where great Achilles, a deserter, lay.
Him Fate had warned to shun the Trojan blows;
Him Greece required – against their Trojan foes.
All the recruiting arts were needful here
To raise this great, this tim'rous volunteer.   10
Ulysses well could talk – he stirs, he warms
The warlike youth. He listens to the charms
Of plunder, fine laced coats, and glitt'ring arms.
Ulysses caught the young aspiring boy,
And listed him who wrought the fate of Troy.   15
Thus by recruiting was bold Hector slain;
Recruiting thus fair Helen did regain.
If for one Helen such prodigious things
Were acted, that they even listed kings;
If for one Helen's artful, vicious charms,   20
Half the transported world was found in arms;

---

11 *warms* Q2 (warns Q1) renders eager, exhorts to valour
15 *listed* enlisted

1–15 Achilles' goddess-mother Thetis learnt that he was fated to a life
either long and obscure, or glorious but brief, and had him hidden on
the island of Scyros, in woman's clothes. The seer Calchas prophesied
that Troy could not be taken without Achilles' help. Verbal echoes
identify the source from which Farquhar took the story of how Ulysses
set off to find him, and recruited him, as Sir Robert Howard's verse
translation of Statius' *Achilleis*, printed in Howard's *Poems* (1660),
pp. 222–59, and *Poems on Several Occasions* (1696), pp. 171–282.

What for so many Helens may we dare,
Whose minds, as well as faces, are so fair?
If, by one Helen's eyes, old Greece could find
Its Homer fired to write – even Homer blind, 25
The Britons sure beyond compare may write,
That view so many Helens every night.

22–3 Ian Donaldson has suggested that these lines allude to the importance
of the presence of women and military officers in the first audiences,
which 'may have had some effect on the design of the play as a whole'
(review of Jeffares, *N&Q*, ccxx (1975), 516–18).

DRAMATIS PERSONAE

Men

MR BALANCE ⎫		*Mr Keen*
MR SCALE ⎬ *three Justices*		*Mr Phillips*
MR SCRUPLE ⎭		*Mr Kent*
MR WORTHY, *a gentleman of Shropshire*		*Mr Williams*
CAPTAIN PLUME, *a recruiting officer*		*Mr Wilks*
CAPTAIN BRAZEN, *a recruiting officer*		*Mr Cibber*
KITE, *Sergeant to Plume*		*Mr Estcourt*
BULLOCK, *a country clown*		*Mr Bullock*
COSTAR PEARMAIN, *a recruit*		*Mr Norris*
THOMAS APPLETREE, *a recruit*		*Mr Fairbank*
[PLUCK, *a butcher*]		
[THOMAS, *a smith*]		
[BRIDEWELL, *a constable*]		

Women

MELINDA, *a lady of fortune*	*Mrs Rogers*
SILVIA, *daughter to Balance, in love with Plume*	*Mrs Oldfield*
LUCY, *Melinda's maid*	*Mrs Sapsford*
ROSE, *a country wench*	*Mrs Mountfort*

Recruits, [drummer,] mob, servants and attendants

Scene *Shrewsbury*

THE RECRUITING OFFICER

Act I, Scene i

The Market-place
DRUMMER *beats the 'Grenadier March'*
Enter SERGEANT KITE, *followed by the* MOB

KITE (*Making a speech*)
If any gentlemen soldiers, or others, have a mind to serve
Her Majesty, and pull down the French king; if any prentices
have severe masters, any children have undutiful parents; if
any servants have too little wages, or any husband too much
wife; let them repair to the noble Sergeant Kite, at the Sign   5
of the Raven, in this good town of Shrewsbury, and they shall
receive present relief and entertainment. – Gentlemen, I
don't beat my drums here to ensnare or inveigle any man;
for you must know, gentlemen, that I am a man of honour.
Besides, I don't beat up for common soldiers; no, I list only   10
grenadiers, grenadiers, gentlemen – pray, gentlemen, observe
this cap – this is the cap of honour, it dubs a man a gentleman in the drawing of a tricker; and he that has the good
fortune to be born six foot high was born to be a great man.
(*To one of the Mob*) Sir, will you give me leave to try this cap   15
upon your head?

0.2 s.d. DRUMMER Ed. (*Drum* Q; i.e., Drummer)
5–6 *the Sign of the Raven* the Raven Hotel, in Castle Street
12 *cap* special headwear of grenadier troops, narrow, with a tall,
      mitre-shaped front
13 *tricker* trigger

0.1–0.2 s.d. '*The* MOB' (*mobile*, crowd), lower-class townspeople and
      countrymen, includes Costar Pearmain and Thomas Appletree. Later
      C18 editions make the entry quasi-processional: '*Enter* Drummer,
      beating the "*Grenadier's March*", *Serjeant* Kite, Costar Pearmain,
      Thomas Appletree, *and* Mob'.
0.2 *Grenadier March.* Not 'The British Grenadiers' but another march;
      its tune and words are reprinted in *The Rambling Soldier*, ed. R. Palmer
      (Harmondsworth, 1977), pp. 18-19.
11 *grenadiers.* Specialist grenade-throwing infantry, chosen for height and
      strength. At this time they formed a separate company within each foot
      regiment, and served as assault troops in siege or trench warfare.

MOB

Is there no harm in't? Won't the cap list me?

KITE

No, no, no more than I can, – come, let me see how it becomes you.

MOB

Are you sure there be no conjuration in it, no gunpowder   20
plot upon me?

KITE

No, no, friend; don't fear, man.

MOB

My mind misgives me plaguily – let me see it. (*Going to put it on*) It smells woundily of sweat and brimstone; pray, Sergeant, what writing is this upon the face of it?   25

KITE

'The Crown, or the Bed of Honour'.

MOB

Pray now, what may be that same bed of honour?

KITE

Oh, a mighty large bed, bigger by half than the great bed of Ware, ten thousand people may lie in't together and never feel one another.   30

---

20 *conjuration* magic spell, conjuring
23 *plaguily* Q2 (plaguely Q1)
24 *woundily* dreadfully, excessively
26 *the Bed of Honour* (death on) the field of battle

---

17 s.p. MOB i.e., one of the mob. Later C18 editions identify him with Costar Pearmain, which may have been Farquhar's final intention. It reflects stage-tradition, and improves dramatic continuity between I.i and II.iii. He is however married, illiterate, and shrewder.

26 *The Crown . . . Honour* Grenadier caps generally bore, on the stiff front, the crown and the royal cipher, or else the motto of the regiment's colonel. No trace has been found of this particular motto's having been associated with any British regiment; apparently it was Farquhar's invention, or a professional jest.

28–9 *the great bed of Ware.* A handsome, carved four-poster, first made famous while in the Crown Inn (some authorities say, the Saracen's Head) at Ware, Hertfordshire, and now in the Victoria and Albert Museum. It measures 10 feet 8½ inches wide, 11 feet 1 inch deep, and was made between 1575 and 1600, though it bears the date '1460'. Literary references to it include those in *Twelfth Night* and Jonson's *Silent Woman.* (See Lawrence Wright, *Warm and Snug: the History of the Bed* [1962], pp. 69–70.)

MOB

My wife and I would do well to lie in't, for we don't care for
feeling one another – but do folk sleep sound in this same bed
of honour?

KITE

Sound! Aye, so sound that they never wake.

MOB

Wauns! I wish again that my wife lay there.   35

KITE

Say you so? Then I find, brother –

MOB

Brother! Hold there, friend, I'm no kindred to you that I
know of, as yet – look'ee, Sergeant, no coaxing, no wheedling,
d'ye see; if I have a mind to list, why so – if not, why 'tis not
so – therefore take your cap and your brothership back   40
again, for I an't disposed at this present writing – no
coaxing, no brothering me, faith.

KITE

I coax! I wheedle! I'm above it. Sir, I have served twenty
campaigns. But sir, you talk well, and I must own that you
are a man every inch of you, a pretty, young, sprightly   45
fellow – I love a fellow with a spirit, but I scorn to coax, 'tis
base; though I must say that never in my life have I seen a
man better built; how firm and strong he treads, he steps
like a castle! But I scorn to wheedle any man – come,
honest lad, will you take share of a pot?   50

MOB

Nay, for that matter, I'll spend my penny with the best he
that wears a head, that is, begging your pardon, sir, and in
a fair way.

KITE

Give me your hand then; and now, gentlemen, I have no
more to say but this – here's a purse of gold, and there is a 55
tub of humming ale at my quarters; 'tis the Queen's money
and the Queen's drink. She's a generous queen and loves
her subjects – I hope, gentlemen, you won't refuse the
Queen's health?

35 *Wauns* dialect-form of 'Wounds', a mild oath; from 'God's
   wounds'
38 *look'ee* Q2 (lookye Q1)
38 *coaxing* includes sense 'persuading by flattery'
42 *faith* in faith, i.e., in truth
48 *man better built* Q2 (better built man Q1)
56 *humming* strong, frothing(?)

ALL MOB

    No, no, no.   60

KITE

    Huzza then! Huzza for the Queen, and the honour of
Shropshire!

ALL MOB

    Huzza!

KITE

    Beat drum.

        Exeunt, drummer beating the 'Grenadier March'

        Enter PLUME *in a riding habit*

PLUME

    By the Grenadier March that should be my drum, and by that   65
shout it should beat with success – let me see – (*looks on his
watch*) – four o'clock – at ten yesterday morning I left
London – a hundred and twenty miles in thirty hours is
pretty smart riding, but nothing to the fatigue of recruiting.

                    Enter KITE

KITE

    Welcome to Shrewsbury, noble Captain: from the banks of   70
the Danube to the Severn side, noble Captain, you're
welcome.

PLUME

    A very elegant reception indeed, Mr Kite, I find you are
fairly entered into your recruiting strain – pray, what
success?   75

KITE

    I have been here but a week and I have recruited five.

PLUME

    Five! Pray, what are they?

KITE

    I have listed the strong man of Kent, the king of the gypsies,

64 s.d. *drummer* Ed. (*drum* Q)
71 *you're* Q2 (you are Q1)

70–1 *from . . . side* Plume is supposed to have recently returned from the
    Battle of Blenheim, fought beside the Danube.
78 *the strong man of Kent.* William Joy, or Joyce, the Kentish strong man,
    known as the Southwark Samson (Ashton, p. 201). He had aroused
    Farquhar's resentment in late 1699 when he had hired the disused
    Dorset Gardens playhouse for exhibitions of 'dexterities of strength',
    competing for audiences with the first run of *The Constant Couple* (see
    its prologue, ll. 32–9, in Stonehill, I, 87–8; *The London Stage, 1660–
    1800*, Part 1, pp. 517, 518, 520).

a Scotch pedlar, a scoundrel attorney, and a Welsh parson.

PLUME

An attorney! Wert thou mad? List a lawyer! Discharge him,   80
discharge him this minute.

KITE

Why, sir?

PLUME

Because I will have nobody in my company that can write;
a fellow that can write, can draw petitions – I say, this
minute discharge him.   85

KITE

And what shall I do with the parson?

PLUME

Can he write?

KITE

Umh – he plays rarely upon the fiddle.

PLUME

Keep him by all means. But how stands the country affected?
Were the people pleased with the news of my coming to   90
town?

KITE

Sir, the mob are so pleased with your honour, and the
justices and better sort of people are so delighted with me,
that we shall soon do our business. But, sir, you have got a
recruit here that you little think of.   95

PLUME

Who?

KITE

One that you beat up for last time you were in the country:
you remember your old friend Molly at the Castle?

PLUME

She's not with child, I hope.

KITE

No, no, sir; she was brought to bed yesterday.   100

PLUME

Kite, you must father the child.

KITE

Humph – and so her friends will oblige me to marry the
mother.

84 *petitions* commonly, for arrears of pay.
102 *friends* relations (as well as modern sense)

98 *the Castle*. Shrewsbury Castle, built in the C13, had lost its status as
a royal fortress during the reign of Charles II, and its use was resident-
ial only.

PLUME

> If they should, we'll take her with us, she can wash, you
> know, and make a bed upon occasion.   105

KITE

> Aye, or unmake it upon occasion. But your honour knows
> that I'm married already.

PLUME

> To how many?

KITE

> I can't tell readily – I have set them down here upon the back
> of the muster-roll. (*Draws it out*) Let me see – *Imprimis*,   110
> Mrs Sheely Snickereyes, she sells potatoes upon Ormonde
> Quay in Dublin – Peggy Guzzle, the brandy-woman at the
> Horse-guard at Whitehall – Dolly Waggon, the carrier's
> daughter in Hull – Mademoiselle Van-bottom-flat at the
> Buss – then Jenny Oakum, the ship-carpenter's widow at   115
> Portsmouth; but I don't reckon upon her, for she was
> married at the same time to two lieutenants of marines, and
> a man of war's boatswain.

PLUME

> A full company – you have named five – come, make 'em half
> a dozen, Kite. Is the child a boy or a girl?   120

KITE

> A chopping boy.

PLUME

> Then set the mother down in your list, and the boy in mine;
> enter him a grenadier by the name of Francis Kite, absent
> upon furlough – I'll allow you a man's pay for his sub-

104 *they* Q2 (*she* Q1)
110 s.d. *Draws it out* Q2 (*Draws out the Muster-roll* Q1)
    Imprimis in the first place
115 *the Buss* 's Hertogenbosch, in North Brabant, Holland
121 *chopping* big and vigorous

---

113 *the Horse-guard*. A guardhouse for the Palace of Westminster, and
    cavalry headquarters, on the site of the present Horse Guards building.
122–4 *set . . . furlough*. J. Burton Hill has drawn attention to an instance
    illustrating the practice of the day, in a letter from the Secretary of War
    to the Paymaster-General dated 28 September 1711: 'Her Majesty
    having been pleased to grant Fitton Minshull, a child, a commission of
    Ensign in Brigadier Stanwix's Regiment of Foot, in order for the sup-
    port of his mother and family . . . has likewise given him a furlough to be
    absent from his duty until further notice' (from Charles M. Clode,
    The Military Forces of the Crown; their Administration and Government
    [1869], II, 610; cited in Hill's *A History of the Reign of Queen Anne*
    [1880], I, 205).

sistence; and now go comfort the wench in the straw.   125

KITE

I shall, sir.

PLUME

But hold, have you made any use of your German doctor's
habit since you arrived?

KITE

Yes, yes, sir; and my fame's all about the country for the
most faithful fortune-teller that ever told a lie; I was obliged   130
to let my landlord into the secret for the convenience of
keeping it so, but he's an honest fellow and will be trusty to
any roguery that is confided to him. This device, sir, will get
you men, and me money, which I think is all we want at
present – but yonder comes your friend Mr Worthy – has   135
your honour any farther commands?

PLUME

None at present.   *Exit* KITE

'Tis indeed the picture of Worthy, but the life's departed.

Enter WORTHY

PLUME

What, arms a-cross, Worthy! Methinks you should hold 'em
open when a friend's so near. The man has got the vapours   140
in his ears, I believe; I must expel this melancholy spirit.

> Spleen, thou worst of fiends below,
> Fly, I conjure thee by this magic blow.
>   *Slaps* WORTHY *on the shoulder*

WORTHY

Plume! My dear Captain, welcome. Safe and sound returned!

PLUME

I 'scaped safe from Germany, and sound, I hope, from   145
London: you see I have lost neither leg, arm nor nose; then
for my inside, 'tis neither troubled with sympathies nor
antipathies, and I have an excellent stomach for roast beef.

125 *in the straw* in her lying-in
130 *faithful* Q2 (famous Q1) veracious
145 *sound* uninfected with syphilis, which caused decay of the nose
148 *stomach* appetite

---

140 *the vapours.* Exhalations supposedly developed within the bodily
    organs; or, the morbid condition caused by them.
142 *Spleen.* Excessive dejection of spirits, gloominess, and irritability;
    melancholia.
147–8 *sympathies nor antipathies.* Excessive affinities, or contrarieties,
    between the different bodily organs, promoting and spreading disorders.

WORTHY

Thou art a happy fellow; once I was so.

PLUME

What ails thee, man? No inundations nor earthquakes in   150
Wales, I hope? Has your father rose from the dead, and
reassumed his estate?

WORTHY

No.

PLUME

Then you are married, surely.

WORTHY

No.   155

PLUME

Then you are mad, or turning Quaker.

WORTHY

Come, I must out with it – your once gay, roving friend is
dwindled into an obsequious, thoughtful, romantic, constant
coxcomb.

PLUME

And pray, what is all this for?   160

WORTHY

For a woman.

PLUME

Shake hands, brother, if you go to that – behold me as
obsequious, as thoughtful, and as constant a coxcomb as
your worship.

WORTHY

For whom?   165

PLUME

For a regiment. – But for a woman! 'Sdeath! I have been
constant to fifteen at a time, but never melancholy for one;
and can the love of one bring you into this pickle? Pray, who
is this miraculous Helen?

WORTHY

A Helen indeed, not to be won under a ten years' siege; as   170
great a beauty, and as great a jilt.

PLUME

A jilt! Pho! Is she as great a whore?

---

158 *thoughtful* moody

---

156 *Quaker.* Ashton (p. 351) notices 'an insane dislike to Quakers in Queen
Anne's reign'; Quaker sobriety was associated inevitably with fanatic
enthusiasm and dishonesty.

WORTHY
  No, no.
PLUME
  'Tis ten thousand pities; but who is she? Do I know her?
WORTHY
  Very well.   175
PLUME
  Impossible! – I know no woman that will hold out a ten
  years' siege.
WORTHY
  What think you of Melinda?
PLUME
  Melinda! Why, she began to capitulate this time twelve-
  month, and offered to surrender upon honourable terms;   180
  and I advised you to propose a settlement of five hundred
  pound a year to her, before I went last abroad.
WORTHY
  I did, and she hearkened to't, desiring only one week to
  consider; when beyond her hopes the town was relieved, and
  I forced to turn my siege into a blockade.   185
PLUME
  Explain, explain.
WORTHY
  My Lady Richly, her aunt in Flintshire, dies, and leaves her
  at this critical time twenty thousand pound.
PLUME
  Oh, the devil! What a delicate woman was there spoiled! But
  by the rules of war now, Worthy, blockade was foolish –   190
  after such a convoy of provisions was entered the place, you
  could have no thought of reducing it by famine – you should
  have redoubled your attacks, taken the town by storm, or
  have died upon the breach.
WORTHY
  I did make one general assault, and pushed it with all my   195
  forces; but I was so vigorously repulsed, that despairing of
  ever gaining her for a mistress, I have altered my conduct,
  given my addresses the obsequious and distant turn, and
  court her now for a wife.

179 *capitulate* negotiate, parley
190 *blockade* Q2 (your blockade Q1)

---

194 *died upon the breach.* Libertine equivoque for premature ejaculation;
    cf. Etherege's 'The Imperfect Enjoyment'.

PLUME

So, as you grew obsequious, she grew haughty, and because   200
you approached her as a goddess, she used you like a dog.

WORTHY

Exactly.

PLUME

'Tis the way of 'em all. Come, Worthy, your obsequious and
distant airs will never bring you together; you must not think
to surmount her pride by your humility. Would you bring   205
her to better thoughts of you, she must be reduced to a
meaner opinion of herself – let me see – the very first thing
that I would do, should be to lie with her chambermaid, and
hire three or four wenches in the neighbourhood to report
that I had got them with child. Suppose we lampooned all   210
the pretty women in town, and left her out? Or what if we
made a ball, and forgot to invite her, with one or two of the
ugliest?

WORTHY

These would be mortifications, I must confess; but we live in
such a precise, dull place that we can have no balls, no   215
lampoons, no –

PLUME

What! No bastards! And so many recruiting officers in
town; I thought 'twas a maxim among them to leave as many
recruits in the country as they carried out.

WORTHY

Nobody doubts your goodwill, noble Captain, in serving your   220
country with your best blood: witness our friend Molly at
the Castle, – there have been tears in town about that
business, Captain.

PLUME

I hope Silvia has not heard of't.

WORTHY

Oh sir, have you thought of her? I began to fancy you had   225
forgot poor Silvia.

201 *used . . . dog* proverbial. Tilley D 514
215 *precise* puritanical

215–16 *no . . . lampoons.* Gaskill's National Theatre production made the
   double entendre explicit by inserting Plume's astonished 'What?' before
   'no lampoons' (Tynan). It was probably intentional already.
220–1 *serving . . . blood.* Probably alluding to the notion that intercourse
   involved a small blood-loss, cf. Donne's 'The Flea'; otherwise, blood:
   mettle.

PLUME

Your affairs had put mine quite out of my head. 'Tis true, Silvia and I had once agreed to go to bed together, could we have adjusted preliminaries; but she would have the wedding before consummation, and I was for consummation before the wedding – we could not agree. She was a pert obstinate fool, and would lose her maidenhead her own way, so she may keep it for Plume.

WORTHY

But do you intend to marry upon no other conditions?

PLUME

Your pardon, sir, I'll marry upon no condition at all, – if I should, I'm resolved never to bind myself to a woman for my whole life, till I know whether I shall like her company for half an hour. Suppose I married a woman that wanted a leg? Such a thing might be, unless I examined the goods beforehand. If people would but try one another's constitutions before they engaged, it would prevent all these elopements, divorces, and the devil knows what.

WORTHY

Nay, for that matter, the town did not stick to say, that –

PLUME

I hate country towns for that reason – if your town has a dishonourable thought of Silvia, it deserves to be burnt to the ground. – I love Silvia, I admire her frank, generous disposition; there's something in that girl more than woman, her sex is but a foil to her – the ingratitude, dissimulation, envy, pride, avarice, and vanity of her sister females, do but set off their contraries in her – in short, were I once a general, I would marry her.

WORTHY

Faith, you have reason; for were you but a corporal, she would marry you. But my Melinda coquettes it with every fellow she sees – I lay fifty pound she makes love to you.

PLUME

I'll lay fifty pound that I return it if she does – look'ee, Worthy, I'll win her and give her to you afterwards.

227 *mine* Q2 (my own Q1)
233 *for Plume* i.e., with no opposition from me
235 *condition* Q2 (conditions Q1)
252 *you have reason* you are right (French: *vous avez raison*)

WORTHY

If you win her you shall wear her, faith; I would not give a
fig for the conquest without the credit of the victory.

Enter KITE

KITE

Captain, Captain, a word in your ear.

PLUME

You may speak out, here are none but friends.　　　　　260

KITE

You know, sir, that you sent me to comfort the good woman
in the straw, Mrs Molly – my wife, Mr Worthy.

WORTHY

Oho! Very well – I wish you joy, Mr Kite.

KITE

Your worship very well may – for I have got both a wife and
a child in half an hour – but as I was a-saying, you sent me　265
to comfort Mrs Molly – my wife, I mean – but what d'ye
think, sir? She was better comforted before I came.

PLUME

As how?

KITE

Why, sir, a footman in a blue livery had brought her ten
guineas to buy her baby clothes.　　　　　270

PLUME

Who in the name of wonder could send them?

KITE

Nay, sir, I must whisper that – (*Whispers*) Mrs Silvia.

PLUME

Silvia! Generous creature.

WORTHY

Silvia! Impossible.

KITE

Here be the guineas, sir; I took the gold as part of my wife's　275
portion. Nay, farther, sir, she sent word the child should be
taken all imaginable care of, and that she intended to stand
godmother. The same footman, as I was coming to you with
this news, called after me, and told me that his lady would
speak with me – I went, and upon hearing that you were　280
come to town, she gave me half a guinea for the news, and

272 s.d. *Whispers* Q2 (*Whispers* PLUME Q1)
276 *portion* dowry
　　word the Q2 (word that the Q1)

ordered me to tell you, that Justice Balance, her father, who
is just come out of the country, would be glad to see you.

PLUME

There's a girl for you, Worthy – is there anything of
woman in this? No, 'tis noble and generous, manly friend-   285
ship; show me another woman that would lose an inch of
her prerogative that way, without tears, fits, and reproaches.
The common jealousy of her sex, which is nothing but their
avarice of pleasure, she despises; and can part with the lover,
though she dies for the man. – Come, Worthy, where's the   290
best wine? For there I'll quarter.

WORTHY

Horton has a fresh pipe of choice Barcelona, which I would
not let him pierce before, because I reserved the maidenhead of it for your welcome to town.

PLUME

Let's away then – Mr Kite, wait on the lady with my humble   295
service, and tell her I shall only refresh a little, and wait
upon her.

WORTHY

Hold, Kite – have you seen the other recruiting captain?

KITE

No, sir.

PLUME

Another? Who is he?   300

WORTHY

My rival in the first place, and the most unaccountable
fellow; but I'll tell you more as we go.   *Exeunt*

---

292 *pipe* winecask holding 105 imperial gallons; or, this quantity
296 *her* I Q2 (her that I Q1)
297 *upon* Q2 (on Q1)

---

292 *Barcelona.* Wine from Barcelona: 'being at war with France, it was
considered patriotic not to drink French wine' (Ashton, p. 151); and in
1706 the name recalled the Allies' capture of the city in the previous
September.

[Act I], Scene ii

MELINDA's *Apartment*
MELINDA *and* SILVIA *meeting*

MELINDA

Welcome to town, cousin Silvia. (*Salute*) I envied you your
retreat in the country; for Shrewsbury, methinks, and all
your heads of shires, are the most irregular places for living;
here we have smoke, noise, scandal, affectation, and pretension; in short, everything to give the spleen, and nothing to   5
divert it – then the air is intolerable.

SILVIA

Oh, madam, I have heard the town commended for its air.

MELINDA

But you don't consider, Silvia, how long I have lived in't!
For I can assure you, that to a lady the least nice in her
constitution, no air can be good above half a year; change of   10
air I take to be the most agreeable of any variety in life.

SILVIA

As you say, cousin Melinda, there are several sorts of airs:
airs in conversation, airs in behaviour, airs in dress; then we
have our quality airs, our sickly airs, our reserved airs, and
sometimes our impudent airs.   15

MELINDA

Psha! I talk only of the air we breathe or more properly of
that we taste – have not you, Silvia, found a vast difference in
the taste of airs?

SILVIA

Pray, cousin, are not vapours a sort of air? Taste air! You
might as well tell me I may feed on air. But prithee, my dear   20
Melinda, don't put on such an air to me; your education and
mine were just the same, and I remember the time when we
never troubled our heads about air, but when the sharp air

0.2 s.d. MELINDA's Ed. (*An* Q)
1   s.d. *Salute* kiss
3   *heads of shires* county towns
8   *in't* Q2 (in it Q1)
13–15 *airs in . . . airs* (*om.* Q2) affectations of manner
16   *Psha*! Q2 (Pshaw, Q1)
20   *might . . . may* Q2 (may . . . might Q1)
21   *an air* Q2 (airs Q1)

from the Welsh mountains made our noses drop in a cold
morning at the boarding-school.   25

MELINDA

Our education, cousin, was the same, but our temperaments
had nothing alike; you have the constitution of a horse –

SILVIA

So far as to be troubled with neither spleen, colic, nor
vapours; I need no salt for my stomach, no hartshorn for my
head, nor wash for my complexion; I can gallop all the   30
morning after the hunting-horn, and all the evening after a
fiddle. In short, I can do everything with my father but drink
and shoot flying; and I'm sure I can do everything my
mother could, were I put to the trial.

MELINDA

You're in a fair way of being put to't; for I'm told your   35
captain is come to town.

SILVIA

Aye, Melinda, he is come, and I'll take care he shan't go
without a companion.

MELINDA

You're certainly mad, cousin.

SILVIA

And there's a pleasure, sure, in being mad,   40
Which none but madmen know.

MELINDA

Thou poor, romantic Quixote, hast thou the vanity to
imagine that a young, sprightly officer that rambles o'er half
the globe in half a year, can confine his thoughts to the little
daughter of a country justice in an obscure corner of the   45
world?

SILVIA

Pshaw! What care I for his thoughts? I should not like a man
with confined thoughts, it shows a narrowness of soul.
Constancy is but a dull, sleepy quality at best, they will
hardly admit it among the manly virtues; nor do I think it   50
deserves a place with bravery, knowledge, policy, justice, and
some other qualities that are proper to that noble sex. In

24 *noses drop* Q1 (fingers ache Q2)
29 *hartshorn* smelling-salts
35 *You're* Ed. (You're are Q1; You are Q2)

40-1 *And ... know.* Torrismond's comment on his apparently hopeless
love for the Queen of Arragon, in Dryden's *The Spanish Friar* (II. ii).

short, Melinda, I think a petticoat a mighty simple thing,
and I'm heartily tired of my sex.

MELINDA
That is, you are tired of an appendix to our sex, that you   55
can't so handsomely get rid of in petticoats as if you were in
breeches. O'my conscience, Silvia, hadst thou been a man,
thou hadst been the greatest rake in Christendom.

SILVIA
I should endeavour to know the world, which a man can
never do thoroughly without half a hundred friendships, and   60
as many amours. But now I think on't, how stands your
affair with Mr Worthy?

MELINDA
He's my aversion.

SILVIA
Vapours!

MELINDA
What do you say, madam?   65

SILVIA
I say that you should not use that honest fellow so in-
humanely. He's a gentleman of parts and fortune, and beside
that he's my Plume's friend, and by all that's sacred, if you
don't use him better, I shall expect satisfaction.

MELINDA
Satisfaction! You begin to fancy yourself in breeches in good   70
earnest. But to be plain with you, I like Worthy the worse for
being so intimate with your captain, for I take him to be a
loose, idle, unmannerly coxcomb.

SILVIA
Oh, madam! You never saw him, perhaps, since you were
mistress of twenty thousand pound; you only knew him when   75
you were capitulating with Worthy for a settlement, which
perhaps might encourage him to be a little loose and unmannerly with you.

MELINDA
What do you mean, madam?

SILVIA
My meaning needs no interpretation, madam.   80

MELINDA
Better it had, madam, for methinks you're too plain.

---

69 *expect satisfaction* i.e., challenge you to a duel

SILVIA

If you mean the plainness of my person, I think your ladyship as plain as me to the full.

MELINDA

Were I assured of that, I should be glad to take up with a
rakehelly officer as you do.   85

SILVIA

Again! Look'ee, madam – you're in your own house.

MELINDA

And if you had kept in yours, I should have excused you.

SILVIA

Don't be troubled, madam, I shan't desire to have my visit
returned.

MELINDA

The sooner therefore you make an end of this the better.   90

SILVIA

I'm easily advised to follow my inclinations – so, madam –
your humble servant.   *Exit*

MELINDA

Saucy thing!

Enter LUCY

LUCY

What's the matter, madam?

MELINDA

Did you not see the proud nothing, how she swells upon the   95
arrival of her fellow?

LUCY

Her fellow has not been long enough arrived to occasion any
great swelling, madam; I don't believe she has seen him yet.

MELINDA

Nor shan't if I can help it; let me see – I have it – bring me
pen and ink – hold, I'll go write in my closet.   100

LUCY

An answer to this letter, I hope, madam. (*Presents a letter*)

MELINDA

Who sent it?

LUCY

Your captain, madam.

MELINDA

He's a fool, and I'm tired of him, send it back unopened.

LUCY

The messenger's gone, madam.   105

85 *rakehelly* Q2 (rakely Q1)

MELINDA

Then how shall I send an answer? Call him back immediately, while I go write.   *Exeunt*

Act II, Scene i

An Apartment [in JUSTICE BALANCE'*s House]*
Enter JUSTICE BALANCE *and* PLUME

BALANCE

Look'ee, Captain, give us but blood for our money, and you
shan't want men. I remember that for some years of the last
war we had no blood nor wounds but in the officers' mouths,
nothing for our millions but newspapers not worth a reading
– our armies did nothing but play at prison bars and hide-   5
and-seek with the enemy; but now ye have brought us
colours and standards and prisoners; odsmylife, Captain, get
us but another Marshal of France, and I'll go myself for a
soldier.

PLUME

Pray, Mr Balance, how does your fair daughter?   10

BALANCE

Ah, Captain, what is my daughter to a Marshal of France?
We're upon a nobler subject. I want to have a particular
description of the Battle of Höchstädt.

107 s.d. *Exeunt* Q2 (*Exeunt severally* Q1)
  8, 11 •*Marshal* Q2 (Mareschal Q1)

2-3 *the last war.* The War of the League of Augsburg (1689–97) 'had been
  sluggish and unexciting' (Archer), made up chiefly of manoeuvring and
  minor sieges, apart from the capture of Marshal Boufflers at Namur in
  1695. The levels of new taxes (e.g., land tax at 4 shillings in the pound)
  to pay for the wars, aroused great resentment; but this was eased in the
  national satisfaction over Marlborough's brilliant victories.
5 *prison bars.* Perhaps a children's game (prisoner's base?), or simply an
  image for the warfare of fortified lines.
7-8 *colours . . . France* The English share of the spoils of Blenheim included 34
  French standards, 128 colours, and 36 high-ranking officers, including the army
  commander Marshal Tallard. The standards and colours were paraded from the
  Tower to Westminster Hall, amid great public rejoicing, on 3 January 1705
  (Winston S. Churchill, *Marlborough, his Life and Times* (1933-8), ii, 516-7).
13 *the Battle of Höchstädt.* i.e., Blenheim, fought on 13 August 1704. The
  Franco-Bavarian forces occupied the villages of Lutzingen and Blen-
  heim, and the ground between them, east of Höchstädt. Here they were
  attacked by the Grand Alliance army under Marlborough and Prince
  Eugene.

PLUME

> The battle, sir, was a very pretty battle as one should desire to
> see, but we were all so intent upon victory that we never   15
> minded the battle; all that I know of the matter is, our
> general commanded us to beat the French, and we did so,
> and if he pleases to say the word, we'll do't again. – But pray,
> sir, how does Mrs Silvia?

BALANCE

> Still upon Silvia! For shame, Captain – you're engaged   20
> already, wedded to the war; victory is your mistress, and it
> is below a soldier to think of any other.

PLUME

> As a mistress, I confess, but as a friend, Mr Balance.

BALANCE

> Come, come, Captain, never mince the matter, would not
> you debauch my daughter if you could?   25

PLUME

> How, sir! I hope she's not to be debauched.

BALANCE

> Faith, but she is, sir, and any woman in England of her age
> and complexion, by a man of your youth and vigour. Look'ee,
> Captain, once I was young and once an officer as you are, and
> I can guess at your thoughts now by what mine were then,   30
> and I remember very well, that I would have given one of my
> legs to have deluded the daughter of an old, plain country
> gentleman, as like me as I was then like you.

PLUME

> But, sir, was that country gentleman your friend and
> benefactor?   35

BALANCE

> Not much of that.

PLUME

> There the comparison breaks; the favours, sir, that –

BALANCE

> Pho, I hate speeches. If I have done you any service, Captain,
> 'twas to please myself, for I love thee; and if I could part with
> my girl, you should have her as soon as any young fellow I   40
> know; I hope you have more honour than to quit the service,

17 *general* Q2 (generals Q1) Marlborough
21 *victory* Q2 (war Q1)   26 *she's* Q2 (she is Q1)

---

18 *and if . . . again.* Not mere rhetoric, but a reflection of the full, and
   justified, confidence his army had in him (see A. L. Rowse, *The Early
   Churchills* [Harmondsworth, 1959], p. 294).

and she more prudence than to follow the camp. But she's
at her own disposal, she has fifteen hundred pound in her
pocket, and so – Silvia, Silvia!   *Calls*

Enter SILVIA

SILVIA
There are some letters, sir, come by the post from London;   45
I left them upon the table in your closet.
BALANCE
And here is a gentleman from Germany. (*Presents* PLUME *to
her*) Captain, you'll excuse me, I'll go read my letters, and
wait on you.   *Exit*
SILVIA
Sir, you're welcome to England.   50
PLUME
You are indebted to me a welcome, madam, since the hopes
of receiving it from this fair hand was the principal cause of
my seeing England.
SILVIA
I have often heard that soldiers were sincere, shall I venture
to believe public report?   55
PLUME
You may, when 'tis backed by private insurance; for I
swear, madam, by the honour of my profession, that whatever dangers I went upon, it was with the hope of making
myself more worthy of your esteem, and if I ever had
thoughts of preserving my life, 'twas for the pleasure of   60
dying at your feet.
SILVIA
Well, well, you shall die at my feet, or where you will; but
you know, sir, there is a certain will and testament to be made
beforehand.
PLUME
My will, madam, is made already, and there it is. (*Gives her*   65
a parchment) And if you please to open that parchment,
which was drawn the evening before the Battle of Blenheim,
you will find whom I left my heir.
                              SILVIA *opens the will and reads*

51–64 So Q2 (Q1, see Appendix 1, A, i)
56 *insurance* (a) assurance; (b) in the modern sense

59–61 The equivoque on 'die' ('experience sexual orgasm') links this
    declaration to their dispute about marriage and consummation; see
    I.i, 229–34.

SILVIA

'Mrs Silvia Balance'. – Well, Captain, this is a handsome
and a substantial compliment; but I can assure you I am   70
much better pleased with the bare knowledge of your
intention than I should have been in the possession of your
legacy; but methinks, sir, you should have left something to
your little boy at the Castle.

PLUME

(*Aside*) That's home. – My little boy! Lack-a-day, madam,   75
that alone may convince you 'twas none of mine; why the
girl, madam, is my sergeant's wife, and so the poor creature
gave out that I was father in hopes that my friends might
support her in case of necessity; that was all, madam. – My
boy! No, no, no.   80

Enter SERVANT

SERVANT

Madam, my master has received some ill news from London
and desires to speak with you immediately, and he begs the
captain's pardon that he can't wait on him as he promised.

PLUME

Ill news! Heavens avert it; nothing could touch me nearer
than to see that generous, worthy gentleman afflicted; I'll   85
leave you to comfort him, and be assured that if my life and
fortune can be any way serviceable to the father of my Silvia,
he shall freely command both.

SILVIA

The necessity must be very pressing that would engage me
to endanger either.   *Exeunt severally* 90

[Act II], Scene ii

Another Apartment
Enter BALANCE *and* SILVIA

SILVIA

Whilst there is life there is hope, sir; perhaps my brother may
recover.

 80 *No, no, no* Q2 (No, no Q1)
 88 *he* Q2 (she Q1)
 90 *endanger* Q2 (do Q1)
  0.2 s.d. *Another Apartment* Ed. (SCENE *changes to another Apartment*
       Q1; SCENE, *Another Apartment* Q2)
  1 *Whilst . . . hope* proverbial. Tilley, L 269

BALANCE

We have but little reason to expect it. Dr Kilman acquaints
me here, that before this comes to my hands he fears I shall
have no son. – Poor Owen! But the decree is just; I was   5
pleased with the death of my father, because he left me an
estate, and now I'm punished with the loss of an heir to
inherit mine. I must now look upon you as the only hopes of
my family, and I expect that the augmentation of your
fortune will give you fresh thoughts and new prospects.   10

SILVIA

My desire of being punctual in my obedience requires that
you would be plain in your commands, sir.

BALANCE

The death of your brother makes you sole heiress to my
estate, which you know is about twelve hundred pounds a
year; this fortune gives you a fair claim to quality and a title; 15
you must set a just value upon yourself, and in plain terms
think no more of Captain Plume.

SILVIA

You have often commended the gentleman, sir.

BALANCE

And I do so still; he's a very pretty fellow; but though I
liked him well enough for a bare son-in-law, I don't approve   20
of him for an heir to my estate and family; fifteen hundred
pound, indeed, I might trust in his hands, and it might do
the young fellow a kindness, but odsmylife, twelve hundred
pound a year would ruin him, quite turn his brain. A
captain of foot worth twelve hundred pound a year! 'Tis a   25
prodigy in nature. Besides this, I have five or six thousand
pounds in woods upon my estate; oh, that would make him
stark mad! For you must know that all captains have a
mighty aversion to timber, they can't endure to see trees

---

11 *punctual* punctilious
14–15 *which you . . . year* Q2 (which three or four years hence will
     amount to twelve hundred pound *per annum* Q1)
15 *fair . . . title* i.e., to marry a man with both
23 *odsmylife* mild oath, from 'God save my life'

24–6 *A captain . . . nature.* A captain of foot received about £100 a year
     (see Stonehill, II, 434).

standing. Then I should have some rogue of a builder by the   30
help of his damned magic art transform my noble oaks and
elms into cornishes, portals, sashes, birds, beasts, gods, and
devils, to adorn some maggoty, new-fashioned bauble upon
the Thames; and then you should have a dog of a gardener
bring a *habeas corpus* for my *terra firma*, remove it to Chelsea   35
or Twit'nam, and clap it into grass-plats and gravel walks.

Enter a SERVANT

SERVANT
Sir, here's one below with a letter for your worship, but he
will deliver it into no hands but your own.
BALANCE
Come, show me the messenger.   *Exit with* SERVANT
SILVIA
Make the dispute between love and duty, and I am Prince   40
Prettyman exactly. – If my brother dies, ah, poor brother!
If he lives, ah, poor sister! – 'Tis bad both ways; I'll try it
again, – follow my own inclinations and break my father's
heart, or obey his commands and break my own; worse and
worse. Suppose I take it thus – a moderate fortune, a pretty   45
fellow, and a pad; or a fine estate, a coach-and-six, and an
ass – that will never do neither.

Enter BALANCE *and* SERVANT

BALANCE
Put four horses into the coach.
                            To the SERVANT, *who goes out*
Ho, Silvia –

---

32 *cornishes* cornices
35 *habeas corpus* literally, writ requiring that a person be brought
    before a judge or into court
36 *Twit'nam* Twickenham
    grass-plats lawns

30–6 *Then . . . walks.* Many of the nobility and gentry were moving to
    London during this decade, building houses in the western quarter.
    Chelsea and Twickenham were then small-town areas to the west. (See
    John Loftis, *Comedy and Society from Congreve to Fielding* [Stanford,
    1959], pp. 12–13).
40–1 *Prince Prettyman.* In Buckingham's *The Rehearsal* (III.ii), where it is
    Volscius who is pulled between the claims of love and honour. Farquhar
    makes the same mistake in *Love and Business* (see Stonehill, II, 305,
    434).

SILVIA

Sir.   50

BALANCE

How old were you when your mother died?

SILVIA

So young that I don't remember I ever had one; and you
have been so careful, so indulgent to me since, that indeed I
never wanted one.

BALANCE

Have I ever denied you anything you asked of me?   55

SILVIA

Never, that I remember.

BALANCE

Then, Silvia, I must beg that once in your life you would
grant me a favour.

SILVIA

Why should you question it, sir?

BALANCE

I don't, but I would rather counsel than command; I don't   60
propose this with the authority of a parent, but as the advice
of your friend, that you would take the coach this moment
and go into the country.

SILVIA

Does this advice, sir, proceed from the contents of the letter
you received just now?   65

BALANCE

No matter; I will be with you in three or four days and then
give you my reasons. But before you go, I expect you will
make me one solemn promise.

SILVIA

Propose the thing, sir.

BALANCE

That you will never dispose of yourself to any man without   70
my consent.

SILVIA

I promise.

BALANCE

Very well, and to be even with you, I promise I will never
dispose of you without your own consent; and so, Silvia, the
coach is ready; farewell. (*Leads her to the door and returns*)   75
Now she's gone, I'll examine the contents of this letter a
little nearer. (*Reads*)

Sir,

   My intimacy with Mr Worthy has drawn a secret from

him that he had from his friend Captain Plume, and my   80
friendship and relation to your family oblige me to give
you timely notice of it: the captain has dishonourable
designs upon my cousin Silvia. Evils of this nature are
more easily prevented than amended, and that you would
immediately send my cousin into the country is the advice   85
of,

Sir, your humble servant,
MELINDA.

Why, the devil's in the young fellows of this age; they're ten
times worse than they were in my time! Had he made my   90
daughter a whore and forswore it like a gentleman, I could
have almost pardoned it; but to tell tales beforehand is
monstrous! Hang it, I can fetch down a woodcock or snipe,
and why not a hat and feather? I have a case of good pistols,
and have a good mind to try.   95

Enter WORTHY

BALANCE

Worthy, your servant.

WORTHY

I'm sorry, sir, to be the messenger of ill news.

BALANCE

I apprehend it, sir; you have heard that my son Owen is past
recovery.

WORTHY

My advices say he's dead, sir.   100

BALANCE

He's happy, and I am satisfied; the strokes of heaven I can
bear; but injuries from men, Mr Worthy, are not so easily
supported.

WORTHY

I hope, sir, you're under no apprehension of wrong from
anybody?   105

BALANCE

You know I ought to be.

WORTHY

You wrong my honour, sir, in believing I could know anything to your prejudice without resenting it as much as you
should.

BALANCE

This letter, sir, which I tear in pieces to conceal the person   110

100 *advices* communications from a distance

that sent it, informs me that Plume has a design upon Silvia,
and that you are privy to't.

WORTHY

Nay then, sir, I must do myself justice and endeavour to find
out the author. (*Takes up a bit*) Sir, I know the hand, and if
you refuse to discover the contents, Melinda shall tell me.   115
                                                    Going

BALANCE

Hold, sir, the contents I have told you already, only with this
circumstance, that her intimacy with Mr Worthy had drawn
the secret from him.

WORTHY

Her intimacy with me! – Dear sir, let me pick up the pieces
of this letter; 'twill give me such a hank upon her pride, to   120
have her own an intimacy under her hand; 'twas the luckiest
accident. (*Gathering up the letter*) The aspersion, sir, was
nothing but malice, the effect of a little quarrel between her
and Mrs Silvia.

BALANCE

Are you sure of that, sir?   125

WORTHY

Her maid gave me the history of part of the battle just now,
as she overheard it.

BALANCE

'Tis probable, I am satisfied.

WORTHY

But I hope, sir, your daughter has suffered nothing upon the
account?   130

BALANCE

No, no – poor girl, she's so afflicted with the news of her
brother's death that to avoid company she begged leave to
be gone into the country.

WORTHY

And is she gone?

BALANCE

I could not refuse her, she was so pressing; the coach went   135
from the door the minute before you came.

WORTHY

So pressing to be gone, sir! – I find her fortune will give her
the same airs with Melinda, and then Plume and I may
laugh at one another.

114 s.d. *bit* Q2 (*piece of the letter* Q1)   120 *hank* hold
128 so, Q1 (speech omitted Q2)
131 *she's* Q2 (she is Q1)

BALANCE

    Like enough; women are as subject to pride as we are, and   140
    why mayn't great women as well as great men forget their old
    acquaintance? But come, where's this young fellow? I love
    him so well it would break the heart of me to think him a
    rascal. – (*Aside*) I'm glad my daughter's gone fairly off
    though. – Where does the captain quarter?   145

WORTHY

    At Horton's; I'm to meet him there two hours hence, and we
    should be glad of your company.

BALANCE

    Your pardon, dear Worthy, I must allow a day or two to the
    death of my son; the decorum of mourning is what we owe
    the world because they pay it to us. Afterwards, I'm yours   150
    over a bottle, or how you will.

WORTHY

    Sir, I'm your humble servant.   *Exeunt severally*

[Act II], Scene iii

The Street

Enter KITE, [*leading* COSTAR PEARMAIN *in one hand, and* THOMAS
          APPLETREE *in the other, both drunk*]

KITE (*Sings*)

          Our prentice Tom may now refuse
          To wipe his scoundrel master's shoes,
          For now he's free to sing and play,
          Over the hills and far away.
             Over, &c.   5
          [APPLETREE *and* PEARMAIN *join in the chorus*]

150 *us. Afterwards, I'm* Ed. (us afterwards. I'm Q)
   0.1–0.2 s.d. *leading . . . drunk* Ed. (*with one of the Mob in each hand,*
     drunk Q1)
  1 KITE (*Sings*) Ed. (0.1 Kite *sings* Q)
  5, 10 *Over,&c* Q2 (*Over the hills*, &c Q1)
  5 s.d. APPLETREE . . . *chorus* Ed. (*The Mob sing the Chorus* Q)

  0.1, s.d. etc. COSTAR PEARMAIN . . . THOMAS APPLETREE. Farquhar's '1st
    Mob' and '2d Mob' give their names in full at the end of the scene, and
    are identified by name in later C18 editions. The speech prefixes in
    Q1–4 are confused: before Plume's entry at l.46, '1st Mob' is clearly
    Thomas, and after it he is addressed as Costar; similarly '2d Mob' is
    Costar initially and then Thomas.
  1–10 Verses 10 and 12 of ''The Recruiting Officer': The chorus is as sung
    by Plume, ll. 48–51 below.

    We all shall lead more happy lives,
    By getting rid of brats and wives,
    That scold and brawl both night and day,
    Over the hills and far away.
        Over, &c.　　　　　　　　　　　　　　　　　10

Hey, boys! Thus we soldiers live; drink, sing, dance, play; we live, as one should say – we live – 'tis impossible to tell how we live. We're all princes – why – why, you're a king – you're an emperor, and I'm a prince – now – an't we? –

APPLETREE

No, Sergeant – I'll be no emperor.　　　　　　　　　　　15

KITE

No?

APPLETREE

No, I'll be a justice of peace.

KITE

A justice of peace, man!

APPLETREE

Aye, wauns will I, for since this Pressing Act they are greater than any emperor under the sun.　　　　　　　　　　20

KITE

Done; you're a justice of peace, and you're a king, and I'm a duke, and a rum duke, an't I?

PEARMAIN

No, but I'll be no king.

KITE

What then?

PEARMAIN

I'll be a queen.　　　　　　　　　　　　　　　　　25

KITE

A queen!

PEARMAIN

Aye, Queen of England, that's greater than any king of 'em all.

KITE

Bravely said, faith! Huzza for the Queen!　　　*All huzza*

15, etc. s.p. APPLETREE Ed. (1st *Mob* Q)
22 *rum* excellent (O.E.D.,a¹)
23, etc. s.p. PEARMAIN Ed. (2nd *Mob* Q1)

---

19 *this Pressing Act.* The Impressment Act of 1703, 2° and 3° Anne, cap. xiii, and others in 1704 and 1705, empowered three justices to impress any man who lacked lawful employment or means of support.

But hark'ee you Mr Justice and you Mr Queen, did you ever   30
see the Queen's picture?

BOTH

No, no, no.

KITE

I wonder at that; I have two of 'em set in gold, and as like
Her Majesty, God bless the mark. (*He takes two broad pieces
out of his pocket*) See here, they're set in gold.   35
Gives one to each

APPLETREE

The wonderful works of Nature!   *Looking at it*

PEARMAIN

What's this written about? Here's a posy, I believe, *Ca-ro-lus*
– what's that, Sergeant?

KITE

Oh, *Carolus*! Why, *Carolus* is Latin for Queen Anne, that's
all.   40

PEARMAIN

'Tis a fine thing to be a scollard – Sergeant, will you part
with this? I'll buy it on you, if it come within the compass of
a crawn.

KITE

A crown! Never talk of buying; 'tis the same thing among
friends, you know, I present 'em to you both; you shall give   45
me as good a thing. Put 'em up, and remember your old
friend, when I'm *over the hills and far away*.   *Singing*
They sing and put up the money

32 *No, no, no* Q2 (No, no Q1)
34 *God bless the mark* exclamation by way of apology, for taking her
name in vain
36 s.d. *Looking at it* Q2 (*Looking earnestly upon the piece* Q1)
37 *posy* short motto, usually in verse
45, 46, 62, 97 *'em* Q2 (them Q1)

---

34 s.d. *broad pieces*. Gold coins, originally valued at 20*s.*; here, doubtless,
hammered unites struck between 1660 and 1662, on which the king's
bust could plausibly be passed off as 'the Queen's picture', unlike that of
the bearded Charles I. The bust of Charles II appears on the obverse,
'in profile to the left, laureate, with long hair, neck bare, and armour
with a scarf over it', together with the legend 'CAROLVS. II. D.G. MAG.
BRIT. FRAN. ET. HIB. REX.', and, initially, no value-designation (Sir
Geoffrey Duveen and H. G. Stride, *The History of the Gold Sovereign*
[London, 1962], pp. 44–8, plate 10c).
47 s.d. N.T. 'Plume's entry is not fortuitous: he enters at a signal from
Kite' (Tynan).

Enter PLUME *singing*

PLUME

> Over the hills, and o're the main,
> To Flanders, Portugal, or Spain;
> The Queen commands, and we'll obey,   50
> Over the hills and far away.

Come on my men of mirth, away with it, I'll make one
among ye. – Who are these hearty lads?

KITE

Off with your hats; ounds, off with your hats; this is the
captain, the captain.   55

APPLETREE

We have seen captains afore now, mun.

PEARMAIN

Aye, and lieutenant captains too; flesh, I'se keep on my nab.

APPLETREE

And I'se scarcely d'off mine for any captain in England; my
vether's a freeholder.

PLUME

Who are these jolly lads, Sergeant?   60

KITE

A couple of honest, brave fellows that are willing to serve the
Queen; I have entertained 'em just now as volunteers under
your honour's command.

PLUME

And good entertainment they shall have; volunteers are the
men I want, those are the men fit to make soldiers, captains,   65
generals.

PEARMAIN

Wauns, Tummas, what's this? Are you listed?

APPLETREE

Flesh, not I; are you, Costar?

PEARMAIN

Wauns, not I.

KITE

What, not listed! Ha, ha, ha, a very good jest, faith.   70

PEARMAIN

Come, Tummas, we'll go whome.

APPLETREE

Aye, aye, come.

51 *hills* Q2 (hill Q1)
57 *nab* hat

KITE

Home! For shame, gentlemen, behave yourselves better
before your captain – dear Tummas, honest Costar –

PEARMAIN

No, no, we'll be gone.   *Going*   75

KITE

Nay, then I command you to stay: I place you both sentinels
in this place for two hours to watch the motion of St Mary's
clock, you, and you the motion of St Chad's; and he that dare
stir from his post till he be relieved shall have my sword in
his guts the next minute.   80

PLUME

What's the matter, Sergeant? I'm afraid you're too rough
with these gentlemen.

KITE

I'm too mild, sir, they disobey command, sir, and one of 'em
should be shot for an example to the other.

PEARMAIN

Shot, Tummas!   85

PLUME

Come, gentlemen, what's the matter?

APPLETREE

We don't know; the noble sergeant is pleased to be in a
passion, sir – but –

KITE

They disobey command, they deny their being listed.

PEARMAIN

Nay, Sergeant, we don't downright deny it neither, that we   90
dare not do for fear of being shot; but we humbly conceive
in a civil way, and begging your worship's pardon, that we
may go home.

PLUME

That's easily known; have either of you received any of the

86 *what's* Q2 (what is Q1)

77–8 *St Mary's . . . St Chad's* St Mary's Church, founded in the C10, and
containing much Norman work, remains intact. It 'has a chiming clock
with . . . four bells' (Jeffares). The old St Chad's, also founded in Saxon
times, was roughly south-west of St Mary's. It collapsed in 1788,
leaving only the lady-chapel standing, and the new St Chad's was built
in 1790–92 farther westward.

83–4 *one . . . other.* N.T.: 'During rehearsals Kite improvised as follows:
". . . and they both should be shot as an example to one another." This
impromptu—a distinct improvement on Farquhar's original—was
retained in performance' (Tynan).

Queen's money?   95

APPLETREE
Not a brass farthing, sir.

KITE
Sir, they have each of 'em received three and twenty shillings
and sixpence, and 'tis now in their pockets.

APPLETREE
Wauns! If I have a penny in my pocket but a bent sixpence,
I'll be content to be listed, and shot into the bargain.   100

PEARMAIN
And I, look'ee here, sir.

APPLETREE
Aye, here's my stock too, nothing but the Queen's picture
that the sergeant gave me just now.

KITE
See there, a broad piece, three and twenty shillings and
sixpence; the t'other has the fellow on't.   105

PLUME
The case is plain, gentlemen, the goods are found upon you:
those pieces of gold are worth three and twenty and sixpence
each.

PEARMAIN
So it seems that *Carolus* is three and twenty shillings and
sixpence in Latin.   110

APPLETREE
'Tis the same thing in the Greek, for we are listed.

PEARMAIN
Flesh, but we an't, Tummas; I desire to be carried before
the mayar, Captain.
                 While they talk, the CAPTAIN *and* SERGEANT *whisper*

PLUME
'Twill never do, Kite; your damned tricks will ruin me at last
– I won't lose the fellows though, if I can help it. – Well,   115
gentlemen, there must be some trick in this; my sergeant
offers to take his oath that you're fairly listed.

APPLETREE
Why, Captain, we know that you soldiers have more liberty
of conscience than other folks, but for me or neighbour
Costar here to take such an oath, 'twould be downright   120
perjuration.

102 *stock* total property
117 *offers to* Q2 (offers here to Q1)

118-9 *liberty of conscience* strictly, freedom of worship other than Church of England,
   while holding public office (historically valid remark) (*N&Q*).

PLUME

Look'ee you rascal, you villain, if I find that you have
imposed upon these two honest fellows, I'll trample you to
death, you dog; come, how was't?

APPLETREE

Nay, then we will speak. Your sergeant, as you say, is a rogue,   125
begging your worship's pardon, and –

PEARMAIN

Nay, Tummas, let me speak, you know I can read. – And so,
sir, he gave us those two pieces of money for pictures of the
Queen by way of a present.

PLUME

How! By way of a present! The son of a whore! I'll teach   130
him to abuse honest fellows like you. Scoundrel, rogue,
villain, *etc.*   *Beats off the* SERGEANT, *and follows*

BOTH

O brave, noble Captain! Huzza! A brave captain, faith.

PEARMAIN

Now, Tummas, *Carolus* is Latin for a beating; this is the
bravest captain I ever saw. – Wauns, I have a month's mind   135
to go with him.

Enter PLUME

PLUME

A dog, to abuse two such honest fellows as you! Look'ee,
gentlemen, I love a pretty fellow; I come among you here as
an officer to list soldiers, not as a kidnapper to steal slaves.

PEARMAIN

Mind that, Tummas.   140

PLUME

I desire no man to go with me, but as I went myself: I went
a volunteer, as you or you may go, for a little time carried a
musket, and now I command a company.

APPLETREE

Mind that, Costar, a sweet gentleman.

---

132 s.d. *Beats . . . follows* Q2 (*Beats the Serjeant off the stage, and
   follows him out* Q1)
135 *a month's mind* an inclination
136 s.d. *Enter* Q2 (*Re-enter* Q1)
137 *honest* Q2 (*pretty* Q1)

---

132 *villain, etc.* An invitation to improvise, to which contemporary actors
   were deplorably prone (see Nicoll, pp. 41–2).

PLUME

'Tis true, gentlemen, I might take an advantage of you; the   145
Queen's money was in your pockets, my sergeant was ready
to take his oath you were listed; but I scorn to do a base thing,
you are both of you at your liberty.

PEARMAIN

Thank you, noble Captain. – I cod, I can't find in my heart
to leave him, he talks so finely.   150

APPLETREE

Aye, Costar, would he always hold in this mind?

PLUME

Come, my lads, one thing more I'll tell you: you're both
young, tight fellows, and the army is the place to make you
men forever: every man has his lot, and you have yours.
What think you now of a purse full of French gold out of a 155
monsieur's pocket, after you have dashed out his brains with
the butt of your firelock, eh?

PEARMAIN

Wauns, I'll have it, Captain – give me a shilling, I'll follow
you to the end of the world.

APPLETREE

Nay, dear Costar, duna; be advised.   160

PLUME

Here, my hero, here are two guineas for thee, as earnest of
what I'll do farther for thee.

APPLETREE

Duna take it, duna, dear Costar.
                              (*Cries, and pulls back his arm*)

PEARMAIN

I wull, I wull – wauns, my mind gives me that I shall be a
captain myself. I take your money, sir, and now I'm a   165
gentleman.

PLUME

Give me thy hand. – And now you and I will travel the world
o'er, and command wherever we tread. – [*Aside to*
PEARMAIN] Bring your friend with you if you can.

PEARMAIN

Well, Tummas, must we part?   170

---

147 *oath you* Q2 (oath that you Q1)
149 *I cod* softened oath, cognate with 'egad'
    can't Q2 (cannot Q1)
151 *always* Q2 (alway Q1)

APPLETREE

    No, Costar, I cannot leave thee. Come, Captain (*crying*), I'll
    e'en go along too, and if you have two honester, simpler lads
    in your company than we twa been – I'll say no more.

PLUME

    Here, my lad. (*Gives him money*) Now your name?

APPLETREE

    Thummas Appletree.   175

PLUME

    And yours?

PEARMAIN

    Costar Pearmain.

PLUME

    Born where?

APPLETREE

    Both in Herefordshire.

PLUME

    Very well. Courage, my lads, now we'll sing *Over the hills*   180
    and far away.

            Courage, boys, 'tis one to ten,
            But we return all gentlemen;
            While conquering colours we display,
            Over the hills and far away.   185
            Over, &c.   *Exeunt*

Act III, Scene i

The Market-place
Enter PLUME *and* WORTHY

WORTHY

    I can't forbear admiring the equality of our two fortunes: we
    loved two ladies, they met us halfway, and just as we were
    upon the point of leaping into their arms, fortune drops into

173 *than* Q2 (that Q1)
180 *we'll* Q2 (we will Q1)
184–6 *While . . . &c.* Ed. (not in Q)
186 s.d. *Exeunt* Q2 (not in Q1)
   0.1 *Enter* Q2 (not in Q1)
   1 *can't* Ed. (can'nt Q1)

184–6 *While . . . &c.* Supplied in later C18 editions, as an alternative to
    'All gentlemen as well as they . . .' in the final verse. Extended end-
    ings to this scene in later C18 editions are outlined in Appendix 1.

their laps, pride possesses their hearts, a maggot fills their
heads, madness takes 'em by the tails, they snort, kick up their   5
heels, and away they run.

PLUME
And leave us here to mourn upon the shore – a couple of
poor, melancholy monsters – what shall we do?

WORTHY
I have a trick for mine; the letter, you know, and the fortune-
teller.   10

PLUME
And I have a trick for mine.

WORTHY
What is't?

PLUME
I'll never think of her again.

WORTHY
No!

PLUME
No; I think myself above administering to the pride of any   15
woman, were she worth twelve thousand a year, and I han't
the vanity to believe I shall ever gain a lady worth twelve
hundred; the generous, good-natured Silvia in her smock I
admire, but the haughty, scornful Silvia, with her fortune,
I despise.   20

A SONG

1

Come, fair one, be kind,
You never shall find
A fellow so fit for a lover;
The world shall view
My passion for you,   25
But never your passion discover.

---

4 *maggot* whim
18 *in her smock* as an unaffected, natural country girl

7–8 *And . . . monsters* Probably alluding to Caliban and his sister Sycorax
    ('Two Monsters of the Isle') in Davenant and Dryden's adaptation of
    The Tempest, who will be left behind when the other characters sail
    away. Sycorax has become Mrs Trinculo.
21–38 This song was omitted in Q2, and dramatically 'is obviously detri-
    mental to the scene' (Archer).

2

I still will complain
Of your frowns and disdain,
Though I revel through all your charms;
The world shall declare,   30
That I die with despair,
When I only die in your arms.

3

I still will adore,
And love more and more,
But, by Jove, if you chance to prove cruel: 35
I'll get me a miss
That freely will kiss,
Though I afterwards drink water-gruel.

What, sneak out o'town and not so much as a word, a line, a
compliment – 'sdeath! How far off does she live? I'll go and   40
break her windows.

WORTHY
Ha, ha, ha; aye, and the window bars too to come at her.
Come, come, friend, no more of your rough, military airs.

Enter KITE

KITE
Captain, sir, look yonder, she's a-coming this way, 'tis the
prettiest, cleanest, little tit.   45

PLUME
Now, Worthy, to show you how much I'm in love – here she
comes, and what is that great country fellow with her?

KITE
I can't tell, sir.

Enter ROSE *and her brother* BULLOCK, ROSE *with a basket on her
arm, crying 'Chickens'*

---

32 *die* experience orgasm   38 *water-gruel* fig., type of insipidness
40 *I'll* Q2 (I'd Q1)   45 *tit* small horse; fig., young woman

---

41 *break her windows*. 'This was frequently done to whores, particularly
   when the angry party had a grudge' (Stonehill, II, 435; cf. *The Twin
   Rivals*, I.i, 27).
42 *window . . . her*. Cf. Lancelot in Malory's *Mort d'Arthur*, Book 19,
   chapter 6, who entered Guinevere's bed chamber by this method.

ROSE

Buy chickens, young and tender, young and tender chickens.

PLUME

Here, you chickens!   50

ROSE

Who calls?

PLUME

Come hither, pretty maid.

ROSE

Will you please to buy, sir?

WORTHY

Yes, child, we'll both buy.

PLUME

Nay, Worthy, that's not fair, market for yourself; come,   55
child, I'll buy all you have.

ROSE

Then all I have is at your sarvice.   *Curtsies*

WORTHY

Then I must shift for myself, I find.   *Exit*

PLUME

Let me see – young and tender, you say?

                                   Chucks her under the chin

ROSE

As ever you tasted in your life, sir.   *Curtsies*   60

PLUME

Come, I must examine your basket to the bottom, my dear.

ROSE

Nay, for that matter, put in your hand; feel, sir; I warrant
my ware as good as any in the market.

PLUME

And I'll buy it all, child, were it ten times more.

ROSE

Sir, I can furnish you.   65

PLUME

Come then; we won't quarrel about the price, they're fine
birds; pray what's your name, pretty creature?

ROSE

Rose, sir; my father is a farmer within three short mile o'th'
town; we keep this market; I sell chickens, eggs, and butter,
and my brother Bullock there sells corn.   70

BULLOCK

Come, sister, haste ye; we shall be liate a wnome.

             All this while BULLOCK *whistles about the stage*

PLUME

Kite! (*Tips him the wink, he returns it*) Pretty Mrs Rose – you have – let me see – how many?

ROSE

A dozen, sir, and they are richly worth a crawn.

BULLOCK

Come, Ruose, Ruose, I sold fifty stracke o'barley today in 75
half this time; but you will higgle and higgle for a penny more than the commodity is worth.

ROSE

What's that to you, oaf? I can make as much out of a groat as you can out of fourpence, I'm sure – the gentleman bids fair, and when I meet with a chapman, I know how to make 80
the best on him – and so, sir, I say for a crawn piece the bargain's yours.

PLUME

Here's a guinea, my dear.

ROSE

I con't change your money, sir.

PLUME

Indeed, indeed but you can – my lodging is hard by, chicken, 85
and we'll make change there.   *Goes off, she follows him*

KITE

So, sir, as I was telling you, I have seen one of these hussars eat up a ravelin for his breakfast and afterwards pick his teeth with a palisado.

BULLOCK

Aye, you soldiers see very strange things – but pray, sir, 90
what is a ravelin?

72 s.d. *Tips . . . it* Q2 (*He tips the wink upon* Kite, *who returns it* Q1)
75 *stracke* (strake Q2) strike(s), usually identical with bushel(s)
76 *higgle* haggle
77 *commodity* could mean 'whore' or 'fēmale pudenda'
80 *chapman* customer
82 *bargain's* Q2 (bargain is Q1)
83 *guinea* then worth 20s
85 *chicken* Q2 (you shall bring home the chickens Q1)
88 *ravelin* in fortification, outwork consisting of two faces forming a salient angle, beyond main ditch and curtain
89 *palisado* one of a row of pointed stakes, an infantry defence against cavalry

78–9 *I can . . . fourpence*. A groat being worth fourpence; 'probably a rustic proverb' (Strauss). Tucker Brooke suggests as a modern equivalent 'I can make as much out of six as you can out of half a dozen'.

KITE
> Why 'tis like a modern minced pie, but the crust is con-
> founded hard, and the plums are somewhat hard of
> digestion!

BULLOCK
> Then your palisado, pray what may he be? – Come, Ruose,   95
> pray ha' done.

KITE
> Your palisado is a pretty sort of bodkin about the thickness
> of my leg.

BULLOCK
> (*Aside*) – That's a fib, I believe. – Eh, where's Ruose?
> Ruose! Ruose! 'sflesh, where's Ruose gone?   100

KITE
> She's gone with the captain.

BULLOCK
> The captain! Wauns, there's no pressing of women, sure?

KITE
> But there is, sir.

BULLOCK
> If the captain should press Ruose, I should be ruined;
> which way went she? – Oh, the devil take your rablins and   105
> palisaders.   *Exit*

KITE
> You shall be better acquainted with them, honest Bullock, or
> I shall miss of my aim.

Enter WORTHY

WORTHY
> Why, thou'rt the most useful fellow in nature to your
> captain, admirable in your way, I find.   110

KITE
> Yes, sir, I understand my business, I will say it; you must
> know, sir, I was born a gypsy, and bred among that crew till
> I was ten year old, there I learned canting and lying; I was
> bought from my mother Cleopatra by a certain nobleman
> for three pistoles, who liking my beauty made me his page,   115
> there I learned impudence and pimping; I was turned off for
> wearing my lord's linen, and drinking my lady's ratafia; and
> then turned bailiff's follower, there I learned bullying and

---

115 *pistoles* Q2 (pistols Q1) Spanish gold coins worth about 18*s*., or
    Scottish £12 pieces, in England worth about £1
117 *ratafia* Q2 (brandy Q1)

swearing. I at last got into the army, and there I learned
whoring and drinking. – So that if your worship pleases to   120
cast up the whole sum, viz., canting, lying, impudence,
pimping, bullying, swearing, whoring, drinking, and a
halberd, you will find the sum total will amount to a
recruiting sergeant.

WORTHY

And pray, what induced you to turn soldier?   125

KITE

Hunger and ambition – the fears of starving and hopes of a
truncheon led me along to a gentleman with a fair tongue
and fair periwig, who loaded me with promises; but I gad
'twas the lightest load that I ever felt in my life – he
promised to advance me, and indeed he did so – to a garret   130
in the Savoy. I asked him why he put me in prison; he called
me lying dog, and said I was in garrison; and indeed 'tis a
garrison that may hold out till doomsday before I should
desire to take it again. But here comes Justice Balance.

Enter BALANCE *and* BULLOCK

BALANCE

Here, you Sergeant, where's your captain? Here's a poor,   135
foolish fellow comes clamouring to me with a complaint, that
your captain has pressed his sister; do you know anything of
this matter, Worthy?

WORTHY

Ha, ha, ha, I know his sister is gone with Plume to his
lodgings to sell him some chickens.   140

BALANCE

Is that all? The fellow's a fool.

BULLOCK

I know that, an't please you; but if your worship pleases to
grant me a warrant to bring her before you for fear o' th'
worst.

BALANCE

Thou'rt mad, fellow, thy sister's safe enough.   145

KITE (*Aside*)

I hope so too.

---

123 *halberd* combination spear and battle-axe, sergeant's symbol of
    authority
127 *truncheon* baton, symbol of authority
131 *Savoy* notorious London military prison, often used to hold recruits.
145 *Thou'rt mad* Q2 (Thou art a mad Q1)

WORTHY

Hast thou no more sense, fellow, than to believe that the captain can list women?

BULLOCK

I know not whether they list them, or what they do with them, but I'm sure they carry as many women as men with   150
them out of the country.

BALANCE

But how came you not to go along with your sister?

BULLOCK

Luord, sir, I thought no more of her going than I do of the day I shall die; but this gentleman here, not suspecting any hurt neither, I believe – you thought no harm, friend, did ye?   155

KITE

Lack-a-day, sir, not I. – (*Aside*) Only that I believe I shall marry her tomorrow.

BALANCE

I begin to smell powder. Well, friend, but what did that gentleman with you?

BULLOCK

Why, sir, he entertained me with a fine story of a great fight   160
between the Hungarians, I think it was, and the Irish.

KITE

And so, sir, while we were in the heat of the battle, the captain carried off the baggage.

BALANCE

Sergeant, go along with this fellow to your captain, give him my humble service, and desire him to discharge the wench,   165
though he has listed her.

BULLOCK

Aye – and if he ben't free for that, he shall have another man in her place.

162–3 assigned to KITE Ed. (part of BULLOCK's speech Q)
165 *and desire* Q2 (and I desire Q1)

160–1 *a great . . . Irish.* Not impossible, between Hungarians in Eugene's army and Irish regiments in the French service, that fought at Blenheim; but 'Hungarians' may be Bullock's mistake for 'hussars' (see l. 87). Later C18 editions 'improve' to 'a great sea-fight between the Hungarians and the wild Irish'.

162–3 *And . . . baggage.* The assigning of this speech to Kite in later C18 editions is clearly right: it exhibits both his command of military idiom and his brand of humour.

KITE

Come, honest friend. – (*Aside*) You shall go to my quarters
instead of the captain's.   *Exeunt* KITE *and* BULLOCK   170

BALANCE

We must get this mad captain his complement of men, and
send him a-packing, else he'll overrun the country.

WORTHY

You see, sir, how little he values your daughter's disdain.

BALANCE

I like him the better; I was much such another fellow at his
age; I never set my heart upon any woman so much as to   175
make me uneasy at the disappointment; but what was very
surprising both to myself and friends, I changed o' th' sudden
from the most fickle lover to the most constant husband in the
world. But how goes your affair with Melinda?

WORTHY

Very slowly. Cupid had formerly wings, but I think in this   180
age he goes upon crutches, or I fancy Venus had been
dallying with her cripple Vulcan when my amour com-
menced, which has made it go on so lamely. My mistress has
got a captain too, but such a captain! As I live, yonder he
comes.   185

BALANCE

Who? That bluff fellow in the sash? I don't know him.

WORTHY

But I engage he knows you, and everybody at first sight; his
impudence were a prodigy, were not his ignorance proportionable; he has the most universal acquaintance of any
man living, for he won't be alone, and nobody will keep him   190
company twice; then he's a Caesar among the women, *veni*,
vidi, *vici*, that's all. If he has but talked with the maid, he
swears he has lain with the mistress; but the most surprising
part of his character is his memory, which is the most

178 *to the* Q2 (to be the Q1)
181 *had* Q2 (has Q1)
186 *sash* worn around the waist by some officers
191–2 *veni, vidi, vici* 'I came, I saw, I conquered'; Julius Caesar,
    after defeating Pharnaces at Zela

184–5 *yonder he comes*. Q1 provides no stage-direction. N.T.: 'Brazen is
    glimpsed crossing the stage, at rear. He disappears [right], only to make
    another "subliminal" entrance and exit, crossing [left] to [right], before
    re-entering [left] and spotting Worthy. This triple entrance helps to
    establish the man's total vagueness and inability to concentrate on
    anything for more than a few moments' (Tynan).

prodigious, and the most trifling in the world.   195

BALANCE

I have met with such men, and I take this good-for-nothing
memory to proceed from a certain contexture of the brain,
which is purely adapted to impertinencies, and there they
lodge secure, the owner having no thoughts of his own to
disturb them. I have known a man as perfect as a chronologer   200
as to the day and year of most important transactions, but be
altogether ignorant of the causes, springs, or consequences
of any one thing of moment; I have known another acquire
so much by travel, as to tell you the names of most places in
Europe, with their distances of miles, leagues, or hours, as   205
punctually as a post-boy; but for anything else, as ignorant
as the horse that carries the mail.

WORTHY

This is your man, sir, add but the traveller's privilege of
lying, and even that he abuses; this is the picture, behold the
life.   210

Enter BRAZEN

BRAZEN

Mr Worthy, I'm your servant, and so forth – hark'ee, my
dear –

WORTHY

Whispering, sir, before company is not manners, and when
nobody's by, 'tis foolish.

BRAZEN

Company! *Mort de ma vie*, I beg the gentleman's pardon,   215
who is he?

WORTHY

Ask him.

BRAZEN

So I will. – My dear, I'm your servant, and so forth, – your
name, my dear?

BALANCE

Very laconic, sir.   220

BRAZEN

Laconic, a very good name truly; I have known several of
the Laconics abroad. Poor Jack Laconic! He was killed at

215 *Mort de ma vie* 'death of my life', softened oath, from 'Mort de
    Dieu'

220 *laconic.* Local family joke (?): the mother-in-law of Francis Berkeley, on whom
    Balance was reputedly based, belonged to the Lacon family; and his daughter
    ('Sylvia') was christened Laconia (*N&Q*).

the battle of Landen. I remember that he had a blue ribband in his hat that very day, and after he fell, we found a piece of neat's tongue in his pocket.   225

BALANCE

Pray, sir, did the French attack us or we them at Landen?

BRAZEN

The French attack us! Oons, sir, are you a Jacobite?

BALANCE

Why that question?

BRAZEN

Because none but a Jacobite could think that the French durst attack us – no, sir, we attacked them on the – I have   230
reason to remember the time, for I had two-and-twenty horses killed under me that day.

WORTHY

Then, sir, you must have rid mighty hard.

BALANCE

Or perhaps, sir, like my countryman, you rid upon half a dozen horses at once.   235

BRAZEN

What d'e mean, gentlemen? I tell you they were killed, all torn to pieces by cannon-shot, except six that I staked to death upon the enemy's *chevaux de frise*.

BALANCE

Noble Captain, may I crave your name?

BRAZEN

Brazen, at your service.   240

BALANCE

Oh, Brazen, a very good name, I have known several of the Brazens abroad.

WORTHY

Do you know Captain Plume, sir?

BRAZEN

Is he anything related to Frank Plume in Northamptonshire?

225 *neat's tongue* ox tongue, a favourite snack
227 *Jacobite* supporter of the dynastic claims of 'James III', the Old Pretender
233 *must have rid* Q2 (rid Q1)
234-5 Unexplained; possibly Mr Evans, a contemporary equestrian acrobat.
238 *chevaux de frise* instruments for repelling cavalry charges, composed of a joist bristling with iron-pointed spears

223 *Landen.* The French attacked William III's army at Landen, about 30 miles south-east of Brussels, on 29 July 1693, and routed it after a long, bitter fight.

– Honest Frank! Many, many a dry bottle have we cracked   245
hand to fist; you must have known his brother Charles that
was concerned in the India Company, he married the
daughter of old Tongue-Pad, the Master in Chancery, a very
pretty woman, only squinted a little; she died in childbed of
her first child, but the child survived, 'twas a daughter, but   250
whether 'twas called Margaret or Marjory, upon my soul I
can't remember – but, gentlemen (*looking on his watch*), I
must meet a lady, a twenty-thousand-pounder, presently,
upon the walk by the water – Worthy, your servant; Laconic,
yours.   *Exit*   255

BALANCE

If you can have so mean an opinion of Melinda, as to be
jealous of this fellow, I think she ought to give you cause to
be so.

WORTHY

I don't think she encourages him so much for gaining herself
a lover, as to set me up a rival; were there any credit to be   260
given to his words, I should believe Melinda had made him
this assignation; I must go see – sir, you'll pardon me.

BALANCE

Aye, aye, sir, you're a man of business.   [*Exit* WORTHY]
But what have we got here?

Enter ROSE *singing*

ROSE

And I shall be a lady, a captain's lady, and ride single upon   265
a white horse with a star, upon a velvet sidesaddle; and I
shall go to London and see the tombs and the lions, and the
Queen. Sir, an't please your worship, I have often seen your
worship ride through our grounds a-hunting, begging your
worship's pardon – pray, what may this lace be worth a yard?   270
Showing some lace

---

248 *Tongue-Pad* talkative person, esp. if smooth and insinuating
248 *Master in Chancery* one of the twelve assistants to the Lord
      Chancellor
264 s.d. *singing* Q2 (*singing what she pleases* Q1)

---

267 *the tombs and the lions.* 'The three great sights of London [were] the lions
      at the Tower, the tombs in Westminster Abbey, and the poor mad folk
      in Bedlam. "To see the lions" is proverbial, and these had to be visited
      by every one new to the City' (Ashton, p. 186; see *Tatler*, No. 30,
      Spectator, No. 26).

BALANCE

Right Mechlin, by this light! Where did you get this lace, child?

ROSE

No matter for that, sir, I come honestly by't.

BALANCE

I question it much.

ROSE

And see here, sir, a fine turkey-shell snuff-box, and fine   275
mangeree, see here: (*takes snuff affectedly*) the captain learnt me how to take it with an air.

BALANCE

Oho, the captain! Now the murder's out – and so the captain taught you to take it with an air?

ROSE

Yes, and give it with an air too – will your worship please to   280
taste my snuff?   *Offers the box affectedly*

BALANCE

You're a very apt scholar, pretty maid. And pray what did you give the captain for these fine things?

ROSE

He's to have my brother for a soldier, and two or three sweet-hearts that I have in the country, they shall all go with the   285
captain. Oh, he's the finest man, and the humblest withal; would you believe it, sir, he carried me up with him to his own chamber with as much familiarity as if I had been the best lady in the land.

---

271 *Mechlin* type of lace made in Mechlin in Belgium
275 *turkey-shell* presumably 'tortoise shell', or 'turtle shell', mis-remembered
276. *mangeree* presumably 'orangery' misremembered: a snuff scented with an extract from orange flowers
  s.d. *takes* Q2 (*She takes* Q1)

---

276 *takes snuff affectedly.* 'The Exercise of the Snuff Box, according to the most fashionable Airs and Motions', by both sexes, is satirized in *Spectators* 138 and 344. The fad arose in England following the capture of a huge amount of Spanish snuff in 1702.

BALANCE

Oh, he's a mighty familiar gentleman as can be.   290

Enter PLUME *singing*

PLUME

But it is not so
With those that go
Through frost and snow
Most apropos,
My maid with the milking-pail.   295

Takes hold on ROSE

How, the justice! Then I'm arraigned, condemned, and executed.

BALANCE

Oh, my noble Captain.

ROSE

And my noble captain too, sir.

PLUME

'Sdeath, child, are you mad? – Mr Balance, I am so full of   300
business about my recruits, that I han't a moment's time to –
I have just now three or four people to –

BALANCE

Nay, Captain, I must speak to you.

ROSE

And so must I too, Captain.

PLUME

Any other time, sir – I cannot for my life, sir –   305

BALANCE

Pray, sir.

PLUME

Twenty thousand things – I would but – now, sir, pray –
devil take me – I cannot – I must –   *Breaks away*

BALANCE

Nay, I'll follow you.   *Exit*

ROSE

And I too.   *Exit*   310

290 f. be/*Enter* Q2 (Q1 reads:

ROSE

But I must beg your worship's pardon, I must go seek out my
brother Bullock.   *Runs off singing*

BALANCE

If all officers took the same method of recruiting with this
gentleman, they might come in time to be fathers as well as captains of their companies.)

291–5 Refrain of a well-known song, 'The Milkmaid's Life'.

[Act III], Scene ii

The Walk by the Severn side
Enter MELINDA *and her maid* LUCY

MELINDA

And pray, was it a ring, or buckle, or pendants, or knots; or
in what shape was the almighty gold transformed that has
bribed you so much in his favour?

LUCY

Indeed, madam, the last bribe I had was from the captain,
and that was only a small piece of Flanders edging for   5
pinners.

MELINDA

Aye, Flanders lace is as constant a present from officers to
their women as something else is from their women to them.
They every year bring over a cargo of lace to cheat the
Queen of her duty, and her subjects of their honesty.   10

LUCY

They only barter one sort of prohibited goods for another,
madam.

MELINDA

Has any of them been bartering with you, Mrs Pert, that you
talk so like a trader?

LUCY

Madam, you talk as peevishly to me as if it were my fault,   15
the crime is none of mine though I pretend to excuse it;
though he should not see you this week, can I help it? But as
I was saying, madam, his friend Captain Plume has so taken
him up these two days –

MELINDA

Psha! Would his friend, the captain, were tied upon his back;   20
I warrant he has never been sober since that confounded
captain came to town; the devil take all officers, I say – they
do the nation more harm by debauching us at home, than
they do good by defending us abroad: no sooner a captain
comes to town, but all the young fellows flock about him,   25
and we can't keep a man to ourselves.

___

1 *knots* bows of ribbon (of gold thread?)
6 *pinners* cap-like headdress with two long flaps
14 *trader* whore
20 *tied . . . back* as a monkey would be tied on a donkey's back, to be
    attacked by dogs, as a comic interlude at the Bear Gardens

LUCY

One would imagine, madam, by your concern for Worthy's
absence, that you should use him better when he's with you.

MELINDA

Who told you, pray, that I was concerned for his absence?
I'm only vexed that I've had nothing said to me these two   30
days: one may like the love and despise the lover, I hope; as
one may love the treason and hate the traitor. Oh! Here
comes another captain, and a rogue that has the confidence
to make love to me; but indeed I don't wonder at that, when
he has the assurance to fancy himself a fine gentleman.   35

LUCY (*Aside*)

If he should speak o' th' assignation, I should be ruined.

Enter BRAZEN

BRAZEN

True to the touch, faith. (*Aside*) I'll draw up all my compliments into one grand platoon, and fire upon her at once.
    Thou peerless princess of Salopian plains,
    Envied by nymphs and worshipped by the swains,   40
    Behold how humbly does the Severn glide,
    To greet thee, princess of the Severn side.
Madam, I'm your humble servant and all that, madam – a
fine river this same Severn – do you love fishing, madam?

MELINDA

'Tis a pretty melancholy amusement for lovers.   45

BRAZEN

I'll go buy hooks and lines presently; for you must know,
madam, that I have served in Flanders against the French,
in Hungary against the Turks, and in Tangier against the
Moors, and I was never so much in love before; and split me,
madam, in all the campaigns I ever made I have not seen so   50
fine a woman as your ladyship.

32 *treason . . . traitor* proverbial. Tilley, K64
33 *confidence* impudence
37 *touch* test
37–42 so, Q1 (all after 'faith' omitted, Q2)
38 *platoon* small group of foot-soldiers, drilled as a unit

39–42 Brazen's use of the quatrain, with Plume's later, serves to emphasize
    its triteness.
48 *in Hungary*. The Imperialist armies drove the Turks out of Hungary
    finally in 1716.
    Tangier. The English garrisoned Tangier between 1661 and 1684.

MELINDA

And from all the men I ever saw I never had so fine a
compliment; but you soldiers are the best-bred men, that
we must allow.

BRAZEN

Some of us, madam, but there are brutes among us too, very   55
sad brutes; for my own part, I have always had the good luck
to prove agreeable – I have had very considerable offers,
madam, I might have married a German princess worth fifty
thousand crowns a year, but her stove disgusted me. – The
daughter of a Turkish bashaw fell in love with me too when   60
I was prisoner among the infidels; she offered to rob her
father of his treasure, and make her escape with me, but I
don't know how, my time was not come; hanging and
marriage, you know, go by destiny; Fate has reserved me
for a Shropshire lady with twenty thousand pound – do   65
you know any such person, madam?

MELINDA

Extravagant coxcomb! – To be sure, a great many ladies of
that fortune would be proud of the name of Mrs Brazen.

BRAZEN

Nay, for that matter, madam, there are women of very good
quality of the name of Brazen.   70

Enter WORTHY

MELINDA

Oh, are you there, gentleman? – Come, Captain, we'll walk
this way, give me your hand.

56 *sad* deplorably bad
60 *bashaw* pasha
63–4 *hanging . . . destiny* proverbial. Tilley, W232

---

59 *her stove* (a) Sitting-room or bedroom heated with a furnace; or (b)
foot-warmer containing burning charcoal, which Dutch women tucked
under their skirts; or possibly (c) sweating-room. In William Cavendish's *The Humorous Lovers* (1677), p. 10, it is said of the character
Furrs, obsessive about keeping warm, that 'A *Dutch* Stove would make
him a most passionate Lover'. The sense here is probably the first.
Jeffares notes that 'English travellers often objected to the overheating
of rooms on the continent'. In Augustin Daly's stage-version of the
play, 'but her stove disgusted me' is replaced by: ' "but the garlic and
onions! Whew!" perhaps from some old prompt-book' (Strauss).

BRAZEN
    My hand, heart's blood, and guts are at your service. –
    Mr Worthy – your servant, my dear. *Exit leading* MELINDA
WORTHY
    Death and fire! This is not to be borne.   75

Enter PLUME

PLUME
    No more it is, faith.
WORTHY
    What?
PLUME
    The March beer at the Raven; I have been doubly serving
    the Queen, – raising men and raising the excise – recruiting
    and elections are rare friends to the excise.   80
WORTHY
    You an't drunk?
PLUME
    No, no, whimsical only; I could be mighty foolish, and
    fancy myself mighty witty; Reason still keeps its throne,
    but it nods a little, that's all.
WORTHY
    Then you're just fit for a frolic?   85
PLUME
    As fit as close pinners for a punk in the pit.
WORTHY
    There's your play then, recover me that vessel from that
    Tangerine.
PLUME
    She's well rigged, but how is she manned?
WORTHY
    By Captain Brazen that I told you of today; she is called   90
    the Melinda, a first rate I can assure you; she sheered off
    with him just now on purpose to affront me, but according

---

78 *March beer* strong beer brewed in March
80 *rare* Q2 (good Q1)
83–4 *Reason . . . little* cf. proverb, 'Let reason rule all your actions',
      Tilley R43
86 *punk in the pit* whore in the pit of the theatre
88 *Tangerine* Tangiers privateer or pirate ship
89 *rigged* pun on slang sense, 'clothed'
90 *she* Q2 (the frigate Q1)
91 *first rate* warship of the highest rating

to your advice I would take no notice, because I would
seem to be above a concern for her behaviour. But have a
care of a quarrel.   95

PLUME

No, no, I never quarrel with anything in my cups but an
oyster wench or a cook maid, and if they ben't civil, I knock
'em down. But hark'ee my friend, I will make love, and I
must make love. I tell'ee what, I'll make love like a platoon.

WORTHY

Platoon, how's that?   100

PLUME

I'll kneel, stoop, and stand, faith; most ladies are gained by
platooning.

WORTHY

Here they come; I must leave you.   *Exit*

PLUME

So – now must I look as sober and demure as a whore at a
christening.   105

Enter BRAZEN *and* MELINDA

BRAZEN

Who's that, madam?

MELINDA

A brother officer of yours, I suppose, sir.

BRAZEN

Aye! – (*To* PLUME) My dear.

PLUME

My dear!   *They run and embrace*

BRAZEN

My dear boy, how is't? – Your name, my dear? If I be not   110
mistaken, I have seen your face.

PLUME

I never see yours in my life, my dear – but there's a face

96 *but an* Q2 (but with an Q1)
100 *Platoon* Q2 (A platoon Q1)
104 *must I* Q2 (I must Q1)
107 *sir* Q2 (not in Q1)

---

101 *kneel, stoop, and stand.* The jest reflects the older firedrill still in use by the
French, of firing by ranks, with the forward ranks kneeling or crouching, in turn,
to reload and allow those behind to fire. Marlborough's field regiments were
trained to fire by platoons: the men stood in three ranks, with those behind firing
over the shoulders of men in front, in concentrated volleys. In the drawn-up
battalion, three series of platoons fired in succession.

well known as the sun's, that shines on all and is by all
adored.

BRAZEN

Have you any pretensions, sir?   115

PLUME

Pretensions!

BRAZEN

That is, sir, have you ever served abroad?

PLUME

I have served at home, sir, for ages served this cruel fair –
and that will serve the turn, sir.

MELINDA (*Aside*)

So, between the fool and the rake I shall bring a fine spot of   120
work upon my hands – I see Worthy yonder, I could be
content to be friends with him would he come this way.

BRAZEN

Will you fight for the lady, sir?

PLUME

No, sir, but I'll have her notwithstanding.
      Thou peerless princess of Salopian plains,   125
      Envied by nymphs and worshipped by the swains—

BRAZEN

Oons, sir, not fight for her!

PLUME

Prithee be quiet, I shall be out –
           Behold how humbly does the Severn glide
           To greet thee, princess of the Severn side.   130

BRAZEN

Don't mind him, madam. – If he were not so well dressed I
should take him for a poet; but I'll show the difference
presently – come, madam, we'll place you between us, and
now the longest sword carries her.

Draws, MELINDA *shrieks*

Enter WORTHY

MELINDA

Oh, Mr Worthy, save me from these madmen.   135

Runs off with WORTHY

PLUME

Ha, ha, ha, why don't you follow, sir, and fight the bold
ravisher?

---

113 *sun . . . all* proverbial. Tilley, S985
118 *fair* beauty

BRAZEN
No, sir, you're my man.

PLUME
I don't like the wages, and I won't be your man.

BRAZEN
Then you're not worth my sword.   140

PLUME
No? Pray what did it cost?

BRAZEN
It cost me twenty pistoles in France, and my enemies
thousands of lives in Flanders.

PLUME
Then they had a dear bargain.

Enter SILVIA *dressed in man's apparel*

SILVIA
Save ye, save ye, gentlemen.   145

BRAZEN
My dear, I'm yours.

PLUME
Do you know the gentleman?

BRAZEN
No, but I will presently. – Your name, my dear?

SILVIA
Wilful, Jack Wilful, at your service.

BRAZEN
What! The Kentish Wilfuls or those of Staffordshire?   150

SILVIA
Both, sir, both; I'm related to all the Wilfuls in Europe,
and I'm head of the family at present.

PLUME
Do you live in this country, sir?

SILVIA
Yes, sir, I live where I stand, I have neither home, house,
nor habitation beyond this spot of ground.   155

BRAZEN
What are you, sir?

SILVIA
A rake.

142–3 *It cost . . . Flanders* Q2 (It cost my enemies thousands of lives,
    sir Q1); pun on 'livres'
153 *this* Q2 (the Q1)
154 *stand* Q2 (should Q1)

PLUME

    In the army, I presume.

SILVIA

    No, but intend to list immediately – look'ee, gentlemen,
he that bids me fairest has me.   160

BRAZEN

    Sir, I'll prefer you, I'll make you a corporal this minute.

PLUME

    A corporal! I'll make you my companion, you shall eat with
me.

BRAZEN

    You shall drink with me.

PLUME

    You shall lie with me, you young rogue.   *Kisses her*   165

BRAZEN

    You shall receive your pay and do no duty.

SILVIA

    Then you must make me a field-officer.

PLUME

    Pho, pho, I'll do more than all this, I'll make you a corporal,
and give you a brevet for sergeant.

BRAZEN

    Can you read and write, sir?   170

SILVIA

    Yes.

BRAZEN

    Then your business is done, I'll make you chaplain to the
regiment.

SILVIA

    Your promises are so equal that I'm at a loss to choose;
there is one Plume that I hear much commended in town,   175
pray which of you is Captain Plume?

PLUME

    I am Captain Plume.

159 *but intend* Q2 (but I intend Q1)
160 *has* Q2 (shall have Q1)
167 *field-officer* officer above the rank of captain and below that of
general; they frequently held additional sinecure posts
169 *brevet* document conferring nominal rank
177 *I am* Q2 (I'm Q1)

165 *lie with me.* Sharing beds was the rule rather than the exception; a
century later Wellington's junior officers were sometimes four to a bed.

BRAZEN
> No, no, I'm Captain Plume.

SILVIA
> Hey day!

PLUME
> Captain Plume, I'm your servant, my dear.   180

BRAZEN
> Captain Brazen, I'm yours. – The fellow dare not fight.

Enter KITE

KITE
> Sir, if you please –   *Goes to whisper* PLUME

PLUME
> No, no, there's your captain. – Captain Plume, your ser-
> geant here has got so drunk he mistakes me for you.

BRAZEN
> He's an incorrigible sot. – Here, my Hector of Holborn,   185
> forty shillings for you.

PLUME
> I forbid the banns – look'ee, friend, you shall list with
> Captain Brazen.

SILVIA
> I will see Captain Brazen hanged first, I will list with
> Captain Plume; I'm a freeborn Englishman and will be a   190
> slave my own way. – (*To* BRAZEN) Look'ee, sir, will you stand
> by me?

BRAZEN
> I warrant you, my lad.

SILVIA
> Then I will tell you, Captain Brazen (*to* PLUME), that you
> are an ignorant, pretending, impudent coxcomb.   195

BRAZEN
> Aye, aye, a sad dog.

SILVIA
> A very sad dog; give me the money, noble Captain Plume.

---

178 *I'm* Q2 (I am Q1)

185 *Hector of Holborn.* Holborn was the route along which criminals were
taken from Newgate to Tyburn to be hanged; the title probably means
'gallows-bird swashbuckler', formed as an analogue of 'Guy of Hampton' and other names of heroes of chivalric romance.
186 *forty shillings.* The bounty for volunteering.

PLUME

Then you won't list with Captain Brazen?

SILVIA

I won't.

BRAZEN

Never mind him, child, I'll end the dispute presently;   200
hark'ee, my dear –

Takes PLUME *to one side of the stage and entertains him in
dumb show*

KITE

Sir, he in the plain coat is Captain Plume; I'm his sergeant
and will take my oath on't.

SILVIA

What! You are Sergeant Kite?

KITE

At your service.   205

SILVIA

Then I would not take your oath for a farthing.

KITE

A very understanding youth of his age. Pray, sir, let me
look you full in the face.

SILVIA

Well, sir, what have you to say to my face?

KITE

The very image and superscription of my brother, two   210
bullets of the same calibre were never so like; sure it must
be Charles, Charles –

SILVIA

What d'ye mean by Charles?

KITE

The voice too, only a little variation in effa ut flat; my dear
brother, for I must call you so, if you should have the   215
fortune to enter into the most noble society of the sword, I
bespeak you for a comrade.

SILVIA

No, sir, I'll be your captain's comrade if anybody's.

198 *Then* Q2 (Hold, hold, then Q1)
204 *You are* Q2 (Are you Q1)
214 *effa ut flat* Q2 (C fa ut flat Q1)

---

214 *effa ut flat.* F fa ut, the fuller name of the note F which was sung to the
syllable *fa* or *ut* according as it occurred in one or other of the hexa-
chords to which it could belong (a hexachord being a diatonic series or
scale of six notes).

KITE

Ambition! There again, 'tis a noble passion for a soldier; by
that I gained this glorious halberd. Ambition! I see a com-   220
mission in his face already; pray, noble Captain, give me
leave to salute you.   *Offers to kiss her*

SILVIA

What, men kiss one another!

KITE

We officers do, 'tis our way; we live together like man and
wife, always either kissing or fighting. – But I see a storm   225
a-coming.

SILVIA

Now, Sergeant, I shall see who is your captain by your
knocking down the t'other.

KITE

My captain scorns assistance, sir.

BRAZEN

How dare you contend for anything and not dare to draw   230
your sword? But you're a young fellow, and have not been
much abroad, I excuse that; but prithee resign the man,
prithee do; you're a very honest fellow.

PLUME

You lie, and you're a son of a whore.
                              Draws, and makes up to BRAZEN

BRAZEN (*Retiring*)

Hold, hold, did not you refuse to fight for the lady?   235

PLUME

I always do – but for a man I'll fight knee deep, so you lie
again.
      PLUME *and* BRAZEN *fight a traverse or two about the stage;*
      SILVIA *draws, and is held by* KITE, *who sounds to arms with his
      mouth, takes* SILVIA *in his arms, and carries her off the stage*

BRAZEN

Hold – where's the man?

PLUME

Gone.

BRAZEN

Then what do we fight for? (*Puts up*) Now let's embrace,   240
my dear.

---

223 *men kiss.* The practice was generally thought foppish and Frenchified or
    intolerably boorish, but was evidently customary among sergeants (see
    Congreve, *The Way of the World*, III.xv, 72–3).

PLUME

With all my heart, my dear. (*Putting up*) I suppose Kite
has listed him by this time.   *They embrace*

BRAZEN

You're a brave fellow. I always fight with a man before I
make him my friend; and if once I find he will fight, I never   245
quarrel with him afterwards. – And now I'll tell you a
secret, my dear friend, that lady we frighted out o'the walk
just now I found in bed this morning, so beautiful, so
inviting – I presently locked the door – but I'm a man of
honour – but I believe I shall marry her nevertheless; her   250
twenty thousand pound, you know, will be a pretty conveniency – I had an assignation with her here, but your
coming spoiled my sport, curse ye, my dear, – but don't do
so again.

PLUME

No, no, my dear, men are my business at present.   255

                                              Exeunt

Act IV, Scene i

The Walk by the Severn side
[*Enter*] ROSE *and* BULLOCK *meeting*

ROSE

Where have you been, you great booby? You're always out
o' th'way in the time of preferment.

BULLOCK

Preferment! Who should prefer me?

ROSE

I would prefer you; who should prefer a man but a woman?
Come throw away that great club, hold up your head,   5
cock your hat, and look big.

BULLOCK

Ah! Ruose, Ruose, I fear somebody will look big sooner
than folk think of; this genteel breeding never comes into
the country without a train of followers. – Here has been
Cartwheel your sweetheart, what will become o' him?   10

ROSE

Look'ee, I'm a great woman and will provide for my rela-

---

242 s.d. *Putting* Q2 (*Puts* Q1)   247 *lady we* Q2 (lady that we Q1)
251–2 *conveniency* Q2 (convenience Q1)
  0.2 *The Walk . . . side* Ed. (SCENE *of the Walk continues* Q)
  6 *look big* attempt an impressive manner

tions; I told the captain how finely he played upon the
tabor and pipe, so he has set him down for drum-major.

BULLOCK

Nay, sister, why did not you keep that place for me? You
know I always loved to be a-drumming, if it were but on a   15
table, or on a quart pot.

Enter SILVIA

SILVIA

Had I but a commission in my pocket I fancy my breeches
would become me as well as any ranting fellow of 'em all;
for I take a bold step, a rakish toss, a smart cock, and an
impudent air to be the principal ingredients in the com-   20
position of a captain. – What's here? Rose, my nurse's
daughter. I'll go and practise. – Come, child, kiss me at
once. (*Kisses* ROSE) And her brother too. – Well, honest
Dungfork, do you know the difference between a horse cart
and a cart horse, eh?   25

BULLOCK

I presume that your worship is a captain by your clothes
and your courage.

SILVIA

Suppose I were, would you be contented to list, friend?

ROSE

No, no, though your worship be a handsome man, there be
others as fine as you; my brother is engaged to Captain   30
Plume.

SILVIA

Plume! Do you know Captain Plume?

ROSE

Yes, I do, and he knows me. – He took the very ribbands
out of his shirtsleeves and put 'em into my shoes – see
there. – I can assure you that I can do anything with the   35
captain.

12 *played* Q2 (could play Q1)
13 *tabor* small drum on which the piper accompanied himself
    for drum-major Q2 (for a drum-major Q1)
19 *toss* quick upward or backward movement of the head
19 *cock* upward or significant turn
34 *'em* Q2 (them Q1)
35 *you* Q2 (not in Q1)

24 *horse cart*. 'To set the cart before the horse' (proverb; Tilley C103)
    itself means to reverse the right order.

BULLOCK

That is, in a modest way, sir. – Have a care what you say, Ruose, don't shame your parentage.

ROSE

Nay, for that matter I am not so simple as to say that I can do anything with the captain, but what I may do with any-   40
body else.

SILVIA

So! And pray what do you expect from this captain, child?

ROSE

I expect, sir! I expect – but he ordered me to tell nobody – but suppose that he should promise to marry me?

SILVIA

You should have a care, my dear, men will promise any-   45
thing beforehand.

ROSE

I know that, but he promised to marry me afterwards.

BULLOCK

Wauns, Ruose, what have you said?

SILVIA

Afterwards! After what?

ROSE

After I had sold him my chickens. – I hope there's no   50
harm in that.

Enter PLUME

PLUME

What, Mr Wilful, so close with my market-woman!

SILVIA

(*Aside*) I'll try if he loves her. – Close, sir! aye, and closer yet, sir. – Come, my pretty maid, you and I will withdraw a little.   55

PLUME

No, no, friend, I han't done with her yet.

SILVIA

Nor have I begun with her, so I have as good a right as you have.

---

51 *that* Q2 (that, though there be an ugly song of chickens and sparagus Q1)

59–82 so, Q2 (alternative version in Appendix 1, Q1)

---

51 The 'song' (Q1) has been identified by Peter Dixon as *The three jovial companions, or the merry travellers, who paid their shot where ever they came, without ever a stiver of money* (ca. 1685), reprinted in *Pills to Purge Melancholy*, ed. T. Durfey (1714), V, 17-19. It is decidedly bawdy.

PLUME
Thou art a bloody impudent fellow.

SILVIA
Sir, I would qualify myself for the service.   60

PLUME
Hast thou really a mind to the service?

SILVIA
Yes, sir; so let her go.

ROSE
Pray, gentlemen, don't be so violent.

PLUME
Come, leave it to the girl's own choice. – Will you belong to
me or to that gentleman?   65

ROSE
Let me consider, you're both very handsome.

PLUME
Now the natural inconstancy of her sex begins to work.

ROSE
Pray, sir, what will you give me?

BULLOCK
Dunna be angry, sir, that my sister should be mercenary,
for she's but young.   70

SILVIA
Give thee, child! – I'll set thee above scandal; you shall have
a coach with six before and six behind, an equipage to make
vice fashionable, and put virtue out of countenance.

PLUME
Pho, that's easily done, – I'll do more for thee, child, I'll
buy you a furbelow scarf, and give you a ticket to see a play.   75

BULLOCK
A play! Wauns, Ruose, take the ticket, and let's see the
show.

SILVIA
Look'ee, Captain, if you won't resign, I'll go list with
Captain Brazen this minute.

PLUME
Will you list with me if I give up my title?   80

---

72 *coach ... behind* six horses before, six footmen on the rear
platform
75 *furbelow* flounced

---

59 *bloody*. As an intensive, has at this time an undertone of high but roistering blood.

SILVIA
I will.

PLUME
Take her: I'll change a woman for a man at any time.

ROSE
I have heard before, indeed, that you captains used to sell your men.

BULLOCK
(*Crying*) Pray, Captain, don't send Ruose to the West   85
Indies.

PLUME
Ha, ha, ha, West Indies! No, no, my honest lad, give me thy hand; nor you nor she shall move a step farther than I do. – This gentleman is one of us, and will be kind to you, Mrs Rose.   90

ROSE
But will you be so kind to me, sir, as the captain would?

SILVIA
I can't be altogether so kind to you, my circumstances are not so good as the captain's; but I'll take care of you, upon my word.

PLUME
Aye, aye, we'll all take care of her; she shall live like a   95
princess, and her brother here shall be – what would you be?

BULLOCK
Ah! sir, if you had not promised the place of drum-major –

PLUME
Aye, that is promised – but what think ye of barrack-master? You're a person of understanding, and barrack-master you shall be. – But what's become of this same   100
Cartwheel you told me of, my dear?

ROSE
We'll go fetch him – come, brother barrack-master. – We shall find you at home, noble Captain?

Exeunt ROSE *and* BULLOCK

PLUME
Yes, yes – and now, sir, here are your forty shillings.

85–6 *West Indies*. Service here was rightly dreaded: 'the men died like flies from tropical diseases and gross neglect, forgotten by the War Office and often by their own absentee officers', who, like the civil contractors, were usually defrauding them of pay, food and clothing (G. M. Trevelyan, *England under Queen-Anne: Blenheim* [London, 1948], pp. 217, 228).

SILVIA

Captain Plume, I despise your listing-money; if I do serve,   105
'tis purely for love – of that wench I mean. For you must
know, that among my other sallies, I have spent the best
part of my fortune in search of a maid, and could never
find one hitherto; so you may be assured I'd not sell my
freedom under a less purchase than I did my estate. – So   110
before I list I must be certified that this girl is a virgin.

PLUME

Mr Wilful, I can't tell how you can be certified in that point,
till you try, but upon my honour she may be a vestal for
aught that I know to the contrary. – I gained her heart
indeed by some trifling presents and promises, and knowing   115
that the best security for a woman's soul is her body, I
would have made myself master of that too, had not the
jealousy of my impertinent landlady interposed.

SILVIA

So you only want an opportunity for accomplishing your
designs upon her?   120

PLUME

Not at all, I have already gained my ends, which were only
the drawing in one or two of her followers. The women, you
know, are the loadstones everywhere: gain the wives and
you're caressed by the husbands; please the mistresses and
you are valued by their gallants; secure an interest with the   125
finest women at court and you procure the favour of the
greatest men; so, kiss the prettiest country wenches and
you are sure of listing the lustiest fellows. Some people
may call this artifice, but I term it stratagem, since it is so
main a part of the service – besides, the fatigue of recruiting   130
is so intolerable, that unless we could make ourselves some
pleasure amidst the pain, no mortal man would be able to
bear it.

SILVIA

Well, sir, I'm satisfied as to the point in debate; but now let
me beg you to lay aside your recruiting airs, put on the man   135
of honour, and tell me plainly what usage I must expect when
I'm under your command.

---

109 *I'd not* Ed. (that I won't Q1; I'd Q2)
130 *main* highly important   130 *fatigue* Q2 (fatigues Q1)

---

111 N.T.: 'Insisting on a virgin is of course evidence of lubricity, not prim-
    ness. Silvia is trying to pass herself off as a thoroughly jaded rake' (Tynan).

PLUME

You must know in the first place, then, that I hate to have
gentlemen in my company, for they are always troublesome and expensive, sometimes dangerous; and 'tis a con-   140
stant maxim amongst us, that those who know the least
obey the best. Notwithstanding all this, I find something
so agreeable about you, that engages me to court your company; and I can't tell how it is, but I should be uneasy to
see you under the command of anybody else. – Your usage   145
will chiefly depend upon your behaviour; only this you
must expect, that if you commit a small fault I will excuse it,
if a great one, I'll discharge you; for something tells me I
shall not be able to punish you.

SILVIA

And something tells me, that if you do discharge me 'twill be   150
the greatest punishment you can inflict; for were we this
moment to go upon the greatest dangers in your profession,
they would be less terrible to me than to stay behind you. –
And now your hand, – this lists me – and now you are my
captain.   155

PLUME

Your friend. (*Kisses her*) 'Sdeath! There's something in this
fellow that charms me.

SILVIA

One favour I must beg – this affair will make some noise, and
I have some friends that would censure my conduct if I
threw myself into the circumstance of a private sentinel of   160
my own head; I must therefore take care to be impressed by
the Act of Parliament; you shall leave that to me.

PLUME

What you please as to that. – Will you lodge at my quarters
in the meantime? You shall have part of my bed.

SILVIA

Oh, fie, lie with a common soldier! – Would not you rather   165
lie with a common woman?

PLUME

No, faith, I'm not that rake that the world imagines; I have

141 *amongst* Q2 (among Q1)   151 *can* Q2 (will Q1)
160 *circumstance* Q2 (circumstances Q1)
    private sentinel private soldier
167 *I'm* Q2 (I am Q1)

167–73 N.T.: 'This is an honest confession on Plume's part—and he makes
    it to Wilful, the professed rake, with some embarrassment' (Tynan).

got an air of freedom which people mistake for lewdness in
me, as they mistake formality in others for religion; the
world is all a cheat, only I take mine which is undesigned to   170
be more excusable than theirs, which is hypocritical; I hurt
nobody but myself, and they abuse all mankind. – Will you
lie with me?

SILVIA

No, no, Captain, you forget Rose, she's to be my bedfellow
you know.   175

PLUME

I had forgot, pray be kind to her.   *Exeunt severally*

Enter MELINDA *and* LUCY

MELINDA

'Tis the greatest misfortune in nature for a woman to want a
confidante: we are so weak that we can do nothing without
assistance, and then a secret racks us worse than the colic;
I'm at this minute so sick of a secret that I'm ready to faint   180
away – help me, Lucy.

LUCY

Bless me, madam, what's the matter?

MELINDA

Vapours only – I begin to recover – if Silvia were in town, I
could heartily forgive her faults for the ease of discovering
my own.   185

LUCY

You're thoughtful, madam; am not I worthy to know the
cause?

MELINDA

You're a servant, and a secret would make you saucy.

LUCY

Not unless you should find fault without a cause, madam.

MELINDA

Cause or no cause, I must not lose the pleasure of chiding   190
when I please; women must discharge their vapours somewhere, and before we get husbands, our servants must
expect to bear with 'em.

LUCY

Then, madam, you had better raise me to a degree above a
servant: you know my family, and that five hundred pound   195
would set me upon the foot of a gentlewoman, and make me
worthy the confidence of any lady in the land. Besides,

172 *and* Q2 (but Q1)
176 *Hunt and Archer start a new scene here*

madam, 'twill extremely encourage me in the great design I
now have in hand.

MELINDA

I don't find that your design can be of any great advantage   200
to you; 'twill please me indeed in the humour I have of being
revenged on the fool for his vanity of making love to me, so
I don't much care if I do promise you five hundred pound
upon my day of marriage.

LUCY

That is the way, madam, to make me diligent in the vocation   205
of a confidante, which I think is generally to bring people
together.

MELINDA

Oh, Lucy, I can hold my secret no longer – you must know
that hearing of the famous fortune-teller in town, I went
disguised to satisfy a curiosity which has cost me dear; that   210
fellow is certainly the devil, or one of his bosom favourites,
he has told me the most surprising things of my past life –

LUCY

Things past, madam, can hardly be reckoned surprising,
because we know them already; did he tell you anything
surprising that was to come?   215

MELINDA

One thing very surprising, he said I should die a maid.

LUCY

Die a maid! Come into the world for nothing! – Dear
madam, if you should believe him, it might come to pass;
for the bare thought on't might kill one in four and twenty
hours. – And did you ask him any questions about me?   220

MELINDA

You! Why, I passed for you.

LUCY

So 'tis I that am to die a maid – but the devil was a liar from
the beginning, he can't make me die a maid – I have put it
out of his power already.

MELINDA

I do but jest, I would have passed for you, and called myself   225
Lucy, but he presently told me my name, my quality, my
fortune, and gave me the whole history of my life; he told me
of a lover I had in this country, and described Worthy
exactly, but in nothing so well as in his present indifference
– I fled to him for refuge here today – he never so much as   230

198 *design I* Q2 (design that I Q1)
204 *upon my day of* Q2 (the day of my Q1)

encouraged me in my fright, but coldly told me that he was
sorry for the accident, because it might give the town cause
to censure my conduct; excused his not waiting on me home,
made a careless bow, and walked off. 'Sdeath, I could have
stabbed him, or myself, 'twas the same thing. – Yonder he   235
comes – I will so slave him.

LUCY
Don't exasperate him, consider what the fortune-teller told
you; men are scarce, and as times go, it is not impossible for
a woman to die a maid.

Enter WORTHY

MELINDA
No matter.   240

WORTHY
I find she's warmed, I must strike while the iron is hot. –
You have a great deal of courage, madam, to venture into the
walks where you were so late frighted.

MELINDA
And you have a quantity of impudence to appear before me,
that you have so lately affronted.   245

WORTHY
I had no design to affront you, nor appear before you either,
madam; I left you here because I had business in another
place, and came hither thinking to meet another person.

MELINDA
Since you find yourself disappointed, I hope you'll withdraw
to another part of the walk.   250

WORTHY
The walk is broad enough for us both. (*They walk by one
another, he with his hat cocked, she fretting and tearing her fan*)
Will you please to take snuff, madam?
*He offers her his box, she strikes it out of his hand; while he is
gathering it up,*

Enter BRAZEN

BRAZEN
What, here before me, my dear!
                              Takes MELINDA *round the waist*

241 *strike . . . hot* proverbial. Tilley, I 94
251 *The walk . . . both* Q2 (The walk is as free for me as you, madam,
        and broad enough for us both Q1)
251–2 s.d. so, Hunt (*continuous, following* snuff, madam Q1)
252–3 s.d. *Enter* BRAZEN/*Takes . . . waist* Ed. (*Enter* BRAZEN *who takes*
        MELINDA *about the middle* Q1; BRAZEN *takes her round the waist* Q2)

MELINDA

What means this insolence?   *She cuffs him*

LUCY

(*To* BRAZEN) Are you mad? Don't you see Mr Worthy?   255

BRAZEN

No, no, I'm struck blind – Worthy! – Adso, well turned,
my mistress has wit at her fingers' ends – madam, I ask your
pardon, 'tis our way abroad – Mr Worthy, you're the happy
man.

WORTHY

I don't envy your happiness very much, if the lady can afford   260
no other sort of favours but what she has bestowed upon
you.

MELINDA

I'm sorry the favour miscarried, for it was designed for you,
Mr Worthy; and be assured, 'tis the last and only favour you
must expect at my hands. – Captain, I ask your pardon.   265

                                        Exit with LUCY

BRAZEN

I grant it. – You see, Mr Worthy, 'twas only a random shot,
it might ha' taken off your head as well as mine; courage, my
dear, 'tis the fortune of war; but the enemy has thought fit
to withdraw, I think.

WORTHY

Withdraw! Oons, sir, what d'ye mean by withdraw?   270

BRAZEN

I'll show you.   *Exit*

WORTHY

She's lost, irrecoverably lost, and Plume's advice has ruined
me; 'sdeath, why should I that knew her haughty spirit be
ruled by a man that's a stranger to her pride.

                        Enter PLUME

PLUME

Ha, ha, ha, a battle royal; don't frown so, man, she's your   275
own, I tell'ee; I saw the fury of her love in the extremity of

256 *Adso* exclamation of asseveration
274 *that's* Q2 (that is Q1)

256–8 Brazen pretends to be the recipient of a blow of wit, 'well fashioned',
       playing on proverbial phrases 'to have wit at will' and 'to have some-
       thing at one's fingers' ends'—(Tilley, W552, F245) Shugrue makes
       'Mr Worthy, you're the happy man' a question; even then these words,
       with Worthy's reply, remain obscure.

her passion, the wildness of her anger is a certain sign that
she loves you to madness. That rogue, Kite, began the
battle with abundance of conduct, and will bring you off
victorious, my life on't; he plays his part admirably; she's to   280
be with him again presently.

WORTHY

But what could be the meaning of Brazen's familiarity with
her?

PLUME

You are no logician if you pretend to draw consequences
from the actions of fools; there's no arguing by the rule of   285
reason upon a science without principles, and such is their
conduct; whim, unaccountable whim, hurries 'em on, like a
man drunk with brandy before ten o'clock in the morning –
but we lose our sport; Kite has opened above an hour ago,
let's away.   *Exeunt*   290

[Act IV], Scene ii

A Chamber

KITE, *disguised in a strange habit, sitting at a table, [whereon are
books and globes;* SERVANT *in attendance]*

KITE (*Rising*)

By the position of the heavens, gained from my observation
upon these celestial globes, I find that Luna was a tide-waiter,
Sol a surveyor, Mercury a thief, Venus a whore, Saturn an
alderman, Jupiter a rake, and Mars a sergeant of grenadiers;
and this is the system of Kite the conjurer.   5

Enter PLUME *and* WORTHY

PLUME

Well, what success?

KITE

I have sent away a shoemaker and a tailor already, one's to be
a captain of marines and the other a major of dragoons, I am

---

279   *conduct* skill in managing affairs
287   *'em* Q2 (them Q1)
   0.3 s.d. *A Chamber* Ed. (*A Chamber with books and globes* Q) pres-
      umably within Kite's quarters; see I.i, 130–3
   0.2 s.d. *a strange habit* the German doctor's habit; see I.i, 127–8
      s.d. *habit . . . table* Q2 (*habit, and sitting at the table* Q1)
2   *tide-waiter* customs official
3   *Saturn* associated with law and order
7   *tailor* proverbially cowardly and insignificant (Tilley, T17–25)

to manage them at night. Have you seen the lady, Mr
Worthy?   10

WORTHY

Aye, but it won't do – have you showed her her name that I
tore off from the bottom of the letter?

KITE

No, sir, I reserve that for the last stroke.

PLUME

What letter?

WORTHY

One that I would not let you see, for fear you should break   15
windows in good earnest.   *Knocking at the door*

KITE

Officers to your post.   *Exeunt* WORTHY *and* PLUME
Tycho, mind the door.

        SERVANT *opens the door, enter* [THOMAS,] *a* SMITH

SMITH

Well, master, are you the cunning man?

KITE

I am the learned Copernicus.   20

SMITH

Well, Master Coppernose, I'm but a poor man and I can't
afford above a shilling for my fortune.

KITE

Perhaps that is more than 'tis worth.

15–16 *break windows* Q2 (break Melinda's windows) cf. III.i, 41
18 *Tycho* (omitted Q2) ex. Tycho Brahe (1546–1601), Danish
    astronomer
19 *cunning* possessing magical knowledge
20 *Copernicus* (1473–1543), Polish astronomer

---

16 *earnest*. Later C18 editions add: 'Here, captain, put it in your pocket-
    book, and have it ready upon occasion'. As Strauss says, 'the purpose of
    this speech evidently was to prepare for the farcical devil scene of Q1';
    see l.237 n.
17 s.d. Hunt's edition has Worthy and Plume retire behind a screen,
    evidently following stage-tradition. This blocking has obvious merits;
    but in Restoration comedies characters offstage, and overhearing, are
    generally in closets, or, as in Vanbrugh's *Provoked Wife*, cupboards.
21 *Coppernose*. Red nose due to disease or intemperance. Rothstein sug-
    gests the smith's blunder may be 'Farquhar's mischievous reminiscence
    of Tycho Brahe's famed golden nose' (p. 129). 'Coppernose' was
    omitted in Q2, perhaps as too farcical.

SMITH

Look'ee, doctor, let me have something that's good for my
shilling, or I'll have my money again.   25

KITE

If there be faith in the stars, you shall have your shilling forty
fold. Your hand, countryman – you are by trade a smith.

SMITH

How the devil should you know that?

KITE

Because the devil and you are brother tradesmen – you were
born under Forceps.   30

SMITH

Forceps, what's that?

KITE

One of the signs; there's Leo, Sagittarius, Forceps, Furnes,
Dixmude, Namur, Brussels, Charleroi, and so forth – twelve
of 'em. Let me see – did you ever make any bombs or
cannon-bullets?   35

SMITH

Not I.

KITE

You either have, or will – the stars have decreed that you
shall be – I must have more money, sir, your fortune's great –

SMITH

Faith, doctor, I have no more.

KITE

Oh, sir, I'll trust you, and take it out of your arrears.   40

SMITH

Arrears! What arrears?

KITE

The five hundred pound that's owing to you from the
government.

SMITH

Owing me!

30 *Forceps* obstetrical instrument, smith's tongs
32 *Furnes* of these Flanders towns, this fell to the French, Jan. 1693
33 *Namur* fell to the French, June 1692, recaptured in September
    1695
33 *Brussels* William frustrated a French attack, 1697
    Charleroi fell to the French, 1693   35 *cannon* Q2 (cannons Q1)

40 *arrears.* Proportion of military pay supposed to be paid at the end of each year,
    after deductions; in practice, frequently overdue (see R. E. Scouller, *The Armies of
    Queen Anne*, Oxford, 1966, 127-8).

KITE

Owing you, sir – let me see your t'other hand – I beg your   45
pardon, it will be owing to you; and the rogue of an agent
will demand fifty per cent for a fortnight's advance.

SMITH

I'm in the clouds, doctor, all this while.

KITE

Sir, I am above 'em, among the stars – in two years, three
months, and two hours, you will be made Captain of the   50
Forges to the Grand Train of Artillery, and will have ten
shillings a day and two servants; 'tis the decree of the stars,
and of the fixed stars, that are as immovable as your anvil.
Strike, sir, while the iron is hot – fly, sir, begone –

SMITH

What! What would you have me do, doctor? I wish the stars   55
would put me in a way for this fine place.

KITE

The stars do – let me see – aye, about an hour hence walk
carelessly into the market-place and you'll see a tall, slender
gentleman cheapening a pen'worth of apples, with a cane
hanging upon his button – this gentleman will ask you what's 60
o'clock – he's your man, and the maker of your fortune;
follow him, follow him. And now go home and take leave of
your wife and children; an hour hence exactly is your time.

SMITH

A tall, slender gentleman, you say! With a cane. Pray, what
sort of a head has the cane?   65

KITE

An amber head with a black ribband.

SMITH

But pray, of what employment is the gentleman?

KITE

Let me see – he's either a collector of the excise, or a pleni-
potentiary, or a captain of grenadiers – I can't tell exactly
which. But he'll call you honest – your name is –   70

SMITH

Thomas.

---

46 *agent* regimental paymaster and clerk; notoriously grasping
49 *Sir . . . 'em* Q2 (So am I sir Q1)
59 *cheapening* bargaining for
68 *excise, or a* Q2 (excise, a Q1)

---

65 f. N.T.: 'Plume, who is hidden behind a screen, brandishes his cane in
front of Kite's face' (Tynan).

KITE

He'll call you honest Tom.

SMITH

But how the devil should he know my name?

KITE

Oh, there are several sorts of Toms – Tom a'Lincoln, Tom-   75
tit, Tom Telltroth, Tom o'Bedlam, Tom Fool. – (*Knocking
at the door*) Begone – an hour hence precisely.

SMITH

You say he'll ask me what's o'clock?

KITE

Most certainly, and you'll answer you don't know, and be
sure you look at St Mary's dial, for the sun won't shine, and
if it should, you won't be able to tell the figures.   80

SMITH

I will, I will.   *Exit*

PLUME ([*Appearing*] *behind*)

Well done, conjurer, go on and prosper.

KITE

As you were.

Enter [PLUCK] *a* BUTCHER

KITE (*Aside*)

What, my old friend Pluck the butcher – I offered the surly
bulldog five guineas this morning and he refused it.   85

BUTCHER

So, Master Conjurer, here's half a crown – and now you
must understand –

KITE

Hold, friend, I know your business beforehand.

72 *He'll* Q2 (Right, he'll Q1)
74 *Tom-tit* blue titmouse
75 *Tom Telltroth* honest man
   Tom o' Bedlam released lunatic, licensed to beg
   Tom Fool (a) half wit (b) buffoon
83 s.d. PLUCK heart, liver, lungs, etc. of a beast, used as food

---

74 *Tom a' Lincoln.* 'The Red Rose Knight', protagonist of Richard Johnson's
romance, *The Most Pleasant History of Tom a Lincolne* (Stationers'
Register, 2 pt., 1599, 1607), of which a new edition appeared in
1705, and also of an unpublished tragi-comedy attributed to Thomas
Heywood. There was a 'famous bear' of the same name (see William
Cavendish, *The Humorous Lovers*, [1677], p. 48), and a large bell in
Lincoln Cathedral.

BUTCHER

You're devilish cunning then; for I don't well know it myself.

KITE

I know more than you, friend – you have a foolish saying,   90
that such a one knows no more than the man in the moon;
I tell you the man in the moon knows more than all the men
under the sun; don't the moon see all the world?

BUTCHER

All the world see the moon, I must confess.

KITE

Then she must see all the world, that's certain. Give me   95
your hand – you're by trade either a butcher or a surgeon.

BUTCHER

True, I am a butcher.

KITE

And a surgeon you will be, the employments differ only in
the name – he that can cut up an ox, may dissect a man, and
the same dexterity that cracks a marrow-bone will cut off a   100
leg or an arm.

BUTCHER

What d'ye mean, doctor, what d'ye mean?

KITE

Patience, patience, Mr Surgeon-General, the stars are great
bodies and move slowly.

BUTCHER

But what d'ye mean by Surgeon-General, doctor?   105

KITE

Nay, sir, if your worship won't have patience, I must beg the
favour of your worship's absence.

BUTCHER

My worship, my worship! But why my worship?

KITE

Nay, then I have done.   *Sits*

BUTCHER

Pray, doctor.   110

KITE

Fire and fury, sir! (*Rises in a passion*) Do you think the stars
will be hurried? Do the stars owe you any money, sir, that
you dare to dun their lordships at this rate? Sir, I am porter
to the stars, and I am ordered to let no dun come near their
doors.   115

91 *the man in the moon* proverbial. Tilley, M240

96 *you're* Q2 (you are Q1)

103 *Surgeon-General* chief surgeon of an expeditionary force

BUTCHER

> Dear doctor, I never had any dealings with the stars, they don't owe me a penny – but since you are their porter, please to accept of this half-crown to drink their healths, and don't be angry.

KITE

> Let me see your hand then once more – here has been gold – five guineas, my friend, in this very hand this morning. 120

BUTCHER

> Nay, then he is the devil – pray, doctor, were you born of a woman, or did you come into the world of your own head?

KITE

> That's a secret – this gold was offered you by a proper, handsome man, called Hawk, or Buzzard, or – 125

BUTCHER

> Kite, you mean.

KITE

> Aye, aye, Kite.

BUTCHER

> As errant a rogue as ever carried a halberd – the impudent rascal would have decoyed me for a soldier.

KITE

> A soldier! A man of your substance for a soldier! Your 130 mother has a hundred pound in hard money lying at this minute in the hands of a mercer, not forty yards from this place.

BUTCHER

> Oons, and so she has, but very few know so much.

KITE

> I know it, and that rogue, what's his name, Kite, knew it, and 135 offered you five guineas to list because he knew your poor mother would give the hundred for your discharge.

BUTCHER

> There's a dog now – flesh, doctor, I'll give you t'other half-crown, and tell me that this same Kite will be hanged.

KITE

> He's in as much danger as any man in the county of Salop. 140

BUTCHER

> There's your fee – but you have forgot the Surgeon-General all this while.

KITE

> You put the stars in a passion.   *Looks on his books*

117 *their porter* Q2 (the porter Q1)

But now they're pacified again – let me see – did you never
cut off a man's leg?   145

BUTCHER

No.

KITE

Recollect, pray.

BUTCHER

I say no.

KITE

That's strange, wonderful strange; but nothing is strange to
me, such wonderful changes have I seen – the second or   150
third, aye, the third campaign that you make in Flanders, the
leg of a great officer will be shattered by a great shot; you will
be there accidentally, and with your cleaver chop off the limb
at a blow; in short, the operation will be performed with so
much dexterity, that with general applause you will be made   155
Surgeon-General of the whole army.

BUTCHER

Nay, for the matter of cutting off a limb, I'll do't, I'll do't
with any surgeon in Europe, but I have no thoughts of
making a campaign.

KITE

You have no thoughts! What matter for your thoughts? The   160
stars have decreed it, and you must go.

BUTCHER

The stars decree it! Oons, sir, the justices can't press me.

KITE

Nay, friend, 'tis none of my business, I ha' done. Only mind
this, you'll know more an hour and a half hence – that's all –
farewell.   *Going*   165

BUTCHER

Hold, hold, doctor, Surgeon-General! What is the place
worth, pray?

KITE

Five hundred pound a year, beside guineas for claps.

BUTCHER

Five hundred pound a year! – An hour and half hence you
say?   170

KITE

Prithee, friend, be quiet, don't be so troublesome, here's

155 *general* Q2 (the general Q1)
166 *What* Q2 (Pray what Q1)
168 *for claps* i.e., for curing gonorrhoea

such a work to make a booby butcher accept five hundred
pound a year. – But if you must hear it – I tell you in short,
you'll be standing in your stall an hour and half hence, and
a gentleman will come by with a snuff-box in his hand, and   175
the tip of his handkerchief hanging out of his right pocket;
he'll ask you the price of a loin of veal, and at the same time
stroke your great dog upon the head and call him Chopper.

BUTCHER

Mercy upon us! Chopper is the dog's name.

KITE

Look'ee there – what I say is true, things that are to come   180
must come to pass. Get you home, sell off your stock, don't
mind the whining and the snivelling of your mother and
your sister, women always hinder preferment; make what
money you can and follow that gentleman, his name begins
with a P – mind that. There will be the barber's daughter,   185
too, that you promised marriage to, she will be pulling and
hauling you to pieces.

BUTCHER

What! Know Sally too? He's the devil, and he needs must
go that the devil drives. – (*Going*) The tip of his handkerchief
out of his left pocket?   190

KITE

No, no, his right pocket; if it be the left, 'tis none of the man.

BUTCHER

Well, well, I'll mind him.   *Exit*

PLUME (*Behind with his pocket-book*)

The right pocket, you say?

KITE

I hear the rustling of silks. (*Knocking*) Fly, sir, 'tis Madam
Melinda.   195

Enter MELINDA *and* LUCY

KITE [*To* SERVANT]

Tycho, chairs for the ladies.

MELINDA

Don't trouble yourself, we shan't stay, doctor.

KITE

Your ladyship is to stay much longer than you imagine.

---

187 *hauling* Q2 (haleing Q1)
188–9 *he needs . . . drives* proverbial. Tilley, D278

MELINDA

　For what?

KITE

　For a husband. – (*To* LUCY) For your part, madam, you　200
won't stay for a husband.

LUCY

　Pray, doctor, do you converse with the stars, or with the
devil?

KITE

　With both; when I have the destinies of men in search, I
consult the stars; when the affairs of women come under my　205
hand, I advise with my t'other friend.

MELINDA

　And have you raised the devil upon my account?

KITE

　Yes, madam, and he's now under the table.

LUCY

　Oh, heavens protect us! Dear madam, let us be gone.

KITE

　If you be afraid of him, why do you come to consult him?　210

MELINDA

　Don't fear, fool. Do you think, sir, that because I'm a woman
I'm to be fooled out of my reason, or frighted out of my
senses? – Come, show me this devil.

KITE

　He's a little busy at present, but when he has done he shall
wait on you.　215

MELINDA

　What is he doing?

KITE

　Writing your name in his pocket-book.

MELINDA

　Ha, ha, ha, my name! Pray, what have you or he to do with
my name?

KITE

　Look'ee, fair lady – the devil is a very modest person, he seeks　220
nobody unless they seek him first; he's chained up like a
mastiff, and can't stir unless he be let loose. – You come to
me to have your fortune told – do you think, madam, that I
can answer you of my own head? No, madam, the affairs of
women are so irregular, that nothing less than the devil can　225
give any account of 'em. Now to convince you of your
incredulity, I'll show you a trial of my skill. – Here, you

Cacodemo del Plumo, exert your power, – draw me this lady's
name, the word Melinda, in the proper letters and character
of her own handwriting. – Do it at three motions – one –	230
two – three – 'tis done – now, madam, will you please to send
your maid to fetch it.

LUCY

I fetch it! The devil fetch me if I do.

MELINDA

My name in my own handwriting! That would be convincing
indeed.	235

KITE

Seeing's believing.	*Goes to the table,* lifts up the carpet
Here Tre, Tre, poor Tre, give me the bone, sirrah. – There's
your name upon that square piece of paper – behold –

MELINDA

'Tis wonderful! My very letters to a tittle.

LUCY

'Tis like your hand, madam, but not so like your hand	240
neither, and now I look nearer, 'tis not like your hand at all.

KITE

Here's a chambermaid now will out-lie the devil.

LUCY

Look'ee, madam, they shan't impose upon us; people can't
remember their hands no more than they can their faces. –

---

228 *Cacodemo del Plumo* Q2 (*Cacodemon del fuego* Q1)
237 *sirrah.—There's* Q2 (11 lines of additional text Q1) see Appendix
    1, A, iii, a
242 *now will* Q2 (now that will Q1)

---

228 *Cacodemo del Plumo.* Q1's '*Cacodemon del fuego*', evil spirit from hell,
    makes ready sense, 'while the use of Plume's name is incautious and out
    of character' (Strauss). It is not needed in Q2 to cue him to be ready to
    hand over the paper; still, it must have come from the theatre, and
    received Farquhar's sanction.
237 *sirrah.* There follows in Q1 the passage in which Plume grabs Kite's
    hand under the table, and makes him believe for a moment that this is
    'the devil in good earnest!' Archer in describing it as an 'outrageously
    farcical passage, which was doubtless found ineffective, and therefore
    omitted in Q2,' is probably right. It seems awkward to stage, without
    the girls catching sight of Plume. As its presence significantly alters the
    effect of the scene towards farce the present edition follows Q2: it, and
    the related passage following l.280 below, have been relegated to
    Appendix 1.

Come, madam, let us be certain, write your name upon this   245
paper, then we'll compare the two names.

Takes out paper and folds it

KITE

Anything for your satisfaction, madam – here's pen and ink.

MELINDA *writes*, LUCY *holds the paper*

LUCY

Let me see it, madam, 'tis the same, the very same. – (*Aside*)
But I'll secure one copy for my own affairs.

MELINDA

This is demonstration.   250

KITE

'Tis so, madam, the word 'demonstration' comes from
Daemon the father of lies.

MELINDA

Well, doctor, I'm convinced; and now pray what account
can you give me of my future fortune?

KITE

Before the sun has made one course round this earthly globe,   255
your fortune will be fixed for happiness or misery.

MELINDA

What! So near the crisis of my fate!

KITE

Let me see – about the hour of ten tomorrow morning you
will be saluted by a gentleman who will come to take his leave
of you, being designed for travel. His intention of going   260
abroad is sudden, and the occasion a woman. Your fortune
and his are like the bullet and the barrel, one runs plump
into the t'other. – In short, if the gentleman travels he will
die abroad, and if he does you will die before he comes home.

MELINDA

What sort of man is he?   265

KITE

Madam, he's a fine gentleman, and a lover – that is, a man of
very good sense, and a very great fool.

MELINDA

How is that possible, doctor?

KITE

Because, madam – because it is so: a woman's reason is the
best for a man's being a fool.   270

247 s.d. LUCY Q2 (*and* LUCY Q1)
262 *plump* directly (muzzle loaded)
266 *he's* Q2 (he is Q1)
269 *a woman's reason* it is so because it is so

MELINDA

Ten o'clock, you say?

KITE

Ten, about the hour of tea-drinking throughout the kingdom.

MELINDA

Here, doctor. (*Gives money*) Lucy, have you any questions
to ask?

LUCY

Oh, madam! a thousand.   275

KITE

I must beg your patience till another time, for I expect more
company this minute; besides, I must discharge the gentleman under the table.

LUCY

Oh, pray, sir, discharge us first.

KITE

Tycho, wait on the ladies downstairs.   280

           Exit MELINDA *and* LUCY

Enter PLUME *and* WORTHY

KITE

Mr Worthy, you were pleased to wish me joy today, I hope
to be able to return the compliment tomorrow.

WORTHY

I'll make it the best compliment to you that ever I made in
my life, if you do; but I must be a traveller, you say?

KITE

No farther than the chops of the Channel, I presume, sir.   285

PLUME

That we have concerted already. (*Knocking hard*) Hey day!
You don't profess midwifery, doctor?

KITE

Away to your ambuscade.   *Exeunt* PLUME *and* WORTHY

273 s.d. *Gives money* Q2 (*Gives him money* Q1)
279 *Oh* Q2 (not in Q1)
280.2 f. so, Q2 (7 lines of additional text Q1) see Appendix 1, A, iii, b
283–4 *ever I made in my* Q2 (you ever made in your Q1)
  compliment pun on sense 'complimentary gift'
285 *chops* entrance to the English channel, approached from the
  Atlantic

---

272 *tea-drinking* Tea was expensive (16*s* to 18*s* a pound in 1706) and the
  tea-table an established female institution (see Ashton, pp. 73, 154;
  Congreve, *The Way of the World*, IV.v, 129f.).

Enter BRAZEN

BRAZEN

Your servant, servant, my dear.

KITE

Stand off, I have my familiar already.   290

BRAZEN

Are you bewitched, my dear?

KITE

Yes, my dear, but mine is a peaceable spirit, and hates
gunpowder – thus I fortify myself; (*draws a circle round
him*) and now, Captain, have a care how you force my lines.

BRAZEN

Lines! What dost talk of lines? You have something like a   295
fishing-rod there, indeed; but I come to be acquainted
with you, man – what's your name, my dear?

KITE

Conundrum.

BRAZEN

Conundrum! Rat me, I know a famous doctor in London of
your name – where were you born?   300

KITE

I was born in Algebra.

BRAZEN

Algebra! – 'Tis no country in Christendom I'm sure,
unless it be some pitiful place in the Highlands of Scotland.

KITE

Right! I told you I was bewitched.

BRAZEN

So am I, my dear, I'm going to be married – I've had two   305
letters from a lady of fortune that loves me to madness, fits,
colic, spleen, and vapours – shall I marry her in four and
twenty hours, aye or no?

KITE

I must have the year and day o'th' month when these
letters were dated.   310

BRAZEN

Why, you old bitch, did you ever hear of love-letters dated
with the year and day o'th' month? Do you think *billets doux*
are like bank bills?

KITE

They are not so good – but if they bear no date, I must
examine the contents.   315

BRAZEN

    Contents, that you shall, old boy, [*pulls out two letters*] here
they be both.

KITE

    Only the last you received, if you please. (*Takes the letter*)
Now, sir, if you please to let me consult my books for a
minute, I'll send this letter enclosed to you with the deter-   320
mination of the stars upon it to your lodgings.

BRAZEN

    With all my heart – I must give him – (*puts his hand in his
pocket*) Algebra! I fancy, doctor, 'tis hard to calculate the
place of your nativity – here. – (*Gives him money*) And if I
succeed, I'll build a watchtower upon the top of the highest   325
mountain in Wales for the study of astrology, and the benefit of Conundrums.   *Exit*

Enter PLUME *and* WORTHY

WORTHY

    Oh! Doctor, that letter's worth a million, let me see it –
and now I have it, I'm afraid to open it.

PLUME

    Pho, let me see it! (*Opening the letter*) If she be a jilt – damn   330
her, she is one – there's her name at the bottom on't.

WORTHY

    How! – Then I'll travel in good earnest – by all my hopes,
'tis Lucy's hand.

PLUME

    Lucy's!

WORTHY

    Certainly, 'tis no more like Melinda's character than black   335
is to white.

PLUME

    Then 'tis certainly Lucy's contrivance to draw in Brazen
for a husband – but are you sure 'tis not Melinda's hand?

WORTHY

    You shall see; where's the bit of paper I gave you just now
that the devil writ 'Melinda' upon?   340

KITE

    Here, sir.

PLUME

    'Tis plain, they're not the same; and is this the malicious

322 s.d. *in his* Q2 (*in's* Q1)
332 *I'll* Q2 (I will Q1)

name that was subscribed to the letter which made Mr
Balance send his daughter into the country?

WORTHY

The very same, the other fragments I showed you just now.   345

PLUME

But 'twas barbarous to conceal this so long, and to continue me so many hours in the pernicious heresy of believing
that angelic creature could change – poor Silvia!

WORTHY

Rich Silvia, you mean, and poor captain – ha, ha, ha; come,
come, friend, Melinda is true and shall be mine; Silvia is   350
constant and may be yours.

PLUME

No, she's above my hopes – but for her sake I'll recant my
opinion of her sex.
　　By some the sex is blamed without design,
　　Light, harmless censure, such as yours and mine,   355
　　Sallies of wit, and vapours of our wine.
　　Others the justice of the sex condemn,
　　And wanting merit to create esteem,
　　Would hide their own defects by censuring them.
　　But they, secure in their all-conqu'ring charms,   360
　　Laugh at the vain efforts of false alarms;
　　He magnifies their conquests who complains,
　　For none would struggle were they not in chains.

Exeunt

Act V, Scene i

An Antechamber [adjoining SILVIA's *bedroom], with a
periwig, hat, and sword upon the table
Enter* SILVIA *in her nightcap*

SILVIA

I have rested but indifferently, and I believe my bedfellow
was as little pleased; poor Rose! Here she comes –

Enter ROSE

Good morrow, my dear, how d'ye this morning?

345　*now* Q2 (now, I once intended it for another use, but I think I
　　have turned it now to better advantage Q1)
361　*false alarms* (presumably) false attacks, feints
363　s.d. *Exeunt* Q2 (not in Q1)
　　Scene i wholly omitted in Q2

ROSE

Just as I was last night, neither better nor worse for you.

SILVIA

What's the matter? Did you not like your bedfellow?   5

ROSE

I don't know whether I had a bedfellow or not.

SILVIA

Did not I lie with you?

ROSE

No – I wonder you could have the conscience to ruin a poor girl for nothing.

SILVIA

I have saved thee from ruin, child; don't be melancholy, I   10
can give you as many fine things as the captain can.

ROSE

But you can't, I'm sure.   *Knocking at the door*

SILVIA

Odso! My accoutrements – (*Puts on her periwig, hat, and sword*) Who's at the door?

[CONSTABLE (*without*)]

Open the door, or we'll break it down.   15

SILVIA

Patience a little –   *Opens the door*

Enter [MR BRIDEWELL, *a*] CONSTABLE *and* WATCH

CONSTABLE

We have 'em, we have 'em, the duck and the mallard both in the decoy.

SILVIA

What means this riot? Stand off! (*Draws*) The man dies that comes within reach of my point.   20

CONSTABLE

That is not the point, master, put up your sword or I shall knock you down; and so I command the Queen's peace.

SILVIA

You are some blockhead of a constable.

CONSTABLE

I am so, and have a warrant to apprehend the bodies of you and your whore there.   25

---

16 s.d. WATCH Ed. (MOB Q1)

22 *command . . . peace* command you to keep the peace (rendering further resistance a breach of it)

ROSE
  Whore! Never was poor woman so abused.

                Enter BULLOCK *unbuttoned*

BULLOCK
  What's matter now? – Oh! Mr Bridewell, what brings you
  abroad so early?
CONSTABLE
  This, sir – (*Lays hold of* BULLOCK) You're the Queen's
  prisoner.   30
BULLOCK
  Wauns, you lie, sir, I'm the Queen's soldier.
CONSTABLE
  No matter for that, you shall go before Justice Balance.
SILVIA
  Balance! 'Tis what I wanted. – Here, Mr Constable, I
  resign my sword.
ROSE
  Can't you carry us before the captain, Mr Bridewell?   35
CONSTABLE
  Captain! Han't you got your bellyful of captains yet? Come,
  come, make way there.   *Exeunt*

                [Act V], Scene ii

                JUSTICE BALANCE'*s house*
                Enter BALANCE *and* SCALE

SCALE
  I say 'tis not to be borne, Mr Balance.
BALANCE
  Look'ee, Mr Scale, for my own part I shall be very tender
  in what regards the officers of the army; they expose their
  lives to so many dangers for us abroad that we may give
  them some grains of allowance at home.   5
SCALE
  Allowance! This poor girl's father is my tenant, and if I
  mistake not, her mother nursed a child for you; shall they
  debauch our daughters to our faces?
BALANCE
  Consider, Mr Scale, that were it not for the bravery of these

  27 *Bridewell* ex. house of correction
  0.1 s.d. *Enter* Q2 (not in Q1)

officers we should have French dragoons among us, that   10
would leave us neither liberty, property, wife, nor daughter. – Come, Mr Scale, the gentlemen are vigorous and
warm, and may they continue so; the same heat that stirs
them up to love, spurs them on to battle; you never knew a
great general in your life that did not love a whore. This I   15
only speak in reference to Captain Plume, for the other spark
I know nothing of.

SCALE

Nor can I hear of anybody that does – oh, here they come.
       Enter SILVIA, BULLOCK, ROSE, *prisoners*; CONSTABLE *and*
                         WATCH

CONSTABLE

May it please your worships, we took them in the very act,
re infecta, sir – the gentleman indeed behaved himself like   20
a gentleman, for he drew his sword and swore, and afterwards laid it down and said nothing.

BALANCE

Give the gentleman his sword again – wait you without.
                         Exeunt CONSTABLE *and* WATCH
(*To* SILVIA) I'm sorry, sir, to know a gentleman upon such
terms, that the occasion of our meeting should prevent the   25
satisfaction of an acquaintance.

SILVIA

Sir, you need make no apology for your warrant, no more
than I shall do for my behaviour – my innocence is upon an
equal foot with your authority.

SCALE

Innocence! Have you not seduced that young maid?   30

SILVIA

No, Mr Goosecap, she seduced me.

BULLOCK

So she did, I'll swear – for she proposed marriage first.

BALANCE

What! Then you're married, child?   (*To* ROSE)

20 *re infecta* the act not having been accomplished
23 s.d. *and* WATCH Q2 (*&c.* Q1)
25 *prevent* anticipate
31 *Goosecap* alluding to his Justice's wig; dolt

---

10 *French dragoons* Englishmen generally were convinced that, subjected
   to Louis XIV, they would have lawless dragoons forcibly quartered on
   them, as had happened to the French Huguenots before the Revocation
   of the Edict of Nantes in 1685, to harry them into conversion to Cath-
   olicism.

ROSE
Yes, sir, to my sorrow.

BALANCE
Who was witness?   35

BULLOCK
That was I – I danced, threw the stocking, and spoke jokes
by their bedside, I'm sure.

BALANCE
Who was the minister?

BULLOCK
Minister! We are soldiers, and want no ministers – they
were married by the Articles of War.   40

BALANCE
Hold thy prating, fool. Your appearance, sir, promises
some understanding; pray, what does this fellow mean?

SILVIA
He means marriage, I think – but that, you know, is so odd
a thing, that hardly any two people under the sun agree in
the ceremony; some make it a sacrament, others a con-   45
venience, and others make it a jest; but among soldiers
'tis most sacred – our sword, you know, is our honour; that
we lay down, the hero jumps over it first, and the amazon
after – leap rogue, follow whore – the drum beats a ruff,
and so to bed; that's all, the ceremony is concise.   50

BULLOCK
And the prettiest ceremony, so full of pastime and prod-
igality –

BALANCE
What! Are you a soldier?

BULLOCK
Aye, that I am. Will your worship lend me your cane, and
I'll show you how I can exercise.   55

---

36 *threw the stocking*. Part of the knockabout fun traditional for weddings:
when the newly-weds are in bed,

> The bridesmen take the bride's stockings, and the bridesmaids the
> bridegroom's; both sit down at the bed's feet and fling the stockings
> over their heads, endeavouring to direct them so as that they may fall
> upon the married couple. If the man's stockings, thrown by the maids,
> fall upon the bridegroom's head, it is a sign she will quickly be married
> herself; and the same prognostic holds good of the woman's stockings
> thrown by the man.

(*M. Misson's Memoirs*, etc., translated by Ozells (1719); cited from
Ashton, p. 33).

BALANCE
> Take it. (*Strikes him over the head*) Pray, sir, what com-
> mission may you bear?   (*To* SILVIA)

SILVIA
> I'm called Captain, sir, by all the coffeemen, drawers,
> whores, and groom-porters in London, for I wear a red
> coat, a sword, a hat *bien troussé*, a martial twist in my cravat,   60
> a fierce knot in my periwig, a cane upon my button, piquet
> in my head, and dice in my pocket.

SCALE
> Your name, pray, sir?

SILVIA
> Captain Pinch; I cock my hat with a pinch, I take snuff
> with a pinch, pay my whores with a pinch; in short, I can   65
> do anything at a pinch, but fight and fill my belly.

BALANCE
> And pray, sir, what brought you into Shropshire?

SILVIA
> A pinch, sir: I knew you country gentlemen want wit, and
> you know that we town gentlemen want money, and so –

BALANCE
> I understand you, sir. – Here, Constable!   70

Enter CONSTABLE

Take this gentleman into custody till farther orders.

ROSE
> Pray your worship, don't be uncivil to him, for he did me no
> hurt; he's the most harmless man in the world, for all he
> talks so.

SCALE
> Come, come, child, I'll take care of you.   75

SILVIA
> What, gentlemen, rob me of my freedom and my wife at
> once! 'Tis the first time they ever went together.

BALANCE (*Whispers*)
> Hark'ee, Constable –

---

58 *coffeemen* coffee-house keepers *drawers* tapsters
59 *groom-porters* royal officers appointed to supervise gaming
60 *a hat* Q2 (not in Q1)
     bien troussé neatly arranged
61 *piquet* card-game
68 *knew you* Q2 (knew that you Q1)
78 s.d. *Whispers* Ed. (*Whispers the Constable* Q)

CONSTABLE
It shall be done, sir. – Come along, sir.
                    Exeunt CONSTABLE, BULLOCK, [ROSE] *and* SILVIA
BALANCE
Come, Mr Scale, we'll manage the spark presently.   80
                              Exeunt BALANCE *and* SCALE

[Act V], Scene iii
MELINDA'S *Apartment*
Enter MELINDA *and* WORTHY

MELINDA
(*Aside*) So far the prediction is right, 'tis ten exactly. –
And pray sir, how long have you been in this travelling
humour?
WORTHY
'Tis natural, madam, for us to avoid what disturbs our quiet.
MELINDA
Rather the love of change, which is more natural, may be the   5
occasion of it.
WORTHY
To be sure, madam, there must be charms in variety, else
neither you nor I should be so fond of it.
MELINDA
You mistake, Mr Worthy, I am not so fond of variety as to
travel for't, nor do I think it prudence in you to run your-   10
self into a certain expense and danger, in hopes of pre-
carious pleasures which at best never answer expectation,
as 'tis evident from the example of most travellers, that
long more to return to their own country than they did to
go abroad.   15
WORTHY
What pleasures I may receive abroad are indeed uncertain;
but this I am sure of, I shall meet with less cruelty among
the most barbarous nations than I have found at home.
MELINDA
Come, sir, you and I have been jangling a great while; I
fancy if we made up our accounts, we should the sooner   20
come to an agreement.
WORTHY
Sure, madam, you won't dispute your being in my debt –

0.2 s.d. MELINDA'S *Apartment* Q2 ([SCENE] *changes to* MELINDA'S
    Apartment Q1)
0.1 s.d. *Enter* Q2 (not in Q1)

my fears, sighs, vows, promises, assiduities, anxieties,
jealousies, have run on for a whole year, without any payment.   25

MELINDA

A year! Oh Mr Worthy, what you owe to me is not to be
paid under a seven years' servitude. How did you use me the
year before, when taking the advantage of my innocence and
necessity, you would have made me your mistress, that is,
your slave? Remember the wicked insinuations, artful baits,   30
deceitful arguments, cunning pretences; then your impudent behaviour, loose expressions, familiar letters, rude
visits; remember those, those, Mr Worthy.

WORTHY

(*Aside*) I do remember, and am sorry I made no better use
of 'em. – But you may remember, madam, that –   35

MELINDA

Sir, I'll remember nothing – 'tis your interest that I should
forget; you have been barbarous to me, I have been cruel to
you; put that and that together, and let one balance the
other. Now if you will begin upon a new score, lay aside
your adventuring airs, and behave yourself handsomely till   40
Lent be over, here's my hand, I'll use you as a gentleman
should be.

WORTHY

And if I don't use you as a gentlewoman should be, may
this be my poison.   *Kissing her hand*

Enter SERVANT

SERVANT

Madam, the coach is at the door.   45

MELINDA

I'm going to Mr Balance's country-house to see my cousin
Silvia; I have done her an injury, and can't be easy till I have
asked her pardon.

WORTHY

I dare not hope for the honour of waiting on you.

MELINDA

My coach is full, but if you will be so gallant as to mount   50

---

27 *seven years' servitude* cf. *Genesis* 29:18–30
41 *Lent* meant figuratively

---

50 *My coach is full.* Separation of Melinda and Worthy is essential for the
subsequent complication, yet its justification is slapdash: 'Lucy,
presumably, is to be Melinda's companion, yet this arrangement clashes
with Lucy's plan concerning Brazen' (Strauss).

your own horses and follow us, we shall be glad to be
overtaken; and if you bring Captain Plume with you, we
shan't have the worse reception.

WORTHY

I'll endeavour it.   *Exit* WORTHY *leading* MELINDA

[Act V], Scene iv
The Market-place
Enter PLUME *and* KITE

PLUME

A baker, a tailor, a smith, and a butcher – I believe the first
colony planted at Virginia had not more trades in their
company than I have in mine.

KITE

The butcher, sir, will have his hands full; for we have two
sheep stealers among us – I hear of a fellow, too, com-   5
mitted just now for stealing of horses.

PLUME

We'll dispose of him among the dragoons. Have we ne'er a
poulterer among us?

KITE

Yes, sir, the king of the gypsies is a very good one, he has an
excellent hand at a goose or a turkey. Here's Captain Brazen,   10
sir – I must go look after the men.   *Exit*

Enter BRAZEN *reading a letter*

BRAZEN

Um, um, um, the canonical hour – um, um, very well. – My
dear Plume! Give me a buss.

PLUME

Half a score if you will, my dear. [*They kiss*] What hast got
in thy hand, child?   15

BRAZEN

'Tis a project for laying out a thousand pound.

PLUME

Were it not requisite to project first how to get it in?

1–2 *first . . . Virginia.* Established at Jamestown, 1607.

5–6 *sheep stealers . . . horses.* Under the Impressment and Mutiny Acts,
  convicted felons could avoid civil punishment by enlisting.

BRAZEN

You can't imagine, my dear, that I want a thousand pound;
I have spent twenty times as much in the service – now, my
dear, pray advise me, my head runs much upon architec-   20
ture; shall I build a privateer or a playhouse?

PLUME

An odd question – a privateer or a playhouse! 'Twill require
some consideration. – Faith, I'm for a privateer.

BRAZEN

I'm not of your opinion, my dear – for in the first place a
privateer may be ill-built.   25

PLUME

And so may a playhouse.

BRAZEN

But a privateer may be ill-manned.

PLUME

And so may a playhouse.

BRAZEN

But a privateer may run upon the shallows.

PLUME

Not so often as a playhouse.   30

BRAZEN

But, you know, a privateer may spring a leak.

PLUME

And I know that a playhouse may spring a great many.

BRAZEN

But suppose the privateer come home with a rich booty, we
should never agree about our shares.

PLUME

'Tis just so in a playhouse – so by my advice, you shall fix   35
upon the privateer.

---

18 *a thousand* Ed. (twenty thousand Q)

---

18 *thousand.* Q1's 'twenty' is clearly caught from the line below; for if
   Brazen said 'twenty thousand' here Plume would not react so sharply
   when he says it at l.37. Even Brazen would scarcely boast of spending
   twenty times this.

20–36 This reflects upon the current problems of the two rival theatres,
   and primarily on those of the Queen's Theatre in the Haymarket,
   opened in April 1705. Sir John Vanbrugh had raised the capital by
   subscription to build a handsome theatre, yet its acoustics were very
   poor, Betterton's acting-company had few good actors left, and the first
   year's productions usually flopped (see *An Apology for the Life of Colley
   Cibber*, op. cit., ch. IX; *The London Stage, Part II*, introduction).

BRAZEN

Agreed – but if this twenty thousand should not be in specie –

PLUME

What twenty thousand?

BRAZEN

Hark'ee –   *Whispers*   40

PLUME

Married!

BRAZEN

Presently, we're to meet about half a mile out of town at the waterside – and so forth – (*Reads*) 'For fear I should be known by any of Worthy's friends, you must give me leave to wear my mask till after the ceremony, which will make me   45 ever yours'. – Look'ee there, my dear dog –
                    Shows the bottom of the letter to PLUME

PLUME

Melinda! And by this light, her own hand! – Once more, if you please, my dear; her hand exactly! – Just now you say?

BRAZEN

This minute I must be gone.

PLUME

Have a little patience, and I'll go with you.   50

BRAZEN

No, no, I see a gentleman coming this way that may be inquisitive; 'tis Worthy, do you know him?

PLUME

By sight only.

BRAZEN

Have a care, the very eyes discover secrets –   *Exit*

Enter WORTHY

WORTHY

To boot and saddle, Captain, you must mount.   55

PLUME

Whip and spur, Worthy, or you won't mount.

WORTHY

But I shall: Melinda and I are agreed; she's gone to visit Silvia, we are to mount and follow, and could we carry a parson with us, who knows what might be done for us both?

PLUME

Don't trouble your head, Melinda has secured a parson   60 already.

57 *she's* Q2 (she is Q1)

WORTHY
    Already! Do you know more than I?
PLUME
    Yes, I saw it under her hand – Brazen and she are to meet
    half a mile hence at the waterside, there to take boat, I sup-
    pose to be ferried over to the Elysian fields, if there be any   65
    such thing in matrimony.
WORTHY
    I parted with Melinda just now; she assured me she hated
    Brazen, and that she resolved to discard Lucy for daring to
    write letters to him in her name.
PLUME
    Nay, nay, there's nothing of Lucy in this – I tell ye I saw   70
    Melinda's hand as surely as this is mine.
WORTHY
    But I tell you, she's gone this minute to Justice Balance's
    country-house.
PLUME
    But I tell you, she's gone this minute to the waterside.

                        Enter a SERVANT

SERVANT (*to* WORTHY)
    Madam Melinda has sent word that you need not trouble   75
    yourself to follow her, because her journey to Justice
    Balance's is put off, and she's gone to take the air another
    way.
WORTHY
    How! Her journey put off?
PLUME
    That is, her journey was a put-off to you.   80
WORTHY
    'Tis plain, plain – but how, where, when is she to meet
    Brazen?
PLUME
    Just now, I tell you, half a mile hence at the waterside.
WORTHY
    Up, or down the water?
PLUME
    That I don't know.   85
WORTHY
    I'm glad my horses are ready. – Jack, get 'em out.
                                            [*Exit* SERVANT]
PLUME
    Shall I go with you?

WORTHY

Not an inch; I shall return presently.

PLUME

You'll find me at the hall; the justices are sitting by this
time, and I must attend them.   [*Exeunt severally*]   90

[Act V], Scene v

A Court of Justice
BALANCE, SCALE *and* SCRUPLE *upon the bench;*
CONSTABLE, KITE, *Mob* [*in attendance*]
KITE *and* CONSTABLE *advance forward*

KITE

Pray, who are those honourable gentlemen upon the bench?

CONSTABLE

He in the middle is Justice Balance, he on the right is
Justice Scale, and he on the left is Justice Scruple, and I
am Mr Constable, four very honest gentlemen.

KITE

Oh dear sir, I'm your most obedient servant. (*Saluting the*   5
CONSTABLE) I fancy, sir, that your employment and mine are
much the same, for my business is to keep people in order,
and if they disobey, to knock 'em down; and then we're
both staff-officers.

CONSTABLE

Nay, I'm a sergeant myself – of the militia. Come, brother,   10
you shall see me exercise – suppose this a musket now.
(*He puts his staff on his right shoulder*) Now I'm shouldered.

KITE

Aye, you're shouldered pretty well for a constable's staff,
but for a musket you must put it on t'other shoulder, my
dear.   15

CONSTABLE

Adso! That's true. – Come, now give the word o'command.

KITE

Silence.

CONSTABLE

Aye, aye, so we will, – we will be silent.

KITE

Silence, you dog, silence –
                    Strikes him over the head with his halberd

0.3 s.d. *and* Q2 (not in Q1)
0.1 s.d. *forward* Q2 (*to the front of the stage* Q1)

CONSTABLE

That's the way to silence a man with a witness! – What d'ye   20
mean, friend?

KITE

Only to exercise you, sir.

CONSTABLE

Your exercise differs so from ours, that we shall ne'er agree
about it; if my own captain had given me such a rap, I had
taken the law of him.   25

Enter PLUME

BALANCE

Captain, you're welcome.

PLUME

Gentlemen, I thank'ee.

SCRUPLE

Come, honest Captain, sit by me. (PLUME *ascends, and sits
upon the bench*) Now produce your prisoners – here, that
fellow there – set him up. [CONSTABLE *brings first prisoner to*   30
the dock] Mr Constable, what have you to say against this
man?

CONSTABLE

I have nothing to say against him, an't please ye.

BALANCE

No? What made you bring him hither?

CONSTABLE

I don't know, an't please your worship.   35

SCRUPLE

Did not the contents of your warrant direct you what sort of
men to take up?

CONSTABLE

I can't tell, an't please ye, I can't read.

20 *with a witness* with a vengeance
37 *take up* seize by legal authority

28 *sit by me.* 'In order that the proceedings' of conscription under the
Impressment Acts 'might be deemed *Civil* and not Military, the statute
provided that no Justice of the Peace having any military office or
employment . . . should execute the Act' (Clode, op. cit., II, 15). As Hill
has noticed, the physical presence of Plume on the bench helps to point
to the possible abuses inherent in obedience to the letter and not the
spirit of the Acts (J. Burton Hill, op cit., I, 203)

SCRUPLE

A very pretty constable truly! I find we have no business
here.   40

KITE

May it please the worshipful bench, I desire to be heard in
this case, as being counsel for the Queen.

BALANCE

Come, Sergeant, you shall be heard, since nobody else will
speak; we won't come here for nothing.

KITE

This man is but one man, the country may spare him and   45
the army wants him; besides, he's cut out by nature for a
grenadier: he's five foot ten inches high, he shall box,
wrestle, or dance the Cheshire Round with any man in the
county, he gets drunk every sabbath-day, and he beats his
wife.   50

WIFE

You lie, sirrah, you lie, an't please your worship, he's the
best-natured, pains-taking man in the parish, witness my
five poor children.

SCRUPLE

A wife! And five children! You, Constable, you rogue, how
durst you impress a man that has a wife and five children? 55

SCALE

Discharge him, discharge him.

BALANCE

Hold, gentlemen. – Hark'ee, friend, how do you maintain
your wife and five children?

KITE

They live upon wild fowl and venison, sir; the husband
keeps a gun, and kills all the hares and partridges within   60
five mile round.

BALANCE

A gun! Nay, if he be so good at gunning he shall have
enough on't – he may be of use against the French, for he
shoots flying to be sure.

SCRUPLE

But his wife and children, Mr Balance!   65

WIFE

Aye, aye, that's the reason you would send him away: you

42 *counsel* punning on 'sergeant': barrister
58 *five* Q2 (not in Q1)
59 s.p. KITE Ed. (PLUME Q)

know I have a child every year, and you're afraid they
should come upon the parish at last.

PLUME

Look'ee there, gentlemen, the honest woman has spoke it at
once; the parish had better maintain five children this year   70
than six or seven the next; that fellow upon his high feeding
may get you two or three beggars at a birth.

WIFE

Look'ee, Mr Captain, the parish shall get nothing by sending
him away, for I won't lose my teeming-time if there be a
man left in the parish.   75

BALANCE

Send that woman to the house of correction – and the man –

KITE

I'll take care o'him, if you please.   *Takes him down*

SCALE

Here, you Constable, the next: set up that black-faced
fellow, he has a gunpowder look; [CONSTABLE *sets up* SECOND
PRISONER] what can you say against this man, Constable?   80

CONSTABLE

Nothing, but that he's a very honest man.

PLUME

Pray, gentlemen, let me have one honest man in my company for the novelty's sake.

BALANCE

What are you, friend?

SECOND PRISONER

A collier, I work in the coal-pits.   85

SCRUPLE

Look'ee, gentlemen, this fellow has a trade, and the Act of
Parliament here expresses, that we are to impress no man
that has any visible means of a livelihood.

KITE

May it please your worships, this man has no visible means
of a livelihood, for he works underground.   90

PLUME

Well said, Kite – Besides, the army wants miners.

BALANCE

Right! And had we an order of government for't, we could
raise you in this and the neighbouring county of Stafford
five hundred colliers that would run you underground like

76 *house of correction* workhouse

77 s.d. *him* Q2 (*the man* Q1)

85 s.p. SECOND PRISONER Ed. (MOB Q)

moles, and do more service in a siege that all the miners in   95
the army.

SCRUPLE

Well, friend, what have you to say for yourself?

SECOND PRISONER

I'm married.

KITE

Lack-a-day, so am I.

SECOND PRISONER

Here's my wife, poor woman.   100

BALANCE

Are you married, good woman?

WOMAN

I'm married in conscience.

KITE

May it please your worship, she's with child in conscience.

SCALE

Who married you, mistress?

WOMAN

My husband – we agreed that I should call him husband to   105
avoid passing for a whore, and that he should call me wife to
shun going for a soldier.

SCRUPLE

A very pretty couple! Pray, Captain, will you take 'em both?

PLUME

What say you, Mr Kite – will you take care of the woman?

KITE

Yes, sir, she shall go with us to the seaside and there if she   110
has a mind to drown herself we'll take care that nobody
shall hinder her. [*Takes down* SECOND PRISONER]

BALANCE

Here, Constable, bring in my man.   *Exit* CONSTABLE
Now, Captain, I'll fit you with a man such as you ne'er listed
in your life.   115

Enter CONSTABLE *and* SILVIA

Oh my friend Pinch, I'm very glad to see you.

SILVIA

Well, sir, and what then?

SCALE

What then! Is that your respect to the bench?

SILVIA

Sir, I don't care a farthing for you nor your bench neither.

SCRUPLE

Look'ee, gentlemen, that's enough, he's a very impudent   120
fellow, and fit for a soldier.

SCALE

A notorious rogue, I say, and very fit for a soldier.

CONSTABLE

A whoremaster, I say, and therefore fit to go.

BALANCE

What think you, Captain?

PLUME

I think he's a very pretty fellow, and therefore fit to serve.   125

SILVIA

Me for a soldier! Send your own lazy, lubberly sons at home,
fellows that hazard their necks every day in pursuit of a fox,
yet dare not peep abroad to look an enemy in the face.

CONSTABLE

May it please your worships, I have a woman at the door to
swear a rape against this rogue.   130

SILVIA

Is it your wife or daughter, booby? I ravished 'em both
yesterday.

BALANCE

Pray, Captain, read the Articles of War, we'll see him listed
immediately.

PLUME (*Reads*)

'Articles of War against Mutiny and Desertion . . .'   135

SILVIA

Hold, sir. – Once more, gentlemen, have a care what you do,
for you shall severely smart for any violence you offer to me;
and you, Mr Balance, I speak to you particularly, you shall
heartily repent it.

PLUME

Look'ee, young spark, say but one word more and I'll build   140
a horse for you as high as the ceiling, and make you ride the
most tiresome journey that ever you made in your life.

SILVIA

You have made a fine speech, good Captain Huffcap, but you

135 PLUME (*Reads*)/*Articles* . . . Ed. (PLUME *reads Articles of War
against Mutiny and Desertion* Q; PLUME *prepares to read Articles* . . .
Jeffares 2)   143 *Huffcap* swashbuckler

141 *horse* 'Riding the great horse', or timber mare, was a military punishment. The crudely shaped horse had a sharp-peaked back, with sloped flat sides.
The soldier was made to sit astride, with bundles of muskets hung from his legs.

had better be quiet, I shall find a way to cool your courage.

PLUME

Pray, gentlemen, don't mind him, he's distracted.   145

SILVIA

'Tis false – I'm descended of as good a family as any in your
county, my father is as good a man as any upon your bench,
and I am heir to twelve hundred pound a year.

BALANCE

He's certainly mad – pray, Captain, read the Articles of War.

SILVIA

Hold, once more. – Pray, Mr Balance, to you I speak: sup-   150
pose I were your child, would you use me at this rate?

BALANCE

No, faith, were you mine, I would send you to Bedlam first,
and into the army afterwards.

SILVIA

But consider my father, sir, he's as good, as generous, as
brave, as just a man as ever served his country; I'm his only   155
child, perhaps the loss of me may break his heart.

BALANCE

He's a very great fool if it does. Captain, if you don't list
him this minute I'll leave the court.

PLUME

Kite, do you distribute the levy-money to the men whilst I
read.   160

KITE

Aye, sir, – silence, gentlemen.

                    PLUME *reads the Articles of War*

BALANCE

Very well; now, Captain, let me beg the favour of you not to
discharge this fellow upon any account whatsoever. –
Bring in the rest.

CONSTABLE

There are no more, an't please your worship.   165

BALANCE

No more! There were five two hours ago.

SILVIA

'Tis true, sir, but this rogue of a constable let the rest escape
for a bribe of eleven shillings a man, because he said that the
Act allows him but ten, so the odd shilling was clear gains.

---

144 *cool . . . courage* proverbial.Tilley, C716
152 *Bedlam* lunatic asylum in London
161 s.d. *the Articles of War* see Appendix 2

ALL JUSTICES
  How!   170
SILVIA
  Gentlemen, he offered to let me get away for two guineas,
  but I had not so much about me. – This is truth, and I'm
  ready to swear it.
KITE
  And I'll swear it, give me the book, 'tis for the good of the
  service.   175
SECOND PRISONER
  May it please your worship, I gave him half a crown to say
  that I was an honest man, – but now since that your wor-
  ships have made me a rogue, I hope I shall have my money
  again.
BALANCE
  'Tis my opinion that this constable be put into the captain's   180
  hands, and if his friends don't bring four good men for his
  ransom by tomorrow night – Captain, you shall carry him to
  Flanders.
SCALE, SCRUPLE
  Agreed, agreed.
PLUME
  Mr Kite, take the constable into custody.   185
KITE
  Aye, aye, sir. – (*To the* CONSTABLE) Will you please to have
  your office taken from you, or will you handsomely lay
  down your staff as your betters have done before you?
                              The CONSTABLE *drops his staff*
BALANCE
  Come, gentlemen, there needs no great ceremony in adjourn-
  ing this court; – Captain, you shall dine with me.   190
KITE
  Come Mr Militia Sergeant, I shall silence you now I
  believe, without your taking the law of me.
                                             Exeunt omnes

---

177 *but now since* Q2 (and now Q1)

187–8 *lay down your staff*. The phrase was used for the resignation of
  ministers of state.

[Act V], Scene vi

The Fields
Enter BRAZEN *leading in* LUCY *masked*

BRAZEN
  The boat is just below here.
        Enter WORTHY *with a case of pistols under his arm*
WORTHY
  Here, sir, take your choice.
                    Going between 'em, and offering them
BRAZEN
  What! Pistols! Are they charged, my dear?
WORTHY
  With a brace of bullets each.
BRAZEN
  But I'm a foot-officer, my dear, and never use pistols, the   5
  sword is my way – and I won't be put out of my road to
  please any man.
WORTHY
  Nor I neither, so have at you.   *Cocks one pistol*
BRAZEN
  Look'ee, my dear, I don't care for pistols; – pray oblige me
  and let us have a bout at sharps; damn't there's no parrying   10
  these bullets.
WORTHY
  Sir, if you han't your belly full of these, the swords shall
  come in for second course.
BRAZEN
  Why then fire and fury! I have eaten smoke from the mouth
  of a cannon, sir, don't think I fear powder, for I live upon't.   15
  Let me see. (*Takes one*) And now, sir, how many paces
  distant shall we fire?
WORTHY
  Fire you when you please, I'll reserve my shot till I be sure
  of you.
BRAZEN
  Come, where's your cloak?   20

0.1–0.2 *The Fields/Enter . . . masked* Q2 ([SCENE] *changes to the*
    Fields, BRAZEN *leading in* LUCY *masked* Q1)
  1 s.d. *arm* Q2 (*arm, parts* BRAZEN *and* LUCY Q1)
  2 s.d. *Going . . . them* Q2 (*Offering the pistols* Q1)
 10 *sharps* duelling swords
 16 s.d. *one* Q2 (*a pistol* Q1)

WORTHY
Cloak! What d'ye mean?

BRAZEN
To fight upon, I always fight upon a cloak, 'tis our way
abroad.

LUCY
Come, gentlemen, I'll end the strife.   *Unmasks*

WORTHY
Lucy! Take her.   25

BRAZEN
The devil take me if I do – Huzza! (*Fires his pistol*) D'ye
hear, d'ye hear, you plaguey harridan, how those bullets
whistle, suppose they had been lodged in my gizzard
now? –

LUCY
Pray, sir, pardon me.   30

BRAZEN
I can't tell, child, till I know whether my money be safe.
(*Searching his pockets*) Yes, yes, I do pardon you, – but if I
had you in the Rose Tavern, Covent Garden, with three or
four hearty rakes, and three or four smart napkins, I would
tell you another story, my dear.   *Exit*   35

WORTHY
And was Melinda privy to this?

LUCY
No, sir; she wrote her name upon a piece of paper at the
fortune-teller's last night, which I put in my pocket, and
so writ above it to the captain.

WORTHY
And how came Melinda's journey put off?   40

LUCY
At the town's end she met Mr Balance's steward, who told
her that Mrs Silvia was gone from her father's, and nobody
could tell whither.

WORTHY
Silvia gone from her father's! This will be news to Plume.
Go home, and tell your lady how near I was being shot for   45
her.   *Exeunt*

24 s.d. *Unmasks* Q2 (*Pulls off her mask* Q1)
34 *napkins* tapsters

33 *Rose Tavern, Covent Garden.* In Russell Street, adjoining the Drury
Lane Theatre, 'a favourite place of resort after the play', also, 'a noted
haunt of bad characters, especially those of the female sex' (Ewald).

[Act V], Scene vii
[BALANCE's *house*]

Enter BALANCE *with a napkin in his hand, as risen from dinner, and* STEWARD

STEWARD
We did not miss her till the evening, sir, and then searching
for her in the chamber that was my young master's, we
found her clothes there, but the suit that your son left
in the press when he went to London was gone.

BALANCE
The white, trimmed with silver!   5

STEWARD
The same.

BALANCE
You han't told that circumstance to anybody?

STEWARD
To none but your worship.

BALANCE
And be sure you don't. Go into the dining-room, and tell
Captain Plume that I beg to speak with him.   10

STEWARD
I shall.   *Exit*

BALANCE
Was ever man so imposed upon? I had her promise indeed
that she should never dispose of herself without my consent.
– I have consented with a witness, given her away as my act
and deed – and this, I warrant, the captain thinks will pass;   15
no, I shall never pardon him the villainy, first of robbing me
of my daughter, and then the mean opinion he must have of
me to think that I could be so wretchedly imposed upon; her
extravagant passion might encourage her in the attempt, but
the contrivance must be his – I'll know the truth presently.   20

Enter PLUME

Pray, Captain, what have you done with your young
gentleman soldier?

PLUME
He's at my quarters, I suppose, with the rest of my men.

BALANCE
Does he keep company with the common soldiers?

0.3 s.d. BALANCE's *house* Ed. (not in Q)
0.1 s.d. *and* STEWARD Q2 (*talking with his* STEWARD Q1)

PLUME

No, he's generally with me.   25

BALANCE

He lies with you, I presume?

PLUME

No, faith, – I offered him part of my bed, but the young
rogue fell in love with Rose, and has lain with her, I think,
since he came to town.

BALANCE

So that between you both, Rose has been finely managed.   30

PLUME

Upon my honour, sir, she had no harm from me.

BALANCE

All's safe, I find. – Now, Captain, you must know that the
young fellow's impudence in court was well grounded; he
said I should heartily repent his being listed, and so I do
from my soul.   35

PLUME

Aye! For what reason?

BALANCE

Because he is no less than what he said he was, born of as
good a family as any in this county, and is heir to twelve
hundred pound a year.

PLUME

I'm very glad to hear it, for I wanted but a man of that   40
quality to make my company a perfect representative of the
whole commons of England.

BALANCE

Won't you discharge him?

PLUME

Not under a hundred pound sterling.

BALANCE

You shall have it, for his father is my intimate friend.   45

PLUME

Then you shall have him for nothing.

BALANCE

Nay, sir, you shall have your price.

PLUME

Not a penny, sir; I value an obligation to you much above a
hundred pound.

BALANCE

Perhaps, sir, you shan't repent your generosity. – Will you   50

34 *said I* Q2 (said that I Q1)   34 *so* Q2 (not in Q1)

please to write his discharge in my pocket-book? (*Gives his book*) In the meantime we'll send for the gentleman. Who waits there?

Enter SERVANT

Go to the captain's lodgings and inquire for Mr Wilful; tell him his captain wants him here immediately.   55

SERVANT

Sir, the gentleman's below at the door inquiring for the captain.

PLUME

Bid him come up – here's the discharge, sir.

BALANCE

Sir, I thank you. – (*Aside*) 'Tis plain he had no hand in't.

Enter SILVIA

SILVIA

I think, Captain, you might have used me better, than to   60
leave me yonder among your swearing, drunken crew; and
you, Mr Justice, might have been so civil as to have invited
me to dinner, for I have eaten with as good a man as your
worship.

PLUME

Sir, you must charge our want of respect upon our ignorance   65
of your quality – but now you're at liberty – I have
discharged you.

SILVIA

Discharged me!

BALANCE

Yes, sir, and you must once more go home to your father.

SILVIA

My father! Then I'm discovered! Oh sir, (*kneeling*) I expect   70
no pardon.

BALANCE

Pardon! No, no, child; your crime shall be your punishment;
here, Captain, I deliver her over to the conjugal power for
her chastisement; since she will be a wife, be you a husband,
a very husband: when she tells you of her love, upbraid her   75
with her folly; be modishly ungrateful, because she has been
unfashionably kind; and use her worse than you would
anybody else, because you can't use her so well as she
deserves.

PLUME

And are you Silvia in good earnest?   80

SILVIA

Earnest! I have gone too far to make it a jest, sir.

PLUME

And do you give her to me in good earnest?

BALANCE

If you please to take her, sir.

PLUME

Why then I have saved my legs and arms, and lost my
liberty; secure from wounds, I'm prepared for the gout;   85
farewell subsistence and welcome taxes. – Sir, my liberty
and hopes of being a general are much dearer to me than
your twelve hundred pound a year – but to your love,
madam, I resign my freedom, and to your beauty my
ambition – greater in obeying at your feet, than commanding   90
at the head of an army.

Enter WORTHY

WORTHY

I'm sorry to hear, Mr Balance, that your daughter is lost.

BALANCE

So am not I, sir, since an honest gentleman has found her.

Enter MELINDA

MELINDA

Pray, Mr Balance, what's become of my cousin Silvia?

BALANCE

Your cousin Silvia is talking yonder with your cousin Plume.   95

MELINDA ⎫
WORTHY ⎭

How!

SILVIA

Do you think it strange, cousin, that a woman should change?
But, I hope, you'll excuse a change that has proceeded from
constancy; I altered my outside because I was the same
within, and only laid by the woman to make sure of my man;   100
that's my history.

MELINDA

Your history is a little romantic, cousin, but since success has
crowned your adventures you will have the world o' your
side, and I shall be willing to go with the tide, provided you
pardon an injury I offered you in the letter to your father.   105

83 s.p. BALANCE Q1 (SILVIA Q2)

___

97 *that a woman should change.* cf. *Æneid*, IV, 569: *Varium et mutabile
semper fœmina.* Also, proverbial. Tilley, W674, W698.

PLUME

That injury, madam, was done to me, and the reparation I
expect shall be made to my friend; make Mr Worthy happy,
and I shall be satisfied.

MELINDA

A good example, sir, will go a great way – when my cousin is
pleased to surrender, 'tis probable I shan't hold out much   110
longer.

Enter BRAZEN

BRAZEN

Gentlemen, I am yours – madam, I am not yours.

MELINDA

I'm glad on't, sir.

BRAZEN

So am I. – You have got a pretty house here, Mr Laconic.

BALANCE

'Tis time to right all mistakes – my name, sir, is Balance.   115

BRAZEN

Balance! Sir, I'm your most obedient. – I know your whole
generation – had not you an uncle that was governor of the
Leeward Islands some years ago?

BALANCE

Did you know him?

BRAZEN

Intimately, sir – he played at billiards to a miracle; you had   120
a brother, too, that was captain of a fireship – poor Dick – he
had the most engaging way with him – of making punch, –
and then his cabin was so neat – but his boy Jack was the most
comical bastard – ha, ha, ha, ha, a pickled dog, I shall never
forget him.   125

PLUME

Well, Captain, are you fixed in your project yet? Are you
still for the privateer?

BRAZEN

No, no, I had enough of a privateer just now, I had like to
have been picked up by a cruiser under false colours, and a
French picaroon for aught I know.   130

PLUME

But have you got your recruits, my dear?

BRAZEN

Not a stick, my dear.

124 *pickled* waggish
130 *French picaroon* pirate or privateer, i.e., whore with the 'French
disease', syphilis

PLUME

    Probably I shall furnish you.

Enter ROSE *and* BULLOCK

ROSE

    Captain, Captain, I have got loose once more, and have
    persuaded my sweetheart Cartwheel to go with us, but you   135
    must promise not to part with me again.

SILVIA

    I find Mrs Rose has not been pleased with her bedfellow.

ROSE

    Bedfellow! I don't know whether I had a bedfellow or not.

SILVIA

    Don't be in a passion, child, I was as little pleased with your
    company as you could be with mine.   140

BULLOCK

    Pray, sir, dunna be offended at my sister, she's something
    underbred – but if you please I'll lie with you in her stead.

PLUME

    I have promised, madam, to provide for this girl; now will
    you be pleased to let her wait upon you, or shall I take care
    of her?   145

SILVIA

    She shall be my charge, sir, you may find it business enough
    to take care of me.

BULLOCK

    Aye, and of me, Captain, for wauns! if ever you lift your
    hand against me, I'll desert.

PLUME

    Captain Brazen shall take care o' that. – My dear, instead of   150
    the twenty thousand pound you talked of, you shall have the
    twenty brave recruits that I have raised, at the rate they
    cost me. – My commission I lay down to be taken up by
    some braver fellow, that has more merit and less good
    fortune, whilst I endeavour by the example of this worthy   155
    gentleman to serve my Queen and country at home.

        With some regret I quit the active field,
        Where glory full reward for life does yield;
        But the recruiting trade, with all its train
        Of lasting plague, fatigue, and endless pain,   160
        I gladly quit, with my fair spouse to stay,
        And raise recruits the matrimonial way.

                                    Exeunt

EPILOGUE

All ladies and gentlemen that are willing to see the comedy
called *The Recruiting Officer*, let them repair tomorrow night by
six o'clock to the sign of the Theatre Royal in Drury Lane, and
they shall be kindly entertained –

We scorn the vulgar ways to bid you come,   5
Whole Europe now obeys the call of drum.
The soldier, not the poet, here appears,
And beats up for a corps of volunteers;
He finds that music chiefly does delight ye,
And therefore chooses music to invite ye.   10

Beat the *Grenadier March* – Row, row, tow! – Gentlemen,
this piece of music, called *An Overture to a Battle*, was composed by a famous Italian master, and was performed with
wonderful success, at the great operas of Vigo, Schellenberg,
and Blenheim; it came off with the applause of all Europe,   15
excepting France; the French found it a little too rough for
their *delicatesse*.

Some that have acted on those glorious stages,
Are here to witness to succeeding ages
That no music like the *Grenadier's* engages.   20

Ladies, we must own that this music of ours is not altogether
so soft as Bononcini's, yet we dare affirm, that it has laid more

---

1–4 Cf. Kite's announcement, I.i, 1–7; this also echoes contemporary
advertisements for concerts.

9–37 The past year had seen the growth of a passionate demand for
Italianate opera.

14 *Vigo, Schellenberg, and Blenheim.* The three proudest Allied victories in
the current war, to this time. On 12 October 1702 Sir George Rooke's
fleet, assisted by Ormonde's army (cf. note, dedicatory epistle, l. 61),
burnt the Spanish and French shipping in Vigo harbour, sacked the
town, and carried off a gratifying array of booty. Marlborough's costly
victory over the Elector of Bavaria's army at Schellenbergh on 2 July
1704 was a necessary preliminary to the decisive triumph at Blenheim
on 17 August (see note to II.i, 13).

22 *Bononcini's* Antonio Maria Bononcini (1675–1726), composer of the
music for *Camilla* (originally, *Il Trionfo di Camilla, regina de' Volsci*).
For the Drury Lane production his score had been adapted by Nicolo
Haym, with Stampiglia's libretto translated by Owen Swiney and
Mr Northam (see Nicoll, p. 274). It was performed on 30 March and
6 April, two days before Farquhar's opening night, and also interrupted
the run of *The Recruiting Officer*, on the 11th.

people asleep than all the *Camillas* in the world; and you'll
condescend to own that it keeps one awake better than any
opera that ever was acted.   25

The *Grenadier March* seems to be a composure excellently
adapted to the genius of the English; for no music was ever
followed so far by us, nor with so much alacrity; and with all
deference to the present subscription, we must say that the
Grenadier March has been subscribed for by the whole Grand   30
Alliance; and we presume to inform the ladies, that it always
has the pre-eminence abroad, and is constantly heard by the
tallest, handsomest men in the whole army. In short, to gratify
the present taste, our author is now adapting some words to
the *Grenadier March*, which he intends to have performed   35
tomorrow, if the lady who is to sing it should not happen to be
sick.

    This he concludes to be the surest way
    To draw you hither, for you'll all obey
    Soft music's call, though you should damn his play.   40

26 *composure* composition
29 *subscription* the arrangement by which the production-costs of
   Camilla were met by public subscription; the people so sub-
   scribing
30–1 *the Grand Alliance* England, the Dutch Republic, the Empire,
   the Spanish supporters of Archduke Charles, and some German
   states in coalition against France

APPENDIX 1

TEXTUAL

(A) *Passages in Q1 deleted in Q2*

Minor Q2 cuts have been noticed in footnotes, and several more substantial passages, notably the song in Act III, scene i, and the entirety of Act V, scene i, retained in the text, being clearly delimited and not distorting their contexts.

(i) First version of part of Silvia-Plume *tête-a-tête*, Act II, scene i, replaced by the present edition's ll. 51–64:

PLUME
> Blessings in heaven we should receive in a prostrate posture, let
> me receive my welcome thus.   *Kneels and kisses her hand*

SILVIA
> Pray rise, sir, I'll give you fair quarter.

PLUME
> All quarter I despise, the height of conquest is to die at your feet.
>   *Kissing her hand again*

SILVIA
> Well, well, you shall die at my feet, or where you will; but first let
> me desire you to make your will, perhaps you'll leave me something.

(ii) First version of Silvia-Plume argument over Rose, Act IV, scene i, replaced in the present edition by ll. 56–82:

PLUME
> . . . Let her go, I say.

SILVIA
> Do you let her go.

PLUME
> *Entendez vous français, mon petit garçon?*

SILVIA
> *Oui.*

PLUME
> *Si voulez vous donc vous enroller dans ma compagnie, la demoiselle
> sera à vous.*

SILVIA
> *Avez vous couché avec elle?*

PLUME
> *Non.*

SILVIA
> *Assurement?*

PLUME
> *Ma foi*

SILVIA

C'est assez. Je serai votre soldat.

PLUME

La prenez donc. I'll change a woman for a man at any time.

(iii) Devil incident in Act IV, scene ii:
(a) Following Kite's 'Here Tre, Tre, poor Tre, give me the bone, sirrah – ', the present l. 237,

> *He puts his hand under the table,* PLUME *steals to the other side of the table and catches him by the hand*[1]

KITE

Oh! oh! The Devil, the Devil in good earnest, my hand, the Devil, my hand!

MELINDA *and* LUCY *shriek, and run to a corner of the stage.* KITE *discovers* PLUME *and gets away his hand*

KITE

A plague o' your pincers, he has fixed his nails in my very flesh. Oh! Madam, you put the Devil in such a passion with your scruples, that it has almost cost me my hand.

MELINDA

It has cost us our lives almost – but have you got the name?

KITE

Got it! Aye, madam, I have got it here – I'm sure the blood comes – but there's your name upon that square piece of paper – behold –

(b) Corresponding passage, at Plume and Worthy's entry, ll. 280 ff. (they enter '*laughing*'):

KITE

Aye, you may well laugh, gentlemen, not all the cannon of the French army could have frighted me so much as that gripe you gave me under the table.

PLUME

I think, Mr Doctor, I out-conjured you that bout.

KITE

I was surprised, for I should not have taken a captain for a conjurer.

PLUME

No more than I should a sergeant for a wit.

(B) *Revisions in 'Works', 1728*

Certain revisions which clearly relate to the current prompt-book and may reflect much earlier stage-practice appear in the 6th edition of *The Works of the Late Ingenious Mr George Farquhar*, etc., of 1728. Presumably the changes were initiated by William Rufus Chetwood, who supplied the biography of the author which first appeared in

---

[1] In Q1, s.d. follows '. . . my hand'; this arrangement is Hunt's.

1728. These revisions do not appear in the editions of the play printed separately till 1736 (the copy, British Museum L.1342.n.27, has 1736 on its title-page though it is catalogued as '1728'), nor in the reprints of *The Comedies of Mr Farquhar* (7th edition, 1736: *The Dramatic Works* . . .). Accordingly, the denotation through the critical notes of 'later C18 editions' means '*Works*, 1728, text and those that follow it'. These changes include, among others:

(i) Act I, scene i: the entry direction has 'Thomas Appletree, Costar Pearmain *and the Mob*', rather than '*the Mob*'; and in this scene '*Costar*' or '*Cost*' appears as a speech-prefix in place of '*Mob*'. In 'Costar's' third speech, he adds, after 'brimstone': 'Smell Tummas', and the latter replies 'Aye, wauns does it'.

(ii) In Act II, scene iii, the first stage direction has '*Enter* Kite, *with* Costar Pearmain *in one hand and* Thomas Appletree *in the other, drunk*', in place of '*Enter* Kite, *with one of the* Mob *in each hand, drunk*'. The speech-prefixes are *Kite*, *Thomas*, and *Costar*, rather than *Kite*, *1st Mob*, and *2d Mob*.

(iii) At the end of Act II, scene iii, when Costar gives his name, Plume replies: 'Well said, Costar. Born where?' in place of 'Born where?' The last verse of the song is complete, as in the present edition, and is followed by:

PLUME
 Kite, take care of 'em.

Enter KITE

KITE
 Ain't you a couple of pretty fellows now! Here have you complained to the captain, I am to be turned out, and one of you will
 be sergeant. But in the meantime, march, you sons of whores.
                                                    Beats 'em off

(iv) An extra gag appears in Act III, scene i: Rose's 'familiarity' (the present l. 288) becomes 'fam-mam-mil-yararality'.

(v) Act V, scene iv, begins with Plume's saying: 'A baker, a taylor, smith, butcher, carpenters and journeyman shoemakers, in all thirty-nine – I believe . . .'

(C) *Bell's acting edition, 1776*, etc.

John Bell's *British Theatre* volumes appeared first in 1776, with *The Recruiting Officer* in volume IV. The text is 'as written by G. Farquhar, Esq. Distinguishing also the variations of the theatre, as performed at the Theatre-Royal in Drury-Lane. Regulated from the prompt-book, by permission of the managers, by Mr Hopkins, Prompter'. Passages for omission in presentation are marked off with inverted commas, apart from a few omitted silently. The version follows Q2, and all changes introduced in the 1728 edition are present.[2]

Another edition 'marked with the variations in the prompter's book' published in the same year by T. Lowndes was probably essentially similar, as the 1792 edition of Bell's text was to be described as that in use at both theatres, Drury Lane and Covent Garden.

Two minor kinds of changes are introduced throughout: 'queen' becomes 'king', 'Queen Anne' becomes 'King George', and Rose in III.i, 267 is going to London to see 'the king and queen'. Also, 'broad pieces' worth 23s. 6d. in Act II, scene iii, become guineas worth 'one and twenty shillings'.

The following are the cuts or revisions of more than a few words:

I.i: 195–6 cut, 'and pushed it with all my forces'; 248–50 cut, 'her sex . . . in her'; 255 'fifty' becomes 'a hundred'.

I.ii: 49–52 cut, 'Constancy . . . noble sex'.

II.i: 2–7 cut, 'I remember . . . prisoners'.[3]

II.ii: 26–36 cut, 'Besides . . . gravel walks'; 149–50 cut, 'the decorum . . . us'.

II.iii: the end, instead of 'But in the meantime, march, you sons of whores', Kite says:

> . . . Which of you is to have my halberd?

BOTH REC [RUITS]

I.

KITE

So you shall – in your guts –
March, you sons of whores.

Beats 'em off

III.i: 4–5 cut, 'a maggot fills their heads'; 111 added, after 'say it'

WORTHY

How came you so qualified?

115 cut, 'who liking . . . page'; 160–1 'fight' and 'Irish' become 'sea-fight' and 'wild Irish'; 162–3 speech assigned to

---

[2] The edition of Bell's text inspected is that of 1792, but the presence of the listed variants in the 1776 edition has been kindly checked by Professor H. F. Brooks. A prompt-book of this era is included in volume 8 of a collection of thirty-eight Covent Garden prompt-books represented in microfilm at the University of North Carolina.

[3] So, 1776. In 1792 the remaining words of the speech, 'Ad's my life [for 'odsmylife'] . . . soldier', were also marked for omission; they may have been intended to be in 1776, and not marked as such by accident.

Kite; 175–9 cut, 'I never . . . world'; 180–3 cut 'Cupid . . .
lamely'; 196–203 cut, 'I have . . . moment'.

III.ii: 15–26 cut, 'Madam . . . ourselves'.

IV.i: 8–9 cut, 'this genteel . . . followers'; 122–33 'the women . . .
bear it'; 138–45 cut, 'You must . . . else'; 188–207 cut, 'You're . . .
together'; 285–7 cut, 'there's . . . conduct'.

IV.ii: 19–195 cut, from Smith's entry to just before Melinda's
entry (i.e., to ' 'tis Madam Melinda'); 308 ff. added, after 'aye or
no'.

KITE
  Certainly.
BRAZEN
  Gadso, aye –
KITE
  – Or no – but I must . . .

V.i: as in Q2, cut completely.

V.ii: 3–15 cut, 'they expose . . . This'; 60–1 cut, '*bien* . . . button'.

V.iii: 12–15 cut, 'which . . . abroad'.

V.iv: 1–3 cut, 'I believe . . . mine'; 19–37 cut, 'now, my dear . . .
Agreed'.

V.vi: scene cut completely.

V.vii: 126–30 cut, 'Well . . . know'.

APPENDIX 2

'ARTICLES OF WAR AGAINST MUTINY AND DESERTION'

Article XIV
No man shall presume so far as to raise or cause the least Mutiny or Sedition in the Army, upon Pain of Death. And if any number of Soldiers shall presume to assemble to take Counsel amongst themselves for the demanding their Pay, or shall at any time demand their Pay in a Mutinous manner, any Inferior Officers accessory thereunto, shall suffer Death for it, as the Heads and Ringleaders of such Mutinous and Seditious Meetings; And the Soldiers shall be punished with Death. And if any Captain, being privy thereunto shall not suppress the same, or complain of it, he shall likewise be punished with Death.

Article XV
No Officer or Soldier shall utter any Words tending to Sedition or Mutiny, upon Pain of Death.
   And whosoever shall hear any Mutinous or Seditious Words spoken, and shall not with all possible speed reveal the same to his Superior Officers, shall likewise be punished with Death.

Article XVI
If any Inferior Officer or Soldier shall refuse to obey his Superior Officer, he shall be punished with Death.

Article XVII
If any Officer or Soldier shall presume to resist any Officer in the Execution of his Office, or shall strike, or lift up his hand to strike, or shall draw, or lift up any Weapon against his Superior Officer upon any Pretence whatsoever, he shall suffer Death.

Article XXII
When any March is to be made, every Man who is sworn shall follow his Colours; and whoever shall without leave stay behind, or depart above a Mile from the Camp, or out of the Army without Licence, shall die for it.

Article XXIII
All Officers or Soldiers that shall desert either in the Field, upon a

shall be reputed and suffer as Deserters, who shall be found a Mile from their Garison or Camp without leave from the Officer Commanding in Chief.

Article XXIV

No Officer or Soldier shall leave his Colours, and List himself into any other Regiment, Troop or Company, without a Discharge from³ the Commander in Chief of the Regiment, Troop or Company, in² which he last served, upon pain of being reputed a Deserter, and suffering Death for it; and in case any Officer shall Receive, or Entertain any Non-Commission Officer or Soldier, who shall have so Deserted or left his Colours without a Discharge, such Officer shall be immediately Cashiered.

From *Rules and Articles for the better Government of Her Majesties Land-Forces in the Low-Countries, and Parts beyond the Seas* (1702), 9-13, all in black letter (O: Vet A4 f. 1286). Which articles would have been read to recruits is uncertain (e.g. No. XVI has the side-title 'Disobedience'). No. XVI has obvious bearing on II. iii. 83-84: 'they disobey command, sir, and one of them should be shot for an example to the other'. Similarly when Kite places Tummas and Costar as sentinels, his threat that 'he dare stir from his post till he be relieved shall have my sword in his guts the next minute' (II. iii, 78-80) has the ostensible authority of Article XXXVI: . . . 'And if a Centinel or Perdue shall forsake his Place, before he be relieved or drawn off . . . he shall suffer Death.' (p. 17).

New Mermaids

New Mermaid drama books

New Mermaids present modern-spelling, fully annotated
editions of classic English plays, including works by Marlowe,
Jonson, Webster, Congreve, Sheridan, and Wilde. Each volume
includes a biography of the writer, a critical introduction to
the play, discussions of dates and sources, and a bibliography.

Arden of Faversham

edited by Martin White,
University of Bristol

160 pages
0 510-33508-X £3.25

Three Late Medieval Morality Plays

(Everyman, Mankind, Mundus et Infans)

edited by Geoffrey Lester,
University of Sheffield

204 pages
0 510-33505-5 £3.50

Francis Beaumont

The Knight of the Burning Pestle

edited by Michael Hattaway,
University of Kent

144 pages
0 510-33202-1 £3.25

George Chapman

Bussy D'Ambois

edited by Maurice Evans

160 pages
0 510-33202-1 £3.25

Chapman, Jonson and Marston

Eastward Ho!

edited by C. G. Petter

192 pages
0 510-33311-7 £3.25

William Congreve

The Double Dealer

edited by John Ross, Massey
University

168 pages
0 510-33504-7 £3.25

Love for Love

edited by Malcolm Kelsall,
University College, Cardiff

158 pages
0 510-33662-0 £3.25

The Way of the World

edited by Brian Gibbons,
University of Zurich

152 pages
0 510-33672-8 £3.25

Thomas Dekker

The Shoemakers' Holiday

edited by David Palmer, University of Manchester

128 pages
0 510-33721-X £3.25

John Dryden

All for Love

edited by N. J. Andrew

144 pages
0 510-33711-2 £3.25

Sir George Etherege

The Man of Mode

edited by John Barnard, University of Leeds

200 pages
0 510-33500-4 £3.25

George Farquhar

The Beaux' Stratagem

edited by Michael Cordner, University of York

160 pages
0 510-33781-3 £3.25

The Recruiting Officer

edited by John Ross, Massey University

184 pages
0 510-33731-7 £3.25

John Ford

'Tis Pity She's a Whore

edited by Brian Morris, University College, Lampeter

128 pages
0 510-34145-4 £3.25

Oliver Goldsmith

She Stoops to Conquer

edited by Tom Davis, University of Birmingham

132 pages
0 510-34142-X £3.25

Jasper Heywood/Seneca

Thyestes

edited by Joost Daalder, Flinders University

144 pages
0 510-39010-2 £3.95

Ben Jonson

The Alchemist
edited by Douglas Brown

176 pages
0 510-33606-X £3.25

Bartholmew Fair
edited by G. R. Hibbard,
University of Waterloo,
Ontario

216 pages
0 510-33710-4 £3.25

Epicoene
edited by R. V. Holdsworth,
University of Manchester

224 pages
0 510-34154-3 £3.25

Every Man in his Humour
edited by Martin Seymour-Smith

160 pages
0 510-33636-1 £3.25

Volpone
edited by Philip Brockbank,
Shakespeare Institute,
University of Birmingham

208 pages
0 510-34157-8 £3.25

Thomas Kyd

The Spanish Tragedy
edited by J. R. Mulryne,
University of Warwick

176 pages
0 510-33707-4 £3.25

Christopher Marlowe

Doctor Faustus
edited by Roma Gill,
University of Sheffield

128 pages
0 510-33821-6 £3.25

Edward the Second
edited by W. Moelwyn
Merchant, University of Exeter

144 pages
0 510-33806-2 £3.25

The Jew of Malta
edited by T. W. Craik,
University of Durham

128 pages
0 510-33836-4 £3.25

Tamburlaine Parts I & II
edited by J. W. Harper,
University of York

208 pages
0 510-33851-8 £3.25

Thomas Middleton and William Rowley

The Changeling

edited by Patricia Thomson, University of Sussex

128 pages
0 510-34106-3 £3.25

A Fair Quarrel

edited by R. V. Holdsworth, University of Manchester

176 pages
0 510-34108-X £3.25

George Peele, Nicholas Udall, etc.

Three Sixteenth Century Comedies

(The Old Wife's Tale, Gammer Gurton's Needle, Roister Doister)

edited by Charles Whitworth, University of Birmingham

240 pages
0 510-33509-8 £4.95

Richard Brinsley Sheridan

The Rivals

edited by Elizabeth Duthie, University College, Cardiff

160 pages
0 510-34141-1 £3.25

OD O level Eng Lit 1983-4-5-6
SU A level Eng Lit 1983

The School for Scandal

edited by F. W. Bateson

200 pages
0 510-34364-3 £3.25

J. M. Synge

The Playboy of the Western World

edited by Malcolm Kelsall, University College, Cardiff

128 pages
0 510-33771-6 £3.25

Cyril Tourneur

The Atheist's Tragedy

edited by Brian Morris, St Davids University College, & Roma Gill, University of Sheffield

144 pages
0 510-33751-1 £3.25

The Revenger's Tragedy

edited by Brian Gibbons, University of Zurich

144 pages
0 510-34206-X £3.25

Sir John Vanbrugh

The Provoked Wife

edited by James L. Smith, University of Southampton

160 pages
0 510-34252-3 £3.25

The Relapse

edited by Bernard Harris, University of York

160 pages
0 510-34262-0 £3.25

John Webster

The Devil's Law-Case

edited by Elizabeth M. Brennan, University of London

192 pages
0 510-34296-5 £3.25

The Duchess of Malfi

edited by Elizabeth M. Brennan, University of London

160 pages
0 510-34306-6 £3.25

The White Devil

edited by Elizabeth M. Brennan, University of London

208 pages
0 510-34321-X £3.25

Oscar Wilde

The Importance of Being Earnest

edited by Russell Jackson, The Shakespeare Institute, University of Birmingham

192 pages
0 510-34143-8 £3.25

Lady Windermere's Fan

edited by Ian Small, University of Birmingham

176 pages
0 510-34153-5 £3.25

Two Society Comedies

(An Ideal Husband, A Woman of No Importance)

edited by Russell Jackson, Shakespeare Institute, University of Birmingham & Ian Small, University of Birmingham

336 pages
0 510-33511-X £4.95

William Wycherley

The Country Wife

edited by John Dixon Hunt, University of London

160 pages
0 510-343521-X £3.25

The Plain Dealer

edited by James L. Smith, University of Southampton

216 pages
0 510-33503-9 £3.25